Research Methodologies
in Supply Chain Management

Herbert Kotzab · Stefan Seuring
Martin Müller · Gerald Reiner
(Editors)

Research Methodologies in Supply Chain Management

In Collaboration with Magnus Westhaus

With 71 Figures and 67 Tables

Physica-Verlag

A Springer Company

Professor Dr. Herbert Kotzab
Copenhagen Business School
Department of Operations Management
SCM-Group
Solbjerg Plads 3
2000 Frederiksberg
Denmark
hk.om@cbs.dk

PD Dr. Stefan Seuring
PD Dr. Martin Müller
Supply Chain Management Center
Institute of Business Administration
Faculty of Business, Economics and Law
Uhlhornsweg
26111 Oldenburg
Germany
stefan.seuring@uni-oldenburg.de
martin.mueller@uni-oldenburg.de

Dr. Gerald Reiner
Vienna University of Economics
and Business Administration
Department of Production Management
Nordbergstraße 15
1090 Vienna
Austria
gerald.reiner@wu-wien.ac.at

Cataloging-in-Publication Data
Library of Congress Control Number: 2005924508

ISBN 3-7908-1583-7 Physica-Verlag Heidelberg New York

This work is subject to copyright. All rights are reserved, whether the whole or part of the material is concerned, specifically the rights of translation, reprinting, reuse of illustrations, recitation, broadcasting, reproduction on microfilm or in any other way, and storage in data banks. Duplication of this publication or parts thereof is permitted only under the provisions of the German Copyright Law of September 9, 1965, in its current version, and permission for use must always be obtained from Physica-Verlag. Violations are liable for prosecution under the German Copyright Law.

Physica is a part of Springer Science+Business Media

springeronline.com

© Physica-Verlag Heidelberg 2005
Printed in Germany

The use of general descriptive names, registered names, trademarks, etc. in this publication does not imply, even in the absence of a specific statement, that such names are exempt from the relevant protective laws and regulations and therefore free for general use.

Softcover-Design: Erich Kirchner, Heidelberg

SPIN 11408475   43/3153-5 4 3 2 1 0 – Printed on acid-free paper

Preface

For reseach in all subjects and among different philisopical paradigms, research methodologies form one of the key issues to rely on.

This volume brings a series of papers together, which present different research methodologies as applied in supply chain management. This comprises review oriented papers that look at what kind of methodologies have been applied, as well as methodological papers discussing new developments needed to successfully conduct research in supply chain management. The third group is made up of applications of the respective methodologies, which serve as examples on how the different methodological approaches can be applied. All papers have undergone a review process to ensure their quality. Therefore, we hope that this book will serve as a valid source for current and future researchers in the field.

While the workshop on "Research Methodologies in Supply Chain Management" took place at the Supply Chain Management Center, Carl von Ossietzky University in Oldenburg, Germany, it is based on a collaboration with the Supply Chain Management Group of the Department of Operations Management at the Copenhagen Business School and the Department of Production Management at the Vienna University of Economics and Business Administration.

We would like to thank all those who contributed to the workshop and this book. We are grateful to all for sharing their work and ideas with us, as we learned a great deal from them. We are happy to have brought together authors from Austria, Brazil, Denmark, England, Finland, France, Germany, Ireland, Italy, New Zealand, Norway, Scotland, South Africa, Spain, Thailand, and the United States of America.

Our gratitude goes to Magnus Westhaus, who organized all the major and minor things for this project over a 14-month period. From the first idea of organizing the workshop to editing the last page of this book, he took responsibility for all processes with great skill and dedication.

We would also like to give a special thanks to our support team in Oldenburg. Dave Kloss did a major review of the text and helped improve the English for the non-native speakers. Before, during and after the workshop, Julia Koplin, Kerstin Siebke, Henning Dettleff, Hendrik Eggers, Hartmut Marx, and Magnus Westhaus did a great job of supporting our efforts by picking up and returning participants to the airport, filling the cookie plates, and all the other little things needed.

Copenhagen, Denmark, Oldenburg, Germany, Vienna, Austria, January 2005

Herbert Kotzab, Stefan Seuring, Martin Müller, Gerald Reiner

Contents

Preface V

Is There a Right Research Design for Your Supply Chain Study? 1
Stefan Seuring, Martin Müller, Gerald Reiner, Herbert Kotzab

Part 1 – Substantive Justification for Theory Building

A Balanced Approach to Research in Supply Chain Management 15
Susan L. Golicic, Donna F. Davis, Teresa M. McCarthy

A Critical Discussion on the Theoretical and Methodological Advancements in Supply Chain Integration Research 31
Dirk Pieter van Donk, Taco van der Vaart

Measuring Supply Chain Integration – Using the Q-Sort Technique 47
Sakun Boon-itt, Himangshu Paul

Supply Chain Management and the Challenge of Organizational Complexity – Methodological Considerations 59
Stig Johannessen

The Configurational Approach in Supply Chain Management 75
Axel Neher

Conducting a Literature Review – The Example of Sustainability in Supply Chains 91
Stefan Seuring, Martin Müller, Magnus Westhaus, Romy Morana

Research Methodologies in Supply Chain Management – What Do We Know? 107
Árni Halldórsson, Jan Stentoft Arlbjørn

Part 2 – Surveys in Supply Chain Management

The Role and Importance of Survey Research in the Field of
Supply Chain Management 125
Herbert Kotzab

Web-based Surveys in Logistics Research: An Empirical Application 139
David B. Grant, Christoph Teller, Wolfgang Teller

SCM Research Methodologies: Employing Structural Equation Modeling 155
Cristina Gimenez, Rudolf Large, Eva Ventura

Structural Equation Modeling as a Basis for Theory Development within
Logistics and Supply Chain Management Research 171
Carl Marcus Wallenburg, Jürgen Weber

Customers' Perceptions of Service Quality by TPL Service Providers in the
United Kingdom – A Confirmatory Factor Analysis 187
Harlina Suzana Jaafar, Mohammed Rafiq

Third Party Logistics in Thailand – From the Users' Perspective 203
Pornpen Setthakaset, Chuda Basnet

A Market-Oriented View of SCM – Researching Criteria and Instruments
in the Public Procurement Process 219
Edeltraud Günther, Ines Klauke

Part 3 – Case Study Research in Supply Chains

Case Study Research in Supply Chains – An Outline and Three Examples 235
Stefan Seuring

A Proposal for Case Study Methodology in Supply Chain
Integration Research 251
Teresa M. McCarthy, Susan L. Golicic

Using Case Study Methods in Researching Supply Chains 267
Marie Koulikoff-Souviron, Alan Harrison

Multilevel Issues in Supply Chain Management 283
Marian Oosterhuis, Eric Molleman, Taco van der Vaart

Cost Management along the Supply Chain – Methodological Implications 299
Richard Chivaka

Case Studies and Surveys in Supply Chain Management Research –
Two Complementary Methodologies 315
Cristina Gimenez

Towards Triangulation – Blending Techniques in Supply Chain
Management Context 331
Ozlem Bak

Part 4 – Action Research in Supply Chains

Action Research in Supply Chain Management – An Introduction 349
Martin Müller

The Application of Action Learning and Action Research in Collaborative
Improvement within the Extended Manufacturing Enterprise 365
Rick Middel, Louis Brennan, David Coghlan, Paul Coughlan

Integrating Environmental and Social Standards into Supply Management –
An Action Research Project.. 381
Julia Koplin

Supply Chain Diagnostics to Confront Theory and Practice –
Re-Questioning the Core of Supply Chain Management................................... 397
Günter Prockl

A Logistics and Supply Chain Approach to Seaport Efficiency –
An Inquiry Based on Action Research Methodology 413
Khalid Bichou, Richard Gray

Part 5 – Modelling Supply Chains

Supply Chain Management Research Methodology Using
Quantitative Models Based on Empirical Data.. 431
Gerald Reiner

Of Stocks, Flows, Agents and Rules – "Strategic" Simulations in
Supply Chain Research... 445
Andreas Größler, Nadine Schieritz

Analysis of Supply Chain Dynamics through Object Oriented Simulation 461
Francesco Casella, Giovanni Miragliotta, Luigi Uglietti

The Potential of Cooperative Game Theory for Supply Chain Management 477
Jörn-Henrik Thun

Modeling the Effect of Product Architecture Modularity in Supply Chains 493
Juliana H. Mikkola

Heuristics in the Multi-Location Inventory System with Transshipments 509
Lars Magne Nonås, Kurt Jörnsten

Contract Typology as a Research Method in Supply Chain Management 525
Alejandra Gomez-Padilla, Jeanne Duvallet, Daniel Llerena

Load Dependent Lead Times – From Empirical Evidence to
Mathematical Modeling 539
Julia Pahl, Stefan Voß, David L. Woodruff

Recovery Network Design for End-of-Life Vehicles 555
Heinz Ahn, Jens Keilen, Rainer Souren

Modeling and Integrated Assessment of Mass and Energy Flows within
Supply Chains 571
Jutta Geldermann, Martin Treitz, Hannes Schollenberger, Otto Rentz

Socrates Thematic Network to Enhance European Teaching and Research of
Operations as well as Supply Chain Management 587
*José A. D. Machuca, Rafaela Alfalla Luque, Macarena Sacristán Díaz,
Gerald Reiner*

Editors 593
Authors 595

Is There a Right Research Design for Your Supply Chain Study?

Stefan Seuring, Martin Müller, Gerald Reiner, Herbert Kotzab

1   Introduction 2
2   Substantive Justification for Theory Building 3
3   Surveys in Supply Chain Management 5
4   Case Study Research in Supply Chains 6
5   Action Research in Supply Chains 7
6   Modelling Supply Chains 8
7   Future Implications for Supply Chain Management Research 10
8   References 11

Summary:
The field of Supply Chain Management has seen rapid advances in recent years. However, questions of how to conduct empirical research are rarely addressed. This volume brings together a number of papers that address both how different research techniques can be applied in conducting research on and in supply chains. As it is shown in this book, the discipline seems to adapt Stock's (1997) suggestion of borrowing by applying a huge variety of research methods in order to study the phenomena of and in supply chains. It also seems that new approaches to empirical research have to be used in order to explore the full meaning of supply chain management. This also means that the applied methods reach beyond the established techniques. This introduction offers some insights into the overall contribution of the papers. Therefore, the structure of this paper mirrors the subsequent sections of the book.

Keywords:
Supply Chain Management, Research Methodology, Theory Building, Models, Survey, Case Study, Action Research

1 Introduction

The heading of this introduction to this collection of papers is a modification Fisher's (1997) classic on supply chain management. Looking at the number of courses thought at business schools, the interest of practioners in the subject and also the number of publications in a wide range of journals, we can argue that supply chain management has come to prominence and can now be called an established concept within management. However, looking at the research level of the discipline, we identified an exciting matter. Interestingly, when we first came about discussing which research methodologies that are used in our research on supply chain management, we realized, that there are hardly any publications on methodological questions in the field. It seems obvious that related research builds on the "usual suspects", such as (Mitroff et al., 1974) for model building, Dillman (1978; 2000) for surveys, Yin (2003) for case study research, or Argyris et al. (1990) for action research, as there is a multitude of further references to draw from.

This raises the question, whether there is a need do develop research methods further so that they in particular deal with supply chain management issues. Or, if this is expressed the other way round, what are key characteristics of supply chain management research that require modified or extended methods. Yet, research methodologies are at the hard of any kind of research, which has let to a multitude of related textbooks for business and management research (e.g. Brewerton & Millward, 2001; Cooper & Schindler, 2003; Saunders et al., 2003).

Furthermore, in all kind of functional research fields, like Operations Management, where specific papers have provided guidance on how research methodologies can be applies. One recent example is the special issues of the International Journal of Operations & Production Management (2002, Vol. 22, No. 2; containing a paper each on surveys: Forza, 2002; case studies: Voss et al., 2002; action research: Coughlan & Coghlan, 2002; and quantitative modeling: Bertrand & Fransoo, 2002).

Additionally papers exist, on how a wider set of research methods can be applied, e.g. in logistics (Mentzer & Kahn, 1995), or operations management (Flynn et al., 1991). So the questions remains, whether there is a real need for further development in research methodologies towards supply chain management? Stock (1997) might have an answer to this, as he suggests to borrow theories from other disciplines. In fact, this can also be interpreted for a call of applying a variety of research methodologies in order to answer the research questions of our discipline.

We might end up with the question of what supply chain management is: a tool, a concept, a theory? In their recent paper, Chen & Paulraj (2004) opt for the wording theory. Yet, it might be too early to call the current status of knowledge in supply chain management a theory.

Which means, that Supply Chain Management is not only an umbrella term for different understandings of the concept, but also allows the application of different research methodologies. The papers in this volume provide evidence that there is no right or wrong supply chain management research methodology. Hence, every research method has its merits in its own, if applied "rigorously". The results rather show the broad-mindedness of the field towards research methodologies.

The remainder of this chapter will provide an overview of the papers presented in the book. They are arranged into five tracks, which will be used to structure this chapter. They are primarily organized according to certain research methodologies:

1. Substantive Justification for Theory Building,
2. Surveys in Supply Chain Management,
3. Case Study Research in Supply Chains,
4. Action Research in Supply Chains,
5. Modelling Supply Chains.

It is acknowledged, that some papers might have been grouped in a different way. This is in particular true for papers providing empirical evidence collected with different methods.

2 Substantive Justification for Theory Building

The section on substantive justification for theory building by literature reviews contains a total of seven papers, which comprise both more methodology related discussions on how research in supply chain management can be conducted, but also provide first examples. These comprise more conceptual contributions as well as more review oriented ones.

As the first paper, Golicic, Davis & McCarthy discuss "A Balanced Approach to Research in Supply Chain Management". It is evident, that a more deductive quantitative and a more inductive qualitative research have both its advantages and shortcomings. In every kind of empirical research trade-offs between control, realism and generalizability have to be made. Therefore, they describe a double cycle research process, where the two approaches are balanced.

A further introductory paper by Van Donk & Van der Vaart offer "A Critical Discussion on the Theoretical and Methodological Advancements in Supply Chain Integration". While the focus is more on a critical assessment of related research, the later part of the paper addresses, how research on supply chain integration can be conducted applying different empirical methods, where specially a multi-case study design is argued for, which might have advantages compared to both a survey or a single case study approach.

Boon-iit & Paul provide an approach for "Measuring Supply Chain Intergration – Using the Q-sort Technique", thereby contribution the single empirical paper in this section. This paper uses a method not often applied in business research, but valuable to address the multi-dimensionality of a construct. It allows to organize single subjective judgments and form a description of an indescribable object.

Methodological issues are again at the core of Johannessens paper. "Supply Chain Management and the Challenge of Organizational Complexity: Methodological Considerations" offers a critical appraisal of logistical systems thinking. While it is frequently named to be at the core of logistical thought, it does not allow to assess organizational change phenomena. Contrastingly, organizational complexity thought is much better able to describe processes of social interaction, but this requires a different ontological position.

Ever since the classical paper of Fisher on the right design of your supply chain, research on "The Configurational Approach in Supply Chain Management" is taken up in Nehers paper. Hence, major contributions to these stream of research are presented. This allows to point of the underlying dimensions, which are then used to suggest a wider, more holistic approach, which is able to integrate previous research.

The section is concluded by two literature reviews, which both present how such reviews might be conducted in a structured way. For a complete review of published research, the issues addressed has to be delimited, as Seuring, Müller & Westhaus outline this in "Conducting a Literature Review - The Example of Sustainability in Supply Chains". Vairous restrictions had to be taken into account to reduce the number of papers reviewed to a suitable and manageable number. This prepares the ground for conducting a content analysis, where both quantitative and qualitative issues of the body of research are assessed.

In a similar manner, Halldorsson & Arlbjørn look at "Research Methodologies in Supply Chain Management – What Do We Know?". One of their major delimitations comes from concentrating on three journals and analyzing, what kind of research methodologies have been published in the respective papers on supply chain management. A particular glimpse is taken at the research methodologies used in the papers. Overall, several limitation of previous research are pointed out.

3 Surveys in Supply Chain Management

A total of seven papers make up this section of the book. This includes critical reviews, method development as well as several applications of survey research.

Kotzab starts the section with a look at "The Role and Importance of Survey Research Methods in the Field of Supply Chain Management", which builds on a meta-analysis of papers published in the Journal of Business Logistics between 1993 and 2003. Thereby, Kotzab is able to identify the typical research design, but also reveals several weaknesses of published research, as quite often basic information, such as the kind of questionnaire used or the sample size is missing.

Grant, Teller & Teller discuss the development of a rather new method of data collection. Their paper on "Web-Based Surveys in Logistics Research: An Empirical Application" outlines and illustrates, how the internet can be used in collecting data. This has several methodological, but also technological advantages compared to more traditional "paper-bound" techniques. Still, they mention, that even though they research on IT-related companies, some problems similar to postal surveys (e.g. response rate) were encountered.

With the next paper by Giménez-Thomsen, Large & Ventura on "Supply Chain Management Research Methodologies – Employing Structural Equation Modeling", the move is towards specific techniques and their application in supply chain research. The paper outlines the basics of structural equation modeling and how it can be applied, as it is typically used to analyze relationships among abstract concepts.

Wallenburg & Weber use the same technique in their paper "Structural Equation Modelling as a Basis for Theory Development within Logistics and Supply Chain Management Research". As with other research methods, survey research can not only be used for theory testing, but also for theory development. This is one key point in their paper, which deals with a conceptual framework for the impact of logistics on overall firm performance.

A third paper applying structural equation modeling is presented by Jaafar & Rafiq on "Customers' Perceptions of Third Party Logistics Service Provider in the United Kingdom". The main aim is to test the logistics service quality instrument. Thereby they use a replication logic building on the original work of Mentzer et al. (1999), who developed the concept.

Related both in content and research method applied, Setthakaset & Basnet discuss "Third Party Logistics in Thailand –From the Users' Perspective". While the previous study is based on UK data, this one presents data from Thailand, a developing country, where the 3PL approach has not received so much attention so far. The strive for competitive advantage contributes much more to companies outsourcing activities than cost reduction. These findings are in line, with the one of Wallenburg and Weber reported earlier on in this volume.

In a further survey paper Günther & Klauke present "A Market-oriented View of SCM – Criteria and Instruments in the Public Procurement Process". So far, supply chain management for public authorities has not received much attention. Yet, specific legal requirements as well as related organizational issues justify to explore the implication of supply chain management in such a context. Therefore, Günther & Klauke offer insights into the public procurement process and show, how specially information deficits in the early market research phase hinder future developments.

4   Case Study Research in Supply Chains

Among the seven papers in this section, three are rather "pure" case study papers, while the further three provide examples, where case study research is mixed with survey research. This is particularly valuable, as it allows to overcome the weaknesses of a particular research approach and enrich the data collection and analysis. This should allow for the research finding to rest on a wider basis.

The first paper by Seuring on "Case Study Research in Supply Chains" is a mixture of some basics on case study research. Structuring the research process allows to conduct rigorous research. Three brief examples how case study research in supply chain management, all taken from the textile industry, are then presented, where each stage of the research process is briefly described.

McCarthy & Golicic write on "Interfirm Demand Integration – A Case Study of Supply Chain Integration Processes". In a first step, they present a conceptual framework for interfirm demand integration, which is informed by various theories. Against this background, three cases are presented which center on a focal firm but where further data has been collect at suppliers and customers. All stages of the research process are documented against guidelines offered in literature, such as Stuart et al. (2002).

Next, Koulikoff-Souviron & Harrison deal with "Designing Robust Comparative Research on Inter- and Intra-Firm Supply Relationships". Also based on some methodological underpinnings on case research. This includes a meta-analysis of nine case study papers recently published in the Journal of Operations Management (2002-2004). Furthermore, they offer insights into pitfalls encountered during their research on inter- and intra-firm supply relationships, which will be helpful for other researchers in avoiding them.

Oosterhuis, Mollemann & Van der Vaart aim to point at "Multilevel Issues in Supply Chain Management (SCM)", which forms a piece of conceptual research that is related to case study research. The authors related to three levels, a theoretical/conceptual one, a methodological one and an analytic one. These levels are then related to aspects of human behavior in supply chain management, which have great impact on supply chain performance.

The paper by Chivaka on "Strategic Cost Management along the Supply Chain – Implications for Empirical Research Methods" mainly presents data collected in the South African textile and food industries. A survey was used to pre-inform the research and collect first data. Further material was collect through interviews, personal observation and document analysis. This allowed to identify, how different cost management techniques are used in the three "three-stage" supply chains studied.

One example, where case study research and surveys are mixed is opened by Giménez-Thomsen, who writes on "SCM Research: Case Studies and Surveys – Two Complementary Methodologies". This paper explicitly discusses how the two different methods can be used to complement each other building on research in the Spanish grocery sector.

Bak also writes on "Towards Triangulation – Blending Techniques in Supply Chain Management Context" and build on case and survey research". In this case, first case study research was conducted on the use of the internet and B2B-commerce in automotive supply chains. This informed a subsequent survey in the same sector aiming to access the changes triggered by the use of e-business applications.

5 Action Research in Supply Chains

Action research is still not so much used in business and management research. Quite often, researchers might be involved in some kind of action research or action learning project without really being aware of it. While four papers deal with action research and action learning explicitly, Prockl's paper implicitly related to it, so it is also contained in this section.

As a start of the section, Müller "Action Research – An Introduction" provides first insights on action research and its historical roots. Further, he points towards the underpinning within the philosophy of science, which are relevant for action research.

Middel, Brennan, Coghlan & Coghlan present in their paper "The Application of Action Learning and Action Research in Collaborative Improvement within the Extended Manufacturing Enterprise", how action research can help in implementing collaborative improvements. As it is also wrought with difficulties, the authors pay attention to the accumulation and development of knowledge of capabilities for learning improvement between organizations.

Koplin writes on "Integrating Sustainability into Purchasing – Developing an Implementation Concept by Using Action Research". Thereby, she builds on a project conducted in the automotive industry. Within this project, a concept was developed, that allows for integrating environmental and social standards into purchasing.

Prockl's paper on "Supply Chain Diagnostics to Confront Theory and Practice" forms part of this section as it reports the results of a project, where researchers and consultants exchanged with practitioners. The aim is to design a tools that allows to diagnose the weak spots of a supply chain. Such practical developments question the underlying theoretical constructs. This is fruitful for both theory reflection and empirical tests.

Bichou & Gray provide a further example with "Logistics and supply chain management approach to seaport efficiency: An inquiry based on action research methodology". Action research is used to present port managers and other experts with a model of port performance appropriate to the role of ports in a logistics and supply chain context.

6 Modelling Supply Chains

This section focuses on the development of quantitative models in the field of supply chain management research. management. A total of ten papers make up this section of the book, which explore a wide array of research issues and quantitative research methods, e.g., systems dynamics, agent-based simulation, object-oriented modeling, discrete event simulation, optimization problems, game theory and queuing networks.

The first contribution is an article, by Reiner on "Supply Chain Management Research Methodology Using Quantitative Models Based on Empirical Data", which describes the importance of empirical quantitative model-driven research methodologies in supply chain management. Furthermore, the relevance of discrete-event simulation models for modeling supply chain risks based on empirical distribution and aspects of mixed model research are discussed. Finally an overview based on the most relevant literature in this field is presented how to conduct empirical quantitative model-driven research.

Within the next article Größler & Schieritz write on "Of Stocks, Flows, Agents and Rules – "Strategic" Simulations in Supply Chain Research" and explores how strategic simulation experiments try to combine the advantages of mathematical modeling with the practical relevance and external validity of empirical research. The approach is demonstrated by a combination of systems dynamics and agent-based simulation in new way. With this simulation model they are able to test the stability of supply chain structures under different levels of uncertainty, in particular stochastic demand.

Supply chain dynamics plays also a major role in the third contribution "Analysis of Supply Chain Dynamics through Object Oriented Simulation". Casella, Miragliotta & Uglietti explain how Modelica, a well-acknowledged modeling language for traditional engineering applications, can be usefully applied to the study of supply chain dynamics. Furthermore, the bullwhip effect for a very simple supply chain was simulated, but all the objects needed to build much more complex models have been developed and illustrated as well.

In the fourth article Thun elaborates on "The Potential of Cooperative Game Theory for Supply Chain Management" and discusses the aspect of profit allocation within Supply Chain Management in the light of cooperative game theory. The illustration analyses example show that cooperative game theory has a great potential to explore cooperation within Supply Chain Management. Furthermore the results should support the development of improved contracts between the supply chain partners.

Subsequently, Mikkola presents in her paper on "Modeling the Effect of Product Architecture Modularity in Supply Chains" ways to mathematical model the effect of product architecture modularity in supply chains at two levels of analyses respectively model settings: supply chain level and focal firm level. Finally, in order to illustrate how the models can be applied, a case example from the automotive industry is presented.

Nonås & Jörnsten write on "Heuristics in the Multi-Location Inventory System with Transshipments" propose a greedy transshipment policy for a multi-location inventory system with transshipments. The usage of an ordering policy based on a greedy transshipment policy is suggested for large problem instances where the computational complexity is intractable; because numerical examples show a near-optimal performance of this heuristic while the solution time can be reduced.

The seventh article, by Gomez-Padilla, Duvallet & Llerena, studies contractual relations in "Contract Typology as a Research Method in Supply Chain Management". The basic elements for understanding and describing a contractual relation have been identified. Then present also a mathematical model of the relationship between an upstream and a downstream supply chain partner.

Pahl, Voß & Woodruff, survey and suggest optimization models that take into account "Load Dependent Lead Times – From Empirical Evidence to Mathematical Modeling". The approach of modeling clearing functions is outlined to deal with load dependent lead times. This approach is implemented in a stochastic framework by using queuing models with the purpose of integrating the problem of stochastic demand and in order to analyze the behavior of load dependent lead times.

Ahn, Keilen & Souren take up the challenge of "Recovery Network Design for End-of-Life Vehicles" and focuses on the specific requirements posed by recovery and recycling regulation in the German automotive industry. Furthermore an optimization approach was developed for solving facility location problems with regard to the positioning of different participants of the automotive recovery network. In order to validate the network structure, an additional discrete event simulation model was developed. The main emphasis is on the interaction of the simulation model and the optimization approach.

Last but not least in this section, Geldermann, Treitz, Schollenberger & Rentz present a paper on "Modeling and Integrated Assessment of Mass and Energy Flows within Supply Chains". They develop a techno-economic approach for modeling and integrated assessment of mass and energy flows in supply chains and stress the importance of considering the technical scope.

As additional information, there is a short introduction to THNEXOM (European Thematic Network for the Excellence in Operations and Supply Chain Management, Education, Research and Practice) by Machuca, Alfalla, Sacristán, Reiner. The network investigates research and teaching in those subjects in European Universities.

7 Future Implications for Supply Chain Management Research

This book brings together a total of 36 papers, which cover a wide range of issues on research methodologies in supply chain management. However, we assess the results rather as the start than the end of related developments in Supply Chain Management research. We strongly believe that for developing research methodologies researchers in the field have to account for new conceptual and theoretical developments. Hence, we look forward to future examples of (empirical) research on supply chain management, where innovative approaches are applied to further our understanding of supply chain management and related issues.

As the papers in this book use all different kinds of research designs, it is straight forward that there is no simple answer to the question raised in the heading. Every methodology has its pros and cons. Hence, there is no simple answer to the question raised as heading of this introduction.

8 References

Argyris, C., Putman, R., McLain, D. (1990): Action science, 3rd print, Jossey-Bass, San Francisco.

Bertrand, J. W. M., Fransoo, J. C. (2002): Operations Management Research Methodologies using quantitative Modelling, in: International Journal of Operations & Production Management, 22(2): 241-264.

Brewerton, P., Millward, L. (2001): Organisational Research Methods, Sage, London.

Chen, I. J., Paulraj, A. (2004): Towards a Theory of Supply Chain Management – The Constructs and Measurement, in: Journal of Operations Management, 22(2): 119-150.

Cooper, M. C., Lambert, D. M., Pagh, J. D. (1997): Supply Chain Management: More than a new name for Logistics, in: The International Journal of Logistics Management, 8(1): 1-14.

Cooper, D. R., Schindler, P. S. (2003): Business Research Methods, 8th edition, McGrawHill, Boston.

Coughlan, P., Coghlan, D. (2002): Action Research for Operations Management, in: International Journal of Operations & Production Management, 22(2): 220-240.

Croom, S., Romano, P., Giannakis, M. (2000): Supply Chain Management: An Analytical Framework for Critical Literature Review, in: European Journal of Purchasing & Supply Management, 6(1): 67-83.

Dillman, D. A. (1978): Mail and Telephone Survey – The Design Method, Wiley & Sons, New York.

Dillman, D. (2000): Mail and Internet Surveys. The Tailored Design Method, Wiley, New York.

Handfield, R. B., Nichols, E. L. (1999): Introduction to Supply Chain Management, Prentice-Hall, New Jersey.

Fisher, M. L. (1997): What is the right Supply Chain for Your Product?, in: Harvard Business Review, 75(2): 105-116.

Flynn, B. B., Sakakibara, S., Schroeder, R., Bates, K. A., Flynn, E. J. (1991): Empirical Research Methods in Operations Management, in:Journal of Operations Management, 9(2): 250-284

Forza, C. (2002): Survey Research in Operations Management: A Process-based Perspective, in: International Journal of Operations & Production Management, 22(2): 152-194.

Mayring, P. (2002): Einführung in die qualitative Sozialforschung – eine Anleitung zum qualitativen Denken (Introduction in Qualitative Social Research), Beltz Verlag, Weinheim und Basel.

Mayring, P. (2003): Qualitative Inhaltanalyse – Grundlagen und Techniken (Qualitative Content Analysis – Basics and Techniques), 8. Edition, Beltz Verlag, Weinheim.

Mentzer, J. T., Kahn, K. B. (1995): A Framework of Logistics Research, in: Journal of Business Logistics, 16 (1): 231-250.

Mentzer, J. T., Flint, D. J. & Hult, T. M. (2001): Logistics Service Quality as a Segment-Customised Process, in: Journal of Marketing, 65(4): 82-104.

Meredith, J. (1993): Theory Building through Conceptual Methods, in: International Journal of Operations & Production Management, 13(5): 3-11.

Mitroff, I., Betz, F., Pondy, L. Sagasti, F. (1974): On Managing Science in the Systems Age: Two Schemas for the Study of Science as whole Systems Phenomenon, in: Interfaces, 4(3): 46-58.

Otto, A., Kotzab, H. (2001): Der Beitrag des Supply Chain Managements zum Management von Supply Chains – Überlegungen zu einer unpopulären Frage (How Supply Chain Management Contributes to the Management of Supply Chains - Preliminary Thoughts on an Unpopular Question), in: Zeitschrift für betriebswirtschaftliche Forschung, 53(3): 157-176.

Saunders, M., Lewis, P., Thornhill, A. (2003): Research Methods for Business Students, Prentice Hall, Harlow.

Schary, P., Skjøtt-Larsen, T. (2001): Managing the Global Supply Chain, 2nd edition, Copenhagen Business School Press, Copenhagen.

Stuart, I., Mc Cutcheon, D., Handfield, R., McLachlin, R., Samson, D. (2002): Effective Case Research in Operations Management: A Process Perspective, in: Journal of Operations Management, 20(5): 419-433.

Voss, C., Tsikriktsis, N., Frohlich, M. (2002): Case Research in Operations Management, in. International Journal of Operations & Production Management, 22(2): 195-219.

Yin, R. (2003): Case Study Research – Design and Methods, 3rd edition, Sage, Thousand Oaks.

Part 1
Substantive Justification for Theory Building

A Balanced Approach to Research in Supply Chain Management

Susan L. Golicic, Donna F. Davis, Teresa M. McCarthy

1 Introduction 16
2 Qualitative Research in Logistics and Supply Chain Management 17
3 The Balanced Approach 19
4 Discussion 24
5 References 27

Summary:
When choosing a research strategy, there are tradeoffs in control, realism and generalizability. Quantitative research methods optimize control and generalizability (external validity), while qualitative research maximizes realism (internal validity). Logistics scholars agree that logistics and supply chain management are steeped in the positivist paradigm and that past research is primarily normative and quantitative. An imbalance exists in the conduct and publishing of rigorous qualitative research studies such as grounded theory, ethnography, phenomenology, semiotics, and historical analysis. At the same time, the business environment in which logistics and supply chain phenomena are located is becoming increasingly complex and less amenable to using just a quantitative approach. In order to accurately describe, truly understand and begin to explain these complex phenomena, research streams should include more studies using qualitative methods. Researchers who exclusively choose one approach or the other seriously delimit the scope of their inquiry and, thereby, their ability to contribute to the body of knowledge.

Keywords:
Supply Chain Management, Inductive Methodologies, Deductive Methodologies, Grounded Theory, Content Analysis, Survey Research, Structural Equation Modeling

1 Introduction

"All research strategies and methods are seriously flawed, often with their very strengths in regard to one desideratum functioning as serious weaknesses in regard to other, equally important, goals" (McGrath, 1982: 70). McGrath goes on to describe tradeoffs in control, realism and generalizability when choosing a research strategy. Quantitative research methods optimize control and generalizability (external validity), while qualitative research maximizes realism (internal validity). Creswell (1998) offers a photograph analogy to illustrate this tradeoff: quantitative research is a wide-angle lens or panoramic shot, while qualitative research presents a close-up view. In order to truly understand and explain a phenomenon, it is necessary to see both views, or as McGrath argues, different problems demand different kinds of choices.

In 1995, Mentzer & Kahn published a framework of logistics research, which followed the positivistic tradition in their description of formulating hypotheses and testing for validity. They summarized the current state of logistics research, primarily published in North American journals, and found it to be heavily quantitative. This finding propelled them to call for more two-study research designs to balance the need for internal and external validity. Näslund (2002) echoed this when stating that both quantitative and qualitative research is needed since all research questions cannot be solved with the same approach.

Scholars agree that logistics and supply chain management are steeped in the positivist paradigm and that past research published in the top, North American journals is primarily normative (theoretical models and literature reviews) and quantitative (modeling and surveys). An imbalance exists in the conduct and publishing of rigorous qualitative research studies such as grounded theory, ethnography, phenomenology, semiotics, and historical analysis. At the same time, the business environment in which logistics and supply chain phenomena are located is becoming increasingly complex and less amenable to using just one type of research approach. In order to accurately describe, truly understand and begin to explain these complex phenomena (such as outsourcing, business-to-business relationships, strategic sourcing, demand management, etc.), research streams should include more studies using multiple methods. Researchers who exclusively choose one approach or the other seriously delimit the scope of their inquiry and, thereby, their ability to contribute to the body of knowledge. There is a need for a more balanced approach to research using inductive research methods (typically qualitative) in addition to deductive methods (typically quantitative) in supply chain management.

The purpose of this paper is to propose a model for a balanced approach to knowledge and to offer guidelines and illustrations for implementing such an approach in supply chain management research. In addition, specific examples of the implementation of the balanced approach in empirical supply chain studies will be described demonstrating the importance of the use of multiple methods. The paper concludes with suggestions for increased implementation of the balanced approach in supply chain management disciplines (i.e., logistics, operations, marketing, etc.).

2 Qualitative Research in Logistics and Supply Chain Management

Qualitative research is best described as a category of research methods rather than a single research framework. Creswell (1998: 13) describes the qualitative approach as "an intricate fabric composed of minute threads, many colors, different textures, and various blends of materials." Studies have shown minimal use of these methods in supply chain management disciplines.

Mentzer & Kahn (1995) reviewed publications in the Journal of Business Logistics (JBL) through 1993. The Journal of Business Logistics is one of the top publications in the logistics discipline. Näslund (2002) reviewed more recent issues of JBL as well as the International Journal of Physical Distribution and Logistics Management (IJPDLM) and the International Journal of Logistics Management (IJLM), but does not provide the results other than the finding that 7% of the articles were based on case studies. Halldorsson et al. (2004) examined only supply chain management articles in these same journals from 1997 through 2004; only 8 of 71 employed qualitative methods. Kotzab (2005) also extended the Mentzer & Kahn review through 2003 and found that quantitative research, primarily surveys, was still the majority in both these journals as well as in German journals. [Transportation and production/operations journals were not examined, as their focus is by nature very quantitative, so it was not expected to find higher usage of qualitative methods than in those journals reviewed. Language issues and limited access to country specific journals prohibited reviews of these as well.

We reviewed all of these journals plus the proceedings from the Logistics Educators Conference (LEC) and Supply Chain Management: An International Journal (SCM) for the time period following Mentzer & Kahn's review (1994-2004). While the use of qualitative research techniques such as interviews to clarify concepts or develop survey measures may be increasing, Table 1 shows that the percentage of qualitative studies published in these journals is still very low. These are studies that follow rigorous qualitative methods, i.e., the specific philosophical tradition and guidelines for the particular methodology (e.g., Yin (1994) for case studies or Strauss & Corbin (1998) for grounded theory). The application of concepts or models in particular contexts or brief interviews prior to survey development is frequently called qualitative research (i.e., a case study); however, the methodology followed is rarely described in the publication. Therefore, while a qualitative technique is used, it is not considered to be rigorous qualitative research so these are shown separately. Although SCM reports a high number of case studies* (102 total), a random sample of these articles (10%) were read and none of them employed a rigorous case study methodology making this large number suspect.

Journal	Total Articles	Qualitative Studies	Qual Technique Applied
JBL	234	4.7%	9.8%
IJPDLM	431	4.2%	8.6%
IJLM	169	4.1%	4.1%
LEC Proceedings	132	4.5%	3.0%
SCM	236	36.0%*	5.9%

Table 1: Qualitative Research in Major Logistics Journals (1994-2004)

In 2002, two issues of IJPDLM were devoted to research using qualitative methods. This was done, according to the editor's note, "in the hopes that it would stimulate further use in logistics research." There is recognition in the discipline that logistics is dominated by quantitative research and that more qualitative research is needed. When discussing this with attendees of the 2004 Research Workshop on Research Methodologies in Supply Chain Management at the University of Oldenburg, it was concluded that research in Europe relies much more heavily on qualitative methods than in North America. However, many scholars still do not see the value of qualitative research due to the tradition of positivism in logistics.

Research methods are grounded in philosophical traditions that stem from the researcher's paradigm or, "basic set of beliefs that guides action" (Guba, 1990: 17). These traditions differ among the various quantitative and qualitative research methods. For example, realist paradigms (empiricists, positivists) view reality as existing in the objective world external to the individual while interpretivist paradigms (relativists, existentialists) view it much more subjectively, existing in individuals as they construct it (Flint et al., 1999). These beliefs or traditions then drive how a researcher obtains knowledge. It is therefore understandable how one set of methods dominates research in a discipline if that discipline has been dominated by one philosophical tradition.

Much of how scholars view the world is a product of their training. In doctoral programs, students are exposed primarily to the traditions that exist in their disciplines – those followed by the researchers they train under and those published in the top journals. Because logistics has followed the positivist paradigm, most North American logistics scholars receive little training in interpretivist or qualitative research methods. The situation in European programs is rarely better as many programs do not offer formal training in any research methods (these programs are generally focused on producing Ph.D.s for industry).

Publishing is a key component for the advance of a discipline. Because established scholars (e.g., university faculty, journal editors and reviewers) in logistics have followed a history of positivism, the traditions and methods of positivism are more accepted for publication, particularly in North American journals. The small amount of qualitative research that has been published in logistics and operations journals supports this. As Näslund (2002: 327) points out, it is therefore easier for younger researchers to "follow the paved way."

Qualitative and quantitative research approaches are not substitutes for one another; rather they observe different aspects of the same reality (McCracken, 1988). However, the two approaches represent very different intellectual frames of mind. Students of one tradition will not be able to master the other by just learning a few methodological techniques. "Learning the qualitative tradition will require the absorption of new assumptions and ways of seeing. It will require new strategies of conceptualizing research problems and data," (McCracken, 1988). This is also true for quantitative methods. This learning needs to begin in doctoral programs related to supply chain management. Education in qualitative AND quantitative research methods should be required as part of these programs. To then promote the application of these methods, the discipline should reward their use through increased acceptance of multiple approaches in research studies, using rigorous qualitative and/or quantitative methods. As Näslund (2002: 328) noted, "If logistics academics want to lead rather than follow practitioners then we must gain extreme relevance in our research." In order to do this, research studies need to utilize qualitative methods in addition to quantitative methods. Future scholars must therefore be trained in both qualitative and quantitative methods, and both must be accepted in the major logistics and supply chain management publications.

3 The Balanced Approach

Imagine two views of a university campus: one is an overhead snapshot taken from an airplane and the other is a ground level video created by a student as she goes about her daily routine. Which provides better information? Obviously, it depends on what you want to know about the campus. Similarly, deductive (typically quantitative) and inductive (typically qualitative) approaches to research provide different views of logistics and supply chain phenomena. Which approach provides better information? Again, it depends on what you want to know about the phenomenon.

At the heart of logistics and supply chain research is the researcher's idea or question about a particular phenomenon (see Figure 1). Once the phenomenon is identified, the researcher sharpens the focus of the proposed study by developing research questions. The choice of research approach (i.e., quantitative and/or qualitative) should depend on what the researcher wants to know as determined by the nature of the phenomenon and the type of research questions. The following sections describe the steps on each path and the integration of these paths in a program of research.

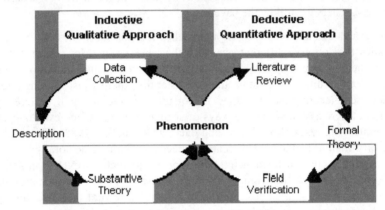

Figure 1: The Balanced Approach Model (Adapted from Woodruff 2003)

3.1 The Qualitative Path

Various terms are used to denote the qualitative research approach such as naturalistic, humanistic, and interpretive. Overlaying these methodological frameworks are traditions of inquiry arising from specific disciplines such as the anthropologist's ethnography, the psychologist's phenomenological interview, and the sociologist's grounded theory. Each methodological framework and disciplinary tradition of inquiry is accompanied by a set of philosophical understandings, tools, and standards for rigor.

Because the aim of the qualitative approach is to "understand the phenomenon in its own terms" (Hirshman, 1986), the first step on the qualitative path is data collection. Typically, the researcher makes several field visits to observe the phenomenon in a natural setting in order to begin to frame an understanding. Researchers who adopt the qualitative approach are interested in first-hand learning about everyday experiences from the informant's perspective, rooted in the philosophical assumption that "knowledge is in the meanings people make of it;

knowledge is gained through people talking about their meanings" (Creswell, 1998: 19). The use of relevant literature does not appear as a separate stage in the qualitative path because it is embedded in various stages of the qualitative approach, depending on the tradition and methodological framework. Although the use of literature varies across traditions, in all cases the substantive theory produced by the qualitative approach emerges from the data rather than the literature.

The second step in the qualitative path is to describe the phenomenon from the point of view of the informants. Qualitative research is designed to explore the deep structure of the phenomenon using "thick" descriptions that explore the multiple dimensions and properties of the phenomenon. Descriptions are generated using qualitative techniques such as asking open-ended questions and examining multiple data sources (Hirschman, 1986), which can take the form of interviews, observations, documents, and audiovisual materials (Maxwell, 1996). Both the data and research design evolve as the researcher gains a first-hand understanding of the phenomenon.

Building a substantive theory -- a theory of the phenomenon -- from descriptive data is the next step in the qualitative path. Qualitative data is analyzed working inductively from detailed parts to more general perspectives that may be called categories, themes, dimensions, or codes, depending on the analytical method prescribed by the methodology selected by the researcher. The analysis yields a substantive theory of the phenomenon, which is typically a process model describing relationships among variables with feedback loops that capture the dynamic nature of the phenomenon. "These relationships emerge late in the study after the researcher exhaustively describes a single idea" (Creswell, 1998: 21), bringing the researcher full-circle to a deeper understanding of the core phenomenon.

3.2 The Quantitative Path

As described previously, the quantitative approach dominates research in logistics and supply chain phenomena. Like the qualitative approach, the quantitative approach is identified with several paradigm terms such as positivism, logical empiricism, and realism. These frameworks are also overlaid by disciplinary traditions such as economics, marketing and psychology. The goal of the quantitative approach is to add to the body of knowledge by building formal theory that explains, predicts and controls the phenomenon of interest.

The first step in the quantitative path is to review appropriate literature in order to develop a conceptual framework that specifies relevant variables and expected relationships among them (Bickman & Rog, 1998). While the researcher may also enter the field to conduct interviews at this stage, it is often for the purpose of developing and refining measures or clarifying the variables and relationships among them rather than generating the conceptual framework as is the case with the qualitative approach.

The next step is to build a formal theory grounded in previous research. Formal theories are general; that is, they "apply to many phenomena and to many people in many places" (Kerlinger & Lee, 2000). The formal theory developed in the quantitative path should be capable of generating predictive statements that can be tested by confronting the theory with real-world data about the phenomenon (Hunt, 1991). Before collecting data, the researcher proposes answers to research questions in the form of hypotheses arising from the theory. These hypotheses are generated through deductive reasoning; that is, the researcher begins with the general view (i.e., the theory) and then moves to particulars in the form of data.

In the third step, data is collected through carefully constructed measurement instruments administered in field surveys or experiments. The purpose of data collection is to verify the formal theory by testing the significance and strength of proposed relationships among the variables expressed in the hypotheses (e.g., increased trust between trading partners increases relationship commitment). The conclusion of a quantitative study brings the researcher full-circle to a higher level of understanding and explanation of the phenomenon, generating more questions to be answered in future research.

3.3 Choosing a Research Approach

When the phenomenon of interest is new, dynamic or complex, relevant variables are not easily identified and extant theories are not available to explain the phenomenon (Creswell, 1998). In this situation, a qualitative approach is often preferred in order to build understanding grounded in a detailed description of the phenomenon generated by collecting field data. The qualitative approach provides researchers with access to deeper levels of understanding of new or complex phenomena by yielding a high level of detail -- a "close-up" view of the topic (Creswell, 1998). For example, the new phenomenon of homeland security regulations in supply chain management would be an appropriate topic for the qualitative approach. Before we can accurately measure the impact of this phenomenon, we must first identify and understand the relevant variables.

Context is intrinsic to the phenomenon in the qualitative approach; therefore, phenomena that involve the exploration of well-known concepts in new contexts (e.g., What is the meaning of "brands" in the supply chain context?) are also a good match for qualitative methods. Qualitative research questions often start with "how" or "what" indicating the researcher's aim to describe a process (e.g., What is the nature of change in a customer's desired value?).

On the other hand, phenomena that have been fully described and documented through previous research frequently lend themselves to a quantitative approach. In this case, the researcher can confidently turn to the literature to identify relevant variables, discover gaps in our understanding that need further attention, and develop measures for research instruments. Research questions aimed at explaining relationships among variables by examining variation are ideal for the quantitative approach (Creswell, 1998). The researcher may want to evaluate the direction or strength of relationships, or determine cause and effect (e.g., Does trust between trading partners increase with the length of the relationship?). These questions aim to determine the degree of variability in the phenomenon by asking "why" or "to what extent." As described subsequently, the quantitative approach allows the researcher to step away from the data in order to develop a more general explanation of the phenomenon, that is, to take a look at the "big picture" in order to build a formal theory.

Another way to think about choosing a research approach is to consider a typical conceptual model comprised of boxes representing variables and arrows signifying relationships among the variables. The purpose of the qualitative approach is to understand the boxes while the focus of the quantitative approach is to explain the arrows. Before choosing a research approach, the researcher is advised to seriously consider the question, "How much do we (the discipline) know about this phenomenon?" If the answer implies the research focus should be "up close" in order to develop an understanding of new or complex phenomena, then the qualitative approach is typically the best path. If the researcher aims to take a more general view in order to explain relationships or demonstrate cause-and-effect among well-researched concepts, then the broader view provided by the quantitative path is often more appropriate.

We join Dunn et al. (1994) in advocating that logistics and supply chain researchers appreciate and encourage methodological diversity in their research programs in order to thoroughly understand the critical issues facing the discipline. The 50,000-foot view provided by traditional quantitative methods generates important insights as does the close-up of qualitative methods; however, heavy reliance on one research approach seriously limits our understanding. Näslund (2002) notes that supply chain phenomena are often "ill-structured, messy" problems especially because they involve more than one and often more than two firms. Given the dynamic, complex nature of these phenomena and the relative newness of scholarly research in this area, many supply chain researchers would be wise to begin their research programs by first gaining deep understandings of their phenomena of interest. Having identified relevant variables by building a substantive theory of the phenomenon grounded in the data, the researcher could then evaluate relationships among variables and determine the boundaries for which the understanding holds.

Balance is achieved in a program of research by tacking back and forth between qualitative and quantitative approaches as shown in Figure 1. An inductive approach is often needed to begin to understand and generate substantive theory about new and/or complex phenomena while a deductive approach is better for developing and then testing formal theory. Research studies should then progress through the circles in the figure, sometimes repeating the same circular path, sometimes crossing over to the other approach.

4 Discussion

In the ongoing debate of the relative merits of quantitative versus qualitative research approaches, there is an inclination to treat this choice as one of incommensurable philosophical beliefs rather than the selection of a research approach responsive to the problem at hand. As noted by Deshpande (1983: 109), "There is a tendency to categorize them (research paradigms) in such a fashion that they seem independent and mutually exclusive. Nothing could be farther from the truth." This is echoed by Hudson & Ozanne (1988: 508) who note, "incommensurability does not mean that the two approaches cannot peacefully coexist or that other middle-ground approaches cannot or should not be developed." As described in this paper, it is entirely feasible -- indeed, it is often advisable -- for individual researchers to adopt a balanced approach in their own research programs. Ellram is one author in the field of supply chain management who has been using a balanced approach in her research for several years (for example, see Ellram, 1994; Ellram, 1996; Ellram & Maltz, 1996; Ellram & Siferd, 1998). Her publications demonstrate how she tacked back and forth through the inductive and deductive cycles in conducting case studies, depth interviews and surveys to answer subsequent research questions in her stream of research on the total cost of ownership in purchasing.

The present authors have also adopted the balanced approach in beginning their individual streams of research. All three conducted supply chain research for their dissertations and used a combination of qualitative and quantitative methods to do so. In each case, high response rates and significant results in the quantitative phase can be attributed to the use of a qualitative phase to answer appropriate research questions. In addition, some of the attendees of the 2004 Research Workshop on Research Methodologies in Supply Chain Management at the University of Oldenburg demonstrated the use of multiple methodologies in the research they presented. More details of these examples follow.

4.1 Balanced Approach Examples

The first author was trying to answer the question, "What is the effect of the level of magnitude on relationship type and on the perception of value from the relationship?" (Golicic, 2003). In order to do this, another question had to be answered first since relationship magnitude is a relatively new phenomenon. How is the magnitude of an interorganizational relationship and value from this relationship perceived by those in the relationship? This required an inductive method. Qualitative interviews were conducted with a sample of fourteen employees in various positions within their firms involved in managing relationships with suppliers and/or customers in three different supply chains (automotive, pharmaceutical, and plastics). It was important to interview representatives of firms that were linked together in a supply chain in order to understand what was happening within a supply chain relationship. Content analysis was used to analyze the interviews. The data helped answer the preliminary research question, develop the model and five hypotheses surrounding the magnitude phenomenon, and create items for the subsequent survey. A survey of customers in relationships and structural equation modelling was then used to answer the question of effect. The five hypotheses were all supported, and the model achieved a good fit (CFI of .998, RMSEA of .066). The success of the theoretical model was attributed to the results of the qualitative study, which helped strengthen the hypotheses and survey items. The researcher is now looking at the suppliers in the relationship to determine if the two sides view relationship magnitude differently and has chosen to stay on the deductive side of the balanced approach and conduct a replicating survey with the different sample.

The second author posed the question, "What is the effect of brand equity in the supply chain?" (Davis, 2003). She, too, first followed the qualitative path then cycled through the quantitative path. In order to first understand the meaning of brand equity as it is experienced by trade partners (a well-researched phenomenon in a new context), the author conducted a grounded theory study with 16 executives from six interconnected firms in three supply chains. The data that emerged from the interviews were used to build a theory with seven primary hypotheses that were subsequently tested using a survey and structural equation modelling. The basic structural equation model achieved a good fit (CFI of .973, RMSEA of .071), and five of the hypotheses were supported. Following different research approaches was critical to properly answering the different research questions.

In trying to answer the questions, "Why and how do firms engage in interfirm demand integration?" the third author also followed a balanced approach (McCarthy, 2003). She began with grounded theory to gain an understanding of the mechanisms involved in integration across firms in a supply chain (a phenomenon in a new context). She interviewed 26 executives representing several different industries at different tiers in the supply chain. The grounded theory analysis led to the development of a theoretical model of interfirm demand integration and its performance outcomes. A survey and structural equation modelling were used to test the model and its six research hypotheses. Four of the hypotheses were supported, and the model achieved a good fit (CFI of .913, RMSEA of .052). Again, using both the qualitative and quantitative paths was pertinent for first understanding and then explaining this phenomenon in a supply chain context. The author is now asking more detailed questions about interfirm demand integration processes across firms in different supply chains. To answer these questions, she is tacking back to the inductive cycle and employing a case study approach.

Gimenez (2004) studied the relationship between internal and external integration and their relationships with logistics performance. She first wanted to explore the integration practices in the context of a supply chain. Thus she accomplished this using a case study method using her context, a grocery supply chain, as a case. The results of this qualitative research helped in the design of a questionnaire. Gimenez then used a survey and structural equation modelling to answer the research question on the effect of integration on performance. She attributed her good results to using these two different, but complementary methods.

Similar to the other examples, Jaafer & Rafiq (2004) conducted a survey and analysed the data using structural equation modelling, but not before using an inductive method to better inform their theory and survey items. The authors were trying to replicate the logistics service quality scale in the context of third party logistics services in the UK. They needed to determine if the scale was appropriate for their context so they first conducted depth interviews with nine customers of third party logistics services. The results helped them refine the scale before distributing the survey to make it appropriate for their population.

Following multiple paths through the balanced approach was important to properly researching the supply chain phenomena presented in each of these cases. If the qualitative/inductive path had not been followed first, the theoretical models may not have been strong enough nor the subsequent survey items reliable enough to attain the successful results that the examples achieved. The specific research techniques chosen depended on the questions asked and the amount of prior research available. For example, the study on relationship magnitude (Golicic, 2003) relied on the vast relationship literature to help formulate research ideas about a relatively new phenomenon; therefore content analysis could be used to analyse the depth interviews. However, the study on integration and performance (Gimenez, 2004) studied an existing phenomenon (integration) in a new context (a supply chain), and therefore a case study was conducted to better understand how the phenomenon behaved in this context.

When investigating new, complex supply chain phenomena, researchers often need to develop a deep understanding of how the phenomenon is experienced in the field, particularly in the context of a supply chain. Qualitative methods are ideal for this. Theory can then be built from the qualitative data, which brings about more questions that can then often be answered through quantitative research. It is expected that the next steps in each of the examples described here will continue cycling through the inductive and deductive paths as more questions arise. It is by following a balanced approach that research in supply chain management can be conducted most effectively.

4.2 Conclusion

Researchers rarely adopt a balanced approach; it is easier to develop research skills in a single approach. However, we argue that researchers who exclusively choose one approach may delimit the scope of their inquiry and, thereby, their ability to consistently and effectively contribute to the body of supply chain management knowledge. Dunn et al. stated that, "a given field may be underachieving if all of its research is being conducted within a narrow methodological domain. When the research in a particular field embraces a balance of methodological types, a higher form of intellectual honesty and content richness can be said to occur," (1994: 123). Selecting a single approach constrains inquiry to only those questions that are amenable to the approach selected. Because methods are driven by their philosophical traditions, it is important to understand the philosophy as well as the methodological steps. Those researchers who feel it is unreasonable or impractical to develop skills in multiple approaches could certainly collaborate with coauthors in order to add the necessary methodological expertise.

In order to teach the balanced approach in Ph.D. programs, supply chain educators need to learn multiple methods through self-directed study, discussions with colleagues, professional conferences, and workshops in order to adopt a balanced approach in their own research programs. Doctoral seminars can draw on expertise of faculty in research traditions outside the college of business, such as sociology and anthropology, as well as those from other universities who are already engaged in balanced research programs. As evidenced by recent calls for qualitative studies in logistics and supply chain journals, there is a growing awareness of the need for a balanced approach in the discipline.

The body of knowledge in logistics and supply chain research needs to grow through the balance of the rich data that can be gained through qualitative methods and the generation of formal theory through the quantitative approach. There is a need to have researchers who have developed profound understandings of their phenomena through the qualitative approach to subsequently engage in building formal theory and putting resulting hypotheses to the test in the quantitative approach. Likewise, there is a need for researchers who have identified insightful questions in their quantitative studies to pursue those questions through the qualitative approach. And of utmost importance, there is a need to develop an appreciation for balancing our approach to research in logistics and supply chain management among the intended audiences of scholarly research. For this to occur, the discipline must seriously consider implementing changes to assure a balanced approach within research streams. It begins with the introduction of multiple philosophies and methods in doctoral programs and continues when journal reviewers, editors, and promotion and tenure committees encourage both qualitative and quantitative studies. It is our hope that logistics and supply chain researchers will thoughtfully consider implementing the balanced approach in their stream of research.

5 References

Bickman, L., Rog, D. J. (1998): Handbook of Applied Social Research Methods, Sage Publications, Thousand Oaks, CA.

Creswell, J. W. (1998): Qualitative Inquiry and Research Design: Choosing Among Five Research Traditions, Sage Publications, Thousand Oaks, CA: 13-26.

Davis, D. F. (2003): The Effect of Brand Equity in Supply Chain Relationships, University of Tennessee Dissertation, Knoxville, TN.

Deshpande, R. (1983): Paradigms Lost: On Theory and Method in Research in Marketing, in: Journal of Marketing, 47(3): 101-110.

Dunn, S. C., Seaker, R. F., Stenger, A. J., Young R. (1994): An Assessment of Logistics Research Paradigms, in: Educators Conference Proceedings, Council of Logistics Management, Chicago, IL: p. 121-139.

Ellram, L. R. (1996): The Use of the Case Study Methodology in Logistics Research, in: Journal of Business Logistics, 17(2): 93-138.

Ellram, L. R. (1994): A Taxonomy of Total Cost of Ownership Models, in: Journal of Business Logistics, 15(1): 171-192.

Ellram, L. R., Maltz, A. B. (1996): The Use of Total Cost of Ownership Concepts to Model the Outsourcing Decision, in: International Journal of Logistics Management, 7(2): 55-66.

Ellram, L. R., Siferd, S. P. (1998): Total Cost of Ownership: A Key Concept in Strategic Cost Management Decisions, in: Journal of Business Logistics, 19(1): 55-84.

Flint, D. J., Haley, J. E., Mentzer, J. T. (1999): Eclectic Marketing Inquiry, working paper, University of Tennessee.

Gimenez, C. (2005): Supply Chain Management Research: Case Studies and Surveys – Two Complimentary Methodologies, in: Kotzab, H., Seuring, S., Müller, M., Reiner, G. (eds.): Research Methodologies in Supply Chain Management, Physica, Heidelberg: p. 315-330.

Golicic, S. L. (2003): An Examination of Interorganizational Relationship Magnitude and Its Role in Determining Relationship Value, University of Tennessee Dissertation, Knoxville, TN.

Guba, E. G. (1990): The Paradigm Dialog, Sage Publications, Newbury Park, CA.

Halldorsson, A., Arlbjorn J. S. (2005): Research Methodologies in Supply Chain Management – What Do We Know? in: Kotzab, H., Seuring, S., Müller, M., Reiner, G. (eds.): Research Methodologies in Supply Chain Management, Physica, Heidelberg: p. 107-122.

Hirshman, E. (1986): Humanistic Inquiry in Marketing Research: Philosophy, Method and Criteria, in: Journal of Marketing Research, 23(3): 237-249.

Hudson, L. A., Ozanne, J. L. (1988): Alternative Ways of Seeking Knowledge in Consumer Research, in: Journal of Consumer Research, 14(1): 508-521.

Hunt, S. D. (1991): Modern Marketing Theory: Critical Issues in the Philosophy of Marketing Science, South-Western Publishing Co., Cincinnati, OH.

Jaafar, H. S., Rafiq, M. (2005): Customer's Perceptions of Third Party Logistics Service Provider in the United Kingdom, in: Kotzab, H., Seuring, S., Müller, M., Reiner, G. (eds.): Research Methodologies in Supply Chain Management, Physica, Heidelberg: p. 187-202.

Kerlinger, F. N., Lee, H. B. (2000): Foundations of Behavioral Research, Fourth Edition, Harcourt College Publishers, Fort Worth, TX.

Kotzab, H. (2005): The Role and Importance of Survey Research Methods in the Field of Supply Chain Management, in: Kotzab, H., Seuring, S., Müller, M., Reiner, G. (eds.): Research Methodologies in Supply Chain Management, Physica, Heidelberg: p. 125-138.

McCarthy, T. M. (2003): Interfirm Demand Integration: The Role of Marketing in Bridging the Gap between Demand and Supply Chain Management, University of Tennessee Dissertation, Knoxville, TN.

McCracken, G. (1988): The Long Interview, Sage Publications, Newbury Park, CA.

McGrath, J. E. (1982): Dilemmatics, The Study of Research Choices and Dilemmas, in: Judgment Calls in Research, J. E. McGrath, J. Martin and R. A. Kulka editors, Sage Publications, Beverly Hills, CA.

Mentzer, J. T., Kahn, K. B. (1995): A Framework of Logistics Research, in: Journal of Business Logistics, 16(1): 231-250.

Näslund, D. (2002): Logistics Needs Qualitative Research – Especially Action Research, in: International Journal of Physical Distribution and Logistics Management, 32(5): 321-338.

Strauss, A., Corbin, J. (1998): Basics of Qualitative Research, Sage Publications, Thousand Oaks, CA.

Woodruff, R. (2003): Alternative Paths to Marketing Knowledge, Qualitative Methods Doctoral Seminar, University of Tennessee.

Yin, R. K. (1994): Case Study Research, Sage Publications, Thousand Oaks, CA.

A Critical Discussion on the Theoretical and Methodological Advancements in Supply Chain Integration Research

Dirk Pieter van Donk, Taco van der Vaart

1 Introduction 32
2 Evaluation of Supply Chain Integration Research 33
3 Antecedents of Supply Chain Integration 36
4 Methodological Issues 40
5 Conclusion 42
6 References 42

Summary:
Integration is one of the central themes in supply chain management research. This paper explores and discusses the constructs and methods used in empirical research with respect to supply chain integration. A large part of the empirical research on integration is characterized by the use of constructs and scales that measure limited, partial aspects of integration. Furthermore, it appears that contextual factors are hardly addressed. This paper develops a broader construct of supply chain integration and sketches the advantages of a multi-case study approach as an alternative methodology to survey research to develop our knowledge of supply chain integration and its antecedents.

Keywords:
Supply Chain Integration, Supply Chain Context, Methodology

1 Introduction

Over the past decade, one of the main themes in the SC literature has been integration as a key factor in achieving improvements (e.g. Tan et al., 1999; Romano, 2003). The general idea is that integrative practices and a high level of integration have a positive impact on corporate and supply chain performance.

Recent empirical work (Frohlich & Westbrook, 2001; Vickery et al., 2003; Childerhouse & Towill, 2003) shows convincing evidence for the relationship between integration and performance. Although some of these studies might be criticized for using a limited description of integration, we think that there are more fundamental problems in both the empirical and the theoretical work on integration. More specifically, Ho et al. (2002) formulate doubts with respect to the relationship between integration and performance in these empirical studies. They state that there is little consistency about the basic definition and content of the constructs used in these studies (Ho et al., 2002: 4415). In future research, we thus need to come up with sound constructs and adequate methodologies that help us to understand the relationship between integrative practices and supply chain performance.

From a methodological point of view, the majority of the empirical studies seem to be either single cases (e.g. Lee et al., 1993; Hewitt, 1997; Childerhouse et al., 2002) or survey-based research (e.g. Frohlich & Westbrook, 2001; Vickery et al., 2003; Tan et al., 1999). Typically, the first type of research describes and analyzes one dyad or single link, is often practitioner-oriented, and shows the advantages of (the introduction of) a new integrative practice. Survey-based research on integration hardly considers single links or relationships. In this type of research, integrative practices and the relationship with performance are studied on a high level of aggregation. Aggregated constructs are used to measure the integrative practices conducted by e.g. a buying company in the links with all their suppliers.

Overall, case studies make it harder to generalize findings, specifically if there is no clear theoretical framework supporting these case studies (Yin, 2003; Meredith, 1998). As opposed to case studies, the surveys incorporate limited aspects of integration and fail to grasp what actually happens in supply chain relationships.

A last critical issue is that much of the empirical work fails to address the context (Ho et al., 2002) or business conditions (Van der Vaart & Van Donk, 2003a; 2003b). Our paper will explain how business conditions and context can be incorporated into a theoretical framework that explains the level of integration in a supply relationship using a broad construct of integration.

The main aim of this paper is to discuss the theoretical framework and the constructs used. Based on an assessment of empirical research, we will present a theoretical model that combines context, level of focus, supply chain integration, and performance. However, we also pay attention to the research methods used to measure integrative practices and discuss our experiences in a recent empirical study using a multi-case study setting. We argue that multi-case studies can help to bridge the gap between single case studies and surveys, and is an appropriate means to develop knowledge in the field of supply chain integration in its current stage of development.

This paper is organized into five sections. In the next section we will evaluate empirical work on integrative practices in supply chains. Then, we will present an alternative framework that addresses the shortcomings in these empirical studies. The fourth section pays attention to the methodological problems in measuring the framework presented. The last section summarizes our conclusions.

2 Evaluation of Supply Chain Integration Research

This section will review the empirical work on supply chain integration. The main point of this section is not to give an overview of all literature in the field, but rather to focus on the constructs used in measuring supply chain integration and its antecedents. More specifically, we address three points of concern regarding the current state of empirical research in the area of supply chain integration. First, we pay attention to the limited scope of the constructs used in measuring supply chain integration. Second, we discuss the role of contextual factors in current empirical work. As a third point, we advocate the measurement of supply chain integration at the level of dyads, instead of measurement at higher aggregated levels.

2.1 Limited Scope of Integration

Supply chain management as a discipline has been inspired by many fields: materials management, quality, industrial markets, purchasing, and logistics. At the core of SCM lies the idea of collaboration between buyer and supplier or the building of a relationship (Ho et al., 2002; Chen & Paulraj, 2004). It is not surprising that integration has been seen as one of the main drivers in establishing good supply chain management. Stevens (1989) was among the first to stress the strategic importance of integration. Other researchers (e.g. New, 1996) mention it as one of the core elements of SCM, describe different types of integration (e.g. Tan, 2001), pay attention to integration of key business processes (e.g. Ho et al., 2002), or describe it in terms of integrating traditional logistical functions (Gustin et al., 1995). Integration can also be discussed as removing barriers (or boundaries) between organizations (Naylor et al., 1999; Romano, 2003).

It is surprising to note that, although the importance of integration is broadly advocated and different areas are mentioned in conceptual contributions, the measures or constructs used (especially in surveys) are rather narrow. The surveys presented in Shin et al. (2000), Carr & Pearson (2002), and Prahinski & Benton (2003) focus on relational and/or strategic issues. Examples of factors that are considered are strategic purchasing, supplier evaluation systems, buyer-supplier relationships, supply management orientation, and supplier development. The aim of another group of surveys is to find out how operational practices help in improving performance in the supply chain. Here, the studies are mostly limited to a few number of aspects mostly related to the flow of goods and information only. Frohlich & Westbrook (2001) measure integration by selecting eight aspects in the two areas that relate to the operational aspects of information and physical flow. Vickery et al. (2003) stress the importance of integrative information technologies as a prime dimension in integration.

Most surprisingly, given the large amount of elements distinguished within supply chain integration research, Chen & Paulraj (2004) built in their broad study a construct of logistics integration around only six items related to how integration is perceived, that is, focused on the flow of goods only. While each of the above-mentioned studies helps in understanding the relationship practices-performance, little has been done at comparing practices (Ho et al., 2002).

2.2 Context and Supply Chain Integration

While the majority of empirical studies focus their attention on the relationship between supply chain management practices or supply chain integration and (improved) performance, Ho et al. (2002) state that these practices are embedded in the context that supports or restricts the use of certain supply chain practices. One of their examples to show that context is relevant is the influence of demand characteristics on the type of practices employed: an issue addressed by Fisher (1997), Mason-Jones & Towill (1998) and Childerhouse & Towill (2002). Ramdas & Spekman (2000) find differences in supply chain practices in functional products supply chains as opposed to those in innovative products chains. Hill & Scudder (2002) link the size of a company to its use of EDI. Van Donk & van der Vaart (2005) show that the process capabilities of a process industry are an important context factor that can pose considerable limitations for integrative practices with buyers. This stream of research partly answers the remark by Frohlich & Westbrook (2001: 185): "Our knowledge is relatively weak concerning which forms of integration manufacturers use to link up with suppliers and customers." Still, the influence of context is not very well investigated.

Uncertainty seems to be one of the most important aspects of the context of supply chain management and a number of studies pay attention to it. Much work has been done on the "bull-whip" effect in a more model-based and limited context (e.g. Lee et al., 1997; DeJonckheere et al., 2003). Others like Childerhouse & Towill (2002) see the importance of uncertainty for integration but regard reducing uncertainty as an equivalent of integration: "An integrated supply chain has minimal uncertainties..." (Ibidem, 2002: 3503). Still, we feel that context and its importance is not valued enough. This is illustrated by the relatively poor attention Chen & Paulraj (2004) give to context. While addressing almost all aspects of supply chain management and developing scales for each concept, context is represented in their research framework by uncertainty, supply network structure (power) and competitive factors.

2.3 Supply Chain Integration as a Dyadic Concept

Supply chain management and the associated idea of seamless coordinated flows of materials and information has aroused such enthusiasm in the literature that one of the often-stated beliefs is that companies no longer compete but that supply chains or supply networks do. This might be true for a number of specific chains, such as the automotive industry where all different partners in a chain are totally attuned. In that specific context, one often encounters supplying plants that deliver all production to one final assembly automotive line. As a result, different supply chains in the automotive industry compete. However, in other industries, suppliers deliver to different (probably competing) companies and have to balance their capacity to be able to deliver to different customers. Often, they will be part of several if not numerous supply chain networks. As a result, we need research on the supply relationship between two companies: a buyer and a supplier. In most cases we do not directly need insight into the whole reverse and forward chain. This might even apply to the automotive industry where agreements are made on the buyer-supplier link as well. For each dyad in the chain, circumstances can be quite different, resulting in link-specific arrangements.

Another argument for focusing on one company and the relationship with either a buyer or a supplier comes from New (1996), who points out the problem of dividing the benefits of an integrated supply chain. He raises the question on whether the end-user will benefit from lower costs or that one of the chain members will raise his profits. The issue of who benefits is even more interesting in the case of two competing customers of one supplier; here one competitor might profit from improved supply chain management practices with the other competitor. Once again, this type of problem needs to be resolved in the dyad of supplier and buyer.

Some recent research explicitly pays attention to the dyadic nature of supply chain management (e.g. Johnston et al., 2004). For a summary of related research we refer to Chen & Paulraj (2004). We strongly believe that supply chain management practices are formed and managed in the one-to-one relationship between a supplier and a buyer. A long-term relationship, which is often seen as part of supply chain management, can only develop and prosper if both the supplier and buyer profit from the relationship. Apparently, a supplier will more compete with other similar suppliers than compete with the competitors of his buyer.

3 Antecedents of Supply Chain Integration

This section will elaborate on the basic building blocks for conceptualizing and measuring integration and the main factors influencing the type and level of integration in a supply link. So far, we have paid little attention to performance, as most research is quite clear on the relationship between integration and performance. In our proposed framework, we see performance as the ultimate outcome (see Figure 1). It should be emphasized that measuring performance is not an easy task as well. With respect to supply chain performance, a large number of performance measures have been used in the literature, stressing that performance is a multi-dimensional concept itself. For further discussion we refer to the specialized performance measurement literature. In the development of our framework we explicitly do not address the relational aspects as power and trust. The main reason is that our intention is to examine the influence of structural factors related to technology and market structure on supply chain integration and integrative practices.

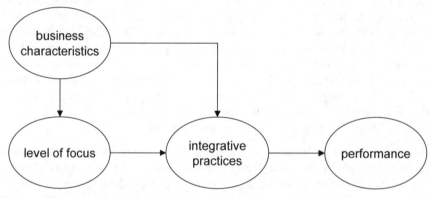

Figure 1: Conceptual Framework

Integrative practices depend on two factors: business characteristics and the level of focus. Business characteristics (context according to Ho et al., 2002) are related to the nature of the production processes and the nature of the products and markets. These factors influence the need for integrative practices. For example, highly innovative products require a high level of attuning between buyer and supplier (Ramdas & Spekman, 2000). The level of focus relates to how the above factors are combined into shaping the production system and the relationship with buyers/suppliers. In principle, two extreme options exist for the level of focus. Resources are shared for all products and all buyers, or resources are singled out to supply products for one buyer. It might be clear that the level of focus determines to some degree the limitations and possibilities for integrative practices. Each part of Figure 1 will be further elaborated in the following subsections.

3.1 Business Characteristics

In contrast to uncertainty, most other business characteristics have been relatively ignored. Of course, a number of context factors have been mentioned: e.g. power, trust, network structure, and knowledge. Another approach is to look more at the structural factors as Ramdas & Spekman (2000) do. Building on Porter (1985), they pay attention to what drives supply chain performance by distinguishing between basically two types of chains: innovative product versus functional product supply chains. The main factors taken into account as business characteristics are: availability of substitutes (limited vs. large), changes in market conditions (rapid vs. slow), changes in technology (rapid vs. slow), market maturity (low vs. high), and product life-cycle length (short vs. long). Other relevant factors that seem to influence both the level of integration and the level of focus are discussed in Van der Vaart & Van Donk (2003a; 2003b). They investigated the influence of order winners (ranking of performance dimensions), the location of the decoupling point (percentage products that are produced using MTO, ATO, MTS), time window for delivery (average, range), batch size (average, range), and the volume-variety ratio (average volume per product). Aitken et al. (2003) investigate the influence of the position in the life cycle of a product and show that products in the early phase of the life cycle need to be treated differently than mature products with respect to the type of SCM.

The above enumeration of characteristics is probably not complete, but in the papers mentioned they provide a good explanation for differences in the type and level of integrative practices. Moreover, the type of industrial sector is probably an important factor as well. For instance, factors like shelf-life constraints and increased consumer attention for safe and environmental-friendly production methods (Van der Vorst & Beulens, 2002) partly explain the focus on transparency and ICT in food supply chains (e.g. Hill & Scudder, 2002). In the automotive industry, the large volumes and relatively stable demand patterns enable lean practices (e.g. Hines et al., 2000), packaging customization and standardization of deliveries (e.g. Van der Vaart & Van Donk, 2003a).

3.2 Level of Focus: Shared or Buyer Focus Resources

Since the seminal article of Skinner (1974), focus has been on the agenda in operations management research. The decision to focus a part of the operations is one of the strategic decisions to be taken within manufacturing strategy. The basic idea in most contributions is that a focused operation (either manufacturing or supply chain) should be matched to the market requirements. Although the strategic nature of supply chain management has been stressed from Stevens' contribution (1989) onwards, supply chain focus has been relatively ignored (Aitken et al., 2003).

Griffiths & Margetts (2000) and Griffiths et al. (2000) fill that gap by introducing a new form of focus: customer or buyer focus, aimed at supply chain integration. Buyer focus can be understood as singling out resources for the purpose of delivering products for one buyer. In that case, integrative practices can easily be achieved along a broad scope and at a high level (see next subsection). While buyer focus enables integrative practices, shared resources can be seen as a barrier. A shared network resource is a common-capacity source in two or more supply chains or networks (see also Hoekstra & Romme, 1992). Shared network resources are resources that are used by a supplier in the network for more than one buyer. Here, buyers competing for the resources seem to be one of the main barriers in achieving integration. This is especially true if the capacity of these resources is scarce (see Van Donk & Van der Vaart, 2005). These two extreme situations that are further explored in Van der Vaart & Van Donk (2004) are part of a continuum that is labeled as "Level of focus." One of the intermediate positions is e.g. the singling out of assembly operations that are performed for one customer, while the core activities are still performed using the shared network resources.

The level of focus will be chosen based on market characteristics and business conditions (as described above) and technology. As with focus in general, this is a strategic decision, that is to some extent restricted by the typical technology employed in a certain industrial sector. Level of focus is also important as it either enables or restricts the possibilities for integrative practices in supplying buyers.

3.3 Supply Chain Integration

Based on the literature, we distinguish three aspects of integration: direction, scope and level. These three aspects already reflect our aim to develop a rich and multi-dimensional construct of integration. We elaborate that concept further by distinguishing five dimensions of the scope of integration.

A first natural distinction is the direction of integration: downstream with suppliers, upstream with customers. This distinction goes back to the separation of inbound and outbound logistics, materials management, and physical distribution or purchasing and distribution. This distinction is widely accepted and documented in the literature (e.g. New, 1996; Tan, 2001; Frohlich & Westbrook, 2001). Integration in supply management can also be external (with other organizations) or internal (within one company). We will limit ourselves to external integration, because we consider that to be the innovative/new element in the philosophy of supply chain management.

A second aspect of integration is the number of different areas in which joint activities are developed. This is labeled as the scope of integration. Based on our critical comments on the narrow scope and level of integration as expressed in the field, we do not restrict ourselves to a few practices, but measure integration across a larger number of possible areas or dimensions from the fields of production management, complemented with concepts from the supply chain theory and logistics management as being among the key antecedent disciplines of supply chain research according to Croom et al. (2000). In line with recent work (Van Donk, 2003; Childerhouse & Towill, 2002; Childerhouse et al., 2002) we distinguish four supply dimensions to which we add product development as a fifth one (based on e.g. Lee et al., 1993; Davis, 1993):

- Physical Flow: typical integrative practices are Vendor Managed Inventories (VMI), packaging customization and common equipment or containers (see also Frohlich & Westbrook, 2001).

- Planning & Control: examples are joint planning or forecasting, Multi-Level-Supply-Control (Van der Vlist et al. (1997) and rolling plans with quantity commitment (Tsay, 1999) (instead of discrete ordering). Advanced practices involve an orchestrated supply chain.

- Organization: this dimension refers to the type of relationship between buyer and supplier (e.g. partnership). Concrete examples are JIT II (i.e. application of JIT concepts to the purchasing function by having a representative of the supplier locate at the buying organization's facility; see Stock & Lambert, 2001: 294), specific account managers, dedicated planners for one buyer, and the creation of quasi-firms (Lamming, 1993).

- Flow of information: integrative practices with respect to information and communication technology (ICT). Examples are EDI and bar coding, the use of MRP/ERP (Vickery et al., 2003).

- Product development: the level of integrative practices with respect to product development can be measured by information shared on technical details, the mutual involvement in product development, and process improvements (e.g. Davis, 1993; Lee et al., 1993).

The third aspect of integration is the Level of Integration. This can be described (in line with Frohlich & Westbrook, 2001) as to what extent integrative activities within one dimension are developed. This can be measured as the number of activities within one dimension, but the level is also higher if more advanced and demanding practices are used. The level of integration applies to each of the areas presented above. As an example, it is clear that a rather high level of integration is reached in planning and control in the case of Multi-Level Supply Control. A low level of integration in this field might be to only inform your supplier about your promotional actions.

4 Methodological Issues

4.1 Surveys and Single Case Studies

While we already pointed out the limited scope of supply chain integration measurements in section 2.1., we have some doubts regarding the way questions are asked. In many surveys respondents are asked to report whether they feel that over a certain period specific practices have grown in importance or not. In most cases this means relying on the perception of respondents instead of relying on real measurements of the effects. The same holds for the effect: the perceived improvement in certain performance measures is measured (e.g. Shin et al., 2000; Vickery et al., 2003; Prahinsky & Benton, 2004).

In general, there is an adverse relationship between the length of a survey (the number of questions and the level of detail asked) and the response rate. When making a survey and sending it out, this puts the researcher in a paradoxical situation. The more you learn from each respondent, the fewer responses one might expect. Still, even with a small number of questions, surveys show a low level of response. Some researchers even state that 15-20% is "normal." A recent example is given by Bagchi & Skjoett-Larsen (2004) who report less than a 20% response rate even in the home country of the second author. In general, this gives a serious limitation to the validity of the results.

With respect to the case studies performed in literature, there are serious doubts as well. Most cases describe improvements of supply chain management practices and are problem driven. Strangely enough, the literature hardly reports on failures, while the successful improvements are numerous. This raises the question regarding whether cases were selected with the purpose of "theoretical replication" (Eisenhardt, 1989) in mind. Actual analysis, case study protocol and other measures of validity and reliability are hardly discussed. Only a few researchers pay attention to case study methodology. Childerhouse & Towill (2003) analyze 32 cases with the same instrument and take care of triangulation of the data, showing their research protocol, etc. However, little can be said about the selection of their sample, which is generally considered to be critical in case study research (e.g. Eisenhardt, 1989). Aitken et al. (2003) take care in the description and analysis of their cases as well.

4.2 Multi-Case Approach

In the introduction we stated that the majority of empirical contributions in supply chain management research falls into one of two categories: survey or single case study. It is not the intention of this contribution to repeat the advantages and disadvantages of both. Meredith (1998) has given a good overview of both methods in the field of operations management that is applicable for supply chain management research. Although not being a description of research methods themselves, two recent articles by Dennis & Meredith (2000a; 2000b) shed some interesting new light on the use and analysis of case studies. In their study, 19 companies are described using a case study approach that combines quantitative and qualitative data as well as observations. These data are reduced to a limited number of variables that are used to perform a statistical analysis along with a cluster analysis. For the interpretation of the clusters, the additional qualitative findings are beneficial for further explanation and understanding of the findings. Here we see a nice combination of survey and case study approaches.

In the field of supply chain management and integration, many questions relate to why supply chain management in certain circumstances works (or not) and how certain practice work (or not). With respect to integration in supply chain management, our knowledge is still in its infancy and we do not yet fully understand and know the antecedents of integration. Despite all efforts in performing single case studies, more comparison seems needed to further develop supply chain management research. A multi case study approach combines a number of aspects. First, each case can be explored in depth, using a variety of research approaches to enhance triangulation. Second, a multi case study approach can be used to find contrasting situations that are based on theoretical concerns. Most preferable are studies that combine cases that show high levels of integration with cases that have an absence of integration. Such choices of the sample (based on conceptual propositions and theoretical constructs) are advocated by Eisenhardt (1989) to enhance the contribution of case study research. Third, the case study approach enables the links between two companies to really be explored, while looking at their (mutual) integrative practices. Integration should be measured at the level of links and not as an organizational concept.

Recently, we conducted a study along 9 units to investigate the integrative practices between suppliers and their key buyers (Van der Vaart & Van Donk, 2003a; 2003b). We gathered data on business characteristics, the level of focus, and the integrative practices using structured interviews with open questions and observation of the production processes. Each unit was visited twice, which took about one day for each unit to collect data and to check and validate our findings. A combination of qualitative and quantitative data enabled and facilitated cross-case comparison, and on the other hand, interpretation of findings for each case and across cases. In line with Dennis & Meredith (2000a), and as suggested by Voss et al. (2002) we rescaled a number of variables. Given the relatively small number we did not use any statistical tools, as different clusters could be identified without such tools. All in all, we strongly believe that this type of study provides rich research material and profound insights, while the investment in time spent on collecting the data is still affordable. Dennis & Meredith (2000a; 2000b) and Childerhouse & Towill (2003) spent more time on data collection (for each company about one week) and probably have a richer set of data. Within a case study framework, some additional data collection instruments such as questionnaires for a larger number of employees can be used. This will result in more reliable data, and moreover, specific concepts can be investigated. In a study by Nauta et al. (2002), questionnaires were used to link personality characteristics to bargaining behavior between sales and production departments. These findings could be linked with findings on the process characteristics, demand patterns, etc. from interviews, data files and observations.

5 Conclusion

This paper has evaluated the advancements in supply chain integration research. The main criticism on the literature can be summarized into four points:

- Supply chain integration has been conceptualized and measured as a too-limited construct;
- Supply chain integration research pays little attention to contextual factors;
- Supply chain integration is measured as an organizational concept instead of as a dyadic concept;
- The methodology used in supply chain integration research does not sufficiently support the necessary explorative character of research.

We develop a conceptual framework that takes into account business characteristics (context) as a main factor for integrative practices. Integration is sketched as a multi-dimensional phenomenon, while level of focus is seen as an intermediate variable. We advocate a multi-case approach as a sound strategy for the further development of the field.

Further research should extend our framework empirically and conceptually. Testing and applying the framework, adding more variables to it and developing scales to measure its concepts and dimensions are among our priorities.

6 References

Aitken, J., Childerhouse, P., Towill, D. (2003): The impact of product life cycle on supply chain strategy, in: International Journal of Production Economics, 85: 127-140.

Bagchi, P. K., Skjoett-Larsen, T. (2004): Supply Chain Integration in Nordic Firms, in: Papers from the Second World POM Conference/15th Annual POMS Conference, Cancun, Mexico, April 30 – May 3: p. 1-23.

Carr, A. S., Pearson, J. N. (2002): The impact of purchasing and supplier involvement on strategic purchasing and its impact on firm's performance, in: International Journal of Operations & Production Management, 22(9): 1032-1053.

Chen, I. J., Paulraj, A. (2004): Towards a theory of supply chain management: the constructs and measurement, in: Journal of Operations Management, 22: 119-150.

Childerhouse, P. Aitken, J., Towill, D. R. (2002): Analysis and design of focused demand chains, in: Journal of Operations Management, 20: 675-689.

Childerhouse, P., Towill, D. R. (2002): Analysis of the factors affecting the real-world value stream performance, in: International Journal of Production Research 40(15): 3499-3518.

Childerhouse, P., Towill, D. R. (2003): Simplified material flow holds the key to supply chain integration, in: Omega, 31: 17-27.

Croom, S., Romano, P., Giannakis, M. (2000): Supply chain management: an analytic framework for critical literature review, in: European Journal of Purchasing & Supply Management, 6: 67-83.

Davis, T. (1993): Effective supply chain management, in: Sloan Management Review, Summer: 35-46.

DeJonckheere, J., Disney, S. M., Lambrecht, M. R., Towill, D. R. (2003): Measuring the Bullwhip Effect: A control theoretic approach to analyse forecasting induced Bullwhip in order-up-to policies, in: European Journal of Operations Research, 147(3): 567-590.

Dennis, D. R., Meredith, J. R. (2000a): An analysis of process industry production and inventory management systems, in: Journal of Operations Management, 18: 683-699.

Dennis, D. R., Meredith, J. R. (2000b): An Empirical Analysis of Process Industry Transformation Systems, in: Management Science, 46(8): 1085-1099.

Eisenhardt, K. M. (1989): Building Theories from Case Study research, in: Academy of Management Review, 14(4):532-550.

Fisher, M. L. (1997): What is the right supply chain for your product?, in: Harvard Business Review, 75(2): 105-116.

Frohlich, M. T., Westbrook, R. (2001): Arcs of integration: an international study of supply chain strategies, in: Journal of Operations Management, 19(2): 185-200.

Griffiths, J., Margetts, D. (2000): Variation in production schedules - implications for both the company and its suppliers, in: Journal of Materials Processing Technology, 103: 155-159.

Griffiths, J., James, R., Kempson, J. (2000): Focusing customer demand through manufacturing supply chains by the use of customer focused cells: An appraisal, in: International Journal of Production Economics, 65: 111-120.

Gustin, C. M., Daugherty, P. J., Stank, T. P. (1995): The effects of information availability on logistics integration, in: Journal of Business Logistics, 16(1): 1-21.

Hewitt, F. (1997): Customer supply assurance management at Xerox, in: Journal of the Canadian Association of Logistics Management, 3(4): 521-530.

Hill, C. A., Scudder, G. D. (2002): The use of electronic data interchange for supply chain coordination in the food industry, in: Journal of Operations Management, 20: 375-387.

Hines, P., Lamming, R., Jones, D., Cousins, P., Rich, N. (2000): Value stream management, strategy and excellence in the supply chain', Pearson Education, Harlow, England.

Ho, D. C. K., Au, K. F., Newton, E. (2002): Empirical research on supply chain management: a critical review and recommendations, in: International Journal of Production Research, 40(17): 4415-4430.

Hoekstra, S., Romme, J. (1992): Integral logistic structures. Developing customer-oriented goods flow, McGraw-Hill Book Company, London.

Johnston, D. A., McCutcheon, D. M., Stuart, F. I., Kerwood, H. (2004): Effects of supplier trust on performance of cooperative supplier relationships, in: Journal of Operations Management, 22: 23-38.

Lamming, R. (1993): Beyond Partnership: strategies for innovation and lean supply Prentice Hall, New York.

Lee, H. L., Billington, C., Carter, B. (1993): Hewlett-Packard gains control of inventory and service through design for localization, in: Interfaces, 23(4): 1-11.

Lee, H. L., Padmanabhan, P., Whang, S. (1997): Information distortion in a supply chain: the Bullwhip Effect, in: Management Science, 43: 543-558.

Mason-Jones, R., Towill, D. R. (1998): Shrinking the supply chain uncertainty circle, in: The Institute of Operations Management Control Journal, 24(7): 17-22.

Meredith, J. (1998): Building operations management theory through case and field research, in: Journal of Operations Management, 16: 441-454.

Nauta, A., De Dreu, C. K. W., Van der Vaart, J. T. (2002): Social value orientation, organizational goals and interdepartemental problem-solving behavior, in: Journal of Organizational Behavior, 23: 199-213.

Naylor, J. B., Naim, M. M., Berry, D. (1999): Leagility: Integrating the lean and agile manufacturing paradigms in the total supply chain, in: International Journal of Production Economics, 62: 107-118.

New, S. J. (1996): A framework for analysing supply chain improvement, in: International Journal of Operations & Production Management, 16(4): 19-34.

Prahinski, C., Benton, W. C. (2004): Supplier evaluations: communication strategies to improve supplier performance, in: Journal of Operations Management, 22: 39-62.

Ramdas, K., Spekman, R. E. (2000): Chain or Shackles: understanding what drives supply-chain performance, in: Interfaces, 30(4): 3-21.

Romano, P. (2003): Co-ordination and integration mechanism to manage logistics processes across supply networks, in: Journal of Purchasing & Supply Management, 9(5-6): 119-134.

Shin, H., Collier, D. A., Wilson, D. D. (2000): Supply management orientation and supplier/buyer performance, in: Journal of Operations Management, 18: 317-333.

Skinner, W. (1974): The focused factory, in: Harvard Business Review, 52(3): 113-121.

Stevens, G. C. (1989): Integrating the supply chain, in: International Journal of Physical Distribution and Material Management, 19(8): 3-8.

Stock, J. R., Lambert, D. M. (2001): Strategic Logistics Management, 4th ed., McGraw-Hill, Boston.

Tan, K. C. (2001): A framework of supply chain management literature, in: European Journal of Purchasing & Supply Management, 7: 39-48.

Tan, K. C., Kannan, V. R., Handfield, R. B., Ghosh, S. (1999): Supply chain management: an empirical study of its impact on performance, in: International Journal of Operations & Production Management, 19(10): pp 1034-1052.

Tsay, A. A. (1999): The quantity flexibility contract and supplier-customer incentives, in: Management Science, 45(10): 1339-1358.

Van der Vlist, P., Hoppenbrouwers, J. J. E. M., Hegge, H. M. H. (1997): Extending the enterprise through multi-level supply control, in: International Journal of Production Economics, 53: 35-42.

Van der Vaart, J. T., Van Donk, D. P. (2003a): Two worlds? Supply chain practices and supply chain theory, in: Spina, G. et al., (eds.): One World? One View of OM? The challenges of integrating research & practice, Proceedings of the 10th International Conference European Operations Management Association, Cernobbio, Lake Como, 16-18 June 2003, Servizi Grafici Editoriali, Padova: p. 351-360.

Van der Vaart, J. T., Van Donk, D. P. (2003b): Explaining buyer-focused operations as a supply chain strategy: empirical findings, in: Pawar, K. S., Muffatto, M. (Eds.): Logistics and Networked Organisations, Proceedings of the 8th International Symposium on Logistics, University of Nottingham, Nottingham: p. 29-34.

Van der Vaart, J.T. & Van Donk, D.P. (2004): Buyer focus: Evaluation of a new concept for supply chain integration, in: International Journal of Production Economics, 92: 21-30.

Van der Vorst, J. G. A. J., Beulens, A. J. M. (2002): Identifying sources of uncertainty to generate supply chain redesign strategies, in: International Journal of Physical Distribution & Logistics Management, 32(6): 409-430.

Van Donk, D. P. (2003): Redesigning the supply of gasses in a hospital, in: Journal of Purchasing & Supply Management, 9: 225-233.

Van Donk, D. P., Van der Vaart, J. T. (2005): A case of shared resources, uncertainty and supply chain integration in the process industry, in: International Journal of Production Economics, 96(1): 97-108.

Vickery, S.K., Jayaram, J., Droge, C., Calantone, R. (2003): The effects of an integrative supply chain strategy on customer service and financial performance: an analysis of direct versus indirect relationships, in: Journal of Operations Management, 21: 532-539.

Voss, C., Tsikriktsis, N., Frohlich, M. (2002): Case research in operations management, in: International Journal of Operations & Production Management, 22(2): 195-219.

Yin, R.K. (2003): Case Study Research: Design and Methods, 3rd Edition, Sage Publications.

Measuring Supply Chain Integration – Using the Q-Sort Technique

Sakun Boon-itt, Himangshu Paul

1	Introduction	48
2	Theoretical Background of Supply Chain Integration	49
3	Q-Sort Technique	51
4	An Application of the Q-Sort Technique	52
5	Conclusion	56
6	References	57

Summary:
Supply chain integration is an important topic for researchers and practitioners. However, the major concerns constraining the full and complete use of this concept in supply chain management research has been that the construct takes on its own meaning depending on individual subjectivity and different points of view. There is a need for researchers to operationalize and measure what it means by "supply chain integration." The basic research question is whether a meaningful measure of supply chain integration could be developed. The Q-sort techniques could be used to cluster stimuli from subjective judgments to form a description of an indescribable object. This paper describes how the Q-sort technique could be used in the scale development process, and applies it to the context of measuring supply chain integration. The results indicate that the Q-sort technique is a useful methodological approach in eliminating the validity and reliability problems particularly in the early scale development stages for defining the construct of supply chain integration.

Keywords:
Supply Chain Integration, Q-Sort Technique

1 Introduction

In an increasingly competitive global marketplace, most firms are competing with a high level of market pressure worldwide. To be successful, they need to develop a better way to ensure that customers are satisfied with high service levels at acceptable prices. Based on this strategy, the focus is now shifting towards effective supply chain management. Instead of doing business with other organizations one by one, firms need to manage a whole network of relationships to include logistics and other business processes, from suppliers to end users.

It is important to recognize that one of the most important prerequisites for successful supply chain management is the integration of information flows, material flows, and all the business processes within a supply chain network (Lambert et al., 1998). Effective and efficient management of the supply chain requires the integration of all processes that go beyond purchasing and logistics activities. In the literature, one can find a considerable number of research areas related to the benefits of supply chain integration: maximized supply chain performance (Frohlich & Westbrook, 2001); reduced ordering cost (Scannell et al., 2000); reduced cycle time and inventory level (Stank et al., 1999); and reduced business uncertainties (Childerhouse et al., 2003).

However, a major obstacle standing between the full and complete use of this concept in supply chain management research has been that the supply chain integration is a construct that takes on its own meaning at a level of individual subjectivity and different points of view. For this reason, it is necessary to find appropriate methodologies to develop robust empirical scales to measure supply chain integration. In other words, there is a need for researchers to operationalize and validate scales to measure the supply chain integration construct. The Q-sort technique could be beneficial in this regard (Ekinci & Riley, 1999).

This paper applies the Q-sort technique to the scale development process to address the reliability and validity problems caused by subjectivity of the supply chain integration concept. In other words, this study provides an overview of the Q-sort technique to test whether these constructs could be described and differentiated at the preliminary stage of scale development. Indeed, the main contribution in this paper is not related much to theoretical concepts; rather, it focuses on the methodological aspects in terms of how to use Q-sort as a tool to pre-validate and measure supply chain integration in a Thai context. This paper is set out in three sections. The first section provides a review of the theoretical background of supply chain integration. This is followed by an explanation of the Q-sort technique. Section three discusses the major findings and how to analyze these results, and certain conclusions are drawn in the last section on the suitability of the Q-sort technique for scale development for supply chain integration.

2 Theoretical Background of Supply Chain Integration

In a competitive environment, an increase in the level of partnership among businesses is required. Spekman et al. (1998) summarize the development of partnership into three stages, starting from cooperation, to coordination, and then to collaboration. Cooperation, whereby firms exchange essential information and engage some suppliers into a long-term contract, has become the threshold level of interaction. In other words, cooperation is a starting point for supply chain management and it has become a necessity for business. However, it is not a sufficient condition. The next stage is coordination whereby specified material and information are exchanged among partners to create seamless linkage among trading partners. Again, this process is important, but it is not a sufficient condition for integration due to the lack of integrated information flow.

At the highest level, collaboration, also known as supply chain integration, requires that all trading partners throughout the supply chain become integrated into their suppliers'/customers' processes. For example, supply chain partners cannot only plan the future production scheduling together, but they also share technology as well as future design, product requirement, and long-term strategic intentions. The movement from coordination to collaboration or integration requires high levels of trust and information sharing among partners. Figure 1 below shows the development of the supply chain integration.

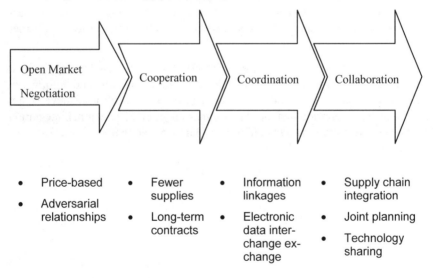

Figure 1: Development of Supply Chain Integration (Spekman et al., 1998)

An increasing ability to compete in the global market expands the domain of business practice to include the notion of integration into supply chain strategy. Consequently, there has been a great deal of attention revealing that supply chain integration is increasingly an important topic for researchers and practitioners (Morash & Clinton, 1998; Frohlich & Westbrook, 2001; Frohlich, 2002; Chandra & Kumar, 2001). There is realization that the basic concept of supply chain management is to integrate production and information flow across the supply chain processes (Lambert et al., 1998). In the supply chain context, integration is defined as the extent to which all activities within an organization, and the activities of its suppliers, customers, and other supply chain members, are integrated together (Narasimhan & Jayaram, 1998). An integrated supply chain is linked organizationally and coordinated with information flow, from raw materials to on-time delivery of finished products to customers. The entire supply chain is linked by information on anticipated and actual demand (Sabath, 1995).

To understand the classification of supply chain integration, Frohlich and Westbrook (2001) describe that there are two interrelated forms of integration that manufacturers regularly employ. The first type of integration involves integrating the forward physical flow of delivery between suppliers, manufacturers, and customers. Studies on the forward physical flow include topics such as Just-in-Time (Richeson et al., 1995; Claycomb et al., 1999; Dong et al., 2001) and delivery integration or postponement strategy (van Hoek et al., 1999). The second type of integration involves backwards integration of information technologies and flow of data from customers to suppliers. This means that the information systems used must be integrated and capable of pushing demand from one level to the next, and that communication among all levels must be both effective and timely (Turner, 1993).

Bowersox et al. (2000) and Stank et al. (2001) further discuss the supply chain integration framework by extending the scope of production and information flows. In their study, six critical areas used in the framework to achieve supply chain logistics integration include: 1) customer integration, 2) internal integration, 3) supplier integration, 4) technology and planning integration, 5) measurement integration, and 6) relationship integration.

3 Q-Sort Technique

The Q-sort technique was originally developed by psychologists as a way to examine personal traits. Its ability to uncover a person's underlying values also makes it ideal for identifying the basic factors that drive purchasing behavior (Brown, 1986). This technique is very versatile. Although it is often directed at priorities and suspected rank orders (Tractinsky & Jarvenpaa, 1995), the technique is especially suited to cases where the very existence of concepts has not been established.

However, although Q-sort addresses problems of this nature, it is not a technique from which results could be generalized to a population without confirmatory factor analysis. This preliminary technique will be followed by more empirical approaches (McKeown & Thomas, 1988). In general, the output of Q-sort could be seen as a proof of reliability or a cognitive pattern (Thomas & Baas, 1992). Essentially, Q-sort is about finding concepts. It categorizes scales, assigning the most appropriate statement to the measured construct while eliminating the meaningless one (content validity) in order to avoid an unambiguous variable definition. By requiring respondents to sort statements into different groups, many problems associated with questionnaires could be avoided (Kendall & Kendall, 1993).

Based on Ekinci & Riley's (1999) study to measure service quality in the hotel industry, there are three stages in the initial application including:

1. Create a set of construct definitions by inductive (literature review) or deductive (expert opinion) methods (Hinkin & Schriesheim, 1989);
2. create sets of statements which nominally represent those definitions; and
3. test, in order to avoid forced choices that would run the risk of a false conclusion, whether subjects are asked to combine the statements with the definitions on a "free sort" basis with the option of "not applicable."

If none or few of the statements qualify, it may be that the definitions are wrong or the construct does not exist. It is also important to state two defining rules in order to judge the final result when using the Q-sort technique. First, a definition only exists if at least two statements legitimately describe it. Second, for a statement to be legitimate, 70 percent of the sample must have allocated it to the same definition. In other words, an entity exists if 70 percent of the sample agrees that the two statements describe it. In addition, at least four to six statements per scale should be obtained in order to get the internal consistency (reliability) of a scale (Hinkin et al., 1997).

4 An Application of the Q-Sort Technique

This technique assumes that there is a theoretical multidimensional concept of supply chain integration. To illustrate the usefulness of this Q-sort methodology, six dimensions of supply chain integration were developed by Bowersox et al. (2000) and Stank et al. (2001) including:

- Customer integration,
- Internal integration,
- Supplier integration,
- Technology and planning integration,
- Measurement integration, and
- Relationship integration.

The objective of this study is to illustrate whether the six dimensions of supply chain integration mentioned above could be verified. Based on the studies of Bowersox et al. (2000) and Stank et al. (2001), this Q-sort technique consisting of six definitions and a "not applicable" (N/A) category and 29 statements representing six dimensions were also written on separate cards. The set of cards for each construct was shuffled and given to the respondents. The respondents were then asked to put each card under one of the dimensions to the best of their knowledge. A "not applicable" category was also included to ensure that the respondents did not force any item into a particular category. Prior to sorting the cards, the respondents were briefed with a set of instructions.

4.1 Samples

Although it is possible to use the Q-sort technique with one individual, Kerlinger (1986) states that Q-sort should have as many subjects as possible. Q-sort could have some bias towards small sample sizes and single case studies (McKeown and Thomas, 1988). Brown (1986) notes that 30 to 50 samples are usually more than adequate for the study using the Q-sort technique. Therefore, in this study, the basic procedure was to have 30 purchasing/production managers and academics acting as respondents. The items were sorted into several groups, with each group corresponding to a factor or dimension, based on the similarities and differences among them.

4.2 Findings

Due to space limitation in this paper, an example of the results for only one dimension (Relationship Integration) is illustrated. Table 1 shows the performance of the statements corresponding to this dimension. The percentage represents the degree of consensus between the samples on how far the statement describes the definition. There are five statements, which means that only two statements were consigned to the acceptable level of Relationship Integration. In other words, the first two statements in the table pass the qualifying criteria of over 70 percent of the sample consensus. After the analysis, it is evident that a dimension such as Relationship Integration exists.

Statements	Frequency (%), n = 30
Relationship Integration	
The capability to provide supply chain arrangements with suppliers and customers that operate under principles of shared rewards and risks	0.80*
The capability to provide guidelines for developing, maintaining, and monitoring supply chain relationships	0.70*
The level of strategic planning to share a common set of expectations with supply chain partners	0.63
The willingness to share strategic information with selected supply chain partners	0.50
The level of joint planning and forecasting with supply chain partners	0.50

*Pass the qualifying criteria with over 70 percent of the sample consensus

Table 1: The Result and Frequency of the Relationship Integration Construct

The overall result illustrated in Table 2 explains the frequency of qualifying to non-qualifying statements for the sample. The output of the Q-sort technique is a set of 21 statements with at least two consigned to each dimension as defined in Table 3. This could support the concept that all dimensions used in this study are valid. However, one dimension (Relationship Integration) has a limited number of statements. In this case, the statements need to be rephrased, and another Q-sort technique should be run to give a second chance. After completing a sufficient number of statements, the next stage of scale development is to transfer the acceptable statements to a questionnaire and test them using a range of scale types.

Final statistics	Number of items
Statements placed on dimensions	
Qualifying statements (Item ≥ 0.70)	21
Rejected statements (Item < 0.70)	8
Total	29

Table 2: The Overall Result from the Q-Sort Technique

Dimensions of statements	Q-sort study Result (%), n =30
Internal Integration	
Integration across functional areas under firm control	1.00
Level of information flow within firm between order and inventory management process	0.87
Level of responsiveness and flexibility to meet internal customers' needs	0.80
Degree of interpersonal, relations, communication activity interaction among functions in firm	0.77
Customer Integration	
Degree of customer involvement in product development	0.93
Degree of joint planning to anticipate demand visibility with customers	0.73
Level of information sharing about market information and inventory stocking point with customers	0.70
Capability to achieve efficient and rapid delivery for customer ordering	0.70

Table 3: The Qualified Statements: Supply Chain Integration Construct

Dimensions of their statements	Q-sort study Result (%), n =30
Supplier Integration	
Degree of supplier involvement in the process of procurement and production	0.93
Degree of supplier involvement in product development	0.90
Level of strategic partnership and long-term relationship with suppliers (single / dual sourcing of supply)	0.73
Technology and Planning Integration	
Level of technology designed to facilitate cross-organizational data exchange	0.90
Capability to provide integrated database and access method to facilitate information sharing	0.87
Capability to obtain available, timely, and accurate information to facilitate use	0.73
Degree of information system that reflects more enterprise-wide integrated processes (i.e. Enterprise Resources Planning)	0.70
Measurement Integration	
Capability to measure supply chain performance in terms of impact on business profit statements	0.90
Performance measurement data across supply chain partners is available on a more timely basis	0.87
Quality of data available for performance measurement in the firm	0.70
Relationship Integration	
Capability to provide supply chain arrangements with suppliers and customers that operate under principles of shared rewards and risks	0.80
Capability to provide guidelines for developing, maintaining, and monitoring supply chain relationships	0.70

Table 3: The Qualified Statements: Supply Chain Integration Construct (Continued from page 54)

5 Conclusion

This case study has shown that determining an appropriate construct in the specific context is a crucial issue in describing the statements or items to measure supply chain integration in Thailand. However, this case study does not aim to offend the supply chain integration concept already proposed in the literature; indeed, this finding seeks to validate the statements or concepts of supply chain integration by other means before using questionnaires as a tool to collect data. It is important to note that the scale development process is very crucial at the beginning to ensure that the researchers are able to get the best information they need from the respondent. It is not necessarily the case that the concepts applied in Western contexts such as the United Kingdom, Europe, and the United States would be appropriate for use in Thailand. Therefore, this Q-sort technique plays the role of applying a theoretical framework combined with considerations of the contextual factors. In this case, the supply chain integration assessment studies encourage a tendency towards eliminating the statements that contain misunderstood or mixed-worded items in a Thai context (8 items), especially in relationship integration. As a result, researchers have to be careful not to use the entire statement proposed in the different context when needing to measure relationship integration. Therefore, it is necessary to re-word or eliminate negative statements in order to avoid the respondents' bias in measurement.

The purpose in this paper has been to illustrate the value and procedures of the Q-sort technique as a preliminary process in scale development. We have attempted to establish a set of statements which have a degree of pre-validation by using the scientific method known as the Q-sort technique. The goal of the Q-sort technique is to match the proposed statements with the appropriate constructs and contexts. By using the concept of supply chain integration, a scaled questionnaire could be used to check the reliability and validity of the dimension and constructs. The case study through this Q-sort application has shown that determining a qualified statement is an important issue in explaining the dimensions of supply chain integration in Thailand. However, it is noted that this technique should be used as a preliminary approach in scale development rather than as a complete process. This process should be viewed only as the means to improve internal consistency reliability in scale development processes.

In conclusion, the objective in this study was to address not only the procedures but also the benefits of the Q-sort technique as a preliminary process in scale development. It may be useful if researchers will use this technique instead of employing an expert opinion or piloted questionnaire to probe validity of the final questionnaire.

This study opens up several directions for future research. First, how do results from this study compare with other key issues studied? Second, why are the results in scale development processes conducted in the Thai context different from other studies, especially in relationship integration? Third, how can we avoid issues or statements which are too subjective due to the theoretical framework?

6 References

Bowersox, D. J., Closs, D. J., Stank, T. P. (2000): Ten Mega-Trends That Will Revolutionize Supply Chain Logistics, in: Journal of Business Logistics, 21(2): 1-16.

Brown, W. (1986): Q Technique and Methods; Principles and Procedures, in: Berry, W., Lewis-Beck, M. (eds.): New Tools for Social Scientists; Advances and Applications in Research Methods, Sage, London.

Chandra, C., Kumar, S. (2001): Supply Chain Management in Theory and Practice: A Passing Fad or a Fundamental Change?, in: Industrial Management and Data System, 100(3): 100-113.

Childerhouse, P., Hermiz, R., Mason-Jones, R., Popp, A., Towil, D. R. (2003): Information Flow in Automotive Supply Chains: Identifying and Learning to Overcome Barriers to Change, in: Industrial Management and Data Systems, 103(7): 491-502.

Claycomb, C., Droge, C., Germain, R. (1999): The Effect of Just-in-Time With Customers on Organizational Design and Performance, in: The International Journal of Logistics Management, 10(1): 37-58.

Dong, Y., Carter, C.R., Dresner, M. E.,(2001): Just in Time Purchasing and Performance: An Exploratory Analysis of Buyer and Supplier Perspectives, in: Journal of Operations Management, 19: 471-483.

Ekinci, Y., Riley, M. (1999): Measuring Hotel Quality: Back to Basics, in: International Journal of Contemporary Hospitality Management, (11)6: 287-293.

Frohlich, M. T. (2002): E-integration in the Supply Chain: Barriers and Performance, in: Decision Science, 33(4): 537-555.

Frohlich, M. T., Westbrook, R. (2001): Arcs of Integration: An International Study of Supply Chain Strategies, in: Journal of Operations Management, 19(2): 185-200.

Hinkin, T. R., Schriesheim, C. A. (1989): Development and Application of New Scales to Measure the Frech and Raven (1959) bases of Social Power, in: Journal of Applied Psychology, (74)4: 561-567.

Hinkin, T. R., Tracey, J. B., Enz, C. A. (1997): Scale Construction: Developing Reliable and Valid Measurement Instruments, in: Journal of Hospitality and Tourism Research, (21)1: 100-120.

Kendall, J. E., Kendall, K.E. (1993): Metaphors and Methodologies: Living Beyond the Systems Machine, in: MIS Quarterly, (17)3: 149-171.

Kerlinger, F. (1986): Foundation of Behavioral Research, 3rd ed., Holy Reinhart and Winston, New York.

Lambert, D. M., Cooper, M. C., Pagh, J. D. (1998): Supply Chain Management: Implementation Issues and Research Opportunities, in: The International Journal of Logistics Management, 9(2): 1-19.

McKeown, B., Thomas, D. (1988): Q Methodology, University Paper 66, Sage, London.

Morash, E. A., Clinton, S. R. (1998): Supply Chain Integration: Customer Value Through Collaborative Closeness Versus Operational Excellence, in: Journal of Marketing Theory and Practice, 6(4): 104-120.

Narasimhan, R., Jayaram, J. (1998): Causal Linkage in Supply Chain Management; An Exploratory Study of North American Manufacturing Firms, in: Decision Science, 29(3): 579-605.

Richeson, L., Lackey, C. W., Stranter, J. W. (1995): The Effect of Communication on The Linkage Between Manufacturing and Suppliers in a JIT Environment, in: International Journal of Purchasing and Materials Management, 31: 21-28.

Sabath, R. (1995): Volatile Demand Calls for Quick Response: The Integrated Supply Chain, in: Logistics Information Management, 8(2): 49-52.

Scanell, T. V., Vickery, S. K., Droge, C. L. (2000): Upstream Supply Chain Management and Competitive Performance in the Automotive Supply Chain Industry, in: Journal of Business Logistics, 21(1): 23-48.

Spekman, R. E., Kamauff, J., Myhr, N. (1998): An Empirical Investigation Into Supply Chain Management: A Perspective on Partnerships, in: Supply Chain Management: An International Journal, 3(2): 53-67.

Stank, T. P., Crum, M., Arango, M. (1999): Benefits of Interfirm Coordination in Food Industry Supply Chain, in: Journal of Business Logistics, 20(2): 21-41.

Stank, T.P., Keller, S. B., Closs, D. J. (2001): Performance Benefits of Supply Chain Logistics Integration, in: Transportation Journal. 41(2/3): 32-46.

Thomas, D. B., Baas, L. R. (1992): The Issue of Generalization in Q Methodology; Reliable Schematics Revisited, in: Operand Subjectivity, (16)1: 18-36.

Tractinsky, N., Jarvenpaa, S. (1995): Information Systems Design Decisions in A Global Versus Domestic Context, in: Management Information Quarterly, December: 507-534.

Turner, J. R. (1993): Integrated Supply Chain Management: What's Wrong With This Picture, in: Industrial Engineer, 14: 190-202.

Van Hoek, R. I., Vos, B., Commandeur, H. R. (1999): Restructuring European Supply Chains by Implementing Postponement Strategies, in: Long Range Planning, 32(5): 505-518.

Supply Chain Management and the Challenge of Organizational Complexity – Methodological Considerations

Stig Johannessen

1	Introduction – Methodology	60
2	Systems Thinking – A Dominating Position in SCM	60
3	Radical Process Thinking and Complexity	64
4	Implications for SCM	68
5	Conclusions	71
6	References	71

Summary:
The dominating organizational perspectives within supply chain management (SCM) are firmly based in a methodological position of holistic systems thinking. From this perspective, it is argued that activities in organizations are best understood and developed when seen as holistic systems, where the various subsystems and processes are seen to interact and constitute a whole. However, holistic systems thinking fails to provide convincing explanations for the change phenomena many people experience in logistics-oriented organizations. Recent organizational complexity research challenges the systems perspective and argues from an ontological position of radical process thinking. Organizational activity is described in terms of processes of local social interaction, creating further interaction and patterns of action with global effects. The causes and explanations are to be found in the experience of these processes and not in some kind of system. There are profound implications from this shift in methodological orientation for organizational research in SCM.

Keywords:
Supply Chain Management, Methodology, Systems Thinking, Radical Process Thinking, Organizational Complexity

1 Introduction – Methodology

One of the foremost methodologists in the social sciences, Herbert Blumer, talked about the methodology of science as the study of the principles which underlie scientific inquiry (Blumer, 1969). This definition implies that methodology reaches into the philosophical provinces of logic, epistemology, and ontology. Blumer's critique was aimed at those who would equate method with methodology. They represent a belief that the essential character and principles of scientific practice are already established and the task narrows to one of application, which essentially is a technical problem of translating scientific method into specific procedures (Baugh, 1990).

This is also very much the situation within the fields of logistics and SCM (Mentzer & Kahn, 1995; Seaker et al. 1993). The debate is often about the contrast between qualitative and quantitative methods and the importance of particular approaches, for instance, case studies (Ellram, 1996) or action research (Naslund, 2002). However, Mears-Young & Jackson (1997); Johannessen & Solem (2002); and Arlbjorn & Halldorsson (2002) provide discussions more focused on the underlying ways of thinking about knowledge creation and research within logistics and SCM.

The present paper is an attempt to contribute further to such discussions. Building on Blumer's definition of methodology, the following will be a reflection and an interpretation of the origin, emergence and problems of systems thinking, which is the dominating ontological and epistemological position within the field of SCM today. This will then be contrasted by a different perspective - radical process thinking - which is the position adopted in the recently developed organizational theory of complex responsive processes. The implications of such a shift of methodological position and theoretical foundation are discussed with respect to management competencies and research method. Finally, some thoughts on future research issues are put forward before making some concluding remarks.

2 Systems Thinking – A Dominating Position in SCM

2.1 Systems Thinking

Johannessen & Solem (2002) describe the ontological and epistemological underpinnings of logistics and point to two systems perspectives. One is a reductionist mechanistic systems perspective (Taylor, 1911), and the other is a holistic systems perspective (von Bertalanffy, 1968). These different perspectives have emerged through history and have led to various ideas, principles and practices about how organizations oriented towards creating value through an effective flow of materials, products, services and information, should be organized and managed.

The two systems perspectives correspond to two organizational paradigms held in logistics and SCM (Christopher, 1998). The "old paradigm" is the organizational thinking typical of the functionally oriented mass-producing industrial companies. Here, logistics is seen to be one of many functions, sometimes with its own department.

The "new paradigm" is to organize according to business processes that cut across functional departments. Such business processes incorporate precise, time-effective and cost-effective ways of supplying a product or a service to a customer. Linking these business processes externally to include several companies in a supply chain or a network brings about the need for effective supply chain management (Hammer, 2001).

It is assumed that this is achieved by looking at the supply chain as a whole system, which in turn requires an "overview" of the organizations and their business processes. Thus, to move the organizations from a functional orientation towards a business process orientation is simultaneously a shift from a reductionist to a holistic way of thinking about systems.

Stacey et al. (2000), Griffin (2002), and Stacey (2003) demonstrate how holistic systems thinking originates from the thoughts of the German philosopher Immanuel Kant. From the 1940s and all the way up until the present day, these thoughts have emerged as dominating ideas in organizational thinking. This origin is therefore of prime importance for a methodological discussion on logistics and SCM.

2.2 The Origins of Holistic Systems Thinking

Kant was trying to resolve a debate in his time concerning the nature of knowledge where on the one hand scientific realists, building on Descartes and Leibnitz, claimed that external reality exists and we are capable of directly obtaining knowledge about this reality. Science was simply understood to be the true knowledge about nature obtained by using the "scientific method" where the individual scientist objectively observes nature, formulates hypotheses about the laws governing it and then tests these laws against quantified data.

Opposing this point of view were the radical skeptics, building on the Scottish philosopher David Hume, who claimed that we cannot know reality directly. Knowledge is relative and unreliable. Ideas result from connections in experience, not from independent reality, and intelligibility reflects habits of mind, not the nature of reality.

Kant's answer to this controversy was to construct a dualism agreeing with both the scientific realists and the radical skeptics. His view is that on one hand there is reality and on the other hand there is the appearance of reality. We can never know reality itself, but only the appearance of reality as sensation.

In talking about living organisms, he saw both the parts and the whole emerge from internal interactions and unfolding what has already been enfolded in them from the beginning, as if there was a purpose for an organism to move towards a mature form of itself. By this, Kant introduced a causality that was formative rather than the linear, "if-then" causality assumed in the mechanistic way of understanding nature.

With regard to human action, Kant held that humans are autonomous and make rational choices. In posing this he introduced a rationalist causality for explaining human behavior. So, nature develops according to a formative causality, where it unfolds what is enfolded through internal interactions. And human action follows a rationalist causality where people can make individual free choices. Humans and nature follow a dualistic causality.

When modern organizational theory developed after the 1940s, it did so at the same time that modern systems thinking developed in the form of cybernetics, general systems theory and systems dynamics. The ideas of Kant were now slightly changed and directly applied to human action. Organizations were thought of as systems with humans being the parts. By the interaction of the parts (humans), the system (organization) could unfold its enfolded nature (purpose). In order to explain change, one must resort to autonomous individuals standing outside the organization and making rational choices for the organization. These individuals are of course the leaders.

2.3 Problems with Holistic Systems Thinking

In holistic systems thinking the duality of being able to be both a part of the organization and also stand outside it is resolved by locating such contradictions in different spaces and time periods, in accordance with the dualistic thinking of Kant. Different spaces are created in the spatial metaphor of a whole separated by a boundary from other systems, or wholes, which leads to the image of an "inside" and an "outside" of organizations. Different time periods are created by leaders seeing themselves operating in sequenced time. First, they are free and can see themselves standing outside the organization and making decisions. Then, they are not free and can see themselves as a part of the organization unfolding according to the decisions that they have made earlier.

This way of thinking creates many problems. Perhaps the most important is the problem of explaining novelty and change. Explanations pointing to "outside pressure," which imply that change is caused by the operation of external factors on the organizations, are unsatisfactory. What does "outside" really mean? If we agree to the assumption that change has to do with human activity, we would face the difficulty of explaining how any human activity in our world could be outside of other human activities.

Another important problem having to do with the separation of the inside and the outside is the epistemological assumption of the "objective observer." The manager or the researcher is seen as being able to gather facts about organizations, supply chains or networks. In doing this they proceed as if they were in some way placed outside of various organizational phenomena, thought of as objects. This separation does not explain what exactly the manager or the researcher is being placed outside of. Organizational aspects like work routines, relationships, knowledge, culture, value creation, strategies, and logistics are all human creations – ongoing human action, which inevitably only can be found in human experience. So if we are going to do research into such human experience, and can place ourselves on the "outside," it would also mean that we have the capacity to place ourselves on the outside of our own experience, an idea that both intuitively and logically is absurd.

2.4 Further Problems with Current SCM Thinking

It is a common view that the essence of logistics-oriented success is cooperation and coordination within and between companies (Stock & Lambert, 2001). Prime importance is placed on relationships between companies (Christopher, 1998). However, there seems to be little attention given to human and social perspectives and explanations about what relationships mean in terms of social interaction. Bypassing these issues represents serious shortcomings within the field of SCM.

Croxton et al. (2001) serve as an example of the dominating attitudes in this respect. Building on the recommendations by the Global Supply Chain Forum, they stress that success in SCM is dependent on managers directing the changes, the creation of agreement on manager's visions, the movement against stated goals, the empowerment of people, and the continuous work on the understanding of change.

According to these statements, managers can simply direct and control changes. There is nothing in the prescriptions to indicate how they deal with difficulties and conflicts that they may face. They are supposed to create agreement on visions, but how is this done? Can people just suspend their personal and social intentions and replace this with the stated visions of managers? The movement against stated goals is also supposedly important, as if the future unfolds in a linear and predicable way. Does this match what we experience? How is it that managers supposedly possess visions of the future, and are able to know the right direction for reaching the associated stated goals? What does direction really mean in terms of social interaction in complex contexts?

The recommendations also suggest that people are to be empowered. But if empowerment means influencing decisions, then this means that people interact and engage in social patterns and political processes that are very unlikely to turn out according to managers' visions, goals and directions. Empowerment and controlled directions are diverging recommendations.

The last point in the recipe for success in SCM is the ongoing work on understanding change. Despite this, no ideas are given about what change might be or how it is produced. Change seems to be rational, planned implementations of certain clear-cut ideas, while the phenomena of unpredictable and unknowable change are not treated, although most companies today struggle to deal with this. Many would think that the stated recommendations are unrealistic ideas of what organizations are and what competencies managers need to have in a turbulent business world.

The theories that are often referred to as being essential in logistics and SCM - transaction cost theory, agency theory, resource-based theory, network theory, and various combinations of these theories – are all confined within the assumptions of holistic systems thinking (Johannessen, 2003). They deal with unpredictable change as something coming from the "outside of the system." Change can be analyzed and acted upon with rational decisions in order to implement adaptations to the observed situation. Again, no attention is given to the way unpredictable change emerges in social interactions and affects the results of organizational activities. The theories of logistics and SCM, and the subsequent prescriptions for SCM success, stand out as extreme simplifications and diversions from everyday experiences and challenges in supply chain organizations.

Let us now turn to a radically different perspective on organizational activity and see how this contrasts and challenges the systems perspective.

3 Radical Process Thinking and Complexity

3.1 Radical Process Thinking

All the central features of systems thinking – the ideas of dual causality, thinking in terms of wholes, boundaries, "insides" and "outsides" – are abandoned in radical process thinking. There is also a movement away from thinking about different hierarchical levels of existence or explanation, such as the notions that certain explanations apply to the individual "level," another to the group, and yet another to phenomena on the organizational "level." In radical process thinking individual and social phenomena are seen as different aspects and expressions of the same basic processes of human interaction.

This thinking can be traced back to the German philosopher Georg W.F. Hegel's critique of Kant (Stacey et al., 2000). Hegel saw knowledge creation taking place through conflict, and the world of our experience is the world we create in our thought. He criticized Kant's position of starting with an isolated individual subject capable of experiencing an outside reality, a system lying outside of experience and causing it, from which the person is separated.

Writing in the late 1930s, the sociologist Norbert Elias was influenced by the thoughts of Hegel. He was concerned about how the evolution of social order and civilization had emerged through history without anyone planning this evolution (Elias, 1939/2000). It seemed to have evolved through self-regulating and self-organizing processes that were paradoxically creating order at the same time, as no one was planning or overseeing the ordering.

Elias found that this phenomenon arose in the interactions between people constantly following their own intentions at the same time as they are being constrained in social action. The long-term consequences cannot be foreseen because the conflict between actions, plans and purposes of many individuals gives rise to contexts and situations that no one has planned, intended or created. Individuals do not pursue their plans separate from others. They are always in some kind of relationship or power configuration with others.

In Elias' process theory, change is self-organizing, emergent processes of perpetually constructing the future as continuity and transformation. Order arises in specific dynamics of social interweaving in particular places at particular times. This process cannot be explained within the causality frameworks of systems thinking, or by looking at the change process as being caused by something outside the process itself, e.g. forces of some kind. Instead, a paradoxical causality is suggested, in which individuals form social relations while being formed by them at the same time. The sociology of Elias provides a distinctive way of thinking about the relationship between the individual and the group as two aspects of the same process of human relating. The relationship between the individual and the group is paradoxical in that each simultaneously forms and is formed by the other.

Bringing Elias' thoughts in contact with more recent developments in the field of complexity research reveals striking mutual support. Complexity research demonstrates that the unpredictable emergence of order from disorder in nature happens through processes of spontaneous self-organization (Prigogine, 1997). This points clearly to an ontological view of transformative process, in which reality changes and evolves within paradoxical order/disorder processes that have inherent organizing potential and do not operate as an effect of some external cause.

Thus, there is only one causality – that of a transformative process. This provides us with the opportunity to use analogues from complexity research in explaining human action from the perspective of this transformative process ontology. This is exactly the point of departure for the newly developed perspective of complex responsive processes (Stacey et al., 2000; Griffin, 2002; Stacey, 2003).

3.2 The Complex Responsive Processes Perspective

The complex responsive processes perspective draws on particular insights from natural scientific complexity research associated with the phenomena of self-organization, paradoxes, simultaneity of stability and change, non-linearity, spontaneous creation of novelty, the collapse of linkage between cause and effects, and the creation of radical unpredictability (Allen, 1998; Casti, 1997; Gell-Mann, 1994; Holland, 1998; Kauffman, 1993; Prigogine, 1997). It also provides a consistent reinterpretation of ideas developed earlier in history concerning human interactions and the structural self-organizing emergence of human consciousness, organizations and societies (Mead, 1934; Elias, 1939/2000). With this perspective, the problem of organizational change is beginning to be addressed from a radically different orientation.

From the complex responsive processes perspective, organizational phenomena are a result of people interacting with each other and the environment. By the responding processes they create, they transform the reality of both themselves and their environment in unpredictable ways. Thus, human reality is described in terms of relational processes of never-ending transformative character - processes that escape systems theoretical terms. The notion of systems is therefore abandoned.

This perspective sets out to explain what creates potential transformational change in terms of self-organizing processes. These are processes born out of human interaction, which means that change does not come from the outside of anything. Every human activity produces change.

The result is a refocusing of attention when thinking about organizations. The focus is on self-organizing processes, emergent results and different qualities such as participation, diversity, conversational life, and living with anxiety, unpredictability and paradox. The quality of relations creates the organizational capacity for change and new patterns.

This different understanding also brings the insight that conversations are the basis for new direction, as the future is constructed from transformative conversational processes. It is from these conversational processes that the form of the organization continuously re-emerges and potentially changes (Shaw, 2002). It is here that basic assumptions and ideas about how and why things are done are explored and challenged. The creation and evolution of organizations happen because of the involvement and interactions of many people, all of whom are constrained and enabled by power relations and shifting degrees of influence.

3.3 Comparing Perspectives

A comparison between the complex responsive processes perspective and the systems perspective are above all a debate about ontological and epistemological positions. As should be clear from the discussion so far in this paper, established ideas of logistics and SCM are based on an ontological assumption of holistic systems thinking, while the theory of complex responsive processes is based on a different ontological assumption, i.e. the assumption of reality as processes in the particular meaning promoted by Hegel and Elias.

Which one is better? This is a question of making sense of the arguments. Many researchers and practitioners find that the complex responsive processes perspective offers explanations that resonate with their experience, and therefore makes more sense than the explanations offered by systems thinking. Others might think differently about it.

Strong criticism about systems thinking and its dominance, and promoting a different view, could be perceived as a wish for such a different view to become dominant. It is therefore important to distinguish between making a critical argument, and the idea that this argument represents the only right way of thinking. On the contrary, it is the absence of criticism that inevitably will mean submission to a dominant view. Today, systems thinking dominates the ideas and perspectives on organizations and their management. This means that critique of systems thinking should be encouraged and welcomed.

It must be appreciated that the theory of complex responsive processes is not the first theory to create a different attitude towards the dominating views of science and research. As shown throughout this paper, critical and alternative ideas to systems thinking have been voiced by philosophers and social thinkers, all the way from Hegel's critique of Kant up until Elias' ideas on social interaction and Blumer's critique of method in social science. The complex responsive processes perspective is the voice raised again today – this time enriched with the fundamental insights from the natural sciences of complexity.

4 Implications for SCM

4.1 Management Competencies

For (supply chain) managers the complex responsive processes perspective implies a different focus of attention. Managers need to become engaged in activities which address people's responses to the meaning and effects of power relations, conflicts, unpredictability, open futures, the processes of making sense, living with paradoxes, self-organizing phenomena, and diversity. This is very different from defining the role of the manager to be about engagement in the creation of strategic plans, common visions, values and goals, performance measurements and other control activities. A shift of attention could mean that managers and others could act in the present towards an uncertain future by accepting that the future is evolving in non-linear, paradoxical and radically unpredictable ways.

For instance, to pay attention to power relations and conflict is about learning to live with conflicts and realize that they simultaneously are the source of both constrained behavior and of change in behavior and action. It is particularly important for managers to develop relationship competencies since it is in the encounters between people that the future of the organization is continuously created and recreated.

Another example of the ability to accept and live with paradoxes is being committed to what one is doing, as one can doubt this at the same time. Traditionally, it does not look good if managers doubt their decisions. They are supposed to be totally committed to their own decisions. However, this could leave them incapable of understanding the importance of unpredictable new patterns that are emerging. On the other hand, doubt renders the risk of paralysis in decision-making. Keeping paradoxes alive is perhaps the most important management competency from the standpoint of complex responsive processes theory, and indeed a great challenge to develop and uphold.

4.2 Research Method

Within the field of SCM, the perspective of complex responsive processes could advance the meaning, explanation and understanding of how the relations between people involved in various activities in logistics oriented organizations affect the patterns of logistical action. Logistics and SCM are about how one can create added value to a product in the flow of materials, services and information. It is about how a product is transformed, stored, transported, sold and recycled. There is some kind of pattern of human action everywhere.

If we, as researchers, enter a particular pattern of logistical action, a possible approach is to try to make sense about how these patterns of action are created in the relations that we, like the other participants, play a part in.

The complex responsive processes perspective suggests that knowledge is about identity, and identity is both personal and social at the same time. Knowledge based on experience in relating must be said to be scientific when given the discussion and theoretical treatment that will seek to explain such experience. Such explanations do not have to be systematized, tabularized and catalogued. They could nevertheless provide insight and value for researchers, managers and others.

The complex responsive processes perspective departs from a view of the detached or objective observer and promotes a research approach of emergent participative exploration (Christensen, 2003). The role of the researcher is seen to emerge from the relations with people engaged in organizational patterns. This means that the result of the researcher's presence can be influential, but carries no guarantee of this. The intention of the researcher is to join ongoing conversations in order to make sense out of the relations he/she participates in (Shaw, 2002). The researcher can obtain knowledge about organizational patterns by engaging in relations with people. The knowledge creation process is not separated from the people the researcher is relating with.

The methods of participative exploration imply documentation by the writing of narratives and stories as accounts of experiences. These accounts, when enriched with theoretical explanation, should form a piece of scientific work from the complex responsive processes perspective. The contribution is to be found in the responses this work might evoke in people, responses that might resonate with their own experiences and so help explain such experiences. If this results in further actions in companies or elsewhere, it is not because of some recipe or specific recommendations, but rather because someone has gained a different insight that will inspire or provoke that person to do something or say something that stimulates a different attention in everyday organizational life.

Narrative documentations provide researchers and others with the possibility to see how everyday conversations in organizational life affect the way meaning and patterns of action are created (Johannessen, 2003). It is the attentive research focus of the "here and now" which escapes conventional scientific criteria, but nevertheless is particularly valuable with respect to understanding organizational developments in terms of processes of change in human action. Hence, the contribution and usefulness of this approach should not be assessed from an ontological position of systems thinking and the epistemological constraint of traditional science. These issues must be evaluated from the ontological and epistemological position of the radical process perspective that the research is based upon.

4.3 Future Research Issues

Some of the important themes in organizational life, which the complex responsive processes theory addresses, are for instance power relations, self-organization, non-linear phenomena, emergence, paradox, complexity, and unpredictability. These issues are experienced and produced by supply chain managers and others every day. In order to learn more about these phenomena, we need to address them specifically in research. Research questions must therefore be formulated and pursued.

Questions such as: what are the global effects of local power differences in the everyday life of managers? In what way are supply chain actors experiencing their everyday situation compared to the plans and strategies made by them and others? How is change produced in supply chains and networks, and what are the effects of this change?

The nature of competition and cooperation can be understood as paradoxical aspects of human relations. One important research issue related to this is: how do such paradoxical patterns of action emerge and transform complex (often global) value-creating structures such as supply chains and networks of organizations?

In this context it is a crucial research focus to explore the co-developmental dynamics between people and technology. People influence and structure technology, while at the same time they are being influenced and structured by technology and wider economic and organizational patterns. Research into these complex interactions and relations have consequences for areas such as product development, electronic business, production, and transportation.

The phenomenon of self-organization is not explained in traditional organizational theory or in any of the theories underlying logistics and SCM. The dynamics and evolution of self-organizational processes are a very important theme for future research initiatives into organizational complexity, logistics and supply chains, because they deal with the non-intended structuring of organizations, that is, patterning without any overall decisions having being made to this effect.

It is also important to explore the interactions between people and resources, such as finance and the time people use, and to investigate the emergence of meaning about corporate responsibility and sustainable development in the global economy.

In order to address, explain and obtain knowledge about these phenomena, we need theory and methods. The complex responsive processes perspective provides us with ideas about this. Theoretically we can be helped with the basic explanations about social interaction. Methodologically, knowledge creation is also understood as interactional patterns between people. Consequently, participative methods are advocated, because they will provide the researcher with the opportunity to interact with people in ways which are relevant with respect to everyday life. The researcher engages in relationships, which in turn are the source of inquiries and explorations.

Thus, the theoretical and methodological perspective of complex responsive processes offer an advancement towards insights about how companies in supply chains and networks emerge as complex self-organizing patterns of action involving people, technology, nature and resources.

5 Conclusions

It is increasingly clear that established theories regarding organizations and development are falling short in the face of rapidly changing organizational realities. There is a great need for new theories and methodologies that can address organizational understanding in different orientations.

The complex responsive processes perspective challenges the systems theoretical foundation of logistics and SCM. It is based on a shift in methodological thinking towards a radical process perspective. Such a process perspective abandons the notion of systems altogether and sees organizations emerging as a result of people interacting with each other and the environment, and by the responding processes they create. People in their social interaction transform the reality of both themselves and their environment.

The complex responsive processes perspective serves as a powerful new theoretical and methodological approach. It constructs explanations concerning logistics and SCM as self-organizing patterns of action perpetually evolving in the experience of everyday conversational life. Future research offers the possibility of further constructing meaningful explanations of the paradoxes associated with the emergence of global value-creating structures such as supply chains and networks.

6 References

Allen, P. M. (1998): Evolving complexity in social science, in: Altman, G. & Koch, W. A. (eds.): Systems: New Paradigms for the Human Sciences, Walter de Gruyter, New York.

Arlbjorn, J. S., Halldorsson, A. (2002): Logistics knowledge creation: Reflections on content, processes and context, in: International Journal of Physical Distribution & Logistics Management, 32(1): 22-40.

Baugh, K. (1990): The Methodology of Herbert Blumer. Critical Interpretation and Repair, Cambridge University Press, New York.

Blumer, H. (1969): Symbolic Interactionism. Perspective and Method, Prentice-Hall, Englewood Cliffs, New Jersey.

Casti, J. (1997): Complexification: Explaining a Paradoxical World through the Science of Surprise, HarperCollins, London.

Christensen, B. (2003): Reframing consulting from within human relating, Unpublished DMan-thesis, University of Hertfordshire, London.

Christopher, M. (1998): Logistics and Supply Chain Management, second edition, Pearson Education, London.

Croxton, K. L., García-Dastugue, S. J., Lambert, D. M., Rogers, D. S. (2001): The Supply Chain Management Processes, in: International Journal of Logistics Management, 12(2): 13-36.

Elias, N. (2000): The Civilizing Process, Blackwell, Oxford. First published 1939.

Ellram, L. M. (1996): The use of the Case Study Method in Logistics Research, in: Journal of Business Logistics, 17(2): 93-138.

Gell-Mann, M. (1994): The quark and the jaguar, Freeman, New York.

Griffin, D. (2002): The Emergence of Leadership: Linking self-organization and ethics, Routledge, London.

Hammer, M. (2001): The superefficient company, in: Harvard Business Review, 79(8): 82-92.

Holland, J. (1998): Emergence from chaos to order, Oxford University Press, New York.

Johannessen, S., Solem, O. (2002): Logistics Organizations: Ideologies, Principles and Practice, in: The International Journal of Logistics Management, 13(1): 31-42.

Johannessen, S. (2003): An Explorative Study of Complexity, Strategy and Change in Logistics Organizations, PhD-thesis 2003:91, Norwegian University of Science and Technology, Trondheim.

Kauffman, S. A. (1993): Origins of order: Self-organization and selection in evolution, Oxford University Press, Oxford.

Mead, G. H. (1934): Mind, Self and Society, Chicago University Press, Chicago.

Mears-Young, B., Jackson, M. C. (1997): Integrated logistics – call in the revolutionaries, in: Omega – International Journal of Management Science, 25(6): 605-618.

Mentzer, J. T., Kahn, K. (1995): A framework for logistics research, in: Journal of Business Logistics, 16(1): 231-250.

Naslund, D. (2002): Logistics needs qualitative research – especially action research, in: International Journal of Physical Distribution & Logistics Management, 32(5): 60-77.

Prigogine, I. (1997): The End of Certainty: Time, Chaos and the New Laws of Nature, The Free Press, New York.

Seaker, R. F., Waller, M. A., Dunn, S. C. (1993): A Note on Research Methodology in Business Logistics, in: Logistics and Transportation Review, 29(4): 383-387.

Shaw, P. (2002): Changing the Conversation in Organizations. A Complexity Approach to Change, Routledge, London.

Stacey, R. D., Griffin, D, Shaw, P. (2000): Complexity and Management - Fad or Radical Challenge to Systems Thinking? Routledge, London.

Stacey, R. D. (2003): Strategic Management & Organisational Dynamics: The Challenge of Complexity, Pearson Education Ltd, London.

Stock, J. R., Lambert, D. M. (2001): Strategic Logistics Management, McGraw-Hill, New York.

Taylor, F. W. (1911): Scientific Management, Harper Brothers, New York.

von Bertalanffy, L. (1968): General systems theory: Foundations, Development, Applications, George Braziller, New York.

The Configurational Approach in Supply Chain Management

Axel Neher

1 Holistic View in Supply Chain Management 76
2 Selected Supply Chain Management Configurations 78
3 Conclusions and Directions for Further Research 85
4 References 88

Summary:
A basic element of logistics and supply chain management is the holistic or system view. Following this perspective, especially on a strategic level, supply chain management has to analyze the supply chain as a whole and must not only concentrate on details or specific elements. The configurational approach is one method for realizing this. A configuration is defined as a commonly occurring cluster of strategy, structure, process and context. The following article analyzes how the configurational approach can be applied in supply chain management and provides a critical overview on the different existing configurational approaches in supply chain management.

Keywords:
Supply Chain Management, Configurational Approach, Logistics Types

1 Holistic View in Supply Chain Management

1.1 Holistic View

Increasing complexity forces supply chain management to concentrate on the essential and characteristic aspects in designing, managing and controlling supply chains. As Khandwalla already pointed out in 1973, not only the optimization of isolated elements, but also the harmony among these elements have a deep impact on performance. It is argued that a better fit between the elements of a system will lead to higher performance.

Although the system or holistic perspective is defined as a main characteristic dimension of logistics and supply chain management, most approaches, methods or instruments still focus on parts of the system, neglecting the relations between the parts. For further improvements in supply chain management, an approach is required which actually applies this system view to the tasks of designing, managing and controlling in supply chains. One approach for such a necessary system or holistic point of view can be seen in the 'configurational approach.'

1.2 Configurational Approach

The configurational approach describes organizations as commonly occurring clusters of attributes of strategy, structure, process and context (Miller, 1981; Macharzina & Engelhard, 1991). Each type of configuration is characterized as a set of variables which fits together including internal aspects of the organization as well as the external environment/context (Figure 1). It is assumed that the parts of a socio-economic system (here: logistics systems or supply chains) take their meaning from the whole and cannot be understood in isolation (Meyer et al., 1993).

In this sense, configurations are composed of tight constellations of mutually supportive elements and there is a harmony among these elements. It is argued that a configuration is dominated by a "theme" which expresses the characteristics of such a configuration (Miller, 1986). By focusing on this theme and in assuring consistency between the internal elements as well as between the internal elements and its environment, a better performance is expected concerning the selected multi-dimensional effectiveness profile.

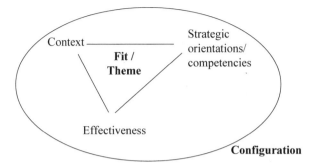

Figure 1: Basic Pattern of a Configuration

In the beginning of configurational approaches, classical organization related aspects like centralization–decentralization of decision making, specialization, functional aspects etc. were focused upon. Famous examples are the five ideal types of organizational configurations by Mintzberg (1979) (simple structure, machine bureaucracy, professional bureaucracy, divisionalized form, adhocracy) or the four transition types by Miles & Snow (1978) (prospector, analyzer, defender, reactor). With growing interest in logistics and supply chain management in the last years and the need for a more holistic perspective in these fields, the configurational approach has been adopted to logistics and supply chain management. Configurations like Lean, Agile, Physically Efficient, Responsive, Risk-Hedging etc. are elaborated upon.

But what does such a supply chain configuration look like? What are the main aspects of such configurations? What is the dominant "theme" of the configuration all elements have to fit to? When applying the configurational approach to supply chain management, these questions have to be answered. In a first step, a clear description of the relevant elements of context, strategic orientation and effectiveness is necessary. In a second step, the relations between these elements have to be analyzed and the dominating "theme" of the configuration has to be shown.

The application of the configurational approach to supply chain management will lead to a better understanding of the relations between the numerous elements of supply chain management, which is an important step towards a supply chain theory. The knowledge of the different configurations spans a field of possible solutions for supply chain management in the sense of equifinality, which means that a functional outcome can be realized via different ways (Gresov & Drazin, 1997). In this sense, configurations are not ideal or normative models but patterns of cohesive elements linked to or expressed by a certain theme. This knowledge will help a supply chain manager to set the details in his organization either by copying or by promoting innovations.

1.3 Supply Chain Management

Although academic definitions of supply chain management differ in details across authors, the overall main aspect can be seen in the definition of supply chain management as the management of the goods and information flow through the supply chain from the raw material supplier to the final customer (Mentzer et al., 2001). The focus of this definition is on the interorganizational coordination of the different actors within a supply chain.

However, even though logistics and supply chain management went through a rapid development in recent years, and in the former development stage logistics or supply chain management was limited to the internal view of an enterprise, this perspective (or definition) of supply chain management continues to be in use. Most of the approaches on supply chain configurations take this perspective and argue from the enterprise's point of view. In most cases a critical reflection concerning the special requirements of an interorganizational management is missing.

In the following chapter selected configurational approaches in supply chain management are presented. The focus is on the main dimensions and the dominant themes of the configurations.

2 Selected Supply Chain Management Configurations

A starting point of the configurational approach in supply chain management can be seen in the article of Fisher (1997), which discusses the question: "What's the right supply chain for your product?" To describe his configurations, he identifies the 'type of product' or 'predictability of demand' as main characteristic elements and differentiates between functional products (predictable demand) and innovative products (unpredictable demand). With a predictable demand environment, a logistics configuration focusing on physically efficient processes is considered as most appropriate, whereas in the case of an unpredictable demand (innovative products), a market-responsive-process configuration fits better (see table 1).

Tan et al. offer a more differentiated approach concerning the market-responsive supply chain configuration (Tan et al., 2000). They divide the market-responsive supply chain configuration into two types: the customizable product type configuration and the innovative product type configuration. The market responsive process configuration for customizable products is characterized by semi-predictable demand pattern and medium life cycles. The key action and goal is to customize products to individual demand. This could be achieved by demand-driven planning processes, assembly-to-order, mass customization, and postponement strategies. The minor differences of the market responsive process configuration for innovative products compared to the customizable product configuration could be seen in unpredictable demand patterns, short life cycles and a make-to-order strategy.

	Physically Efficient Process	**Market-Responsive Process**
Primary purpose	supply predictable demand efficiently at the lowest possible cost	respond quickly to unpredictable demand in order to minimize stockouts, forced markdowns, and obsolete inventory
Manufacturing focus	maintain high average utilization rate	deploy excess buffer capacity
Inventory strategy	generate high turnover and minimize inventory throughout the chain	deploy significant buffer stocks of parts or finished goods
Lead-time focus	shorten lead time as long as it doesn't increase cost	invest aggressively in ways to reduce lead time
Approach to choosing suppliers	select primarily for cost and quality	select primarily for speed, flexibility, and quality
Product-design strategy	maximize performance and minimize cost	use modular design in order to postpone product differentiation for as long as possible

Table 1: Efficient vs. Market-Responsive Supply Chain Configuration (Fisher, 1997: 108)

The three differentiated configurations by Tan et al. provide only vague information on how to design or manage the supply chain. The main differences between the configurations are characterized by the demand management policies of make-to-stock, assembly-to-order, and make-to-order. The information concerning the other characteristic elements of the configuration like strategy or information sharing are closely related to the demand management policy. This differentiation provides some information concerning which parts of supply chain processes should be standardized or individualized (see the standardization-individualization continuum of Lampel & Mintzberg, 1996 or the comparable postponement concept (Bucklin, 1965; Bowersox et al., 1986; Ciou et al., 2002)).

Another more production oriented configuration approach is shown by Christopher. He distinguishes two types of supply chain configurations, the 'Agile Supply Chain' and the 'Lean Supply Chain' (Christopher, 2000). Differentiating dimensions are the variability of demand/variety of products offered and the volume of production (see Figure 2).

If the environment is not very predictable (volatile demand) and the requirement for variety is high, then an 'Agile Supply Chain' is needed. In high volume, low variety and predictable environments, 'Lean Supply Chains' work best. As turbulent and volatile markets are becoming the norm, Christopher feels that agile supply chains are more likely to survive.

Unfortunately, Christopher only provides little information describing the agile supply chain configuration. He states that agile supply chains should be market sensitive (pull-oriented), virtual, process integrating and network based, and he stresses that the information technology is vital for agile supply chains. For the management of such a supply chain configuration, this information is limited.[1] Furthermore he notes that pure configurations might be appropriate on some occasions, but there will often be situations where hybrid configurations are appropriate. "A supply chain may need to be lean for part of the time and agile for the rest" (Christopher, 2000: 40).

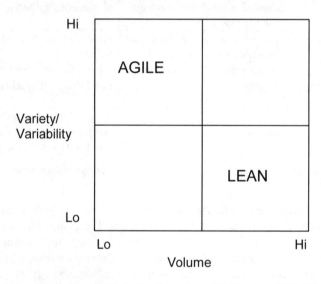

Figure 2: Lean and Agile Supply Chain Configurations (Christopher, 2000: 39)

Others call this hybrid-configuration 'Leagile' as the combination of Lean and Agile (see Mason-Jones, Naylor & Towill, 2000). Referring to the postponement concept, they characterize the 'leagile' supply chain configuration as a combination of a lean process part before the decoupling point and an agile process part after the decoupling point (see Figure 3).

---

[1] In a later article (Christopher & Towill, 2002) a more detailed description of these two configurations is given, but the information concerning the management of such configurations is still limited.

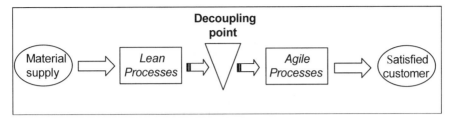

Figure 3: Leagile Supply Chain Configuration (Mason-Jones et al., 2000: 4065)

The approaches presented above concentrate on the customer/demand side. As Lee argued, this is correct but not sufficient (Lee, 2002). In order to design the right supply chain strategy, it is necessary to take all uncertainties into account; on the demand side as well as on the supply side. Lee's configurations are determined by the two dimensions of demand uncertainty and supply uncertainty.

Recurring to Fisher, Lee describes the demand side as 'functional products' (low demand uncertainty) and 'innovative products' (high demand uncertainty) and the supply side as 'stable' processes (low supply uncertainty) and 'evolving' processes (high supply uncertainty).

Combining these two dimensions, Lee distinguishes four types of supply chains: 'Efficient', 'Risk-hedging', 'Responsive', and 'Agile' (see Figure 4). In the case of low demand and low supply uncertainty, the 'efficient supply chain configuration' is appropriate. The focus should be on economies of scale, non-value-added activities should be eliminated, and optimization techniques should be deployed (Lee, 2002). 'Risk-hedging supply chain' configurations are appropriate for low demand uncertainty and high supply uncertainty. The main characteristic of this type is to pool and share resources in a supply chain to reduce and share risks. In the situation of high demand uncertainty and low supply uncertainty, the 'responsive supply chain' configuration is considered the most appropriate. This configuration is characterized by build-to-order and mass customization processes, and order accuracy is considered the key to success. The 'agile supply chain' configuration is proposed in highly uncertain demand and supply environments. This configuration can be seen as a combination of the strengths of hedging and responsive supply chain configurations and aims "at being responsive and flexible to customer needs, while the risks of supply shortages or disruptions are hedged by pooling inventory or other capacity resources" (Lee, 2002: 114).

	Demand Uncertainty	
	Low (Functional Products)	High (Innovative Products)
Low (Stable Process)	**Efficient supply chains** (Grocery, basic apparel, food, oil and gas)	**Responsive supply chains** (Fashion apparel, computers, pop music)
High (Evolving Process)	**Risk-hedging supply chains** (Hydro-electric power, some food products)	**Agile supply chains** (Telecom, high-end computers, semiconducter)

(Supply Uncertainty on vertical axis)

Figure 4: Uncertainty-based Supply Chain Configurations (Lee, 2002: 108, 114)

The advantage of Lee's approach is that it focuses on uncertainty, which can be identified as one of the prevailing problems in supply chains. In comparison with other approaches, he not only concentrates on demand uncertainty, but also takes supply uncertainty into account. He also provides some examples on how to design the different configurations. However, there is no clear structure for describing the organizational structure or physical and management processes of each configuration. A direct comparison of the different configurations is not possible and the practical use for managers could be considered limited.

Another configurational approach is presented by Corsten and Gabriel (2002). They use the dimensions "product structure" and "demand uncertainty" to describe supply chain configurations (Corsten & Gabriel, 2002). For physical-assembled products in a stable demand environment they propose a 'Lean Supply Chain Design' as most appropriate, whereas in unstable demand environments an 'Agile Supply Chain Design' is probably most successful. For chemical-biological products in a stable demand environment 'Connected Supply Chain Designs' are proposed, and in unstable environments 'Speed Supply Chain Designs' are suggested (see Figure 5).

	Product structure	
	Physical-assembled	Chemical-Biological
Stable	**Lean** **Supply Chain Design** Automobile Industry	**Connected** **Supply Chain Design** Chemical- and Pharmaceutical Industry
Dynamic	**Agile** **Supply Chain Design** Electronic Industry	**Speed** **Supply Chain Design** Consumer Goods

Demand (row label spanning between Stable and Dynamic)

Figure 5: Supply Chain Configurations by Corsten & Gabriel
(Based on Corsten & Gabriel, 2002: 235)

In contrast to the configurational approaches mentioned before, Corsten and Gabriel provide a more detailed and structured description of the different configurations. Based on the SCOR-Model, which is a process reference model that describes supply chains using the five main processes of source, make, deliver, return, and plan, they give an overview of consequences for these processes in each configuration. These descriptions provide supply chain managers with information on how to design these processes. However, the descriptions are relatively vague, and key words like "Efficient Consumer Response" or "Lean Production" are used.

Another approach is provided by Klaas (2003). He integrates most of the aspects of the other approaches. The main dimensions describing a configuration are the strategic goals on the one hand and the mechanisms of coordinating the flow of goods and information in the supply chain on the other hand. Strategic goals are cost and flexibility. Coordination mechanisms are differentiated on a first level into forecast-driven (anticipative) and demand-driven (reactive) mechanisms, and on a second level further subdivided into push and pull systems.

The combination of these dimensions leads to four types of configurations as shown in Figure 6. Klaas calls these types 'logistics segments' to point out that in a supply chain, different logistics segments, for example related to different customers or products, could exist at the same time.

While the other approaches do not explicitly relate to configuration theory, Klaas' approach is theoretically based on the configuration theory. As a configuration is defined as a cluster of context, strategy, structure, and processes, he describes the four different types of logistics segments using the dimensions 'mechanism of coordination', 'logistics processes and infrastructure', 'formal organizational structure', and 'logistics context'. The dimension 'mechanism of coordination' includes aspects of push or pull oriented coordination of the flow of goods as well as how tight the different parts of the supply chain (supply, production, distribution) are connected. 'Logistics processes and infrastructure' includes aspects of postponement/speculation, bundling of materials' flow, and the question of centralizing/decentralizing. The dimension 'formal organizational structure' is broadly described and includes all aspects of formal organization structure like specialization, standardization, delegation, etc. The 'logistical context' includes all aspects of demand (predictable/unpredictable, required service level, quantity required), product (volume, weight), production technology (flexibility, economies of scale) and competitive strategy (cost leader; differentiation).

	strategic goal	
	cost	flexibility
forecast driven	**Tight logistics segment** functional standard products 'anticipative push-controlling'	**Agile logistics segment** innovative standard products 'anticipative pull-controlling'
coordinating mechanism		
demand driven	**Modular logistics segment** modular system products 'reactive pull-controlling'	**Individual logistics segment** individual single products 'reactive push-controlling'

Figure 6: Supply Chain Configurations by Klaas (Klaas, 2003: 277)

Table 2 gives a summarizing overview on the selected configurational approaches presented above.

Authors	Dimensions	Configurations
Fisher, 1997	- uncertainty of demand - product	- Physically efficient process - Market responsive process
Tan et al., 2000	- uncertainty of demand - product	- Physically efficient process - Market responsive process • *customizable product* • *innovative product*
Christopher, 2000	- Variety/Variability - Volume	- Agile - Lean
Mason-Jones/ Naylor/Towill, 2000	- various	- Leagile
Lee, 2002	- Demand characteristics - Supply characteristics	- Efficient supply chain - Responsive supply chain - Risk-hedging supply chain - Agile supply chain
Corsten & Gabriel, 2002	- Demand uncertainty - Product structure	- Lean Supply Chain - Connected Supply Chain - Agile Supply Chain - Speed Supply Chain
Klaas, 2003	- strategic goal - coordination mechanism	- Tight logistics segment - Agile logistics segment - Modular logistics segment - Individual logistics segment

Table 2: Overview on Supply Chain Configuration Approaches

3 Conclusions and directions for further research

The analysis of the supply chain configuration approaches shows that they are all based on an individual (enterprise) point of view. Although the different approaches focus on varying aspects, most approaches use similar main dimensions to extract the different configurations and use comparable labels to describe the prevailing themes of the configurations.

Dominant dimensions influencing the theme of a configuration are the uncertainty of demand (and supply), volume, and (either explicitly or implicitly mentioned) generic competitive strategies like cost leadership or differentiation (by quality or flexibility). A comparison of the different approaches based on these dimensions leads to three clusters of configurations (Figure 7) which can be labeled:

- Lean (low uncertainty, high volume, cost orientation)
- Agile (high uncertainty, low volume, differentiation orientation,
- Leagile (hybrid of Lean and Agile).

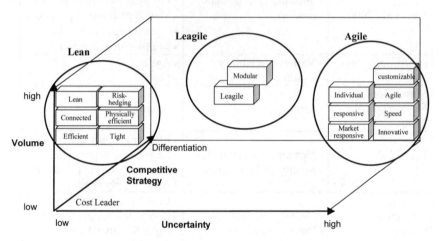

Figure 7: Three Configuration Clusters

Although the presented approaches do not focus on interorganizational aspects of supply chains, they are nevertheless helpful for supply chain management. The knowledge of the individual configuration of the main (focal) actor and the other actors in the supply chain is very helpful in the process of aligning all actors to an overarching theme or vision as a means of coordinating and assessing the right governance form for supply chains.

Abers, Gehring & Heuermann (2003) for example focus on these cooperation aspects and present two forms of supply chain governance, 'unilateral governance' and 'bilateral governance', which are related to the supply chain configurations proposed by Fisher (efficient process configuration, market-responsive configuration). They propose a unilateral supply chain governance for an efficient supply chain configuration and a bilateral supply chain governance for a market-responsive configuration. The description of the supply chain governance configuration is based on dimensions like command structure/authority system, incentive system, standard operating procedures, dispute resolution and pricing systems.

Whereas the differentiation of distinct configurations like efficient and market-responsive or Lean and Agile seems to be relatively easy, the discussion about the Leagile configuration clearly showed that almost all supply chains consist of a certain kind of combination of Lean and Agile or, more generally, of cost-oriented and differentiation-oriented parts. The main task for supply chain management is to clearly determine the split-off point between these two dominating views, i.e. which actor in the supply chain is acting lean and which actor is acting agile.

Another challenge occurs when the perspective of supply chain management changes from an OEM to a supplier who is an actor in several supply chains. How should his configuration look like when he is serving a customer in a predictable environment on the one hand, and a customer with an unpredictable environment on the other hand? Is the right configuration in such a case an agile one which includes the possibility to be lean as well? Is the solution a multi-configuration management in the sense of logistics segments?

In summary, it can be stated that the presented configurational approaches use different variables to describe the configurations and the different approaches are more or less detailed. Further research is needed to elaborate a set of dimensions and variables for the description of configurations which take all aspects of supply chain management into account, i.e. structure, process, management activities, and context. A first step in this direction could be seen in the work of Corsten and Gabriel using the processes of the SCOR model as a framework, or the approach presented by Klaas with the dimensions 'mechanism of coordination', 'logistics processes and infrastructure', 'formal organizational structure', and 'logistics context'.

Based on such a catalogue of dimensions and variables, future research is needed to find configurations empirically. This will lead to the question of what relevant supply chain definition the configurational approach will concentrate on (i.e. which actors in the chain should be considered).

Most of the approaches are intuitively appealing concerning the results and propositions for designing and managing supply chains. But none of them (except Klaas) recurs to a theoretical basis. Most of the approaches implicitly argue in the classical structure-conduct-performance framework of industrial organization theory or can be linked to Porter's generic competitive strategies (Porter, 1980). However, a more profound theoretical basis is needed.

In addition, for a holistic view on supply chain management, this outside-in perspective in industrial organization theory should be supplemented by an inside-out perspective as proposed by resource-based-view approaches (see Barney, 1997; Wernerfelt, 1984; Penrose, 1959). Following these approaches, the gain and retaining of sustainable competitive advantages is based on resources (or core competencies) which are rare, cannot be transferred, and cannot be imitated. These resources or core competencies can be seen as the initial point for an orchestrating theme of a supply chain configuration. The identification of supply chains' core competencies will be a crucial aspect of future supply chain management.

4 References

Albers, S., Gehring, M., Heuermann, C. (2003): A Configurational Approach to Supply Chain Governance, in: Seuring, S., Müller, M., Goldbach, M., Schneidewind, U. (Eds.): Strategy and Organization in Supply Chains, Physica Verlag, Heidelberg, New York: 99-113.

Barney, J. B. (1997): Gaining and Sustaining Competitive Advantage, Addison-Wesley, Reading (Mass.).

Bowersox, D. J., Closs, D. J., Helferich, O. K. (1986): Logistical Management. A System of Integration of Physical Distribution Management, Manufacturing Support, and Materials Procurement, 3rd ed., Macmillan, New York.

Bucklin, L. P. (1965): Postponement, Speculation and the Structure of Distribution Channels, in: Journal of Marketing Research, 2(1): 26-31.

Chiou, J.-S., Wu, L-Y., Hsu, J. C. (2002): The Adoption of Form Postponement Strategy in a Global Logistics System: The Case of Taiwanese Information Technology Industry, in: Journal of Business Logistics, 23(1): 107-124.

Christopher, M. (2000): The Agile Supply Chain – Competing in Volatile Markets, in: Industrial Marketing Management, 29(1): 37-44.

Christopher, M., Towill, D. R. (2002): Developing Market Specific Supply Chain Strategies, in: The International Journal of Logistics Management, 13(1): 1-14.

Corsten, D., Gabriel, Chr. (2002), Supply Chain Management erfolgreich umsetzen. Grundlagen, Realisierung und Fallstudien (Successful Implementation of Supply Chain Management. Basics, Realization, Case Studies), Springer Verlag, Berlin.

Fisher, M. L. (1997): What is the right Supply Chain for your product?, in: Harvard Business Review, March-April: 107-116.

Gresov, C., Drazin, R. (1997): Equifinality: Functional Equivalence in Organization Design, in: Academy of Management Review, 22(2): 403-428.

Khandwalla, P.N. (1973): Viable and effective organizational designs of firms, in: Academy of Management Journal, 16(3): 481-495.

Klaas, T. (2003): Logistik-Organisation. Ein konfigurationstheoretischer Ansatz zur logistikorientierten Organisationsgestaltung (Logistics Organization. A configurational approach towards a logistics-oriented Organization), Gabler Verlag, Wiesbaden.

Lampel, J., Mintzberg, H. (1996): Customizing Customization, in: Sloan Management Review, 38, Fall: 21-30.

Lee, H. L. (2002): Aligning Supply Chain Strategies with Product Uncertainties, in: California Management Review, 44(3): 105-119.

Macharzina, K., Engelhard, J. (1991): Paradigm Shift in International Business Research: From Partist and Eclectic Approaches to the GAINS Paradigm, in: management international review, 31(special issue): 23-43.

Mason-Jones, R., Naylor, B., Towill, D. R. (2000): Lean, agile or leagile? Matching your supply chain to the marketplace, in: International Journal of Production Research, 38(17): 4061-4070.

Mentzer, J. T., DeWitt, W., Keebler, J. S., Min, S., Nix, N. W., Smith, C. D., Zacharia, Z. G. (2001): Defining Supply Chain Management, in: Journal of Business Logistics, 22(2): 1-25.

Meyer, A. D., Tsui, A. S., Hinings, C. R. (1993): Configurational Approaches to Organizational Analysis, in: Academy of Management Journal, 36(6): 1175-1195.

Miles, R. E. and Snow, C. C. (1978): Organizational strategy, structure, and process, MacGraw-Hill, New York.

Miller, D. (1981): Toward a new contingency approach – the search for organizational gestalts, in: Journal of Management Studies, 18(1): 1-26.

Miller, D. (1986): Configurations of Strategy and Structure: Towards a Synthesis, in: Strategic Management Journal, 7: 233-249.

Mintzberg, H. (1979): The structuring of organizations, Prentice Hall, Englewood Cliffs, N.J.

Penrose, E. G. (1959): The Theory of the Growth of the Firm, New York.

Porter, M. E. (1980): Competitive Strategy, Free Press, New York.

Tan, G. W., Shaw, M. J., Fulkerson, W. (2000): Web-based Global Supply Chain Management, in: Shaw, M., Blanning, R., Strader, T., Whinston, A. (Eds.): Handbook of Electronic Commerce, Springer, Berlin: 457-478.

Wernerfelt, B. (1984): A resource-based view of the firm, in: Strategic Management Journal, 5: 171-180.

Conducting a Literature Review –
The Example of Sustainability in Supply Chains

Stefan Seuring, Martin Müller, Magnus Westhaus, Romy Morana

1 Introduction 92
2 Literature Reviews as Content Analysis 93
3 The Example of Sustainability in Supply Chains 96
4 Conclusion 103
5 References 104

Summary:
Literature reviews are an essential part of all kinds of research. Their importance is frequently emphasized in introductory texts on research methodology as well as in methodological papers. The methodological basis for a literature review is usually a document analysis conducted as a content analysis. Therefore, criteria have to be chosen which allow the search for and the categorization of relevant literature. Such classification forms part of the structured analysis. Yet, not all aspects can be assessed this way, so conceptual research must also be a part of the research. Using the example of sustainability in supply chains, this paper offers insights on how a literature review might be conducted. This field provides and interesting example, as it is a young field of academic writing, so a total analysis of all relevant work published since 1990 is feasible.
Qualitative issues as observed in literature on environmental and sustainability management as well as supply and supply chain management are used to identify criteria to review the literature.

Keywords:
Literature Review, Document Analysis, Qualitative Content Analysis, Supply Chain Management, Sustainability

1 Introduction

Rigorous research can only be conducted in relation to existing knowledge. Literature reviews are therefore an essential part of the research process, as is frequently pointed out by both textbooks on research methodologies (e.g. Easterby-Smith, 2002: 159; Brewerton & Millward, 2001: 36; Saunders et al., 2003: 46) or methodological papers in high quality journals (e.g. Eisenhardt, 1989; Mentzer & Kahn, 1995). It fulfills two specific functions: First, it helps to generate ideas for research and summarizes existing research by identifying patterns, themes and issues. This way, the literature review provides a starting point for research, which justifies why review papers are frequently cited (Easterby-Smith et al., 2002: 159). Second, any contribution to research, be it from conceptual or empirical work, has to be enfolded against existing theories (Saunders et al., 2003: 46) as a means of thought organization (Brewerton & Millward, 2001: 36).

"A literature review is a systematic, explicit, and reproducible design for identifying, evaluating, and interpreting the existing body of recorded documents" (Fink, 1998). The analysis of documents pursues the aim of opening up material that does not have to be created on the basis of a data collection by the researcher. The design comprises the aim and the course of research (Meredith, 1993). One problem derives from the challenge that it is impractical to read everything. Only for emerging or narrowly defined issues might it be possible to provide complete reviews. One example is the analysis presented by Dangayach & Deshmukh (2001), who reviewed 260 papers from 31 journals. This might be at the upper level of workload that can be taken within a wider research project.

1.1 Aim and Outline

The aims of this paper are to outline the basics on how to conduct a literature review and more particularly how a structured content analysis can be carried out. Using the example of "sustainability in supply chains," a topic that is central to our research at the Supply Chain Management Center at the University of Oldenburg, the paper will provide an example of how a literature review can be conducted and results obtained. From the wider review carried out, selective issues will be presented whose form examples how the research process can be carried out. Therefore, the paper is organized into two related sections. The subsequent discussion will focus on aspects of the qualitative content analysis, which is applied a as method to evaluate the collected literature and provides the wider methodological framework. Details on general aspects of the literature review, as well as supportive tools (e.g. how to search the databases or the internet) can be found in the aforementioned textbooks, so they are not presented in detail. This also applies to quality criteria for such research, which are comparable to those of qualitative research in general (Mayring, 2003: 109).

1.2 Basic Terminology and Delimitations

Before continuing into the main sections of the paper, basic terms need to be defined. "Purchasing is obtaining from external sources of all goods, service, capabilities and knowledge which are necessary for running, maintaining and managing the company's primary and support activities at the most favorable conditions" (van Weele, 2002: 14). Purchasing mainly takes the interface between two companies into account. Supply chain management is defined in a broader manner. "The supply chain encompasses all activities associated with the flow and transformation of goods from raw materials stage (extraction), through to the end user, as well as the associated information flows. Material and information flow both up and down the supply chain. Supply chain management (SCM) is the integration of these activities through improved supply chain relationships, to achieve a sustainable competitive advantage" (Handfield & Nichols, 1999: 2). These two definitions alone already highlight search terms used later on such as purchasing, sourcing, supply, and supply chain.

Sustainable development is defined as "a development that meets the needs of the present without compromising the ability of future generations to meet their own needs" (WCED, 1987: 43). Regarding corporate sustainability, Dyllick & Hockerts (2002: 131) state: "Corporate sustainability can accordingly be defined as meeting the needs of a firm's direct and indirect stakeholders (such as shareholders, employees, clients, pressure groups, communities etc), without compromising its ability to meet the needs of future stakeholders as well." One central concept helping to operationalize sustainability is the triple bottom line approach, where a minimum performance is to be achieved in the economic, environmental and social dimension (Elkington, 2002; also Dyllick & Hockerts, 2002: 132). Related keywords for the literature search are sustainable, sustainable development, sustainability, environment(al), ecology, ecological, green, social, and ethics. Keywords from the supply chain management side and from the sustainability side were combined for the search.

2 Literature Reviews as Content Analysis

As mentioned, a literature review is a valid approach and necessary step towards structuring a research field, and forms an integral part of any research conducted (Mentzer & Kahn, 1995; Easterby-Smith et al. 2002). This helps to identify the conceptual content of the field (Meredith, 1993) and can contribute to theory development. Therefore, a (qualitative) content analysis can be used (Ryan & Bernard, 2000; Mayring 2003). Brewerton & Millward (2001: 151) distinguish qualitative, quantitative and structural content analysis, which are not mutually exclusive. A structural "content analysis involves the development of a representation of the relationships between elements in the target material. In order to do this, both qualitative and quantitative aspects of the data have to be considered" (Brewerton & Millward 2001: 153).

Quantitative and qualitative methods do not constitute oppositional and contradicting methods. In fact, quantitative methods can successfully support the qualitative methods (Brewerton & Millward, 2001: 151; Mayring, 2003: 19). For example: "The classification of text sections to (qualitative generated) categories can be quantitatively evaluated. It can be assessed what kind of category is most encoded" (Mayring, 2002: 117). It is important to mention that quantitative results always have to be interpreted qualitatively against the background of the original research objective. Mayring (2003: 19) characterizes such a research process as follows: "From quality to quantity and back to quality."

A structuring content analysis can capture formal aspects as well as content aspects. Mayring (2003: 13) characterizes content analysis (QCA) as a method for analyzing communication (e.g. as embedded in documents) by applying a systematic procedure. The research is driven by theoretical pre-considerations and follows a clear process, as this allows conclusions to be drawn on the analyzed material. A process model for content analysis (Mayring, 2003: 54) comprises the following steps:

1. Material collection:
   The material to be collected is defined and delimitated. This might include taking a look at how the material emerged. Furthermore, the unit of analysis (i.e. the single paper) is defined.

2. Descriptive analysis:
   Formal aspects of the materials are assessed, e.g. the number of publications per year. This description forms the background upon which the theoretical analysis is conducted.

3. Category selection:
   Now, structural dimensions and related analytic categories are selected, which are to be applied in the literature review to structure the field. Structural dimensions form the major topics of analysis, which cover various analytic categories, e.g. the single year across a time period.

4. Material evaluation:
   The material is analyzed and sorted according to the structural dimensions and categories built (for details see Figure 1, which will be discussed below). This should allow identification of relevant issues and interpretation of results.

For the analysis of the material (steps 3 and 4), Figure 1 provides a detailed description of the process. While it includes a feedback loop for the analysis of the collected material, such a loop might be needed for the overall process.

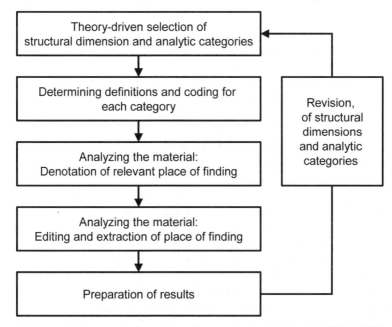

Figure 1: Research Process of a Structuring Content Analysis (Mayring, 2002: 120)

Structural dimensions and related analytic categories which allow classification of the reviewed literature can be derived deductively or inductively. In a deductive approach they are selected before the material is analyzed; when using an inductive method, they are developed from the material by means of generalization (Mayring, 2003: 75). In either case, they should have a clear relation to existing theory. Still, "content analysis is reliant on the multiple judgments of a single analyst [...] keen to find support for a particular view of the data" (Brewerton & Millward 2001: 153). This means that the analyst makes various decisions about how the paper is comprehended. Such risk can be reduced by involving two or more researchers when searching for and analyzing the data. Yet, the revision of the structural dimension and analytic categories might be necessary.

After this short overview on the research design of a document analysis and the method of qualitative content analysis, this is applied to the body of literature on sustainability in supply chain management.

3 The Example of Sustainability in Supply Chains

3.1 Relevance and Previous Reviews

In the debate on sustainable development, companies are increasingly seen as central actors. This extends further to the focal companies of supply chains, which are held responsible for the environmental and social performance of their suppliers (Seuring, 2004; Seuring et al., 2004). Focal companies are thereby such companies that either rule or govern the supply chain or provide the direct contact to the customer (Handfield & Nichols, 1999: 18; Schary & Skjott-Larsen, 2001: 24). This is especially the case for companies that own brands, as they are likely to come under pressure from stakeholders, e.g. non-governmental organizations (NGOs). These companies are asked to consider environmental and social problems observed in their supply chain. For example, apparel distributors such as Nike, Disney, Levi Strauss, Benneton, Adidas or C&A were blamed in recent years for problems occurring during the production of their clothing. Inhumane working conditions or spillage of toxic substances into the environment are frequently mentioned as problems (Seuring, 2001). Various companies have pursued proactive approaches to sustainable supply chain management (Bowen et al., 2001; Seuring, 2004).

Such triggers have increased interest in green/environmental or sustainable supply chain management, which has so far been dispersed into various lines of research. The literature is still limited in quantity, and no major reviews of the field have been presented. Only three journal papers (de Burgos & Lorente, 2001; Zsidisin & Siferd, 2001; Baumann et al., 2002) and one additional paper in conference proceedings (Alfaro et al., 2003) that attempt to review this part of the literature were found. Alfaro et al. (2003) focus on remanufacturing and reverse logistics and take only publications from operations and supply chain management journals into account. A specific focus also prevails in the review of Baumann, Boons & Bragd (2002), who concentrate on green product development. The third review deals with environmental performance as an operations objective, where supply chain issues are only secondarily addressed (de Burgos & Lorente, 2001). Zsidisin & Siferd (2001) provide a review, but it is only based on 38 publications, i.e. it does not aim to cover all related publications. Hence, a literature review was conducted in the second half of 2003 aiming to collect and analyze all relevant papers in the field by means of a structured search for literature (Easterby-Smith et al., 2002: 159).

3.2 Material Collection

While the intersection between supply chain management and sustainable development has increased in recent years, the number of related publications are still limited. Against this background, a literature review as a total analysis was seen as an adequate and practicable research methodology (Easterby-Smith et al., 2002: 159). Basic definitions of purchasing, supply chain management and sustainable development and relevant search terms have already been presented in Section 1. For a literature review it is particularly important to define clear boundaries to delimitate the research. In this context three notes are made:

- Publications with the main topic of public purchasing are not considered. This debate includes strong public law aspects and differs from the discussion of supply (chain) management in companies.
- Articles focused only on ethical demands placed on purchasing staff (e.g. acceptance of gifts) are excluded. Respective papers mainly discuss codes of conduct for purchasers, so there is no direct link to sustainable development.
- Papers focusing on reverse-logistics and remanufacturing, but also closed-loop supply chains are not included. Often, arguments center on end-of-the-product life cycle issues, while the presented research concentrates on forward supply chains. Meanwhile, there is a rich body of literature here which has already been reviewed by other researchers (Guide et al., 2000).

3.3 Search for Related Papers

This analysis aims at scientific publications with clear conceptual or empirical content. Practitioner papers which only provide anecdotal evidence were not to be considered. The relevant period was set from 1990 onwards. Pre-knowledge of the field seemed to indicate that research on sustainability in supply chains emerged around that time, which is also supported by the fact that sustainable development was established in 1987, as noted above (WBCSD, 1987).

The work presented forms part of a wider search of literature, where German and English publications were analyzed, including books and edited volumes. Here, the discussion is limited to peer-reviewed journal papers published in English.

Two lines for searching were followed. A total of 19 selected journals, published in English, were seen as particularly relevant, e.g. *International Journal of Operations & Production Management* (IJOPM), (European), *Journal of Purchasing and Supply Management, Greener Management International* or *Business Strategy and the Environment* were completely checked. This included all major international journals where research is published on supply chain management and environmental/sustainability management respectively. All issues published since 1990 were scanned for relevant papers. Furthermore, eight databases were used to search for further articles, such as those provided by major publishers, e.g. Elsevier (www.sciencedirect.com), Emerald (www.emeraldinsight.com), Kluwer (www.wknp.nl), Wiley (www.wiley.com) or library services (e.g. ebsco.com, subito-doc.de, www.gbv.de or www.vlb.de). Thereby, related edited volumes and single papers in other journals could also be found. As an additional means, literature cited in identified papers was checked.

After a first quick content check, identified articles were in- or excluded from the analysis. To increase the reliability of the research, databanks and journals as well as the single papers were checked by a second researcher. Reading the papers, cited references were used as a secondary source, but did not yield many additional papers, which can be taken as proof of the validity of the research. A total of 92 papers were identified.

3.4 Descriptive Analysis

In a first step of the evaluation, descriptive dimensions were used to classify the papers. Such descriptions provide first insights into the material. As presented here, the analysis was based on the following criteria, where each paper was assigned to exactly one category (for details see Seuring & Müller, 2004):

1. How is the distribution of publications across the time period?
2. In which journals are such articles published?
3. What research methodologies are applied?

The distribution of the publication in the researched period (1990 – 2004) is displayed in Figure 1. While the search started in 1990, the first published paper was found for 1994. There are some even older papers, but these were not taken into account as mentioned above.

A particularly high number of publications is found in 2001. This is easily explained. In 2001 a special issue of *Greener Management International* was published with eight articles. A further special issue of *Greener Management International* was published in 2003, containing another seven papers. It is important to note that for 2003 and 2004, not all relevant publications could have been acquired, so these numbers are expected to be considerably higher. The continuity of publication shows that related issues are considered to be of interest.

Among the journals, *Greener Management International* alone accounts for 21 papers (22.8% of all publications). Second are the *International Journal of Operations & Production Management* and *Supply Chain Management* with six papers each. There is a dominance of environmental management-related journals, but in recent years, traditional operations and supply chain management journals have increasingly been used as a publication channel.

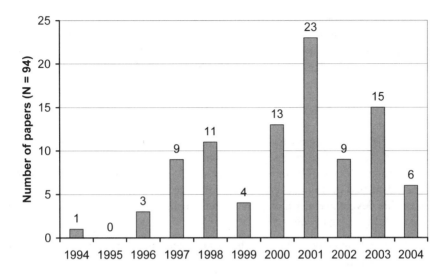

Figure 2: Allocation of the Articles across the Analyzed Period 1994-2004

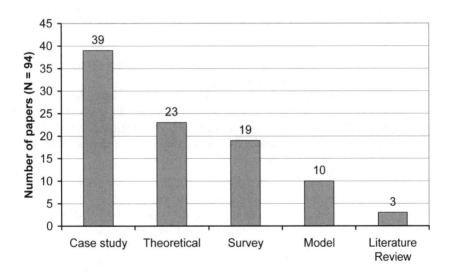

Figure 3: Research Methodologies Applied in the Papers

Five research methodologies were differentiated: case studies, models, empirical surveys, literature reviews, and theoretical and conceptual papers. Figure 3 shows the assignments of the papers to the methodologies. The case study category captures 39 articles. For a new, unexplored field, this is not surprising, as this allows the field to be explored and provide illustrative evidence (Yin, 2003). It must however be mentioned that most of the case papers are rather case examples than clear case studies. Evidence is often presented in a rather illustrative mode that employs the methodological rigor asked for in a case study (Yin, 2003: 34).

3.5 Category Selection

For an initial structuring content analysis, the following dimensions and categories were used. They form a basic set of the dimensions and categories used (see Seuring & Müller, 2004). The dimensions presented offer first insights into how the papers identified deal with the two key fields, i.e. supply chain management and sustainable development, which provide the overall backbone of the research field "sustainability in supply chains."

1. Supply Chain Dimension: Does the paper focus on purchasing or supply chain management issues?
   Based on the above-presented definitions and related theory, the structural dimension of supply chain management was built into the related analytic categories "purchasing" or "supply chain management." The criteria for assigning the papers to either category was whether problems and solutions addressed deal with the interface between two companies (dyads i.e. purchasing or supply management) or with a chain of companies, where related problems are at least considered.

2. Sustainability Dimension: Which dimension of sustainable development beyond economic arguments is included?
   Three categories were defined: (1) environmental, (2) social or (3) sustainability related papers, requiring that both environmental and social issues are addressed. As only management related papers were included, it was assumed (and confirmed by the analysis) that the economic dimension is, as least to a certain degree, present in every paper.

3. Performance Interrelation Dimension: How are the performance relations between the three dimensions of sustainability addressed?
   As a third dimension for the content analysis, which will be discussed subsequently, the relation between environmental and social issues and the economic performance of the supply chain will be used. Three categories are distinguished: Win-win situations apply when environmental and/or social measures improve business performance, while trade-offs are the opposite. It was also necessary to define a third category, which is described as "minimum performance for environmental and social welfare."

For the supply chain and the sustainability dimension, the categories are unambiguous, so each paper is assigned to one category only. This does not apply to the third dimension, as a paper e.g. can present evidence for both win-win or trade-off situations.

- Supply Chain Dimension

Based on the definitions of purchasing or supply chain management provided above, 25 articles focus on purchasing and supply management related topics. Papers were classified in this category if they only took the perspective of sourcing materials from one prior stage in the supply chain. The majority of 69 papers are classified as attempting to capture supply chain management by dealing with more than two stages of the supply chain. This points towards the wider consideration of cooperation between the partners in the supply chain.

- Coverage of Sustainable Development

The articles were differentiated into three categories in relation to sustainable development. The majority of the articles (70) deal with environmental issues. Only 12 papers focused on the social dimension or integrated environmental and social issues, thereby addressing all three dimensions of sustainability. This reveals a clear deficit in supply chain management literature regarding social problems. Additionally, the full meaning of sustainable development is rarely accounted for. This offers clear evidence of a research deficit identified through the literature review.

Dimensions of Sustainable Development	Numbers of Articles
Environmental	70
Social	12
Sustainable	12

Table 1: Dimensions of Sustainable Development

- Goal Relation between Business Objectives and Sustainable Development

For furthering sustainability in companies, if is of great importance that this be in line with business objectives. If environmental and social achievements help to increase business performance, this would be a clear win-win situation. Besides this "ideal" category, the second category is opposed to this, as trade-off situations between these objectives exist. This has a clear relation to both the classic arguments on trade-offs (Corbett & Van Wassenhove 1993) as well as the environmental management-based discussion (Wagner et al. 2001). Finally, a third category was found where a minimum performance for environmental and social issues is demanded, which can be seen as an order qualifier, while the economic dimension or business performance enables companies and supply chains to win orders (Hill, 2000). This reflects debates going on in environmental management literature (Newton & Hartge, 1997; Seuring & Müller, 2004), but was only identified during the research process. Results are shown in Table 2. As can be seen, most papers point out win-win situations and trade-offs. Yet, as papers can mention two or even all three of the identified relations (as well as none of them), the total number does not add up to the number of papers (N = 94).

Dimensions of Sustainable Development	Number of Articles
Win-win situation	58
Trade-off situation	44
Minimum performance for environmental and social issues	13

Table 2: Goal Relations between Economic and Sustainability Objectives

3.6 Interpreting Results of the Literature Review

The literature review is especially interesting for identifying research gaps. While quantitative evidence was presented for all categories, such counting is only a first step, which is not sufficient for the content analysis and reaching conclusions in the literature review. In the presented case, the following main conclusions could be drawn. The papers mentioned are exemplary ones, seen as good examples for the arguments made:

- Case examples and conceptual papers are what is mostly published. A theoretical basis is often missing, so hardly any paper uses typical theories that are frequently applied in wider literature on supply chain management, such as new institutional economics (Meisner Rosen et al., 2001; Zsidisin & Siferd, 2001; Goldbach et al., 2004) or the resource-based view (de Bakker & Nijhoff, 2002).

- The supply chain focus is evident, so not just dyadic relationships are addressed. Still, empirical data collection on more than one stage of the supply chain is rare (Kogg, 2004; Seuring, 2004).

- Environmental aspects clearly dominate. Social issues and integrative debates of sustainable aspects are neglected. One stream in environmentally related literature captures technical issues of solving specific environmental problems such as introducing greener or cleaner production and related managerial systems or measures (de Groene & Hermans, 1998; Clift, 2003). Furthermore, environmental management systems, specially ISO 14001, also play a prominent role (Beamon, 1999; Corbett & Kirsch, 2001; Pesonen, 2001).

- Among the triggers for sustainability in supply chains, legal requirements (Walton et al., 1998; Min & Galle, 2001) and the pressure of customers and stakeholders (Pesonen, 2001; Preuss, 2001; Seuring et al., 2004) are most important. This explains why environmental and social issue are increasingly perceived as dimensions where a minimum performance has to be achieved. This is often a risk avoidance-driven approach, as it limits the liabilities a focal company might face from problem occurring at suppliers.

- The publication output in the field has considerably increased in recent years and can be expected to at least stay on this level.

From a general perspective, there is a deficit in the take-up of theories, both from within supply chain or operations management, as well as from a wider perspective, such as new institutional economics or strategic management. Future research should take this into account. In particular, empirical research, as carried out in case studies and surveys, needs to build on a stronger theoretical basis.

The comprehension of sustainable development is often very simple. Mostly the Brundtland definition, cited above, is referred to, but it is not discussed if a more technical, positivist comprehension or a social science-based approach is taken, where sustainability is comprehended as a regulative idea. Consequently, the understanding of sustainable development is fragmented and mostly one-dimensional, i.e. environmentally based. An integrated perspective is needed for future research.

In supply chain management, risk and benefit sharing between the partners in the chain is widely discussed. But how such sharing has to be extended to capture environmental and social issues requires further analysis, as this is hardly discussed in the analyzed literature. All of the discussed issues can be taken up in future research to enrich the emerging field of sustainability in supply chains.

4 Conclusion

The paper outlines how a literature review can be conducted. From the methodology perspective this is a structure-content analysis. Here, the approach was a deductive one, where identified dimensions and related categories were used to assess publication. As a topic, sustainability in supply chains proves to be suitable, as it is a young field of research and publication and therefore allows complete analysis. The dimensions and categories discussed show how this can be conducted. Furthermore, these examples show how quantitative and qualitative aspects complement each other and support, but cannot substitute the creative imagination and interpretation of the researcher in understanding the field.

5 References

As listing all papers contained in the review would take up several papers, interested readers are advised to contact Stefan Seuring (stefan.seuring@uni-oldenburg.de) to obtain a full list of references.

Alfaro, J. A., Alvarez, M. J., Montes, M. J., Viguier, R. (2003): "Green Light" for Supply Chain Research: What is on Regarding Environmental Issues?, in: Spina, G., Vinelli, A., Cagliano, R., Klachschmidt, M., Romano, P., Salvador, F. (eds.): One World? One View of OM? - The Challenges of Integrating Research & Practice, Proceedings of the 10th International Conference EurOMA, 16-18 June 2003, Como, Italy: p. 949-958.

Baumann, H., Boons, F., Bragd, A. (2002): Mapping the green product development field: engineering, policy and business perspectives, in: Journal of Cleaner Production, 10(5): 409-425

Bowen, F. E., Cousins, P. D., Lamming, R. C., Faruk, A. C. (2001): The Role of Supply Management Capabilities in Green Supply, in: Production and Operations Management, 10(2): 174-189.

Brewerton, P., Millward, L. (2001): Organisational Research Methods, Sage, London.

Clift, R. (2003): Metrics for Supply Chain Sustainability, in: Cleaner Technology and Environmental Policy, 5: 240-247.

Corbett, C. J., Kirsch, D. A. (2001): International Diffusion of ISO 14000 Certification, in: Production and Operations Management, 10(3): 327-342.

Corbett, C. J., Van Wassenhove, L. N. (1993): Trade-Offs? What Trade-Offs? Competence and Competitiveness in Manufacturing Strategy, in: California Management Review, 35(4): 107-122.

Dangayach, G. S., Deshmukh, S. G. (2001): Manufacturing Strategy: Literature Review and Some Issues, in: International Journal of Operations & Production Management, 21(7); 884-932.

de Bakker, F., Nijhof, A. (2002): Responsible Chain Management: A Capability Assessement Framework, in Business Strategy and the Environment, 11(1): 63-75.

de Burgos, J., Lorente J. J. C. (2001): Environmental performance as an operations objective, in: International Journal of Operations & Production Management, 21(12): 1553-1572.

Easterby-Smith, M., Thorpe, R., Lowe, A. (2002): Management Research – An Introduction, Sage Publications, London.

Elkington, J. (2002): Cannibals with Forks: The Triple Bottom Line of 21st Century Business, Reprint (originally published 1997), Capstone, Oxford.

Fink, A. (1998): Conducting Research Literature Reviews: From Paper to the Internet , Sage, Thousand Oaks.

Goldbach, M., Seuring, S., Back, S. (2003): Coordinating sustainable cotton chains for the mass market - The case of the German mail order business OTTO, in: Greener Management International, Issue 43: 65-78.

Guide, V. D. R., Jayaraman, V., Srivastava, R., Benton, W. C. (2000): Supply Chain Management for Recoverable Manufacturing Systems, in: Interfaces, 30(3): 125-142.

Handfield, R. B., Nichols, E. L. (1999): Introduction to Supply Chain Management, Prentice-Hall, New Jersey.

Hill, T. (2000): Manufacturing Strategy, Text and Cases, 3. edition, McGraw-Hill, Boston.

Kogg, B. (2003): Greening a Cotton-textile Supply Chain: A Case Study of the Transition towards Organic Production without a Powerful Focal Company, in: Greener Management International, Issue 43: 53-64.

Mayring, P. (2002): Einführung in die qualitative Sozialforschung – eine Anleitung zum qualitativen Denken (Introduction to Qualitative Social Research), Beltz Verlag, Weinheim und Basel.

Mayring, P. (2003): Qualitative Inhaltanalyse – Grundlagen und Techniken (Qualitative Content Analysis – Basics and Techniques), 8th Edition, Beltz Verlag, Weinheim.

Meisner Rosen, C., Bercovitz, J., Beckman, S. (2001): Environmental Supply-Chain Management in the Computer Industry, in: Journal of Industrial Ecology, 4(4): 83-104.

Mentzer, J. T., Kahn, K. B. (1995): A Framework of Logistics Research, in: Journal of Business Logistics, 16(1): 231-250.

Meredith, J. (1993): Theory building through conceptual methods, in: International Journal of Operations & Production Management, 13(5), 3-11.

Min, H., Galle, W. P. (2001): Green purchasing practices of US firms, International Journal of Operations & Production Management, 21(9): 1222-1238.

Newton, T., Harte, G. (1997): Green Business: Technicist Kitsch?, in: Journal of Management Studies, 34(1): 75-98.

Pesonen, H.-L. (2001): Environmental Management of Value Chains, in: Greener Management International, Issue 33: 45-58.

Preuss, L. (2001): In Dirty Chains? Purchasing and Greener Manufacturing, in: Journal of Business Ethics, 34(3/4): 345-359.

Ryan, G. W., Bernard, H. R. (2000): Data Management and Analysis Methods, in: Denzin, N.K., Lincoln, Y.S. (eds.): Handbook of Qualitative, Research, Sage, Thousand Oaks: p. 769-802.

Saunders, M., Lewis, P., Thornhill, A. (2003): Research Methods for Business Students, Prentice Hall, Harlow.

Schary, P., Skjøtt-Larsen, T. (2001): Managing the Global Supply Chain, 2nd edition, Copenhagen Business School Press, Copenhagen.

Seuring, S. (2004): Integrated Chain Management and Supply Chain Management – Comparative Analysis and Illustrative Cases, in: Journal of Cleaner Production, 12(8-10): 1059-1071.

Seuring, S., Goldbach, M., Koplin, J. (2004): Managing time and complexity in supply chains: two cases from the textile industry, in: International Journal of Integrated Supply Management, 1(2): 180-198.

Seuring, S., Müller, M. (2004): „Beschaffungsmanagement & Nachhaltigkeit – Eine Literaturübersicht" (Supply Management and Sustainable Development – A Literature Review): in: Hülsmann, M., Müller-Christ, G., Haasis, H.-D. (eds.): Betriebswirtschaftslehre und Nachhaltigkeit - Bestandsaufnahme und Forschungsprogrammatik, (Business Administration and Sustainability), Gabler, Wiesbaden: p. 117-170.

van Weele, A. J. (2002): Purchasing and Supply Chain Management – Analysis, Planning and Practice, 3rd Edition, Thomson Learning, London.

Wagner, M., Schaltegger, S., Wehrmeyer, W. (2001): The Relationship between the Environmental and Economic Performance of Firms, Greener Management International, Issue 34: 95-108.

Walton, S. V., Handfield, R. B., Melnyk, S. A. (1998): The Green Supply Chain: Integrating Suppliers into Environmental Management Processes: in: International Journal of Purchasing and Materials Management, 34(2): 2-11.

WCED (World Commission on Environment and Development) (1987): Our Common Future, Oxford University Press, Oxford.

Yin, R. (2003): Case Study Research – Design and Methods, 3rd edition, Sage, Thousand Oaks.

Zsidisin, G. A., Siferd, S. (2001): Environmental purchasing: a framework for theory development, in: European Journal of Purchasing and Supply Management, 7(7): 61-73.

Research Methodologies in Supply Chain Management – What Do We Know?

Árni Halldórsson, Jan Stentoft Arlbjørn

1	Background and Objectives	108
2	Scoping SCM	109
3	On Research Methods in Logistics and SCM	110
4	Research Methodology and Framework	111
5	Current Research Methods Within SCM	113
6	Conclusion	118
7	References	120
8	Appendix	122

Summary:
Investigates the methodology applied in supply chain management (SCM) research published in three academic journals from 1997 to 2004. The objective is to analyze and discuss by what research methods our current knowledge of SCM has been generated. 71 papers are identified as containing SCM. Empirical evidence is limited to approximately half of the articles, share of which is frequently generated by quantitative approaches. Conceptual work is weak on discussing fundamental assumptions of SCM (theory, methodology, philosophy of science). Theoretical foundations from a philosophy of science perspective are still unquestioned. Actor and level of analysis are primarily the manufacturing company and a supply chain perspective albeit the empirical evidence usually resides in the particular, focal company. Applications of non-logistics theories or concepts are not navigated by a more fundamental discussion of methodology.

Keywords:
Supply Chain Management, Logistics, Methodology, Research

1 Background and Objectives

SCM cuts across several disciplines such as logistics, operations management, marketing, purchasing, and strategic management, to name few. The four-perspective model on SCM by Larson & Halldórsson (2004) implies that SCM is of a fragmented and multidisciplinary nature. Although the level of analysis – the supply chain – seems to be a constant, the units of analysis differ. To Lambert et al. (1998), SCM is about integration of "key business processes," heavily inspired by the interest of business process reengineering in the early 1990s. Christopher (1998), referring to marketing, views SCM from a "relationship management" point of view. But the disciplinary level (the one that informs the unit of analysis) is not the only way of portraying the nature of SCM. Arlbjørn & Halldórsson (2002) point out that understanding of both the nature of theory and philosophy of science perspectives are important for further fertilization of logistics into SCM. Halldórsson & Aastrup (2003) consider the methodological dimension of logistics research by providing a frame of reference for assessing qualitative inquiries in logistics, as opposed to the dominance of quantitative approaches in the current literature. What still is missing, however, is an overview of the epistemological dimension of how knowledge of SCM "comes about"; not only the general role of research methodology to generate knowledge, but rather how the type of research methodology informs the knowledge of practice we create through research. This assumption of interconnectedness is similar to the interrelationship of the types of research question and research design, respectively, which is an essential feature of the case study approach as presented by Yin (1994).

Based on the assumption that a coherence must exist between research questions, objectives, methods, theories, and ultimate presumptions, the use of a particular research method may provide us with an understanding of what aspects of reality SCM has so far been concerned with, and not least, what role research methods play in further enrichment of the field of SCM. The constituent components of this paper focus on two research issues in order to answer the main question of the paper "What do we know about SCM"?

- Which research methods have been used to create new knowledge on SCM?

- Seen from an epistemological point of view, how does this determine our understanding of SCM?

The objective is to analyze and discuss the research methods by which our current knowledge of SCM has been generated, and hence demonstrate that the epistemological level of research influences our understanding of the phenomenon.

2 Scoping SCM

In 1969, Bowersox (1969) stated: "As with any emerging field, physical distribution [logistics, SCM, eds.] currently suffers from a lack of standardized definitions and vocabulary. The overall field would gain significantly from a clear definition of subject matter and issues." Despite attempts to stabilize the various aspects of logistics/SCM reality into models and methods, it still seems to be an ever-moving target. Logistics and supply chain management (SCM) have both received immense management attention during the last decades as a means to improve company performance. In 2001, Mentzer et al. (2001) argued that: "SCM has become such a "hot topic" that it is difficult to pick up a periodical on manufacturing, distribution, marketing, customer management, or transportation without seeing an article about SCM or SCM-related topics."

Both logistics and SCM grasp a wide range of activities and processes both within a single company and between different companies in chains and networks. Since the introduction of SCM in 1982 by two consultants (Oliver & Webber, 1982), much has been written in the logistics literature about its content, scope and implementation issues.

Over time, the concept has matured and has received acceptance in academic environments and in practice; as a new name for logistics (re-labelers), as a widespanning umbrella that includes logistics (unionists), a new attribute of logistics (traditionalists), or as integrating aspects from other disciplines (intersectionists) (Larson & Halldórsson, 2004). Despite this, the difference or similarity between the concepts appears often more as one of a semantic nature rather than based on the substance itself. On one hand, it can be argued that SCM is a broader concept than logistics because SCM deals with "integrating and managing key business processes across the supply chain" (Cooper et al., 1997). According to Lambert et al. (1998) the confusion between logistics and supply chain management probably is "due to the fact that logistics is a functional silo within companies and is also a bigger concept that deals with the management of material and information flow across the supply chain." On the other hand, it can be argued that differences between the concepts are difficult to outline, since both concepts deal with the same content and scope (Persson, 1997; Arlbjørn, 1999, 2000; Halldórsson & Larson, 2000). The scope of this paper is not to add further views to the academic discourse concerning similarities and differences between logistics and SCM. Instead, the paper focuses on research methodologies applied in SCM research.

3 On Research Methods in Logistics and SCM

Arlbjørn & Halldórsson (2002) assign methodology an important role in generating logistics knowledge, and in particular, facilitating an interplay between philosophy of science, theoretical perspectives and practice. The primary basis for that observation is the following statement by Mentzer & Kahn (1995): "Much of logistics literature and research remains largely managerial in nature and lacks a rigorous orientation in theory development, testing and application". They offer a framework for logistics researchers in which methodology is assumed to be "greatly influenced by previous research, study objectives, the researcher's competencies, and the level of sophistication of the constituency for which the knowledge is intended" (Mentzer & Kahn, 1995). This argument is supported by Mentzer & Flint's (1997) focus on various dimensions of validity. And the path is further emphasized by Garver & Mentzer (1999), who suggest structural equation modeling to test for construct validity. Seaker et al. (1993) discuss the need for more formal contributions of research to theory, and argue that "…application of more scientific research methodologies" is to be preferred. In particular, the application of both quantitative and qualitative methods in business logistics research is recommended. Since 1993, the qualitative path of research has been re-emphasized in several logistics contributions. Ellram (1996) argues that logistics research may benefit from the use of case studies as a methodology, in particular "…for theory building, for providing detailed explanations of "best practices" and providing more understanding of data gathered." By this, we may assume that the actual use of the case study methodology in current research on SCM will provide an indicative evidence of the extent of which e.g. "theory building" has taken place, or whether "best practices" have been revealed. Similar to logistics, operations management has a long tradition of using statistical analysis and mathematical modeling for research purposes. Based on this observation, Voss et al. (2002) provide comprehensive guidelines for approaching case studies in operations management. Gammelgaard (1997) describes how the evolution of a joint Ph.D. program in logistics includes "methods in logistics research," and suggests furthermore that such a course may "…stimulate the innovativeness of logistics methodology as well as to encourage the application of infrequently used methods in logistics research." An example of such infrequently used methods is the quest of Näslund (2002) for use of the action approach for research design in logistics. Gammelgaard (2003) also documents the use of case study methods in logistics, both for quantitative and qualitative research designs.

Borrowed from Larson & Halldórsson (2004) who surveyed international researchers in logistics in 2000, Table 1 provides a quantitative picture on a scale of one to five of the use of various research methods in logistics and SCM. It is noteworthy that compared to articles published in the *Journal of Business Logistics* (JBL) from 1978-1993, both case studies and interviews are increasingly to be applied by the year 2000.

Method	Mean	Std. Deviation	*JBL* 1978-1993
Survey	3.78	1.13	54.3%
Interview	3.78	1.11	13.8%
Case Study	3.76	1.24	3.2%
Archival/Secondary Data	3.33	1.20	9.6%
Simulation/Modeling	3.08	1.63	19.2%
Focus Groups	2.29	1.48	n/a
Experiment	2.07	1.57	n/a

Table 1: Preferred Research Methods (Larson & Halldórsson, 2004)

In logistics, opinions of the multiplicity of research methods seem to point in two directions. First, the statement of Mentzer & Kahn (1995) "Those methodologies that have been successfully employed in previous research in the substantive area are more likely to give the current study a higher degree of acceptability within the researcher's community" seems to favor an application of methods that have already gained certain acceptability. On the other hand, this seems to stand in some contrast to the suggestion of Gammelgaard (1997) of a joint Nordic Ph.D. program, in which – as mentioned above - a course on research methods aims to "…encourage the application of infrequently used methods in logistics research."

As a consequence of such a friction, Halldórsson & Aastrup (2003) suggest an alternative of reliability and validity in assessing research quality: truth-value, transferability and contextualism, and trackability and explicity. A common three dimensional view of quality of the research method asserted by Seaker et al. (1993) encompasses generalizability, internal validity and simplicity.

4 Research Methodology and Framework

The collection of theoretical evidences in this paper was made through the following five steps:

1. Selecting journals
2. Assessing review time frame
3. Search for papers
4. Paper validation (contents must be about SCM)
5. Paper review based on review criteria

4.1 Selecting Journals

To achieve the objective of the paper, articles of SCM in three selected academic journals of logistics and supply chain management from 1997-2003 were reviewed: 1. *International Journal of Logistics Management* (IJLM), 2. *International Journal of Physical Distribution & Logistics Management* (IJPD&LM), 3. *Journal of Business Logistics* (JBL). These are among the top five academic journals within logistics and supply chain management (Gibson et al., 2003).

4.2 Assessing Review Time Frame

The year 1997 was chosen as the starting point for selecting papers for reviews since the first coherent frameworks of supply chain management were published in this year (Bechtel & Jayaram, 1997, Cooper et al., 1997). Bechtel & Jayaram (1997) proposed a framework for supply chain management analyses based on a comprehensive literature review. The framework contains different SCM themes that are grouped in either content or process literature areas. Cooper et al. (1997) provided the first conceptual model for supply chain management consisting of business processes, management components and supply chain structure. The overall time frame for reviewing journal papers was January 1st, 1997 to January 27th, 2004.

4.3 Search for Papers and Paper Validation

The "Proquest" database was applied with the following search criteria: "Supply Chain Management" or "SCM" as an exact phrase in the title or abstract. A second search was completed with the following criteria: "Supply-Chain Management" with the exact phrase in the title or abstract.

	Number of papers published	Number of papers including SCM in title or abstract	Number of papers percieved as dealing with SCM
IJLM	109	29	26
IJPD&LM	290	39	34
JBL	147	17	11
Total	**546**	**85**	**71**

Table 2: Number of Articles Published and Reviewed

In all, 546 articles were published in the period from 1997 to 2004 in the three journals. During the review process each paper was validated concerning their content focus on SCM. A few papers mention SCM in either the title or abstract without really containing SCM and thus fail this validation test. A total of 85 of these articles do contain supply chain management in either the title or abstract, and the result of the first four steps of the entire review process is a net sample of 71 articles to be reviewed according to the framework. As shown in Table 2, 14 papers were excluded form further data analysis due to lack of SCM content. Papers only dealing with e.g. IT technology, education, and mathematical models are examples of papers that have been excluded.

4.4 Paper Review Based on Review Criteria

A sheet containing elements for review was developed. The review criteria were chosen with inspiration from Gubi et al. (2003). The review elements were: Primary actor of analysis; Level of analysis; Main purpose of the article; Research design applied; Time frame for the empirically based articles; and Containing elements of philosophy of science? The range of variation (measures) of each review criteria can be found in the appendix at the end of the paper.

4.5 Limitations

The discussion and conclusions of this paper are not without limitations. First, a total of three academic journals were included in the research. Adding more journals might have altered the result or validated the conclusions made in this paper. Related to this, targeting 'SCM' is difficult, as it has not only been assigned a central role in logistics journals, but also publications within purchasing, transportation, operations managements and marketing. Second, risk of subjective review of the particular article by the researcher was another hazard. To calibrate the review process, the authors and an assistant reviewed four articles. Third, the parameters in the research framework are not directly measurable from the particular article reviewed, and are therefore dependent upon estimation.

5 Current Research Methods Within SCM

Based on the article sample, this section seeks to answer the question: What research methods have been used to create new knowledge on SCM? The presentation is based on the structure of the analytical framework referred to in a previous section.

5.1 Primary Actor of Analysis

The category of "primary actor of analysis" denotes what type of company the "focal firm" is in the particular study. As such, Table 3 shows the number of papers citing different types of primary actors of analysis.

	IJLM	IJPD&LM	JBL	Total
Manufacturer	8	8	4	20
Carrier	0	3	0	3
Wholesaler	0	3	1	4
Retailer	2	4	1	7
Warehousing	1	2	0	3
n/a	15	14	5	34
Total	**26**	**34**	**11**	**71**

Table 3: Primary Actor of Analysis

In most cases, the articles do not point out a "focal company" (n/a in Table 3) that is related to the problem of the article. The reason may be that much of the literature is still of a conceptual nature, and thus provides a contextualization for a particular framework. IJPD&LM has actors in all categories, but also has the largest sample in the study. The overall view seems to be that manufacturers are the most common company studied in SCM and of these, most are supported by empirical evidence. In JBL, all four articles taking the manufacturers' perspective rely upon a quantitative approach, which in general is the case for four articles in IJLM and three articles in IJDP&LM. Qualitative studies of manufacturing companies appear in three articles in each of these two latter journals. Only two examples of methodological triangulation were found, both in IJPD&LM.

5.2 Level of Analysis

A major difference between logistics and supply chain management is the ability of the latter to penetrate the functional silos within the particular firm, and to involve suppliers and customers in the logistics coordination (Lambert & Cooper, 2000). A formal definition of a supply chain complies with at least three actors (Mentzer et al. 2001). From a researchers' point of view, the question is how this extension applies in current research designs. Is research conducted in a "supply chain" perspective? In this study, the level of analysis is viewed in a broad sense, not only including those who include actual data from inter-connected buyers and suppliers, but also those who study a focal company and its interaction with external organizations, ultimately both customers and/or suppliers. Table 4 presents the current scope of the sample, and the number of articles referring to the various levels of analysis. Not surprisingly, the "supply chain" is by far the most common level of analysis in all three logistics journals, followed by the "dyad", which is the label typically used in studies on buyer/supplier relationships.

	IJLM	IJPD&LM	JBL	Total
Function	0	0	0	0
Firm	1	2	0	3
Dyad	5	2	2	9
Chain	13	13	6	32
Network	1	1	0	2
n/a	6	16	3	25
Total	26	34	11	71

Table 4: Level of Analysis

A closer look at the research design behind these studies reveals that almost half of the studies on "supply chains" are of a conceptual nature. The data also reveals that the remaining methods are divided almost equally between qualitative and quantitative approaches, though in terms of number, are in the favor of the latter one. It was impossible to derive a level of analysis from several articles (cf. "n/a" in Table 4), but nevertheless these results seem to confirm that the literature seeks to comply with the ideal of a "supply chain" by defining the scope of the study – the level of analysis as the "supply chain." As noted before, this study does not consider the extent to which the particular article includes data from more than one member of the supply chain. It must, however, be noted that especially in qualitative and contextualized studies, the inclusion of more than one level of the supply chain will enhance the validity of that particular study.

5.3 Main Purpose, Research Design and Time Frame

Table 5 shows the number of articles on different purposes, research design and time frame across the three journals. The majority of articles have a descriptive, explorative or explanative purpose both overall (53 out of 71) and within each of the three journals (IJLM: 15 out of 26; IJPD&LM: 30 out of 34 and JBL: 8 out of 11). Thus, taking these purposes as one group they feature greater critical distance, more observation and less involvement directly with the field. A second group, including articles with the main purpose to understand, diagnose, be normative or to intervene, features a more active involvement and closer proximity to the field of study. Together, this group constitutes 18 out of 71 reviewed articles. The highest number (absolute and percentage) of normative purposes is found in IJLM. Research designs applied in the reviewed articles are also summarized in Table 5.

	IJLM	IJPD&LM	JBL	Total
Purpose				
To describe	8	14	3	25
To explore	4	6	4	14
To explain	3	10	1	14
To understand	4	0	0	4
To diagnose	1	0	2	3
To be normative	6	3	1	10
To intervene	0	1	0	1
Purpose total	*26*	*34*	*11*	*71*
Research design				
Desk research – literature review	7	6	5	18
Desk research – literature review and empirical qualitative analysis	2	4	0	6
Desk research – literature review and empirical quantitative analysis	5	6	1	12
Desk research – literature review and empirical analysis based on triangulation	1	2	1	4
Desk research – theorizing	5	8	0	13
Desk research – theorizing and empirical qualitative analysis	4	3	1	8
Desk research – theorizing and empirical quantitative analysis	1	3	3	7
Desk research – theorizing and empirical analysis based on triangulation	1	2	0	3
Research design total	*26*	*34*	*11*	*71*
Time frame				
Snapshot	13	19	6	38
Longitudinal	1	1	0	2
n/a	12	14	5	31
Time frame total	*26*	*34*	*11*	*71*

Table 5: Main Purpose, Research Design and Time Frame

Table 5 differentiates between two types of desk research: literature review and theorizing. "Literature review" denotes articles discussing and referring to what already has been published in the field. In "theorizing," earlier developed or new theoretical elements are combined to constitute new theoretical insight. The major distinction between the two types of desk research and theorizing is a form of development which does not take place with literature review. Both types of desk research may be combined with three types of empirical research designs: qualitative, quantitative or triangulation. As the data in Table 5 shows, the total bulk of articles involved in this research are grounded in empiricism (40 out of 71). In turn, the majority of these articles are based on quantitative methods (19 out of 40). The third part of Table 5 classifies the empirically oriented articles (40 of 71) relative to the time frame in which they operate. As the table clearly indicates, the data collection process is geared to generate a snapshot in almost every one of the applicable articles (38 out of 40). Inherently, this places a severe limit on the researcher's ability to analyze data according to a progressive perspective. A similar result was obtained by Gubi et al. (2003) in their study of Nordic doctoral dissertations. The lack of longitudinal studies is not a trivial concern considering the fact that the implementation and development of logistics systems often is a very complex and long-term process (Gubi et al., 2003).

5.4 Theoretical Area

SCM is often explained further by referring to theories or concepts from both logistics as well as non-logistics disciplines. These theories or concepts can be understood in an SCM perspective, but more importantly, if supported by empirical evidence over time, they might appear as constituent elements of SCM. In the sample articles, theories or concepts related to logistics and SCM include purchasing, operations management, operations research, location theory, reverse logistics, inventory management, materials management, inter-modal transport, order release theory, e-business, customer service, manufacturing and just-in-time. To borrow theories from other disciplines, the multiplicity of theories and concepts from non-logistics disciplines seems to confirm to some extent the proposal of Stock (1997).

5.5 Containing Elements of Philosophy of Science

Several researchers have called for more debate on philosophy of science within logistics. This may help perpetuate or be a part of the borrowing of theories from non-logistics disciplines (Stock, 1997), help logistics to mobilize beyond its functionalistic paradigm (Mears-Young & Jackson, 1997), and even improve the current understanding of what logistics knowledge is and how it comes about (Arlbjørn & Halldórsson, 2002). To investigate to what extent the current literature on SCM may be following such paths, the sample articles were reviewed for references to the literature on philosophy of science. This was the case in a total of four articles. Skjøtt-Larsen (1999) touches upon these elements by suggesting the cross-fertilization of SCM with the transaction cost approach and the resource-based perspective. In addition, the work of Waller et al. (2000) on developing mathematical models for postponement and product customization refers to two sources of philosophy of science.

5.6 References to Methodology

As in the previous section, we found it interesting to investigate further to what extent studies of SCM refer to literature dedicated to methodological issues. A few articles cite a number of references on methodology. For example, Gimenez & Ventura (2003) mention 9 such references in their study of the competitive advantage of SCM in the Spanish grocery sector, and Wisner (2003) applies 13 references when using a structural equation model of the relationship between supply chain management strategies and firm performance. Few sample articles refer to other studies in logistics and SCM and their use of particular methods and research designs. But the majority of the sample articles, both quantitative and qualitative, does not refer to this particular literature at all. The conceptual contributions by Goldsby & Garcia-Dastugue (2003) explicitly point out that their study of one particular SCM process, i.e. manufacturing flow management, is "contextual-neutral."

6 Conclusion

SCM has received great attention from both research and practice. What do we know about SCM? "Not much," would be an honest but immeasurable answer. This study reviewed 71 journal articles spanning three large logistics journals. The results in the previous sections draw conclusions on methodologies applied in SCM as well as related attributes of every research design. The overall conclusion of this paper is that the current knowledge of SCM is contingent on the variables in Table 6's application in the research process.

Starting with the two latest bullet points, previous claims of the lacking empirical support of SCM seem to be consistent with rather limited methodological references in the sample. Furthermore, the proportion of conceptual work seemed to not be justified by a discussion of the fundamental assumptions of SCM (theory, methodology, philosophy of science), as references to this literature are limited in the sample, to say the least. Theoretical foundations from a philosophy of science perspective are still unquestioned, with the exception of Mears-Young & Jackson (1997) and Arlbjørn & Halldórsson (2002).

- Primary actor of analysis: Manufacturer mentioned most frequently.
- Level of analysis: Primarily supply chain
- Main purpose: Majority of articles have a descriptive, explorative or explanative purpose
- Research design: 40 of 71 articles are grounded by empirical evidence
- Time frame: Primarily "snapshots"
- Theoretical area: Primarily other articles of logistics/SCM, but also references to non-logistics theories, under fields both related and not related to logistics
- Containing elements of philosophy of science: Four of 71 articles
- References to methodology: A majority of the articles do not refer to methodological literature

Table 6: Summary of Review Elements

The results of the analysis of methodology applied in papers about SCM presented here may have implications for future research. We can outline four implications. First, two central decisions of a research design, actor and level of analysis seem to concentrate on one particular variable: manufacturing company and supply chain perspective, respectively. Accordingly, they indicate a gap in current research and knowledge on SCM. The primary actor of analysis is the manufacturer, and only to a limited extent other actors in the supply chain; this study does not distinguish between types of manufacturers, process characteristics, nor their industrial context. However, it can be questioned whether all the models and frameworks generated by the manufacturer's perspective also apply equally among other members of the supply chain. Second, besides empirical evidence, we also want to advocate a contextualization of the current managerial frameworks. Although the empirical evidence is most frequently collected by one company in the particular supply chain, the "supply chain" itself is the most frequent level of analysis. In terms of validity, this represents a weakness of the concurrent studies: not only logistics objectives may differ among the members of the supply chain, but also their perception of each other. Third, in terms of time, these studies primarily provide a static, snapshot picture of reality. Thus, a future research opportunity exists both by including more members of the supply chain in the particular study, and following their interactions over time. Ultimately, this might confirm or affirm the sustainability of SCM as a competitive solution. Finally, this study observed non-logistics concepts applied to SCM related problems. However, we should be cautious of terming this application as "cross-fertilization" because it is rarely navigated by a more fundamental discussion of the nature of the discipline by e.g. discussing the fundamentals of methodology and philosophy of science perspectives.

7 References

Arlbjørn, J. S. (1999): Logistik og supply chain management: Er der et teoretisk ståsted? (Logistics and Supply Chain Management: Is there a Theoretical Point of Departure?), in: Ledelse & Erhvervsøkonomi, 63(3): 177-189.

Arlbjørn, J. S. (2000): A Comparative Logistical Analysis: A Search for a Contingency Theory, Ph.D. thesis, Odense University Press, Odense.

Arlbjørn, J. S., Halldórsson, A. (2002): Logistics Knowledge Creation: Reflections on Content, Processes and Context, in: International Journal of Physical Distribution & Logistics Management, 32(1): 22-40.

Bechtel, C., Jayaram, J. (1997): Supply Chain Management: A Strategic Perspective, in: International Journal of Logistics Management, 8(1): 15-34.

Bowersox, D. J. (1969): Physical Distribution Development, Current Status, and Potential, in: Journal of Marketing, 33(1): 63-70.

Christopher, M. (1998): Logistics and Supply Chain Management: Strategies for Reducing Cost and Improving Service, Pitman Publishing, London.

Cooper, M. C., Lambert, D. M., Pagh, J. D. (1997): Supply Chain Management: More than a new name for logistics, in: International Journal of Logistics Management, 8(1): 1-14.

Ellram, L. M. (1996): The Use of the Case Study Method in Logistics Research, in: Journal of Business Logistics, 17(2): 93-138.

Gammelgaard, B. (1997): A Joint-Nordic Ph.D. Program in Logistics, in: Masters, J. (ed.): Proceedings of The Twenty-Sixth Annual Transportation and Logistics Educators Conference, Council of Logistics Management, Chicago.

Gammelgaard, B. (2003): Case studies in logistics research, in: Juga, J. (ed.): Proceedings of the 15th Annual Conference for Nordic Researchers in Logistics NOFOMA, Oulu, Finland: 556-567.

Garver, M. S., Mentzer, J. T. (1999): Logistics Research Methods Employing Structural Equation Modeling to test for Construct Validity, in: Journal of Business Logistics, 20(1): 33-57.

Gibson, B. J., Hanna, J. B. (2003): Periodical Usefulness: The U.S. Logistics Educator Perspective, in: Journal of Business Logistics, 24(1): 221-240.

Gimenez, C., Ventura, E. (2003): Supply Chain Management as a Competitive Advantage in the Spanish Grocery Industry, in: International Journal of Logistics Management, 14(1): 77-88.

Goldsby, T. J., Garica-Dastugue, S. J. (2003): The Manufacturing Flow Management Process, in: International Journal of Logistics Management, 14(2): 33-52.

Gubi, E., Arlbjørn, J. S., Johansen, J. (2003): Doctoral Dissertations in Logistics and Supply Chain Management: A Review of Scandinavian Contributions from 1990 to 2001, in: International Journal of Physical Distribution & Logistics Management, 33(10): 854-885.

Halldórsson, A., Aastrup, J. (2003): Quality Criteria for Qualitative Inquiries in Logistics, in: European Journal of Operational Research, 144: 321-332.

Lambert, D. M., Cooper, M. C., Pagh, J. D. (1998): Supply Chain Management: Implementation Issues and Research Opportunities, in: International Journal of Logistics Management, 9(2): 1-19.

Lambert, D. M., Cooper, M. C. (2000): Issues in Supply Chain Management, in: Industrial Marketing Management, 29(1): 65-83.

Larson, P. D., Halldórsson, A. (2004): Logistics versus Supply Chain Management: An International Survey, in: International Journal of Logistics: Research and Applications, 7(1): 17-31.

Mears-Young, B., Jackson, M. C. (1997): Integrated Logistics – Call in the Revolutionaries, in: Omega – International Journal of Management Science, 25(6): 605-618.

Mentzer, J. T., Flint, D. J. (1997): Validity in Logistics Research, in: Journal of Business Logistics, 18(2): 199-216.

Mentzer, J. T., Kahn, K. (1995): A Framework for Logistics Research, in: Journal of Business Logistics, 16(1): 231-250.

Mentzer, J.T., DeWitt, W., Keebler, J. S., Min, S. (2001): Defining Supply Chain Management, in: Journal of Business Logistics, 22(2): 1-25.

Näslund, D. (2002): Logistics Needs Qualitative Research – Especially Action Research, in: International Journal of Physical Distribution & Logistics Management, 32(5): 321-338.

Persson, U. (1997): A Conceptual and Empirical Examination of the Management Concept of Supply Chain Management, Licentiate Thesis, Division of Industrial Logistics, Luleå University of Technology.

Oliver, R. K., Webber, M. D. (1982): Supply Chain Management: Logistics Catches up With Strategy in: Christopher, M. (ed.): Logistics: The Strategic Issues, Chapman & Hall, London.

Seaker, R. F., Waller, M. A., Dunn, S. C. (1993): A Note on Research Methodology in Business Logistics, in: Logistics and Transportation Review, 29(4): 383-387.

Skjøtt-Larsen, T. (1999): Supply Chain Management: A New Challenge for Researchers and Managers in Logistics, in: International Journal of Logistics Management, 10(2): 41-53.

Stock, J. R. (1997): Applying Theories from Other Disciplines to Logistics, in: International Journal of Physical Distribution & Logistics Management, 27(9/10): 515-539.

Voss, C., Tsikriktsis, N., Frolich, M. (2002): Case Research in Operations Management, in: International Journal of Operations & Production Management, 22(2): 195-218.

Waller, M. A., Dabholkar, P. A., Gentry, J. J. (2000): Postponement, Product Customization, and Market-Oriented Supply Chain Management, in: Journal of Business Logistics, 21(2): 133-160.

Wisner, J. D. (2003): A Structural Equation Model of Supply Chain Management Strategies and Firm Performance, in: Journal of Business Logistics, 24(1): 1-26.

Yin, R. (1994): Case Study Research Design and Methods, Sage Publications, London.

8 Appendix

Review element	Range of variation
Primary actor of analysis	1. Manufacturer; 2. Carrier; 3. Wholesaler; 4. Retailer; 5. Warehousing; 6. n/a
Level of analysis	1. Function 2. Firm 3. Dyad 4. Chain 5. Network 6. n/a
Main purpose of article	1. Describe 2. Explore 3. Explain 4. Understand 5. Diagnose 6. Normative 7. Intervene
Research design applied	1. Desk research – literature review 2. Desk research – literature review and empirical qualitative analysis 3. Desk research – literature review and empirical quantitative analysis 4. Desk research – literature review and empirical analysis based on triangulation 5. Desk research – theorizing 6. Desk research – theorizing and empirical qualitative analysis 7. Desk research – theorizing and empirical quantitative analysis 8. Desk research – theorizing and empirical analysis based on triangulation
Time frame of the empirically based articles	1. Snapshot; 2. Longitudinal or 3. n/a
Containing elements of philosophy of science	1. Yes 2. No
Number of references dealing with science	Number
Number of references dealing with methodology	Number
Does the paper contain SCM?	1. Yes 2. No

Table 7: The Frame of References Used in Rating the Individual Articles

Part 2
Surveys in Supply Chain Management

The Role and Importance of Survey Research in the Field of Supply Chain Management

Herbert Kotzab

1 Introduction 126
2 A State-of-the-Art Survey Research in the JBL from 1993 to 2003 127
3 Conclusions and Outlook 136
4 References 136

Summary:
The following paper continues the work of Mentzer & Kahn (1995) by examining 99 'survey' articles that have been published in the Journal of Business Logistics *between Volume 14 (2) and Volume 24. In order to identify certain tendencies in the methodological development in the field, the assessment includes the analysis of the methods used for collecting data, the sampling procedures, the response rates, the data format, and research. Although survey research seems to be an accepted research approach in the field of logistics and Supply Chain Management, the information given in the articles is unsatisfactory, as no article contains all the necessary data that allow conclusions towards reliability, validity and objectivity of the study.*

Keywords:
Supply Chain Management, Research Methodologies, Survey Research

1 Introduction

1.1 The Importance of Surveys in the Field of Business and Logistics Research

Survey research plays an important role in many disciplines when it comes to collecting primary data (Zikmund, 2000: 167). Choosing a survey strategy allows the collection of large amounts of data in an efficient manner. Typically, this is done by using questionnaires with which researchers bring together standardized data that can be compared easily (Saunders et al. 2004). Surveys, for example, are very important for marketing research as they are "normally associated with descriptive and causal research situations" (Hair, et al. 2003: 255). The study conducted by Krafft et al. (2003) showed that 60% of the empirical papers presented between 1990 and 2002 in the German journals Die Betriebswirtschaft (DBW), Zeitschrift für Betriebswirtschaft (ZfB) and Zeitschrift für betriebswirtschaftliche Forschung (zfbf) refer to surveys. In his study, where he examined 513 articles that had been published in leading academic German journals between 1997 and 2000, Hausschildt (2003) identified a 'market share' of empirical papers of 32%. Within this sample, marketing is the leading discipline, followed by finance and capital markets, organization, and human resources.

Survey research also seems to be important for research in the field of logistics Supply Chain Management (SCM) and logistics research (Larson & Poist 2004). Large & Stölzle (1999) showed that 19 of 88 German doctoral dissertations (published between 1990 and 1997) used surveys as the method of choice. In comparison to a US study conducted by Dunn et al. (1993), this share was lower.

In 1995, Mentzer & Kahn (1995) proposed a research framework for logistics research and reviewed all articles that had been published in the *Journal of Business Logistics* (JBL) from Vol. 1 (1978) to Vol. 14, issue 1 (1993) in order to assess the application of their suggestion. One conclusion has been that mail surveys are made out as the "methodology of choice in logistics" (Mentzer & Kahn, 1995: 241). The study by Larson & Poist (2004), which examined all volumes of the *Transportation Journal* between 1992 and 2003, also showed that 30 to 60% of all articles report on mail surveys.

1.2 Methodology

The following article continues this assessment by presenting a review of all articles published in the JBL from Volume 14, issue 2 (1993) to Volume 24, issue 2 (2003). In order to identify certain tendencies in the methodological development in the field, the assessment includes the analysis of the methods used for collecting data, the sampling procedures, the response rates, the data format and research designs (in accordance with Krafft et al., 2003). The results of this analysis are compared with the results of the studies by Krafft et al. (2003) and Larson & Poist (2004).

2 A State-of-the-Art Survey Research in the JBL from 1993 to 2003

2.1 Description of the Population and the Sample

A total of 223 articles have been published in the Journal of Business Logistics (JBL) from Volume 14, issue 2 (1993) to Volume 24 (2003). Key word searches in the Business Source Premier database and "leaping through" the hard copies of the journals resulted in an identification of 99 articles that report on survey research. This means that the reader of the JBL will find about 5 articles that present results based on surveys (n=223; standard deviation: 1.15) in every issue (see Table 1).

Volume	Total number	Survey articles	'market share'
14 (issue 2 only)	9	3	33.33%
15	26	12	46%
16	26	11	42%
17	26	9	35%
18	22	9	41%
19	22	10	45%
20	21	8	38%
21	20	9	45%
22	18	10	56%
23	13	7	54%
24	20	11	55%
Total	223	99	44 %
Total without Vol. 14 (2)	214	96	45 %

Table 1: Total Number of Articles per Volume of JBL and Number of Articles

The 'market share' of survey research presented in the JBL within the observed period can therefore be calculated with 44%. Compared with the findings of Mentzer & Kahn (1995), one could expect a decline. However, the authors did not comment on the computation of their Table 2 that presents the research methodologies used between JBL Volume 1 (1) and Volume 14 (1). These results, however, match the results of Larson & Poist (2004) very well.

2.2 Types of Questionnaires – The Research Design

The distinctive research instrument of the survey is the questionnaire, which is understood as a data collection technique where different persons (= respondents) are asked to respond to the same set of questions in a prearranged order (deVaus, 2002 or Zikmund, 2000). For research efficiency reasons, questionnaires are very widely used for descriptive (e.g. attitudes, opinions, organizational practices) and/or explanatory/analytical research (e.g. cause-and-effect relationships) (e.g. Saunders et al., 2004: 92). However, there are also some pitfalls that have to be considered, resulting in specific errors such as random sampling errors or systematic errors (Zikmund, 2000: 169).

When it comes to differentiation of questionnaires, Saunders et al. (2004: 282) differ between self-administered and interviewer-administered questionnaires. The distinction is dependent on the amount of contact researchers have with their respondents. In the case of self-administered questionnaires, respondents usually complete the questionnaire without any interaction with a second person, while in the case of interviewer-administered questionnaires, an interviewer records the answers of the respondents (Scholl 2003: 139).

The specific choice for a special questionnaire type is reliant on some factors such as the characteristics of the respondents, the importance of reaching the respondents, the importance of respondents' answers not being contaminated or distorted, the size of the sample the researcher needs, the types of questions a researcher needs to ask, and the number of questions a researcher needs to ask (Saunders et al., 2004).

Table 2 shows the results of the identified types of questionnaires in the examined JBL articles. A total number of 106 questionnaire approaches were identified in 93 articles. In five cases, the authors did not explicitly present their type of questionnaire. The results also show that the self-administered questionnaire is the dominant questionnaire type. Within this category, the postal questionnaire is the most chosen one. This is due to the fact that the majority of the research is executed amongst managers in a business-to-business setting (see also 3.3). These results are not surprising, as Krafft et al. (2003) could also identify the dominance of self-administered surveys in their study, as well as identifying nebulous information on the design.

Questionnaire					
Self-administered				Interviewer-administered	
online		postal (+ fax)	delivery and collection questionnaire	telephone questionnaire	structured interview
email	web site				
1	2	83 (+3)	4	9	4
93				13	
106					

Table 2: The Types of Questionnaires in JBL Research

2.3 The Sampling Procedures

- **The Philosophy of Sampling**

Samples are defined as subsets or parts of a larger population (Zikmund, 2000). The population or universe is seen as a complete group of entities that share some common set of characteristics. Sampling is characterized as the process of using a small number of items or parts of a larger population to make conclusions about a whole population. Whenever the objective is to estimate an unknown population, value researchers choose sampling due to pragmatic reasons such as time and budget constraints. Samples are typically drawn from a list of population elements, which is also called the *sampling frame*. Such frames can be found in mailing lists, directories, membership rosters, etc. (see Zikmund, 2000: 342).

It seems that in the case of the analyzed JBL articles, not every article presents this clear approach in its section on methodology. This critique e.g. refers to the information on the population on which the results can be generalized. Only 20 out of 106 studies inform the reader on the relevant population that ranges from 68 to 10,000 elements (!). In another share of 24 studies, no information on the population or a sample frame is presented at all. For the rest, the samples were mainly drawn from a membership roster where the CLM membership roster dominated (see Figure 1). However, this drawback has also been recognized by Krafft et al. (2003) in their German study, where every fifth article did not inform the reader on the sample procedures.

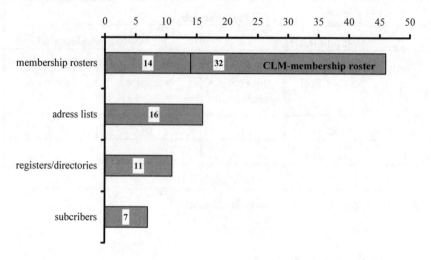

Figure 1: Sampling Frames Most Frequently Used in JBL Survey Studies

The second largest group refers to various address lists, followed by directories/registers and subscribers of journals. While the samples of 39 studies refer to one specific type of organization (e.g. manufacturers or retailers only), the sample of 53 studies is drawn from several stages of a logistics chain. The remaining 20 studies do not inform regarding this issue. Looking at the involved industries, 68 studies surveyed across industries while 24 studies examined inside one industry. The remaining articles gave no further information on this. The majority of the studies refer to B2B.

The potential respondents refer to a broad range of different professions and job titles. Figure 2 shows those groups that had been addressed in most of the cases; the rest of the 115 job/function titles refer to functional management groups such as marketing, materials or finance managers. Interestingly enough, truck drivers, employees and even professors had been the object of interest for some studies.

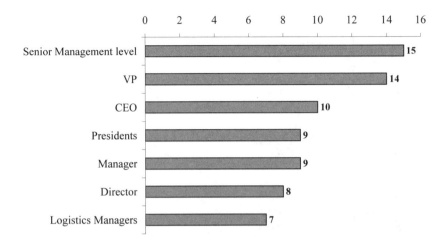

Figure 2: Typical Respondent in a JBL Survey Study

- **Planned and Actual Sample Sizes**

Not all studies report on the number of questionnaires sent out, as this information is given for 102 of 112 studies. The number of total research designs sent out was calculated at 105,609. The 'average' JBL survey study refers to approximately 1,035 sampling units (n=102; standard deviation: 2,128).

The minimum number of questionnaires was 11 (Edwards et al., 2001; interviewer administered questionnaire) and the maximum number of questionnaires was 16,920 (Mentzer et al., 1999; no information on the type of questionnaire). The average response rate over all examined studies was calculated with 38.94% (n=101; standard deviation 26.99%), varying between 4% and 100%. This number is not surprising, as Larson & Poist (2004) report on 106,300 surveys that were mailed by the authors of *Transportation Journal*. The average response with 26% is, in the case of the *Transportation Journal*, a little bit lower.

Following Larson & Poist's (2004) idea of correlating the response rate with the number of sent questionnaires (see Figure 3), we identified a weak, but significant, negative relationship between the size of the sampling fraction and the response rate; including all those cases where both information on the sample and the questionnaires sent were given (n=101). A moderate, but also significant, negative relationship was identified even when excluding all cases where the number of questionnaires sent out was over 5,000 (n=97). These results confirm Larson & Poist's notions.

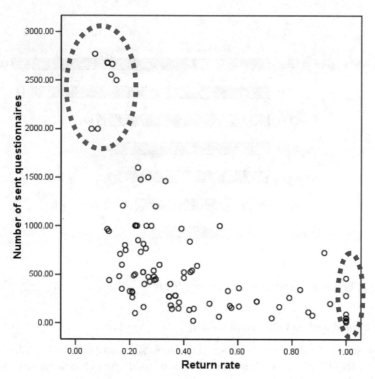

Correlations (all cases, N = 101)		VAR00002	VAR00003
VAR00002	Pearson Correlation	1	-.299**
	Sig (2-tailed)	,	.002
	N	101	101
VAR00003	Pearson Correlation	-.299**	1
	Sig (2-tailed)	.002	,
	N	101	102

** Correlation is significant at the 0.01 level (2-tailed)

Correlations (excluded cases, N = 97)		VAR00002	VAR00003
VAR00002	Pearson Correlation	1	-.544**
	Sig (2-tailed)	,	.000
	N	97	97
VAR00003	Pearson Correlation	-.544**	1
	Sig (2-tailed)	.000	,
	N	97	97

** Correlation is significant at the 0.01 level (2-tailed)

Figure 3: Relation between Response Rate and Total Number of Questionnaires in the JBL Studies

As response rate is also dependent on certain activities, we wondered whether this information would be found in the articles (see Jobber & O'Reilly, 1996). Although not all studies report on the process of how the questionnaire was administered, 15 studies present information on the pre-survey contact, 50 studies report on first follow-up, another 16 on second follow-up, and in 2 studies we observed third follow-up activities (see Figure 4).

Although we could identify a difference in the response rates between those studies that use such methods and those which do not apply them, the difference cannot be acknowledged as being significant. This is contrary to the findings of Larson & Poist (2004), who observed significant differences in response rates when certain techniques such as pre-notification, follow-up mailings, and monetary incentives had been used.

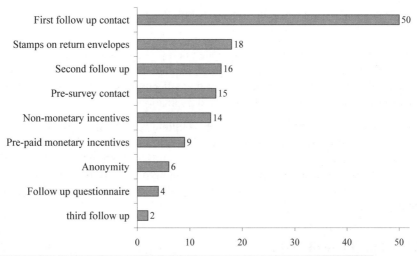

Figure 4: Applied Techniques to Increase Response Rates as Indicated in the JBL Studies

- **Type of Sampling**

Table 3 shows the results of the identified sampling techniques. 93 articles give insight on a total of 106 sampling techniques. Six articles do not specify the sampling technique.

Sampling techniques									
Probability sampling					Non-probability sampling				
1.	2.	3.	4.	5.	6.	7.	8.	9.	10.
17	3	5	18	0	0	30	7	12	14
43					63				
106									

(1 = simple random; 2 = systematic; 3 = stratified random; 4 = cluster; 5 = multi-stage; 6 = quota; 7 = purposive/judgmental; 8 = snow ball; 9 = self-selection; 10 = convenience; multiple responses)

Table 3: Sampling Techniques as Presented in the JBL Studies

The majority of logistics researchers applied non-probability sampling techniques, out of which judgmental sampling had been applied most often. The disadvantage of such samples is that the findings from the collected data cannot be considered to be statistically representative for the total population.

In the case of probability sampling, cluster sampling was mainly applied, followed by simple random sampling. Interestingly enough, no survey research has been published in the JBL using quota sampling. This differs from the results of Krafft et al. (2003: 93), where the most common sampling procedure is simple probability sampling, while only 11.8% of all survey studies applied convenience sampling.

2.4 The Type of Data

The goal for any self-administered survey is to develop a research design that all the respondents will interpret in the same manner (Dillman, 2000: 32). Survey questions are therefore often posed as closed questions in order to obtain lists, rankings, categories, ratings or quantities (Saunders et al., 2004: 292). From a research point of view, this is a question of measuring in different levels or scales of measurement, especially when it comes to the assessment of quantitative data (Ghauri & Grønhaug, 2002: 66; see also Table 4).

Level of measurement/scale	Characterization
nominal level (scale)	lowest level of measurement; typically used for classification
ordinal level (scale)	used for variables that cannot be classified but can be ranked in an order
interval level (scale)	used for variables where a distance between the observations is constant and exact
ratio level (scale)	used for variables with a natural or absolute zero and where a distance between the observations is constant and exact

Table 4: Levels of Measurement (Ghauri & Grønhaug, 2002: 66)

Saunders et al. (2004) classify these levels into two groups – categorical (nominal and ordinal level) and quantifiable (continuous and discrete) and show how the precision of the data increases when data is obtained in a discrete manner. There is also a need for a specific scale level when it comes to applying certain analysis tools, as not all scales are suited for specific multi-variable analysis (Hair et al., 1998).

Table 5 shows the results of the assessment of the data types as presented in the JBL studies.

Quantitative data type			
categorical data		quantifiable data	
nominal	ordinal	continuous	discrete
28	89	19	18

Table 5: Types of Data and Levels of Numerical Measurement as Outlined in the JBL Studies (multi-responses)

The majority of the measurements used in the published articles referred to ordinal scale levels. This is therefore very interesting, as a preliminary analysis of the applied statistical analysis tools showed the use of sophisticated tools such as structuring equation modeling, although the indicated scale level seemed to be inappropriate for such analysis, because data has to be at least on an interval scale level and normally distributed (see Hair et al., 1998).

3 Conclusions and Outlook

Overall we have seen that survey research plays an important role in the field of logistics and supply chain research. The results of the presented approach can be summarized as follows:

- The 'market share' of survey research in the JBL is over 40%, which is higher than in other comparable logistics journals;
- the self-administered interview is the method of choice in logistics and supply chain survey research;
- within this category, the postal questionnaire is the most preferred one;
- not all studies report on the population, the number of questionnaires sent out, or the sample size, which limits the reliability and the validity of the presented results;
- the most used sampling frame are membership rosters – especially the one from CLM;
- the 'president's view' dominates;
- the majority of logistics researchers applied non-probability sampling techniques out of which judgmental sampling had been applied most;
- response rate management seems to be a key issue, but there might be other more important effects.

A comparison of these findings with the main results of Krafft et al. (2003) and Larson & Poist (2004) confirms a specific pattern, especially when it comes to the presentation of some key information, as it seems to be standard not to report on all issues of this research strategy. There is the impression that quoting standard references like Dillman (2000) is the equivalent of guaranteeing a quality standard when doing survey research.

4 References

de Vaus, D. (2002): Surveys in Social Research, 5th edition, Taylor & Francis Books, London.

Dillman, D. (2000): Mail and Internet Surveys. The Tailored Design Method. Wiley, New York et al.

Dunn, S., Seaker, R., Stenger, A., Young, R. (1993): An Assessment of Logistics Research Paradigms. In: Masters, J. (ed.): Current Topics in Logistics Education and Research. The Transportation and Logistics Research Fund. The Ohio State University: p. 121-139.

Hair, J., Anderson, R., Tatham, R., Black, W. (1998): Multivariate Data Analysis, 5th edition. Prentice-Hall International, London et al.

Hair, J., Bush, R., Ortinau, D. (2003): Marketing Research. Within a changing information environment, McGraw-Hill Irwin, Boston et al.

Hauschildt, J. (2003): Zum Stellenwert der empirischen betriebswirtschaftlichen Forschung (State of the Art of empirical research in business administration). In: Schwaiger, M., Harhoff, D. (eds.): Empirie und Betriebswirtschaft. Entwicklungen und Perspektiven (Empiricism and Business Administration. Development and Perspectives), Schäffer-Poeschel, Stuttgart: p. 3-24.

Jobber, D., O'Reilly, D. (1998): Industrial Mail Surveys: A Methodological Update, in: Industrial Marketing Management, 27(2): 95-107.

Krafft, M., Haase, K., Siegel, A. (2003): Statistisch-ökonometrische BWL-Forschung: Entwicklung, Status Quo und Perspektiven (Statistical-econometric business research: Development, Status Quo and Perspectives), in: Schwaiger, M., Harhoff, D. (eds.): Empirie und Betriebswirtschaft. Entwicklungen und Perspektiven (Empiricism and Business Administration. Development and Perspectives), Schäffer-Poeschel, Stuttgart: p. 83-104.

Large, R, Stölzle, W. (1999): Logistikforschung im Spiegel wissenschaftlicher Publikationen. Eine empirische Untersuchung auf der Basis betriebswirtschaftlicher und ingenieurwissenschaftlicher Dissertationen (Examination of scientific logistics publications – an empirical investigation by comparing business and engineering Ph.D. theses). In: Pfohl, H.-C. (ed.): Logistikforschung. Entwicklungszüge und Gestaltungsansätze (Logistics research. Development and Approaches), Erich Schmidt Verlag, Berlin: p. 3-35.

Larson, P., Poist (2004): Improving Response Rates to Mail Surveys: A Research Note, in: Transportation Journal, 43(4): 67-75.

Mentzer, J., Flint, D., Kent, J. (1999): Developing a logistics service quality scale, in: Journal of Business Logistics, 20(1): 9-32.

Mentzer, T., Kahn, K. (1995): A framework of logistics research. Journal of Business Logistics, 16(1): 231-250.

Saunders, M., Lewis, P., Thornhill, A. (2004): Research Methods for Business Students, FT-Prentice-Hall, Harlow et al.

Scholl, A. (2003): Die Befragung. Sozialwissenschaftliche Methode und kommunikationswissenschaftliche Anwendung (Surveys. A method of social science and its use in communication studies). UTB, Konstanz.

Zikmund, W. (2000): Business Research Methods, 6th edition. Harcourt, Fort Worth et al.

Web-based Surveys in Logistics Research: An Empirical Application

David B. Grant, Christoph Teller, Wolfgang Teller

1 Introduction 140
2 Literature Review 141
3 Application of Web-based Survey Methodology 143
4 Survey Findings 146
5 Study Limitations 151
6 Conclusions 151
7 References 152

Summary:
The use of surveys continues to lead logistics and supply chain management research. We discuss the use of Internet or Web-based surveys as an alternative to traditional survey methods in the context of a Web-based empirical study to identify advantages, disadvantages and limitations of this approach. We demonstrate that this approach has numerous technological and methodological advantages to improve not only internal validity but also external validity. Based on a literature survey, we identify different advantages and validate them by presenting the results of a Web-based survey that was conducted in a typical logistics research setting.

Keywords:
Web Research, Web-Based Surveys, Logistics, Research Methods

1 Introduction

Surveys are the most frequently used method for empirical research in the social sciences (Bortz & Döring, 2002), particularly logistics and supply chain management (SCM) research (Mentzer & Kahn, 1995, Large & Stolzle, 1999, Griffis et al., 2003). Self-administered postal or mail surveys have been the usual application in these contexts as they provide inexpensive and easily administered results from a large number of respondents (Berekoven, et al., 2001; Griffis et al., 2003). However, this method has a number of disadvantages including low return and high non-response rates leading to a lack of external validity for samples, and no control over the survey situation regarding the way questionnaires are completed and how respondents are motivated to give their respective answers (Atteslander, 2000).

Most logistics respondents are practitioners in enterprises and are surveyed on facts pertaining to their complex business practices (Mentzer & Kahn, 1995), thus this research tends to be in the business-to-business (B2B) domain rather than business-to-consumer (B2C). Further, the lack of consistent comprehension of terms and an inability to clarify them reduces the internal validity of such surveys (Mentzer & Flint, 1997). The widespread use of the survey method suggests logistics researchers are aware of its shortcomings but cannot see an alternative to its cost effectiveness as an empirical approach. However, the Internet or world wide web (Web) and its growing penetration into enterprises provides a fresh opportunity to overcome these shortcomings by using Web-based surveys that provide many improvements, some of which follow (Pincott & Branthwaite, 2000; Brown et al., 2001; Cobanoglu et al., 2001; Tuten et al., 2002; Illieva et al., 2002):

- A context-driven interview situation,
- A combination of survey and limited observation,
- The digitization of information,
- Dramatization of stimuli.

We consider the topic of Web-based surveys and their use for logistics research in the context of an empirical survey of information and education services for Austrian computer retailers conducted with a Web-based survey in conjunction with the Austrian Chambers of Commerce (ACC). We review extant literature on surveys in section 2 focusing on mail or postal surveys versus Internet or Web-based surveys. We then discuss the methodology of our Web-based survey in section 3 and follow with findings in section 4. We identify limitations of our methodological approach in section 5, and lastly in section 6 we draw conclusions and provide suggestions for logistics researchers conducting Web-based surveys. It must be noted that electronic surveys - even a Web-based questionnaire used together with a web-database tool - do not revolutionize the empirical survey methodology but represent a new technique to collect data and mitigate the disadvantages of self-administered questionnaires (Illieva et al., 2002).

2 Literature Review

2.1 Mail or Postal Surveys

Prior to the telephone facsimile and Internet eras, three methods of consumer and customer surveys were prevalent: personal interview or administration by trained interviewers, telephone surveys conducted by trained interviewers, and mail or postal surveys completed solely by respondents. Mail surveys continue to be the most widely used amongst these three methods (Diamantopoulos & Schlegelmilch, 1996), particularly in logistics or SCM research (Mentzer & Kahn, 1995).

The advantages of mail surveys include concentration of process control, no clustering of interviews, no interviewer bias and low administration costs (Whitley, 1985). However, the distance involved between respondent and the surveyor leads to low response rates overall and high non-responses to questions within the survey (Diamantopoulos & Schlegelmilch, 1996).

Suggested techniques to increase overall response rates include pre-notification of respondents (Schlegelmilch & Diamantopoulos, 1991), personalization of respondents and addresses (Wunder & Wynn, 1988), providing self-addressed, stamped envelopes (SASE) and using professional survey documents and cover letters (Whitley, 1985), using first-class postage (Harvey, 1986) and providing incentives for respondents (Whitley, 1985). However, these suggestions have not all proven satisfactory. Two survey-on-surveys studies provide similar evidence about the effectiveness of these various techniques. Diamantopoulos & Schlegelmilch (1996) surveyed 200 market research agencies and 200 company executives and received 79 (40% response rate) and 81 (41% response rate) responses respectively. Greer et al. (2000) surveyed 344 and 355 company executives in two samples and received 76 (25% response rate) and 64 (20% response rate) responses respectively.

A majority of respondents in each study indicated that survey sponsorship, SASE and personalization, short versus long surveys, and survey content all positively influenced respondent participation. Responses were however mixed regarding the effectiveness of survey pre-notification and follow-up, as well as incentives and survey timing, i.e. what day of the week the survey is received by respondents.

Greer et al.'s (2000) study also found that "noncomparative scales or open-ended questions should be used when asking respondents for facts whereas comparative scales or fixed alternatives should be used when asking respondents for opinions or numbers." This finding regarding survey content should be considered when designing all types of surveys, including those that are Internet or Web-based.

2.2 Internet or Web-based Surveys

The Web provides new opportunities to conduct research by using e-mail or Web-based surveys. A concern is that all households and businesses do not have access to e-mail or the Web (Dillman, 1999). But with two-thirds of UK small and medium enterprises (SMEs) having Internet access and one-quarter of the world's B2B purchases soon being made online (Brown et al., 2001), the Web is fast becoming a medium of choice for researchers. Web-based surveys provide a mechanism for collecting data more quickly which should lead to increased response rates in a cost-effective manner (Griffis et al., 2003).

However, there has not been much research investigating technology-based survey methodologies within this new medium. The few studies published focus either on mixing e-mail and Internet methods (Griffis et al., 2003) or using e-mail messages as the delivery method as opposed to a Web-based platform (Cobanoglu et al., 2001). Some e-mail studies appear narrow in focus regarding the Web's potential; for example Dommeyer & Moriarty (2000) only investigated whether paper-type surveys would generate better response rates if imbedded within or attached to a solicitation e-mail. Such a focus may be the result of researchers continuing to slavishly apply Dillman's (1978) original Total Design Method (TDM) that suggests a one-size-fits-all approach whereby survey implementation methods are the same regardless of medium (Cobanoglu et al., 2001; Dillman, 1999).

However, Web-based surveys have four main technological advantages over face-to-face, mail and telephone alternatives that should influence and increase response rates relative to these methods (Pincott & Branthwaite, 2000; Brown et al., 2001; Cobanoglu et al., 2001; Tuten et al., 2002; Kent & Lee, 1999). These advantages are summarized as follows:

- **A context-driven interview situation:** The use of 'pop-up' windows in a Web-based survey enables a demand-driven dialogue with the respondent. This can be important to control the flow of stimuli, i.e. order of questions, to provide support if necessary, and is a substitute for interviewer control in face-to-face interviews (Tuten et al., 2002). The strength of such visual and verbal information can lead to considered and reasoned responses (Pincott & Branthwaite, 2000).

- **A combination of survey and limited observation:** In traditional mail or postal surveys the process between sending and receiving surveys has been a 'black-box' for researchers. With Web-based surveys it is possible to not only observe the recording of question answers, but also who the respondent is, the date of response(s), and the duration of question answers (Tuten et al., 2002). While there are issues of confidentiality, such observation provides information about the involvement, the reliability and the accuracy of the respondent and should also help monitor response speed, which has been found to be more than 64% faster than traditional mail surveys (Cobanoglu et al., 2001).

- **The digitization of information:** Since all information is on a digital basis the gap between paper and analysis software is removed. This leads to savings in time and money, as there are no variable costs for copying and mailing, and in reductions of input data error (Cobanoglu et al., 2001). Additionally, the survey response can be observed in real time, so the researcher can take actions, for example re-sending a letter of motivation, if the response rate does not turn out to be satisfactory (Tuten et al., 2002).

- **Dramatization of stimuli:** The use of proper quality colors, figures, tables, and images enhances the appearance of the stimuli within a Web-based survey (Brown et al., 2001). This improves respondent interest, motivation and interactivity compared to paper-based surveys (Pincott & Branthwaite, 2000) and should lead to increased response rates, which have been found to be almost 65% higher than mail surveys (Cobanoglu et al., 2001); thus improving internal and external validity (Mentzer & Flint, 1997; Tuten et al., 2002).

In summary, the adoption of Web-based surveys utilizing the above suggested techniques may mitigate shortcomings found in traditional mail or postal survey methods. We employed such techniques in an empirical B2B study that is discussed in sections 3 and 4.

3 Application of Web-based Survey Methodology

In this section we present the methodological application of our Web-based survey. The context of the survey is typical of research in logistics or SCM and ideal for choosing the Internet as a transmission and processing medium of the questionnaire. The framework of our survey can be characterized as follows:

- B2B context.
- Identified population and respondents.
- High degree of involvement of the research subject.
- High degree of reachability via the Internet.

The results may contribute to the use of Web-based surveys for logistics research problems.

3.1 Survey Context and Research Objectives

Our empirical study surveyed all Austrian IT retailers and wholesalers (N=4,828). From our point of view the research goal was twofold. On the one hand we were investigating satisfaction with information and education services provided by the ACC, and on the other hand we evaluated the potential of our Web-based questionnaire in a B2B context; we are only reporting the latter here. The target group provided an excellent opportunity to conduct a Web-based survey because of the following professional or legal reasons and intuitive assumptions:

- Respondents have a comparably high affinity to the Internet medium.
- All of them are expected to have access to and use the Internet including e-mail on a daily basis.
- They can all be reached by postal contact and identified through the ACC membership list.
- Austrian companies in general are highly involved in the topic regarding the ACC.

Referring to the aforementioned technological advantages of Web-based surveys, this specific target group would find it easier and more convenient to reply to such an e-questionnaire (Tse, 1998).

Research Method	Internet-based (Web site/HTML) survey
Duration of Data Collection	July 14 – October 21 2003
Research Design	Standardized questionnaire including closed and open-ended questions
Respondent Population	-Compulsory members of the ACC (Division: Trade/professional guild): IT retailer/whole-seller -4,828 population size
Research Topic	-Evaluation of services provided by the ACC -Evaluation of advantages and pitfalls of Web-based surveys
Instrument Pretest	July 1 – July 7 2003 with selected (15) members of ACC
Resultant Sample Size	506 (11%) for completed questionnaires
Analysis Software	SPSS 11.0, MS-Access, QSR N6 V6.0

Table 1: Research Design

Since every Austrian company must be a member of the ACC by law, the sample was drawn from the ACC's membership list and was thus a census. Although this list contains the official postal address of each company, only a limited number of e-mail addresses were available. Table 1 provides a general overview of the research design applied. This survey was a follow up study of a face-to-face survey including 222 personal interviews of Viennese IT-companies in 2002. The most relevant information generated by this previous study was that this trading sector is dominated by small and medium sized enterprises selling almost solely to professionals (B2B). This provided a basis for the formulation of questions and the setting up of the online questionnaire dramaturgy.

3.2 Web-based Questionnaire – Design and Features

- **Research tool:** The research tool can be characterized as a web-based questionnaire consisting of primarily four technical components. One component is the front end or client interface where the visual part of an HTML program contains numerous JavaScript programs that control the questionnaire, e.g. the flow of stimuli. At the back end or server interface there is a mySQL database where the results are edited for the researchers in real time. A third component at the server represents CGI-scripts required to control programs to generate HTML sites and replenish the database with data from respondents. Lastly, the tool contains a control panel capable of controlling answers given by respondents and editing the results in a real time setting on the Web site.

- **Appearance:** The questionnaire was designed according to guidelines of the corporate design (color, logos, fonts, etc.) for the Vienna University of Economics and Business Administration in order to provide an independent, non-commercial and respectable appearance.

- **Questions and scales:** We used a mixture of closed and open-ended questions and applied numerous kinds of scales. The scales were partly aided by graphical elements. We used 'radio buttons' and 'check boxes' for closed questions and description fields for open-ended questions to increase respondent convenience in completing the questionnaire.

- **Guidance and dialogue driven interview situation:** The respondent was guided through the questionnaire by using 'submit-buttons.' If he/she forgot to answer one or more questions, an alert window appeared and the missing answer was highlighted by a colored frame. If the respondent refused to answer the question he/she had to choose between the response categories 'do not know' and 'not willing to give an answer.' This guaranteed a high item response rate and a differentiated missing value analysis. Apart from the principle that questions have to be as short, as precise and as simple as possible, we provided the opportunity to retrieve explanations for terms which can be misunderstood such as 'service,' 'net-sales,' 'new members of the EU,' etc. Respondents had only to move the cursor over the term (i.e. a 'mouse-over effect') and they received a small description field looking like 'pop-up' window that provided brief explanations. Additionally, this text included links to websites where further information could be retrieved on demand.

- **Abandonment prevention:** Each site contained buttons with which the respondents could choose to abandon the survey. After using that opportunity he/she got an alert window indicating what he/she was going to do. This included an instruction to confirm their intention and make them aware of the opportunity to continue the survey whenever they were willing to do so. The 'cookies' saved on the local hard disk stored all information provided to this point by the respondent that enabled him/her to continue right away from where the abandonment took place.

- **Completion rate:** Each Web page or window in the questionnaire contained a status bar giving information on what percent of questions had already been answered.

- **Humanization of the questionnaire:** Anonymity is one of the major characteristics driving the development of the Internet. In order to differentiate our survey from a growing number of other e-questionnaires and to emphasize the scientific and official character of our study, a button was placed on each Web page or window providing the opportunity to contact the authors of the study via e-mail or other means of communication. The intention behind this was to give the respondents the ability to identify a human being behind the program. However, only 15 respondents (3%) used this feature.

4 Survey Findings

4.1 Notification and Incentive Strategy

Based on the findings from our literature survey regarding the problem of low response rates in mail or postal surveys we applied the following techniques (Dillon et al., 1994; Schlegelmilch & Diamantopoulos, 1991): pre- and post- survey notification including a reference to the e-questionnaire Web site via a postal newsletter of the ACC, personal notification by ACC representatives of each Austrian federal state, and notifications in IT-journals. Additionally, vouchers for training courses amounting to €5,000 were offered as a raffle prize to respondents. Lastly, the link to the questionnaire Web site was transmitted via e-mail stemming from the ACC database and an electronic e-mail database service. Thus, each IT retailer and wholesaler was contacted and notified by both electronic and non-electronic media. While 1,112 respondents entered the Web site (23%), the resulting response of 506 (11%) that fully completed the questionnaire in a timely manner was disappointing given these notification strategies and incentives.

In our final question we evaluated the importance of the various contact media used and found that more than three-quarters of respondents (78%, n=438) indicated e-mail was the transmission medium that triggered them to complete the questionnaire. Only 14% (n=71) were notified by the postal newsletter. A reason for this discrepancy appears to be the effort involved between two different media, e.g. paper and the Internet. The clicking on a Web link sent via e-mail may be more convenient than keying in a short URL into a Web browser. Lastly, 80% of respondents (n=405) participated in the voucher raffle even though personal information had to be disclosed. Therefore we conclude that e-mail notification and the attractiveness of incentives offered for participation are of relevance and importance to respondents.

4.2 Response Quality

As noted above, postal surveys lack information regarding response behavior compared to face to face interviews. Web-based surveys provide the opportunity to combine the survey method with elements of the observation method. This is done by recording time stamps in the database during the self-administered completion process of the questionnaire. This information enables researchers to generate findings about various behavioral aspects and feedback regarding the research design. Following are such findings from our survey.

- **Mortality curve:** No information can be obtained with paper surveys as to why respondents fully completed or did not complete the questionnaire. Since every click is recorded in a Web-based survey, we obtained a completion overview and respondent fatigue effect during the survey process. We experienced a high abandonment rate after the first introduction window (from n=1,112 to n=840) that included information about the research team and the aim of the survey. The main part consisting of 15 windows experienced a continuous abandonment from n=760 to n=548. Interestingly, most of the respondents that survived this far were also willing to answer the most sensitive questions dealing with the characterization of their companies (sales, employees, assortment, clients/customers, etc.). While 506 completed the questionnaire to allow for data analysis, only 457 participated at the raffle stage. The curve leads to the conclusion that the first Web site pages did not attract respondents' attention to a satisfactory degree. The length of the questionnaire, especially the part with questions regarding service evaluation, may have turned out to be too long or too complicated to retain respondent interest. Both of these factors may have affected our response rates. Therefore, we agree with the literature that Web-based surveys should be short and sharp to attract and retain respondents' attention and encourage survey completion.

- **Survival of the most carefully completed questionnaires:** The number of completed questionnaires included in the analysis sample was 506. These were selected on the basis of time records serving as an indicator, together with an inspection of the results of the open-ended questions for analysis and assessing quality. We inspected all questionnaires which were completed in less than eight minutes by looking at the number of 'do not know' or 'do not want to answer' entries and whether they made any notes on open-ended questions. If the respondent did not complete it carefully and spent less than eight minutes completing it, we excluded it from the analysis. We knew from pre-testing the instrument that a carefully completed questionnaire (i.e. reading, understanding and clicking or typing) could not be undertaken in less than eight minutes. Indeed, such pre-test questionnaires included almost no entries for open-ended questions and contained an extensive number of missing values (e.g. 'do not know' and 'not willing to answer').

Additionally, we excluded any inadvertent duplicate entries by inspecting the IP addresses and cookie entries. By analyzing the time periods spent on completing the questionnaire we found that half of the respondents (median) completed it in less than 14.3 minutes. Therefore we consider the analysis of response duration together with inspection of the open-ended questions serves as a reliable indicator for excluding questionnaires that would have a negative effect on the validity of results.

4.3 Time to Respond

According to Illieva et al. (2002) one of the advantages of online surveys is a short time to respond. The experience of our survey agrees with that supposition. Figure 1 shows the distribution of answers over the survey period.

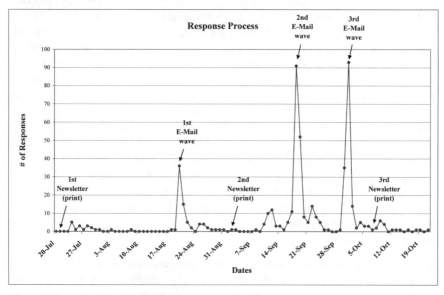

Figure 1: Response Process (n=506)

The peaks in the graph indicate the immediate reaction to the pre- and post-notification e-mails. Thus, respondents either reacted immediately or not at all. Interestingly, 67% (n=338) completed the questionnaire during their usual working hours from 8:00 AM to 6:00 PM. Therefore, we agree with Illieva et al.'s (2002) supposition that the speed of data collection via a Web-based questionnaire is a considerable advantage.

4.4 Degree of Question Difficulty and Appropriateness of Questionnaire Length

Time stamps were also recorded between the various windows containing different numbers and kinds of questions. This gave us the opportunity to compare the degree of length and difficulty of bundles of questions in each Web page or window by comparing the average time spent for working through them. Figure 2 provides a total overview of the different time values per question, the average number of characters keyed in the description fields, and the average number of clicks on each window. This analysis can enable a researcher to gather information about the appropriateness of each question in terms of length and difficulty of each question and of the total questionnaire. The time recorded and illustrated in Figure 2 includes the time for reading, understanding, clicking and typing. Regarding closed questions, the time component for clicking can be neglected to a certain degree.

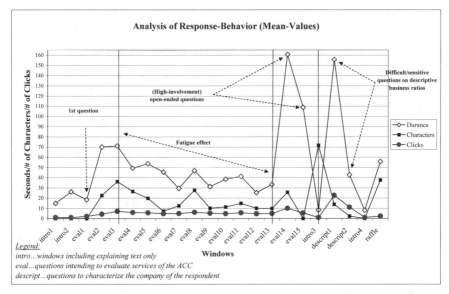

Figure 2: Response Behavior

In our questionnaire we recognized a fatigue effect between the windows 'eval3' and 'eval13.' Those windows include the same number and type of questions. The number of keyed-in characters declines with the length of the questionnaire. The peak at 'eval14' in terms of time and number of characters can be explained by the fact that this window almost exclusively contains open-ended questions. The peaks at windows 'descript1' and 'descript2' are caused by the sensitive and difficult character of the questions. There we asked respondents to characterize their companies by ratios such as sales volume, number of employees, etc.

We conclude that researchers should aim to minimize the time span for completing questions on each window and at the same time maximize the number of characters keyed in description fields if open-ended questions are part of the study.

4.5 Convenience and Capability for Collecting Qualitative Data

Mehta & Sivadas (1995) emphasized the convenience of e-mail-based questionnaires regarding the receipt, completion and shipment of the questionnaire from the respondents' point of view. Additionally, they emphasized that the perceived anonymity of the e-mail medium encourages respondents to write longer answers. This is also true for Web-based surveys where even the shipment of the document has become unnecessary. The transfer of data takes place every time a respondent clicks on a 'submit' button when proceeding within the questionnaire. However, the question remains whether clicking on a keyboard button is faster and more convenient than ticking answers with a pencil. This factor is likely very dependant on the skill of a respondent to use a mouse or a keyboard. We found a high response in terms of the number of figures keyed in description fields. In total, our respondents (n=506) wrote 27,105 words, which equals 122 words per respondent. This amount also equaled 181,385 keyed characters (358 characters per respondent). This volume of qualitative data enabled us to conduct a text analysis using qualitative analysis software.

We conclude that a Web-based questionnaire offers an opportunity to apply a mixed-method approach since the affinity and propensity to use the keyboard is connected to the use of computers in general, and should provide a faster response and richer qualitative data than that found when using traditional survey methods.

4.6 Costs

Costs for conducting a Web-based survey are comparably high when it comes to designing and producing the program and Web database. Therefore fixed costs dominate such projects (Cobanoglu et al., 2001). However, once the program is up and running the gathering of data is quite cheap since there is no need to print, copy and ship the questionnaire (Mehta & Sivadas, 1995). The researcher does not even have to overcome a media gap by coding and transferring the data into an electronic format. It should also be noted that the respondent pays for the completion of the Web-based questionnaire since he/she provides the infrastructure and undertakes the online fees. Nonetheless the usability and functionality turn out to be crucial for the success of such a survey, thus the availability of technical expertise is rather important (Cobanoglu et al., 2001).

5 Study Limitations

Notwithstanding the foregoing advantages of Web-based questionnaires compared to paper or e-mail questionnaires, our approach did suffer from a few limitations:

As noted above the overall response rate of 11% for completed and usable questionnaires can be considered relatively low. Reasons for that may be low involvement by the subject, reluctance to participate in surveys and lack of reachability because of false e-mail addresses. The latter reason stems from continual changes of Internet service providers that quickly makes e-mail addresses obsolete. Approximately 15% of e-mails were undeliverable and returned immediately after sending them out. In hundreds of cases the e-mail was sent to non-personalized 'office' addressees, which reduced the probability that the right respondent received the notification e-mail (Cobanoglu et al., 2001).

We do not know whether we overcame the 'information overflow' problem, i.e. the growing number of solicited and unsolicited (SPAM) e-mail that users receive every day.

Lastly, many Internet users are reluctant to click on links transferred via e-mails because of the fear of getting viruses that could damage the software on personal computers. The use of Internet panels could serve as a solution to that problem although we are not aware of any such B2B panels so far.

6 Conclusions

We have presented empirical evidence investigating whether Web-based surveys are a substantial improvement over traditional mail surveys for logistics or SCM research. We applied our surveying technique in a typical logistics research context. Since the Internet has not penetrated the entire business community in most countries, we chose computer retailers and wholesalers as an ideal type of respondent because of their experience and affinity with this medium, and their likely Internet penetration compared favorably to other business sectors. We identified similar advantages and disadvantages of online market research as stated in the literature (see Kent & Lee, 1999; Mehta & Sivadas, 1995; Illieva et al., 2002) and shown in Table 2.

Apart from these features we also demonstrated two potential benefits of Web-based questionnaires compared to e-mail or postal questionnaires:

First, a researcher has the opportunity to analyze the response behavior during completion due to time-data recording during the completion process by every respondent. This can be used to identify low quality questionnaires and to improve questions or formulations for further research. By inspecting the mortality curve the effect of the introductory texts, icebreaker questions or raffles can easily be detected. Such response behavior can serve as an indicator of the appropriateness of the research tool design.

Advantages	Disadvantages
Short response time	Low questionnaire response rate
Low variable costs	High fixed costs at the beginning
Convenience for respondents and researchers	Little sample control
No media gap to overcome	Coverage error
Willingness to answer open-ended questions exten-	
High item response rate	

Table 2: Advantages and Disadvantages of Web-based Surveys

Second, interactivity offers the largest and most important potential for Web-based questionnaires compared to all other self-administered survey techniques. Difficult terms can be explained using 'pop-up' windows, respondents can be reminded if he/she forgot to complete single questions and assistance can be provided if needed through a 'help' function. Interactivity can also be used to guide respondents through the questionnaire.

In summary, we support Illieva et al. (2002) that there are substantial technological and methodological improvements to be gained using Web-based surveying. However, we also consider that methodological concepts underlying it are the same as those for other survey approaches. Thus, we agree with Miller (2001) that it is necessary for logistics researchers to understand not only the survey method itself but also the technical context of Web-based research. By doing so logistics researchers who utilize a Web-based questionnaire approach have an opportunity to significantly improve the internal and external validity of their research results.

7 References

Atteslander, P. (2000): Methoden der empirischen Sozialforschung (Methods of empirical social research), 9th ed., deGruyter, Berlin.

Berekoven, L., Eckert, W., Ellenrieder, P. (2001): Marktforschung: Methodischen Grundlagen und praktische Anwendung (Market research – methodical basics and practical application), 9th ed., Gabler, Wiesbaden.

Bortz, J., Doring, N. (2002): Forschungsmethoden und Evaluation für Human- und Sozialwissenschaftler (Research methods and evaluation for social researchers), 3rd ed., Springer, Berlin.

Brown, J., Culkin, N., Fletcher, J. (2001): Human factors in business-to-business research on the Internet, in: International Journal of Market Research, 43(4): 425-440.

Cobanoglu, C., Warde, B., Moreo, P. J. (2001): A comparison of mail, fax and web-based survey methods, in: International Journal of Market Research, 43(4): 441-452.

Diamantopoulos, A., Schlegelmilch, B. B. (1996): Determinants of Industrial Survey Response: A Survey-on-Surveys Analysis of Researchers' and Managers' Views, in: Journal of Marketing Management, 12: 505-531.

Dillman, D. A. (1978): Mail and Telephone Surveys: The Total Design Method, Wiley-Interscience, New York.

Dillman, D. A. (1999): Mail and Internet Surveys: The Tailored Design Method, 2nd ed., John Wiley & Sons, New York.

Dillon, W. R., Madden, T. J., Firtle, N. F. (1994): Marketing Research in a Marketing Environment, 3rd ed., Irwin, Boston.

Dommeyer, C. J., Moriarty, E. (2000): Comparing two forms of an e-mail survey: imbedded vs. attached, in: International Journal of Market Research, 42(1): 39-50.

Greer, T. V., Chuchinprakarn, N., Seshadri, S. (2000): Likelihood of Participating in Mail Survey research: Business Respondents' Perspectives, in Industrial Marketing Management, 29: 97-109.

Griffis, S. E., Goldsby, T. J., Cooper, M. (2003): Web-Based and Mail Surveys: A Comparison of Response, Data and Cost, in: Journal of Business Logistics, 24 (2): 237-258.

Harvey, L. (1986): A research note on the impact of class-of-mail on response rates to mailed questionnaires, in: Journal of the Market Research Society, 28 (3): 299-300.

Illieva, J., Baron, S., Healey, N. M. (2002): Online surveys in marketing research: pros and cons, in: International Journal of Market Research, 44 (3): 361-376.

Kent, R., Lee, M. (1999): Using the internet for market research: a study of private trading on the internet, in: Journal of the Market Research Society, 41 (4): 377-385.

Large, R., Stölzle, W. (1999): Logistikforschung im Spiegel wissenschaftlicher Publikationen: Eine empirische Untersuchung auf der Basis betriebswirtschaftlicher und ingenieurwissenschaftlicher Dissertationen (Logistics research characterized by scientific publication), in: Pfohl, H. (ed.): Logistikforschung, Entwicklungszüge und Gestaltungsansätze, Erich Schmidt Verlag, Berlin: p. 3-35.

Mentzer, J. T., Flint, D. J. (1997): Validity in Logistics Research, in: Journal of Business Logistics, 14(1): 27-42.

Mentzer, J. T., Kahn, K. B. (1995): A framework of logistics research, in: Journal of Business Logistics, 16(1), 231-251.

Mehta, R., Sivadas, E. (1995): Comparing response rates and response content in mail versus electronic mail surveys, in: Journal of the Market Research Society, 37 (4): 429-439.

Miller, T. W. (2001): Can we trust the data of online research? in: Marketing Research, 13 (2): 26-32.

Pincott, G., Branthwaite, A. (2000): Nothing new under the sun? in: International Journal of Market Research, 42(2): 137-155.

Schlegelmilch, B. B., Diamantopoulos, A. (1991): Prenotification and mail survey response rates: a quantitative integration of the literature, in: Journal of the Market Research Society, 33(3): 243-255.

Tse, A. C. B. (1998): Comparing the response rate, response speed and response quality of two methods of sending questionnaires: e-mail vs. mail, in: Journal of the Market Research Society, 40 (4): 353-361.

Tuten, T. L., Urban, D. J., Bosnjak, M. (2002): Internet Surveys and Data Quality: A Review, in: Batinic, B., Reips, U., Bosnjak, M. (eds.): Online Social Science, Hogrefe & Huber, Seattle.

Whitley, E. W. (1985): The case for postal research, in: Journal of the Market Research Society, 27(1): 5-13.

Wunder, G. C., Wynn, G. W. (1988): The effects of address personalisation on mailed questionnaires response rate, time and quality, in: Journal of the Market Research Society, 30(1): 95-101.

SCM Research Methodologies: Employing Structural Equation Modeling

Cristina Gimenez, Rudolf Large, Eva Ventura

1	Introduction	156
2	What is SEM?	156
3	An Example	161
4	Final Comments	166
5	References	167
6	Appendix	170

Summary:
Supply Chain Management research very often involves an analysis of relationships among abstract concepts. For this type of analysis, Structural Equation Modeling (SEM) is a very powerful technique because it combines measurement models (confirmatory factor analysis) and structural models (regression analysis) into a simultaneous statistical test. The objective of this paper is to show how SEM can be employed in theory testing. We will also describe a process regarding its implementation and show an example of a research paper based on this methodology.

Keywords:
Supply Chain Management, Structural Equation Modeling, SEM

1 Introduction

The field of Supply Chain Management (SCM) has seen rapid advances in recent years. It is a topic of interest among logistics managers and researchers because it is considered a source of competitive advantage (Christopher, 1998). However, how to conduct empirical research in this area has rarely been addressed.

SEM is a statistical technique that combines measurement models (confirmatory factor analysis) and structural models (regression analysis) into a simultaneous statistical test (Byrne, 2001). An increasing number of SCM researchers have recently employed SEM in their works. Some examples include Autry & Daugherty (2003); Gimenez & Ventura (2003, 2005); Large (2003, 2005); Stank et al. (2001) and Wisner (2003).

The SCM area involves abstract concepts such as integration, collaboration, coordination, competitive advantage and many others, which might be related among them. Such concepts can be represented by latent variables. Since the latent variables (also called factors) are not directly observable or measurable, it is necessary to have a set of measures (or indicators) to account for the abstract concepts of interest. The fact that SEM can analyze structural and measurement models simultaneously makes it especially valuable to researchers in SCM.

The objective of this paper is to show how SEM can be employed in theory testing and what its main benefits are. We hope this will encourage more researchers to employ this powerful statistical technique. This paper describes SEM and shows an example of a research paper based on this methodology.

The paper is structured as follows: First, we describe the main characteristics of SEM and a process very useful for its implementation. In the following section, we provide an example of how SEM methodology was employed in an SCM research project. The last section brings together some final comments.

2 What is SEM?

SEM is a collection of related techniques that share some common characteristics. Briefly, SEM requires that the researcher considers an underlying model that depends on some structural parameters and then uses the covariances (and sometimes the means) of observed data to test hypotheses about those parameters. SEM developed around several different research disciplines, and currently represents the integration of two different statistical traditions: factor analysis and simultaneous equation modeling.

SEM's origins can be traced back to Spearman (1904) with the development of what we now call exploratory factor analysis but it was some years later when

Wright (1921, 1934) developed and applied path analysis to the study of causal effects in the field of genetics. Later, the path analysis technique was spread to the fields of economics, sociology, and psychology. It was not until the early 1970s that path and factor analyses were integrated into a unique framework. And since then (especially during the last two decades), we have witnessed a rapid expansion of the SEM techniques to more diverse areas such as genetic behavior, education research, marketing, management, and psychiatry. Jöreskog (1973) outlined the general structural equation model as the combination of two distinct parts: the measurement part that links observed variables to latent variables across a confirmatory factor model, and the structural part that describes the relationships among the different latent variables of the model.

The usefulness of SEM lies in its ability to test hypotheses that are difficult if not impossible to evaluate with other analytical methods. This is due to the fact that SEM uses a very general framework that may encompass many standard statistical techniques. For example, combining factor analysis and structural equation modeling allows complex interrelated dependence relationships to be assessed, while simultaneously incorporating the presence of measurement error in the data. Another advantage of employing SEM is that there are currently many statistical software options that make SEM very easy to specify and estimate. Among the available programs we can mention are AMOS, CALIS, EQS, LISCOMP, LISREL, MX, RAMONA and SEPATH. Some of these programs offer the possibility of "drawing" the model that one wants to estimate. The program then translates the drawing into code and performs an analysis. It is not necessary to say how appealing this is, although one must of course be very cautious in light of such automated alternatives.

Many excellent introductory and advanced books have been written on the SEM technique, and we will make no attempt to cite them all. There are also several annotated bibliographies; see for example Austin & Wolfe (1991), Austin & Calderón (1996), and Wolfe (2003). The next subsections offer a brief (non-exhaustive) inventory of SEM's special features that make it an interesting and useful technique for SCM research.

2.1 Characteristics of SEM

We now follow Kline (1989) and describe some of the most important characteristics of SEM. SEM is a member of what is known as the general linear model. More standard statistical techniques such as regression analysis, simultaneous equations, factor analysis, or ANOVA can be contemplated as special cases of SEM. One must notice, nevertheless, that some flexible extensions of the basic SEM exist that allow the incorporation of some nonlinear relations. See for example Cohen & Cohen (1983).

The researcher needs to have some basic model in mind before using SEM. However, SEM analysis is not just a confirmatory analysis. A model can be as simple as stating which variables are assumed to affect others and the direction of such effects. The model can be then tested with SEM and might or might not be supported by the data. In the last case, the technique can guide the researcher towards useful and meaningful modifications of the initial model to improve its appropriateness without sacrificing its theoretical foundations. See Jöreskog (1993).

SEM can discern between observed and latent variables, which certainly widens the type of models that can be studied. For instance, abstract concepts such as "level of integration" or "quality of information" can be represented as latent variables (or factors) in SEM. It is then of course necessary to create accurate measurements of these factors. Issues concerning measurement errors in variables are thus easily distributed within the framework of SEM. Bollen (1989) or Lomax (1986) offer a discussion about the effects of measurement error in SEM.

Many standard analysis techniques are based on the modeling of individual observations. For instance, a residual analysis looks at the differences between observed and fitted values for every observation in the sample. SEM on the other hand considers and models all the sample observations simultaneously. Consequently, it attempts to minimize the function of the difference between the sample covariances and the predicted (by the model) covariances. The technique attempts to understand the correlations among a set of variables and tries to explain as much of their variance as possible with the model specified by the researcher. However, it can also handle other types of analysis, such as analysis of means including between-group and within-group mean comparisons. See Bollen (1989) or Browne & Arminger (1995) for a discussion of these topics.

2.2 How Can We Use SEM?

SEM is extremely flexible and powerful. It is also easy to use once one gets acquainted with it. But it is very important to be especially careful when addressing the specification of the model, the preparation of the data, the analysis, and possible re-specification of the model and the final interpretation of the estimation results. It is useful to follow a sequence of steps when conducting a SEM analysis. Figure 1 shows a process adapted from Kaplan (2000).

The first stage of the process consists of developing the theoretical model, specifying the variables and the causal relationships among them. Here, the researchers express their hypotheses in the form of a structural equation model, either by "drawing" the model and using a program capable of translating the picture into code, or by writing the set of equations by themselves. The equations define: (1) the structural equations that link the constructs (dependent-independent variable relationships), and (2) the measurement model specifying which variables measure each construct. It is also necessary to specify a set of matrices indicating any hypothesized correlation among the constructs.

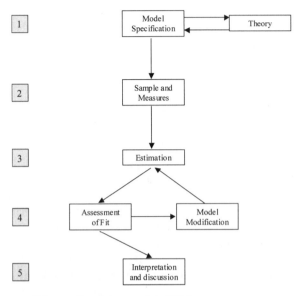

Figure 1: Diagram of Conventional Approach to SEM

The model must be identified in the sense that it should be possible for the computer to derive a unique estimate of every parameter in the model. Unfortunately, there is no simple rule for guaranteeing the identification of the model. It is necessary to consider different rules for different types of SEM (see for example Bollen, 1989). It is essential to understand that the model should be specified before the data is collected and not the other way around. Otherwise it would be too late when problems are encountered, derived from the omission of relevant variables or that the model is not identified. The omission of relevant explanatory variables that are correlated with other variables of the model can lead to biased estimations of causal effects (see Kline, 1998). The specification of the model should be guided by the objective of parsimony. Any model can fit the data perfectly providing that it is sufficiently complex and unrestricted. But in this case, the model does not test any particular hypothesis and becomes useless (see MacCallum et al., 1993).

In the second stage, the researcher has to select the measures of the latent variables of the model and collect the data. This is one of the most important aspects in SEM estimation, and sometimes also one of the most neglected ones. It is impossible to obtain good estimates of the parameters of a model if the observed variables do not really measure what the researcher intends to measure. See Kap-

Ian & Sacruzzo (1993) for information on how to construct good measures from the psychometric point of view, and Dunn et al. (1994) for scale development and validation in logistics.

SEM requires large samples, since it relies on asymptotical distribution assumptions for significance tests, consistency and efficiency. Nevertheless it is very difficult to make a quantitative assessment of what a large sample means. An optimal sample is between 100 and 200 observations, but samples with a number of observations between 50 and 400 are also acceptable (Hair et al., 1992). There are cases in which very good results have been obtained with only 22 observations (Hayduk, 1987). The complexity of the model one wants to evaluate and the algorithm used in the analysis affect sample size requirements. Simpler models may do well with smaller samples.

SEM assumes independent observations, random sampling and linearity of all relationships. In addition, it has to be stated that SEM is very sensitive to the distributional characteristics of the data, particularly the departure from multivariate normality. This implies that it is necessary to be careful when handling missing observations (make sure that the pattern of missing observations is random) and multi-collinearity (large correlation values can deliver unstable solutions and even crash the fitting program). If the data violate the assumption of multivariate normality, a set of transformations of the data (when appropriate) may remedy part of the problem. It is true that the values of the parameter estimators are relatively robust against non-normality, but tests of significance are positively biased (that is, one tends to reject the null hypothesis more often). If the data is severely abnormal it will be necessary to use corrected statistics (see Satorra, 1992) or an estimation method that does not assume normality (usually this may require still larger samples). In the case of abnormality it seems to be advisable to additionally conduct an estimation procedure based on bootstrapping (see Stine, 1990 and Yung & Bentler, 1996). If the differences between the bootstrap mean that estimates and the traditional estimates are very small, the effects of non-normality tend to be negligible (see for example Large & Giménez, 2004).

The third stage is devoted to the estimation of the model. There are different estimation procedures: Maximum Likelihood, Ordinary Least Squares, Weighted Least Squares, etc. The researcher's choice has to be based on its adequacy to the data and model being analyzed (see Bollen, 1989). It is important to analyze the different parts of a model separately. For instance, if the fit of our estimated model is poor we have to be able to determine whether we have committed a mistake in the specification of the structural part of the model, or in the measurement part of the model. It is a good idea to perform confirmatory factor analysis of the measurement structures first and use them to assess the unidimensionality, reliability and validity of that part of the model. Next, we can add the structural part and estimate the complete model (see Anderson & Gerbing, 1988).

Stage 4 of this model requires an analysis of the "appropriate fit" of the model. This has to be addressed at two levels: First, for the overall model, and then for the measurement and structural models separately. There are different measures to test the appropriate fit of the overall model such as the CFI (Comparative Fix Index), the RMSR (Root Mean Square Residual), etc. Hair et al. (1998) provide a description of several measures. Once the overall model has been evaluated, the measurement of each construct has to be assessed for unidimensionality and reliability. Finally, the structural model has to be evaluated. This can be done through an overall coefficient of estimation (R^2) for the entire structural equation or through the significance of the estimated coefficients. If the model does not fit the data very well, it will be necessary to modify the model and repeat the estimation until an adequate fit is attained. As with the initial specification of the model, its revision should be guided by the researcher's hypotheses based on theory. One should never re-specify the model based entirely on statistical criteria, since the resulting model may be completely nonsensical even when the data fits perfectly well.

The last stage (Stage 5) of the process involves interpreting the results. This means determining if the relationships established in the theoretical model are supported or not. To that purpose, one should examine the whole output of the estimation process, and not only the overall fit indexes. It could be the case that the fit indexes are correct but some parts of the model are not properly explained. Careful examination of the significance tests of the coefficients, and especially of the correlations among the estimation residuals can help evaluate the model. See Hoyle & Panter (1995) for a discussion on reporting SEM analyses.

It has to be stated that SEM is very useful for rejecting a false model, but it does not really tell us whether a given model is true or not. Almost any structural equation model we can think of has an equivalent version that generates the same observed correlations or covariances. Sound theory is the key to defending our particular option as opposed to other alternatives.

In summary, it is true that SEM is a very powerful and sophisticated method. But using SEM does not compensate for a deficient work regarding the design and accomplishment of a research project.

3 An Example

We have chosen to illustrate the use of SEM by means of an example that represents a compromise between simplicity and the non-trivial application of the methodology. The example is based on an analysis performed by Gimenez & Ventura (2005) in which the authors raise several hypotheses regarding the relationships between the Logistics-Production and Logistics-Marketing interfaces and the external integration process. The study also investigates the causal impact of these internal and external relationships on the company's logistical service absolute performance ("performance" for short).

This paper aims to offer a brief introduction to the use of SEM in practical applications, and it is not intended to discuss any aspects of SCM in detail. The reader can consult Gimenez & Ventura (2005) to obtain details on the generation of the model and the exact numerical results of the estimation.

3.1 Stage 1: Model Specification

An exploratory case study reveals itself as a very useful mechanism to help develop a model with its corresponding hypotheses. Gimenez (2004) conducted such a study. A thorough review of the existing literature is also necessary for such a process.

Stevens (1989) suggests that companies internally integrate first and then extend integration to other supply chain members. This indicates that internal integration influences external integration. However, our exploratory case study showed that one company (out of fifteen analyzed) initiated internal integration after the implementation of an external integration program. This led us to hypothesize that both levels of integration may influence each other. This was incorporated in our model by establishing a positive correlation between internal and external integration (see Hypotheses H1a and H1b in Figure 2).

The existing literature (see Ellram & Cooper, (1990); Christopher, (1998); and more recently Stank et al., (2001)) and the results of the exploratory study (Gimenez, (2004)) suggested hypothesizing a positive impact of internal and external integration on performance (see Hypotheses H3a, H3b and H4).

- Hypothesis H1a: There is a positive relationship between the level of internal integration in the Logistics-Production interface and the level of external integration.

- Hypothesis H1b: There is a positive relationship between the level of internal integration in the Logistics-Marketing interface and the level of external integration.

- Hypothesis H2: There is a positive relationship between the level of internal integration in the Logistics-Production interface and the level of internal integration in the Logistics-Marketing interface.

- Hypothesis H3a: The level of internal integration in the Logistics-Marketing interface has a positive effect on the logistics performance.

- Hypothesis H3b: The level of internal integration in the Logistics-Production interface has a positive effect on the logistics performance.

- Hypothesis H4: The level of external integration has a positive effect on the logistics performance.

Figure 2 shows the proposed relationships between Internal and External Integration, and the performance of the firm.

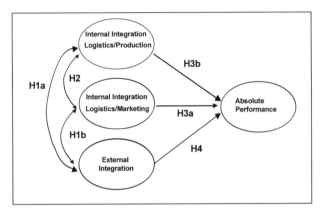

Figure 2: Theoretical Model (Gimenez & Ventura, 2005)

3.2 Stage 2: Sample and Measures

The data survey included seven questions intended to measure the level of internal integration for each company in the Logistics-Production and Logistics-Marketing interfaces. These measures were defined from the literature (Stank et al., 1999). The questionnaire also included eight variables to measure the level of external integration. These variables were designed adapting the internal integration variables used by Stank et al. (1999) to a supply chain relationship. As companies usually strategically segment their relationships (Kraljic, 1983), we decided to measure the level of external integration, in particular manufacturer-retailer relationships. Each respondent was asked to choose two manufacturer-retailer relationships: the first relationship had to be the most collaborating relationship, while the second had to be the least collaborating. Finally, the questionnaire included five items intended to measure the absolute performance. These variables were designed according to the literature and the results of the exploratory case study (Gimenez, 2004). All the items used to measure the integration and performance constructs are shown in the appendix (Table 1a). Questions were designed using a ten-point Likert scale.

Potential participants were identified from a Spanish company's database (Fomento de la Producción 25,000). Manufacturers from the food and perfumery-detergent sectors with sales figures higher than 30 million euros were selected to make up the sample (199 companies). As prenotification increases the response rate (Fox et al., 1988), all the companies in the sample were telephoned before mailing the questionnaire. During the Spring of 2001, the questionnaire was sent to the supply chain or logistics director of each firm. 64 companies returned the questionnaire, which represents a 32.3% (64/198) response rate. Despite the high response rate, we conducted an analysis of non-response bias based on the procedure described by Armstrong & Overton (1977) and Lambert & Harrington (1990), and did not find any noticeable pattern among the variables that could indicate the existence of a non-response bias.

It has to be stressed that in order to minimize the potential pitfalls related to measurements, we selected them based on the literature and the results of the exploratory case study.

3.3 Stage 3: Estimation

The estimation was based on "Maximum Likelihood" and "Normal" theory. We estimated the model twice, with data from the strongest and the weakest collaborating relationship.

Close examination of the data revealed that using Maximum Likelihood based on Normal theory could be justified, given that the Likert scales used to measure the variables were wide enough and the sample distribution did not show excessive skew.

3.4 Stage 4: Assessment of Fit and Model Modification

According to the CFI measure of fit, the model was accepted when estimated with data from the most collaborating relationship. The results were different when we estimated the model with data from the least collaborating relationship. The fit of the model in this latter case was a little worse, but very close to the acceptance boundary of 0.9 (the exact value was 0.897).

Although the measurement and the construct parts are estimated simultaneously, the appropriate fit of the model has to also be addressed for the measurement and structural models separately.

- The Measurement Model

Garver & Mentzer (1999) suggested that researchers should perform and report all kinds of construct validity tests in order to increase the research rigor. Following this, we performed some exploratory and confirmatory factor analysis before attempting the estimation of the complete model. Our exploratory analysis computed the correlation matrix of the variables in each construct and calculated their eigenvalues. Close examination of these eigenvalues suggested discarding variable II1 for the Logistics-Production interface, since it was not associated with the construct of interest. The rest of the groups of measurement variables behaved well and each group of variables measured just one factor. Next, following Garver & Mentzer (1999), we conducted a separate confirmatory factor analysis for each of the four groups of measures in order to assess unidimensionality, validity and reliability of the model. We observed that all the factor loadings had the right sign and magnitude, and were highly significant. As for scale reliability, we reported three measures: the Cronbach's α (which was always greater than the benchmark value of 0.9), the Construct Reliability Test (which was always greater than the acceptance level of 0.7), and the Variance Extracted Test (which was always greater than 0.5, as it should be). All these tests and statistics constitute a previous check of the adequacy of the measurement model.

- The Structural Model

The structural model (regression analysis) showed that there were some significant relationships between the factors. All the covariance figures were statistically significant, except for the Internal Integration Logistics-Marketing and External Integration covariance, which was not statistically significant in the least collaborating relationship model. Regarding the regression coefficients, it has to be stated that External Integration had a direct positive effect on performance in both models (the most and the least collaborating relationship models). However, regarding internal integration, only Internal Integration in the Logistics-Production interface had a statistically significant effect on performance (this impact being positive). Figure 3 shows some of these results for the most collaborating relationship.

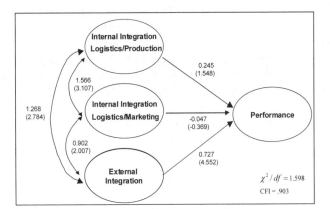

Figure 3: Path Coefficients, Covariances and Measures of Fit

These findings led us to the following contrast of hypotheses:

Hypothesis	MOST collaborating relationship model	LEAST collaborating relationship model
H1a	Accept	Accept
H1b	Accept	Reject
H2	Accept	Accept
H3a	Reject	Reject
H3b	Reject	Accept
H4	Accept	Accept

Table 1: Contrast of Hypotheses

In order to minimize the pitfalls in the assessment of fit and interpretation of the model, we examined the whole output of the estimation process, and not only the overall fit indexes. Checking the correlation residuals matrix was emphasized.

3.5 Stage 5: Interpretation and Discussion

We can now summarize the results derived from our analysis. Internal integration influences external collaboration and vice versa. The levels of internal integration in the Logistics-Production and Logistics-Marketing interfaces positively influence each other. With respect to the impact of internal integration on performance, we have to distinguish between the Logistics-Marketing and the Logistics-Production interfaces. When companies achieve a high level of integration in the Logistics-Marketing interface, this level of internal integration does not lead to a better absolute performance. When a firm achieves a high level of integration in the Logistics-Production interface, its effect on performance depends on whether there is external integration. The level of Logistics-Production integration leads to a better absolute performance when there is no external integration. However, when firms are externally integrated, the level of external integration has such an important effect on performance that it annuls (or reduces) the effect of the Logistics-Production integration. External collaboration among supply chain members contributes to achieving cost, stock-out, and lead-time reductions. The greatest influence on firms' logistical service performance is found in external integration.

4 Final Comments

SCM usually involves analyzing relationships among abstract concepts. We have shown how SEM can be very useful in this type of analysis. By combining measurement and construct models, it allows complex interrelated dependence relationships to be assessed. We have suggested a sequence of steps that can be followed when conducting SEM. We have also illustrated the implementation of this process and the use of SEM by means of an example of a particular SCM research project. We believe that this paper will be both informative and insightful to researchers in the SCM field who are willing to use SEM to test their theoretical models.

5 References

Anderson, J., Gerbing, D. (1988): Structural Equation Modeling in Practice: A Review and Recommended Two-Step Approach, in: Psychological Bulletin, 103(3): 411-423.

Armstrong, J. S., Overton, T. S. (1977): Estimating Non-response Bias in Mail Surveys, in: Journal of Marketing Research, 14(3): 396- 402.

Autry, C., Daugherty, P. J. (2003): Warehouse Operations Employees: Linking Person-Organization Fit, Job Satisfaction, and Coping Responses, in: Journal of Business Logistics 24(1): 171-198.

Austin. J. T., Calderón, R. F. (1996): Theoretical and Technical Contributions to Structural Equation Modeling: An Updated Annotated Bibliography, in: Structural Equation Modeling, 3: 105-175.

Austin. J. T., Wolfe, L. M. (1991): Annotated Bibliography of Structural Equation Modeling: Technical Work, in: British Journal of Mathematical and Statistical Psychology, 44: 93-152.

Bollen, K. A. (1989): Structural Equations with Latent Variables, A Wiley-Interscience publication.

Browne, M. W., Arminger, G. (1995).: Specification and estimation of mean- and covariance-structure models, in Arminger, G., Clogg, C. C., Sobel, M. E. (eds.): Handbook of statistical modeling for the social and behavioral sciences, Plenum Press, New York: p. 185-241.

Byrne, B. M., (2001): Structural Equation Modeling with AMOS – Basic Concepts, Applications and Programming, Lawrence Erlbaum Associates, Mahwah.

Christopher, M. (1998): Logistics and Supply Chain Management: Strategies for Reducing Cost and Improving Service, Financial Times Pitman Publishing, London.

Cohen, J., Cohen P., (1983): Applied multiple regression/correlation analysis for the behavioral sciences, Lawrence Erlbaum, Hillsdale.

Dunn, S., Seaker, R., Waller, M. (1994): Latent Variables in Business Logistics Research: Scale Development and Validation, in: Journal of Business Logistics, 15(2): 145-172.

Ellram, L. M., Cooper, M. C. (1990): Supply Chain Management, Partnerships, and the Shipper-Third Party Relationship, in The International Journal of Logistics Management, 1(2): 1-10.

Fox, R. J., Crask, M. R., Kim, J. (1988): Mail Survey Response Rate: A Meta-analysis of Selected Techniques for Inducing Response, in: Public Opinion Quarterly, 52(1): 467-491.

Garver, M. S., Mentzer, J. T. (1999): Logistics Research Methods: Employing Structural Equation Modelling to Test for Construct Validity, in: Journal of Business Logistics, 20(1): 33-57.

Gimenez, C., Ventura, E., (2003): Supply Chain Management as a Competitive Advantage in the Spanish Grocery Sector, in: The International Journal of Logistics Management, 14(1): 77-88.

Gimenez, C., Ventura, E. (2005): Logistics-Production, Logistics-Marketing and External Integration: Their Impact on Performance, in: International Journal of Operations & Management, 25(1), 20-38.

Gimenez, C. (2004): Supply Chain Management Implementation in the Spanish Grocery Sector: An Exploratory Study, in: International Journal of Integrated Supply Management, 1(1): 98-114.

Hair, J. F., Anderson, R. E., Tatham, R. L., Black, W. C. (1992): Multivariate Data Analysis with Readings, Macmillan Publishing Company, New York.

Hair, J. F., Anderson, R. E. Tatham, R. L., Black, W. C. (1998): Multivariate Data Analysis, Prentice-Hall International, London.

Hayduk, L. A. (1987): Structural Equation Modeling with LISREL – Essentials and Advances, The Johns Hopkins University Press, Baltimore.

Hoyle, R. H., Panter, A. T. (1995): Writing about structural equation models, in Hoyle, R.H. (Ed): Structural equation modeling, Sage, Thousand Oaks, CA: p. 158-176.

Jöreskog, K .G. (1973): A General Method for Estimating a Linear Structural Equation System, in Goldberger, A. S. , Duncan, O.D. (Eds.), Structural Equation Models in the Social Sciences, Seminar, New York: 85-112.

Jöreskog, K. G. (1993): Testing Structural Equations Models. In K.A. Bollen, J.S. Lang (Eds.): Testing structural equations models, Sage, Newbury Park, CA: p. 294-316.

Kaplan, D. (2000): Structural Equation Modeling: Foundations and Extensions, Sage Publications, California.

Kaplan, R. M., Sacruzzo, D. P. (1993): Psychological testing, 3rd edition, Brooks/Cole, Pacific Grove, CA.

Kline, R. B. (1998): Principles and Practice of Structural Equation Modeling, Guilford Press, New York.

Kraljic, P. (1983): Purchasing Must Become Supply Management, in: Harvard Business Review, 61: 109-117.

Lambert, D.M., Harrington, T.C. (1990): Measuring Non-Response in Customer Service Mail Surveys, in: Journal of Business Logistics, 11(2): 5-25.

Large, R., Giménez, C. (2004): Oral Communication Capabilities of Purchasing Managers, in: International Purchasing & Supply Education & Research Association (ed.): The Purchasing Function: Walking a Tightrope. 13th Annual IPSERA Conference 2004. Catania: p. C-191-C-204.

Large, R. (2003): Communication Behavior and Successful Supplier Management, in: Proceedings of the Logistics Research Network Annual Conference, London: p. 268-277.

Large, R. (2005): Communication Capability and Attitudes towards External Communication of Purchasing Managers in Germany, in: International Journal of Physical Distribution & Logistics Management, forthcoming.

Lomax, R.G. (1986): The effect of measurement error in structural equation modeling, in: Journal of Experimental Education, 54: 157-162.

McArdle, J.J. (1994): Structural factor analysis experiments with incomplete data, in: Multivariate Behavioral Research, 29: 409-454.

MacCallum, R. C., Wegener, D. T., Uchino, B. N., Fabrigar, L. R. (1993): The problem of equivalent models in applications of covariance structure analysis, in: Psychological Bulletin, 114: 185-199.

Satorra, A. (1992): Asymptotic Robust Inference in the Analysis of Mean and Covariance Structure Analysis: a Unified Approach, in: Psychometrika, 50: 83-90.

Spearman, C. (1904): The Proof and Measurement of Association between Two Things, in: American Journal of Psychology, 15: 72-101.

Stank, T. P., Keller, S., Daugherty, P. (2001): Supply Chain Collaboration & Logistical Service Performance, in: Journal of Business Logistics, 22(1): 29-48.

Stank, T., Daugherty, P., Ellinger, A. (1999): Marketing/Logistics Integration and Firm Performance, in: The International Journal of Logistics Management, 10(1): 11-25.

Stevens, G. C. (1989): Integrating the Supply Chain, in: International Journal of Physical Distribution and Materials Management, 19(8): 3-8.

Stine, R. (1990): An Introduction to Bootstrap Methods: Examples and Ideas, in: Sociological Methods and Research, 8: 243-291.

Wisner, J. D. (2003): A Structural Equation Model of Supply Chain Management Strategies and Firm performance, in: Journal of Business Logistics, 24(1): 1-26.

Wolfe, L. M., (2003): The Introduction of Path Analysis to the Social Sciences, and Some Emergent Themes: An Annotated Bibliography, in: Structural Equation Modeling, 10(1): 1-34.

Wright, S. (1921): Correlation and Causation, in: Journal of Agriculture Research, 20: 557-585.

Wright, S. (1934): The method of Path Coefficients, in: Annals of Mathematical Statistics, 5: 161-215.

Yung, Y., Bentler, P. M. (1996): Bootstrapping Techniques in Analysis of Mean and Covariance Structure, in: Marcoulides, G. A., Schumacker, R. E. (Eds.): Advanced Structural Equation Modeling. Issues and Techniques, Erlbaum, Mahwah: 195-226.

6 Appendix

II: Internal Integration (scale of 1 to 10)
II1: Informal teamwork
II2: Shared ideas, information and other resources
II3: Established teamwork
II4: Joint planning to anticipate and resolve operative problems
II5: Joint establishment of objectives
II6: Joint development of the responsibility's understanding
II7: Joint decisions about ways to improve cost efficiencies
EI: External Integration (scale of 1 to 10)
EI1: Informal teamwork
EI2: Shared information about sales forecasts, sales and stock levels
EI3: Joint development of logistics processes
EI4: Established work team for the implementation and development of continuous replenishment program (CRP) or other ECR practice
EI5: Joint planning to anticipate and resolve operative problems
EI6: Joint establishment of objectives
EI7: Joint development of the responsibility's understanding
EI8: Joint decisions about ways to improve cost efficiencies
AP: Absolute Performance (scale of 1 to 10)
AP1: My company has achieved a reduction in costs to serve this customer
AP2: My company has achieved cost reductions in transportation to this customer
AP3: My company has achieved cost reductions in the order process of this customer
AP4: My company has achieved stock-out reductions in the products this customer buys
AP5: My company has achieved a lead-time reduction for this customer

Table 1a: Variables

Structural Equation Modeling as a Basis for Theory Development within Logistics and Supply Chain Management Research

Carl Marcus Wallenburg, Jürgen Weber[1]

1	Introduction	172
2	Structural Equation Modeling within Research	172
3	Impact of Logistics on Firm Performance	177
4	Conclusion	184
5	References	184

Summary:
Despite the recent debate on theories, logistics and SCM research still lacks a focus on theory development. Research will undoubtedly advance through rigorous empirical approaches, such as the use of structural equation modeling (SEM) within theory construction. SEM is well established in many fields of economic research, as it allows for validity of the structures and constructs in proposed theoretical models to be tested. This paper discusses the contribution of SEM to theory development and presents guidelines for the application of SEM to analyze both measurement and structural models. It exemplifies the use of SEM to capture and analyze the impact of logistics on the performance of companies. Based on a sample of 245 German companies, it emerges that logistics service levels have a greater impact on the performance of companies than logistics costs.

Keywords:
Structural Equation Modeling, Theory Development, Firm Performance, Logistics Services, Logistics Costs

---

[1] The authors thank Wolfdieter Keppler, WHU – Otto-Beisheim Graduate School of Management for his input in the process of developing the conceptual framework on the impact of logistics on overall firm performance.

1 Introduction

Logistics and SCM have won widespread recognition both in practice and management science. The respective research shows a broad scope of approaches and a high degree of interdisciplinarity. However, as Mentzer & Kahn (1995: 231) pointed out almost a decade ago, much of logistics and SCM research is managerial in nature. This holds true even today. Despite the recent debate on logistics theories, research still lacks a focus on methodology and theory development and testing. Undoubtedly, theory development will advance, as shown in the field of marketing research, through a rigorous empirical research approach.

In this context, Bagozzi (1984; 1998) distinguishes between theory construction as structure and as process. The structure of theory construction presents the concepts, constructs, hypotheses, observations and measures of a theory and their organization in an overall representation, whereas the process applies logical principles and scientific methods. To model the structure, the concept of Structural Equation Modeling (SEM) has been introduced. At the same time, SEM allows for validity in the process of theory construction to be tested.

To date, SEM is well established in many fields of economic research, whereas only few logistics researchers are employing this valuable method (Garver & Mentzer, 1999: 33), probably due to its complexity. However, as research matures, the use of SEM can bring logistics research to a more sophisticated level.

To support this development, the paper discusses the contribution of SEM to theory development and describes its principles. Additionally, we present comprehensive guidelines for the application of SEM. To conclude, we exemplify the use of SEM to capture and analyze the impact of logistics on the overall performance of companies. Our model, which has been validated and replicated in independent settings, shows that the level of logistics services has a far greater impact on the overall performance of companies than logistics costs.

2 Structural Equation Modeling within Research

The SEM approach has its roots in the beginning of the last century. However, it was not until the 1960s that sociologists in particular discovered the full potentials of path analysis. Based on this, Jöreskog (1973), Keesling (1972) and Wiley (1973) developed SEM to a general concept, usable for all causal relationships. Its use within economics, and especially within marketing research was promoted by Bagozzi and is to date standard in most economic disciplines.

2.1 Contribution of SEM to Theory Development

The contribution of SEM to theory construction is mostly seen within the process of empirical analysis of proposed causal relationships. However, as Bagozzi (1984) stressed two decades ago, it also enriches the possibilities to model theories and their structure. Although the process and the structure of theory construction interact, we separate them for exposition purposes and because an in-depth view of the structure of theory construction is beyond the scope of this article.

- **Theory Construction as Structure**

The structure of theory construction comprises the concepts of a theory, the hypotheses made by the theory, the observations and measurements included in the theory, and the formal organization of all these elements in an overall representation (Bagozzi, 1998: 47). In this context, SEM offers a holistic approach that aims at closing the gap between philosophical and statistical traditions. It offers a representation of both theoretical and observational terms and their corresponding rules. At the same time, it accounts for the possibility of measurement errors in the variables and the equations. SEM incorporates manifest variables as indicators at the observable level, and unobserved, latent or emergent variables (theoretical constructs) at the theoretical level. The relationship between constructs and indicators are modeled by measurement models, which specify how the constructs are measured by the indicators. The theoretical relationships between the constructs are represented by equations in the structural model.

- **Theory Construction as Process**

Once formulated, a theoretical model can be confronted with empirical data. In this process, SEM is currently the state-of-the-art technique used for multivariate statistical analysis. Although most researchers equate SEM with covariance structure analysis, other approaches like Partial Least Squares (PLS) exist. Despite widespread use within industrial application, PLS has gained attention within research only in recent years (Tobias, 1995: 1; Götz & Liehr-Gobbers, 2004: 1).

The covariance-based SEM analyzes the data based on the covariances of all observable variables. In this point it differs fundamentally from methods like regression analysis, where individual cases are viewed. The empirical covariance matrix is used to estimate all free parameters from the models. This is done iteratively with the aim of minimizing the difference between the empirical covariance matrix and the covariance matrix derived from parameter estimates.

The covariance-based SEM is designed to test the validity of a priori specified models and is primarily confirmatory. It requires a theoretical basis and its contribution to theory construction lies in the ability to assess the validity of measurement models, the discriminate validity of different constructs and the theoretical validity of causal relationships. This means that this type of SEM comes into the process of theory construction after the conceptual work.

PLS is based on multiple regression analysis and estimates all free parameters from the structural and measurement models successively in an iterative process. The aim is to minimize the variances of the residual variables. Thus, the explanatory power of the structural model is maximized (Götz & Liehr-Gobbers, 2004: 4). This approach is designed to construct predictive models and analyze the predictive power of exogenous variables; the emphasis, however, is not on analyzing the underlying causal relationships (Tobias, 1995: 1). Thus, PLS is a primarily explorative approach complementary to the covariance-based SEM. This type of SEM comes into the process of theory construction at an early stage when theories have not been developed or adapted sufficiently to propose causal relationships. It is rather the starting point for conceptual work aimed at developing a theoretical model before the covariance-based SEM is used in a later stage.

2.2 Advantages and Disadvantages of SEM

Generally, different multivariate statistical methods based on the principles of regression analysis are suitable for analyzing causal relationships. In comparison to most other methods, both the covariance-based SEM and the PLS approach to SEM offer various advantages as outlined below:

- **Covariance-based SEM**

The covariance-based SEM not only allows incorporation of theoretical constructs as latent variables, but also correlations between different exogenous variables, as well as causal effects and correlations between different endogenous variables. These are clear advantages over the multiple regression analysis which requires independent exogenous variables and can only include one endogenous variable in each analysis. In contrast to this, SEM permits the modeling of complex structures and even includes mediating variables. In this way, all hypotheses can be tested simultaneously and indirect and direct effects on the endogenous variables can be separated. Additionally, covariance-based SEM facilitates the explicit consideration of measurement errors and its separation from other sources of errors (i.e. specification errors). Another advantage is that the model fit can be assessed using statistical tests and a variety of goodness-of-fit criteria.

Disadvantages of the covariance-based SEM lie especially in the necessity of large sample sizes, in most cases exceeding 200 individual cases. Further, most of the established estimation functions used within the process require metrically scaled indicators and a multivariate normal distribution of the analyzed data. However, the maximum-likelihood estimation proves to be robust against violations of the latter prerequisite (Boomsma, 1982: 157; Bentler & Chou, 1987: 89). Generally, covariance-based SEM allows both reflective and formative indicators. However, know-how for the use of formative indicators is limited.

- **PLS Approach**

The PLS approach matches the covariance-based SEM in most of its advantages. Additionally, PLS has no prerequisites regarding the data distribution and only requires small sample sizes. Sample size should, however, at least exceed ten times the number of indicators of the most complex construct and ten times the largest number of exogenous variables loading on a single endogenous variable (Chin, 1998: 311). In contrast to the covariance-based SEM, there are no problems dealing with formative indicator within PLS.

Clear disadvantages of PLS lie in the weaknesses of the parameter estimations with respect to consistency of estimations and to systematic measurement errors. Therefore, PLS should only be used when the study focuses on exploration rather than confirmation, when sample size is small, data is not normally distributed, formative indicators are to be included, or predictive power is to be maximized. When this is the case, PLS is a very useful and powerful approach to data analysis.

2.3 Guidelines for the Use of the Covariance-Based SEM

Due to its high complexity, the covariance-based SEM creates room for improper use and misspecifications. Therefore, a brief guideline for its application is given in the following. However, due to the scope of this paper, we have to refer to works like Kline (1998) for detailed and operationally orientated insights into SEM and Chin (1998) for a comprehensive describtion of PLS.

Even though SEM allows the simultaneous analysis of both measurement and structural models, a two-step approach – proposed by Anderson & Gerbing (1988) – represents established proceeding. In a first step, the measurement models are assessed with the objective to ensure that each scale measures what it intends to measure (Garver & Mentzer, 1999). In a second step, the structures are tested.

To obtain valid measurements, theoretical constructs are modeled as latent variables and measured by manifest variables. When using the covariance-based SEM, these indicators should be measured on continous scales or on rating scalea of at least five points. Further, all indicators ought to be truly reflective. Many researchers do not consider this prerequisite sufficiently, which in turn reduces the validity of the measurement models (Eggert & Fassot, 2003).

To ensure construct content validity, a thorough review of the literature and interviews with researchers and business professionals are to be conducted. According to Homburg & Giering (1996), validity of measurement models should additionally be assessed in a process using first generation criteria in a first phase and second generation criteria thereafter. If necessary, indicators reducing the validity are to be eliminated. To identify this, they recommend the use of exploratory factor analysis (EFA), Cronbach alpha and item-to-total-correlation first, and the use of confirmatory factor analysis (CFA) in the second phase.

However, if indicators are eliminated in the first phase (as proposed), on the basis of item-to-total-correlation, only convergent validity is taken into account. Therefore we suggest using the second generation criteria parallel. In this way, the reliability of each indicator can also be considered when deciding on elimination.

When analyzing the indicators of a construct with EFA, all indicators should load on one single factor. Otherwise convergent validity is violated as the indicators do not measure the same, but rather different dimensions. Cronbach alpha ought to yield values exceeding 0.7 or at least 0.6. Otherwise indicators have to be eliminated that show a low reliability. Within CFA, a one factorial structure is assumed and analyzed. Within literature, a large number of criteria to assess goodness-of-fit have been proposed. To obtain a comprehensive impression of the model fit, we suggest combining the recommendations of Homburg & Giering (1996) and Garver & Mentzer (1999) and consider the χ^2/df, the Tucker-Lewis-Index (TLI), the Goodness-of-Fit-Index (GFI) and the root mean squared error of approximation (RMSEA) as global fit indices. Acceptable fit requires a χ^2/df below 2.5, a RMSEA below 0.08 and both TLI and GFI to exceed 0.9. Additionally, local fit indices ought to be considered with the aim of composite reliability exceeding 0.6 and variance extracted exceeding 0.5. If multiple indices do not meet the requirements, indicators have to be eliminated from the measurement model.

To test for discriminant validity between the constructs, we recommend the Fornell/Larcker criterion (Fornell & Larcker, 1981). It states that discriminant validity is given for all pairs of constructs with a shared variance lower than the respective variance extracted.

The validity of the structural models is assessed with the same global fit criteria as above. Additionally, the squared multiple correlation (R^2) shows the explanatory power with respect to each endogenous variable. It states the degree to which their variance is explained by the variance of the exogenous variables.

When the fit shows to be insufficient, this can be due to inadequate data quality, misspecifications within the model, or model complexity that is too high. Within applications like AMOS or EQS, misspecifications can be identified on the basis of the modification indices. For each fixed parameter, and especially for all relationships not included in the model, they estimate the change in χ^2 when the parameter is estimated freely. Model fit can be improved by including not-modelled relationships. This should, however, only be done when theoretical justification for this is strong. Otherwise the danger is great that the model is just tailored to fit the data, without chance of replication in later studies. The other possibility is to reduce complexity by eliminating constructs from the structural model – either single endogenous variables or exogenous variables that offer a very limited contribution to explaining the endogenous variables.

3 Impact of Logistics on Firm Performance

To exemplify the use of SEM, we view logistics performance. There are different approaches to capture the performance of logistics as described by Weber (2003). Traditionally, performance has been related to the input, the processes or the output of logistics and measured in different ways. When viewing a company as a whole, however, it seems more appropriate to view the effects logistics have on the firm and its performance.

During the last years, some research aimed at illuminating this. The results from Inis & La Londe (1994), Bowersox (1995), Daugherty et al. (1998), Bowersox et al. (1999); Wisner (2003); Stank et al. (2003) and others, however, only offer an ambiguous picture of the impact logistics have on firms' performance. The link between logistics and overall firm performance has not been established yet.

In order to do this, we developed a two-dimensional structure as a conceptual framework for further discussion. These two dimensions span a two-by-two matrix of four possible types of logistics impact on firms' performance.

On the one hand, the logistics can be discussed based on the productivity-oriented paradigm, along with the effects of its input and output as the two sources of impact that logistics processes can have on their environment:

- *Effects of input.* Input directly relates to the consumption of resources including personnel, tangibles and intangibles, as well as services provided by third parties such as LSPs. Resource consumption by a process causes effects on the surrounding system typically equated with costs.

- *Effects of output.* Output represents the result of business processes and includes modifications in logistical properties of objects (e.g., time and location). In the surrounding system, the delivered output causes certain effects, referred to as *outcome*. Typical examples include enabling other operations, and direct or indirect revenues from customers.

On the other hand, we can distinguish the effects of logistics on firm performance by the degree their uncertainty differentiates between two main perspectives:

- The *operative perspective* refers to those effects of logistics on which comprehensive and reliable information are available. Thus, uncertainty is low. These effects materialize within a short time from when the logistics services are rendered, leaving little doubt about their exact amount. For example, logistics costs have an operative effect in the way that they are incurred when the respective service is rendered.

- In contrast, the *strategic perspective* refers to effects that are difficult to predict for the individual firm, and where uncertainty is high. The strategic effects usually materialize after a long time and may differ to a great extent from the initial expectations. A good example of this is the impact of superior logistics on customer loyalty and other aspects of market performance.

3.1 Impact of Logistics' Input

Regarding the input side, logistics' main contribution to firms' success is delivering predetermined logistical services (the four Rs) with minimum resources. Reduction of resource consumption by logistics has various operative and strategic effects.

- **Operative Perspective**

One major operative effect of logistics input is direct profit contribution through reduced resource consumption, as this translates into reduced cost. At constant revenues, these savings directly increase profits for the respective company.

Another operative effect is indirect profit contribution through increased revenues. Whenever demand for a firm's product is elastic in price, reduced prices – afforded by lower costs – will lead to increased sales quantities. In combination with constant or even higher margins, this yields additional profits.

The general potentials of cost reduction through logistics are well established in theory (e.g. Lambert & Stock, 1993: 25) and practice and is seen to be the most significant operative contribution to firm performance. Therefore we hypothesize:

> *H 1: Cost-effective management of logistics contributes to firms' operative performance.*

- **Strategic Perspective**

Logistics cost reductions also have a strategic impact on firm performance – especially with relational clients and when following a cost leadership strategy.

In relational client settings, cost effective management of logistics enhances stability of relationships. When cooperating over a long time period, customers typically expect cost savings. Building capabilities for cost reduction can help a firm to secure its competitive position. This effect is limited, however, as other elements display a greater impact on customer loyalty (Stank et al., 2003; Wallenburg, 2004: 259-263).

Pursuing an overall cost leadership strategy means outperforming competitors in overall cost. This requires – among others – aggressive pursuit of cost reductions (Porter, 1998: 35). In this context, the contribution of each business function is limited to its share of total costs. Only in few industries (such as retail) do logistics actually account for high cost shares. In the industries that account for the main value added in modern economies, however, the typical share of logistics in overall cost is low (Baumgarten & Thoms, 2002: 14). In general, the direct impact of logistics within a cost leadership strategy is very limited.

From the preceding arguments we conclude:

> *H 2: Cost-effective management of logistics does not contribute significantly to firms' strategic performance.*

3.2 Impact of Logistics' Output

Logistics output can influence the cost and revenue position of a firm, as well as its competitive positioning in different ways – both operative and strategic.

- **Operative Perspective**

Logistics can have a multitude of operative effects on a firm's short-term financial performance, affecting both the cost and the revenue side. This perspective is not unusual in literature (e.g. Beamon, 1999; Gunasekaran et al., 2001).

By meeting logistical requirements, costs in other functions are avoided, e.g. destruction or deterioration of goods through inadequate transport handling or warehouse management. Additionally, losses from unfilled orders are avoided. This is relevant when customers turn to competitors if demand is not fulfilled directly. In most cases, these possible costs associated with logistics faults are already avoided, as competition generally has led to a high level of logistics. Therefore, further improvement of logistics service here only offers limited potential.

By meeting logistical requirements of customers that could not yet be served, additional revenues can be generated. When customer segments differ in their service levels expectations, logistics can be used as an enabler to address new customer segments. This effect, however, is limited to only a few industries.

Furthermore, in markets with no market-specific service present, firms can yield price premiums for superior logistics services. Higher service levels lead to an increased fulfillment of customer demand and higher willingness to pay. In this way, price premiums can generate additional revenues. Unless the firm is a logistics service provider, however, revenues from logistics play only a limited role.

To conclude, the operative effects of improved logistics are limited to only a few industries. Thus, we hypothesize:

> *H 3: The level of logistics service does not contribute significantly to firms' operative performance.*

- **Strategic Perspective**

Besides the operative perspective, logistics output also induces a variety of mid- and long-term strategic effects on the firm.

By improving logistics service levels and meeting logistical requirements of customer segments not servable yet, the customer base can still be extended. This additional business immediately improves a company's market position.

Offering reliable logistics services that constantly meet service level requirements builds customer loyalty. Customers that are used to always receiving the logistical quality that is promised are more likely to be loyal to their supplier than those who become frequently dissatisfied by insufficient logistics services, such as late or damaged delivery, or impolite service personnel. Offering premium logistics services can further enhance customer loyalty – in markets without specific logistics service level standards. Sometimes, logistics service features can even serve as attractive elements (Kano, 1979), and in this way enhance loyalty.

When viewing market performance over time, superior logistics support adaptation to market changes. Additionally, responsive and adaptive logistics functions can tremendously improve firms' time-to-market for new products and in turn help secure their market position. Based on the above arguments we hypothesize:

H 4: The level of logistics service contributes to firms' strategic performance.

3.3 Empirical Analysis of Logistics' Impact

We use SEM to model our conceptual framework and test the proposed hypotheses in order to find empirical evidence for the differentiated impact of logistics. Because of the confirmatory nature of this process, we use the covariance-based SEM as described in chapter 2.

- **Research Model**

To capture the possible impacts of logistics, a well-established approach from marketing research was used (Irving, 1995; Ruekert et al., 1985). This approach distinguishes three different components of firm performance: financial performance, market performance, and responsiveness (adaptiveness).

Financial performance refers to the generated profit and serves as a short-term, operative indicator of firm performance. In contrast, market performance – as an antecedent to financial performance – has a strategic character. The same is true for responsiveness, which is regarded as the capability of a company to adjust to environmental developments, and serves as an antecedent to market performance.

Following our conceptual framework, the research hypotheses translate into the research model as follows. The level of logistics services – as a measure of the output dimension of logistics – positively influences responsiveness and market performance as strategic components within a firm. It has, however, no direct effect on the short-term financial performance as an operative component of firm performance. In contrast, the level of logistics costs – as a measure of the input dimension – has no influence on responsiveness and market performance, but a positive direct effect on the short-term financial performance.

- **Sample Design of the Empirical Study**

The research model was evaluated on the basis of a survey conducted by our research center in 2002 on 7,800 companies from various industries (food, chemicals, plastics, pharmaceuticals, industrial machines, automotive, electronics, optics, retail and other). The sample was drawn randomly from the subscribers of the German logistics journal "Logistik Heute". The survey was addressed to logistics managers, considered as key informants for the specific topic. The response rate was 3.2 percent. Still, no non-response bias was detected when tested for it following Armstrong & Overton (1977), by using late informants as proxies for non-respondents, and comparing them with early respondents. Additional analysis also showed that the sample is representative and unbiased (Engelbrecht, 2004: 80-85). Out of a total of 245 returned surveys, 216 were usable to test the proposed model.

- **Measurement Scales Used in the Study**

Each construct in this study was modeled as a latent variable and measured by several items on a five-point Likert-Scale, as shown in Table 1.

The short-term-oriented financial performance was measured using indicators referring to the "return on sales" (RoS). The informants assessed the RoS in comparison to their competitors. Such a subjective measurement generally shows high consistency with both objective internal data (Dess & Robinson, 1984) and external secondary data (Venkatraman & Ramanujam, 1986).

Construct	Item (relative to respective competitors)	Item-to-Total Correlation	Item reliability	t-Value
Financial Performance	(FP 1) Return on sales last year	0.78	0.85	11.10
	(FP 2) Return on sales last 3 years	0.70	0.99	10.95
	(FP 3) Development of RoS last 3 years	0.66	0.53	-
Market Performance	(MP 1) Customer satisfaction	0.60	0.51	7.26
	(MP 2) Customer value	0.72	0.81	7.50
	(MP 3) Customer loyalty	0.56	0.41	6.84
	(MP 4) Acquisition of new customers	*Item dropped*		
	(MP 5) Growth of market share	0.48	0.27	-
	(MP 6) Market share	*Item dropped*		
Responsiveness	(RS 1) Adoption of products/services to customer demands	0.65	0.50	10.50
	(RS 2) Reaction to market developments	0.79	0.94	10.59
	(RS 3) Utilization of market opportunities	0.65	0.51	-
Logistics Services	(LS 1) Lead (cycle) time	0.59	0.56	5.35
	(LS 2) Delivery time	0.56	0.52	5.34
	(LS 3) Delivery capacity	*Item dropped*		
	(LS 4) Delivery flexibility	0.50	0.35	5.03
	(LS 5) Process quality	0.36	0.18	-
Logistics Costs	(LC 1) Logistics costs with respect to sales	0.55	0.66	4.64
	(LC 2) Overall costs of transport	0.51	0.46	5.21
	(LC 3) Inventory level	*Item dropped*		
	(LC 4) Logistic-specific costs of personnel	0.36	0.18	-

Table 1: Item Overview and Statistical Measures

Market performance was measured using a scale developed by Irving (1995), which is well established in German research. It captures how successfully a firm operates in its markets. Out of originally six items, two (MP 4 and 6) were dropped and not considered in the analysis, because the CFA had shown a high correlation of its measurement error with other measurement errors.

Following Ruekert et al. (1985), responsiveness was understood as the company's ability to adapt to changes in its environment and measured by three items that contain a subjective assessment of the fulfillment of different aspects of responsiveness in comparison to the respective competitors.

In order to measure the level of logistics service as a proxy for the output dimension of logistics, a scale consisting of five items was developed. All of them comprise different aspects of logistics services from a customer's perspective as well as internal cycle times and process stability and refer to the company's relative position with respect to its competitors.

Since the perception of which costs are logistics costs differs widely between companies, a scale of four items was developed to account for this problem and to focus on the core of logistics costs. Respondents were asked to report how they assess their logistics costs compared to their competitors.

Construct	Cr. Alpha	χ^2/df	TLI	GFI	RMSEA	Composite reliability	Variance extracted
Financial Performance	0.85	-	-	-	-	0.99	0.98
Market Performance	0.78	0.68	1.01	1.00	0.00	0.78	0.48
Responsiveness	0.83	-	-	-	-	0.85	0.65
Logistics Service	0.71	2.44	0.96	0.99	0.08	0.72	0.40
Logistics Costs	0.66	-	-	-	-	0.68	0.42

Table 2: Statistical Measures for Constructs

Following the proposed two-step approach the measurement models were tested before analyzing the structural model. Convergence validity was assessed by calculating Cronbach Alpha for each construct and item-to-total correlations for each item. Furthermore, a CFA was performed on all scales using AMOS 4.0. The results from the CFA show a high degree of reliability and convergent validity (see Table 2). For all scales the different goodness-of-fit-criteria exceed the established requirements. Additionally, the constructs show discriminant validity according to the Fornell/Larcker criterion. Thus, all constructs qualify for use in testing and evaluating our hypothesis.

- **Analysis of the Structural Model and the Hypotheses**

The structural model was analyzed based on the described measurement models above. All goodness-of-fit-criteria as shown in Figure 1 indicate that the research model fits the sample data well. For each path, the path coefficient was calculated and its statistical significance assessed. The model shows three non-significant and three significant paths at the .01 level and two at the .10 level.

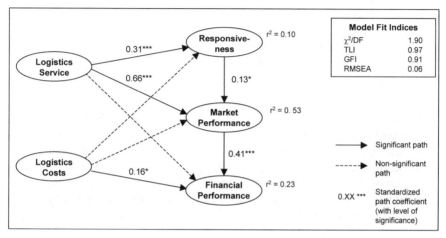

Figure 1: Results of the Causal Model

Logistics costs only show a significant direct effect on short-term financial performance and no influence on responsiveness and market performance. This likewise supports our hypotheses that logistics input only has an operative and no strategic effect on firm performance.

In contrast to this, the level of logistics services has a strong direct effect on responsiveness and on market performance, and no direct effect on the short-term financial performance. This supports our research hypotheses that logistics output only has a strategic effect, whereas the operative effect on firm performance can be neglected. Financial performance is only affected in the long run, when superior services lead to increased market performance. This indirect effect however has a standardized value of 0.30 and thus surpasses the direct effect of logistics costs on financial performance. Overall, the level of logistics services has a greater impact on firm performance than logistics costs.

The presented results – which might be surprising in their clarity – hold even truer in a longer perspective than another study at our research center (Dehler, 2001) which was conducted in 1999 aiming at a different research topic. It showed the same relationship between logistics service and logistics costs on the one hand and responsiveness, market performance and financial performance on the other hand.

4 Conclusion

This paper clearly shows the comprehensive contribution structural equation modeling (SEM) has to offer to theory development and testing. SEM offers a holistic approach to represent the elements and structures of a theoretical model based on equations. Further, it serves as a statistical method to confront theoretical models with empirical observations and assess their validity on this basis. Within this process, PLS serves as an exploratory approach to gain an understanding of causal relationships, whereas the covariance-based SEM offers a confirmatory approach used after a conceptual framework and a theoretical model have been developed. In comparison to most other multivariate statistical methods, SEM offers various advantages – especially the capability to assess complex structures and causal relationships.

In addition, the paper gives detailed guidelines for the use of the covariance-based SEM and exemplifies its use through the impact of logistics on the overall performance of companies. The basis for this is a conceptual framework that differentiates between the input and output dimensions on one hand and the operative and the strategic perspective on the other hand. The results from the SEM conducted on a sample of 216 German companies prove that logistics have a significant impact on overall firm performance. Additionally, they show that the level of logistics service in this respect has a far greater importance than the logistics costs.

5 References

Anderson, J., Gerbing, D. (1988): Structural Equation Modeling in Practice: A Review and Recommended Two-Step Approach, Psychological Bulletin, 103(3): 411-423.

Armstrong, S., Overton, T. (1977): Estimating Nonresponse Bias in Mail Surveys, Journal of Marketing Research, 14(8): 396-402.

Bagozzi, R. P. (1984): A Prospectus for Theory Construction in Marketing, in: Journal of Marketing, 48(Winter): 11-29.

Bagozzi, R. P. (1998): A Prospectus for Theory Construction in Marketing: Revisited and Revised, in: Hildebrandt, L.; Homburg, C. (eds.): Die Kausalanalyse: Ein Instrument der empirischen betriebswirtschaftlichen Forschung, Schäffer, Stuttgart: p. 86-115.

Baumgarten, H., Thoms, J. (2002): Trends und Strategien in der Logistik: Supply Chains im Wandel (Trends and Strategies within Logistics), Bereich Logistik, Institut für Technologie und Management, Technische Universität Berlin, Berlin.

Beamon, B. M. (1999): Measuring Supply Chain Performance, International Journal of Operations and Production Management, 19(3): 275-292.

Bentler, P. M., Chou, C. P. (1987): Practical Issues in Structural Modeling, in: Sociological Methods & Research, 16: 78-117.

Boomsma, A. (1982): The robustness of LISREL against small sample sizes in factor analysis models, in: Jöreskog, K.G.; Wold, H. (eds.): Systems under indirect observation: Causality, structure, prediction, Amsterdam: p. 149-173.

Bowersox, D. J. (1995): World Class Logistics: The Challenge of Managing Continuous Change, Council of Logistics Management, Oak Brook, IL.

Bowersox, D. J., Closs, D. J., Stank, T. P. (1999): 21st Century Logistics: Making Supply Chain Integration a Reality, Council of Logistics Management, Oak Brook, IL.

Chin, W. W. (1998): The partial least squares approach for structural equation modeling, in Marcoulides, G.A. (eds.): Modern methods for business research, Lawrence Erlbaum, Mahwah, NJ: p. 295-336.

Daugherty, P. J., Stank, T. P., Ellinger, A. E. (1998): Leveraging Logistics/Distribution Capabilities: The Effect of Logistics Service on Market Share, Journal of Business Logistics, 19(2): 35-51.

Dehler, M. (2001): Entwicklungsstand der Logistik. Messung, Determinanten, Erfolgswirkungen, (Logitics Development – Measurement, Determinants, Success), Gabler/DUV, Wiesbaden.

Dess, G., Robinson, R. (1984): Measuring Organizational Performance in the Absence of Objective Measures, Strategic Management Journal, 5(3): 265-73.

Eggert, A., Fassott, G. (2003): Zur Verwendung formativer und reflektiver Indikatoren in Strukturgleichungsmodellen (On the use of formative and reflective indicators in SEM) Paper at the 65. Annual Confernece of the VHB e.V. (Pfingsttagung), Zürich 2003.

Engelbrecht, C. (2004): Logistikoptimierung durch Outsourcing (Optimizing Logistics through Outsourcing) DUV, Wiesbaden.

Fornell, C., Larcker, D. (1981): Evaluating Structural Equation Models with Unobservable Variables and Measurement Error, Journal of Marketing, 45(2): 39-50.

Garver, M. S., Mentzer, J. T. (1999): Logistics Research Methods: Employing Structural Equation Modeling to Test for Construct Validity, Journal of Business Logistics, 20(1): 33-57.

Götz, O., Liehr-Gobbers, K. (2004): Der Partial-Least-Squares (PLS)-Ansatz zur Analyse von Strukturgleichungsmodellen (The Partial Least Squares Approach to SEM), Workingpaper of the Institute for Marketing at the University of Münster, Nr. 2, March 2004.

Gunasekaran, A., Patel, C., Tirtiroglu, E. (2001): Performance Measures and Metrics in a Supply Chain Environment, International Journal of Operations and Production Management, 21(1): 71-87.

Homburg, C.; Giering, A. (1996): Konzepualisierung und Operationalisierung komplexer Konstrukte – Ein Leitfaden für die Marketingforschung (Conceptualisation and Operationalisation of complex constructs – A Guideline), in: Marketing – ZFP, 18(1): 5-24.

Innis, D. E., La Londe, B. J. (1994): Customer Service: The Key to Customer Satisfaction, Customer Loyalty, and Market Share, Journal of Business Logistics, 15(1): 1-28.

Irving, E. (1995): Marketing Quality Practices, Dissertation, University of North Carolina.

Jöreskog, K. (1973): A General Method for estimating a linear Structural Equation System, in: Goldberger, A. S.; Duncan, O. D. (eds.): Structural Equations in the Social Sciences, Seminar Press, New York.

Kano, N. (1979): On M-H Property of Quality", in Nippon QC Gakka, 9th Annual Presentation Meeting, Abstracts, Japanese Society of Quality Control: p. 21-26.

Keesling, J.W. (1972): Maximum Likelihood Approaches to Causal Flow Analysis, Dissertation, University of Chicago, Chicago.

Kline Rex B. (1998): Principles and Practice of Structural Equation Modeling, Guilford Press, N.Y.

Lambert, D. M., Stock, J. R. (1993): Strategic Logistics Management, Irwin, Homewood.

Mentzer, J.T.; Kahn, K.B. (1995): A Framework of Logistics Research, in: Journal of Business Logistics, 16(1): 231-249.

Porter, M. E. (1998): Competitive Strategy: Techniques for Analyzing Industries and Competitors, The Free Press, New York.

Ruekert, R. W., Walker Jr., O. C., Roering, K. J. (1985): The Organization of Marketing Activities: A Contingency Theory of Structure and Performance, Journal of Marketing, 49(1): 13-25.

Stank, T. P., Goldsby, T. J., Vickery, S. K., Savitskie, K. (2003): Logistics Service Performance: Estimating its Influence on Market Share, Journal of Business Logistics, 24(1): 27-55.

Tobias, R. (1995): An Introduction to Partial Least Squares Regression, in: Proceedings of the 20. Annual SAS Users Group International Conference, Cary, NC: 1250 -1257.

Venkatraman, N., Ramanujam, V. (1986): Measurement of Business Performance in the Absence of Objective Measures, Strategic Management Review, 11(4): 801-814.

Wallenburg, C. M. (2004): Kundenbindung in der Logistik - Eine empirische Untersuchung zu ihren Einflussfaktoren (Customer Loyalty within Logisitics – An empirical study on its determinats), Haupt Verlag, Bern et al.

Weber, J. (2003): Macht Logistik erfolgreich? – Konzeptionelle Überlegungen und empirische Ergebnisse (Does Logistics make successfull? Conceptual thoughts and empirical results), in: Logistik Management, 5(3): 11-22.

Wiley, D. E. (1973): The Identification Problem for Structural Equation Models with Unmeasured Variables, in: Goldberger, A. S.; Duncan, O. D. (eds.) Structural Equation Models in the Social Sciences, Seminar Press, New York: p. 69-83.

Wisner, J. D. (2003): A Structural Equation Model of Supply Chain Management Strategies and Firm Performance, Journal of Business Logistics, 24(1): 1-26.

Customers' Perceptions of Service Quality by TPL Service Providers in the United Kingdom - A Confirmatory Factor Analysis

Harlina Suzana Jaafar, Mohammed Rafiq

1	Introduction	188
2	Logistics Service Quality	189
3	Methodology	189
4	Results	194
5	Discussion	198
6	Conclusion	199
7	References	200

Summary:
Structural Equation Modeling (SEM), including Confirmatory Factor Analysis (CFA) is a statistical tool that is becoming increasingly popular in logistics research. The intent of this paper is to demonstrate the application of CFA in logistics research particularly in testing Mentzer et al. (1999) Logistics Service Quality (LSQ) instrument, a scale developed in the United States. This paper displays the value of CFA for scale development and testing with particular reference to dealing with missing data. The study is based on cross-sectoral mail survey of the customers of Third Party Logistics (TPL) providers in the United Kingdom (UK). With some improvement, it demonstrates the generalizability of LSQ scale across industries in the UK.

Keywords:
Third Party Logistics, Logistics Service Quality, Confirmatory Factor Analysis, Missing Data, Testing and Mail Survey

1 Introduction

Structural Equation Modeling (SEM) is one of the multivariate techniques that has been widely used in disciplines disparate as psychology, marketing, education, sociology and organizational behavior (Hair, 1998). The process of SEM follows two stages; (1) validating the measurement model, and (2) fitting the structural model. The former is achieved primarily through confirmatory factor analysis (CFA), while the latter is accomplished through path analysis with latent (unobserved) variables. CFA plays an important role in SEM. It is used to confirm that the indicators measure the corresponding latent variables, represented by the factors. It is also used to assess the role of measurement error in the model, to validate a multifactorial model and to determine group effects on the factors. SEM is becoming more popular in logistics research (Keller et al., 2002) as this technique allows the development of valid, robust and generalizable measures, thus increasing external validity (e.g. Hubbard & Vetter, 1996; Thacker et al., 1989). Joreskog (1974) suggests that one should attempt CFA in the replications of factor structure. According to Lindsay and Ehrenberg, (1993: 219) research findings, including those with "high" levels of statistical significance would remain "virtually meaningless and useless" in themselves until they were generalized. Mentzer & Flint (1997) highlight that there is no single study that can ensure external validity. Instead, the external validity can only be enhanced through studies conducted under varying conditions of time and place. Thus, they suggest that replications in logistics journals should be encouraged.

Third party logistics (TPL) services provision emerged as a significant topic in the mid 1980s. The fact that the UK has the highest rate of outsourcing among the European countries reflects the level of the industry's development (Anonymous, 1999). In 2002, the contract logistics market reached a value of approximately GBP 12.5 billion, doubling its share since 2000. Despite its growth, customers' perception of UK logistics outsourcing has received relatively little attention in academic literature.

This paper demonstrates the value of CFA in testing the generalizability of Logistics Service Quality (LSQ) scale (Mentzer et al., 1999) to the customers of TPL providers in the United Kingdom. With the exception to Mentzer et al. (2001), LSQ scale has not been tested in any existing study. If it measures the true logistics service quality, it is imperative that the customers' perceptions of service quality in logistics should be understood. It will also reinforce the important aspect of increased rigor in logistics research by testing the LSQ scale in a different context.

This paper is structured as follows. First, the LSQ scale is discussed followed by the explanation of the methodology. The results of testing the scale are then presented and discussed. The paper closes with a discussion of the implications of the methodology used in this research.

2 Logistics Service Quality

Logistics Service Quality (LSQ) is a scale for measuring logistics service quality. It was developed and empirically validated on a single large logistics provider firm, Defense Logistics Agency (DLA) in the United States that provides logistics services to internal customers (Mentzer et al., 1999; 2001). By following the general methodology used by Bienstock et al. (1997) to develop the Physical Distribution Service Quality (PDSQ) scale that measures technical quality, Mentzer et al. (1999) extended the concept of service quality into logistics context by incorporating the functional quality aspects of logistics services. It is conceptualized as a set of nine interrelated constructs from the perspective of customers that is valid across customer segments (construction, electronics, fuels, industrial supplies, medical supplies, textiles and general). The nine constructs are information quality, ordering procedures, order release quantities, timeliness, order accuracy, order quality, order condition, order discrepancy handling and personnel contact quality (Mentzer et al., 1999). Mentzer et al. (2001) extended Mentzer et al.'s (1999) study by conceptualizing the nine constructs of LSQ as a process by which perceptions of logistics service components affect one another and eventually lead to satisfaction in four customer segments (general, textiles, electronics and construction). This paper, however, focuses on the first stage of testing the LSQ scale (Mentzer et al., 1999), rather than testing LSQ process model.

3 Methodology

Since the LSQ scale has not been tested outside of its original context, it is useful to examine closely the research procedures of the original study. This helps to establish whether it has the potential to be generalized more widely. This study seeks to ensure that the variations in this study are not great enough to encourage significantly different results than those found in the original study. Table 1 summarizes the procedures used in the present study compared with Mentzer's (1999) study.

LSQ US (Mentzer et al., 1999)	LSQ UK study
Purpose: To investigate a particular focal organization with multiple market segments in order to determine whether the general methodology used by Bienstock et al. (1997) results in a similarly valid, reliable scale of logistics service quality, LSQ.	Purpose: To test the applicability and generalizability of Logistics Service Quality (LSQ) scale across industrial sectors in the UK.
Sample: Customers from various segments of one single organization that perform logistical functions in the US.	Sample: Customers of TPL providers from across industrial sectors throughout the UK
Exploratory research: Focus group: 13 focus group discussions with key buyers of logistics services.	Exploratory research: In-depth interviews: 7 logistics-related managers from TPL customers' companies of various industries and 2 managers from a large TPL company
Pre-test: Using one out of ten respondents' data set in the final survey for scale purification.	Pre-test: A mail survey was sent to a random sample of 50 logistics-related managers throughout the UK
Main survey: DLA personnel distributed survey instruments to 16920 DLA customers. Response rate: 32.7 percent (n=5531)	Main survey: Mail survey to 1258 logistics-related managers throughout the UK Response rate: 16.4 percent (n=183)
Instrumentation: 5-point Likert scale with 25 items	Instrumentation: 7-point Likert scale with 32 items

Table 1: Comparison of Methodologies between the Current Study and Mentzer's Study (1999)

3.1 Qualitative Study and Instrumentation

For the purpose of testing the generalizability of the LSQ scale, several procedures were followed. An exploratory study was conducted consisting of seven interviews with logistics managers of TPL customer firms and two with logistics managers of a leading TPL company. A mixture of experts reviewed the research instrument to ensure the content validity. They consisted of 4 academics, a logistics consultant and a TPL customer, who had twelve years' experience in his current position. The instrument was then pre-tested using a random sample of 50 firms. Six (6) usable questionnaires were obtained. The findings from the qualitative fieldwork and the pilot test of this study suggested several changes. First, in order to improve the LSQ scale, two constructs (information quality and ordering procedures) that were tapped with only two items needed to be expanded. Particularly with the information quality construct, it was found that the concept was not applicable because for the managers of a TPL customer firm, there was no catalogue information. Mentzer et al. (1999) argued that the information that is contained in the service provider's catalogue should be available and of adequate quality in order to make decisions. The results from the exploratory study reflected that the logistics practice heavily involves inter-organizational information systems such as the Internet and Electronic Data Interchange (EDI) in exchanging information due to the complexity of logistics operations and interorganizational relationships. Thus, the quality of information should be evaluated in a more rigorous manner. The information quality measures, developed by Mohr & Spekman (1994) were found to be appropriate in this study and were therefore adopted (see Table 2).

The second two-item construct was ordering procedures. In Mentzer et al.'s (1999) study, ordering procedures refer to the efficiency and effectiveness of the order placement procedures. In a cross-sectoral context, the situation is more complex and ordering procedures measures used by Mentzer et al. (1999) do not fully reflect the ordering procedures in certain industries. Instead, measures such as effectiveness, ease, simplicity, flexibility of the ordering procedures as well as time and effort taken are deemed to be important (Dabholkar, 1994). Thus, a wider concept of ordering procedures was used in this study (see Table 2).

Besides the modification of these two-item scales, the results from the exploratory and pilot study found that an exact application of the scale would generate some complications in the responses and analysis of the results due to the specific type of measures that were developed within the DLA organization. The LSQ scale was also confined specifically to inbound logistics. It was expected that the complex procedures of the logistics operations among industries and the specific type of services used by customers would also contribute to the problems.

LSQ US (Mentzer et al., 1999)	LSQ UK study
Information Quality Customers perceive the availability and adequacy of information on products that is contained in the catalogs.	**Information Quality** Quality of information exchange includes such aspects of accuracy, timeliness, adequacy and credibility.
Operational measures: Catalog information is available. Catalog information is adequate.	Operational measures: The information communicated by this TPL provider is timely. The information communicated by this TPL provider is accurate. The information communicated by this TPL provider is adequate. The information communicated by this TPL provider is complete. The information communicated by this TPL provider is credible.
Ordering procedures Refers to the efficiency and effectiveness of the procedures followed by the supplier.	**Ordering procedures** Customers concern not only the efficiency and effectiveness of the procedures, but it includes time and effort in placing the order, the complexity of the procedures, the accuracy of the order, the reliability of the ordering system and the flexibility in any event of changing the order.
Operational measures: Requisitioning procedures are effective. Requisitioning procedures are easy to use.	Operational measures: Requisitioning procedures are effective. Requisitioning procedures are easy to use. Requisitioning procedures are simple. Requisitioning procedures are do not take much effort. Requisitioning procedures do not take much time. Requisitioning procedures are flexible.

Table 2: Changes in the Definitions and Operational Measures of Information Quality and Ordering Procedures

In this study, it is argued that the logistics managers would be the best people to assess logistics services provided by their TPL providers as compared to those involved in purchasing as used by Mentzer et al. (1999) as they are assessing the logistics services of the supplying firms that are delivered by a TPL provider. Although it is difficult to segregate the logistics managers to inbound and outbound categories as the use of inbound and outbound logistics was unknown, it was decided that the logistics managers would provide the best data for this study.

As proposed by Mentzer et al. (1999), the number of scale responses was increased from 5-point Likert "agree/disagree" scale to 7-point scale to allow wider discrimination of the responses. A larger number of scale points leads to larger variances, resulting in increased reliability. Due to the expected problems of filling in the questionnaire, the scales of "don't know" and "not applicable" as used by Mentzer et al. (1999) were not incorporated in the questionnaire. It is argued that excluding these options discloses the largest amount of information (Malhotra, 1998).

3.2 Sampling and Survey Procedures

The survey was mailed to 1258 logistics related managers from across industrial sectors selected from the Institute of Logistics and Transport (ILT) Members' Directory 2000. It employed the Total Design Method by Dillman (2000). The respondents were contacted via three waves of questionnaire mailings together with a pre-notification letter and postcard reminder. A total of 336 (26.7%) managers responded. However, by excluding the wrongly delivered, unusable responses and non-TPL customers from the original sample, the usable responses came from 183 TPL customers giving an effective response rate of 16.4%. The survey was conducted from November 2003 through February 2004. The responding firms were asked to report their views on the services that they received from their main TPL providers. The majority of the respondents were logistics-related managers (68.8 percent). Most respondents (70.5 percent) had more than six years of working experience in the current position as well as having more than 6 years experience working with TPL providers (62.1 percent). This reflects positively on the reliability of the information obtained, given that the respondents would have familiarity with the subject matter. More than half (56.3 percent) of the companies that responded were manufacturers followed by wholesalers/distributors (27.7 percent), retailers (9.8 percent) and others (6.2 percent). The largest number of respondents (27.3 percent) came from food, beverages and the tobacco sector.

To test for non-response bias, as recommended by Armstrong & Overton (1977), early respondents were compared with late respondents on the variables in the study. The results showed that there were only two items with p less than 0.05 level of significance. Therefore, with the exception of the two items in the order release quantities construct, there was no difference in the opinion between the early and late respondents, suggesting that the response bias was not a problem.

4 Results

In the light of the problems with LSQ measures that were specific to one single organization that were highlighted in section 3.1, as expected some respondents had difficulties in filling in part of the questionnaire. As a result, the responses generated 15.83 percent of incomplete data. Order quality, order release quantities, and order accuracy constructs were the constructs that were largely affected. Most respondents who were using TPL providers for outbound logistics only or using specific types of logistics services indicated that those constructs' measures were not applicable. Enders (2001) states that missing data is a common problem in applied research settings. McArdle (1994) emphasizes that although the term missing data typically represents an image of negative consequences and problems; such missingness can provide a wealth of information in its own right and, indeed, often serves as a useful part of the analyses. Researchers who have attempted to deal with incomplete data have used various approaches such as listwise deletion, pairwise deletion and imputation. However, the modern approaches such as multiple imputation and maximum-likelihood methods are proven to produce unbiased estimates of the population values, thus improving both the accuracy and often the statistical power of results. AMOS 5.0, which is used in this study, represents a direct approach that is based on maximum likelihood (ML) estimation (Byrne, 2001; Arbuckle, 1996). Byrne (2001) demonstrated that despite 25 percent data loss in a sample, the overall χ^2 and the goodness-of-fit statistics such as RMSEA and CFI are relatively close. These findings provide strong evidence for the effectiveness of the direct ML approach in addressing the problem of missing data values.

The strength lies in the consistency and efficiency of ML estimates when the unobserved values are Missing Completely At Random (MCAR), provides unbiased estimates when the unobserved values are Missing At Random (MAR) and ML estimates provide the least bias when the missing values are Non-ignorable Missing At Random (NMAR) (Byrne, 2001; Enders, 2001). However as noted earlier, the missingness of data in this study was because certain measures simply did not apply to particular respondents. Therefore, literally there are no missing data in this problem. As according to Schafer & Graham (2002), if responses to these measures were available from some other respondents, the observations may denote responses for those who claimed that the measures were applicable and the missing ones represents hypothetical responses for those who think that the measures were not applicable. Thus, the hypothetical missing data could be regarded as MAR. They argued that researchers do not have to worry whether the missingness depends on the characteristics of those who think the measures as not applicable, but the missing values are introduced merely as a mathematical device to simplify the computations. Based on this argument, the incomplete data in this study would be regarded as MAR, therefore, ML method appears to yield an accurate assessment of model fit especially when normality assumptions are met (Enders, 2001).

4.1 Measurement Model Evaluation

Confirmatory Factor Analysis (CFA) was conducted on the indicators measuring the nine constructs in the LSQ model in order to examine the scales' psychometric properties more closely. The analyses conceptualized LSQ as a second-order construct comprised of information quality, ordering procedures, order quality, order condition, order accuracy, order discrepancy handling, personnel contact quality, order release quantities and timeliness. A second order factor model is one with one or more latent constructs whose indicators are also latent. Table 3 reports the results of the measurement model of this study. The unidimensionality, reliability, convergent and discriminant validity were then assessed.

Unidimensionality refers to the existence of a single construct underlying a set of measures (Gerbing & Anderson, 1988). It is important to ensure that a set of items forming the instrument measures one thing in common. Unidimensionality is considered as the most critical and basic assumption of measurement theory and should be assessed for all multiple-indicator constructs before assessing their reliability (e.g. Hair et al., 1998). Loadings on all 32 items range from 0.518 to 0.969 underlining the unidimensionality of all constructs. Anderson & Gerbing (1982) suggest that unidimensionality using the confirmatory analysis reflects internal and external consistency. In evaluating the overall model fit, the same fit indices as in Mentzer et al. (1999) were used so as to compare the differences clearly. Thus, Normed Fit Index (NFI), Comparative Fit Index (CFI), and Root Mean Square Error of Approximation (RMSEA) were used to analyze and compare the results. The Bentler-Bonett (1980) normed fit index (NFI) evaluates the estimated model by comparing the χ^2 value of the model to the χ^2 value of the independence model. It has the tendency to underestimate fit in small samples, thus Bentler (1990) revised the NFI to take sample size into account and proposed the Comparative Fit Index (CFI). CFI assesses fit relative to other models and employs the noncentral χ^2 distribution with the noncentrality parameters. He found that using the ML method, CFI had no systematic bias when the sample size was small. High values (greater than .90) are indicative of a good-fitting model for both NFI and CFI (Bentler, 1990). However, he suggests that the CFI should be the index of choice. Loehlin (1998) proposed that the value of CFI of less than 0.9, but close to 0.9 is also appealing. RMSEA estimates the lack of fit in a model compared to a perfect (saturated) model (Browne & Cudeck, 1993) and is relatively insensitive to sample size (Loehlin, 1998). Browne & Cudeck (1993) suggest that a value of RMSEA below 0.05 indicates close fit and that value up to

0.08 are reasonable or less indicates a reasonable error of approximation. Thus, the LSQ model fitted the data reasonably well in this study with a chi-square of 868.318 (df = 455, p < 0.001), χ/df <2, RMSEA = 0.071, CFI = 0.910 and NFI = 0.83. It is important to note that the low value of NFI is likely to have been influenced by sample size (e.g. Bollen, 1986), thus it is not a good indicator for evaluating model fit when N is small (Hu & Bentler, 1995). A better measure, TLI, which is less affected by sample size, (e.g. Hu & Bentler, 1999) demonstrated an adequate fit, as the TLI value is .895 (close to 0.9).

Constructs	Alpha LSQ US	Alpha LSQ UK	*Composite Reliability	*Average Variance Extracted
Information Quality (IQ)	-na-	0.9586	0.9604	0.8293
Ordering procedures (OP)	-na-	0.9575	0.9636	0.8161
Order Release Quantities (ORQ)	0.7328	0.8149	0.8184	0.6020
Timeliness (TI)	0.7956	0.8488	0.8743	0.7008
Order Accuracy (OA)	0.8232	0.8743	0.8856	0.7245
Order Quality (OQ)	0.7611	0.6914	0.7257	0.4756
Order Condition (OC)	0.8245	0.8695	0.8774	0.7070
Order Discrepancy Handling (ODH)	0.8851	0.9167	0.9212	0.7965
Personnel Contact Quality (PCQ)	0.8902	0.8876	0.8918	0.7339

	Chi-square	Degrees of freedom	RMSEA	CFI	NFI	TLI
LSQ US	329.452	266 (p = 0.00484)	0.0316	0.977	0.893	na
LSQ UK	804.315	428 (p < 0.001)	0.070	0.918	0.842	0.898

* Composite reliability, average variance extracted and R-squared were not available in Mentzer et al. (1999) for comparison

Table 3: The Measurement Model

In evaluating the components of the measurement model, none of the items could be deleted because the entire original LSQ constructs (Mentzer et al., 1999) had only three items. Also, none of the measures of information quality and ordering procedures needed deletion because the results showed that all measures were excellent. Baumgartner & Homburg (1996) recommend that a latent variable should be assessed with a minimum of three or four indicators each because having two measures per factor might be problematic (Bentler & Chou, 1987), and with one measurement would ignore the unreliability of measurement. The second order factor loading values of LSQ in Table 4 were better except for order release quantities and order quality, which loaded quite weakly on LSQ (0.380 in each item). As mentioned earlier, these were the two constructs that were largely affected by those customers who claimed that the measures were not applicable, i.e. most respondents using TPL provider for outbound logistics only. Owing to the fact that LSQ was originally developed specifically for inbound logistics, the constructs that loaded weakly on LSQ could be affected by the proportion of outbound logistics respondents. Consistent with Mentzer et al. (1999), the other seven constructs loaded quite well on LSQ. Consequently, LSQ served well as a second-order construct.

	IQ	OP	ORQ	TI	OA	OQ	OC	ODH	PCQ
LSQ US	0.516	0.626	0.551	0.610	0.612	0.671	0.537	0.703	0.621
LSQ UK	0.852	0.836	0.380	0.747	0.615	0.380	0.695	0.765	0.766

Table 4: Second-Order Factor Loadings of LSQ

4.2 Reliability and Validity

Unidimensionality alone is not sufficient to ensure the usefulness of the scale. According to the scale development paradigm as in Gerbing & Anderson (1988), the reliability of the composite score should be assessed after the unidimensionality has been acceptably established. All Cronbach alpha values exceeded .70 except for order quality, which was 0.69, indicating an acceptable reliability levels. Second, as can be derived from the confirmatory factor results, all composite reliability measures were also above 0.7, exceeding the minimum values of .60 (Bagozzi & Yi, 1988). Composite reliability is superior to Cronbach alpha due to several limitations associated with it such as the tendency to underestimate scale reliability and assuming that all items have equal reliabilities (e.g.. Fornell & Lacker, 1981).

Convergent validity was supported as all loadings were highly statistically significant ($p < .01$) and that the squared multiple correlation (R^2) were larger than 0.50 except for IQ1, which is 0.268. R^2 is the percent variance explained in each endogenous variable in the scale (Dunn et al., 1994). Discriminant validity for a construct's measure was indicated by average variance extracted estimates of .50 or higher (Fornell & Larcker, 1981). The results demonstrated that all constructs exceeded the estimates of .50 except for order quality, which was .47. It implies that the variance accounted for by each construct was greater than the variance accounted for by the measurement error (Hair et al., 1998). The intercorrelations among the factors were all less than .743 suggesting all nine factors demonstrated discriminant validity. A correlation between two factors that is very close to one or minus one indicates poor discriminant validity.

Predictive validity was also tested by correlating LSQ to customer satisfaction construct. Measures of customer satisfaction developed by Mentzer et al. (2001) were used. Previous studies (e.g. Mentzer et al., 2001; Bienstock et al., 1997) have demonstrated that there is a link between LSQ and customer satisfaction. A high correlation value of .79 was obtained, which showed a strong support for the test of predictive validity.

5   Discussion

Lindsay & Ehrenberg (1993) argue that, when assessing the status of replication, it is essential to consider whether differences between the two studies are expected to prompt different results. With a "close replication", the differences are not expected to prompt different results; with a "differentiated replication", the differences are expected to influence the data in a different way than the original. When differentiated replication produces similar results, this is stronger evidence of theory generalisability because, despite important differences between the studies, the same results emerge. As the intent of this study was to make comparisons in a different operational and cultural context, it was necessary to keep the scales identical in both studies in the first attempt at replication (Lindsay & Ehrenberg, 1993) of LSQ. Consistent with Mentzer et al. (1999), by improving the two two-item' constructs and using exactly the same seven out of nine LSQ measures, the results provide a strong support for LSQ scale as a valid and reliable scale across industrial sector in the UK. The composite reliabilities of the seven constructs range from .72 to .92, exceeding 0.70 cutoff levels and both improved constructs were .96 each. Although, there was a slight problem with the order quality construct where Cronbach alpha, average variance extracted and R^2 were slightly lower than the acceptable levels (.69, .47 and .268), it is argued that it is reliable and valid in this study as the composite reliability demonstrated is at an acceptable level of .72. In an extension study that conceptualized LSQ as a process of nine interrelated quality constructs, Mentzer et al. (2001) found that order quality was the only construct with composite reliability below .79. It could be concluded that the results in both studies were consistent. The results provide evidence that LSQ can be regarded as an excellent scale for measuring logistics service quality in both studies. This could be the outcome of using a 7-point Likert scale as compared to a 5-point Likert scale in the original study as the reliability of a scale increases with an increase in the number of response categories (Churchill & Peter, 1984).

It is well known that the SEM is a large-sample technique. Bentler & Chou (1987) suggested that under normal distribution theory, the ratio of sample size to number of free parameters should be at least 5:1 to get trustworthy parameter estimates and in order to get appropriate significance tests although a ratio of 10:1 would be preferred. In a review of studies between 1975 and 1994 in a marketing and consumer context, Baumgartner & Homburg (1996) found that the median ratio of sample size to number of free parameters was about 6:1, while 86 percent of the models had a ratio of less than 10:1. While this study had a ratio of 5.71:1, it is considered reasonable as it is within the range of previous studies.

Goodness of fit tests determine whether the model being tested should be accepted or rejected. Although sample size has to be large for the parameter estimates and test statistics to be valid, based on the three indices CFI, TLI/NNFI and RMSEA that least affected by sample size (Fan et al., 1999), LSQ scale appears to fit the data reasonably well in this study. Moreover, all other things being equal, a model with fewer indicators per factor will have a higher apparent fit than a model with more indicators per factor. Thus, if only three items that demonstrated the highest loading in information quality and ordering procedures are employed, the goodness-of-fit measures tend to be better (CFI increases from .910 to .941; NFI from .830 to .871; TLI from .895 to .922 and RMSEA from .071 to .062).

Based on the above discussion, by overcoming several limitations of LSQ scale as highlighted in Mentzer et al. (1999), we concluded that LSQ is a robust, valid and reliable scale in the context of this study.

6 Conclusion

This study illustrates the use of confirmatory factor analysis (CFA) in testing the LSQ scale. CFA allows the estimation of reliability of the LSQ individual items, constructs and the overall instrument. It demonstrated the applicability and generalizability of the LSQ scale to a sample of TPL providers' customers in the UK. Although this study generated 15.83 percent of missing data, full information maximum likelihood (FIML) method estimation in AMOS 5.0 program made it possible to make full use of the incomplete data. Thus, evidence supports that the model adequately fits the data.

Although the results suggest that the LSQ scale is generalizable across the sample in this study, in reality, several measures especially those associated with technical quality of the scale such as order quality, order release quantities, order accuracy seemed to be developed specific to the inbound logistics operations and may not be appropriate to outbound logistics. The diversity of logistics operation across different industries has also caused some technical quality measures not to be fully generalized. This was due to the tendency of TPL providers to customize their services to specific industries/customers. Other dimensions, especially functional quality measures, personnel contact quality, ordering procedures, order discrepancy handling and information quality could be regarded as excellent for measuring logistics service quality. Further investigation of the generalizability of LSQ by using the CFA warrants a discussion. Future research should examine closely the logistics operations of the industry involved, the inbound and outbound logistics and the type of logistics services used by the customers. Also, the development of measures for outbound logistics appears worthy of research consideration as outbound logistics constitute higher proportion as compared to inbound logistics.

In using the CFA as the method of analysis, it is important to interpret the CFA results with caution. This is because the criteria for judging goodness-of-fit are relative rather than absolute and there are no standard cutoff values for evaluating model-data fit. A good fit does not mean each particular part of the model fits well. Many equivalent and alternative models may yield as good a fit, that is fit indexes rule out bad models but do not prove good models.

Finally, the validation of the instrument allows the managers to have a better understanding and use the instrument with confidence in assessing the service quality provided by TPL service providers.

7 References

Anderson, J. C., Gerbing, D. W. (1982): Some Methods for Respecifying Measurement Models to Obtain Unidimensional Construct Measurement, in: Journal of Marketing Research, 19: 453-460.

Anonymous (1999): UK Top on Outsourcing, in: Supply Management, 4(14): 13.

Arbuckle, J. L. (1996): Full Information Estimation in the Presence of Incomplete Data, in: Marcoulides, G. A. and Schumacker, R. E. (Eds): Advanced Structural Equation Modeling, Mahwah, NJ: p. 243-277.

Armstrong, J., Overton, T. (1977): Estimating Non-response Bias in Mail Surveys, in: Journal of Marketing Research, 14: 396-402.

Bagozzi, R. P., Yi, Y. (1988): On the Evaluation of Structural Equation Models, in: Journal of Academy of Marketing Science, 16 (Spring): 7-94.

Baumgartner, H., Homburg, C. (1996): Applications of Structural Equation Modeling in Marketing and Consumer Research: A Review, in: International Journal of Research in Marketing, 13: 139-161.

Bentler, P. M. (1990): Comparative Fit Indexes in Structural Models, in: Psychological Bulletin, 107: 238-246.

Bentler, P. M., Bonett, D. G. (1980): Significance Tests and Goodness-of-Fit in the Analysis of Covariance Structures, in: Psychological Bulletin, 88: 588-606.

Bentler, P. M., Chou, C. P. (1987): Practical Issues in Structural Modeling, in: Sociological Methods & Research, 16: 78-117.

Bienstock, C. C., Mentzer, J. T., Bird, M. M. (1997): Measuring Physical Distribution Service Quality, in: Journal of Academy of Marketing Science, 25(1), 31-44.

Bollen, K. A. (1986): Sample size and Bentler and Bonett's Non-normed Fit Index, in Psychometrika, 51: 375-377.

Browne, B. M., Cudeck, R. (1993): Alternative Ways of Assessing Model Fit, in: Bollen, K. S., Long, J. S. (eds): Testing Structural Models, Sage Publications, Newbury Park.

Byrne, B. M. (2001): Structural Equation Modeling with AMOS – Basic Concepts, Applications and Programming, Lawrence Erlbaum Associates, Inc., Publishers, New Jersey.

Churchill, G. A., Peter, J. P. (1984): Research Design Effects on the Reliability of Rating Scales: A Meta Analysis, in: Journal of Marketing Research, 21(November): 360-75.

Dabholkar, P. A. (1994): Incorporating Choice into an Attitudinal Framework: Analysing Models of Mental Comparison Processes, in: Journal of Consumer Research, 21 (June): 100-118.

Dillman, D. A. (2000): Mail and Internet Surveys – The Tailored Design Method, John Wiley, New York.

Dunn, S. C., Seaker, R. F., Waller, M. A. (1994): Latent Variables in Business Logistics Research, in: Journal of Business Logistics, 15(2), 145-172.

Enders, C. K. (2001): The Impact of Nonnormality on Full Information Maximum-Likelihood Estimation for Structural Equation Models with Missing Data, in: Psychological Methods, 16(4), 352-370.

Fan, X., Thompson, B., Wang, L., (1999): Effects of Sample Size, Estimation Methods, and Model Specification on Structural Equation Modeling Fit Indexes, in: Structural Equation Modeling, 6(1), 56-83.

Fornell, C., Larcker, D. F. (1981): Evaluating Structural Equation Models with Unobservable Variables and Measurement Error, in: Journal of Marketing Research, 18(3), 39-50.

Gerbing, D. W., Anderson, J. C. (1988): An Updated Paradigm for Scale Development Incorporating Unidimensionality and Its Assessment, in: Journal of Marketing Research, 25(May), 186-192.

Hair, J. F., Rolph, E. A., Ronald, L. T., William, C. B. (1998): Multivariate Data Analysis, Prentice Hall, Upper Saddle River, NJ.

Hu, L. T., Bentler, P. M. (1995): Evaluating Model Fit, in Hoyle, R.H. (Ed): Structural Equation Modeling: Concepts, Issues and Applications, Sage, Thousand Oaks, CA: 76-99.

Hu, L. T., Bentler, P. M. (1999): Cutoff Criteria for Fit Indexes in Covariance Structure Analysis: Conventional Criteria versus New Alternatives, in: Structural Equation Modeling, 6(1), 1-55.

Hubbard, R., Vetter, D. E. (1996): An Empirical Comparison of Published Replication Research in Accounting, Economics, Finance, Management and Marketing, in: Journal of Business Research, 35: 153-164.

Joreskog, K. G. (1974): Analyzing Psychological Data by Structural Analysis of Covariance Matrices, in: Atkinson, R.C., Krantz, D.H., Luce, R.D., and Suppes, P. (Eds): Contemporary Development in Mathematical Psychology II, Freeman, San Francisco: p. 1-54.

Keller, S. B., Savitskie, K, Stank, T. P., Lynch, D. F., Ellinger, A. E. (2002): A Summary and Analysis of Multi-Item Scales Used in Logistics Research, in: Journal of Business Logistics: 23(2), 83-270.

Lindsay, R. M., Ehrenberg, A. S. C. (1993): The Design of Replicated Studies, in: The American Statistician, 47 (August), 217-228.

Loehlin, J. C. (1998): Latent Variables Models: An Introduction to Factor, Path and Structural Analysis, Lawrence Erlbaum Associates, 3rd Ed. Mahwah, NJ.

Malhotra, N. K. (1998): Marketing Research: An Applied Orientation, Prentice Hall, Upper Saddle River, New Jersey.

McArdle, J. J. (1994): Structural Factor Analysis Experiments with Incomplete Data, in: Multivariate Behavioral Research, 29: 409-454.

Mentzer, J. T., Flint, D. J., Kent, J. L. (1999): Developing A Logistics Service Quality Scale, in: Journal of Business Logistics, 20(1), 9-32.

Mentzer, J. T., Flint, D. J. (1997): Validity in Logistics Research, in: Journal of Business Logistics, 18(1), 199-216.

Mentzer, J. T., Flint, D. J., Hult, T. M. (2001): Logistics Service Quality as a Segment-Customised Process, in: Journal of Marketing, 65 (October), 82-104.

Mohr, J., Spekman, R. (1994): Characteristics of Partnership Success: Partnership Attributes, Communication Behavior and Conflict Resolution, in: Strategic Management Journal, 15: 135-152.

Schafer, J. L., Graham, J. W. (2002): Missing Data: Our View of the State of the Art, in: Psychological Methods, 7(2), 147-177.

Thacker, J. W., Fields, M. W., Tetrick, L.E., (1989): The Factor Structure of Union Commitment: An Application of Confirmatory Factor Analysis, in: Journal of Applied Psychology, 74(April): 228-232.

Third Party Logistics in Thailand – From the Users' Perspective

Pornpen Setthakaset, Chuda Basnet

1	Introduction	204
2	Literature Review	205
3	Research Question and Methodology	208
4	Findings and Discussion	210
5	Conclusion	216
6	References	216

Summary:
The practice of outsourcing logistics services is spreading with the increase in globalization and the increasing emphasis on core competence. This so-called third party logistics (3PL) includes various logistics services such as transportation, inventory management, distribution, warehousing services, customs and kitting. Previous studies have shown widespread adoption of 3PL in the USA and Western Europe. The goal of this paper is to explore 3PL in a developing country, Thailand, particularly from a user's perspective. A survey of 3PL users was conducted in Thailand. Results show that 3PL is gaining acceptance in Thailand, and that users are generally satisfied with the service.

Keywords:
Outsourcing, Logistics Services, Third Party Logistics, Survey

1 Introduction

The concept of supply chain management encompasses holistic integration of multiple upstream and downstream processes in the provision of goods and services. While the terms "supply chain management" and "logistics management" are often used interchangeably, the latter is generally understood to have a narrower focus – the internal integration of processes within a firm. Logistics management has significant impacts on the costs and customer satisfaction of manufacturing firms. It may even give an organization competitive advantages in the market. Third party logistics (3PL) is the employment of outside companies whose expertise is in the logistics area of handling a firm's logistical processes. With the increasing emphasis on downsizing and outsourcing in today's global economy, 3PL is being embraced by many firms. These outside companies are called 3PL providers. By outsourcing logistics functions to 3PL providers, companies can focus on their core activities and leave logistics functions to 3PL providers to manage.

There are several advantages cited for companies using 3PL. First, 3PL enables user firms to gain competitive advantages (Daugherty et al., 1995). Second, 3PL providers have the expertise to do their job more effectively (Troyer et al., 1995; Richardson, 1993; Byrne, 1993; Dillon, 1989). Third, 3PL providers have better processes and resources to handle operations (Byrne, 1993; Richardson, 1990; Bask, 2001). Lastly, 3PL can assist user firms to save on their logistics costs (Kasilingam, 1998).

3PL has been widely used in the USA, European countries and Australia (Lie 1992; Lieb et al., 1993; Millen et al., 1997). Recently, 3PL has begun spreading to some Asian countries that have, gradually, been shifting to an industrialized and manufacturing based economy in recent decades. The increase in international trade in these countries has led to an increase in demand for logistics services. Thailand is one of the new industrial developing countries (NIC) and is one of the five "tigers" of the Southeast Asia region. Also, the export potential in Thailand is strong and will continue to grow in the future. Therefore, the 3PL industry is expected to play a significant role in this developing country. Nevertheless, there is not much research that has been conducted about 3PL in the Southeast Asia region. The aim of this paper is to investigate 3PL in Thailand, particularly from the users' perspective. The research reported in this paper seeks to determine the extent of the use of 3PL in Thailand, and to evaluate the performance of Thai 3PL in terms of their service quality.

To answer these research questions, a survey of Thai businesses was conducted by distributing questionnaires. We report on the results of this survey, and begin with a review of the relevant literature in the next section. Section 3 presents the research question and the methodology. In Section 4 we discuss the findings of the research. Finally, Section 5 presents concluding remarks.

2 Literature Review

Lieb (1992) defines 3PL as involving "...the use of external companies to perform logistics functions that have traditionally been performed within an organization. The functions performed by the third party can encompass the entire logistics process or selected activities within that process." 3PL providers add value to their customers by providing services that range from transportation activities to integrated warehousing, distribution, forwarding, packaging, customs handling, kitting, and information management activities. As the adoption of outsourcing of logistics functions has increased, so has the research on this phenomenon.

2.1 Reasons for Outsourcing Logistics Activities

Many researchers have explored the reasons for the growth in 3PL. Due to expansion of global markets, each firm has to develop and provide better products and services while reducing operating costs to allow them to gain competitive advantage. Most authors appear to agree that the main driving force behind outsourcing is the globalization of business (Byrne, 1993).

Another frequently cited reason for the growth in 3PL is the increasing focus on core competencies, and the consequent outsourcing of all none-core services to outside partners (Troyer & Cooper, 1995). 3PL providers have the ability to provide their clients with expertise and experience that would be difficult to acquire, or costly to have in-house (Byrne, 1993; Dillon, 1989). According to Richardson (1993), expertise gained from working with other clients allows user firms to benchmark against other companies and may lead to opportunities to lower costs and improve customer service.

Often the 3PL providers have not only the expertise but also the requisite resources to handle logistics operations for their clients. Most 3PL providers have better processes and knowledge in their core areas compared to their user firms. As a result, providers can deliver a high quality operation including maintaining and developing their systems. They have the ability to adapt quickly to business forces and/or changes, which leads to faster delivery and less damage (Byrne, 1993).

A major benefit of 3PL is the cost savings provided by them. Kasilingam (1998) clarifies some reasons why outsourcers can operate some functions cheaper than in-house operation. 3PL providers can combine business from several companies and offer frequent pick ups and deliveries. Moreover, companies are able to reduce capital investment in facilities and equipment. Survey research conducted by Lieb et al. (1993) reported that some current users have logistics costs up to 30 - 40 percent lower than previously.

3PL is even seen as contributing to competitive advantage, adding more value to products, enhancing customer services, and assisting to access new markets (Daugherty & Pittman, 1995).

2.2 Selection of 3PL Providers

Another avenue of research in this field has been the selection of 3PL providers by the user firms. Research conducted by Lieb et al. (1993) shows that reputation, experience and price are considered the most important factors in the selection process. Therefore, he suggests that user firms need to trade off between service and cost. If companies want to employ 3PL providers having a high reputation and quality, they should prepare for high costs. Byrne (1993) revealed that reputation is on the top of participants' lists of third party selection factors. Byrne (1993) also adds compatibility in approach, attitude and culture, financial strength, flexibility, and customer references.

Harrington (2000) and Bradley (1994b) found that reputation and business expertise were the second factors in their study. The pricing factor was the first determinant for participants to pick a 3PL provider. Other factors that have been mentioned by Harrington (2000) and Bradley (1994c) in selecting 3PL providers are cost/inventory savings, product/business expertise, and technological capability. Sink et al. (1996) noted that credibility and trust were the imperatives in the selection of third party providers.

2.3 Critical Success Factors of 3PL

What are the factors that need to be considered during and after the implementation of the outsourcing process? This question has concerned quite a few investigators. Boyson et al. (1999) surveyed logistics professionals to investigate how companies plan and operate 3PL relationships. They concluded that, in the opinion of the professionals, the prerequisites for a successful 3PL operation are: non-biased identification of 3PL providers, evaluation of costs and improvements, sound contracts, centralized control, and proper monitoring of the 3PL operations.

Bowman (1995) has stressed the importance of communication and coordination between logistics users and providers. Richardson (1990) and Maltz (1995) agree on the importance of educating management on the benefits of contract logistics, which is one factor that helps outsourcing be successful. Management needs to be convinced of the necessity of outsourcing and view it as a strategic activity. Companies need to select third party logistics providers wisely and maintain control while building trust and respect (Richardson, 1994). Trust is fundamental in long term relationships. Mutual trust is a crucial aspect of successful outsourcing because users have to give enough relevant information to enable the service provider to reduce total logistics costs (Bowman, 1995). Additionally, McKeon

(1991) stressed the importance of understanding each other's cultures and organizational structure.

2.4 Impacts of the Use of 3PL Providers on User Firms

Many researchers agree that outsourcing has had strong positive impacts on costs, system performance, response time, enhanced flexibility, and customer satisfaction (Sohail & Sohal., 2003; Lieb, 1992; Bhatnagar et al., 1999). Also, the use of outsourcing has a high positive impact on employee morale. Researchers have also cited some reasons that discourage the use of 3PL. Lieb & Randall (1996) conducted research into the risk of using 3PL services. Survey respondents identified three common concerns about the use of 3PL providers. First, they are afraid of losing control to service providers (Bowman, 1995; Byrne, 1993). Second, management often lacks confidence to use a 3PL firm to deliver products or services to their customers. There is uncertainty about whether third party capabilities are adequate to meet user's expectations. Third, they question the true costs of using third party providers. Other concerns are: 3PL providers do not meet their customers' expectations (Lieb et al., 1996), lack of advanced technology (Byrne, 1993), unreliable promises of providers, inability to respond to changing requirements, and lack of understanding of buyers' business goals (Bradley, 1995).

2.5 Measurement of Logistics Service

Beamon (1999) presented a framework for measuring performance of a supply chain that included measures of resource usage, supply chain outcomes, and flexibility. However, this framework was geared not particularly towards logistics service measurement, but towards general supply chain performance. Lai et al. (2002) devised a construct for measuring transport logistics performance, which included service effectiveness measures for the shippers and the consignees as well as performance efficiency measures for the transport providers. The first two service measures were derived from the reliability and responsibility dimensions of the SERVQUAL instrument of Parasuraman et al. (1988). These two dimensions can be used to measure 3PL services. However, the measures in Lai et al. (2002) are concerned with perceptions of the service, rather than with the expectation-perception gap as suggested in Parasuraman et al. (1988). Whereas Parasuraman et al. (1988) measure the expectation-perception gap on predefined attributes of service, Mentzer et al. (1997) advocate starting from the logistics service values desired by the logistics customers and identifying the logistics service attributes directly through the customers.

2.6 Regional Studies of the 3PL Industry

Many authors have investigated the use of 3PL services in particular regions around the world and made comparisons across the regions. Lieb (1992) studied the use of 3PL services in the USA. Respondents in this research were asked to indicate the level of satisfaction they felt with 3PL's performance, and generally reported positive experiences. He concluded that third party participation in this region had been accepted because many manufacturers are increasingly focusing on reducing logistics costs, fostering productivity increases and improving service quality. Lieb et al. (1993) have compared practices and experiences of long term users of third party logistics services across the USA and Western Europe. Results showed that European manufacturers are more committed to the use of third party providers than their counterparts in the US. There are three main differences between the continents. First, European manufacturers use 3PL for both domestic and international transactions. Second, European companies allocate more of their total logistics budget to these firms and use more services than large US manufacturers. Third, European manufacturers will make long-term contracts with the third party which improves the working relationship. Dapiran et al. (1996) researched 3PL usage by large Australian firms. Millen et al. (1997) compared Australian 3PL usage against American and Western European practices. Randall (1991) reported on 3PL in Europe.

Researchers have also examined the use of 3PL in developing countries. Goh & Pinaikul (1998) reported on the general state of affairs regarding logistics management in Thailand. They reported deficiencies in information systems, road infrastructure, and logistics expertise. Similarly, Kim (1996) has reported on logistics management in Korea. Sohail & Sohal (2003) conducted an empirical research study about the usage of 3PL providers in Malaysia. Results indicated that logistics service providers play an important role in Malaysian industry. It shows that many Malaysian firms are utilizing the services of contract logistics providers, and have been doing so for quite a few years. These companies do not rely solely on one contract logistics provider. However, they prefer to use many logistics providers to enhance their services. Bhatnagar et al. (1999) conducted similar research on Singapore firms. They found that Singapore companies are satisfied with 3PL providers' performance and believe that 3PL have been a positive development within their organizations. Major benefits realized by user firms were cost reductions and improved quality of service.

3 Research Question and Methodology

The review of literature above shows that logistics management currently plays a significant role in many industries. The 3PL industry has been widely researched in the USA, Europe and Australia, and it has been found that they flourish in these environments. The authors note that European countries are leaders in the 3PL industry because they were early users of 3PL services. Further, 3PL is spreading to countries in Asia. After the economic crisis in the late 1990s, many Asian countries such as Singapore, Malaysia and Thailand have gradually transformed into an industrialized, manufacturing based economy. Many firms are employing new logistics techniques to improve their productivity and performance. Thus, logistics operations have started to play an important role in this region. However, there are few researchers whose research is specifically focused on logistics in Southeast Asia. There is scant research examining particularly the experience of logistics user firms toward 3PL. This paper reports on a research aiming to fill this gap. The objectives of the research reported in this paper were:

- To examine the significance of the role played by 3PL in Thai manufacturing.
- To evaluate the performance of Thai 3PL in term of service quality.
- To investigate the impact of 3PL in Thai manufacturing operations.
- To examine prospects of 3PL in a Thai organizational context.

These questions are of an exploratory nature, intending to elicit generalizations that would apply to the population in question – Thai business organizations. There are two potential methodologies that could be adopted for this study. These are: survey research and case study research. Survey research methodology involves the collection of information from a large group of entities by selecting a sample from the target population. Data is collected by using questionnaires and interviews. The case study methodology allows researchers to investigate contemporary phenomenon within a real-life context, focusing on understanding the dynamics present within a single setting and gaining more insight into the unique situation based on a particular context. Both methods have their distinct characteristics and research purposes. However, a survey methodology appears more suitable than the case study methodology in answering the above research questions. Case study methodology was not deemed appropriate because this research did not seek to understand the dynamics present in particular contexts. Instead, this research sought to examine the overall picture of 3PL in Thailand. Thus, every Thai firm should have had a chance to participate. Survey methodology is also more appropriate since the topic matter being investigated is not strictly behavioral and therefore cannot/need not be observed.

For these reasons, a survey methodology was followed in this study. The list of respondents was drawn from the Stock Exchange of Thailand. These listed firms are indicative of the most progressive firms in Thailand, and have their headquarters located in Bangkok. The "nth" (every 3rd) name sampling technique was used for random selection. The survey questionnaires were sent by mail to respondent firms. The questions contained within were based on the above research questions and focused directly on the topic specified in this research. The respondents were required to indicate their level of agreement with a particular statement using 5-point Likert scales. Furthermore, open-ended questions were also provided in order to allow managers to express their thoughts. The questionnaires were designed in English, but were translated into Thai for Thai organizations. Reminder postcards were sent to non-respondents as a follow-up to the first questionnaires. Out of a total of 200 firms, 52 (26%) questionnaires were returned, but only 48 (24%) questionnaires were usable.

The responding firms were in various lines of business as follows:

Lines of Business	Count	Percentage
Packaging Manufacturing	4	8.3
Textiles	6	12.5
Chemicals	2	4.2
Agribusiness	7	14.6
Food & Beverage	4	8.3
Electrical Product	3	6.3
Import-Export	7	14.6
Others (e.g. Pulp & Paper business, automotive products, retail store)	14	29.2

Table 1: The Characteristics of the Responding Firms

These responding firms reported annual sales ranging from $20 million to more than $80 billion, with over 39.5% having revenues of at least $10 billion.

4 Findings and Discussion

4.1 The Role of 3PL in Thai Manufacturing

Third party logistics have started to play a significant role in Thai organizations as a whole. Among our respondents, the number of current users is 54.2%, while 45.8% are non-user firms. These figures indicate that many companies have realized the importance of employing third party logistics providers and using them in a strategy to gain competitive advantage. Of those firms currently outsourcing logistics functions, 80.8% indicated that their firms have been using third party logistics for more than 2 years. This represents a significant amount of experience with third party logistics among Thai companies.

Most of the respondents (70.8%) indicated that they employ only 1-3 providers. Twenty-five percent employ 4-6 providers and only 4.2% employ more than 6 providers. It appears that many companies employ a small number of logistics providers because they want to have a close relationship with their logistics providers. As Goh & Pinaikul (1998) mentioned, Thai firms are more concerned with having a close relationship with their suppliers, which enables them to have a good understanding of organizational structure, better communication, information sharing, and reduction of logistics costs. This result differs from the result of Sohail & Sohal (2003), who found that Malaysian companies do not rely on one or two logistics providers. They appear to prefer employing many logistics providers to enhance their services.

To determine why user companies employed third party logistics providers, respondents were asked to identify their reasons for outsourcing logistics functions. Table 2 presents the reasons given for contracting out logistics functions. Respondents rated the methods using a 5-point Likert scale from strongly disagree (1) to strongly agree (5). The combined percentages of respondents who agreed or strongly agreed with the reasons are shown in the table.

The most important strategic reasons for user firms to be interested in outsourcing their logistics activities are obtaining competitive advantages, and receiving customized services. Gaining the use of sophisticated technology and using the expertise of third party logistics providers are other strong reasons why companies outsource logistics functions. Unlike previous studies, the ability to focus on core activities is not very high on the list. Saving money (funding) is also not considered a prime reason. Globalization, another reason frequently cited in the literature, is not rated highly by our respondents.

Reasons for Employing 3PL	Agree / Strongly Agree
Gaining the competitive advantage	88%
Receiving customised service	85%
Gaining the use of sophisticated technology	85%
Using the expertise of a third party	81%
Ability to focus on your core activities.	81%
Coping with reductions in the resources (i.e. funding)	77%
Reducing inventory	73%
Becoming more active in international shipping	66%
Penetrating markets	58%

Table 2: Reasons for Contracting out Logistics Functions

4.2 Performance of Thai 3PL in Regard to Service Quality

The survey showed that firms used 3PL providers for a wide variety of logistics services. The majority of user firms buy multiple services from 3PL providers. The range of those services is shown in Table 3. Transportation is the most frequently outsourced logistics function at 56.8%. It is also the most frequently outsourced logistics function in the USA (Harrington, 2000). This was followed by packaging (18.2%), and warehousing operation (11.4%). The functions that are least outsourced include inventory management, information systems and other services (such as customs formalities).

Services	Count	Percentage
Transportation	25	56.8
Packaging	8	18.2
Warehousing Operations	5	11.4
Inventory Management	4	9.1
Information Systems	1	2.3
Others (customs formalities)	1	2.3

Table 3: Services Employed by 3PL Users

Natejumnong et al. (2002), in his study of Thai 3PL providers indicated that most outsourced logistics contracts focused on physical processes such as storage, materials handling, cycle counting, picking and packing, dispatching, customer delivery, and returns collection. Thai 3PL providers are able to offer many logistics services such as: warehousing, cargo handling, inventory management, relocating services, freight handling, etc. Bhatnagar et al. (1999) found that the activities contracted out most frequently by firms in neighboring Singapore were: shipment consolidation, order fulfillment, carrier selection, freight payment, and rate negotiation. However, in our study, transportation stands out as the primary service used by 3PL users, followed by packaging. Warehousing is a distant third service contracted out. This is perhaps indicative of the state of development of the Thai 3PL industry, where a few primary logistics services are popular, and more sophisticated and integrative services have yet to gain widespread acceptance.

In the follow-up question, respondents were asked to indicate the level of their satisfaction with the 3PL services (1 = strongly disagree; 5 = strongly agree). The result is presented in Table 4.

Service Attribute	Agree / Strongly Agree
Your 3PL providers are approachable and easy to contact	88%
When your 3PL providers promise to do something by a certain time, they do so.	85%
Your 3PL providers are flexible.	85%
You have a high level of satisfaction with the 3PL's services.	81%
Your 3PL providers provide a prompt service when your firm needs their help.	81%
Your 3PL providers have the required skills and knowledge to perform the service.	77%
You are satisfied with the quality of service for the money invested.	73%
Usage of third party logistics providers has a positive impact on your firm's development.	66%
You have high level of satisfaction with the 3PL's technology.	58%

Table 4: Satisfaction Ratings of 3PL Services

The result of the surveys demonstrated that respondents were satisfied with their logistics providers' services. As can be seen, more than 80% of the respondents agree that 3PL providers are easy to communicate with, do what they said they would do, and are flexible. Respondents appear satisfied with the services rendered by the 3PL providers. It shows that Thai 3PL providers provide good service quality to user firms. However, the level of satisfaction with the 3PL's technology was not very high (58%). Thus, Thai 3PL providers need to be concerned in this regard.

4.3 Impact of 3PL on Thai Manufacturing Firms Using 3PL

Respondents were asked to rate the impacts of outsourcing on their firm. The results are summarized in Table 5. It is apparent that user firms believe that 3PL does have a strong positive impact on their businesses.

Impact Attribute	Agree / Strongly Agree
It provides better delivery.	88%
Your firm has been able to focus on the core business.	77%
It has increased your firm's productivity and efficiency.	70%
It has improved your service quality level.	66%
It has given access to up date technology and special expertise from the 3PL.	66%
It has reduced logistics costs.	62%
It has enhanced your firms' flexibility.	62%
It has increased customer's satisfaction.	58%
Your firm can utilize the space better.	54%
It has improved internal logistics performance.	54%
Your firm has been able to offer new services	50%
It has given access to new markets.	43%
It has increased the number of employee lay-offs.	39%
Its capabilities are inadequate to meet customer's expectations.	27%
Your firm has lost profits to 3PL.	16%
Your firm has lost the direct control of logistics activities to 3PL.	15%

Table 5: Impact of 3PL on User Firms

Companies using 3PL services experience many benefits. The most significant impact appears to be that using 3PL enabled the respondents to achieve better delivery and to focus on their core business. The user firms also believed that using 3PL improved their productivity and efficiency, improved their service quality, gained access to up-to-date technology and enhanced their flexibility. Sixteen (50% agree, 12% strongly agree) of the 26 user firms indicated that 3PL helped them reduce their logistics costs. Respondents reported positive impacts with respect to improved customer satisfaction and internal logistics performance. Some Thai firms are also able to reduce the number of full time logistics employees by using 3PL providers.

Thai firms do not appear to be concerned about losing control of some aspects of their business to 3PL providers (42% disagree, 12% strongly disagree). This differs from the results of Lieb & Randall (1996), who mentioned that one of the common concerns about the use of 3PL is losing control to service providers. Only 16% believe that their company has lost profits on account of using 3PL services, so this does not appear to be a concern.

4.4 Acceptance of 3PL by Thai Organizations

As pointed out before, among our respondents, the number of current 3PL users is 54.2%, while 45.8% are non-user firms. This alone indicates substantial acceptance of 3PL among Thai firms.

User firms were asked to predict the trend of 3PL in the future. They believed that 3PL business will have high growth (57.7%), or moderate growth (34.6%), and slight or no growth (7.6%). Thus the user firms were optimistic about the growth of 3PL services in Thailand.

Among the 22 non-user respondents, 19 (86.4%) respondents are aware of 3PL, while only 3 of them have never heard of it. Almost half of non-user firms are big companies, which have annual sales of more than 1,000 million Baht. They indicated little interest in 3PL. Among the non-users, only 13.6% intend to use 3PL in the near future.

Thus our finding is that large companies do not generally employ 3PL. Many of these large companies do not employ 3PL because they are big enough to have their own logistics department (37% of the non-users), and apparently don't want to give up the control. Most companies who employ 3PL are medium to small companies. These firms apparently do not want to invest money in a logistics department, and would rather employ an outside company with expertise in logistics. This differs from the result of Natejumnong et al. (2002), who found that large companies had experience in utilizing 3PL.

4.5 Findings Summary

Although more than half of the respondents are current users, 3PL in Thailand is still far behind when compared with 3PL in the USA and European countries. Both these regions have been using 3PL for many years. 3PL in these two regions is in the maturity stage while 3PL in Thailand is in the emerging industry stage. 3PL has begun to take an important part in many businesses in Thailand within the last few years.

The most frequent services employed by the respondents are transportation, packaging and warehousing operations. Inventory management and information systems are the least popular services for Thai firms. We found that 3PL providers in Thailand have provided good services to customers, with the majority of respondents being satisfied with the services they received.

Furthermore, current users accepted that 3PL allows them to gain many benefits and believe that 3PL has more positive impacts than negative. With a high level of satisfaction, a large number of user firms are likely to increase the use of 3PL in the near future. In our judgment, 3PL has a bright future in Thailand.

5 Conclusion

The objective of this study was to investigate the experiences of logistics user firms toward the development and implementation of 3PL in Thailand. The study took a unique user's perspective.

It is apparent from the study that 3PL has been accepted by Thai organizations, with more than half of the respondents using 3PL. Most of the current users have been utilizing third party logistics for over 2 years. The study provided evidence that the most frequently used services are transportation, packaging and warehousing operations. In contrast, inventory management and information systems are the least popular services for Thai firms. In addition, the majority of Thai organizations indicated that 3PL providers in Thailand provided a good service to customers, and most respondents are satisfied with the services they receive.

Current users reported many benefits from using 3PL. They believe that 3PL has more positive impacts than negative. The analysis of the experience of Thai organizations in their usage of 3PL activities has revealed that the 3PL industry has a potential for further development in Thailand. Many respondents intend to increase their use of 3PL in the near future. They believe the 3PL industry will have a prosperous future, although there are many local firms that do not employ third party logistics providers.

Future research might focus on decision making processes for selecting 3PL providers. This could include the factors involved in the selection of the 3PL providers. Another avenue for research is the extent of the technology and expertise provided by 3PL and the user perceptions in this regard.

6 References

Bask, A. H. (2001): Relationships among TPL Providers and Members of Supply Chains: A Strategic Perspective, in: The Journal of Business & Industrial Marketing, 16(6): 470-486.

Beamon, B. M. (1999): Measuring Supply Chain Performance, in: International Journal of Operations & Production Management, 19(3): 275–292.

Bhatnagar, R., Sohal, A. S., Millen, R. (1999): Third Party Logistics Services: A Singapore Perspective, in: International Journal of Physical Distribution & Logistics Management, 29(9): 569-587.

Bowman, R. J. (1995): A High-Wire Act, in: Distribution, 94(13): 36-39.

Boyson, S., Corsi, T., Dresner, M., Rabinovich, E. (1999): Managing Effective Third Party Logistics Relationships: What Does it Take?, in: Journal of Business Logistics, 20(1): 73-100.

Bradley, P. (1994b): What Really Matters, in: Purchasing, 117(1): 66-71.

Bradley, P. (1994c): Contract Logistics: It's All about Costs, in: Purchasing, 117(6): 56(A3)-A14.

Bradley, P. (1995): Third Parties Gain Slow, Cautious Buyer Support, in: Purchasing, 118(8): 51-52.

Byrne, P. M. (1993): A New Road Map for Contract Logistics, in: Transportation & Distribution: 34(4): 58-62.

Daugherty, P. J., Pittman, P. H. (1995): Utilization of Time-Based Strategies: Creating Distribution Flexibility/Responsiveness, in: International Journal of Operations & Production Management, 15(2): 54-60.

Dapiran, P., Lieb, R., Millen, R., Sohal A. (1996): Third Party Logistics Services Usage by Large Australian Firms, in: International Journal of Physical Distribution & Logistics Management, 26(10): 36-45.

Dillon, T. F. (1989): Third Party Services-New Route to Transportation Savings, in: Purchasing World, 33(6): 32-33.

Goh, M., Pinaikul, P. (1998): Research Paper: Logistics Management Practices and Development in Thailand, in: Logistics Information Management, 11(6): 359-369.

Harrington, L. H. (2000): Outsourcing Boom Ahead?, in: Industry Week, 249(1): 30-36.

Kasilingam, R. G. (1998): Recent Trends in Logistics, in: Logistics And Transportation Design And Planning. London, Kluwer Academic Publishers.

Kim, J. I. (1996): Logistics in Korea: Current State and Future Directions, in: International Journal of Physical Distribution and Logistics Management, 26(10): 6-21.

Lai, K. H, Ngai, E. W. T., Cheng, T. C. E. (2002): Measures for Evaluating Supply Chain Performance in Transport Logistics, in: Transportation Research Part E, 38(6): 1366-5545.

Lieb, R. C. (1992): The Use of Third-Party Logistics Services by Large American Manufacturers, in: Journal of Business Logistics, 13(2): 29-42.

Lieb, R. C., Millen, R. A., van Wassenhove, L. N. (1993): Third Party Logistics: A Comparison of Experienced American and European Manufacturers, in: International Journal of Physical Distribution & Logistics Management, 23(6): 35-46.

Lieb, R. C., Randall, H. L. (1996): A Comparison of the Use of Third-Party Logistics Service by Large American Manufacturers, 1991, 1994, and 1995, in: Journal of Business Logistics, 17(1): 305-320.

Maltz, A. (1995): Why You Outsource Dictates How, in: Transportation & Distribution, 36(3): 73-80.

McKeon, J. E. (1991): Outsourcing Begins In-House, in: Transportation & Distribution, 25(8): 24-28.

Mentzer, J. T., Rutner, S. M., Matsuno K. (1997): Application of the Means-End Value Hierarchy Model to Understanding Logistics Service Value, in: International Journal of Physical Distribution & Logistics Management, 27(9/10): 630-643.

Millen, R., Sohal, A., Dapiran, P., Lieb, R.C., Van Wassenhove, L.N. (1997): Benchmarking Australian Firms' Usage of Contract Logistics Services - a Comparison with American and Western European Practice, in: Benchmarking for Quality Management & Technology, 4(1): 34-46.

Natejumnong, P., Byrne, R., Niruntasukkarat, K. (2002, July 31): 2002 Current Status and Future Prospects of the Third Party Logistics Industry in Thailand from Provider Perspectives, Retrieved August 11, 2003, from www.logisticsbureau.com.

Parasuraman, A., Zeithaml, V. A., Berry, L. L. (1994): Reassessment of Expectations as a Comparison Standard in Measuring Service Quality: Implications for Future Research, in: Journal of Marketing 58 (1): 201–230.

Randall, H. L. (1991): Outsourcing Logistics in Europe, in: Journal of European Business, 12(6): 21-26.

Richardson, H. L. (1990): Explore Outsourcing, in: Transportation & Distribution, 31(7): 17-20.

Richardson, H. L. (1993): Why Use Third Parties?, in: Transportation & Distribution, 34(1): 29-32.

Richardson, H. L. (1994): Building Trust, But Audit Too, in: Transportation & Distribution, 35(3): 17-20.

Sink, H. L., Langley, C. J. Jr., Gibson, G. J. (1996): Buyer Observations of the US Third-Party Logistics Market, in: International Journal of Physical Distribution & Logistics management, 26(3): 36-46.

Sohail, M. S., Sohal, A. S. (2003): The Use of Third Party Logistics Services: a Malaysian Perspective, in: Technovation, 23(5): 401-408.

Troyer, C., Cooper, R. (1995): Smart Moves in Supply Chain Integration, in: Transportation and Distribution, 36(9): 55-62.

A Market-Oriented View of SCM – Researching Criteria and Instruments in the Public Procurement Process

Edeltraud Günther, Ines Klauke

1   Introduction 220
2   The Theoretical Background 221
3   Design of the Survey 224
4   Analysis 226
5   Applicability of the Method for Researching Problems in SCM ... 229
6   References 230

Summary:
Supply Chain Management is mostly analyzed in the context of private companies as suppliers and private companies or individuals as customers. This article focuses on the specific issues that have to be integrated in an SCM analysis if the end user is a public authority. The presented research project focuses on the specific end user public authority, the specific information flows due to highly standardized structures, specific goods and services relevant for public authorities as end users, and specific critical success factors for companies to gain competitive advantages within a supply chain dominated by public sector issues.

Keywords:
Supply Chain Management, Purchasing Criteria and Instruments, Environmental Criteria, Public Procurement

1 Introduction

Supply Chain Management. "The supply chain encompasses all activities associated with the flow and transformation of goods from raw material stage (extraction), through to the end user, as well as the associated information flows. ...Supply Chain Management (SCM) is the integration of these activities through improved supply relationships, to achieve a sustainable competitive advantage." (Handfield & Nichols, 1999: 2).

Seuring 2001 analyses three main aspects of supply chain management in literature:

1. The market or customer orientation: All activities in the supply chain have to draw to the customer's benefit.
2. The integration aspect: In SCM the whole supply chain as a unit has to be considered.
3. The efficiency aspect: SCM leads to an optimization of the whole supply chain (Seuring, 2001: 19).

- Public authorities as customers: This paper addresses the first aspect regarding public authorities as important customers and their needs. Total public procurement amounted to 1,500 billion € in 2002, accounting for 16% of the European Union's Gross Domestic Product (GDP). This share has remained stable over the last years. This importance of total public procurement by Member States varies significantly: from 11.9% of GDP in Italy to 21.5% in the Netherlands. It depends on the definition of public procurement in national statistics (EC, 2004: 4).

- Importance: In Germany, public authorities spent approximately 250 billion € per year purchasing goods and services as well as for construction – 11 to 12% of the German GDP in 2002 [Statistisches Bundesamt Deutschland (Federal Statistical Office Germany), 2003]. 44% of this share belongs to municipalities [Bundesministerium für Finanzen Deutschland (Federal Ministry of Finance Germany) ,2002: see pp. 132]. Therefore municipality's procurement and the procurement behavior have an important influence on the market as well as on potential suppliers and should be considered in the supply chain. Moreover, having to deal with specific legal constraints and information flows are specific due to highly standardized structures.

With their market power, public authorities and especially municipalities could represent an important stakeholder to their suppliers. Public procurement therewith can encourage the development and market penetration of environmental innovations. But measures that have been taken so far to encourage environmental and moreover sustainable procurement have not yet had a substantial impact on production processes and products. The question for the authors was then: What is hindering this SCM process between municipalities and suppliers of (green) product and services?

- Information flow: An important factor in that process – from the authors' point of view – is the flow of information. Public procurement and therefore green public procurement is hindered by an information deficit on the suppliers' side. Companies do not know which requirements municipalities set on their suppliers. The definition above already showed the importance of information in supply chain management. (Goldbach, 2003) explains the importance of information flows in the supply chain concerning power in supply chain interaction. "Information constitutes both an authoritative and allocative resource. On the one hand, information is part of a company's knowledge and therefore an allocative resource. On the other hand, it allows authority to be exerted" (Goldbach, 2003: 53).

- Starting point for a survey: With this background it seemed necessary to investigate how public procurement is organized and if municipalities already implement environmental aspects in their procurement decisions. Municipalities, like other public authorities, are characterized by the public procurement process with its legal restrictions and bureaucratic structures. Transparent and predictable procurement procedures are important to improve economic efficiency by promoting competition among suppliers (European Commission (EC), 2004: 6). This specific issue of SCM was not considered. Therefore the authors decided on a survey as an appropriate method. 170 local authorities in Saxony, Germany, were queried by choosing a standardized questionnaire. We decided to restrict our empirical analysis to Saxon municipalities because of legal and regional constraints in the German *Länder*. So restricting the analysis to one *Land* guaranteed a homogenous setting. Specific products and services (IT, office furniture, interior lighting, buildings, electricity and cleaning services) – identified as important by an European research project – were chosen for the survey.

The article will explain the approach, the analysis and the importance of the survey for SCM.

2 The Theoretical Background

Public procurement process. Public procurement could be described as the supply chain system for the acquisition of all necessary goods, works and services by the state and its organs when acting in pursuit of public interest (Bovis, 1998: 11; OECD 2001: 16f., European Commission (EC), 2004: 3).

Although public procurement can be organized in different ways depending on the respective product or service, the process of public procurement can be broken down into four steps: demand management, market research, award and procurement processing (BME, 2000: 7; Guenther & Scheibe, 2004: 5f.).

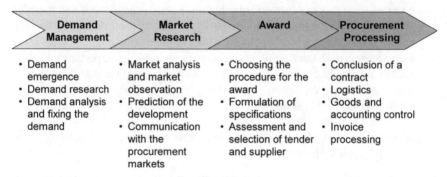

Figure 1: Public Procurement Process. (BME, 2000: 14)

In the *demand management phase* the demand in the municipality regarding a product or service is detected and then specified. During this phase the purchasing officer or purchasing unit examines what is needed, and will describe it as exactly as possible (BME, 2000: 7, OECD, 2001: 41).

The *procurement market research* contains the systematic search, collection and preparation of current and future relevant information for the procurement decision. Market research is important for increasing the transparency and supporting the procurement decision. With market analyses, observation, communication, and managing the gained market data, market research has the aim of obtaining potentials and trends (BME, 2000: 7; Günther & Scheibe, 2004: 6).

The most important phase in the public procurement process is the *award*. This phase reflects the legal framework of public procurement, which should prevent a monopolistic position of the public sector against private companies (Barth & Fischer, 2003: 52; Trionfetti, 2003: 223). In this phase the subject matter of a contract has to be defined (OECD, 2001: 43).

Specific legal issues. With the development of the European Union, the European public procurement directives presented certain thresholds, which should comply with the estimated costs of the relevant service. Above the thresholds (200,000 € for the award of public supply contracts and 5 mio. € for the award of public work contracts), the EU procurements directives apply. Below the thresholds, German public procurement law has to be applied. In the German as well as in the European public procurement law, different award procedures are available: *Open procedures* means those procedures whereby any interested economic operator may submit a tender. *Restricted procedures* mean those procedures in which any economic operator may request to participate and whereby only those economic operators invited by the contracting authority may submit a tender. *Competitive* *dialogue* is a procedure in which any economic operator may request to participate and whereby the contracting authority conducts a dialogue with the candidates admitted to that procedure, with the aim of developing one or more suitable alternatives capable of meeting its requirements, and on the basis of which the candidates chosen are invited to tender (Directive 2004/18/EC Art. 1 (11), BME, 2000: 11; Kosilek & Uhr, 2002: 34f.). Open procedures have been placed in the official journal of the EU beside regional or supra-regional information sources (BME, 2001: 12, Directive 2004/18/EC Art. 36).

The next stage of a procurement procedure is the *determination of the selection criteria* for the bidders. The decision for the appropriate bidder is then followed by the transaction phase. The procurement process ends up with signing and fulfilling the contract (BME, 2000: 1ff.; OECD, 2001: 43ff.).

Publication of the tender as well as of the final outcome of the public procurement procedure is an important element of transparency in EU procurement markets. Competitors can monitor the results of tendering processes and can improve their future bids (EC, 2004: 7).

This shows that public authorities are very specific end users with the supply chain.

Existing empirical studies. As the procurement process in municipalities was identified as the object to be analyzed within the survey, the next step was to get an overview on existing empirical studies. So far empirical research analyzed the efficiency of the procurement process, especially with regard to developments in new public management and e-procurement in public procurement (Kommunale Gemeinschaftsstelle für Verwaltungsvereinfachung [Municipal Community Center for New Public Management] (KGST), 2003). The following studies focusing on public procurement in Germany and with an empirical research design have been analyzed in the research project:

- Hirsch & Gayer Consulting (1998),
- Hirsch & Gayer Consulting (2000),
- Bundesverband für Materialwirtschaft, Einkauf und Logistik e.V. [Federal Association for Material's Management, Purchasing and Logistics] (BME) in cooperation with Booz, Allen & Hamilton (2000),
- Graßl, S. (2001)
- Kosilek, E.; Uhr, W. (2002).

The focus on German studies was chosen because the legal conditions vary so much between the European countries that the analysis would be too general and no conclusions for supply chain management could be drawn. All these studies examined the state of the art of procurement in the public sector in Germany to derive possibilities for efficiency improvement. They analyzed procurement-relevant criteria, procurement methods, tender methods, the quality of tenders, involved hierarchies, the efficiency of procurement, procurement syndicates, the degree of centralization, and the splitting-up of procurement expenses and media used, to name the most relevant for the research targets.

3 Design of the Survey

Defining research questions. The aim of this presented survey was to get an overview on instruments, strategies and hurdles of public procurement to decrease the information gap between municipalities and suppliers of green goods and services and to contribute to a better information flow within the supply chain. Therefore the authors decided to design a survey with a standardized questionnaire. The following research questions were essential for the design of the questionnaire in order to investigate this specific end user within SCM:

- How is the public procurement process structured in municipalities?
- Which strategies and instruments do municipalities use for market research?
- Which requirements do suppliers have to confirm, i.e. which criteria do municipalities consider as the most important for the tender?
- Which ecological criteria do municipalities consider in procurement?
- Which obstacles exist in the procurement process referring to procurement of environmental products and services?
- Can procurement syndicates encourage environmental procurement of municipalities?

Establish a hypothesis. The central focus for the interpretation of the results should be the innovation potential of procurement by municipalities. Furthermore, the following hypothesis above all questions has been tested: *There is a measurable correlation between the examined questions and the size of a municipality.* The idea behind that hypothesis was that it could be necessary for later strategy recommendations to develop different strategies for different categories of municipalities.

Respondents' structure. The investigation addressed decision makers in the central administration of municipalities as key persons within SCM. They were asked about public procurement in general and especially for selected product groups and services. To achieve a comparable population, especially referring to legal and economic conditions, the survey was restricted to Saxon municipalities. The authors all chose municipalities with more than 5,000 inhabitants (basis year 2000). These 170 identified municipalities can be described by the following classification based on the Statistical Yearbook 2000:

Category 1 (5,000 – 9,999 inhabitants):	contains	100 municipalities
Category 2 (10,000 – 19,999 inhabitants):	contains	41 municipalities
Category 3 (20,000 – 49,999 inhabitants):	contains	22 municipalities
Category 4 (50,000 – 99,999 inhabitants):	contains	3 municipalities
Category 5 (100,000 or more inhabitants):	contains	4 municipalities
Sum:		170 municipalities

Selection of the product groups. The questionnaire was planned to contain questions about public procurement in general and especially to selected product groups and services. These selected product groups were information technology, furniture, lighting systems, buildings, electricity and cleaning services.

The choice of these specific product groups and services is based on the European research project RELIEF - Environmental relief potential of urban action on avoidance and detoxification of waste streams through green public procurement. The researchers of this project decided on the product groups *personal computers, buses, photocopiers, furniture (wooden tables), electricity, water saving devices, food*. In a first step they collected the data for the expenditures of every product group in the municipalities participating in the research project (Stuttgart and Hamburg in Germany, Kolding in Denmark, Malmö in Sweden, Zurich in Switzerland and Miscolc in Hungary). In a second step the involved municipalities and explorers assessed the product group's relevance for green public procurement. The selected product groups above are the result of a comparison and discussion within the RELIEF project (Erdmenger, 2003: 117). For the planned survey presented here, buses were excluded, assuming that most Saxon municipalities have separate public transportation companies. Food could be relevant for schools, but the administrations have only very basic staff canteens carried out by the municipalities themselves. Additionally, the authors decided for their survey to analyze the field of construction, and as a part of this, interior lighting. For this field the authors assumed a high economic relevance that should also be reviewed by the survey.

Structure of the questionnaire. The questionnaire contained 26 questionnaires divided into 7 parts, marked from A to G. Part A enclosed three pages on the topic of procurement in general. This part was oriented on the most important steps of the procurement process (demand management, market research, award) concerning the information gap between procurers and suppliers. Parts B to G contained one page each on the consideration of criteria for a potential green purchasing in the named product categories and services. These parts were each printed on another piece of colored paper. By doing this, it was possible for the addressed person to transmit the relevant part to the expert in the municipality.

For most of the questions concerning the opinion or perception of the respondents, the authors chose a four-step Likert-Scale. Depending on the content of the question, the categories passed from "unimportant" to "rather unimportant" and from "rather important" to "important."

The questionnaire was tested in several pre-tests with a purchasing officer in a municipality, a former employee of the head department in a local authority, a member of management in the Saxon *Städte- und Gemeindetag e.V.* (SSG) and a scientist.

The questionnaire was sent out on the 20th of August, 2003. The deadline for sending back the questionnaire was the 30th of September, 2003. One week before the fixed date the authors reminded the respondents of the deadline by phone. Because of the summer holidays in Saxony, some of the respondents did not fill out the questionnaire, so the authors decided to prolong the reply.

4 Analysis

Response rate. Overall, decision makers in 77 municipalities (45.3 % of the population) took part in the survey. 43 municipalities belonged to category 1, 22 municipalities to category 2, 8 municipalities to category 3, 2 municipalities to category 4, and 2 municipalities to category 5. As the population is structured similarly, the survey can be called *representative*.

	population	responses	response rate in %
Category 1: 5,000 – 9,999:	100	43	43.0
Category 2: 10,000 – 19,999:	41	22	53.6
Category 3: 20,000 – 49,999:	22	8	36.4
Category 4: 50,000 – 99,999:	3	2	66.6
Category 5: 100,000 or more	4	2	50.0
	170	77	45.3

Table 1: Response Rate of the Survey

Analysis of the approach. The analysis was carried out on four levels. First the general information, e.g. about the size of the municipality or the expenditures in public procurement was collected. Then the steps of the procurement process –

demand management, market research and award were analyzed for every product group or service. Afterwards the results concerning the consideration of environmental criteria when purchasing the chosen goods and services was inquired. The relevance of the environmental criteria was compared with the relevance of the award criteria.

The descriptive data analyses were realized by frequency tables in SPSS. For testing the thesis (*There is a measurable correlation between the examined questions and the size of a municipality*) the Spearman Rho-coefficient for rank correlation was chosen. That was possible because the classes of municipalities were indicated as "from" and "to". Thus, the data could be seen as ordinal-scaled (Guenther & Klauke 2004: 12). The correlation was tested for each question.

Results. The results will be summarized here briefly by answering the initial research questions (see part 4) to see what the specific characteristics of municipalities as end-users in the supply chain are.

- How is the public procurement process structured in municipalities?

    Centralized organization does not, as is often assumed, exist in the past (Kosilek/ Uhr, 2002:28). In the survey mentioned here, the majority (82%) of the respondents declared not to hold a central procurement department. A weak correlation ($\rho = 0{,}295$, Sig. $= 0{,}011$) exists between the organization of procurement and the size of municipality measured by the number of inhabitants. Moreover, the authors asked for the responsible procurer for the selected product groups. For most product groups, the so-called "Hauptamt" (head department) or a similar department and the so-called "Bauamt" (building department) or a similar department were named as responsible for the coordination of the procurement. For encouraging green procurement in the municipalities, it is necessary to convince these coordinating departments and then provide conditions for passing down information of green procurement (e.g. about the market or characteristics of green products and services) to the users.

- Which strategies and instruments do municipalities use for market research?

    In Germany, public procurement consulting agencies exist, which act as a link between the public procurement departments and the companies. Their task is to specify adequate companies for municipalities on request and to provide companies participating in tenders by informing them about modalities etc. (Verdingungsordnung für Leistungen (VOL), Teil A [Procurement regulations for public supplies and service contracts, Part A (VOL/A)], 2002 §4 (2)). In the presented analysis, the authors found out that approximately 10% of municipalities use the agencies. Therefore the authors assume that the municipalities appreciate this kind of assistance for market investigation. The correlation analysis indicates that there is just as significant a correlation between the size of the municipality and the use of consulting agencies for the product group "furniture" ($\rho = -0.283$, Sig. $= 0.018$). That means the bigger the municipality, the more seldom it uses the consulting agency for the product group "furniture."

Looking at the most important media public procurers use to get an overview of the procurement market, the survey found out that Saxon procurers prefer the personal contact (40% for electricity, 60% for cleaning, 50% for lighting and buildings and 70% for IT and office furniture). This means that suppliers of green products and services should come to the municipalities and introduce their services. A correlation between the size of the municipality and the used information sources was found out only partially for the product group IT (fair: $\rho = 0.244$; Sig. $= 0.038$; personal contact: $\rho = -0.231$; Sig. $= 0.049$).

- Which requirements do suppliers have to confirm, i.e. which criteria do municipalities consider as the most important for the tender?

The Procurement Law determines general criteria for the public procurement act: price, technical know-how, capability and reliability (VOL/A, 2000 §2 no. 3) but do not specify this criteria. It is assumed that public procurers know what specific criteria they have to enlist. For the current analysis, the authors wanted to find out if there are differences between the product groups and services. Using results of former studies, the authors decided to inquire into the product-related criteria capability of the product, longevity, repair friendliness, (equipment) safety, operating costs; and as supplier-related criteria economic bids, technical know-how of the supplier, deadline, promptness of supply, maintenance and installing services, complaint behavior and management, and guaranteed services. Economic bids were the most important criteria for all product groups. Over all product groups and services, the criteria "most economic bid" was the most relevant. For the areas "office furniture" and "interior lighting," municipalities included criteria like "long life of the product" in their procurement decision. A statistically significant correlation between the size of the municipality and the procurement criteria could not be assessed.

- Which ecological criteria do municipalities consider in procurement?

The survey shows that municipalities already consider environmental criteria in their procurement decisions, especially in the product groups furniture, lighting and buildings. For the product group "furniture" the most important criteria is the longevity of the furniture. The aspect of waste disposal is not weighted so much although the costs for the disposal will accrue later. In the product group "lighting" energy efficiency is the most relevant criteria when planning lighting systems. This is not surprising, taking into mind that this aspect also has a great economic relevance. Municipalities could consider further technical developments, like light sensitivity control switches and electronic ballasts. Energy efficiency is also seen as the most important criteria in the use phase of buildings, which is already considered when planning new buildings. Therefore new concepts in the areas of heating technologies, lighting and facilities management meet the needs of the municipalities.

- Which obstacles exist in the procurement process referring to procurement of environmental products and services?

  Basically, the municipalities are interested in green public procurement. The biggest hurdle for green procurement observed by the surveyed procurers is the financial situation. Suppliers should point out the characteristics of green product alternatives, which lead to a cost advantage, e.g. energy efficiency. Costs along the whole life cycle should be considered.

- Can procurement syndicates encourage environmental procurement of municipalities?

  By bundling demand, 15% of expenditures could be saved (Gehrmann & Schinzer, 2002: 19; Schmidt, 2002: 312). Procurement syndicates are allowed within limits, because in some cases public authorities could have strong market power and therefore threaten the existence of small suppliers (KGST, 2003: 40). To set up procurement syndicates, two or more municipalities bundled their demand by putting out tenders together. By doing this, they achieved a better negotiating power towards their suppliers (Graßl, 2002: 84). For green procurement, this kind of syndicate could be of interest because they encourage environmental innovation by increasing the municipalities' power of demand. In the current study, between 45 and 67% of the Saxon municipalities with less than 50,000 inhabitants state that procurement syndicates are not helpful. The product group "electricity" was the area with the most agreement (19.2%). This means that there is still a lack of information that has to be bridged. There was no statistically significant correlation between the size of the municipality and the willingness to bundle the demand.

5 Applicability of the Method for Researching Problems in SCM

As described, this research focuses on public authorities as specific users within SCM, the specific goods and services relevant in public procurement, the information between municipalities as consumers on the market, and the suppliers of (green) products and services as an important factor in supply chain management.

Upon analyzing the results, the critical success factors for companies to gain competitive advantages can be deduced. The results of the approach have shown that most of the criteria determining the information problem lie in the market research phase (instruments applied for the market investigation) and in the award phase (the award criteria and the consideration of environmentally relevant criteria).

Another important issue is the strategies used by municipal procurers, and here especially the question of whether they are already bundling the volume of their purchases (procurement syndicates). The test of the correlation between all results and the size of the municipalities brought the experience that the size is in most cases not relevant for the results. This means that a great distinction does not have to be made in handling different-sized municipalities.

Looking at the results of the study, the specific characteristics of public procurement have to be considered. There are differences between public procurement and procurement in private companies. These differences affect the way purchasing decisions are made and influenced.

One of the greater differences is that the decision maker of a purchasing act – the purchasing officer or agency – is not the end user of the product. He is acting as a buying agent in the organization (OECD, 2000: 38).

Another aspect is the number of people who participate in the decision. In every element of the procurement process, different external stakeholders and decision-makers within a municipality are acting. Every actor along the decision process makes decisions that influence the process itself as well as its final results (Guenther & Scheibe, 2004: 6; OECD, 2000: 38).

Finally, public purchasers rely on highly structured and formalized processes. This is also an important result of the study showing that legal conditions are a relevant hurdle in SCM. Public authorities organize competition between firms. They have to verify that they meet demand in an economically efficient manner. Financial but also political constraints are high as well.

For further B2G research, the specific characteristics of public procurement, especially legal constraints, political constraints, the number of people involved, highly standardized structures, and the financial situation should be considered by private companies.

6 References

Bundesverband für Materialwirtschaft, Einkauf und Logistik e.V. (Federal Association for Material's Management, Purchasing and Logistics) (BME) in Cooperation with Booz, Allen & Hamilton (2000): Chancen und Entwicklungen im Public Procurement. Eine Studie des Bundesverbandes für Materialwirtschaft, Einkauf und Logistik e.V. in Zusammenarbeit mit Booz-Allen & Hamilton (Chances and Development in Public Procurement. A Study of the BME in cooperation with Booz-Allen & Hamilton), Berlin.

Bovis, C. (1998): The Liberalisation of Public Procurement and its Effects on the Common Market. Ashgate Publishing Ltd, Aldershot, Brookfield USA, Singapore, Sydney.

Directive 2004/18/EC of the European Parliament and of the Council of 31 March 2004 on the coordination of procedures for the award of public works contracts, public supply contracts and public service contracts, published 30th of April 2004 in the Official Journal of the European Union, L 134/114.

Erdmenger, C. (2003): The financial power and environmental benefits of green purchasing, in: Erdmenger, C. (ed.): Buying into the environment. Greenleaf Publishing, Sheffield: p. 116-133.

European Commission (EC) (2004): A report on the functioning of public procurement markets in the EU: Benefits from application of EU directives and challenges for the future.03/02/2004, Brussels.

Handfield, R. B., Nichols E. L. (1999): Introduction to Supply Chain Management, Prentice Hall, Upper Saddle River, NJ.

Hirsch & Gayer Consulting (1998): Public Procurement in der Bundesrepublik Deutschland. Kaufentscheidende Kriterien institutioneller (öffentlicher) Entscheidungsträger (Public Procurement in the German Federal Republic. Purchase-determining Criteria of Instititutional (Public) Decision Maker), Rheinbreitenbach/ Essen.

Hirsch & Gayer Consulting (2000): Optimierung der Methode des Einkaufs der öffentlichen Hand. Abschlußbericht. Angefertigt für: Bundesministerium für Wirtschaft und Technologie; Referate I B 3 und I A 2 (Optimizing the purchasing method of the public sector. Final Report. Made for: Federal Ministry of Economy and Technology, Departments I B 3 and I A 2), Rheinbreitenbach/ Essen.

Goldbach, M. (2003): Coordinating Interaction in Supply Chains – The Example of Greening Textile Chains, in: Seuring, S., Müller, M., Golbach, M., Schneidewind, U. (eds.): Strategy and Organization in Supply Chains. Physica-Verlag, Heidelberg, New York: p. 47-63.

Graßl, S. (2001): Die Auswirkungen des E-Procurement auf die Organisation der Beschaffung der Kommunalverwaltung - Möglichkeiten und Grenzen der Einbindung von E-Procurement in das New Public Management. Diplomarbeit an der Universität Konstanz (Consequences of E-Procurement on Municipality's Procurement Organisation – Potentials and Boundaries of Implementing E-Procurement in New Public Management. Diploma Thesis at the University of Konstanz), Konstanz.

Guenther, E., Klauke, I. (2004): Umweltfreundliche Beschaffung in sächsischen Kommunen - Auswertung einer Befragung. Dresden 2004. (= Dresdner Beiträge zur Betriebswirtschaftslehre. 82) Parallel als wissenschaftliches elektronisches Dokument veröffentlicht auf dem Hochschulschriftenserver der Sächsischen Landesbibliothek - Staats- und Universitätsbibliothek Dresden (SLUB) unter: http://hsss.slub-dresden.de/hsss/servlet/hsss.urlmapping.MappingServlet?id=1080136741765-6190 (Green Procurement in Saxon Municipalities – Analysis of a Survey), Dresden 2004.

Guenther, E., Scheibe, L. (2004): The Hurdles Analysis – A Method to identify and analyse Hurdles for Green Procurement in Municipalities. Dresden 2004. (= Dresdner Beiträge zur Betriebswirtschaftslehre. 80):Parallel published as a scientific electronic document on the Online Document Server (HSSS) of the Saxon State and Dresden University of Technology Library (SLUB) under: http://hsss.slub-dresden.de/hsss/servlet/hsss. urlmapping.MappingServlet?id=1074594203546-4130, Dresden 2004.

Kommunale Gemeinschaftsstelle für Verwaltungsvereinfachung [Municipal Community's Center for New Public Management] (KGST) 2003: Elektronische Vergabe und Beschaffung in Kommunalverwaltungen – KGSt-Bericht Nr. 4/2003 (Electronic tender and procurement in municipal administration – KGSt-report no. 4/2003), Köln 2003.

Kogg, B. (2003): Power and Incentives in Environmental Supply Chain Management. in: Seuring, S., Müller, M., Golbach, M., Schneidewind, U. (eds.): Strategy and Organization in Supply Chains, Physica-Verlag, Heidelberg, New York, p. 65-81.

Kosilek, E.; Uhr, W. (2002): Die kommunale elektronische Beschaffung. Bericht zum Forschungsprojekt „KeB" (E-Procurement in Municipalities. Report on the Research Project „KeB"), Dresdner Beiträge zur Wirtschaftsinformatik 37, Dresden.

Seuring, S. (2001): Supply Chain Costing – Kostenmanagement in der Wertschöpfungskette mit Target Costing und Prozesskostenrechnung (Supply Chain Costing with Target Costing and Activity Based Costing), Verlag Franz Vahlen, München.

Trionfetti, F. (2003): Home-biased Government Procurement and International Trade: Descriptive Statistics and Empirical Evidence, in: Arrowsmith, S.; Trybus, M. (eds.): Public Procurement: The Continuing Revolution, Kluwer Law International, The Hague, p. 223-233.

Part 3
Case Study Research in Supply Chains

Case Study Research in Supply Chains – An Outline and Three Examples

Stefan Seuring

1 Introduction 236
2 Supply Chain Management 237
3 Case Study Research 238
4 Three Examples of Case Research in Supply Chains 240
5 Conclusion 247
6 References 248

Summary:
Supply chain management implies that companies cooperate in delivering products and services to customers. As a consequence, related empirical research should collect data from more than one stage of the supply chain. This has rarely been the case so far, as often only one company is approached, implicitly carrying the problem that statements on the supply chain cannot be validated by a view from other participants. Therefore, it is important to select appropriate supply chains and companies for empirical research on supply chain management. One research method that can be applied in such a setting is case study research. This method allows a flexible data collection, which is appropriate for analyzing supply chains and managerial issues therein. While research in supply chain management imposes further difficulties, it also carries the chance to validate collected data by triangulating information obtained at different stages of the supply chain. This paper will outline some basic issues on case study research, and also portray three examples of how such research has been conducted.

Keywords:
Supply Chain Management, Case Study Research, Research Methodology, Qualitative Research, Validity, Empirical Research

1 Introduction

In the past few years, supply chain management has seen a rise both in practical application and academic interest. The rapid development of supply chain management as a field of research has so far not been matched by related developments in research methodologies. While a full range of research methodologies can be and is applied in supply chain management, the use of case study research is an interesting option. Frequently, the analysis of a supply chain and managerial issues therein are highly unstructured problems which can be dealt with in an exploratory research design using case studies (Yin, 2003). Stuart et al. (2002) suggest that case studies are an appropriate research methodology to map the field of supply chain management, as they allow identification and description of critical variables.

This argument is central to the question of which type of research methodology is appropriate, where e.g. Morgan & Smircich (1980) state: "Qualitative research is an approach rather than a particular set of techniques, and its appropriateness derives from the nature of the social phenomenon to be explored." Meredith (1993; 1998) has argued for this in the field of operations management and outlined how case and field research can be used for related theory building. As supply chain management is a rather young field of research, the need for further conceptual and theory building research is frequently highlighted (e.g. Croom et al., 2000; Müller et al., 2003) as a means to continue to shape the contours of supply chain management (Mouritsen et al., 2003).

Against this background, the aim of the paper is to outline when case study research in supply chain management can be used and how it can be conducted, especially in collecting case related information at several stages of the supply chain. Based on the issues raised, the paper will be presented using the following structure: The first section provides a background on supply chain management and reflects on the need for further empirical research therein and the appropriateness of case study-based research. The second chapter will briefly discuss case study research, and concentrate on a few issues seen as particularly relevant for application in supply chain management. Third, a process of conduction case research in supply chains will be put forward (Stuart et al., 2002), which will be used later on in the case studies. On this basis, the next section illustrates this by presenting three cases where the author was involved (e.g. Seuring, 2001; 2002; Goldbach, 2003; Goldbach et al., 2004; Morana & Seuring, 2003a; 2003b). A conclusion will sum up major findings and provide hints for future research.

2 Supply Chain Management

"The supply chain encompasses all activities associated with the flow and transformation of goods from raw materials stage (extraction), through to the end user, as well as the associated information flows. Material and information flow both up and down the supply chain. Supply chain management (SCM) is the integration of these activities through improved supply chain relationships, to achieve a sustainable competitive advantage" (Handfield & Nichols, 1999: 2). This definition is taken as an exemplary one, while several others have been proposed. A number of reviews and systemizations have been provided (e.g. Bechtel & Jayaram, 1997; Cooper et al., 1997; Ganeshan et al., 1998; Croom et al., 2000; 2000; Mentzer et al., 2001; Seuring, 2001a; Otto & Kotzab, 2001; Müller et al., 2003). While these contributions point towards different definitions and conceptualizations, at least two recurring themes can be observed: (1) Supply chains deal with material and information flows, which (2) have to be managed in a cooperative way by all partners involved in the supply chain.

Several authors have pointed toward the problems in even establishing a central content of supply chain management (Mouritsen et al., 2003; Chen & Paulraj, 2004) as well as observed problems practitioners face in aiming at implementing supply chain management (Fawcett & Magnan, 2002). One central issue is identifying which entities are constitutive for a supply chain. It is not trivial to decide which companies form certain supply chains and how far integration has to reach. As Frohlich & Westbrook (2001) argue in their survey-based research, companies to this point have predominantly looked a stage up or down the supply chain. Furthermore, few examples exist where information from different stages, especially more than two stages of the supply chain, have been collected (e.g. Cooper & Slagmulder, 2004; Seuring, 2001; 2002).

Related to this, Stuart et al. (2002: 431) emphasize the need for a "customer focused approach" in management research, where practitioners' perceptions of research are taken into account. In this regard, they highlight that case studies can be a "powerful, influential, and useful contribution to both management practice and theory development" (Stuart et al., 2002) and have a high validity with practitioners (Voss et al., 2002: 195). Some problems faced in supply chain management can be perceived as complex, unstructured situations, where a mapping of major variables (Stuart et al., 2002) or exploration to uncover areas for research and theory development (Voss et al., 2002) are suitable research strategies. These are typical situations where a case study approach seems appropriate (Yin, 2003; Saunders et al., 2003). Hence, two central questions in related research are:

- How can a suitable supply chain which can serve as a case be identified?

- How can access be gained to the different stages of the supply chain to allow data collection at some or all relevant stages?

3 Case Study Research

"A case study is an empirical enquiry that (1) investigates a contemporary phenomenon within its real life context, especially when (2) the boundaries between phenomenon and context are not clearly evident" (Yin, 2003: 13). Case studies are used as a research method if contextual factors are taken into account, but at the same time limit the extent of the analysis (Eisenhardt, 1989; Voss et al., 2002). This allows in-depth insights into emerging fields (Meredith, 1993), yielding a basic comprehension of fuzzy and messy issues (Swamidass, 1991). The strength of the case study method rests on its ability to capture conceptual developments (Meredith et al., 1989; Meredith, 1993), while not immediately proposing broad theories (Weick, 1995; Swamidass, 1991; Wacker, 1998). Therefore, it is particularly appropriate if new fields of research are emerging (Yin 2003). The advantage of the case study approach is its ability to address "Why?" and "How?" questions in the research process (Yin, 2003: 1; Ellram, 1996: 98; Meredith, 1998: 444). Applying a flexible, sometimes even opportunistic research strategy (Yin, 2003) is one of its major strengths, but might also be a major weakness of case study research (Stuart et al., 419). This makes it necessary to briefly look at the related research purpose as well as the research process.

3.1 Research Purpose

Linking this to the research cycle of description, explanation and testing (Meredith, 1993), one can look at what kinds of insights can be gained from case study research. It is evident that case study research investigates a contemporary phenomenon in its real life context (Yin, 2003), so that e.g. existing theories might be taken up to gain a first insight into the phenomenon studied (Swamidass, 1991). Case studies can be used for different purposes. Yin (2003: 3) distinguishes three types of case studies: (1) An exploratory case study is aimed at defining the questions and hypotheses of a subsequent study (not necessarily a case study) or at determining the feasibility of the desired research procedure. (2) A descriptive case study presents a complete description of a phenomenon within its context. (3) An explanatory case study comprises data bearing on cause-effect relationships – explaining how events happened.

Furthermore, Yin (2003: 40-47) suggests case selection based on the following criteria. A single case can serve as a critical example (1) if it forms an extreme or unique case, e.g. if not many cases are available; (2) if it forms a typical or representative case, standing as an example of a wider group of cases; (3) if it is a revelatory case, where the investigator has an opportunity to observe and analyze a phenomenon so far inaccessible to scientific investigation; (4) if it provides a longitudinal case studying two or more points in time; (5) if it stands as a pilot in a multi-case setting. In contrast, multiple cases often use a replication logic, but can also be used to select typical cases within a certain domain (Eisenhardt, 1989).

Furthermore, within a certain case, one or more units of analysis can be studied (Yin, 2003: 40), providing a second replication logic, which can be used to ensure appropriate analytic generalizability of the research conducted (Eisenhardt, 1989).

In relation to this, Handfield & Melynk (1998: 324-325) have outlined how research strategies and theory building activities can be matched. Their list of categories has been modified by Voss et al. (2002: 198), who distinguish four major purposes: exploration, theory building, theory testing, and theory extension/refinement. Case studies can be used for all four purposes, but when the single strategies apply must be carefully evaluated.

3.2 Research Process

The research process for case studies is similar to those used for other (empirical) research (Yin, 2003; McCutcheon & Meredith, 1993). Stuart et al. (2002: 420) propose a five-stage research process (see Figure 1) and explain in detail how each step should be carried out when conducting case study research. As several wider and more detailed accounts for conducting case studies have been presented, this is not reproduced here (see e.g. Yin, 2003; Eisenhardt, 1989; Mentzer & Kahn, 1995; Ellram, 1996; Voss et al., 2002).

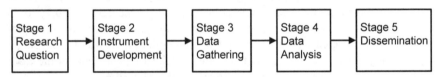

Figure 1: The Five-Stage Research Process Model (Stuart et al., 2002: 420)

One major reason for the great importance of the research process is that the quality of the research is often flawed by a lack of rigor in the research process (Stuart et al., 420). Hence, research quality issues in case study research are briefly addressed.

3.3 Ensuring Quality of Case Study Research

The quality of research designs is ensured by aiming for validity (i.e. is the stated evidence valid?), and reliability (i.e. is the stated evidence correct?) (Mayring, 2002: 140; Yin, 2003: 34). Mayring (2002: 141) emphasizes the specific problems in ensuring objectivity and reliability of qualitative research and measure-related performance. The excellence of qualitative research is addressed especially through procedural reliability and validity (Stuart et al., 2002). This has led to a debate on related quality factors (Mayring, 2002: 144; Maxwell, 1992; Mentzer &

Flint, 1997). In line with other authors, Mayring (2002: 144) proposes six quality factors for qualitative research: (1) process documentation, (2) safeguarding interpretations by arguments, (3) research process structured by rules of conduct, (4) closeness to the study item, (5) communicative validation, (6) triangulation.

For case study research, Yin (2003: 34) outlines how validity of the research can be ensured. He proposes three types of validity: construct validity, internal validity, and external validity. These three types of validity are applied during different stages of the research process, as reliability and validity are ensured by a clearly structured research process. The issues outlined in this section will be taken up in the three cases presented below to illustrate such research.

4 Three Examples of Case Research in Supply Chains

After this brief outline of case study research methodology, special issues will be addressed that have to be taken into account when conducting case study research in supply chain management. Related papers have touched upon this for logistics (e.g. Mentzer & Kahn, 1995; Ellram, 1996) and for operations management (e.g. McCutcheon & Meredith, 1993; Meredith, 1998; Stuart et al., 2002; Voss et al., 2002). While all of these papers carry a reference to logistics or operations management in their title, they mainly describe research procedures that apply to all kinds of management. Furthermore, as Müller et al. (2003) state, few examples exist where data for case study research has been collected at two or more stages of the supply chain. Therefore, it is interesting to take a look at some of the cases published so far and see how data was gathered and evaluated.

In the above section on supply chain management, two specific issues in related case research have been identified which arise from the specific content of supply chain management: the identification of suitable examples, and access to case study companies. In order to provide more detailed insights, the subsequent section will address these two questions using three examples of case study research in supply chains that I took part in. The three cases are sorted according to the number of companies (entities), and data was gathered from the time the case study was conducted. Therefore, the case of Otto is one where only staff from the focal company provided insight, while in the two other cases, data was gathered in various companies or stages of the supply chain. Subsequently, the above outlined five-stage research process (Stuart et al., 2002) will be described for each of the three cases.

4.1 Otto – Introduction of Organic Cotton Apparel

Founded in 1949 in Hamburg, Germany, Otto GmbH & Co. is the largest mail order business in the world. While the headquarters are still there, the Otto group presently consists of 86 companies in 21 countries, employing more than 65,000 people worldwide with a turnover of € 19.2 billion in 2002. The products traded by OTTO cover a wide range, including clothing, electronics and household appliances. For more than two decades, Otto has been an environmentally proactive company. This has led to the strategic decision to introduce apparel produced from organic cotton.

1. Research Question: The research question was how to organize supply chains to be able to introduce organic cotton apparel (Goldbach, 2003; Goldbach et al., 2004). Organic cotton is not readily available on commodity markets, so in order to be able to provide such products, Otto had to start and operate a "new" supply chain from the cradle of raw material production, i.e. cotton farming. Therefore, the case presents (1) an extreme case, as such it is an example of an environmental product innovation, but also (2) a representative case (Yin, 2003: 42), as Otto encountered the typical problems companies face when entering a new product field. Access to Otto was guaranteed by means of a joint, publicly funded research project. Otto provided the business case, while the research team offered academic advice.

2. Instrument Development: In this specific case, but also in most cases, all of the cotton supply chain is operated outside Europe. This issue implied that direct contact to suppliers of Otto in e.g. Turkey or India was not possible. Consequently, the case could only be researched by having access to staff and documents at Otto. As the first mode of access, semi-structured interviews were chosen, as they provide a flexible instrument to get into the field and become familiar with the object studied, while also providing a flexible mode of data gathering (Yin, 2003: 89; Saunders et al., 2003: 246). A second method was taken up later in the research process, as it became evident that a detailed understanding of related product examples was needed. Therefore, document analysis and joint data analysis with staff members of Otto were conducted.

3. Data Gathering: For data collection, 12 semi-structured face-to-face interviews with employees of Otto were conducted. They provided initial insights into the historical development of the field. Furthermore, two specific example model products (a T-shirt and a bathrobe) were selected to gather quantitative data on their production at the single stages and the cost incurred for this. Again, data was only accessible through Otto's staff. The two products analyzed as examples formed two embedded units in the case study research. They are representative of the related product range offered by Otto.

4. Data Analysis: Data analysis was carried out by transcribing the interview data and checking interview protocols with the participants. Furthermore, in an ongoing process, the findings were discussed with Otto staff to validate the findings. A second important mode of data analysis was seen in comparing the results of the research to those of other research groups addressing similar questions (see the case comparison in Seuring, 2004), which served as an additional mode of triangulation (Yin, 2003: 97; Saunders et al., 2003: 99).

5. Dissemination: The material collected in the case study research was related to a different theoretical basis, allowing different insights to be gained. As cost played a central role, cost management was a first means to achieve this, but as the research advanced, it was revealed that costs are not only about reporting data, but carry implications regarding the organizational settings in which they are used (Goldbach, 2002). Furthermore, related transaction costs of the modes of cooperation and coordination they reflect play an important role (Goldbach et al., 2004). This theory-based analysis was extended by building on principal-agent theory and structuration theory (Goldbach, 2003b). Furthermore, the management of time and complexity represented objectives that were employed to systemize measures taken by Otto (Seuring et al., 2004).

This case provides one of exploration, which was later extended to theory building. At the onset of the project, the factors influencing the design and operation of the supply chain were vaguely assumed. Building on existing theories allowed them to be applied in supply chain settings. Access to the case study material was only available through the focal company.

4.2 Steilmann – Supply Chain Target Costing for Polyester Linings

The company Klaus STEILMANN GmbH & Co. KG was founded in 1958 in Wattenscheid, Germany, in the Ruhr region. Company headquarters are still located there today. The core business of STEILMANN is clothing design and sale, and production is carried out at suppliers around the world. Major customers include Marks & Spencer and C&A. In 2001, the company had a turnover of over € 700 million and employed about 14,500 people, mainly in Rumania, where currently about 12,000 (mostly female) employees work. The company pursues an environmentally proactive strategy, which includes the constant aim of improving product quality and environmental performance.

1. Research Question: The research question was how to introduce a new kind of technically and environmentally optimized polyester into apparel products (Seuring, 2001). Polyester is used in a diverse range of products, from bottles, to seat belts, to apparel. This case offers a representative example of new product introduction where existing supply chains have to be overcome (Seur-

ing, 2001). Similar to the Otto case, this formed part of a joint, publicly funded research project.

2. Instrument Development: This case was particularly interesting, as it was possible to access three stages of the supply chain. These three stages form the total relevant supply chain: tier-2 supplier, tier-1 supplier, and focal company. The tier-2 supplier was a chemical company polymerizing the polyester and spinning the yarn. The tier-1 supplier was a textile company conducting weaving and finishing of the apparel. Access to the suppliers was provided by Steilmann, which helped establish contact to the suppliers.

3. Data Gathering: Data gathering was conducted by means of 19 semi-structured face-to-face interviews. In 14 cases, Steilmann staff was interviewed, while in the other five cases, staff of the companies operating the two preceding stages of the supply chain were questioned. Site visits and document analysis formed further modes of data collection. Data collection was carried out at one point in time, where the development over time was taken into account.

4. Data Analysis: In data analysis, the insights gained at the three stages could be validated, and thereby allowed for triangulation of information gathered at the three companies, as well as from further sources, e.g. company websites and secondary material such as related publications. As in the Otto case, interviews were transcribed and checked by the interviewees.

5. Dissemination: Target costing provided a conceptual framework to comprehend the data collected. In the analysis, it became evident that the three companies took an approach that can be described as *supply chain target costing* (Seuring, 2002). None of the companies used the term "target costing," but all of them operated with a clear focus on costs for the final product, which were not to exceed conventional polyester apparel. They even took joint measures to reduce costs, which covered direct costs, administrative processes (activity-based costs) as well as the costs of cooperation (transaction costs) (Seuring, 2001; 2002). As mentioned, access to (all) three stages of the supply chain allowed insight into companies' actions as well as their interaction. While they operate in a competitive environment and each of them has to compete on cost in their particular market, it was interesting to observe how they implemented joint measures in this particular supply chain. Target costing in supply chains has been established before (Cooper & Slagmulder, 2004), but the theoretical framework was extended and tested in the case study.

The Steilmann case operates in a typical manufacturing setting where three companies operate. But the picture changes again if customers form a further stage of the supply chain.

4.3 Ecolog – A Closed-loop Supply Chain for Polyester Apparel

The Ecolog Recycling Network GmbH is a textile recycling network residing in Tettnang on Lake Constance, Germany. The network was founded in 1994 by two German clothing manufacturers for sports wear and outdoor wear: VAUDE and Sympatex Technologie GmbH. Today, it remains a very small company, employing only one person. The Ecolog network has different actors: producers, retailers, consumers, and recycling companies of polyester textiles. The objective of this collaboration is market introduction of apparel manufactured from a homogenous polyester only, which can be recycled. This includes the development and supply of polyester apparel, the collection of post-consumer products by retailers, and the recycling of these products into a granulate that serves as virgin polyester material. This network provides a label for all textiles made entirely of the same homogenous polyester. Since 1994 they have sold about 800,000 labels equaling this number of articles of clothing. Once they are retired from use, these textiles are taken back by Ecolog Recycling GmbH and integrated into a recycling process. Thereby, Ecolog organizes all stages of a closed-loop supply chain (Morana & Seuring, 2003a).

1. Research Question: The research question addressed was how a closed-loop supply chain involving customers as one stage of the supply chain operates and why success of the Ecolog network has so far been very limited. The aim of establishing the network was combining environmental improvements (recycling on the same quality level) with economic feasibility. All major technical problems had been solved before the Ecolog network and label were introduced. By operating a closed-loop supply chain, it forms an extreme example of a textile recycling network (Thierry et al., 1995; Guide et al., 2003). This case was selected, as it is one of the very few examples where such an attempt has ever been made.

2. Instrument Development: Access to the supply chain was first made by contact to the person working at Ecolog, who acts as a network coordinator. Ecolog provided contact to the companies. Again, semi-structured interviews and document analysis proved to be appropriate options for data collection.

3. Data Gathering: A total of 58 interviews were carried out mainly from October 2002 to March 2003 using semi-structured interviews, which were conducted either in person or by telephone. The people interviewed cover four stages of the supply chain, such as producers (four interviews), retailers (23 interviews, seven also related to apparel take-back), consumers (21 interviews), the employee of Ecolog regarding the coordination of the recycling network and collection, as well as nine interviews with related experts. A special issue was identifying customers that purchased such apparel, as the company does not keep a record of its sales. Various e-mail lists were used to post

a search for people owning such apparel and willing to take part in an interview. The different sources, as well as data gathered from literature and other available information on textile recycling created the basis for validating and triangulating single observations.

4. Data Analysis: Collecting data from all stages of this particular closed-loop supply chain allowed for triangulation of the information obtained from the single informant. While interviews were transcribed, only those conducted with the Ecolog staff directly were checked by interviewees. Furthermore, the Ecolog employee, acting as the central coordinator, was contacted several times to discuss findings derived from other interviews.

5. Dissemination: The manufactured and sold apparel products, such as outdoor jackets or occupational safety/weather wear, are products with a use life of several years. Consequently, one major problem identified in the overall operation of the Ecolog closed-loop supply chain was that products do not return. This applies to both private as well as institutional customers. This might be comprehendible for private consumers, who just forget about the option to return the jacket at the end of its life to the place they bought it. Furthermore, they often donate jackets to charities, which gives them "a good feeling." Interestingly, the institutional customers (e.g. DaimlerChrysler AG) somehow had the same problem, as the purchasing decision and the end-of-life decision were taken by different staff members. Information about the recycling option was not passed on and/or stored, so these customers also often opted to donate to charities.

The Ecolog case offered interesting insight into the problems of operating an "ideally" designed supply chain. Guide & Van Wassenhove (2003: 3) characterize closed loop supply chains by a set of activities: "product acquisition, reverse logistics, inspection and disposition (contesting of test, sort and grade), reconditioning (which may include remanufacturing) and distribution and selling of the recovered products." Major aspects are product acquisition and reverse logistics, which are essential for being able to close the loop. As mentioned, in the Ecolog case the technical solution is feasible. Still, the network did not achieve economic success due to organizational or personal failure during product return. This could partly be explained by building on transaction cost analysis, as e.g. the transaction frequency is very low, while the required take-back action is very specific. One measure would have been to introduce an incentive for take back.

The Ecolog case stands as an example where only by inclusion of the customers in the analysis can the picture of the supply chain become complete. Yet, access to this information was the most difficult to get. Furthermore, 21 customers might be seen as too small a number. The evaluation of the interviews conducted clearly provided the stated insight as a uniform explanation.

Ecolog forms a case of theory refinement. In the context of closed-loop supply chains, which serve as the theoretical background, it provides one of the first accounts for data gathering from customers in closed-loop supply chains.

4.4 Comparing the Research Methods in the Three Cases

Table 1 provides an overview of the three case studies and relates the findings presented to the major issues addressed in the section on the case study method. The cases show that data collection can take different forms and has to be customized to the needs of the individual cases. The requirements of each company studied in such a case have to be kept in mind. This might limit access to suppliers and customers, which inevitably has an impact on the data collected in the case study.

Case	**Otto**	**Steilmann**	**Ecolog**
Industry	Textile / Apparel	Textile / Apparel	Textile / Apparel
Access to case	Focal company in joint project	Focal company in joint project, suppliers through focal company	Active search for cases, contact to focal company, search for customers
Case Selection	Extreme / Exemplary case	Exemplary case	Extreme case
Data Gathering in Supply Chain	Focal company	Three (all) stages of the supply chain	Four stages of the supply chain including customers
Method of Data Collection	Interviews, documents	Interviews, documents	Interviews, documents
Validity	Multiple interviews, two embedded examples for detailed analysis	Information from all relevant supply chain partners	Information from all relevant supply chain partners
Research purpose	Exploration and theory building	Theory testing / extension	Theory extension

Table 1: Comparing the Three Case Examples

One issue not addressed in this paper is how to link findings to literature and to enfold them into previously published work (Eisenhardt, 1989). This is of great importance to both the design of the research as well as the dissemination of reaching closure. This issue applies to any kind of research, so it is not specific here and therefore was not addressed.

5 Conclusion

This paper discusses why case study research proves to be an interesting option for empirical research in supply chain management. It is not intended to rewrite or reinvent case study research, as numerous, comprehensive accounts of such research already exist. In contrast, the three cases briefly outlined here show examples of how the research process was carried out in such projects.

In section 2, two questions were raised, which will not be discussed against the background of the cases presented.

- How can a suitable supply chain which can serve as a case be identified?

As discussed in literature (e.g. Yin, 2003: 21), case selection often has to be opportunistic. As the example of Ecolog shows, it might be difficult to find suitable examples at all. In this case only a second suitable case study could be identified, which is now research to provide insight in a cross-case analysis. Still, the active search for appropriate cases that allow insight into how supply chain management works across several stages of the supply chain will be very useful.

In general, case studies often emerge from existing contacts a researcher has to industry. This was the case for the Otto and Steilmann examples, as presented in this paper. While this is justifiable, the researcher still needs to assess why these cases are useful and what the main purpose for researching them would be. This way, one central critique of case study research (that it lacks the rigor of other approaches) could be avoided or at least mitigated.

- How can access be gained to the different stages of the supply chain to allow data collection at some or all relevant stages?

A key approach therefore might be starting at a focal company. From this point onwards, suppliers could be identified. In the Steilmann case, focus was provided by the particular product studies, so there were only two suppliers involved and no further selection possible. A different example is provided in the paper of Chivaka (2005, in this volume). Initially identifying focal companies (as we did), he asked them to identify suitable first-tier suppliers. By repeating this at the supplier, he was able to reach a second-tier supplier, which finally allowed him to research three different three-stage supply chains.

As the reach is beyond a single organization, more flexible and opportunistic approaches of getting access to and collecting data from various stages of the supply chain have to be used.

As a final comment, it has to be admitted that the written findings of such research always idealize the research process, but one strength of the case study method is its flexibility (Yin, 2003; Stuart et al., 2002). Rigor, as expressed in valid and reliable research, stems from process documentation. Triangulation of findings by using multiple sources of evidence is a second important measure. Case study research in supply chain management can help to further explore the field, but is also valid for theory building, testing and extension.

6 References

Bechtel, C., Jayaram, J. (1997): Supply Chain Management: A Strategic Perspective, in: The International Journal of Logistics Management, 8(1): 15-34.

Chivaka, R. (2005): Cost Management along the Supply Chain: Methodological Implications, in: Kotzab, H., Seuring, S., Müller, M., Reiner, G. (eds.): Research Methodologies in Supply Chain Management, Physica, Heidelberg: p. 299-314.

Cooper, M. C., Lambert, D. M., Pagh, J. D. (1997): Supply Chain Management: More than a new Name for Logistics, in: The International Journal of Logistics Management, 8(1): 1-14.

Cooper, R., Slagmulder, R. (2004): Interorganizational cost management and relational context, in: Accounting, Organizations and Society, 29(1): 1-26.

Croom, S., Romano, P. Giannakis, M. (2000): Supply chain management: An analytical Framework for Critical Literature Review, in: European Journal of Purchasing & Supply Management, 6(1): 67-83.

Eisenhardt, K. M. (1989): Building Theory from Case Study Research, in: Academy of Management Review, 14(4): 532-550.

Ellram, L. M. (1996): The Use of the Case Study Method in Logistics Research, in: Journal of Business Logistics, 17(2): 93-138.

Fawcett, S. E., Magnan, G. M. (2002): The Rhetoric and Reality of Supply Chain Integration, in: International Journal of Physical Distribution & Logistics Management, 32(5): 339-361.

Frohlich, M., Westbrook, R. (2001): Arcs of Integration: An International Study of Supply Chain Strategies, in: Journal of Operations Management, 19(2): 185-200.

Ganeshan, R., Jack, E., Magazine, M. J., Stephens, P. (1998): A Taxonomic Review of Supply Chain Management Research, in: Tayur, S., Ganeshan, R., Magazine, M. (eds.): Quantitative models for supply chain management, Kluwer, Dordrecht, p. 839-879.

Goldbach, M. (2003): Coordinating Interaction in Supply Chains – The Example of Greening Textile Chains, in: Seuring, S., Müller, M., Goldbach, M., Schneidewind, U., (eds.): Strategy and Organization in Supply Chains, Physica, Heidelberg: p. 47-63.

Goldbach, M. (2003a): Koordination von Wertschöpfungsketten durch Target Costing und Öko-Target Costing: Eine agentur- und strukturationstheoretische Reflexion (Coordination of Supply Chains by Target Costing and Eco-Target Costing: An Principal-agent and Structuration Theory based Reflection), Deutscher Universitäts-Verlag, Wiesbaden.

Goldbach, M., Seuring, S., Back, S. (2004): Co-ordinating Sustainable Cotton Chains for the Mass Market: The Case of the German Mail-order Business Otto, in: Greener Management International, Issue 43, forthcoming Autumn 2004.

Guide, V. D. R., Harrison, T. P. Van Wassenhove, L. N. (2003): The Challenge of Closed-Loop Supply Chains, in: Interfaces, 33(6): 3-6.

Handfield, R. B., Melnyk, S. A. (1998): The Scientific Theory-building Process: A Primer using the Case of TQM, in: Journal of Operations Management, 16(4): 321-339.

Maxwell, J.A. (1992): Understanding and Validity in Qualitative Research, in: Harvard Educational Review, 62(3): 279-300.

McCutcheon, D.M., Meredith, J.R. (1993): Conducting Case Study Research in Operations Management, in: Journal of Operations Management, 11(3): 239-256.

Mentzer, J. T., Kahn, K. B. (1995): A Framework of Logistics Research, in: Journal of Business Logistics 16(1): 231-250.

Mentzer, J. T., DeWitt, W., Keebler, J. S., Min, S., Nix, N. W., Smith, C. D., Zacharia, Z. G. (2001): Defining Supply Chain Management, in: Journal of Business Logistics, 22(2): 1-26.

Mentzer, J. T., Flint, D. J. (1997): Validity in Logistics Research, in: Journal of Business Logistics, 18(2): 199-216.

Meredith, J. (1993): Theory building through conceptual methods, in: International Journal of Operations & Production Management, 13(5): 3-11.

Meredith, J. (1998): Building operations management theory through case and field research, in: Journal of Operations Management, 16(4): 439-452.

Morana, S., Seuring, S. (2003a): Organizing a Closed-loop Supply Chain - The ECOLOG Case Study, in: Seuring, S., Müller, M., Goldbach, M., Schneidewind, U. (Eds.): Strategy and Organization in Supply Chains, Physica, Heidelberg, p. 369-384.

Morana, R., Seuring, S. (2003): "Analysing and Comparing two Subsets of the ECOLOG Closed-Loop Supply Chain", in: Spina, G., Vinelli, A., Cagliano, R., Klachschmidt, M., Romano, P., Salvador, F. (eds.): One World? One View of OM? - The Challenges of Integrating Research & Practice, Proceedings of the 10th International Conference European Operations Management Association, 16-18 June 2003, Como, Italy, Volume II, p. 1035-1044.

Morgan, G., Smircich, L. (1980): The Case of Qualitative Research, in: Academy of Management Review, 5(4): 491-500.

Mouritsen, J., Skjøtt-Larsen, T., Kotzab, H. (2003): Exploring the Contours of Supply Chain Management, in: Integrated Manufacturing Systems, 14(8): 686-695.

Müller, M., Seuring, S., Goldbach, M. (2003): Supply Chain Management – Neues Konzept oder Modetrend? (Supply Chain Management – New Concept or Fashion Trend?, in: Die Betriebswirtschaft, 63(4): 419-439.

Otto, A., Kotzab, H. (2001): Der Beitrag des Supply Chain Managements zum Management von Supply Chains – Überlegungen zu einer unpopulären Frage (The Contribution of Supply Chain Management to the Management of Supply Chains – Thoughts on an Unpopular Question), in: Zeitschrift für betriebswirtschaftliche Forschung, 53(3): 157-176.

Saunders, M., Lewis, P., Thornhill, A. (2003): Research Methods for Business Students, Prentice Hall, Harlow.

Seuring, S. (2001): Green Supply Chain Costing - Joint Cost Management in the Polyester Linings Supply Chain, in: Greener Management International, Issue 33: 71-80.

Seuring, S. (2002): Supply Chain Target Costing – An Apparel Industry Case Study, in: Seuring, S., Goldbach, M. (eds.): Cost Management in Supply Chains, Physica, Heidelberg, p. 111-125.

Seuring, S. (2004): Integrated Chain Management and Supply Chain Management – Comparative Analysis and Illustrative Cases, in: Journal of Cleaner Production, 12(8-10): 1059-1071.

Seuring, S., Goldbach, M., Koplin, J. (2004): Managing Time and Complexity in Supply Chains - Two Cases from the Textile Industry, in: International Journal of Integrated Supply Management, 1(2): 180-198.

Stuart, I., Mc Cutcheon, D., Handfield, R., McLachlin, R., Samson, D. (2002): Effective Case Research in Operations Management: A Process Perspective, in: Journal of Operations Management, 20(5): 419-433.

Swamidass, P. M. (1991): Empirical science: New frontier in Operations Management Research, in: Academy of Management Review, 16(4), 793-814.

Thierry, M., Salomon, M., Nunen, J., Van, Wassenhove, L. (1995): Strategic Issues in Product Recovery Management, in: California Management Review, 37(2): 114-135.

Voss, C., Tsikriktsis, N., Frohlich, M. (2002): Case Research in Operations Management, in: International Journal of Operations & Production Management, 22(2): 195-219.

Wacker, J. G. (1998): A Definition of Theory: Research Guidelines for Different Theory-building Research Methods in Operations Management, in: Journal of Operations Management, 16(4): 359-382.

Yin, R. K. (2003): Case Study Research – Design and Methods, 3rd edition, Sage, Thousand Oaks.

A Proposal for Case Study Methodology in Supply Chain Integration Research

Teresa M. McCarthy, Susan L. Golicic

1	Introduction	252
2	Research Purpose and Questions	254
3	Theoretical Justification	255
4	Methodology	258
5	Contributions	263
6	References	265

Summary:
This paper describes a case study research proposal designed to explore how and why firms chose to integrate process activities with supply chain partners. Previous quantitative studies suggest that integrating demand management, collaborative forecasting, and demand planning activities can lead to competitive advantage and improved supply chain performance. This qualitative research fills a gap in previous research by exploring the phenomenon of Interfirm Demand Integration in a true supply chain context, garnering perceptions from multiple supply chain partners. Results are expected to contribute to managerial, theoretical, and methodological knowledge.

Keywords:
Case Study, Supply Chain Management, Demand Management, Collaborative Forecasting, Qualitative Research

1 Introduction

In practice, many firms plan and execute supply and demand activities separately (Vokurka & Lummus, 1998). Shankar (2001: 76) asserts supply chain management has traditionally focused on "back-end operational functions, while marketing has addressed front-end, or customer-facing functions". The gap that exists between these two areas limits the potential for competitive advantage in the marketplace. As firms recognize that competition is no longer limited to company versus company, but rather supply chain versus supply chain, reliance on trading partners to help bridge the supply-demand gap and achieve competitive advantage becomes more important. As such, it is essential for trading partners to understand how to integrate supply and demand activities in order to deliver superior customer value. The purpose of this paper is to present a proposal to investigate why and how firms integrate business processes with their supply chain partners in order to bridge the gap between supply and demand activities. An additional objective is to offer a detailed description of the process followed when designing a supply chain research project to foster rigor in methodological approach and execution.

Achrol (1997) suggests that, as firms move toward a more strategic, precise focus on core competencies resulting in vertical disaggregation and outsourcing of non-core competencies, networks of trading partners become more critical for gaining access to resources not controlled within the firm. These "opportunity networks" (Achrol, 1997: 62) represent nonequity modes of governance (Tsang, 2000) in which each trading partner brings a specific strategic resource to the network, and trading partners cooperate on mutually important activities.

One mode of nonequity governance that has been explored in the interfirm literature is joint action arrangements, which is defined as "the extent to which parties undertake activities jointly rather than unilaterally" (Heide & John, 1990: 29). Joint action (JA) has been tested as a single construct representing the degree to which manufacturers and suppliers cooperate on certain activities that are important for both parties, such as: component testing, long-range planning, and forecasting (Heide & John, 1990), marketing strategy, new product launches, and premium volumes (Zaheer & Venkatraman, 1995); cost cutting, product redesign, new product development (Joshi & Stump, 1999).

McCarthy (2003) suggests the concept of undertaking activities jointly in an interfirm governance situation is more complex than that which has been measured in previous studies. McCarthy refined the JA construct and conceptualized *Interfirm Demand Integration Process* as a higher-order construct comprised of three first-order constructs. *Interfirm Demand Integration* (IDI) is a nonequity mode of governance defined as, "the systemic, strategic coordination of the customer-focused functions and tactics across businesses within the supply chain, for the purposes of improving the long-term performance of the individual companies and the supply chain as a whole" (McCarthy, 2003: 9). *IDI Process* is comprised of three distinct process activities coordinated among trading partners, each of which has been shown to improve supply chain performance (McCarthy, 2003): Demand Management (DM), Collaborative Forecasting (CF), and Demand Planning (DP) (see Figure 1).

Demand management (DM) is the mutual modification or creation of demand across firms in the supply chain. Demand management activities are used to modify or create demand to optimize supply. This can take many forms, such as: exclusive products, packaging, and bundling options; the nature and timing of co-branded or trade brand promotions; and mutual decisions regarding market segmentation and positioning. These types of activities appear to parallel traditional marketing functions known as the "4 P's", but they are coordinated between firms rather than developed within one firm.

Collaborative forecasting (CF) is a purposive exchange of specific and timely information (e.g., quantity, level, time horizon, location, probability of new business, etc.) between trading partners to develop a single shared projection of demand. The level of involvement of each partner varies, but the end result is a forecast of demand that both partners agree to and trust.

Demand planning (DP) is coordination of the flow of dependent demand through companies in the supply chain. Dependent demand is demand for component parts or "bill of materials" that is derived from end-user demand for the finished product, taking into account production and shipping lead times. This integrated process is similar to the traditional Sales and Operations Planning (S&OP) processes that occur within firms, which plan for the flow of products within a firm. However, DP integrates the processes across firms in the supply chain.

McCarthy's (2003) quantitative test of the IDI model explored the manufacturer's perception of manufacturer-retailer integration of DM, CF, and DP in the Consumer Packaged Goods industry. Results revealed a positive relationship between integration of these activities and improved supply chain performance under conditions of high interdependence.

However, Cannon & Perreault's (1999) research on buyer-seller relationships revealed some customer firms do not want or need close ties with all of their suppliers. Their results show different types of governance modes are adopted when operational elements (e.g., information exchange, legal bonds, cooperative norms, operational linkages) of the relationship vary. Their results show that governance modes differ based on the level and types of operational elements present in the relationship. Each relationship requires different types and degrees of integration resulting in different outcomes. Cannon & Perrault's results were based on a survey capturing the customer's perception of the buyer-seller relationship. When exploring interfirm relationships, Weitz & Jap (1995) emphasize the importance of refocusing research efforts from the individual firm perception toward dyadic perceptions.

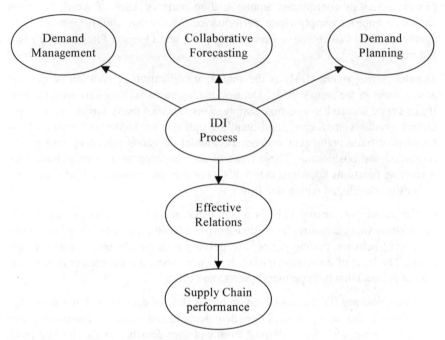

Figure 1: Model of IDI Process and Outcomes

2 Research Purpose and Questions

Many studies exploring interfirm governance modes have surveyed one trading partner's perceptions of a bilateral relationship (Cannon & Perrault, 1999; Heide & John, 1990; Joshi & Stump, 1999; McCarthy, 2003). While results of these studies of integration are important, a deeper understanding of the complex phenomena of interfirm integration requires capturing the perspectives of all trading partners involved in the integrative activities. Therefore, the purpose of this study is to explore the IDI Process model from a true supply chain context – that is, from the perspective of several trading partners within a supply chain. More specifically, this research asks the questions:

- Why do firms to choose to integrate DM, CF, and DP activities with trading partners versus executing these activities autonomously?

- How do firms integrate DM, CF, and DP activities with trading partners?

Regarding the first question, the research will also look to understand if perceptions of and attitudes toward integration with trading partners vary based on a firm's role in the supply chain (e.g., manufacturer, wholesaler, retailer, etc.). Also, which trading partner initiates the move toward integration and why? Do trading partners tend to engage in all three IDI Process activities (DM, CF, DP), or are one or two activities more commonly integrated than others?

Regarding the second research question, the study will attempt to determine if there is a particular pattern of these activities that typically occurs in a business cycle that is more effective in improving supply chain performance than alternative patterns. For example, are all three activities integrated to the same degree or are some more often practiced autonomously? Is integration of DM, CF, and DP practiced in a sequential, iterative, or concurrent manner? Answers to these complex questions can only be understood by gaining the perspectives of all trading partners involved.

3 Theoretical Justification

The literature on formation of interfirm relationships presents both economic and behavioural theories. Three theories that are suggested to explain decisions related to the formation of governance structures – transaction cost analysis (economic based), relational exchange theory (behavioural based), and resource dependence theory/resource based view (behavioural based), – are used to frame this research. Table 1 provides a summary of the approach, motivating variables, and assumptions associated with each of these theories.

Transaction cost analysis (TCA) theories explain choices firms make in organizing transactions and mode of governance (Heide, 1994; Williamson, 1985). The basic motivation of TCA is minimization of transaction costs through the most efficient governance structure. TCA theorists describe governance structures as falling on a continuum ranging from market-based transactions (arms-length) to hierarchies (vertical integration). Researchers have suggested the presence of relational exchange norms allows for a hybrid governance falling between markets and hierarchies (Macneil, 1985).

Under TCA logic, uncertainty and asset specificity are two primary factors contributing to transaction costs and, thus, choice of governance structure. Markets will generally prevail as the mode of choice unless conditions of uncertainty or asset specificity cause transaction costs to increase, resulting in a shift toward hierarchical governance (Williamson, 1985). Hybrid modes of governance prevail when asset specificity is of an intermediate degree (Tsang, 2000). A key behavioural assumption of TCA presumes firms engaged in relationships are motivated

Theory (Key contributors)	Approach	Motivating Variables	Assumptions
Transaction Cost Economics (Coase, 1937; Williamson, 1985)	• Economic	• Uncertainty • Asset specificity	• Governance structure is driven by minimization of transaction cost • Firms are motivated by economic self-interest and will behave opportunistically
Relational Exchange Theory (Granovetter, 1985; Macneil, 1980; Thibaut and Kelley, 1959)	• Behavioral	• Trust • Embeddedness	• Firms enter into a relationship with the expectation that it will be rewarding • Transactions occur within a historical and social context • Embeddeness in a relationship diminishes the need for formal governance mechanisms
Resource Dependency Theory (Pfeffer and Salancik, 1978) and Resourced Based View (Barney, 1991)	• Behavioral	• Uncertainty about supply of resources and competencies • Dependence	• Few organizations are self-sufficient • Firms develop relationships with other firms to obtain needed resources • Firms core competencies are built around resources that are valuable, rare, inimitable, and not easily substitutable

Table 1: Interfirm Governance Theories

by economic self-interest and will thus behave opportunistically when the opportunity arises (Williamson, 1985).

However, relational exchange theory (RET) offers the notion of embeddedness in a relationship (Granovetter, 1985), which evokes a "moral control" (Larson, 1992: 96) that diminishes the desire for opportunism between trading partners. Relational exchange theory proposes the nature of the exchange relationship between entities is directed by the level of expectation that the relationship will be rewarding (Thibaut & Kelley, 1959). The concept of embeddedness in social relationships explains the departure from "pure economic motives" as firms "become overlaid with social content that carries strong expectations of trust and abstention from opportunism," (Granovetter, 1985: 490). Hill (1990) explains that relationships devoid of trust will be less efficient due to the energies expended to focus on safeguarding activities necessary to check opportunism. Thus, relationships characterized by lack of trust are less likely to survive in the marketplace as competitive pressures "select out inefficient relationships and firms that enter into them, leaving behind the more efficient, trust-based ones" (Zaheer & Venkatraman, 1995: 375). Joshi & Stump (1999) suggest the presence of trust in a dyadic relationship allows partners to focus more on developing and sustaining ongoing relations rather than focusing on the present transaction. The possibility of a long-term relationship is conducive to a governance mode characterized by cooperation rather than a transactional, arms-length relationship.

The third relationship theory explaining choice of governance modes is based on possession of and dependence on resources. Resource dependence reflects the importance to a firm of obtaining resources from another firm to accomplish objectives (McCann & Galbraith, 1981). An underlying assumption of resource dependency theory is that most organizations are not self-sufficient, resulting in dependence upon other firms to obtain critical resources (Emerson, 1962; Hunt & Morgan, 1995). One strategy for reducing environmental uncertainty and managing dependence is to purposively structure bilateral governance forms with other organizations in which coordinated efforts enhance the effectiveness of both firms (Heide, 1994).

Similarly, the Resource-Based View (RBV) of the firm suggests firms possess valuable, firm-specific resources that enable them to achieve relative advantage leading to superior performance (e.g., Day, 1994; Hunt & Morgan, 1995). RBV contends the achievement and sustainability of competitive advantage is a function of the firm's core competencies (Barney, 1991; Hunt & Morgan, 1995). Barney (1991) proposes that core competencies are built around resources that are valuable, rare, difficult to imitate, and not easily substitutable.

Transaction Cost Economics, Relational Exchange Theory, and the Resource-Based theories explain various choices in interfirm governance. This research will shed light on the circumstances under which economic-based theories and/or behavioural-based theories explain integration behaviours.

4 Methodology

We follow a research process similar to those suggested by Miles & Huberman (1991) and Stuart et al. (2002). Specifically, the following steps will guide the research design and promote rigor in execution of the research:

1. Define the research question
2. Methodology
    a. Select research structure
    b. Select the sample
    c. Develop the instrument
    d. Collect data
3. Analyze data
4. Disseminate

The first step in the process – defining the research question(s) – must be completed prior to determining the research methodology, and has been presented above. The remainder of this section will describe steps two and three; methodology and data analysis.

4.1 Research Structure

The first step in designing the methodology for any research is selection of the research structure. The chosen methodological structure should be guided by the research question(s). Guidelines for matching research questions with the appropriate methodology have been offered by several researchers (Ellram, 1996; Handfield & Melynk, 1998; Stuart et al., 2002; Yin, 2003). Table 1 (adapted from Handfield & Melynk, 1998; and Stuart et al., 2002) is useful for identifying the appropriate research structure based on the research purpose and questions. Our research purpose and questions are similar to the relationship building category in Table 1 in that we are looking for patterns and linkages between variables, and a better understanding of why the relationships exist. Handfield & Melynk (1998) identify multiple-case study and/or best-in-class case study as appropriate methodological design for the research questions being explored in this study. Näslund (2002) and Yin (2003) also suggest case study methodology is well suited to meet the requirements of answering "why" and "how" questions such ours that examine contemporary phenomena in-context where control over behavioural events is not required. Therefore, a best-in-class, multiple-case design will be adopted.

4.2 Sampling

For multiple case studies, each case must be carefully selected to achieve replication of results (Yin, 1994). Thus, one pilot study and three case studies will be selected that are known a priori to integrate activities with trading partners. As such, a small number of cases is acceptable as results should illustrate replication of findings (Yin, 1994). The pilot and each case will represent one supply chain, each in a different industry. Choice of supply chains for the study will begin with selection of a focal firm (e.g., manufacturer). To achieve best-in-class sampling, the focal firm must be one that has been identified as best-in-class in supply chain integration in publications such as trade journals, academic journals, or popular press (Stuart et al., 2002). The focal firm for each supply chain will be asked to identify one strategically important supplier (e.g., component parts supplier or contract manufacturer) and two customers (e.g., retailers) that would be willing to participate in the study. The supplier will supply goods or services that are intended for the downstream retail customers involved in the study. One of the retail customers will be a highly strategic customer, the other will be one with whom the focal firm has a less strategic relationship. The rationale for including two different types of customers, as well as including supply chains in different industries, is to create variance in patterns of response to the research questions.

4.3 Instrumentation

In case study research, the measurement instrument used to maintain consistent focus and a rigorous approach is the study protocol (Yin, 2003; Stuart et al., 2002). The protocol is more than just a list of questions to be asked during data collection. It is a tool to be used by the researchers to guide them through the entire research process. Yin (2003) suggests the case study protocol should include the following four sections:

1. Overview of the case study project

This section acts as a reference to keep the researchers targeted on the subject of the case study. It includes the conceptual framework, research purpose, and research questions. Relevant readings can also be included in this section.

2. Field procedures

This section includes a list of the companies comprising each case (supply chain) included in the study. A list of the types of people that should be interviewed within each company is included in this section. Ideally, these informants should be described by job responsibility rather than title or position. In addition, introductory letters should be written describing the research project and the

Purpose	Research Question	Research Structure
Discovery: uncover areas for research and theory development	What is going on? Is it interesting enough to research?	In-depth case study (unfocused) Longitundinal case study
Description: explore territory	What is there? What are the key issues?	In-depth case study (unfocused) Longitudinal case study
Mapping: identify and describe critical variables	What are the key variables? What are the key patterns or categories?	Focused case studies In-depth field studies Multi-site case studies Best-in-class cases
Relationship building: identify linkages between variables, causal understanding	What are the patterns that link the variables? Can an order in the relationships be identified? Why do these relationships exist?	Focused case studies In-depth field studies Multi-site case studies Best-in-class cases
Theory validation: test the developed theories, predict future outcomes	Are the theories robust? Is predictive capability validated? Are there unexpected behaviours?	Experiment Quasi-experiment Large-scale sample Refutation case study
Theory extension/refinement: expand the map of the theory, better structure the theories in light of observed results	How widely applicable are the developed theories? What are the constraints?	Quasi-experiment Large-scale sample Contextual case studies

Table 2: Matching Research Question and Structure (Stuart et al., 2002: 422)

participating companies' responsibilities in the research process. For the current study, three introductory letters will be written, each targeted at a trading partner at a different level in the supply chain (i.e., a retailer letter, a focal firm letter, as supplier letter). This section will also describe the variety of evidence that should be collected during the site visit and data collection process. For case study methodology, the primary form of data collection is systematic interviewing and direct observation. Additional data includes any documents collected during the site visits, observation of the physical locations, company websites, plant tours, etc.

3. Case study questions

The questions for this case study protocol are designed to tap the phenomenon of IDI to elicit answers to the research questions presented above, and to evoke responses that will inform the theoretical issues related to TCE, RET, and RBV. Separate protocols will be developed for the focal firm, supplier, and customer to include questions appropriate for each firms' position in the supply chain. Examples of the types of questions designed to tap the constructs of the IDI model include:

- How is demand estimated for this customer (collaborative forecasting example)?
- How are production schedules determined for products sold to this customer (demand planning example)?
- What types of marketing activities are currently employed with this customer (eg., personal selling, sales promotions, advertising, public relations)? Which are most successful? (demand management example)?

4. Guide for case study report

Because a multiple case study involves collection of large amounts of documentary evidence, such as company reports, memoranda, publications, and field notes, these data need to be organized and filed in such a way as to make them easily retrievable for later use. The organizational system should be documented in this section. A specific list of materials needed for the data collection process (e.g., tape recorders, audio tapes, microphones, batteries, copy of non-disclosure agreement) should be included as part of the protocol. In addition, a contact record must be maintained listing all informants by company with their contact information, date and location of interview, and name of researcher conducting the interview.

4.4 Collect Data

For the current project, a team of two researchers will visit each site to conduct pre-arranged depth interviews using a consistent protocol across all cases. Interviews will be arranged to include boundary-spanning personnel involved in supply and demand side activities, such as buyer/purchasing/procurement, inbound and outbound logistics, supply chain management, new product development, marketing, sales, forecasting, demand planning/replenishment, and production. Interviews with informants not present during the site visit will be conducted by telephone as soon as possible following the site visit. Interviews will be transcribed verbatim, and any additional documentation collected during the process will be filed according the protocol.

4.5 Data Analysis

This research will employ pattern-matching logic as the method of analysis (Yin, 1994). In an exploratory multiple case study, this logic seeks to determine if answers to the research questions produce patterns that coincide across cases. *Literal replication* is expected to occur when comparing supply chain cases involving retailers at the same level of strategic importance, while *theoretical replication* is expected to occur when comparing results across cases with different levels of strategic importance (Yin, 1994). Literal replication occurs when patterns are identical across multiple cases. Theoretical replication exists when results from one group of cases fails to occur in a second group of cases due to predictably different circumstances, such as those suggested by TCA, RET, and RBV theories posited to explain choices in governance modes.

Transcribed interviews will be analyzed using NVivo Software. Before identifying patterns, categories of meaning relevant to the study must be identified and defined. Categories – also referred to as nodes (QSR International, 2002) – can represent constructs, concepts, processes, people, actions, or any other ideas relevant to the research. Examples of nodes that will be used in this research include each of the constructs in the IDI Model (Figure 1), and the variables associated with the interfirm governance theories (Table 1), to name a few. For this study, the research team will develop a list of nodes before analysis begins. Analysis in NVivo involves coding, a method of "linking data and ideas" by linking "selected passages of text to the category created for the coding" (QSR International, 2002: 64). Coding will be completed independently by each of the two researchers present during the interview, and subsequently compared to reconcile coding and resolve discrepancies by consensus. A third member of the team will review the reconciled transcripts to verify reliability of the codes. Upon completion of the pilot study, the team will meet to discuss general themes into which the nodes can be linked, and to identify patterns that emerge from the themes. Pattern-matching will occur as the data analysis for the three remaining case studies is completed. In a multiple case study, each case should be analyzed independently for within-case themes, patterns and conclusions before moving onto across-case analysis.

Identification of patterns can be facilitated by rearranging the order in which the data is organized. For example, the data can be arrayed by tier in the supply chain (i.e., retailer, manufacturer, supplier) with each tier in the supply chain analyzed separately, or by strategic versus non strategic relationships, or by informant position. Reorganization of the data can reveal patterns that otherwise would be difficult to discern.

4.6 Data Quality

When designing any research project, four elements must be addressed to ensure quality results (Yin, 1994). The first, internal validity is relevant when testing for causal relationships and is therefore not applicable for the present exploratory study.

Second, construct validity ensures the measures being used correspond to the research concepts. Construct validity is achieved through triangulation of multiple data sources, a chain of evidence, and key informant reviews (Yin, 1994). This research will use interviews, observation, field notes, company documents, and websites as multiple sources of data. The chain of evidence is realized when an independent observer is able to follow the analysis from original data, to coding and theme development, and to pattern matching. For this study, one team member not involved in the interviews or coding will independently review the analysis for chain of evidence. Key informant reviews – also called member checks – involve having the interview participant review a summary interpretation of the interviews. Member checks will be conducted with each company involved in the research.

External validity addresses generalizability of the results. External validity is supported by replication of findings. This replication logic will be sought in the multiple-case design whereby pattern-matching approach is adopted. Replication of results in case study design achieves analytic generalization (versus statistical generalization) from which theoretical implications can be drawn (Yin, 1994).

The fourth test for quality is reliability, which is the ability to repeatedly yield similar results across similar situations (Mentzer & Kahn, 1995). Reliability will be established in the research design by using the protocol consistently across interviews, and a common database for collecting and analyzing data. In addition, the interviews will be conducted by a team of two members of the research team and will be audiotaped for subsequent transcription to minimize researcher bias and support data quality and reliability.

Incorporating these tests into the design of qualitative research is essential to ensure quality data collection and results. Incorporating and following the tactics outlined above will lead to credible, valid, and reliable results.

5 Contributions

Results are expected to add value to both the practitioner and academic communities. Implications for managers are found in the prescriptive insights that can result from this research. Although the importance of supply chain integration is widely recognized, may firms struggle with decisions related to how and when to manage integrative processes, and with which trading partners they should enter into integrative relationships. Weitz & Jap (1995) called for research that would lead to a better understanding of what firms are doing to effectively manage inter-firm relationships, and this research answers that call. For trading partners wishing to improve management of their supply chain, results will reveal effective approaches to interfirm demand integration resulting in improved supply chain performance. More specifically, results will help firms understand how, when, and with whom to integrate supply and demand activities in order to deliver superior customer value and achieve differential advantage.

From a theoretical perspective, gaining insights into how and why relationships are forged and maintained from the perspective of multiple supply-chain trading partners will broaden our understanding of choices and outcomes in governance structure. For example, how and when do TCE, RET, and RBV theories guide decisions to develop integrative governance processes within supply chains as opposed to adopting arms-length transactional relationships? How does the corporate culture of each trading partner affect which approach (behavioural or economic) is adopted? Are cost-based and behavioural-based approaches mutually exclusive, or is some hybrid approach more common? Are governance decisions determined at a firm level, or do different divisions adopt different approaches? What is the impact of corporate structure (e.g., level of centralization) on such decisions? The current research seeks to answer these questions

The current research also makes a methodological contribution. Supply chain management research has been largely conducted from the positivist paradigm (Mentzer & Kahn, 1995; Näslund, 2002). A paucity of rigorous qualitative research has been conducted and published addressing issues related to supply chain management. In order to accurately describe, truly understand, and begin to explain these complex phenomena, supply chain scholars are calling for more studies using qualitative methods (Mentzer and Kahn, 1995), specifically more case study research (Näslund, 2002). In addition, Weitz and Jap (1995) urge interfirm relationship scholars to employ research methods that will collect data from multiple trading partners.

The present study answers these calls for qualitative research in the supply chain context by adopting a qualitative case study approach described in detail below. In doing so, the research will contribute to the body of knowledge by triangulating results from McCarthy's (2003) quantitative study while gaining a deeper, richer understanding of the complex phenomenon of IDI. Finally, the research will result in development of hypotheses that can be tested in future research to further refine our knowledge of integrative processes such as demand management, collaborative forecasting, and demand planning.

6 References

Achrol, R. S. (1997): Changes in the Theory of Interorganizational Relations in Marketing: Toward a Network Paradigm, in: Journal of the Academy of Marketing Science, 25(1): 56-71.

Barney, J. (1991): Firm Resources and Sustained Competitive Advantage, in: Journal of Management, 17(1): 99-120.

Cannon, J. P., Perreault, W. D. (1999): Buyer-Seller Relationships in Business Markets, in: Journal of Marketing Research, 36 (November): 439-460.

Coase, R. H. (1937): The Nature of the Firm, in: Economica N.S., 4: 386-405.

Day, G. S. (1994): The Capabilities of Market-Driven Organizations, in: Journal of Marketing, 58 (October): 37-52.

Ellram, L. M. (1996): The Use of the Case Study Method in Logistics Research, in: Journal of Business Logistics, 17(2), 193-138.

Emerson, R. M. (1962): Power-Dependence Relations, in: American Sociological Review, 27: 31-41.

Granovetter, M. (1985): Economic Action and Social Structure: The Problem of Embeddedness, in: American Journal of Sociology, 19 (November): 481-510.

Hanfield, R. B., Melnyk, S. A. (1998): The Scientific Theory-Building Process: A Primer Using the Case of TQM, in: Journal of Operations Management, 16, 321-339.

Heide, J. B. (1994): Interorganizational Governance in Marketing Channels, in: Journal of Marketing, 58 (January): 71-85.

Heide, J. B., John G. (1990): Alliances in Industrial Purchasing: The Determinants of Joint Action in Buyer-Supplier Relationships, in: Journal of Marketing Research, 27(1): 24-36.

Hill, C. W. L. (1990): Cooperation. Opportunism, and the Invisible Hand: Implications for Transaction Cost Theory, in: Academy of Management Review, 15, 500-513.

Hunt, S D., Morgan R. M. (1995): The Comparative Advantage Theory of Competition, in: Journal of Marketing, 59 (April): 1-15

Joshi, A. W., Stump, R L. (1999): The Contingent Effect of Specific Asset Investments on Joint Action in Manufacturer-Supplier Relationships: An Empirical Test of the Moderating Role of Reciprocal Asset Investments, Uncertainty, and Trust, in: Journal of the Academy of Marketing Science, 27(3): 291-305

Larson, A. (1992): Network Dyads in Entrepreneurial Settings: A Study of the Governance of Exchange Relationships, in: Administrative Science Quarterly, 37: 76-104.

Macneil, I. (1980): The New Social Contract. Yale University Press, New Haven, CT.

McCann, J., Galbraith, J. R. (1981): Interdepartmental Relations, in: Handbook of Organizational Design, 2: 60-84.

McCarthy, T. M. (2003): Interfirm Demand Integration: The Role of Marketing in Bridging the Gap between Demand and Supply Chain Management, Unpublished Doctoral Dissertation, The University of Tennessee.

Mentzer, J. T., Kahn, K. B. (1995): A Framework of Logistics Research, in: Journal of Business Logistics, 16(1): 231-250.

Miles, M. B., Huberman, A. M. (1984): Qualitative Data Analysis: A Sourcebook of New Methods; Sage, Newbury Park.

Näslund, D. (2002): Logistics Needs Qualitative Research – Especially Action Research, in: International Journal of Physical Distribution and Logistics Management: 32(5), 321-338.

Pfeffer, J, Salancik G. R. (1978): The External Control of Organizations: A Resource Dependence Perspective; Harper & Row, New York.

QSR International (2002): Nvivo Qualitative Data Analysis Program, third edition, Melbourne, Australia.

Shankar, V. (2001): Integrating Demand and Supply Chain Management, in: Supply Chain Management Review, (September): 76-81.

Stuart, I., McCutcheon, D., Handfiled, R., McLachlin, R., Samson, D. (2002): Effective Case Research in Operations Management: A Process Perspective, in: Journal of Operations Management, 20: 419-433.

Thibaut, J. W., Kelley, H. H. (1959): The Social Psychology of Groups, Wiley, New York.

Tsang, E. W. K. (2000): Transaction Cost and Resource-Based Explanations of Joint Ventures: A Comparison and Synthesis, in: Organization Studies, 21(1): 215-242.

Vokurka, R. J., Lummus, R. R. (1998): Balancing Marketing and Supply Chain Activities, in: Journal of Marketing Theory and Practice, 6(4): 41-50.

Weitz, B. A., Jap, S. D. (1995): Relationship Marketing and Distribution Channels, in: Journal of the Academy of Marketing Science, 4: 305-320.

Williamson, O. E. (1985): The Economic Institutions of Capitalism: Firms, Markets, and Relational Contracting, The Free Press, New York.

Yin, R. K. (2003): Case Study Research: Design and Methods, third edition, Sage Publications, Thousand Oaks.

Zaheer, A., Venkatraman N. (1995): Relational Governance as an Interorganizational Strategy: An Empirical Test of the Role of Trust in Economic Exchange, in: Strategic Management Journal, 16: 373-392.

Using Case Study Methods in Researching Supply Chains

Marie Koulikoff-Souviron, Alan Harrison

1	Introduction	268
2	The Case Research Process in Supply Chains	268
3	Critical Decisions Within Case Research on Supply Relationships	276
4	Conclusion	281
5	References	281

Summary:
This article aims to contribute to a better understanding of the use of case-based methodologies when researching supply chains. We first draw on Stuart et al. (2002) as well as other researchers in the operations management (OM) field and pioneering authors (Eisenhardt, 1989; Yin, 1993; Miles & Huberman, 1994) to examine the process of conducting case based research. We proceed from its theoretical foundations to the eventual dissemination of the research findings. We also examine how six other researchers have dealt with each stage of the research process as part of their case studies within supply chains. Finally, we illustrate this by presenting the critical decisions made in our research on supply relationships (inter- and intra- firm) and the key pitfalls we encountered.

Keywords:
Supply Chain Management, Case Study, Supply Relationship, Partnership

1 Introduction

Because of their potentially very broad scope and multi-functional perspectives, supply chains present obvious challenges to the researcher. Attempts to engage with these challenges have presented a body of knowledge that will benefit from consolidation and rationalization, as well as from closer engagement with more established bodies of knowledge. For supply chain management (SCM) to be viewed as a discipline, 'there is a need to build up clear definitional constructs and conceptual frameworks' (Croom et al., 2000). Because of the need for continuing exploratory research and theory building in what is still largely a fuzzy area, case study research presents itself as a key research strategy to engage with phenomena that have yet to be tightly identified and defined. A case study is defined as "an empirical inquiry that investigates a contemporary phenomenon within its real-life context, especially when the boundaries between phenomenon and context are not clearly evident" (Yin, 1993: 13). Such a methodology is particularly relevant for research into supply chains because it can help gather better information about the realities of supply chains and develop better, more complete theories about them (Eisenhardt, 1989; Yin, 2003).

Our own perspective on research into SCM is from an Operations Management (OM) point of view. A number of authors have investigated case based research in the OM field (for example, McCutcheon & Meredith, 1993; Meredith, 1998; Stuart et al., 2002; Voss et al., 2002). However, there is an opportunity to extend its application to the more recent and very broad concept of SCM (Cigolini et al, 2004), thus broadening the scope of operations from a single business unit or company to the whole supply chain.

This article aims to contribute to a better understanding of the application of case-based research into SCM. We first draw on Stuart et al. (2002) and pioneering authors (Eisenhardt, 1989; Yin, 1994 and 2003; Miles & Huberman, 1994) to examine the process of conducting case research, from its theoretical foundations to the eventual dissemination of the research findings. We examine each stage of the research process by referring to six articles from the Journal of Operations Management which apply case study methods to researching aspects of SCM. Finally, we provide further evidence from our own research into supply chain relationships and the key pitfalls we encountered in relation to the supply chain context.

2 The Case Research Process in Supply Chains

We have adopted Stuart's 5-stage process model in order to present our perspectives on researching supply chains (see Figure 1). Each stage will be reviewed, from the perspective of case study research and will concurrently highlight specificities of the supply chain context.

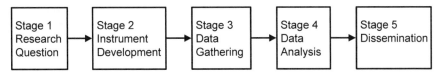

Figure 1: The Five Stage Research Process Model (Stuart et al., 2002)

2.1 Stage 1: Defining the Research Question

Within supply chains, research questions can be asked at different levels of analysis depending on the scope of the study: the internal supply chain, the dyadic supply relationship, the chain and the network (Harland, 1996). It is interesting to note from Table 1 that three out of the six articles listed are located in the internal supply chain, thus highlighting the focus on internal operations still prevailing within operations management research.

There is an ongoing debate on the extent to which a pre-determined framework should guide case investigations. Yin (1994) clearly positions theory development as an inherent feature of case study research design and a necessary step prior to the collection of any data. This is a point of difference between cases and related methods such as ethnography or grounded theory. Thus a-priori identification of constructs from the literature can help provide a better grounding for the emergent theory (Eisenhardt, 1989). Moreover, "a loose, inductive design may be a waste of time" (Miles & Huberman, 1994: 17). However, a strong theoretical framework also raises issues, in that the data collection in the field may be limited by the pre-determined decisions of what to look at. A middle position may also be advocated whereby there is no strict adherence either to "no theory ideal" or to "strong a-priori explanation", but rather a continuous interplay between the two.

Within supply chain management, there is a lack of significant body of a-priori theory (Croom, 2000). In this context of paucity of theory, the use of case studies should be favored as a way to develop stronger theory (Stuart et al., 2002). Research in SCM draws on various bodies of literature, which have been categorized by Croom et al. (2000) as: Strategic management, logistics, marketing, relationship/partnership, best practices and organizational behavior. Table 1 shows the different theory bases used in recent articles, which draw on operations research as well as theories from other fields – this confirms a mixture of OM academic and non-OM academic spread of theories identified in previous works (Stuart et al., 2002).

Case Study	Purpose	Theoretical base	Question	Level of analysis	Number of cases/units of analysis
Pagell, 2004	Theory building Explanatory	Operations research and strategy	What are drivers of internal integration?	Internal supply chain	11 plants from 11 distinct companies
Salvador et al., 2002	Theory testing Explanatory	Design theory/engineering management	How to reduce the product variety- operational performance trade-off?	Internal supply chain	6 product families
Guide et al., 2003	Theory building and testing Explanatory	Operations research and strategy	What problems with descriptions of re-manufacturing?	Internal supply chain	3 cases of closed loop supply chains
Choi & Hong, 2002	Theory building Explanatory		What does a network look like? How does it behave?	Supply network	3 different product families
Heikkila, 2002	Theory building Testable hypothesis	Operations research	What is the architecture of a performing demand chain?	Supply chain	6 customer cases of Nokia demand chain
Williams et al., 2002	Theory testing Explanatory	Value chain, TCE and resource based theory	What strategic capabilities? Where should they be located?	Supply chain	4 case studies manufacturing programs aircraft ind.

Table 1: A Sample of Case Study Research in Supply Chain Management[1]

2.2 Stage 2: Instrument Development and Case Selection

An important element in case-based research is to select cases from an appropriate population in order to avoid, as much as possible, extraneous variations (Eisenhardt, 1989). This involves considering the potential effects of industry, organization size, manufacturing processes and inter-organizational effects (Stuart et al., 2002). Unlike survey design, the choice of case study sites should follow theoretical rather than statistical reasons. Hence cases often are not aimed to be representative but rather exemplary. Pettigrew (1990) proposes three criteria for case selec-

---

[1] Table 1 was compiled from a keyword search on 'case study' and 'supply chain' in the Operations Management Journal. Out of the nine articles that were listed, three were discarded because they did not explicitly refer to Yin's (1989, 1994 or 2003) methodology. The Operations Management Journal was chosen specifically as a reference because of its recent call (Meredith, 2002) for more case study research.

tion: (a) Go for extreme situations (b) Go for polar types as a way of disconfirming patterns from one case study to the other. (c) Go for high experience levels. Pettigrew (1990: 274) also describes as "planned opportunism" the practicalities of the process of choosing and gaining access to research sites. Thus a rationale for the selection of multiple case studies is provided, as opposed to the single case (Yin, 1994). Within SCM research, a single case may be chosen in order to research in great depth exemplary practices, such as cooperative buyer supplier relationships at Toyota.

In the selection of case studies from Table 1, it is interesting to note that all of the researchers have favored a multiple-case design (from three to eleven cases). One explanation is that evidence from multiple cases is considered more compelling and the overall study more robust. Moreover, researchers may have looked for increased generalizability from multiple cases (Leonard-Barton, 1990). The sampling rationale was argued on the basis of: polar types (Heikkilä, 2002) – high or low performance; (Salvador et al., 2002) – high or low product variety and production volume); exemplar cases (Choi & Huong, 2002) case study of Honda, Acura and DaimlerChrysler; (Guide Jr. et al., 2003) case of Kodak, Xerox and US Navy) or comprehensiveness (Williams et al., 2002) argue that their cases cover almost all of the main aerospace market segments. One case only (Pagell, 2004) used planned opportunism as a rationale for case selection: the selected sites were located within 200 miles of the researcher's place of employment.

Defining the unit of analysis, or "defining what the 'case' is" can be problematic in researching supply chains because of the potentially extensive scope of the phenomenon under study (Yin, 2004). Beside the main unit of analysis, cases can also have embedded designs with subunits (Yin, 1993: 39). In the six articles, presented in Table 1, subunits of analysis are: different organizations (Choy and Hong, 2002; Heikkilä, 2002), stages of the value chain (Williams, 2002; Guide et al., 2003), production processes (Salvador et al., 2002), individual functional managers (Pagell, 2004).

The case study protocol contains the instruments, procedures and rules that should be used (Yin, 1994). The protocol is a major tactic in increasing the reliability of case study research and is intended to guide the researcher in conducting each case. Three of the researchers from Table 1 specifically referred to the research protocol in their methodological review (Pagell, 2004; Heikilla, 2002; Choi, Huong, 2002).

2.3 Stage 3: Data Gathering

"Sampling is crucial for later analysis. As much as you might want to, you cannot study everyone, everywhere doing everything" (Miles & Huberman, 1994: 27). The case study protocol needs to document which persons should be interviewed as well as the other sources of information (Yin, 1994). However, "sampling is iterative, working in progressive "waves" as the study progresses" (Miles & Huberman, 1994: 29). Thus one characteristic of case studies is the flexible data collection, which typically draws on multiple data collection methods (Eisenhardt, 1989) to allow triangulation (Jick, 1979). Eisenhardt (1989) argues for joint data collection and analysis; as themes emerge from the field, then the researcher has freedom to add more data.

Case Study	Number of informants	Number of functions	Number of levels within each firm	Number of organizations
Pagell, 2004	Not available	Purchasing, operations, logistics	Several levels in 7 out of 11 plants	Single organization
Salvador et al., 2002	Not available	Product development, manufacturing, purchasing, human resources	Middle and high level managers	Single organization
Guide et al., 2003	Less then 10	Not available	Senior managers	Single organization
Choi & Hong, 2002	Not available	Purchasing, sales representatives, operations	Managers	Final assembler, 3 top-tier and 3 second-tier suppliers
Heikkila, 2002	35 informants; 27 from Nokia, 8 from customers	Not available: members of the demand chain	Not available: members of the demand chain	Supplier-customer representatives
Williams et al., 2002	260 people	Different functional areas	Multiple level	96 organisations

Table 2: Levels of Interview Data Collection within Supply Chains

When dealing with other companies, firms can choose to adopt different types of relationships, which involve very few or multiple ties between organizations. Hence, when collecting data on supply chains, decisions have to be made on the number of individuals interviewed (one "key informant" or several), the number of functions and levels within each individual organization. Moreover, analysis of supply chain configuration requires an identification of the number of organizations and the number of sites per organization (Rudberg & Olhager, 2003). Table 2 shows the different levels of interview data collection in the articles reviewed.

When collecting interview data, researchers should consider the trade-off between efficiency and richness of data (Voss et al., 2002). The richness of a broad sampling allows convergence and clarification (Jick, 1979) but it is also very resource intensive and takes a lot of time. The logic for stopping data collection is when saturation is achieved, that is the point where additional data is only adding incremental value (Eisenhardt, 1989).

Although the authors from our sample have provided extended information about their study design, it is interesting to note from Table 2 that half of them have failed to provide the exact number of interviews that they have conducted. The research sample shows a range of functional scope, some of them limited to the traditional arena of logistics and operations, whereas others have a broader scope including product development, human resource or sales. Finally, the predominance of input sought from senior or middle managers points to what Miles & Huberman (1994) label "elite bias", which, depending on the research question may affect the representativeness of the informants sampling.

The length and protocol for conducting interviews and the extent to which the researcher sticks to the initial interview guide should be provided to the reader, while only two authors mention detailed interviews briefly (Choi & Huong, 2002; Pagell 2004) (see Table 3).

Case Study	Survey	Documentation	Observation	Other data
Pagell, 2004	No	No	Plant tour	No
Salvador et al., 2002	No	Company profiles, industry press, commercial documents	No	Archival data; video tapes. IS
Guide et al., 2003	No	No	No	Internal supply chain
Choi & Hong, 2002	No	Bill of Materials, Vendor agreements	Plant tour	No
Heikkila, 2002	Questionnaires (43 responses for 63 – rate: 73%)	Quantitative data: forecasting and delivery; order-to-delivery cycles, inventory	No	No
Williams et al., 2002	104 face to face interviews	No	No	No

Table 3: Other Data Collection Methods within Supply Chains

A strong feature of case studies as a research strategy is the ability for the researcher to combine multiple data collection methods as a way to have a stronger substantiation of constructs through triangulation. All researchers in our sample drew on at least one additional method, beside interviews, as a way to provide construct validity. Another source of triangulation is data collection by multiple researchers. This was explicitly used by Pagell (2004) and Williams et al. (2002).

2.4 Stage 4: Data Analysis

An iterative, cyclical process characterizes the interaction between data collection and the three components of data analysis: data reduction, data display and conclusions drawing (Miles & Huberman, 1994). Data reduction refers to the process of selecting, focusing, simplifying, abstracting, and transforming the data that appear in written-up field note or transcriptions. This form of analysis sharpens and organizes the data in preparation for conclusion drawing and verification. Data displays allow the researcher to concentrate on a reduced set of data as a basis for thinking about its meaning. The displays help the researcher see patterns. Then the process of writing up conclusions calls for further analytic moves in the data displays, which in turn drive further conclusions. Thus displayed data and the emerging written text influence each other (Miles & Huberman, 1994).

The aim of comparative research is to understand, explain and interpret the phenomenon of interest by identifying similarities and differences across cases. Indeed, "it is not difficult to make sense of an individual case (…). The challenge comes in trying to make sense of the diversity across cases in a way that unites similarities and differences in a single, coherent framework" (Ragin, 1987: 19).

Case Study	Within case analysis	Cross-case analysis
Pagell, 2004	Field notes, data analysis and coding. Reduction through tables. *Coding validity check*	Looking for patterns across organizations.
Salvador et al., 2002	Coding technique	Looking for patterns across cases.
Guide et al., 2003	Presentation of each individual case finding. Validity check	Cross-case conclusion
Choi & Hong, 2002	Within case analysis – no data on actual analysis technique provided. *External validity check: sampling*	Looking for patterns across cases.
Heikkila, 2002	Detailed case study write-ups – Review by informants and survey data. *Reliability and construct validity check*	Search for cross-case patterns: similarities and differences. Case comparison across initial groups
Williams et al., 2002	Qualitative software package. Hierarchical structure	No cross-case analysis

Table 4: Data Analysis Techniques within Supply Chains

One characteristic of comparative research is that cases need to be viewed as "combinations of characteristics" and investigated as wholes (Ragin, 1987). This involves as well understanding and comparing the contextual elements of the cases, which Pettigrew describes as encompassing a "vertical level" including the higher and lower levels of analysis as well as the time dimension, labeled "horizontal level" (Pettigrew, 1990).

Most researchers drew on Miles & Huberman (1994) as a reference for within and cross-case analysis, however little detail was provided on the replication logic used (Yin, 1993; Eisenhardt, 1989) for the multiple cases. Table 4 shows that most researchers have used cross-case patterns as a tactic to build up stronger theories.

2.5 Stage 5: Disseminating the Research Findings

Miles & Huberman (1994) stress the multi-facetted issues related to the 'quality' of qualitative research: "How will you, or anyone else, know whether the finally emerging findings are good? That term has many possible definitions: possibly or probably true, reliable, valid, dependable, reasonable, confirmable, credible, useful, compelling, significant, empowering..." (1994: 277).

A major concern with case study research is rigor in its design. Yin (1994: 33) introduces four tests to safeguard the quality and the overall validity of case study research.

- Construct validity requires that investigators develop "a sufficiently operational set of measures" that preclude "subjective judgments" (Yin, 2003: 35). Convergent validity stems from the accumulation of evidence that converges on a single, well-defined construct whereas discriminant validity stems from the establishment of a conceptual dissimilarity between two constructs (Leonard-Barton, 1990).

- Internal validity requires investigators to establish whether the right cause and effect relationships have been established. One tactic consists in validating conclusions through "pattern matching" where patterns expected from the theory are compared with patterns in the empirical data. This involves the use of "logic" as a test (McCutcheon & Meredith, 1993).

- External validity deals with the question of the applicability of findings beyond the population under study. Yin (1994) argues for analytical generalization by comparing findings against a broader theory. This can be achieved either by literal replication, where, based on the theory, similar results would be expected across cases or by theoretical replication where, based on the theory, different results would be expected.

- Reliability can be increased through documenting the research process to such an extent that data could be duplicated even if collected at another time or through another researcher. This is facilitated through the use of a case study protocol to ensure the trail of evidence is thoroughly documented and a case data base to ensure traceability of all data (Yin, 1994).

Table 4 shows that in the six articles reviewed, Yin's (1994) four quality measures have not been systematically reviewed by each author, although as we have seen throughout the four other stages of the research process, they have been rather explicit on other features of their research.

3 Critical Decisions Within Case Research on Supply Relationships

This section highlights methodological issues related to the research design we developed in support of a cross-case comparison of two dyadic supply relationships. The first was between two partners in the chemical industry in the UK (inter-firm), the second between French and English sites of a pharmaceutical firm that worked on different stages in the manufacture of a drug (intra-firm). Thus we elected to focus the scope of our study onto dyadic rather than onto broader-based supply relationships.

Yin (1994, 55) argues that conducting case study research is not easy in that its demands on a person's intellect, ego and emotions are far greater than those of any other research strategy. The aim of this introspective section is to identify and reflect upon such difficulties in relation to case study research. Following the logic of Stuart et al. (2002), we present our design decisions and present the pitfalls of the research design, in order to share the difficulties encountered in the course of the fieldwork and the potential biases inherent in the research design. For each element, possible tactics are proposed to overcome these pitfalls, which may be valuable wisdom for other researchers conducting case studies.

3.1 Design Decision 1: A-priori Theoretical Framework

This study focused on the 'relationship' as a conceptual framework for the study of inter- and intra-firm relationships. A set of dimensions and their related human resources issues were developed from the literature to characterize operational aspects of managing supply relationships within inter- and intra-firm contexts. These dimensions comprised the intellectual 'bins' (Miles & Huberman, 1994) that guided the researcher as to what information should be collected and analyzed.

There is a direct step from conceptual framework to research questions (Miles & Huberman,1994: 22). The following questions were articulated to conduct this research: (1) In what ways do supply relationships exhibit "specific" characteristics of reciprocal supply relationships and related HR issues? (2) In what ways do HR practices influence supply relationships? (3) How do the inter- and intra-firm contexts influence the supply relationship? The research questions operationalized the conceptual framework in that they aimed at investigating the relationship, its characteristics, HR elements and the inter- and intra-firm comparison. The first question was more deductive in that it sought to compare characteristics of supply relationships in practice with "specific" characteristics derived from the literature. The second and third questions had a more exploratory nature in that there was a gap in the literature on HR within relationships and also little qualitative research had been conducted on intra-firm buyer-supplier relationships.

- Pitfall 1: Data Collection May Be Limited and Biased

Issues related to a strong conceptual framework include the fact that the investigators may be blind to the information or cues that were outside the framework, so that the findings may be just results of a self-serving process.

Our study had an exploratory feature, firstly because little research has sought to compare inter- with intra-firm relationships and secondly because there is a paucity of studies on HR within supply relationships. Therefore, the conceptual framework, developed from the literature review, provided a first list of constructs, which loosely guided the data collection process. This initial framework was iteratively modified based on empirical data from the first (inter-firm), and then the second (intra-firm) study. One example of this was removing the concept of "HR philosophy" as a construct because it appeared as an internal construct that did not explain what was happening in the supply relationship.

3.2 Design Decision 2: "Relationship" as Heart of the Case

This research sought to reduce extraneous variation by selecting cases based on strategic supplier-manufacturer relationships, involving large multinational companies, in the chemical industry (Wheatco and Chemco) and in the closely related pharmaceutical industry (Tyrenco). The second case was selected based on a contrast with the first case: i.e. intra-firm instead of inter-firm, and separate location rather than geographically close. The 'relationship' became the unit of analysis in each case. Moreover, the site selection also drew on "planned opportunism" (Pettigrew, 1990). The fact that one of us was a past employee of Wheatco enabled the access to the first case, whilst privileged contacts between the University School of Management and Tyrenco facilitated access to the second case study.

The focus on the "relationship" involves having a clear description of the unit of analysis in terms of its conceptual nature (the 'relationship'), its social size (the individuals who participate in the relationship), its physical location (the locations where the main activities pertaining to the relationship take place) and its temporal extent (Miles & Huberman, 1994). The bounding of the unit of analysis was based on the main physical product flows, related to the strategic product lines that were at the core of the relationships. Anchoring the qualitative sampling for the 'relationship' on physical flows provided a rationale for excluding other processes, such as secondary flows, which were less central to the study.

- Pitfall 2: Side Tracking into the Subunit of Analysis

"An embedded design (...) has some pitfalls. A major one occurs when the case study focuses only on the subunit level and fails to return to the larger unit of analysis" (Yin, 1994: 44). The focus on the 'relationship' as the main unit of analysis was a central feature of the research design. However, other embedded units of analysis also needed to be considered, such as the partner organizations, the specific units that are in contact (manufacturing units), and the individual employees. This implied a risk of shifting the focus of analysis from the main to the sub-unit.

Such a pitfall was encountered with the intra-firm research, which went off track for the first three months. The study of the relationship between French and English sites of a pharmaceutical firm shifted from the inter-site to the English sub-unit. The original intent was to allow the researcher to become familiar with the background and culture of the overall company and to better understand the context of the site and of its manufacturing unit, which underwent difficulties, both in terms of process performance and people management issues. This "side-tracked" study resulted in a short summarized analysis, which was not part of the final report on the supply relationship. Such indecision has been described by Leonard-Barton (1990) as a shortcoming attributable to operationalization.

3.3 Design Decision 3: Broad Sampling

This research drew on four data collection methods: the main one was semi-structured interviews, supplemented with documentation and archival data, observation and, for one case only, a survey.

We sought to adopt a multi-perspective approach, and to avoid 'elite-bias' by drawing on the perspective of informants at different levels in the relationships studied. The rationale for the choice of informants was to have a broad range of interviewees from each of the units involved in the supply relationships, as well as broad functional representation across levels (manufacturing, quality, logistics) from operating room to site and corporate management. A total of 66 persons were interviewed in the course of the two stages of research, some of them on several occasions. Thus the total number of interviews was 84. In each case study, individuals from each 'side' of the relationship were identified as "key informants" and constituted throughout the research, a resource, to provide access to data or get feedback on emerging themes. Between-firm sampling was a source of verification and triangulation in that it allowed a comparison of points of view.

The Wheatco-Chemco relationship was characterized by a high involvement from operators, who had to be in contact in order to operate the joint production process on a continuous basis. Due to the size of the population (43 operators), the opportunity was grasped to organise a survey of their perception of the other site, as triangulation for the qualitative data. This provided a very useful tactic as it helped confirm some key HR requirements for working across firms.

Thus, one strength of this study was that, thanks to the broad sampling and the time perspective, it could draw on triangulation by data source, which include persons, times, places as well as triangulation by method (interviews, survey, documentation, observation).

- Pitfall 3: Data Overload

A major pitfall of qualitative research is the sheer amount of data that the researcher has to deal with (Miles & Huberman, 1994). Indeed, as argued by Leonard-Barton (1990), "it is difficult to identify critical data in a real-time study, while one is in the midst of the research".

The use of software is all the more appropriate when the amount of data is rather large. Eighty-four interviews, lasting between 1 to 3 hours, were conducted, and more than a hundred other electronic documents were collected. Therefore, from the point of view of data management, software package were relevant. In this research, a computer-assisted qualitative data analysis software (CAQDAS) was used as a tool. N'Vivo® allowed storage and retrieval of the qualitative data, coding, memo writing, sorting and searching.

3.4 Design Decision 4: Use of Similar Protocols to Converse across Studies

Following Miles & Huberman, matrix displays were used extensively in this study as a way to reduce the data and make sense out of it. The purpose was to follow the analytic progression from the descriptive, which aims at making a clear account of the phenomena, through to the explanatory, which seeks to show how concepts fit together, thus allowing some theoretical insights to emerge (Miles & Huberman, 1994). Starting from the raw data, i.e. the node in NVivo (from the coded texts), intermediary tables were produced in order to reduce and categorize the main themes within the node (following a cluster tactic in Miles & Huberman, 248-252). Several iterations were required before developing the final displays. The matrix data was kept as close as possible to the in-vivo text, in order to ensure the context was well rendered.

Interim case reports were used in both cases. They were submitted to key informants. An early version of the case study report on Wheatco-Chemco was developed as a teaching case; it was useful to provide a first synthesis of the case. A draft case study report was written including a return to the literature to tie back the findings. A similar approach was used for Tyrenco.

- Pitfall 4: Seeking Data to Corroborate Own Convictions

A potential weakness of the chosen design pertains to its reliance on qualitative research, which is dependent on the researcher herself as an observant agent, and therefore is prone to be impregnated by the researcher's personal bias. Indeed, the quality of the study depends on whether the study design precludes the investigators from consciously or unconsciously seeking and collecting data to corroborate their preconceived positions among other things. This requires detailed information on how the investigations were carried out and demonstrate that these investigations revealed the relevant picture.

The inter-firm interview guide was the result of several iterations; it was originally longer and more structured but soon evolved to be less constraining. We developed more flexible approaches to the way of asking and sequencing the questions, and to segment them appropriately for different informants. Interviews generally began with an introductory phase, where key objectives of the research were presented. The informant's role in the relationship was then discussed, together with the extent of his interface with the other firm. The intent of the first, rather broad, open-ended questions was to encourage the informants to discuss the supply relationship as much as possible without being influenced by the researcher. Confirmatory questions on the constructs derived from the conceptual framework were generally asked later. Exploratory questions on HR were by and large asked at the end of the interview, although very often themes related to HR would emerge in relation to other questions about the supply relationship.

This interview guide was later used with little modification to run interviews at the intra-firm site. A specific issue was raised in respect to the use of the word 'HR' as in the intra-firm case it was very much referring to the individual HR function, which was not the topic of the study. Therefore all questions were reworded to discuss 'people management', which better fit the informal processes that took place within the internal supply relationship.

3.5 The Rigor of Case-Based Research

This section focuses on construct validity as an illustration of the rationale used for enhancing the quality of the research.

- Construct validity requires that investigators develop "a sufficiently operational set of measures" that preclude "subjective judgments" (Yin, 2003: 35). One of the intent of the research was to better understand different characteristics of supply relationships. One of the constructs was "shared relationship goal", which was operationalized as "strategic" (corporate) vs. "operational" (local relationship) goals. Multiple measure of the construct included "objective" measures (e.g. availability or not of written communication on shared goal) to more "subjective" measures (e.g. the individual's perception of "win-win" but "implicit" goal). The contrast between the inter- and intra-firm case studies showed interesting differences – whereby the intra-firm goals were joint at overall strategic level – but very separate at local level, whereas it was the opposite with the inter-firm relationship, with no stated joint goals at strategic level, but very clear measurable goals at local level. Moreover, the construct of "shared relationship goal" was clearly differentiated from the individual unit or firm "internal goals", that pertained to the individual operational results of the unit or firm. One interesting outcome of this distinction was that in the inter-firm case study, a imbalance stemmed from the fact that one of the partners had aligned their internal goal setting on the relationship goals, whereas the other partner had not. The study thus provided corroborating evidence of both convergent and divergent validity for the construct. Moreover, as indicated by Leonard-Barton (1990), the measures of the construct varied across time and relative to different interviewees.

4 Conclusion

This article has sought to contribute to a better understanding of the role of case study research within supply chains. Following a five stage research process model, we have presented the features of the case study methodology. We have concurrently illustrated those through an in depth review of six articles from the Journal of Operations Management. This allowed us to draw some conclusions about the practice of case studies to research supply chains. Researchers have provided in-depth information about their methodologies to demonstrate the need for rigor in conducting case studies.

Our own research into supply chain relationships has been presented with a review of key pitfalls we have encountered. We believe that our lessons will be of benefit to other researchers.

5 References

Choi, T., Huong, Y. (2002): Unveiling the structure of supply networks: Case studies of Honda, Acura, and Daimler Chrysler, in: Journal of Operations Management, 20: 469-493.

Cigolini, R., Cozzi, M., Perona, M. (2004): A new framework for supply chain management: Conceptual model and empirical test, in: International Journal of Physical Distribution and Logistics Management, 24(1): 7-41.

Croom, S., Romano, P., Giannakis, M.. (2000): Supply Chain Management: An Analytical Framework for Critical Literature Review, in: European Journal of Purchasing and Supply Management, 6(1) : 67-83.

Eisenhardt, K. M. (1989): Building Theories from Case Study Research, in: Academy of Management Review, 14(5): 532-50.

Guide Jr., V. D. R., Jayaraman, V., Linton, J. (2003): Building contingency planning for closed-looped supply chains with product recovery, in: Journal of Operations Management, 21: 259-79.

Harland, C. M. (1996): Supply chain management: relationships, chains and networks, in: British Journal of Management, 7 (Special Issue): S63-S80.

Heikkilä, J. (2002): From supply to demand chain management: efficiency and customer satisfaction, in: Journal of Operations Management, 20: 747-67.

Jick, T. (1979): Mixing Qualitative and Quantitative Methods: Triangulation in Action, in: Administrative Science Quarterly, 24: 602-11.

McCutcheon, D.,Meredith, J. (1993): Conducting case study reserch in Operations Management, in: Journal of Operations Management, 11: 239-56.

Meredith, J. (1998): Building Operations Management theory through case and field research, in: Journal of Operations Management, 16: 441-54.

Miles, M., Huberman, A. (1994): Qualitative data analysis: an expanded sourcebook, SAGE, Thousand Oaks, Ca.

Pagell, M. (2004): Understanding the factors that enable and inhibit the integration of operations, purchasing and logistics, in: Journal of Operations Management, 22: 459-487.

Pettigrew, A. (1990): Longitudinal field research on change: theory and practice, in: Organization Science, 1(3): 267-292.

Salvador, F., Forza, C., Rungtuséannatham, M. (2002): Modularity, product variety, production volume, and component sourcing: theorizing beyond generic prescriptions, in: Journal of Operations Management, 20: 549-75.

Stuart, I., McCutcheon, D., Handfield, R., McLachlin, R., Samson, D. (2002): Effective Case Research in Operations Management: A Process Perspective, in: Journal of Operations Management, 20: 419-33.

Voss, C., Tsikriktsis, N., Frohlich, M. (2002): Case research in Operations Management, in: International Journal of Physical Distribution and Logistics Management, 22(2): 195-219.

Williams, T., Maull, R., Ellis, B. (2002): Demand chain management theory constraints development from global aerospace supply webs, in: Journal of Operations Management, 20: 691-706.

Yin, R. K. (1994): Case study research: design and methods, Sage, Thousand Oaks, CA.

Multilevel Issues in Supply Chain Management

Marian Oosterhuis, Eric Molleman, Taco van der Vaart

1 Introduction 284
2 Behavioral Issues in Supply Chain Management 285
3 The Specification of Levels and Their Interrelatedness 287
4 Construct at Different Levels and Measurement Issues 289
5 Data Structures and Analysis 293
6 Summary and Conclusion 295
7 References 295

Summary:
This study focuses on possible contributions of the multilevel approach to research in supply chain management. Supply chains consist of multiple organizations comprising different departments with people who are interacting inside and across organizations. Factors at different levels may thus influence chain performance in different ways. What is more, the multilevel approach recognizes that concepts may have different or similar meanings at different levels. Finally, the multilevel approach makes nested data structures, for instance data of ten purchasers nested in a purchasing department, more apparent and analyzable. A multilevel approach to SCM may contribute to this field in at least three ways: (1) conceptually/theoretically, (2) in a methodological sense and (3) in an analytical way. In this paper we will elaborate on these issues and we will apply them to our own research on human behavior in supply chains.

Keywords:
Supply Chain Management, Multilevel Theory, Organizational Behavior

1 Introduction

Long before a multilevel approach became popular in organizational studies, it was used in educational research to help find answers to questions such as 'does it matter to which school I send my child?', 'what is the impact of class size on the performance of individual pupils?', or 'what is the impact of the didactical style of a teacher on the learning outcomes of individual students?' (see, for example, Burstein, 1980; Cronbach & Webb, 1979; Raudenbush & Bryk, 1986; for an overview, see Hox, 2002). It was clear that the performance of individual pupils was not only dependent on characteristics of these pupils themselves, such as, for example, intelligence, but also depended on the class or school they were in. This actually means that the performance of individual pupils from the same school and/or class, at least partly, depends on their shared context. From a statistical point of view this means that the results of students within the same class and school are not independent, which is an assumption to apply traditional ways of analyzing and explaining the variance of variables, such as school success. Multilevel analysis does not hold this assumption and takes the interdependence of observations into account.

Later on, a multilevel approach was used to find answers to organizational questions, such as 'what impact does being in a team have on individual motivation?' or 'what is the impact of reward policies on individual motivation?' (for an overview, see Klein & Kozlowski, 2000). The goal of this contribution is to extend the application area of multilevel methodology to the field of supply chain management (SCM). For illustrative purposes we will focus on the area in which we do research ourselves, i.e. behavioral issues in supply chain management. In several places we will include examples that we have borrowed from a case study that we recently conducted in a large manufacturing firm.

As stated above, a multilevel approach has consequences for the way in which empirical material should be analyzed. However, the implications of a multilevel approach are more far-reaching than only these analytical consequences. It also affects theory building, the design of the study, the definition of concepts and the composition of measurement instruments (e.g. Chan, 1998; Klein & Kozlowski, 2000). Therefore, multilevel research brings with it several critical issues and considerations. The following three issues (e.g. Hox, 2002; Klein & Kozlowski, 2000; Snijders & Bosker, 1999) have especially been signposted as key issues in multilevel research, i.e. (1) the specification of levels and their interrelations, (2) constructs at different levels and measurement issues, and (3) data structures and analysis. In this paper we will highlight these three issues. However, before doing this we will briefly introduce our research subject, i.e. behavioral issues in SCM and the case study we will use for illustrative purposes.

2 Behavioral Issues in Supply Chain Management

Research suggests that close collaboration within supply chains leads to improved performance, for example reductions in capital investments, improvements in conformance quality, risk reduction (Lado et al., in Johnston et al, 2004) and improved process technology adoption (Johnston & Linton, in Johnston et al., 2004). However, in current supply chain research little attention seems to be paid to the way collaboration takes place and to the behavior of people that might stimulate or hinder collaboration. The scant research that does exist seems to focus on concepts such as trust or commitment without paying much attention to the people involved who actually expose this behavior. We want to study how different chain types initiate human behavior that is beneficial or disadvantageous for supply chain performance. For example, the behavior of purchasing managers might be disadvantageous when purchasing managers are rewarded for getting the best price out of suppliers, thereby hindering the development of longstanding relationships (Beth et al., 2003).

In our study we distinguish two chain types: innovation-oriented chains and cost-oriented chains (Darr & Talmud, 2003; Lamming et al., 2000; Randall et al., 2003). Innovation-oriented chains create unique products and are characterized by the ability to coordinate technological developments (Kumpe & Bolwijn, 1994). Activities are non-routine and non-repetitive and are often performed in multidisciplinary teams that are well equipped with far-reaching power. Cost-oriented chain types are distinguished by large-scale facilities, long production lead times, large batch sizes, low product variety, standard procedures and routine tasks (Randall, 2003; Kumpe & Bolwijn, 1994). Buyers and sellers in innovation-oriented chains will experience uncertainty regarding product design and product application and will have to interact in order to arrive at shared ideas about the product and eventually its development (Darr & Talmud, 2003). Darr & Talmud (2003) proved that interaction in the sales process of innovation-oriented chains primarily occurs between technical experts on the work floor, without the brokerage of distributors or sales representatives. However, in cost-oriented chains, properties of the product were clear and the sales process was arranged in formal sales contracts at the strategic level of sellers' and buyers' organizations. A lot less interaction was needed in order to exchange the product, and interaction primarily occurred by means of formal forms and letters and strict protocols based on clauses in the sales contract.

We expect that these differences between innovation-oriented chains and cost-oriented chains influence the level at which behavioral issues predominantly influence chain performance, as well as influence the direction of behavior within firms that are involved (either bottom-up or top-down). In line with Darr & Talmud (2003) we suppose that innovation-oriented chains' interaction between supply chain partners will mainly take place at the operational level and that consequently, performance will be influenced by human behavior at the operational level. On the other hand, based on Darr & Talmud (2003) it is expected that interaction within cost-oriented chains will predominantly occur at the strategic level and that therefore human behavior will influence performance at the strategic level. Furthermore, we expect that in innovation-oriented chains, behavior at the operational level affects decisions at higher levels, much more than the other way around. In other words, behavioral issues between suppliers and buyers at the operational level will influence decisions at the tactical and strategic level of buyer's and seller's organizations. For example, if a buying assistant in an innovation-oriented chain is rewarded for buying at high speed, this will affect the decisions of the supplier's technical experts and will hence influence strategic decisions regarding the supplier's product development process. Contrastingly, we expect that in cost-oriented chains, strategic decisions will influence behavior at the operational level. Figure 1 presents our multilevel view of on the one hand the interactions between buyers and suppliers and thus the levels at which behavioral issues influence performance (horizontal arrows), and on the other hand the cross-level processes within firms that evolve out of the interactions between buyer and supplier (vertical arrows). Of course, in most situations interaction occurs on other levels as well, and there might be both top-down as well as bottom-up processes at the same time, but these will be less dominant and are therefore presented with gray dashed arrows. In the next three sections dealing with the before-mentioned three multilevel issues, we will refer to this conceptual model.

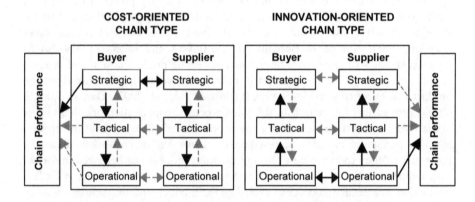

Figure 1: Multilevel Model of Supply Chain Management in Two Chain Types

Our mini case study involves a large manufacturer with a substantial supplier base and clients all over the world. We chose to study this company because it comprises two supply chains: a cost-oriented chain where mature products are manufactured and an innovation-oriented chain where new products are developed. We are in an early stage of studying these chains and we will now only report on data gathered in the cost-oriented chain. Within the cost-oriented chain we conducted five semi-structured interviews with managers involved in supply chain management. These managers were asked to indicate how human behavior played a role and influenced chain performance. In the following sections we will provide examples from this mini-case, and for each multilevel issue we will specify to what extent this issue played a role in the mini case and in what way.

3 The Specification of Levels and Their Interrelatedness

Supply chains essentially consist of several firms with people cooperating across boundaries. These people behave, act and make decisions within various levels of the supply chain. At the strategic level, for example, purchasing management specifies goals and develops differentiated strategies towards their supply market (Kraljic, 1983). At a tactical level, a senior buyer will implement these strategies, select the right suppliers, negotiate, and draw up supply arrangements. These decisions are made within the goals and policies set at the strategic level, and therefore are nested therein. At the operational level of the supply chain, a materials planner or buying assistant place their specific orders with certain delivery times. Again, such decisions will be framed within the higher level arrangements.

> In our case study, supply chain coordination is arranged at the strategic and tactical level with the use of long-term contracts. In these contracts the approximate amount of material delivered and at which price, is affirmed. In the case of large suppliers, the plant manager is the first one to have contact with a supplier. Senior buyers (at the tactical level) wait for the plant manager's approval to start the negotiation process and to draw up contracts. After these contracts have been arranged, interaction with suppliers will mainly occur at the operational level by procurement assistants. The purchasing manager made clear that procurement assistants act within the bounded space of the strict contract clauses. They are not allowed to make slight price changes, or to negotiate about product specifications. If procurement assistants signal any problems then they have to communicate these with the senior buyers at the tactical level. The senior buyers will then have contact with the supplier and will try to solve the problems.
>
> It becomes clear that in this chain, important decisions are taken at the strategic level and that these decisions reduce the space people at lower levels have to operate freely. The relationship between this manufacturer and its suppliers is mainly influenced by interaction at the strategic and tactical level and by top-down processes between these levels and the operational level.

The different levels at which SCM actually takes place has not received specific attention from many researchers in the field of SCM. Most often, researchers do not specify their level of interest or they mix up different levels (Klein et al., 2000). A large part of SCM research primarily considers issues on the macro level, such as the actions of an entire supply network (e.g. Uzzi, 1997) or, the way characteristics of the supply relationship influence the outcomes of the supply relationship (e.g. Wilson, 1995, in Klein et al., 2000). A moderate amount of SCM research is focused on the micro level and deals with phenomena such as trust (e.g. Johnston, 2004; Zaheer et al. 1998) and personal ties (e.g. Ford et al., 1986). There is of course a premise that macro-level SCM practices influence the attributes and behavior of the individual worker, and that in turn, micro level variables contribute to higher-level variables. For instance, individual performance will contribute to supply chain performance, and supply chain cooperation may emerge from the activities of the individual workers. However, multilevel research in the field of SCM that exclusively focuses on the link between the different levels is scarce, whereas it is exactly this link between different levels that could add to our understanding of supply chain performance. The multilevel approach explicitly recognizes that micro phenomena are embedded in macro contexts and that macro contexts often originate from interactions of microelements (Kozlowski & Klein, 2000). According to Koslowski & Klein (2000), a multilevel model must indicate how variables at multiple levels influence each other. Thus, in our study, in order to get to know how human behavior influences the performance of a chain, we have to know at which decision-making levels (strategic, tactical or operational) chain performance is influenced by behavior, and how these different levels are related to each other. Levels can be related to each other either top-down or bottom-up.

In top-down processes, lower levels are influenced by higher-level factors, which form the context for lower level variables. For instance, arrangements made between supply chain partners at the strategic level will certainly influence the day-to-day buying behavior of buying assistants at operational levels. If at the strategic level it is decided that efficiency and cost reduction are important indicators for deliveries in the chain, you wouldn't expect buying assistants to discuss new product development possibilities.

In bottom-up processes, lower level actions affect higher-level phenomena. Many group and organizational phenomena are formed by the behavior, cognition and characteristics of individuals who interact (Kozlowski & Klein, 2000). The interaction of individuals gives rise to a collective behavior pattern, e.g. group norms, which transcends the individuals who produced it. These collective behavior patterns form the basis for collective phenomena (Morgeson & Hofmann, 1999). For instance, if material planners increasingly have to deal with a sequence of missed delivery dates, a set of rules and procedures to deal with malfunctioning suppliers will emerge. Or, to take another example, buying assistants may signal that another supplier delivers at a lower price and inform their senior buyer, thus influencing the choice of suppliers at the tactical level. As a final example: When a team of buying assistants is trained on communication effectiveness, this might influence the higher-level construct of overall procurement performance.

In our conceptual model (Figure 1) we distinguish three decision-making levels with cross-level processes between them; one of these levels dominantly influences chain performance, i.e. the strategic level in a cost-oriented chain type and the operational level in the innovation-oriented chain type. Additionally, it is reasonable to believe that in the different decision-making levels, different people are involved. Day-to-day operational decisions will often be made by buying or procurement assistants, whereas tactical decisions are more likely to be taken by senior purchasers and the strategic decisions by purchasing or procurement managers. It is important that constructs are measured at the appropriate level of theoretical and analytical interest. In our research it is not only important to know at which level chain performance is influenced by human behavior, but also whether top-down processes or bottom-up processes are dominant. This will influence the way data is gathered and more importantly, where it is gathered. If it becomes clear that the relationship between buyer and supplier is mainly coordinated by means of formal contracts at a strategic level and there is little interaction involved at other levels, then it will be more useful to gather data among the people involved at the strategic level, for instance a purchasing manager or a materials manager. Contrastingly, if the relationship is coordinated by means of day to day cooperation between technicians, then it is reasonable that human behavior will mainly influence chain performance at the operational level, thus information might best be gathered at that level. In the next section we will further discuss these measurement issues.

4 Construct at Different Levels and Measurement Issues

The multilevel approach acknowledges that concepts may have different meaning at different levels. Thus, the same SCM concept may have a different meaning depending on the level a researcher is focusing on. Concepts such as performance, trust or power may have a different meaning for people involved at the strategic level as compared with people involved at the operational level. On the strategic level, for example, performance may refer to chain effectiveness, profit or turnover, while at the operational level it may refer to on time deliveries of a supplier. This immediately makes clear that constructs in SCM research may refer to completely different variables depending on the level that is considered (e.g., chain effectiveness vs. on time delivery). What is more, Boyer & McDermott (1999) make clear that the perceptions of people regarding operations strategy differ between different levels of a firm. Employees at the operational level, for instance, exposed significant manufacturing priorities different from those found by their managers at the strategic level.

> While talking with the managers involved in our case study, it became evident that trust was given quite a different meaning depending on the decision-level being discussed. At a strategic level it was mentioned twice that in order to trust supplier organizations or, the other way around, to win the trust of client organizations, there had to be made some significant adaptations. For example, in order to increase the cooperation with a large and important buyer organization, the manufacturing organization of our case study, had to make large flexibility enhancements. On the strategic level, it was promised that in high seasons production capacity would be fully used to serve this client organization. The supply chain manager indicated that this was a matter of winning trust and that otherwise cooperation would be difficult to arrange. At the operational level, totally other trust issues seemed to play a role. At this level, communication skills and knowing your contact person personally were indicated to be essential in order to win trust and to get things done. The materials manager offered an example of a very critical situation in which a supplier had to be asked to deliver a large quantity of extra material on a very short notice. Although he was aware of the current capacity situation at the supplier's plant, the procurement assistant nevertheless phoned his counterpart within the supplying organization. The procurement assistant was very familiar with his contact person and started to talk about family issues and other personal subjects. After a while, the procurement assistant dared to ask for the extra delivery and he was told that the extra material would be delivered within the requested lead-time.
>
> The above examples point out how one construct, in this case trust, can have different meanings depending on the level the researcher is focusing. At the strategic level trust was defined as 'buying in a relationship': trust was developed by proving that the organization was willing to make some important strategic adaptations. However, interviewing the materials manager it became clear that trust was of a totally other meaning at the operational level where day-to-day decisions were made, although trust was regarded equally important at that level as well. Communication skills, knowing and even liking each other, were indicated as important aspects of trust.

We will further stress the issue that constructs have different meanings at different levels by using the work of Klein & Kowzlowski (2000). They distinguish three basic types of constructs in multilevel modeling: global properties, shared properties, and configural or compositional properties. In the rest of this section we will highlight these three types of constructs, and we will give the implications for empirical research for each of the three constructs.

Global characteristics are directly manifested at the higher level. Examples of such attributes are number of suppliers, size of an organization, the function of a department (e.g. sales), and the physical location of a unit. These attributes can mostly be easily observed and lead to rather objective and reliable data.

In our own study we could argue that the supply chain type, either innovative or cost-oriented, is a global property. In order to distinguish whether a supply chain is more cost-oriented or more innovation-oriented, we can make use of rather objective data. For example, we could look at the investments made by chain partners in innovation projects, the presence and size of a research and development department, or the amount of product variety (Fisher, 1997) in order to decide upon the degree of innovativeness. To determine the degree of cost-orientation of a supply chain, we could look at the length of the product life cycle or the investments made in standardizing and automating work processes.

Global properties are relatively easy to measure because they do not emerge from the behavior and actions of lower-level entities (e.g. individuals). Global properties are observable characteristics of a higher-level phenomenon. Therefore, data concerning such properties can ordinarily be collected from a single source, for example a supervisor or a management information system and, consequently, there is no need to collect data from all the lower level entities (Klein & Kozlowski, 2000).

Shared properties are attributes that stem from the perceptions and attributes of lower level units - mostly individual workers - but it is supposed that these lower units share these attributes (Klein & Kozlowski, 2000), hence there is intra-unit agreement. Shared properties may refer to experiences, attitudes, values, norms, cognitions, or behaviors that are held in common by the members of the organizational unit in question. Corporate identity or group cohesion are well-known examples of a shared characteristic. The more that senior buyers for example perceive themselves to be part of the organization or purchasing department instead of being a single individual, the stronger the organizational identity, and the more cohesive the department. Cohesion or identity can be important properties for supply chain management, because employees are more willing to show cooperative behavior if the ties that bind them are stronger (Mullen & Copper, 1994). To give another example of a shared property, boundary spanners of a buying organization can collectively trust their strategic suppliers. Klein et al. (2000) propose that the perceptions, attitudes and actions of boundary spanners are shared and held in common when the benefits of cooperation with suppliers are clearly positive. When the benefits of cooperation are not clear, then members of the focal organization could differ in their trust in suppliers.

Unlike global properties, shared properties do emerge from the attributes, behavior and actions of individuals. For these types of constructs, employees must be in consensus, for it is essential for the property to be held in common or shared. Chan (1998) refers to a 'referent-shift consensus model'. This concerns constructs that are measured at the lower (individual) level, but the construct itself and the wording of items refer to a higher level. Measures of such concepts take the higher level as the point of reference, for example, "In our purchasing department we collectively trust this supplier" and not "I trust this supplier". As stated above, it is assumed that members share perceptions. Hence, in practice there must be sufficient consensus to justify the aggregation of individual perceptions to represent the value of the higher-level variable. When it is certain that intra-unit variance is low, then the mean value of the measure can be assigned to the higher-level construct. A low within-unit variance does not exclude inter-unit variance, and thus, different organizational units may hold different perceptions of a similar concept. If the higher level e.g. refers to a purchasing department or a top-management team, it may well be that the same concepts have different meanings (see, for example, the above mentioned results presented by Boyer & McDermott (1999).

Similar to shared properties, **configural properties** stem from measures at a lower level. In contrast, there is no condition of intra-unit agreement (Klein & Kozlowski, 2000: 217). For instance, if individual employees represent the lower level with attributes like age, skills or personality traits, then it is not supposed that employees share these attributes. An example of a configural property is the performance of a supply chain. The performance of a supply chain cannot easily be attributed to the single organizations and workers involved, because efforts of single organizations and individuals in the chain will merge in a complex way into chain performance. Hence, these properties cannot simply be averaged out (as is the case with shared properties). What matters is the theory that guides the higher-level construct, and which technique is most helpful in capturing configural properties. Kozlowski & Klein (2000) mention a variety of data-combination techniques that can be used: indices of variation, using the minimum or maximum, multidimensional scaling, network analyses, neural nets, systems dynamics, etc. To give an example, in order to measure chain performance, a researcher could use the weakest organization's contributions as a measurement, in the case that it is reasonable to assume that 'the chain is as strong as its weakest link'.

The three property types that we considered in this section are rather static. Chan (1998) has argued that constructs may change over time from one type to another. Collective trust in a supplier may be minimal when a supply relationship has just started, but likely will increase over time, thus changing from a configural construct into a shared construct. The same may be true for norms or supply-related procedures that may primarily be at the individual level when people start working together, but converge into shared constructs when assistant buyers encounter problems upon which they jointly have to react.

5 Data Structures and Analysis

A key feature of nested or hierarchical data structures is that clusters of individual units are contained within higher-level units, for example, procurement assistants within procurement departments, departments within organizations, or organizations within chains. As people may sometimes be nested in higher-level entities, so may other factors be nested as well. All the suppliers of one single firm are nested in that firm. And to give another example, as we have mentioned before, decisions can also be nested: day-to-day decisions regarding procurement are often nested in higher-level time-frames such as tactical contracts with suppliers, regarding price and product volume. These tactical price and volume decisions are likely to be nested in longer time-framed strategic plans in which e.g. cost-reduction or flexible product delivery are the long-term goals. As a consequence, day-to-day decisions cannot be dissociated from tactical and strategic plans, since they will likely be influenced by the long-term plans in which they are nested.

> In our mini case study we did not collect quantitative data. However, our qualitative material indicates the presence of nesting phenomena.
>
> The purchasing manager and material manager of this supply chain mentioned a problem, which indicated the existence of a nested data structure. Recently, there were difficulties in the communication processes towards suppliers. The procurement assistants and the senior buyers told the suppliers different stories with respect to dominant performance objectives. Where the senior buyers were focused on price issue, the procurement assistants emphasised the importance of mix and product flexibility. It turned out that procurement assistants had little contact with senior buyers and the other way around. Procurement assistants did merely cooperate with their colleagues from the procurement department and senior buyers mainly cooperated with people from the purchasing department. Procurement assistants and senior buyers had thus developed separately their own set of rules and customs to deal with suppliers, thereby influenced by their own departments differently. This problem was solved by setting up special cooperation structures between senior buyers and procurement assistants apart from the existing departments. This is a nice example how people may well be influenced by higher-level entities in which they are nested. As illustrated, this might even directly influence chain performance.

Nested data structures can be problematic, as they violate a key assumption in statistical testing, namely the assumption that observations are independently sampled from one another. In nested data structures this assumption is likely to be broken, since the 'clusters' or 'groups' of lower-level units (contained within the higher level units) can be expected to contain more similar responses, attitudes or behaviors than if the lower-level units would have been sampled randomly (Jones & Duncan, 1998; Snijders & Bosker, 1999). If one has gathered data about all the suppliers of a number of companies, the observations belonging to different suppliers delivering to the same buyer company are not independent, because, at least to some extent, they have the same context. Individuals within the same purchasing department, to give another example, work in the same environment, can potentially influence one another, have the same boss and, consequently, their responses will have communalities. Because the observations are in this way not 'truly' independent of one another, they can be expected to have a group level random error component and thus be auto-correlated (Bryk & Raudenbush, 1992). When relationships between variables are consequently tested using traditional single-level analysis techniques whereby a hierarchical data structure is neglected, there is a risk of 'spurious' significant results (e.g. Snijders & Bosker, 1999). Multilevel analytical techniques explicitly model or take into account the effect of a nested data structure and correct for design effects (Jones & Duncan, 1998; Snijders & Bosker, 1999; Hox, 2002).

In multilevel analytical techniques, regression models are tested that essentially are a multilevel version of the familiar multiple regression model, the distinction being that a multilevel regression model includes a separate equation for each higher-level unit (see Hox, 2002; Snijders & Bosker, 1999). To test multilevel models there is specialized software available such as MLwiN (Goldstein et al., 1998). Multilevel analysis takes place by following a two-step procedure (see Hox, 2002; Snijders & Bosker, 1999). First, a basic model is tested without any explanatory or independent variables. Suppose we are interested in predicting the trust of buyers and material planners in suppliers. If we have gathered data in several firms and we have a data structure with three levels (individual, department, firm), this first step decomposes the variance in trust into variance that should be attributed to the firm, to the department and to the individual employee. The second step involves fitting a second model that elaborates on the basic model by adding predictors. In multilevel analysis it is possible to introduce variables from different levels simultaneously. For example, the chain type may be a variable at the firm level, the presence of specific planning software may be a variable at the department level, and skills are at the individual employee level. Of course, this second step depends on the theoretical model one wants to test. For a further reading on the procedures of multilevel analysis we refer to Hox (2002).

6 Summary and Conclusion

In this paper we have focused on three situations in SCM research in which the multilevel approach might prove useful. First, supply chains consist of multiple levels that are linked by cross-level processes. In order to learn something about the performance of supply chains, these multiple level structures and processes should be conceptualized and included in a theoretical SCM research model. Second, the meaning of constructs such as trust, performance, or power can shift depending on the level that is considered. The multilevel approach takes this into account and distinguishes three construct types that vary in meaning and affect the way empirical research is conducted. Third, supply chains are nested systems. The behavior of people or the day-to-day decisions cannot be seen apart from the context in which they occur. Multilevel analysis explicitly models these nested data structures and takes the statistical effects of these structures into account.

By using our own research on human behavior in chains as an example, we have tried to show that SCM research may benefit substantially by integrating or, at the very least, recognizing multilevel structures and processes. Of course, it is hardly possible to incorporate all the issues addressed in one research model, nor do we intend to do so. However, by presenting the effects of human behavior on supply chain performance as a multilevel phenomenon, we have identified several difficulties that arise when building SCM models. We believe that awareness of multilevel issues and the usage of a multilevel approach will considerably contribute to theory building and empirical research in SCM.

7 References

Beth, S., Burt, D. N., Copacino, W., Gopal, C., Lee, H. L., Lynch, R. P., Morris, S. (2003): Supply Chain Challenges: Building Relationships, in: Harvard Business Review, 81(7): 64-73.

Boyer, K. K., McDermott, C. (1999): Strategic Consensus in Operations Strategy, in: Journal of Operations Management, 17(3): 289-305.

Bryk, A. S., Raudenbush, S. W. (1992): Hierarchical Linear Models, Sage, Newbury Park, CA.

Burstein, L. (1980): The Analysis of Multilevel Data in Educational Research in Evaluation, in: Review of Research in Education, 8(1): 158-233.

Chan, D. (1998): Functional Relations among Constructs in the Same Content Domain at Different Levels of Analysis: a Typology of Composition Models, in: Journal of Applied Psychology, 83(2): 234-246.

Cronbach, L. J., Webb, N. (1979): Between Class and Within Class Effects in a Reported Aptitude by Treatment Interaction, in: Journal of Educational Psychology, 67(6): 717-724.

Darr, A., Talmud, I. (2003): The Structure of Knowledge and Seller-Buyer Networks in Markets for Emergent Technologies, in: Organization Studies, 24(3): 443-461.

Fisher, M. L. (1997): What is the Right Supply Chain for your Product?, in: Harvard Business Review, 75(2): 105-117.

Ford, D., Hakansson, H., Johanson, J. (1986): How Do Companies Interact?, in: Industrial Marketing and Purchasing, 1(1): 26-41.

Goldstein, H., Rasbash, J., Plewis, I., Draper, D., Browne, W., Yang, M., Woodhouse, G., Healy, M. (1998): A User's Guide to MlwiN, Version 1.0.: January.

Hox, J. J. (2002): Multilevel Analysis: Techniques and Applications, Lawrence Erlbaum, Mahwah.

Johnston, D. A., McCutcheon, D. M., Stuart, F. I., Kerwood, H. (2004): Effects of Supplier Trust on Performance of Cooperative Supplier Relationships, in: Journal of Operations Management, 22(1): 23-28.

Jones, K., Duncan, C. (1998): Modelling Context and Heterogeneity: Applying Multilevel Models, in: Scarbrough, E., Tannenbaum, E. (eds.): Research Strategies in the Social Sciences, Oxford University Press, New York.

Klein, K. J., Palmer, S. L., Conn, A. B. (2000): Interorganizational Relationships: a Multilevel Perspective, in: Klein, K. J., Kozlowski, W. J. (eds.): Multilevel Theory, Research, and Methods in Organizations: Foundations, Extensions and New Directions, Jossey-Bass, San Francisco: p. 267-307.

Klein, K. J., Kozlowski, W. J. (2000): From Micro to Meso: Critical Steps in Conceptualizing and Conducting Multilevel Research, in: Organizational Research Methods, 3(3): 211-236.

Kozlowski, S. W. J., Klein, K. J. (2000): A Multilevel Approach to Theory and Research in Organizations: Contextual, Temporal, and Emergent Processes, in: Klein, K. J., Kozlowski, W. J. (eds.): Multilevel Theory, Research, and Methods in Organizations: Foundations, Extensions and New Directions, Jossey-Bass, San Francisco: p. 3-90.

Kraljic, P. (1983): Purchasing Must Become Supply Management, in: Harvard Business Review, 61(5): 109-117.

Kumpe, T., Bolwijn, P. T. (1994): Toward the Innovative Firm: Challenge for R&D Management, in: Research Technology Management, 37(1): 38-45.

Lamming, R., Johnsen, T., Zheng, J., Harland, C. M. (2000): An Initial Classification of Supply Networks, in: International Journal of Operations & Production Management, 20(6): 675-691.

Morgeson, F. P., Hofmann, D. A. (1999): The Structure and Function of Collective Constructs: Implications for Multilevel Research and Theory Development, in: Academy of Management Review, 24(2), 249-265.

Mullen, B., Copper, C. (1994): The Relation between Group Cohesiveness and Performance: An Integration, in: Psychological Bulletin, 115(2): 210-227.

Radenbush, S. W., Bryk, A. S. (1986): A Hierarchical Model of Studying School Effects, in: Sociology of Education, 59(1): 1-17.

Randall, T. R., Morgan, R. M., Morton, A. R. (2003): Efficient Versus Responsive Supply Chain Choice: an Empirical Examination of Influential Factors, in: Journal of Product Innovation Management, 20(6): 430-443.

Snijders, T. A. B. Bosker, R. J. (1999): Multilevel Analysis: an Introduction to Basic and Advanced Modelling, Sage Publications, London.

Uzzi, B. (1997): Social Structure and Competition in Interfirm Networks: The Paradox of Embeddedness, in: Administrative Science Quarterly, 42(1): 35-67.

Zaheer, A., McEvily, B., Perrone, V. (1998): Does Trust Matter? Exploring the Effects of Interorganizational and Interpersonal Trust on Performance, in: Organization Science, 9(2), 141-159.

Cost Management along the Supply Chain – Methodological Implications

Richard Chivaka

1 Introduction 300

2 Research Method 301

3 Results 305

4 Findings 310

5 Contribution of Research 310

6 Conclusion 311

7 References 311

Summary:
The strategic importance of supply chain management in creating value is attracting the attention of both practitioners and academics. The potential of strategic cost management to support related value creation has been highlighted. However, very little research using case studies has been done to demonstrate how cost management is implemented along supply chains. The few case studies investigating the application of cost management along the supply chain have largely focused on single cases where supply chain participants have a dyadic relationship. In addition, limited research has focused on supply chain relationships in developing countries. This research uses multiple case studies to investigate and gain insight into the manner in which strategic cost management is applied along a product's supply chain involving both first-tier suppliers, manufacturers, as well as retailers in the developing country of South Africa.

Keywords:
Supply Chain Management, Cost Management, Advanced Management Accounting, Case Study, Developing Country

1 Introduction

Several researchers have highlighted the strategic importance of supply chain management on the one hand (Johnson & Lawrence, 1988; Harland 1996; Margretta, 1998; Chandra & Kumar, 2000; Bagchi & Skjoett-Larsen, 2002), and on the other hand, the role that strategic cost management can play in supply chain management (Bromwich & Bhimani, 1989; Shank & Govindarajan, 1989; Cooper & Slagmulder, 1998; Seuring, 2002b). However, very little research using multiple case studies has been done to demonstrate how cost management is implemented along supply chains beyond a dyadic relationship. In addition, research investigating the application of cost management in developing countries in the context of supply chain relationships is scarce. The few studies investigating the application of cost management along the supply chain have focused on single cases where supply chain participants have a dyadic relationship (see for example Cooper & Yoshikawa, 1994; Dekker, 2003 & 2004; Hakansson & Lind, 2004), with the exception of Choi & Hong, (2003) and Cooper & Slagmulder (2004). These studies have ignored the fact that supply chain management (SCM) involves management processes that transcend legal organizational boundaries, hence requiring more explicit consideration of the integration of actions within networks of organizations (Hopwood, 1996). This research uses multiple case studies to investigate and gain insight into the manner in which strategic cost management is applied along a product's supply chain involving first-tier suppliers, manufacturers, as well as retailers in the developing country of South Africa.

1.1 Literature Review

Whereas much has been said about the inability of traditional management accounting to support strategic decision-making processes (Kaplan, 1984; Johnson & Kaplan, 1987; Ezzamel et al., 1990; Seuring, 2002b), the potential of strategic cost management to support strategic decisions and inter-company operations has been widely recognized (Bromwich & Bhimani, 1989; Shank, 1989; Shank & Govindarajan, 1989; Cooper & Slagmulder, 1998). Additionally, the strategic importance of supply chain management has been highlighted by a number of researchers (Johnson & Lawrence, 1988; Harland 1996; Margretta, 1998; Chandra & Kumar, 2000; Bagchi & Skjoett-Larsen, 2002). SCM is seen as a way of transforming companies into enterprises that are more responsive to customer demand (Dekker & van Goor, 2000; Bommer, O'Neil & Treat, 2001; Bagchi & Skjoett-Larsen, 2002).

Although both cost management and SCM have one thing in common – the management of costs – very little empirical research has been done to investigate the transfer and application of cost management concepts and instruments to SCM. Cost management involves a proactive management of costs by influencing cost structures and cost behavior, and it covers the assessment, planning, controlling and evaluation of costs along the supply chain (Seuring, 2002b). Cost management is seen as achievable along the supply chain through the use of management accounting tools such as target costing (Lockamy III & Smith, 2000; Axelsson et al., 2002), activity-based costing/management (Shank, 1989; Lin et al., 2001; Axelsson et al., 2002; Dekker 2003), balanced scorecard (Kaplan & Norton, 1992; Axelsson et al., 2002), just-in-time (JIT) (Agrawal & Mehra, 1998; Blocher et al., 1999) and total quality management (TQM) (Agrawal & Mehra, 1998; Blocher et al., 1999). These tools are seen as capable of supporting cost management along the supply chain because they are process-oriented and inter-organizational in that they cross traditional company boundaries. Cost management is also seen as being supported by practices such as top management support (Agrawal & Mehra, 1998), open book accounting (Cullen et al., 1999; Seal et al., 1999), inter-company multi-functional teams, collaborative planning, trust (Tomkins, 2001; Dekker, 2003), and sharing of costs and benefits. These practices create an environment that allows supply chain partners to take a total supply chain perspective that facilitates cost management. However, while there has been parallel research in SCM and cost management, research integrating these topical issues has been largely ignored in the accounting research literature (Hopwood, 1996; Axelsson et al., 2002; Cooper & Slagmulder, 2004). As Seuring (2002a: 1) puts it:

"......if costs are to be reduced, companies increasingly turn their attention to their supply chain partners, so both suppliers and customers reach out for new frontiers of competitiveness and profitability. Yet, few approaches exist so far addressing how cost management in a supply chain can be carried out."

This paper uses a multiple case study approach to contribute to the body of knowledge that addresses the question: How is cost management executed among supply chain partners? The paper is organized as follows: The next section discusses the methodology chosen for data collection and case analysis. The main results of the multiple case studies are then presented, followed by a discussion of the contribution of the methodology used in this research in generating the results. The paper concludes with the implications of the research findings on future research methods in cost management along supply chains in the context of the developing world.

2 Research Method

The focus of this research was to understand how cost management is applied along a product's supply chain, where the supply chain involved more than two companies. This implies that the companies involved are intertwined in a complex relationship network, and that an element of cooperative coordination exists in the application of cost management along the supply chain (Hakansson & Lind, 2004). Companies along these supply chains create 'partnerships' with an implied sense of sharing in knowledge, decision making and collective rewards (Tomkins,

2001). Given the focus of this research and the characteristics of supply chains as described above, the case study method of research was utilized for a number of reasons. First, case studies are the preferred strategy when 'how' or 'why' questions are being posed, and when the investigator has little control over behavioral events within a real-life context (Yin, 1989). Second, case study research allows the collection of perceptions of 'unobservable' external world phenomena, for example social bonds, as argued by Tomkins (2001). Case study research also enables the adoption of intimate, contextually sensitive knowledge of actual management practices (Keating, 1995).

Third, the research focused on the application of cost management along supply chains in a developing country. Little, if any, prior empirical research had examined this issue. Achieving deduction in an emerging field is difficult for a number of reasons: the lack of existing principles of a paradigm, the dearth of established principles and constructs, or inadequate accepted principles and constructs (Perry, 1998). Case study research areas are usually contemporary (Yin, 1989; Perry, 1998), thus an exploratory case study approach was considered an appropriate research design, given the lack of previous studies (Yin, 1989; Dekker 2003; Cooper & Slagmulder, 2004). Finally, by studying multiple supply chain cases, it is possible to obtain better insights into the manner in which cost management is applied along the supply chain of a product. It is also possible to identify patterns emerging from these cases (Yin, 1989; Eisenhardt, 1989; Nieto & Perez, 2000).

2.1 Sample Size

Using a 'snowball' approach (Dewhurst et al., 2003), three retailers who jointly control about 80% of the South African retail market were selected for an in-depth study of how they apply cost management along their supply chains for the purpose of value creation. Each retailer was then asked to choose one key manufacturer. The key manufacturer chosen was in turn asked to choose one of its key suppliers (Tier I Supplier, hereinafter referred to as 'supplier'). The suppliers, manufacturers and retailers chosen numbered nine companies in all and constituted a sample size of three separate supply chains. Supply chain 1 is in the textile industry. On the supply side, it consists of Supplier 1 (trim supplier) and Manufacturer 1. On the demand side it consists of Retailer 1. Supply chain 2 is composed of Supplier 2, a garment manufacturer (known as a 'cut-make-and-trim firm', i.e. CMT), Manufacturer 2 (an apparel design and supply company), and Retailer 2. The structure of supply chain 2 is unique in that Manufacturer 2 is part of the Retailer 2 group of companies and is responsible for the design of garments and the outsourcing of their manufacture. Manufacturer 2 supplies garments to three of its sister companies on the retail end of the supply chain, of which Retailer 2 is one. Furthermore, Manufacturer 2 does not perform the actual manufacture of the garments. Its joint focus is on research into current overseas trends (with Retailer 2) and the manufacture of sample garments. Supplier 3 (key ingredients supplier),

Manufacturer 3, and Retailer 3 constitute supply chain 3. Within this supply chain, the retailer has a strong influence on the activities and processes undertaken because the products produced and sold bear its brand name. A survey of the supply chain management practices in the South African retail industry revealed that relationships along the supply chains have moved from arms-length towards more collaborative relationships (Chivaka, 2003).

2.2 Data Collection

Data collection along the three supply chains started in October 2002 and ended in April 2003, and was achieved by way of interviews, personal observations and the perusal of relevant company documents. In order to investigate cost management from both the demand and supply side of the supply chain, interviews were based on a focal company – the manufacturer – and then extended to the manufacturer's supplier and customer (retailer). A tailor-made interview guide facilitated the collection of information on cost management tools and practices pertinent to each major function (e.g. finance, sales, purchasing, logistics and production). The typical time spent with each informant was $1\ ^1/_2$ hours. The interview guide contained semi-structured questions which allowed informants to discuss related issues outside the interview structure in order to permit broader responses, thereby increasing the chances of the researcher gathering data that were relevant to the issues under investigation (Abernethy et al., 1999). The interview guide was divided into sections as follows: The first section covered general company information, the length of time the informant had been with the company, the informant's function and the period of service in that particular function. Subsequent sections contained cost management information specific to the function, explored from the supplier-facing, intra-function and customer-facing perspectives. Questions focused on cost management tools and practices used by the particular function in each company which facilitated value creation (1) within its operations, (2) with its supplier and (3) with the retailer. The details of the informants in the three supply chains are given in Table 1.

The purpose of the interview guide was to ensure the adequate coverage of important themes and at the same time to avoid researcher bias. The questions and probes in each section were non-directive in order to minimize unplanned, non-neutral questions and probes while interviewing (Lillis, 1999). However, the interview guide was used in a reasonably flexible way so as to elicit full but undirected responses from informants on the cost management issues under study.

Company	Sector	Company position	Informants	Position of informants	Period in position
Supplier 1	Textile	Supplier	2	Branch Manager	2 years
				Accountant	5 years
Supplier 2	Textile	Supplier	2	Managing Director	14 years
				Accountant	7 years
Supplier 3	Food	Supplier	2	Production Manager	8 years
				Accountant	4 years
Manufacturer 1	Textile	Manufacturer	4	Purchasing Manager	9 years
				Operations Director	20 years
				Sales Manager	4 years
				Finance Manager	11 years
Manufacturer 2	Textile	Manufacturer	4	Sourcing Director	5 years
				Senior Logistics Manager	10 years
				Senior Production Manager	7 years
				Senior Finance Manager	22 years
Manufacturer 3	Food	Manufacturer	3	Purchasing Director	6 years
				Operations Director	11 years
				Finance Manager	6 years
Retailer 1	Textile	Retailer	4	Supply Chain Executive	4 years
				Chief Accountant	9 years
				Senior Manager	7 years
				Technology Manager	10 years
Retailer 2	Textile	Retailer	2	Design Manager	3 years
				Senior Finance Manager	22 years
Retailer 3	Food	Retailer	2	Supply Chain Executive	4 years
				Chief Accountant	9 years
				Supply Chain Manager	4 years
9			25		

Table 1: Summary of Informants' Details

All interviews were taped, and the transcribed notes were sent to the respective informants for review and comments (Cooper & Slagmulder, 2004). Corrected or amended transcripts were then used as evidence of the application of cost management along the supply chain studied. Personal observations involved visits to stores and distribution centers operated by retailers. The visits each lasted for half a day and were meant to provide the researcher with physical evidence of the products traded along the supply chains, details of the key processes involved in receiving finished products from the manufacturers, as well as those processes relating to returns to the manufacturers. Visits to manufacturers and their suppliers' factories were done, lasting for the whole day in each case. The tours of factories were guided by factory managers and engineers and enabled the researcher to observe the intra- and inter-company processes involved in the (i) product design, (ii) receipt of inputs, (iii) product manufacture and (iv) finished product delivery.

2.3 Case Analysis

Data gathered through interviews were analyzed using a pattern of behavior strategy (Eisenhardt, 1989; Nieto & Perez, 2000) that involved (i) within-case analysis to identify cost management tools in each individual company (ii) cross-case analysis to identify cost management tools across company boundaries within the same supply chain and (iii) cross-case analysis to identify patterns of cost management tools and practices common to multiple companies and supply chains (Choi & Hong, 2002; Cooper & Slagmulder, 2004). The principal unit of analysis (Nieto & Perez, 2000; Rowley, 2002) was the entire three-party supply chain, as opposed to one participant along the supply chain. Each company along the supply chains studied was the intermediate unit of analysis, as it was seen as the "natural field of a combination of factors [tools and practices in each function or multidisciplinary area] which are specific, as well as related to the principal unit" (Nieto & Perez, 2000: 726). The collective results from these sub-sets produced an overall picture (Rowley, 2002) of the cost management tools and practices applied by companies along the supply chains studied.

3 Results

Tables 2 to 4 summarize the cost management tools and practices applied along all three of the supply chains studied. The tools and practices are shown according to whether their emphasis is on intra-company or inter-company cost management.

3.1 Discussion

The results of the three case studies all show that cost management is being implemented (in varying degrees) along the supply chains studied. Tables 2 to 4 shows that (i) budgetary control and variance analysis are the common intra-company cost management tools in all three supply chains, (ii) target costing and continuous improvement are the most common inter-company cost management tools applied in all three supply chains, (iii) advanced management accounting tools are not widely applied and (iv) cost management along the three supply chains appears to be achieved largely through the application of practices rather than tools. This is contrary to expectations raised in the management accounting literature that suggests the use of advanced management accounting tools such as ABC, JIT, TQM and life cycle costing. However, an analysis of the results yields some interesting insights.

	Supplier		Manufacturer		Retailer	
	Tool	Practice	Tool	Practice	Tool	Practice
Intra-Co.	Budgetary control Variance analysis		Budgetary control Variance analysis Work-study		Budgetary control Variance analysis	
Inter-Co.	Target costing Continuous improvement	Quality focus Product delivery scheduling Sharing of cost savings Training & assistance	Target costing Continuous improvement Returns analysis	Quality focus Team-based approach Training & assistance Customer-approved suppliers Delivery scheduling Sharing of cost savings Joint product design	Target costing Continuous improvement	Quality focus Team-based approach Sharing of cost savings Joint product design Delivery scheduling

Table 2: Cost Management Tools and Practices in Supply Chain 1

	Supplier		Manufacturer		Retailer	
	Tool	Practice	Tool	Practice	Tool	Practice
Intra-Co.	Budgetary control Profitability analysis		Budgetary control Variance analysis Work-study	Bulk buying	Budgetary control Variance analysis	
Inter-Co.	Target costing Continuous improvement	Quality focus Team-based approach Open book policy Delivery scheduling Joint product design Sharing of cost savings Training & assistance	Target costing Continuous improvement	Quality focus Team-based approach Training & assistance Joint product design Delivery scheduling Open book policy Sharing of cost savings	Target costing Continuous improvement	Quality focus Team-based approach Joint product design Open book policy Delivery scheduling Sharing of cost savings

Table 3: Cost Management Tools and Practices in Supply Chain 2

	Supplier		Manufacturer		Retailer	
	Tool	Practice	Tool	Practice	Tool	Practice
Intra-Co.	Budgetary control Variance analysis		Budgetary control Variance analysis		Budgetary control Variance analysis	Bulk buying
Inter-Co.	Target costing Continuous improvement	Quality focus Team-based approach Delivery scheduling Joint product design Sharing of cost savings Open book policy Training & assistance	Target costing Continuous improvement	Quality focus Team-based approach Training & assistance Shared transport Customer-approved suppliers Open book policy Sharing of cost savings	Target costing Continuous improvement	Quality focus Team-based approach Sharing of cost savings Open book policy Delivery scheduling Joint product design

Table 4: Cost Management Tools and Practices in Supply Chain 3

First, there appears to be a link between the widespread use of practices along the three supply chains studied and the stage of development of these supply chains. As pointed out earlier, relationships among supply chain partners in the South African retail industry have evolved from arms-length towards more collaborative relationships. Inter-organizational settings along these supply chains are changing as relationships become closer and are aimed at improving the competitiveness of the entire supply chains. In the present study, such changes appear to be initially supported by practices such as information sharing through open book policy, joint product design, inter-company teams and sharing of cost savings. These changes create an environment that supports the application of tools that require a 'common language' such as activity-based costing, so as to avoid incompatibility of accounting data from companies along these supply chains as a result of different accounting systems (Dekker & van Goor, 2000). Also, common terms applicable to inter-company processes need to be developed and understood by all key players along the supply chains. As such, the application of inter-company cost management tools across company boundaries may not be easily achievable during the early stages of supply chain development. Cost management tools may be more readily applied along the supply chain once the requisite changes have facilitated an 'intimacy' between supply chain participants. It appears that in this study, companies in the supply chains are focusing on the application of practices that draw them together as a possible precursor to the application of advanced management accounting tools on a wider scale. As argued by Goldbach (2002), the application of cost management tools and the involvement of the 'actors' along supply chains need to be embedded in the organizational setting of the supply chains. It appears that the supply chain participants are reconfiguring their inter-organizational settings through the deployment of collaborative practices, thereby creating a climate in which the adoption and application of most of the inter-organizational cost management tools can flourish.

Second, an examination of some of the approaches applied along the supply chains studied reveals the application of cost management through tools whose characteristics mimic those of the advanced management accounting tools or at least some aspects thereof. Below are some examples of these approaches.

- **Work-study & ABC**

Garment costs in supply chains 1 and 2 are managed by focusing on the activities performed. The work-study departments in these supply chains produce activity information used to refine the way the activities are performed, all as a way of reducing garment costs. The target costing approach that is commonly applied across the supply chains studied requires the understanding of activities performed to facilitate the re-engineering of products where the target costs are below the actual costs. The activity analysis approach adopted to enable the management of garment costs is similar to ABC/M, in that activity information is obtained from the work-study departments and is then used to reduce costs through the elimination of non-value added activities and processes. The ABC/M approach involves the management of activities as the route towards improving the value received by the customer (Maccarrone, 1998). The labor cost of a garment is determined from the activities that must be performed, i.e. in terms of the time per activity, and the time is then converted into labor cost. An ABC system involves the measurement of time and resources spent on work processes and then the conversion of such time to cost data (Driver, 2001).

- **Delivery scheduling & JIT**

The attributes of the delivery scheduling are similar to the JIT approach. JIT aims at synchronizing the operations of companies along the supply chain, where suppliers deliver inputs of the right quality, quantity and at the right time (Agrawal & Mehra, 1998; Drury, 2000). Its emphasis is on the reduction of non-value added costs by seeking to achieve 100% on-time delivery, along with other goals such as zero inventories, zero defects and zero breakdowns (Drury, 2000). In supply chain 3 for example, Supplier 3 has specific days and times for the delivery of inputs to Manufacturer 3. The manufacturer along supply chain 3 also knows the exact times at which to deliver to the retailer's distribution center (each manufacturer has a 15 minute window within which to arrive at the distribution center to offload at a specific bay). In supply chain 2, the retailer and the manufacturer work on a delivery calendar that specifies the dates and times when garments will be delivered to the retailer's stores.

- **Quality focus & TQM**

The quality focus practice commonly applied along all three supply chains has characteristics similar to TQM. The focus of TQM is the identification and reduction of quality-related costs (Agrawal & Mehra, 1998; Drury, 2000). Its emphasis is on preventive measures, hence the aim is to 'design and build quality in', rather than trying to 'inspect it in' (Drury, 2000: 901). TQM focuses on satisfying the customer, striving for continuous improvement, involvement of all employees, active support and the involvement of top management, clear objectives, and continuous training focused on quality (Blocher et al., 2002). The quality initiatives along the supply chains are focused on preventative measures (testing of input quality) rather than rectification of quality problems. This approach is supported by the selection of key suppliers (especially in supply chains 1 and 3), who are also quality conscious and have the capability to produce good quality inputs and products. Manufacturers in these supply chains are required to source inputs only from suppliers that have been approved by the retailers on the basis of, among other criteria, quality of inputs. A lot of effort is spent in creating an awareness of the importance of quality among factory employees. In supply chains 1and 2, this is achieved through employee training, as well as by the strategic placement of large notices in the factories, encouraging employees to 'do it right first time.' In addition, the analysis of returns-to-manufacturers (RTMs) due to quality problems is done right down to the particular department where the garments were manufactured. Employees are thus made aware of quality-related problems and the concomitant costs. Therefore, the quality focus spans both the horizontal dimension (from suppliers of inputs right up to the retail shop) and the vertical dimension (from the shop floor employees to top management). The involvement of teamwork (both intra- and inter-company teams) also makes this approach very similar to TQM.

- **Other approaches & Life cycle costing**

Some form of life cycle costing is being applied along the supply chains studied. Life cycle costing involves understanding and managing the total costs of a product incurred throughout its life cycle (Drury, 2000). The total cost of a product over its life cycle can be broken down into upstream costs (research & development and design), manufacturing costs (purchasing, direct manufacturing costs and indirect manufacturing costs), and downstream costs (marketing & distribution, and service and warranty costs such as recalls, service, product liability and customer support) (Blocher et al., 2002). Linkages between manufacturers and suppliers (through training & assistance and joint product design), and between manufacturers and retailers (through delivery scheduling and shared transport), assist in managing upstream and downstream costs, respectively. Also, one of the purposes of life cycle costing is to reduce the costs that end-use customers incur after they have bought the product. The lower the after-sales cost, the stronger the competitive advantage of a company. In supply chains 1 and 2, life cycle costing involves tests conducted on fabric to assess how the fabric reacts when (i) washed, either in cold or hot water, (ii) ironed, and (iii) bleached. A 'care label' is then produced to assist end-use customers with the best way of looking after their garments. In supply chain 3, life cycle costing takes the form of shelf-life tests that are used to prescribe 'sell-by' and 'use-by' dates, as well as refrigeration conditions, thus helping end-use customers to reduce costs that could be caused by waste. These quality-related approaches are particularly important in the retail industry, which is one of the industries where upstream and downstream costs account for a significant portion of total life cycle costs (Bloecher et al., 2002).

4 Findings

The application of management accounting tools appears to be preceded by the deployment of collaborative practices that draw together participants along the supply chain. These practices create the environment within which common process terms can be defined and understood. They also create the framework within which tools that require common language can be applied to support cost management. A closer examination of some of the approaches applied along the three supply chains studied shows the application of tools having characteristics similar to advanced management accounting tools. These approaches are activity analysis (through work-study) which is similar to ABC/M, quality focus which is similar to TQM, delivery scheduling which is similar to JIT, and RTMs analysis and quality focus which are similar to life cycle costing. It is the submission of this research that some practitioners are intuitively applying these advanced management accounting tools or parts thereof without referring to conventional terms used in the management accounting literature. Also, it is the submission of this research that if specific terms (e.g. ABC) are used to analyze the presence and hence the application of a tool, it is possible to conclude that such a tool is not being applied. However, if attention is given to the characteristics of the approaches that practitioners are using, and these characteristics are then compared with those of the tools known in the management accounting literature, a better conclusion is likely to be made.

5 Contribution of Research

The major contributions of this research derive from the empirical research method adopted. First, the empirical research on the application of cost management was conducted by gathering data from three supply chains among three different participants along the supply chains, as opposed to gathering data from one stage of the supply chain only. Through multiple case studies and the application of the pattern of behavior approach, the research revealed that some practitioners are intuitively applying advanced management accounting tools or parts thereof to achieve cost management without using textbook definitions. Second, the case studies allowed the understanding of intimate, contextually sensitive knowledge of the manner in which supply chain participants are configuring their relationships through practices (such as open book policy, joint product design, training and assistance) as a precursor to the adoption and application of tools that require common language and a high level of intimacy. Third, case studies facilitated the observation of actual management practices that have an impact on cost management, hence they enabled a gain in insight into this important, emerging and yet ill-defined area from an exploratory perspective.

6 Conclusion

The use of multiple case studies facilitates the understanding of the execution of cost management among supply chain partners from the perspective of characteristics of approaches applied by practitioners. Also, the way in which management accounting tools are applied to support cost management along the supply chains in developing countries should be interpreted in terms of the stage of evolution of the supply chains, as well as the practices deployed in the process of creating more collaborative relationships. This research was exploratory in nature; hence more case studies need to be conducted to increase the extent to which findings can be generalized. Also, other case studies focusing on issues such as the impact of the use of power (i.e. its effects on the nature of co-operation achieved between supply chain participants), and how this affects the manner in which cost management is implemented need to be explored.

7 References

Abernethy, M. A., Chua, W. F., Luckett, P. F, Selto, F. H. (1999): Research in Managerial Accounting: Learning from others' experiences, in: Accounting and Finance 39: 1-27.

Agrawal, S. P., Mehra, S. (1998): Cost Management System: An Operational Overview, in: Managerial Finance, 24(1): 60-78.

Axelsson, B., Laage-Hellman, J., Nilsson, U. (2002): Modern Management Accounting for Modern Purchasing, in: European Journal of Purchasing & Supply Management (8): 53-62.

Bagchi, P. K., Skjoett-Larsen, T. (2002): Organizational Integration in Supply Chains: A Contingency Approach, in: Global Journal of Flexible Systems Management, 3 (1): 1-10.

Blocher, E.J., Chen. K. H., Lin, T.W. (2002): Cost Management – A Strategic Emphasis, Second Edition, McGraw-Hill, Boston.

Bommer, M., O'Neil, B., Treat, S. (2001): Strategic assessment of the supply chain interface: a beverage industry case study, in: International Journal of Physical Distribution and Logistics Management, 31(1): 11-25.

Chandra, C., Kumar, S. (2000): Supply chain management in theory and practice: a passing fad or a fundamental change? in: Industrial Management and Data Systems, 100(3): 100-114.

Chivaka, R. (2003): Value Creation Through Strategic Cost Management along the Supply Chain: Ph.D. thesis, University of Cape Town, South Africa.

Choi, T. Y., Hong, Y. (2003): Unveiling the structure of supply networks: case studies in Honda, Acura, and DaimlerChrysler, in Journal of Operations Management, 20: 469-493.

Cooper, R., Slagmulder, R. (2004): Inter-organizational cost management and relational context, in: Accounting, Organizations and Society, 29 (1): 1-26.

Cooper, R., Slagmulder, R. (1998): Strategic Cost Management, in: Management Accounting, February: 16-18.

Cooper, R., Yoshikawa, T. (1994): Inter-organizational cost management systems: The case of the Tokyo-Yokohama-Kamakura supplier chain, in: International Journal of Production Economics 37: 51-62.

Cullen, J., Berry, A. J., Seal, W., Dunlop, A., Ahmed, M., Marson, J. (1999): Interfirm Supply Chains – the Contribution of Management Accounting, in: Management Accounting, 77(6): 30-32.

Dekker, H. C. (2004): Control of inter-organizational relationships: evidence on appropriation concerns and coordination requirements, in: Accounting, Organizations and Society, 29(1): 27-49.

Dekker, H. C., van Goor, A. R. (2000): Supply Chain Management and Management Accounting: A Case Study of Activity-Based Costing, in: International Journal of Logistics and Applications, 3(1): 41-52.

Dekker, H. C. (2003): Value chain analysis in interfirm relationships: a filed study, in: Management Accounting Research, 14: 1-23.

Dewhurst, F. W., Martinez-Lorente, A. R., Sanchez-Rodriguez, C. (2003): An initial assessment of the influence of IT on TQM: a multiple case study, in: International Journal of Operations & Production Management, 23(4): 348-374.

Driver, M. (2001): Activity-based costing: a tool for adaptive and generative organizational learning? in: The Learning Organization, 8(3): 94-105.

Drury, C. (2000): Management and Cost Accounting, Fifth Edition, Business Press, Thompson Learning, UK.

Eisenhardt, K. (1989): Building theories from case study research, in: Academy of Management Review, 14(4): 532-550.

Ezzamel, M. Hoskin, K., Macve, R. (1990): Managing It All By numbers: A Review of Johnson and Kaplan's 'Relevance Lost', in: Accounting and Business Research, 20(78): 153-166.

Goldbach, M. (2002): Organizational Settings in Supply Chain Costing: in Seuring, S., Goldbach, M. (eds.): Cost Management in Supply Chains, Physica, Heidelberg: p. 89-108.

Hakansson, H., Lind, J. (2004): Accounting and network coordination, in: Accounting, Organizations and Society, 29(1): 51-72.

Hansen, D. R., Mowen, M. M. (2000): Management Accounting, 5th Edition, South-Western College Publishing.

Harland, C. (1996): Supply Chain Management: Relationships, Chains and Networks, in: British Journal of Management, 7(Special Issue): S63-S80.

Hopwood, A. G. (1996): Looking across rather than up and down: On the need to explore the lateral processing of information, in: Accounting, Organizations and Society, 21(6): 589-590.

Johnson, H. T., Kaplan, R. S., (1987): The Rise and Fall of Management Accounting, in: Management Accounting, January, p. 22 – 30.

Johnston, R., and Lawrence, P. R. (1988): Beyond Vertical Integration – the Rise of the Value-Adding Partnership, in: Harvard Business Review, July and August, 66(4): 94-104.

Kaplan, R. S., Norton, D. P. (1992): The Balanced Scorecard – Measures that Drive Performance, in: Harvard Business Review, January-February: 71-79.

Kaplan, R. S. (1984): Yesterday's Accounting Undermines Production, in: Harvard Business Review, July-August, 62(4): 95-101.

Keating, P. J. (1995): A framework for classifying and evaluating theoretical contributions of case research in management accounting, in: Journal of Management Accounting Research, Fall: 65-86.

Lillis, M. A. (1999): A framework for the Analysis of Interview Data from multiple field research sites, in: Accounting and Finance 39(1): 79-105.

Lin, B., Collins, J., Su, R. K. (2001): Supply chain costing: an activity-based perspective, in: International Journal of Physical Distribution & Logistics Management, 31(10): 702-713.

Lockamy III, A., Smith, I. W. (2000): Target costing for supply chain management: criteria and selection, in: Industrial Management & Data Systems, 100(5): 210-218.

Maccarrone, P. (1998): Activity-based management and the product development process, in: European Journal of Innovation Management, 1(3): 148-156.

Margretta, J. (1998): Fast, Global, and Entrepreneurial: Supply Chain Management, Hong Kong Style. An Interview with Victor Fung, in: Harvard Business Review, September – October 76(5): 103-114.

Nieto, M., Perez, W. (2000): The development of theories from the analysis of the organization: case studies by patterns of behavior, in: Management Decision 38(10): 723-733.

Perry, C. (1998): Processes of a case study methodology for postgraduate research in marketing, in: European Journal of Marketing, 32(9/10): 785-802.

Rowley, J. (2002): Using Case Studies in Research, in: Management Research News, 25(1): 16-27.

Seal, W., Cullen, J., Dunlop, A., Berry, T. and Ahmed, M. (1999): Enacting a European supply chain: a case study on the role of management accounting, in: Management Accounting Research, 10: 303-322.

Seuring, S. (2002a): Cost Management in Supply Chains – Different Research Approaches, in: Cost Management in Supply Chains, Physica-Verlag, Heidelberg, p. 1-11.

Seuring, S. (2002b): Supply Chain Costing – A Conceptual Framework, in: Cost Management in Supply Chains, Physica-Verlag, Heidelberg, p. 16-30.

Shank, J. K., Govindarajan, V. (1992): The Strategic Cost Management: The Value Chain Perspective, in: Journal of Management Accounting Research, Fall 1992, 4: 179-197.

Tomkins, C. (2001): Interdependencies, trust and information in relationships, alliances and networks, Accounting, Organizations and Society, 26(2):161-191.

Yin, R. K. (1989): Case Study Research: Design and Methods, Applied Social Research Methods Series, 5, Sage Publications, Thousand Oaks.

Case Studies and Surveys in Supply Chain Management Research – Two Complementary Methodologies

Cristina Gimenez

1	Introduction..	316
2	Case Studies and Surveys: Complementary Methodologies......................	318
3	A SCM Research Project: "Does SCM Lead to a Better Performance?"....	319
4	Case Studies and Surveys: Advantages and Disadvantages........................	327
5	Conclusions..	328
6	References..	329

Summary:
The objective of this paper is to provide Supply Chain Management (SCM) researchers with an example of how to conduct empirical research using two different methodologies (case studies and surveys). The paper examines the methodology used to investigate a particular SCM topic: the SCM-performance relationship. The research design will be outlined and used to carry out the investigation as an illustration of how case studies and surveys can be used as complementary methodologies. These methodologies will be described, along with their role within the research and the contribution they were able to make to the investigation. A summary of the main advantages and disadvantages related to each one of these methodologies will be provided as well.

Keywords:
Supply Chain Management, Case Study, Survey, Grocery Industry

1 Introduction

Supply Chain Management (SCM) is a topic of interest and importance among logistics managers and researchers because it is considered a source of competitive advantage (Christopher, 1998: 4; Gimenez & Ventura, 2003: 84). While this field has seen rapid advances in recent years, empirical research on how to conduct it has been rarely addressed.

In the literature of SCM and related areas such as Logistics and Operations Management, there are some papers that describe how to conduct empirical research using the case study methodology (McCutcheon & Meredith, 1993; Ellram, 1996; Meredith, 1998; Beach et al., 2001; Stuart et al., 2002; Voss et al., 2002). There are other papers which provide guidelines for conducting surveys (Dunn et al., 1994; Mentzer & Flint, 1997; Williams Walton, 1997; Malhotra & Grover, 1998; Meredith, 1998; Forza, 2002), and others which define a framework for Logistics research (Mentzer & Kahn, 1995). However, none of the existing studies present these two different methodologies (case studies and surveys) as complementary tools to conduct a research project. Table 1 summarizes the existing papers.

The objective of this paper is to provide SCM researchers with an example of how to conduct empirical research using two different methodologies (case studies and surveys). The paper examines the methodology used to investigate a particular SCM topic: the SCM-performance relationship. It outlines the research design used to carry out the investigation as an illustration of how case studies and surveys can be used as complementary methodologies. These methodologies, their role within the research, and the contribution they were able to make to the investigation will all be described. The paper also provides a summary of the main advantages and disadvantages related to each of these two methodologies.

Our contribution to the existing SCM literature is to provide an example of how to conduct empirical research using two different but complementary methodologies. We believe that this paper will be both informative and insightful to researchers in the SCM field.

The remainder of the paper is structured as follows: Section two briefly examines the main characteristics of the case study and survey methodologies. Section three describes the research methodology followed in a particular SCM research project. Section four presents the main advantages and disadvantages related to each one of the methodologies. Section five draws conclusions.

Paper	Summary	Methodology described
LOGISTICS/SCM JOURNALS		
Dunn et al. (1994)	Suggests a logistics research methodology for scientific analysis and testing of latent variables	Survey
Mentzer & Kahn (1995)	Presents a framework for understanding logistics research	General framework
Ellram (1996)	Shows how the case study method can be used in business research, with a particular focus on purchasing and logistics research	Case study
Mentzer & Flint (1997)	Addresses ways of increasing logistics research rigor	Case study/ survey
Williams Walton (1997)	Elaborates on the appropriateness of the telephone survey methodology to logistics research	Survey
OPERATIONS MANAGEMENT JOURNALS		
McCutcheon & Meredith (1993)	Offers an introduction to the case study method and provides an outline of the procedure	Case study
Malhotra & Grover (1998)	The authors provide a normative perspective on "good survey research practices"	Survey
Meredith (1998)	Elaborates on methods for increasing the generalizability of both rationalist and case/field research methodologies	Case study/ survey
Beach et al. (2001)	Describes the role of the case study in a research project (of a complex and intangible subject) and the contribution it made to the investigation	Case study
Forza (2002)	The author provides guidelines for the design and execution of survey research in operations management	Survey
Stuart et al. (2002)	The authors examine the process of conducting case research, from its theoretical foundations to the eventual dissemination of the research findings, and provide guidance in each step of the process	Case study
Voss et al. (2002)	This paper provides guidelines and a roadmap for operations management researchers wishing to design, develop and conduct case-based research	Case study

Table 1: Literature Review on Research Methodologies

2 Case Studies and Surveys: Complementary Methodologies

A case study is a an empirical methodology that typically uses multiple methods and tools for data collection from a number of entities by a direct observer(s) in a single, natural setting that considers temporal and contextual aspects of the contemporary phenomenon under study, but without experimental controls or manipulations. The methods and tools employed include both quantitative and qualitative approaches: financial data, interviews, memoranda, questionnaires, organization charts, etc. (Meredith, 1998: 442). The goal is to understand the phenomenon using "perceptual triangulation" (Bonoma, 1985: 203).

On the other hand, survey research involves the collection of information from individuals (through mailed questionnaires, telephone calls, interviews, etc.) about themselves or about the social unit to which they belong by using a structured format. Survey research is usually a quantitative method that requires standardized information in order to define or describe variables, or to study relationships between variables (Malhotra & Grover, 1998: 409). The information is gathered via a sample, which is a fraction of the population.

Case studies and surveys are both field-based methods in which data is gathered from the business context. However, there are some main differences between them (see Table 2).

	Case research	**Survey research**
Orientation	Usually qualitative oriented	Usually quantitative oriented
Variables	Are often not predefined	Are predefined
Data collection	Using structured and unstructured formats (Financial data, interviews, memoranda, questionnaires, organization charts, etc.)	Using a structured format (Questionnaire)
Results	In-depth examination of a phenomenon but not a generalization	Usually allows findings to be generalized from the sample to the population

Table 2: Main Differences between Case Research and Survey Research

Case studies and surveys also differ in the research purpose for which they are normally used. Case studies are appropriate for exploring new areas of research and generating hypotheses, while surveys are a very useful methodology in the "hypotheses testing" stage. Case studies are appropriate for uncovering areas of research (exploration) or identifying key variables or linkages between variables (theory building). This is due to the fact that case studies provide the type of knowledge that cannot be gleaned purely from the statistical analysis of pre-formatted questionnaires. On the other hand, survey research is very useful to test any theory that has been developed in the previous stages of the research. For these reasons, we present both methodologies as complementary tools. They are not mutually exclusive and, if combined, can offer greater potential for enhancing new theories than either method alone.

Eisenhardt (1989), Jick (1979) and Campbell & Fiske (1959) among others suggest that the use of multiple methods (both quantitative and qualitative) can create better assurances that variances are trait-related and not method-related. Dunn et al. (1994) suggested conducting research within the field of Logistics through the application of multiple methods (quantitative and qualitative). We claim that this multiple-method approach should also be applied in SCM research.

In the following section we provide an example of a research project as an illustration of how the case study and survey methodologies were used to conduct empirical research in the SCM field.

3 A SCM Research Project: "Does SCM Lead to a Better Performance?"

3.1 Research Objectives

SCM "is the integration of key business processes from end user through original suppliers, that provides products, services, and information that add value for customers and other stakeholders" (Cooper et al., 1997: 2). This means that SCM implies internal and external integration along the supply chain. Internal integration refers to the coordination, collaboration and integration of different functional units within each organization of the supply chain, while external integration refers to the integration of activities from different supply chain members.

The objectives of the research project presented here were:

- To analyze the relationship between the levels of external and internal integration.
- To study the impact of internal and external integration on performance.

We decided to focus this study on one industry (the grocery sector) because different levels of SCM development may be associated with it. For example, at the time of designing this research project (Spring 1999), the automotive industry was supposed to be very advanced in SCM because the JIT philosophy (which shares many principles with the SCM approach) had been present for decades. On the other hand, the Spanish grocery industry was supposed to have lower levels of SCM implementation due to the fact that the ECR philosophy (which shares many principles with the SCM approach) had been implemented very recently (the first pilot programs started in April 1997, see http://www.ecr-spain.com, accessed April 19th, 1999).

3.2 Research Methodologies and Research Purpose

The empirical research undertaken to analyze the objectives of this project was divided into two phases. The first one comprised an exploratory study based on the case study methodology (Yin, 1994). The aims of this exploratory phase were (1) to obtain an in-depth knowledge of the SCM practices in the Spanish grocery sector, (2) to explore the integration process and (3) to identify the main benefits and barriers found in its implementation. With the results of this exploratory stage of the research, we built a theoretical model.

The second phase involved an explanatory research based on the results of a survey. The aim of this second phase was to test the model built in the exploratory stage of the research. The survey was designed using some integration and performance variables grounded in the literature and some others identified in the exploratory case study. The objective of this second phase was to find causal relationships among the integration constructs (internal and external integration), as well as between them and the performance constructs. Figure 1 summarizes the causal relationships we attempted to analyze.

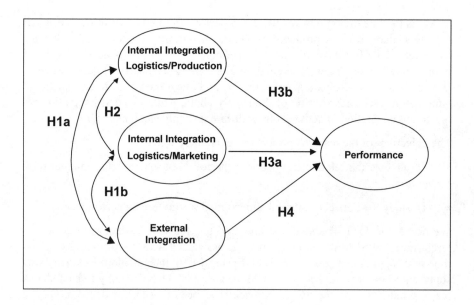

Figure 1: Theoretical Model (Gimenez & Ventura, 2003b: 7)

3.3 The Exploratory Multiple Case Study

This phase was conducted during the Spring/Summer of 1999. The process followed for designing and implementing this methodology was adopted from Yin (1994) and is illustrated in Figure 2.

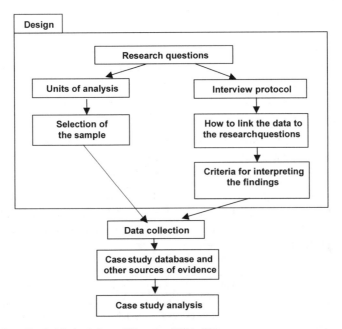

Figure 2: Case Study Methodology (Gimenez, 2001: 89)

The first step in the case study methodology was to define the research questions. As stated before, the research objectives of this exploratory phase were: (1) To determine the extent of SCM development in the Spanish grocery sector, (2) to explore the integration process and (3) to identify the main benefits and barriers found in its implementation.

The following steps refer to the process of determining the units of analysis. As SCM involves integration along the supply chain, the most appropriate approach in our study would have been to consider all elements in this chain such as retailers, third party logistics providers, food manufacturers, wholesalers, purchasing centers, manufacturers' suppliers, etc. But, due to the need of limiting the scope of the study, we focused on the manufacturer-retailer relationship. The units of analysis chosen were manufacturers and retailers from the Spanish grocery sector. The most appropriate approach for analyzing these relationships would have been to analyze particular manufacturer-retailer dyads, but this approach was not possible due to the reticence of the interviewees to identify the supply chain partner they were talking about.

In order to increase the reliability of the case study analysis, it was decided to create an interview protocol and a case study database. With respect to "how to link the data to the research questions," a chain of evidence was established in order to allow any external observer to follow the derivation of any evidence from initial research questions to ultimate case study conclusions.

After establishing the interview protocol and how to link the data to the research questions, interviews with fifteen companies (nine manufacturers and six retailers) were conducted. Initially, ten manufacturers and ten retailers were contacted, but one manufacturer and four retailers declined to participate in the study. Manufacturers were companies among the leaders in different product categories, and retailers were selected among the top twelve Spanish retailers.

Data collected was introduced in the case study database, which was analyzed to obtain the conclusions. Other sources of evidence such as newspaper clippings and articles were used to corroborate and augment evidence.

The results of this exploratory study (which are shown in Table 3) were used to build the theoretical model shown in Figure 1 and to design the questionnaire used to test this model. For further information about the results of this multiple case-study analysis see Gimenez (2004).

Case study findings	Implications in the second phase
Our multiple case study showed that only one of the fifteen companies analyzed had initiated an external integration process without being internally integrated.	Hypothesize that there is a positive relationship between both levels of integration.
The existing studies consider a general internal integration level without taking into account the interaction between departments (for example, Vargas et al. 2000; Stank et al., 2001). Our results showed that companies could have different levels of internal integration in different internal interfaces.	In our model, in order to analyze the level of internal integration we considered different internal interfaces: Logistics-Marketing and Logistics-Production.
The existing studies consider a general level of external integration for each company (for example, Stank et al., 2001). We found that companies, as Kraljic (1983) proposes, strategically segment their relationships.	We decided to analyze the level of external integration in particular supply chain relationships. In the questionnaire, each manufacturer was asked about two manufacturer-retailer relationships.
The literature suggests that high levels of integration are associated with high levels of performance (Frohlich & Westbrook, 2001). Our case study showed that the main benefits companies can achieve with the implementation of SCM are cost reductions and service improvements.	In our questionnaire, we included the measures of service and costs stated by the companies interviewed.

Table 3: Exploratory Case Study Results and Their Implications in the Second Phase

3.4 The Explanatory Survey Research

This phase was conducted during the Spring/Summer of 2001. It involved an explanatory survey research devoted to finding causal relationships among the integration and performance constructs shown in Figure 1. In this second phase, the process followed to design and implement the survey analysis as shown in Figure 3.

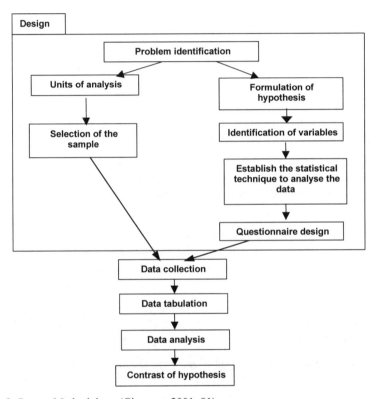

Figure 3: Survey Methodology (Gimenez, 2001: 91)

The first step in the survey methodology was to define the research questions. As stated before, the research questions of this phase were:

1. Is there any relationship between the levels of internal and external integration?
2. Is there any relationship between the level of internal integration in the Logistics-Production interface and the level of internal integration in the Logistics-Marketing interface?

3. Is there any relationship between the levels of internal integration within a company and its logistics performance?
4. Is there any relationship between the level of external integration in a supply chain relationship and the performance of the company in this relationship?

The following are hypotheses related to each of these research questions as shown in Figure 1.

- Hypothesis H1a. There is a positive relationship between the level of internal integration in the Logistics-Production interface and the level of external integration.

- Hypothesis H1b. There is a positive relationship between the level of internal integration in the Logistics-Marketing interface and the level of external integration.

- Hypothesis H2. There is a positive relationship between the level of internal integration in the Logistics-Production interface and the level of internal integration in the Logistics-Marketing interface.

- Hypothesis H3a. The level of internal integration in the Logistics-Marketing interface has a positive effect on the logistics performance. The higher the level of internal integration in the Logistics-Marketing interface the better the logistics performance.

- Hypothesis H3b. The level of internal integration in the Logistics-Production interface has a positive effect on the logistics performance. The higher the level of internal integration in the Logistics-Production interface the better the logistics performance.

- Hypothesis H4. The level of external integration has a positive effect on the logistics performance. The higher the level of external integration the better the logistics performance.

The units of analysis in this second phase were the manufacturer-retailer relationships. However, the survey was designed to be answered only by the manufacturers. Retailers were not included in this stage due to the reduced number of companies in this industry, a highly concentrated sector, which would have led to a very small sample size. Manufacturers of the Spanish grocery sector were asked about their level of internal integration in two internal interfaces, their level of external integration in two relationships, and their performance in these two relationships.

Potential participants were identified from a Spanish company's database (Fomento de la Producción 25,000). Manufacturers from the food and perfumery-detergent sectors with a sales figure higher than €30 million were selected to make up the sample (199 companies).

The questionnaire was designed containing three parts: internal integration, external integration and performance. In the internal integration part of the questionnaire we asked each manufacturer to measure the level of integration in two internal interfaces: Logistics-Marketing and Logistics-Production. The variables used to measure these integration levels were defined from the literature (Stank et al., 1999) and based on expert opinion to provide respondents with a common understanding of the questions.

Part two of the questionnaire was designed to measure the level of external integration. As companies usually strategically segment their relationships (Kraljic, 1983, and the results of the exploratory case study), we decided to measure the level of integration, in particular manufacturer-retailer relationships. Each manufacturer was asked to choose two manufacturer-retailer relationships. The first relationship had to be the most collaborating relationship, while the second should be the least collaborating. The variables used to measure the level of external integration were designed adapting the internal integration variables used by Stank et al. (1999) to a supply chain relationship. Therefore, instead of asking about the collaboration between different functional areas, we asked about the collaboration between the logistics area of one company and the logistics area of its customer (the retailer). The eight questions related to external integration were asked to each manufacturer twice, i.e. for the most and for the least collaborating relationship.

Performance variables were designed according to the literature and the results of the exploratory case study (Gimenez, 2004), which showed that the benefits associated with SCM were service improvements and costs and stock-out reductions. As performance data was difficult to obtain because of the reticence of participants to give confidential data, performance in this study was operationalized by using senior management's perceptions of performance improvements. In order to analyze the integration-performance link, performance had to be related to the external integration level achieved in each relationship. Accordingly, the five questions related to performance were asked for relationship 1 (the most collaborating relationship) and relationship 2 (the least collaborating relationship).

Questions were designed using a ten-point Likert scale. A preliminary survey instrument was pre-tested with three logistics professors and five logistics managers, who were asked to comment on the wording, presentation and face validity of items. Suggestions for rewording and repositioning were incorporated into the final survey instrument.

As pre-notification increases the response rate (Fox et al., 1988), all the companies in the sample were telephoned before mailing the questionnaire. We informed each company's logistics or supply chain director about the study and asked for their participation. Only one company refused to participate in the survey.

During the Spring of 2001, the questionnaire was sent to the supply chain or logistics director of each firm. The mailing included postage stamps for returning the questionnaires and a personalized request on university letterhead. These are factors that increase response rate (Fox et al., 1988). 64 companies returned the questionnaire, which represents a 32.3% (64/198) response rate. This response rate was considered very satisfactory, as potential participants were asked to provide sensitive and confidential data about their performance.

We conducted an analysis of non-response bias based on the procedure described by Armstrong & Overton (1977) and Lambert & Harrington (1990). We numbered the responses sequentially in the order they were received and compared late responses with early responses to all model variables using T-tests. We did not find any noticeable pattern among the variables that could indicate the existence of a non-response bias.

The theoretical model illustrated in Figure 1 was subjected to analysis using Structural Equation Modelling (SEM). SEM is a very general linear statistical modeling technique that encompasses factor analysis, regression, and many other estimation methods as special cases. The proposed model had four latent variables or constructs: internal integration in the Logistics-Production interface, internal integration in the Logistics-Marketing interface, external integration, and company performance. These constructs were not observed directly. Instead, they were measured with error by instrumental variables. Typically, a model of structural equations has two distinct parts which are analyzed simultaneously: the measurement part and the construct part. The measurement part focuses on the relationship between the observed measures and the latent constructs, while the construct part focuses on the relationship between the latent variables.

The measurement part of our model showed that our variables were good indicators of the constructs, and the construct part showed that there were some significant relationships among the constructs (the fit of the models[1] was very good: greater than 0.9, as measured by the Comparative Fit Index). For further information about the analysis conducted in this second phase see Gimenez & Ventura (2003b).

The main conclusions of this study were: (1) Internal integration influences external collaboration and vice versa. (2) The levels of internal integration in the Logistics-Production and Logistics-Marketing interfaces positively influence each other. (3) A high level of internal integration in the Logistics-Marketing interface does not lead to a better absolute performance. (4) The level of Logistics-Production integration leads to a better absolute performance when there is no external integration. When firms are externally integrated, the level of external integration has such an important effect on performance that it nullifies (or reduces) the effect of the Logistics-Production integration. Finally, (5) external collaboration among supply chain members contributes to achieving costs, stock-outs and lead-time reductions.

---

[1] We estimated the theoretical model shown in Figure 1 twice, first with data from the most collaborating relationship, and then with data from the least collaborating relationship.

4 Case Studies and Surveys: Advantages and Disadvantages

Tables 4 and 5 summarize the advantages and disadvantages we found in the methodologies we employed. As can be appreciated, some of the disadvantages of one methodology could be minimized by using the complementary one. For example, in the case study, we obtained complete information about the subject of study, but the sample size was not big enough to generalize the findings; in the survey, we obtained information that was model-limited, but the sample size was big enough to generalize.

Advantages	Disadvantages
• Provided complete information because the data collection was not constrained by the rigid limits of a questionnaire • Led to new and creative insights • We were able to explore relationships • We obtained a good understanding of the relationships between the constructs object of study (integration and performance) • It increased our contact to real life • It had high validity among practitioners[2]	• We were not able to generalize the results because of the reduced sample size • The case study method is usually criticized for its subjectivity. We reduced this limitation by triangulation • It was very time and money intensive (due to the need to travel around Spain to conduct personal interviews)

Table 4: Advantages and Disadvantages of the Case Study Methodology

---

[2] All companies participating in the study received a summary of the findings, and some of them even contacted us for further information.

Advantages	Disadvantages
• We obtained higher precision and reliability • We were able to generalize results because the sample size was big enough • Objectivity • We were able to confirm or refute relationships among the constructs • Reduced expenses in comparison with the case study • We obtained the data we needed because the questionnaire was designed while taking the results of the exploratory phase into consideration	• We asked about perceptions of other people. Therefore, we were not penalized for our subjectivity • The information obtained was model-limited • This method usually has a low response rate. But in our case, it was very high in comparison to other studies. The reasons for this high response rate: prenotification, postage stamps included to return the questionnaire, and the relevance of the topic (SCM was a very hot topic in the Spanish grocery industry when we conducted the survey)

Table 5: Advantages and Disadvantages of the Survey Methodology

5 Conclusions

This paper calls for a multiple-method approach to empirical research in SCM. The paper suggests conducting empirical research within the field of SCM through the application of multiple methods, both quantitative and qualitative. The reasons for using multiple methods are twofold: first, the use of multiple methods can create better assurances that variances are trait-related and not method-related. And secondly, each methodology is more appropriate for a particular research purpose. For example, case studies are more appropriate for the development or exploratory "hypotheses generating" stage of a research, while surveys are more useful to test the theory developed in the previous stages of the research.

We have described the methodology followed in a SCM research project as an illustration of how multiple methods can be used to build and test theory. We have shown the interrelation of both methods: the case study method was used to build a model, while the survey methodology was used to test it.

This paper is intended as a recommendation to SCM researchers to use multiple methods to conduct their research, because it increases the research outcomes' quality and rigor (Mentzer & Flint, 1997), which are very important for creating knowledge.

6 References

Armstrong, J. S., Overton, T. S. (1977): Estimating Non-response Bias in Mail Surveys, in: Journal of Marketing Research, 14(3): 396- 402.

Beach, R., Muhlemann, A. P., Price, D. H. R., Paterson, A., Sharp, J. A. (2001): The Role of Qualitative Methods in Production Management, in: International Journal of Production Economics, 74(1-3): 201-212.

Bonoma, T. V. (1985): Case Research in Marketing: Opportunities, Problems, and a Process, in: Journal Marketing Research, 22(2): 199-208.

Cambell, D., Fiske, D. (1959): Convergent and Discriminant Validation by the Multitrait – Multimethod Matrix, in: Psychological Bulletin 56: 81-105.

Christopher, M. (1998): Logistics and Supply Chain Management: Strategies for reducing cost and improving service, Financial Times Pitman Publishing, UK.

Cooper, M. C., Lambert, D. M., Pagh, J. D. (1997): Supply Chain Management: More than a New Name for Logistics, in: The International Journal of Logistics Management, 8(1): 1-13.

Dunn, S. C., Seaker, R. F., Waller, M. A. (1994): Latent Variables in Business Logistics Research: Scale Development and Validation, in: Journal of Business Logistics, 15(2): 145-172.

Eisenhardt, K. M. (1991): Building Theories from Case Study Research, in: Academy of Management Review, 16 (3): 532-550.

Ellram, L. M. (1996): The Use of the Case Study Method in Logistics Research, in: Journal of Business Logistics, 17(2): 93-137.

Forza, C. (2002): Survey Research in Operations Management: A Process-Based Perspective, in: International Journal of Operations & Production Management, 22(2): 152-194.

Fox, R. J., Crask, M. R., Kim, J. (1988): Mail Survey Response Rate: A Metaanalysis of Selected Techniques for Inducing Response"; Public Opinion Quarterly, 52(1): 467-491.

Frohlich, M., Westbrook, R. (2001): Arcs of integration: an international study of supply chain strategies, in: Journal of Operations Management, 19(2): 185-200.

Gimenez, C. (2001): Competitive Advantage Through Supply Chain Management, PhD Thesis, Universitat de Barcelona, Spain.

Gimenez, C. (2004): Supply Chain Management Implementation in the Spanish Grocery Sector: An Exploratory Study, in: International Journal of Integrated Supply Management, 1(1): 98-114.

Gimenez, C., Ventura, E., (2003): Supply Chain Management as a Competitive Advantage in the Spanish Grocery Sector, in: The International Journal of Logistics Management, 14(1): 77-88.

Gimenez, C., Ventura, E. (2003b): Logistics-Production, Logistics-Marketing and External Integration: Their Impact on Performance, UPF Working Paper # 657.

Jick, T. (1979): Nixing Qualitative and Quantitative Methods: Triangulation in Action, in: Administrative Science Quarterly, 24: 602-611.

Kraljic, P. (1983): Purchasing Must Become Supply Management, in: Harvard Business Review, 61: 109-117.

Lambert, D. M., Harrington, T. C. (1990): Measuring Non-Response in Customer Service Mail Surveys, in: Journal of Business Logistics, 11(2): 5-25.

Malhotra, M. K., Grover, V. (1998): An Assessment of Survey Research in POM: From Constructs to Theory, in: Journal of Operations Management, 16(4): 407-425.

McCutcheon, D. M., Meredith, J. R. (1993): Conducting Case Study Research in Operations Management, in: Journal of Operations Management, 11(3): 239-256.

Mentzer, J. T., Flint, D. J. (1997): Validity in Logistics Research, in: Journal of Business Logistics, 18(1): 199-216.

Mentzer, J. T., Kahn, K. B. (1995): A Framework of Logistics Research, in: Journal of Business Logistics, 16(1): 231-249.

Meredith, J. (1998): Building Operations Management Theory through Case and Field Research, in: Journal of Operations Management, 16(4): 441-454.

Stank, T., Daugherty, P., Ellinger, A. (1999): Marketing/Logistics Integration and Firm Performance, in: The International Journal of Logistics Management, 10(1): 11-25.

Stank, T., Keller, S., Daugherty, P. (2001): Supply Chain Collaboration and Logistical Service Performance, in: Journal of Business Logistics, 22(1): 29-48.

Stevens, G. C. (1989): Integrating the Supply Chain, in: International Journal of Physical Distribution and Materials Management, 19(8): 3-8.

Stuart, I., McCutcheon, R., Handfield, R., McLachlin, R., Samson, D. (2002): Effective Case Research in Operations Management: A Process Perspective, in: Journal of Operations Management, 20(5): 419-433.

Vargas, G., Cardenas, L., Matarranz, L. (2000): Internal and External Integration of Assembly Manufacturing Activities, in: International Journal of Operations and Production Management, 20(7): 809-822.

Voss, C., Tsikriktsis, N., Frolich, M. (2002): Case Research in Operations Management, in: International Journal of Operations & Production Management, 22(2): 195-219.

Willians Walton, L. (1997): Telephone Survey: Answering the Seven Rs to Logistics Research, in: Journal of Business Logistics, 18(1): 217-231.

Yin, R. K. (1994): Case Study Research: Design and Methods, Sage Publications, USA.

Towards Triangulation – Blending Techniques in Supply Chain Management Context

Ozlem Bak

1 Introduction 332
2 Grounded Theory Overview 332
3 Conclusion 340
4 References 344

Summary:
Supply chain relationships are impacted by the use of the Internet and the transformation through its technologies (Bak, 2004). Although an area of growing interest, little research has focused on the impact of the Internet and on understanding how different approaches for creating supply chains are suitable for different supply chain requirements (Pant et al., 2003). Similar to MacPherson et al. (1993) and Sherif & Vinze (2003), a case study research method with grounded theory approach was used. The findings of the case study (Phase A), the so-called derived theory, allowed the researcher to establish a follow up questionnaire for a second investigation (Phase B) in similar settings with a wider spectrum. In this study, blending was particularly helpful in eliciting the controversial findings and proved to be a useful source.

Keywords:
Internet, Supply Chain Management, Transformation, Case Study, Grounded Theory, Blending Techniques

1 Introduction

The commencement of e-business technologies in supply chain propelled companies towards the "Internet-enabled supply chain," i.e. the "e-supply chain" and converted the way companies are conventionally organized (Bak, 2003). Several researchers have identified measures for successful transformation based on: behavioral changes and long-term financial success (Ross & Beath, 2002); economic value, shareholder value, and organizational capacity (Beer & Nohria, 2000); past experience and past performance levels (Venkatraman, 1994; Prahalad & Oosterveld, 1999); and on how well programs across organizations are managed and monitored (Sharma, 2000). With any of these success indicators, companies might differ, as some may choose market share, whereas others choose quality or innovation (Bak, 2004). Thus, companies can be successful on any of these levels.

Returning to our question of transformation, if success depends on each organization's or business unit's goal, which are different when compared to each other, how can we undertake this research? With this aim of answering our research question, the current paper introduces a case study where grounded theory was applied and blended with a questionnaire as a source of triangulation. Therefore, in the first section, grounded theory and its use in supply chain management are explored. This is followed by asking the question of why there was a particular need to introduce the blending techniques to test and verify the findings of this phenomenon within similar settings.

2 Grounded Theory Overview

The grounded theory attempts to generate new theories or conceptual propositions from/with the phenomenon (Glaser & Strauss, 1967; Goulding, 1999; Lee, 1999). The grounded theory research defines (a) where the findings are derived from, (b) how core concepts were elicited, and (c) how empirical links among core concepts were achieved. The main procedure is built upon: (a) Open coding, in which the researcher identifies "naturally occurring" categories depicted from the phenomenon in order to organize, explain and label the empirical data to these categories; (b) Axial coding, where empirical data is assigned to a category and where it is controlled whether data fits within the selected category and any relationships exist between the categories (this process is repeated until all data have been examined and classified (Lee, 1999: 48); and (c) Selective coding, in which categories are arranged according to their importance. The most powerful/important core category is assigned and linked to other categories. This repeats until all the data have been categorized (Lee, 1999: 48-49) and when further data collection is unlikely to add an additional understanding (theoretical saturation) (Lee, 1999: 49-50).

In this context, empirical observation plays an important role, as the role of the researcher in these settings differs when using different versions of grounded theory. These range from the initial Glaser & Strauss (1967) to the Strauss & Corbin (1990) renditions, followed by the Glaser (1987, 1992) interpretation. The key differentiator between these versions is the role of the researcher. Strauss (1987) defines an active role for the researcher as an "imposer of interpretations", wherein "... one makes theoretical comparisons based on what one knows, either from experience or from literature" (Straus & Corbin, 1988: 95). On the other hand, Glaser (1987, 1992) defines the researcher as a passive interpreter whose investigation is solely based on what the researcher could read out of the collected data, not from the literature or his/her prior knowledge (Lee, 1999: 45-46). The ongoing debate on grounded theory indicates, "...there has been no resolution to this issue" as it still "...remains a matter of personal comfort" (Lee, 1999:45-46). This debate will not be a part of this paper, as several researchers have covered this extensively (Charmaz, 1983; Glaser, 1987, 1992; Strauss & Corbin, 1998; Douglas, 2003; Goulding, 1998, 1999; Lee, 1999). Therefore, based on the literature and study carried out by the author, this paper instead attempts to identify the benefits and difficulties of using grounded theory with other methods in the SCM context, where there are no hard-and-fast rules on how to blend.

2.1 SCM and the Use of Grounded Theory

Generally, research papers in supply chain management indicates three ways of conducting research: a) holistically, based on the entire supply chain from the supplier to end customer (Houlihan, 1984; Narsimhan & Jayrum, 1998); b) from the unit level perspective, based on the business units or particular segments (Hakansson & Johansson, 1993; Emberson et al., 2001); and c) specific technologies, based on specific applications such as internet-enabled ERP (Ash & Burn, 2003), EDI (Johnston & Mak, 2000) and B2B (Golilic et al., 2002).

The use of any of these levels depends on research questions and the phenomenon under investigation. For example, considering a recent phenomenon where gaps are identified in literature calls for closeness between the researcher and the setting (environment) of the phenomena where it could be observed (Golilic et al., 2002). The current investigation on Internet applications for supply chains requires tremendous resources, time and energy, as it stretches from supplier to partners where a "one size fits all" approach does not suit all types, because different supply chains have different needs and environmental conditions (Pant et al., 2003). In such cases we have to clearly define our boundaries and our unit of analysis. In instances where this is not possible from the beginning, grounded theory helps to introduce a structural framework on how to analyze the unstructured data sets and define the context and boundaries of the analysis.

When studies are explored that examine the impact of the Internet and its applications; the use of grounded theory was limited to a few cases. One such study was conducted by Golicic et al. (2002), and was a qualitative study commenced with eight e-commerce companies using a grounded theory approach to understand and explore the impact of e-commerce on supply chain relationships. One of the instances where such examination seems to be useful is the impact of Internet applications on company organization and why some business partners agreed and others were reluctant to adopt e-supply chain systems (Pant et al., 2003). Lancioni et al. (2000) undertook research on how and to what extent firms use the Internet in their supply chains. When examining "processes people use to cope with, respond to or alter their environment" (Golilic et al., 2002), grounded methodology can be seen as appropriate. Thus, the importance of the grounded theory approach in the present study was that it incorporated the complexities of environmental conditions of the supply chain under investigation without discarding, ignoring, or assuming away relevant variables.

The complexity of conducting research in SCM remains an important point to be considered. Studies that combine methods with aspects of theory testing, triangulation, and verification incorporate a process known as *blending* (Lee, 1999). However, it is questionable whether there are any rules on how to and when to blend. The following section gives a brief outline of the literature on blending techniques, followed by an example of blending grounded theory with a questionnaire on SCM.

2.2 Blending Techniques

To ground data in one specific setting where phenomena exist might exclude similar settings with similar phenomena due to time, resources and the complexity of such an investigation. In such instances, additional data to verify, test, and validate the outcome might be needed in order to triangulate the data in other settings. This calls for blending methods such as surveys, questionnaires, and interviews.

In some research settings, to test the quality of the process of grounding, two or more researchers are assigned for the coding process to see whether there are discrepancies and, if so, to what extent. Another way of verification can be achieved by allocating another researcher to review the transcripts and verify the reliability (Golilic et al., 2002). Therefore, this paper introduces a case study where grounded theory was applied and blended with another method.

2.3 Case Study Description

An important distinction between case research and other empirical findings is that the variables of interest that explain the phenomena are not identified prior to the study. Both of the variables and the relationships between them emerge as the data is collected or analyzed. This case study embedded two case studies: two applications, namely Extranet and B2B, in an automotive manufacturers supply chain, where data was collected through a variety of methods, including semi-structured interviews, meeting minutes, document review and participant observation.

These various techniques of data collection are beneficial in theory generation, as they provide multiple perspectives on an issue, supply more information on emerging concepts, and allow for cross-checking and triangulation (see Appendix C for quality criteria used in this study) (Orlikowski, 1993; Glaser & Strauss, 1967). Therefore, similar to McPherson et al. (1993) and Sherif & Vinze (2003), a case study research method with grounded theory approach was used. The findings of the case study (Phase A), the so-called "derived theory," allowed the researcher to create a follow up questionnaire for a second investigation (Phase B) in similar settings with a wider spectrum.

The literature review took place mainly before, during, and after the project participation. As a result of the review and experiences of the participant observation, the research methodology decisions were finalized and formalized. The case study process included a research model process focusing on data analysis based on the grounded theory approach by Straus & Corbin (1989) and Eisenhardt (1989). (See Appendix B)

1. Method—The Grounded Theory Approach

By following a grounded theory approach, the first step was to create conceptual categories and establish a context. The categories were drawn from the transformation literature and in particular studies from IT-enabled change. However, being aware of the possibility of introducing bias through a priori constructs, in theory development it is important to review the emergent theory against the existing literature (Strauss & Corbin, 1989: 135). While reviewing the theory "... an extreme dimension or variation of the phenomenon in question" (Strauss & Corbin, 1989: 135) can be searched for, asking what is similar, what is different, and why (Eisenhardt, 1989). From transformation literature, a matrix was derived from Vollman (1996). Transformation levels (challenges, strategic intent, strategic response, competencies and capabilities, processes, resources, outputs) and Graham & Hardaker's (Graham & Hardaker, 2000; based on Rayport & Svioklia, 1994) dimensions of Internet-enabled supply chains (content, context, infrastructure) and elicitation were broken down into 24 categories with additional sub-categories. Data that would contradict was consciously searched for. It soon became clear that the initial concepts generated from the literature did not accommodate some of the findings emerging from the data. Accommodating different experiences led to some elaborations and clarifications in the emerging theoretical framework and forced reconsideration. This ability to incorporate unique insights during the course of study is one of the benefits of a grounded theory research approach, what Eisenhardt (1989: 539) labels "controlled opportunism," where "researchers take advantage of the uniqueness of specific case and the emergence of new themes to improve resultant theory."

Emerging concepts were checked for representativeness by examining them across participants and multiple methods. Triangulation across data sources and data collection methods (interviews, participant observation, and documentation) strengthened the emerging concepts. The results illustrated that some elements showed contradicting/common patterns, indicating that some elements might also have more impact on a certain aspect of transformation than others.

2. Qualitative Data

The data collection and analysis involved in this grounded theory study included approximately four and a half months of participant observation over two projects, 10 hours of semi-structured interviews, 30 personal meeting notes, document analysis, and the distribution of a questionnaire.

The case study involved a business unit incorporated major Internet-mediated tools with organizational implications at rollout phase, and focused on cross-functional business activities. The formal semi-structured interviews were carried out with eight interviewees and lasted between one and two hours. These interviews were taped and transcribed, then entered into N6 software to assist with analysis. These interviews were conducted during and after the participant observation. The content of these semi-structured interviews consisted of interpretation of incidents that were occurring at the time, and were based around the phenomenon of concern. Theoretical sampling was conducted concurrently with data analysis. This meant that the researcher would theorize and write up ideas about the categories as they emerged (Straus & Corbin, 1989, 1994). Handwritten personnel meeting minutes were taken during these interviews and entered into N6 software that helped with indexing, searching and theorizing (package designed by Qualitative Research and Solutions (QSR, 2002). It was used for: (a) storage, categorizing of interview transcripts, personnel meeting minutes, and other documents; (b) creation of categories, moving and linking data through computer-assisted coding; (c) conducting searches relevant to analysis; and (d) creating basic hierarchical models of codes.

3. Quantitative Data

An additional data source was a quantitative questionnaire. The questionnaire contained the results of the qualitative data analysis. The postal questionnaire was distributed to 4 multinational companies' business units; 120 questionnaires were sent out and an initial response rate of 37.5% was achieved. Questionnaires were returned with the stamped envelope included in the questionnaire package.

The reason for using a quantitative instrument alongside the qualitative data was to provide an in-depth understanding of the phenomenon from multiple angles. This blending with the questionnaire allowed the researcher to detect similarities and to compare differences in similar settings with similar applications. The results of the questionnaire advocate what the grounded theory should encompass in some instances, such as similar phenomena and settings, and research techniques that can improve the rigor and explanation of the results achieved. Following theoretical saturation, further Phase B blending should add to or modify the ideas presented here. This data triangulation has been described as "multiple methods" (Denzin, 1970). Similarly, Bryman (1988) noted that triangulation could enhance the quality of information if the multiple methods can provide mutual confirmation. The use of the questionnaire to complement the qualitative data analysis was seen as an effective way to achieve the triangulation of data.

2.4 Analysis

Analysis of qualitative data was conducted in several iterations in order to determine the relationships between categories, i.e. there were a number of coding "families" (Glaser, 1978). By asking the following questions on the data, and seeking answers, categories were compared and abstracted further until all the categories were saturated; that is, no new categories relating to the emerging core category or main theme emerged. What are the relationships between the categories and their consequences? Are the events evident in the phenomenon? Is a category bearing another category as dependent? (Strauss & Corbin, 1990) Is there covariance (when one category changes with the changes in another category) between the categories (which reflect dependency and independency)?

2.5 Findings

The following preliminary findings represent only the conflicting issues stemming from the results of case studies with grounded theory approach and the questionnaire.

1. **Conflicting Questionnaire Results: Change vs. Transformation**

A very interesting finding emerged during the early stages of analysis. This was that the questionnaire data provided contrasting findings when compared with the findings from qualitative analysis of the interview and observation data. If only the questionnaire data were analyzed, they would have concluded that supply chain-wide shifts in industry occur by adapting e-business applications in general. By contrast, if we were to have used only the qualitative data, we would have concluded that they are related to one specific applications and not the other.

One example is that the business unit defined change as transformational: "Its transformational nature, because we have a complete new system.... [It] has a direct effect on how we did the things around here... including structural changes ... training of the employees to use the system...new job definitions and division of tasks... some see that as an extra workload but some see that as a necessity to compete...." One distributor commented on the new system referring to the extent of change "[it] will effect the salesman, when he goes to the customer he would just need his laptop and to connect into the network to do his presentation or to answer any sort of question, and to get our full support... paperless environment... no catalogues... technical sheets...price list...just a click ... you have all the information you need to have." Whereas another interviewee said for the same e-business applications "we haven't changed the way we do business around here...it's just another tool...we have still the same routines."

Such a contradictory finding necessitated further iterations of analysis and interpretation within the principles of theoretical coding and theoretical sampling. Another example stemmed when, considering solutions to change incidents, one team leader noted, "e-business solutions are quite personal because a lot of what we are dealing with is how the individual employee makes use of them." Similar comments on handwritten comments on some questionnaires strengthened this argument. Consequently, we found high mean frequency, relatively high standard deviation, but certainly considerable variation in responses between the items that constituted individualized consideration.

2. Emergence of Categories at Higher Levels of Abstraction

Many lower order categories appeared early in the coding process. One example is the set of lower order categories representing higher order category "disbelief-resistance to change." During coding, it was found that categories possessed similar characteristics in terms of their causes and consequences with other categories. Consequently, another higher order category called "pressure" was found to have a role similar to the other higher order category, and in contributing to change. In fact, the emerging theme was a lack of pressure, more so than a manifestation of change. Those higher order categories are all examined briefly within the context of change.

3. Pressure—Near-Core Category

Another higher order category consequently was found to be, "role defining". Overcoming the effects of pressure requires a shift in order to improve understanding and support for the changing role. When interviewed, one interviewee commented on pressures being "accountable for budget, success of the e-business application, and employee satisfaction." Another interviewee regretted being "pressured from upper management" and carrying several different tasks along with his work.

4. Quantitative Data

However, as the qualitative data analysis progressed, themes emerged from the data to support the interpretation that transformation is affected by more factors than the matrix has included. These themes are now considered from within the context of qualitative analysis of the questionnaire data.

Findings indicated that upper management was seen as not well informed about the extent and workload of the change concept. However, the overall mean score in the samples remained low in an absolute sense (0.9) and the factor was reliable (a=0.9). Answers to these items on the questionnaire reflected this dilemma. Comments written on the questionnaires provided insights into what was perceived by the respondents, and how the ability of those change was inhibited or repressed by the system. For example, with "comments on the problems," one respondent wrote, "Even if the team leader makes decisions, he gets overruled. Therefore we have to wait for the decision of upper management in order to move on." Interpretation of these written comments was central to the grounded theory data analytic process. The high standard deviation factor (0.98 on a scale of 0–5) indicated a considerable variation of responses, although the overall mean was relatively low. The organization practice remains highly procedural.

The questionnaire and case study data provided contrasting views of transformation in the context of a complex and changing organizational environment. This was only achieved with the results being examined qualitatively in conjunction with other methods.

5. Multiple Change-Transformation Realities—Near-Core Category

As well as the identification of the process, it became apparent at the middle stages of analysis that two cases each perceived different realities about the nature of the change process. Extranet was seen as requiring an incremental change, whereas B2B required an abrupt-radical shift in the same business unit. Understanding the multiple realities of these two played a large role in understanding the phenomenon of transformation under investigation. Therefore, the relationships between these groups were investigated in the questionnaire within the context of organizational change and transformation.

Comments made by interviewees provided evidence for a lack of understanding on the part of management. For example, frequently made comments like "...I don't know if they understand the extent of the problems here," or, in another example, the focus on issues by the external staff was found to cause tense disagreement. Although both groups aimed for the same goal, each group's understanding of the other group's issues was found as limited or disregarded. The communication challenges associated with multiple realities were typified by the perceptions found in this research that "the communication from the top on down about organizational changes is inconsistent". Another interviewer said, "There has been no discussion with [management]." It is important to note that change resistance from within the business unit is also responsible for repressing the ability to move toward visions and collaboration. In fact, their relationship was found to be reciprocal and high covariance was found between the two near-core categories; communication and pressure. Throughout these change/transformation processes, employees were not only required to continue to provide excellent tasks, but to enhance the use of new tools in the organization and maximize positive outcomes.

Identifying paradox also met the criteria for being labeled a basic social process because identifying paradox occurred over time under various conditions (Glaser & Strauss, 1967). This process requires either reconciling or legitimizing paradox. Realities between different groups became divergent and subsequent changes were more likely to be perceived as negative. Actors may perceive organizational changes as positive or negative. Depending on the way in which the change is perceived, change is followed by multiple realities.

3 Conclusion

The present study offers implications for organization practice. These implications shall be discussed in line with the terms regarding the objectives of this paper. The first objective of this paper was to create an understanding of why blending techniques were useful in this study. The mainstream research practices in supply chains have traditionally tended to control variables in order to comply with the positivist tradition. By contrast, the grounded theory, and the emergence of abstract concepts have traditionally been difficult to measure with mainstream research methods. The triangulation of the data through the use of blending techniques in this study assisted the researcher in generating more complex and explanatory insights. Therefore, it was particularly helpful in eliciting the findings proven to be a useful source of descriptions and evaluations for research processes. In particular, the contrast in findings between the qualitative and quantitative data forced the researchers to explain the nature of the contrast and its implications.

The second objective of this research was to better understand transformation. As part of the theoretical sampling in this study, employees across all hierarchical levels were formally interviewed, observed, and surveyed. A recurring theme in this study was that managers had the potential to achieve greater influence and change within the organizational environment. However, an equally recurring theme was that this potential was repressed by cultural and societal factors within and outside the organization. The resistance to negatively perceived change sometimes resulted in managers repeating the same steps that resulted in resistance in the first place. It is not enough for studies to express the need for more collegial work practice, a favorable work culture, or for managers to be more proactive and committed.

The third objective of this research was to determine the basic social process. Reflecting paradox does not provide an all-encompassing formula for effective change or transformation. However, it does explicitly identify the underlying causes of the present issues for organizations and offers an in-depth insight into the processes leading to both negative and positive perceptions of change efforts and promotes a greater understanding of the dynamics between subcultures within the organization.

The present research has shown[1] how useful the blending technique was in providing new insights from alternative angles. We analyzed a case where the grounded theory was used and subsequently blended together with a questionnaire. Further research needs to be conducted on the present substantive theory to generalize these findings to other areas.

Appendix A: Introductory questions asked in semi-structured interviews.

Questions relating to change occurring through e-business applications in critical incidents:

- What are the major changes that have taken place?
- What is changing and to what extent is it changing?
- How would you describe these changes (radical or incremental)?
- How do these changes affect your work?
- Who has had the greatest effect in driving these changes?
- How have they had that effect?
- What effect have you had on these changes?
- What initiated this change?
- How has this change impacted your business unit?
- Which other business units were influenced in your organization?
- How did you get through the change process?
- Expand upon and give detail on incidents, processes, and the impact of change on your business unit while comparing it other business units.
- Specify the role of people in your business unit and in the organization.

Questions relating to implicit theories and their effect:

- What does change mean to you?
- Have you seen evidence of such change/transformation in this organization and/or business unit?
- Compare and contrast two e-business-related change efforts in the organization.
- If you were running this change/transformation in this organization, what would you include?

---

[1] The exact wording, and the wording of intervening and supplementary questions, was determined by the direction of the interview and the responses of interviewees.

Appendix B: Evidence, quality and substantiation criteria of this study.

	Corresponding phases in the process of this study		
Processes	Grounded theory (Strauss & Corbin, 1990)	Case researcher responsibilities (Stake, 1994)	Inducing theory using case studies (Eisenhardt, 1989)
Research questions	Defining research questions in the light of former research		Defining research question and possible a priori constructs
Literature review	Contrasting with prior theories	Evaluation in the light of previous research	Conflicting and similar former research in literature
Case selection		Conceptualization of phenomena, themes or issues to be explored	A priori constructs and possible research question
Data collection	Familiarization with data for creating first thoughts		Entering field: data collection
Methodology formulation	Defining concepts and elements that are important for understanding		Crafting instruments and protocols: data collection methods
Systematic data analysis	Categorization, seeking patterns in the data	Triangulate key observation and interpretation	Analyzing data within/ between embedded cases
Empirical results and their evaluation	Linking, connection and recognition of contradictions	Illustrating and evaluating patterns, generalizations in case	Former research: Conflicting and similar

Appendix C: Evidence, quality and substantiation criteria of this study.

	Quality criteria	Quality measures in this study
Construct validity	Iterative and constant comparison (Strauss & Corbin, 1994; Eisenhardt, 1989). Establishing a chain of evidence between research questions, evidence and conclusions (Yin, 1994; Eisenhardt, 1989).	Respondents (feedback supplied) review the case and the results. Use of multiple sources and collection methods. Comparison with conflicting theories
Internal validity	Establishing causal relationship (Yin, 1994). Pattern-matching, explanation building (Yin, 1994) Comparison with conflicting literature (Strauss & Corbin, 1994; Eisenhardt, 1989)	Matching data with constructs based on participant observation, interviews and questionnaire. Comparison with conflicting theory. (Strauss & Corbin, 1994; Eisenhardt, 1989)
External validity	Expert comments on preliminary findings establishes findings to be generalized. Comparison with similar literature (Eisenhardt, 1989) Comprehensive description for the reader's own judgment (Stake, 1994)	Analytical generalizations by reflecting enfolding literature. Embedded case design inside the main unit of analysis (Yin, 1994) Precise and comprehensive case description allowing for reader's own judgment
Reliability	The accuracy of the research methods and techniques. Use of case study protocol (Yin, 1994)	Demonstrating that data collection procedures can be repeated. N6 database containing data used in this study
Validity of interpretations	To demonstrate: concepts can be identified, observed, measured in the same way (Mason, 2002:39)	Similar to the process of internal and external validity.
Distance to phenomena	Drawing an unclear initial line for this study gave the researcher objectivity (Mason, 2002:120)	Participant observation in the case company for four and a half months
Flexibility	Flexibility in the research (Mason, 2002:120)	Advantages of objectivity to phenomenon under study (Mason, 2002: 120)
Data	Collected data through different sources (Eisenhardt, 1989; Yin, 1994)	Multiple data sources and collection methods

4 References

Bak, O. (2003): A framework for Transformation of Supply Chain Management: A just in time investigation in organizations, in: Pawar, K. S., Muffatto, M. (eds.): Proceedings of 8th International Symposium on Logistics, Published by the Centre for Concurrent Enterprise – University of Notthingham, UK, p. 59-63.

Bak, O. (2004): Performance measurement in the transformation context: A case from the automotive supply chain, in: Neely, A., Kennerly, M., Walters, A (eds.): Performance Measurement and Management: Public and Private, The fourth international conference on theory and practice in performance measurement, Edinburgh, UK, p. 67-73

Beer, M., Nohria, N. (2000): Cracking the Code of Change, in: Harvard Business Review, May-June: 133-141.

Blumenthal, B., Haspeslag, P. (1994): Toward a Definition of Corporate Transformation, in: Sloan Management Review, Spring: 101-106.

Boyson, S., Corsi, T., Verbraeck, A. (2003): The e-supply chain portal: a core business model, in: Transportation Research Part E: 175-192.

Bryman, A. (1988): Quality and quantity in social research, Hyman, London.

Charmaz, K. (2000): Grounded Theory: Objectivist and constructivist methods, in: Denzin, N., Lincoln, Y. (eds.) The Handbook of qualitative research, Sage Publications, p. 509-535.

Denzin, N. K. (1970): The research act in sociology: A theoretical introduction to sociological methods, Aldine Press, Chicago.

Easterby-Smith, M., R. Thorpe, A. Lowe (1991): Management Research: an Introduction, Sage, London, UK.

Eisenhardt, K. (1989): Building theories from Case Study research, in: Academy of Management Review, 14 (4): 532-550.

Eisenhardt, K. (1989b): Making fast strategic decisions in high-velocity environments, in: Academy of Management Journal, 14 (4): 543-576.

Fisher, M. L. (1997): What is the Right Supply Chain for your Product, in: Harvard Business Review, March-April: 105-116.

Glaser, B. G., Strauss, A. L. (1967): The discovery of grounded theory, Aldine Press, Chicago.

Glaser, B. G. (1978): Theoretical sensitivity, Sociology Press, Mill Valley, CA.

Glaser, B. G. (1992): Basics of grounded theory analysis, Sociology Press, Mill Valley, CA.

Golilic, S. L., Davis, D. F., McCarthy, T., Mentzer, J. T. (2002): The impact on e-commerce on supply chain relationships, in: International Journal of Physical distribution and logistics management, 32(10): 851-871.

Graham, G., Hardaker, G. (2000): Supply-Chain management across the Internet, in: International Journal of Physical Distribution & Logistics Management, 30(3/4): 286-295.

Jick, T. D. (1979): Mixing Qualitative and Quantitative Methods: Triangulation in Action, in: Administrative Science Quarterly, 24(4): 602-611.

Lancioni, R. A., Smith, M. F., Olivia, T. A. (2000): The Role of the Internet in Supply Chain Management, in: Industrial Marketing Management, 29: 45-56.

N6 Reference Guide (2002): 1st Edition, QSR International Pty. Ltd., Melbourne.

MacPherson, S. J., Kelly. J. R., Webb, R. S. (1993): How designs develop: Insights from case studies in building engineering services, Construction Management and Economics, 11: 475-485.

Miles, M. B., Huberman, A. M (1994): Qualitative Data Analysis: An Expanded Sourcebook, Sage, Thousand Oaks, California.

Pant, S., Sethi, R., Bhandari, M. (2003): Making sense of the e-supply chain landscape: an implementation framework, in: International Journal of Information Management, 23: 201-221.

Parkhe, A. (1993): Messy Research, Methodological Predispositions and Theory Development in International Joint Ventures', in: Academy of Management Review, 18(2): 227-68.

Prahalad, C. K., Oosterveld, J. P. (1999): Transforming Internal Governance: The challenge for multinationals, in: Sloan Management Review, Spring: 31-39.

Rayport, J. F., Sviokla, J. J. (1994): Managing in the Marketspace, in: Harvard Business Review, November-December: 141-150.

Ross, J. W., Beath, C. M. (2002): Beyond the Business Case: New Approaches to IT Investment, in: Sloan Management Review, Winter: 51-59.

Sherif, K., Vinze, A. (2003): Barriers to adoption of software reuse A qualitative study, in: Information and Management, 41:159-175.

Strauss A., Corbin J. (1990): Basics of Qualitative Research – Grounded Theory Procedures and Techniques, Sage, London.

Strauss, A., Corbin, J. (1994): Grounded Theory Methodology: in Denzin, N., Lincoln, Y. (eds.): The Handbook of qualitative research, Sage Publications, Thousand Oaks: p. 273-285.

Venkatraman, N. (1994): IT-Enabled Business Transformation: From Automation to Business Scope Redefinition, Sloan Management Review, Winter: 73-87.

Vollmann, T. E. (1996): The Transformation Imperative, Harvard Business School Press, Boston, Massachusetts.

Weick, K. E. (1989): Theory construction as disciplined imagination, in: Academy of Management Review, 14 (4): 516-531.

Yin. R. K. (1994): Case Study Research: Design and Methods, Sage Publications, Thousand Oaks.

Part 4
Action Research in Supply Chains

Action Research in Supply Chain Management – An Introduction

Martin Müller

1	Introduction	350
2	The History of Development of Action Research	350
3	Basics of Action Research	355
4	Problems and Perspectives of Action Research	357
5	Conclusion	361
6	References	362

Summary:
This paper will outline some basic issues on action research. It aims to provide an overview of the development of action research methodology. In this context, scientific theoretical discussions play an important role. Action research is less used in supply chain management research when compared to other methodologies. Against this background, it will also be discussed what approaches are used for problems and perspectives for using action research in supply chain management. Action research has a special philosophy of science background, namely that this is not the preferred science philosophy in supply chain management or operations management. The use of action research causes problems, but so does the use of other research methodologies. Therefore, there are a lot of opportunities to create knowledge by using action research.

Keywords:
Supply Chain Management, Action Research, Research Methodology

1 Introduction

Research in supply chain management in on the rise in practical and academic fields. In this context, a wide range of research methodologies are applicable. Surveys, modeling, and case studies are often found in literature. Action research is less used compared to these other methodologies, and when looking at the field of operations management, there is no change in this statement. Reviewing Scudder and Hill's (1998) empirical operation management papers during the period 1985-1995, and from Pannirselvam et al. (1999) who examined papers from the period 1992-1997, no specific reference to action research was made. A review of the conference proceedings of the three most recent annual meetings by Coughlan & Coghlan (2002) found a low but increasing incidence of applications of action research. In sum, Coughlan & Coghlan (2002) found "little evidence of AR as a methodology applied in published empirical research in operation management, but some evidence of applications in the pipeline." There is no doubt that the situation in the field of supply chain management is much better. But in literature it is also discussed that action research has the potential to contribute to knowledge and practice (for example Kaplan 1998, Coughlan & Coghlan 2002). Wood-Harper (1985) argued that action research is thought to be most effective for technique development or theory building, and Westbrook (1995) described action research as an approach that could avoid the main deficiencies associated with traditional research methodology.

Against this background, the aim of this overview paper is to discuss the possible problems and perspectives for using action research in supply chain management. Based on the issues raised, the paper will be presented using the following structure: The first chapter will describe in detail the historical development of action research methodology. In this context, philosophies of science basics play an important role. The second section will briefly give an overview of the basic elements of action research. On this basis, the next chapter will discuss the most debated criticisms of action research in literature. This will be reflected in the concept of supply chain management. The aim is to identify perspectives of action, and how to apply research in supply chain management. A conclusion will sum up all major findings.

2 The History of Development of Action Research

Science produces paradigms to explain reality. "Paradigm" means accepted examples for academic practice, theories, models and utilities. These build a strong tradition for academic research (Kuhn, 1967). Central elements of paradigms include meanings, values and techniques shared by members of the scientific community. In this sense, action research has been labeled as a paradigm since the

1970s (Moser, 1977; Hron, 1979). According to this, action research means a new understanding of social research with a specific access to reality.

On the one hand, action research originates from the human relation trend in the US; Kurt Lewin (1963) is mentioned as the founder of action research. On the other hand, action research is rooted in the "positivistic conflict" between positivistic science (Popper, 1971) and critical theory (Apel, 1973; Habermas, 1965). Against this background, action research is part of a critical answer to the positivistic science paradigm. For a deeper understanding of this science theoretical aspect, it is important to present briefly the main assumptions of positivist science.

Positivistic research started with building hypotheses which are often based on theories. The proof of a hypothesis takes place in confrontation with reality. Reality rests on facts and events. This means that the production of knowledge is based on monitoring, i.e. the criteria for knowledge. The result of this process produces scientific theories and rejected hypotheses. Nevertheless, scientific theories are temporary and corrigible. In other words, different scientific theories can explain the same real phenomenon. In the context of this relativistic position, it is not the accordance with reality that is the criteria, but the transparency of the method. The methodological postulate of positivistic science is reliability, validity and objectivity. That means (Friedrichs, 1973: 6):

- the used method does not change the object of research;
- the field of research is unchanged;
- the used method should identify relationships between the variables in the field;
- it is necessary that the method produces results that are inter-subjectively revisable.

The method fulfills these requirements when (Friedrichs, 1973: 6):

- the researcher and activities in the field are determined and the relationships of the researched objects are controlled,
- the research design is clear and the test person has no influence,
- it is possible for the researcher to vary the research process in the case, allowing the effect on single variables to be identified.

These requirements necessitate a strict separation between the object and the subject of research. A change of reality is not a part of the research process.

Lewin (1963) developed his field theory opposite to this paradigm. In his theory, the behavior of individuals is dependent on their direct environment. Motivational change by individuals causes dynamics in the field. These dynamics should be researched using experimental projects. Experiments with corresponding variations (actions) in a field should bring new research experience. The researcher influences the social process and the observed results. Here, changes take place during the research process. According to this, the "action" is one important aspect of research. So Lewin's concept differs from positivistic science. In the foreground, there is no longer the subject-object relationship. Subject-subject relationships characterize the new paradigm. In context with this, the active influence of the researcher by actions in a field is another important aspect of the new methodology. There is no distinction between theory and action. It is however important, as Coughlan & Coghlan (2002) pointed out, that "the challenge for action researchers is to engage in both making the action happen and stand back from the action and reflect on how it happens in order to contribute theory to the body of knowledge."

In this context, Sievers (1979) pointed out that action research is a paradigm change compared to traditional social science, especially in three aspects:

1. Strong cooperation between theory and practice,
2. new conditions for sourcing, use and validity for empirical data, and
3. new design and alternative strategies for science processes.

In the 1960s in Germany, during the positivistic conflict between positivistic science (Popper, 1971) and critical theory (Apel, 1973; Habermas, 1965), action research became more popular. The initial point was criticism of positivistic positions, especially:

- the absence of reflection on the effect of science in social processes,
- reduction of the understanding of action to identify and prove principles and formulate directions,
- the absence of the researcher from the field,
- the isolation of variables,
- the reduction of cognition by empirical instruments.

Based on this background, Moser (1975) developed in contrast to empirical research a more discourse-oriented research, incorporating action research. Theoretical and practical knowledge influence the research process, so a discourse is necessary. For the research process, a cycle with the phases of collecting information and discourses rotate.

Another important characteristic of action research is a cooperation between the researcher and the persons in the field. Action research is interactive and discourse-oriented. The philosophy of science behind it is not instrumental but reflexive, because it involves the implementation process. A subject-object relation is not typical for the positivistic social science, but a subject-subject relation is typical for action research. With cooperation among the relevant people, the results of action research are direct action (Sievers, 1979).

There is a strong link between the science theoretical side of pragmatism to action research (Oquist, 1975). One important aspect of pragmatism is that reality is not an unchangeable object. Knowledge not only exists right now, but will also be created by action (Dewey, 1920). Dewey saw a strong connection between knowledge and action. The pragmatic theory asserted that knowledge is built by active actions. In this case, it makes no difference if theory or practice comes first; knowledge is a result of human behavior. The "production" of new knowledge starts in this context with a practical problem, and research is a sort of practical action. The only target of knowledge is the solution of problematic situations. Knowledge is no target in and of itself, it is only a means to an end. The problems result from practice (James, 1994).

Action research started with praxis problems, and the change of reality is a central aspect of pragmatism. In action research, the planning and implementation of change in companies is fundamental.

The core of action research is the integration of the praxis as a component of social science research (see Krüger et al., 1975: 8). The methodology of action research implements the result of the research during the science process. Science finally engages into practice (Gunz, 1986).

The process of action research focuses on the practical situation. First, the problem must be defined and the target of the practical change discussed. This is the basis of the cooperation between researcher and practitioner (Kemmis & McTaggart, 2000). The following project process is characterized as an oscillation between information accumulation, discourse, and practical action. The information is the basis for the discourse (Moser, 1977: 12). Action research is very applicable when praxis problems require change (Mayring, 2002: 53).

From a philosophy of science perspective, pragmatism is the science theory of action research. In other words: Action research is the research methodology for pragmatism. Positivistic scientists argue that a change of reality is a mistake in research. The change of the object of research is non-scientific.

The following table shows the main difference between positivistic science and pragmatism.

	Positivistic science	**Pragmatism (action research)**
Aim of research	Universal knowledge Theory building and testing	Knowledge in action Theory building and testing in action
Type of knowledge acquired	Universal Covering law	Particular Situational practice
Nature of data validation	Context free Logic, measurement Consistency of prediction and control	Contextually embedded Experiential
Researcher's role	Observer	Actor Agent of change
Researcher's relationship to setting	Detached neutral	Immersed

Table 1: Comparison of Positivism and Pragmatism (Coughlan & Coghlan 2002: 224)

The main characteristics of action research are summarized as follows (Coghlan, 1994; Argyris et al., 1985; Greenwood & Levin, 1998; Gummesson, 2000; McDonagh & Coghlan, 2001):

- The process of action research started by praxis problems.
- Action research takes action.
- Action research is discourse-oriented.
- Action research is embedded in the field.
- The researcher is an agent of change.
- Action research is mainly based on a dialectical theory.

In the next chapter, the basic aspects for conducting an action research project are described.

3 Basics of Action Research

Action research is applicable with highly unstructured problems which can be dealt with in an exploratory research design. Coughlan & Coghlan (2002: 227) recommend the use of action research "when the research question relates to describing an unfolding series of action over time in a given group, community or organization; understanding as a member of a group how and why their action can change or improve the working of some aspects of a system; and understanding the process of change or improvement in order to learn from it" (see also Coghlan & Brannick, 2001).

Action research follows a cyclical process which is illustrated in Figure 1.

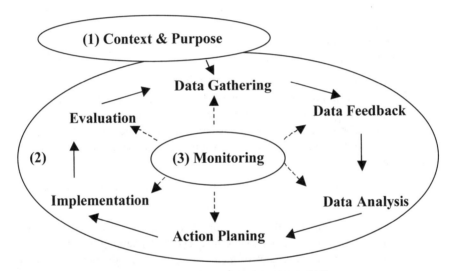

Figure 1: Action Research Cycle (Coughlan & Coghlan 2002: 230)

The action research cycle comprises three types of meta steps (see in Coughlan & Coghlan, 2002: 230):

(1) A pre-step: In this step, two questions are important: What is the rationale for action and what is the rationale for research? In the context of the first question, on the one hand the source, the potential, and the demands for the system is necessary, while on the other hand the economic, political, social and technical forces for driving the need for action are important. The second question is about the appropriate methodology and the worthiness of the project to generate knowledge.

(2) This main step is divided into six other steps:

- Data gathering: Data is gathered in different ways. In companies, financial accounts and reports are one source, while observation, discussing and interviewing are another important source of data. Directly observable behavior is very decisive for action research. The observation of communication patterns, use of power in groups or elements of culture provide an understanding of underlying assumptions and their effects on the work of groups (Schein, 1999).

- Data feedback: The researcher takes the gathered data and "feeds" it to the people in the company. In this step, a discourse-oriented procedure is important (Moser, 1977).

- Data analysis: Both the researcher and members of the company analyze the data together. This collaborative approach is based on the participative aspect of action research, so it is the best way to use the knowledge of the members of the organization.

- Action planning: Beckhard & Harris (1987) recommend six key questions which are important to answer in this step: What needs to change? In what parts of the organization? What types of change are required? Whose support is needed? How is commitment to be built? How is resistance to be managed? These questions need to be answered by action planning.

- Implementation: The members of the organization implement the planned action.

- Evaluation: This involves reflection on the outcomes of the action. The aim of the evaluation is that the next cycle of planning and action may benefit from the experience of the cycle before it. Evaluation is important for learning in the action research process.

(3) The last meta step is monitoring. Monitoring occurs through all the cycles, and all action research cycles continually monitor. In this process, mainly the researcher is engaged, because monitoring of the entire project is the core of the research.

This process of three main steps is the basis for a good implementation of an action research project. But the quality of an action research project is also dependent on research criteria, i.e. validity. Researchers must consciously enact the action research cycle and test their own assumptions (Agyris et al., 1985). Coughlan & Coghlan (2002: 237) point out that "the principal threat to validity for action research is the lack of impartiality on the part of the researcher. As action researchers are engaged in the shaping and telling of a story, they need to consider the extent to which the story is a valid presentation of what has taken place and how it is understood, rather than a biased version." In this background Fisher & Torbert (1995) formulate four parts of speech as useful in action research:

- *Framing* means explicitly stating the purpose of speaking for the present occasion.
- *Advocating* means explicitly stating the aim to be achieved and option, perception, feeling or proposal for action.
- *Illustrating* means telling the concrete story that makes the advocacy clear.
- *Inquiring* means questioning participants to understand perspectives.

The main topic of quality in action research is transparency of the whole action research process (Moser, 1977; Sievers, 1979). This is the guarantee that other researchers can reconstruct the research process, enabling the possibility to reflect the solutions of the action research project.

In this chapter, only the basic characteristics of action research were described. In the next chapter problems and perspectives in connection to supply chain management will be presented. Here, the basic foundations of supply chain management are specified.

4 Problems and Perspectives of Action Research

Different articles exist that analyze the basic elements of supply chain management. In this case SCM, goals and implementation measures of these goals are the focus. SCM goals will be presented based on the surveys of Boutellier (1999), Otto & Kotzab (2001), Wildemann (2001) and Seuring (2001). Table 2 presents an overview of the SCM goals:

As many overlapping goals exist, common features in all SCM analyses can be identified:

- the chain's orientation to various customer needs,
- cooperation along the chain,

With the first goal of supply chain management (problems in interacting with customers), the following can be observed: Detecting customer needs can be perceived as a complex, unstructured situation where a mapping of major variables is required. For example, new products or product service combinations are tested and may be developed together with partners in the supply chain. This is a typical situation where action research projects seem appropriate.

Authors	Supply Chain Characteristics
Boutellier (1999)	Partnership, Individualization, Pull, Postponement, Planning
Otto/Kotzab (2001)	Compression, Speed, Cooperation, Integration, Optimization, Individualization, Modularization, Leveling, Postponement
Wildemann (2001)	Cutting cycle time, Individualization, Core competence, Reducing information asymmetries
Seuring (2001)	Individualization, Integration and Effectiveness, Efficiency

Table 2: Supply Chain Management Goals

A second overlapping goal relates to cooperation along the entire chain. In this connection it is not trivial to decide which companies form certain supply chains and how far integration has to reach. The question arises of which coordination form is preferred in supply chain management. Seuring's (2001: 13) analysis finds that many publications are based on customary instruments and methods focusing on concrete operational situations. For example, Vollmann et al. (1998: 379) present a coordination-based ABC analysis for supply chain cooperation. As a result, there is a theoretical gap regarding coordination forms for supply chain management (Otto & Kotzab, 2001: 161) as well as a lacking empirical basis (see also Croom et al., 2000: 74). With this in mind, it is easy to see why this would be another situation where action research projects seem appropriate and/or better suited.

This short introduction to supply chain management has displayed a general appropriateness for action research projects in supply chain management. How is it then, that action research is so much less used in supply chain management?

As we pointed out in the previous chapter, action research has followed another research paradigm. But is this the reason why this methodology is so much less used in supply chain management research? In this chapter, other action research problems (see Table 3) will be discussed which are often addressed in literature.

The first problem constantly discussed in literature (Heinze, 2001; König, 1983) is the subject-subject relation of action research, i.e. it is argued that the research process is distorted. The initiative for action research projects is often started by researchers. With this in mind, the danger exists that not the practical problem or the subject of research is in the foreground, but instead that the pre-analytic vision and the interpretations of the researcher determine the action research project (König, 1985). Here, an unconscious manipulation of the client might occur (Heinze, 2001: 81).

This is a serious problem, so it is important that the researcher remember that the improvement of the project comes from the acting people, not from himself. For successful action research projects in supply chain management, it is necessary that a synthesis between discoursed theoretical cognition and practical implementation is realized. In other words, the legitimization of action research in general (especially in supply chain management) depends on the question of whether it is possible for researchers to take the changing moment of the action back to the client.

A second critique of action research relates to the discourse or dialogue with the clients. According to this theory, the dialogue takes place without hierarchical or power variations (Heinze, 2001: 85). But this is an idealistic perception of discourse situations (König, 1985). Supply chain management takes place in and between organizations, and it is not a realistic perception to remove it from power-influenced situations, i.e. it is idealistic to think that power structures do not matter between organizations. This critique has a strong link to the one on positivistic science which does not consider the social context in its research. The recommendation for researchers in action research projects in supply chain management is not to wait for a consensus. Hierarchical and power structures are a part of an action research project. Such situations must take into account that they are a part of the socially embedded process. Monitoring the dialogue and reflecting on the result in a later step with the clients is important.

A third argument against action research is that such projects are dominated by action and not by reflection (Heinze, 2001: 86), i.e. that more action than research is the focus of the project. To avoid such situations, it is important for supply chain projects to begin by starting a discussion on the cooperation about the research process. An open discussion about the aims and the content of the project between researcher and client is important. It must articulate which competencies and interests researchers and clients take into the project. The aim of the dialogue is that clients learn theoretical categories connected with practice, and that researchers learn about the problems and the complexity of practice.

This problem has a strong connection to the opinion that action research is rather a consulting process and has nothing to do with research. The clients are only interested in consulting to solve their problems. In a new field of supply chain management where knowledge about implementation is highly interested in practice, this is a serious problem. There are several arguments against this statement (Westbrook, 1995: 10; Gummesson, 2000; Coughlan & Coghlan, 2002):

- A consultant's engagement is only oriented towards solving the problem and of the result for the client. The action researcher's aim is the discovery of new knowledge, and this is reflected in the process of action research. Researchers keep an open mind regarding the process, not only the result.
- Consultants are more rigorous in their inquiries and documentation compared to researchers.

- In a consultant's project timescale, costs and attendance days are specified and the consultant works under strict time and budget constraints. In an action research project, such issues are also necessary but not as important.
- A consultant uses established techniques and is not interested in developing new knowledge. The action researcher on the other hand develops and tests new approaches.
- Researchers require theoretical justifications. Consultants require empirical justifications.
- The process of consultation is frequently in line with a clearly stated point and a fixed result. Action research is cyclical.

Above all, there are important differences between an action research project and consultation. Thus it is no problem for a supply chain researcher to explain what the distinctions are:

Problems of action research projects	Possible solution in supply chain management projects
The practical problem or the subject of research is in the foreground	Necessary is a synthesis between discoursed theoretical cognition and practical implementation
Dialogue without hierarchical or power variations	Monitoring the dialogue and reflecting on the result in a later step with the client
Projects are dominated by action and not by reflection	Open discussion about the aims and the content of the project between researcher and client
Action research is rather a consulting process	• Researchers keep an open mind regarding the process, not only the result • The action researcher develops and tests new approaches • Researchers require theoretical justifications • Action research is cyclical

Table 3: Problems of Action Research Projects and Possible Solutions

In general, supply chain management is a rather young field of research, and the need for further conceptual and theory-built research is frequently highlighted (e.g. Croom et al., 2000; Müller et al., 2003; Otto & Kotzab, 2001). Action research projects can contribute to generating new knowledge.

The process of action research focuses on the practical situation. First the problem must be defined and the target of the practical change discussed. This is the basis of the cooperation between researcher and practitioner (Kemmis & McTaggart, 2000). In this context, the possibility of using supply chain management is important. This concept is relatively new and there are fewer implementations along the chain (Müller et al., 2003). Supply chain management is based on real, practical problems, often e.g. the inefficiency of cooperation in the chain. So the concept of supply chain management has strong requirements for action research projects. Surveys or case study design predict that supply chain management is already implemented in organizations; these methodologies may be useful in a later step of concept development. The project process of action research is characterized as an oscillation between information accumulation, discourse, and practical action. Information is the basis for the discourse (Moser, 1977: 12). Action research is very applicable when practical problems need changes (Mayring, 2002: 53). Implementing supply chain management demands a change in the work flow of staff and employer, so it makes sense to participate with these people and integrate them into the research process. It is possible that in several discourse processes with all relevant members of the supply chain, the best solutions will be found. In sum, there are a lot of interesting perspectives of action research projects in supply chain management. Important here is that an unstructured problem in a new research field and the willingness to change is available.

5 Conclusion

Although action research is confronted with a lot of criticism, this criticism is based on a different scientific theoretical understanding. Most scientists in operations management and logistics follow the positivistic paradigm. This is probably the main reason why action research is not so often used in operation and supply chain management research. Against the other critique, there exist arrangements which, as discussed above, avoid such critiques. Important for a good action research project is a clear agreement with the client organization about the aim of the research project to avoid misunderstandings. Oscillation between information accumulation, discourse and practical action as well as the monitoring of the entire cycle described in the last chapter is the core of a successful action research project. Supply chain management as a young field of research is a good area of application for action research projects.

6 References

Apel, K. O. (1973): Szientistik, Hermeneutik, Ideologiekritik (szientitic, hermeneutic, critic of ideology) in: Apel, K.-O. (ed.): Transformation der Philosophie (transformation of philosophy), Band II, Suhrkamp, Frankfurt: p. 96-127.

Argyris, C., Putnam, R., Smith, D. (1985): Action Science, Jossey-Bass, San Francisco.

Beckhard, R., Harris, R. (1987): Organizational Transitions: Managing Complex Change, second edition, Addison-Wesley, Reading, MA.

Bichou, K., Gray, R. (2004): A Logistics and Supply Chain Approach to Seaport Efficiency: An Inquiry Based on Action Research Methodology, in: Kotzab, H., Seuring, S., Müller, M., Rainer, G (eds.): Research Methodologies for Supply Chain Management, Physica, Heidelberg, p. 413-428.

Coghlan, D. (1994): Research as a process of change; action science in organizations, in: Irish Business and Administrative Research, 15: 119-130.

Coghlan, D., Brannick, T. (2001): Doing Action Research in Your Own Organisation, Sage, London.

Coughlan, P., Coghlan, D. (2002): Action research for operations management, in: International Journal of Operations & Production Management, 22(2): 220-240.

Croom, S., Romano, P. Giannakis, M. (2000): Supply chain management: An analytical Framework for Critical Literature Review, in: European Journal of Purchasing & Supply Management, 6(1): 67-83.

Dewey, J. (1920): Reconstruction in Philosophy, Southern Illinois University Press, New York.

Fisher, D., Torbert, W. (1995): Personal and Organizational Transformation: The True Challenge of Continual Quality Improvement, McGraw-Hill, London.

Friedrichs, J. (1973): Methoden der empirischen Sozialforschung (Methods of Empirical Research in Social Sciences), Reinbeck.

Greenwood, D., Levin, M. (1998): Introduction in Action Research, Sage, Thousand Oaks.

Gummeson, E. (2000): Qualitative Methods in Management Research, second edition, Sage, Tausand Oaks, CA.

Gunz, J. (1986): Handlungsforschung: Vom Wandel der distanzierten zur engagierten Sozialforschung (Action Research – The change from distances to involved research in social sciences), Braumüller, Wien.

Habermas, J. (1965): Erkenntnis und Interesse (Perception and concern), Suhrkamp, Frankfurt.

Heinze, T. (2001): Qualitative Sozialforschung, Einführung (Qualitative Social Science, Introduction), Opladen, München, Wien.

Hron, A. (1979): Aktionsforschung zur Entwicklung eines Paradigmas (Action research as a development to paradigm), in: Hron. A., Kompe, H., Otto, K.-P., Wächter, H. (eds.): Aktionsforschung in der Ökonomie (Action Research in Economics), Campus Verlag, Frankfurt, New York, p. 14-48.

James, W. (1994): Was ist Pragmatismus? (What is pragmatismn?), Beltz, Frankfurt.

Kemmis, S., McTaggart, R. (2000): Participatory Action Research, in: Denzin, N. K., Lincoln, Y. S. (Ed.): Handbook of Qualitative Research, second edition, Sage Thousand Oaks: p. 567-605.

König, E. (1983): Methodenprobleme der Handlungsforschung (methodic problems of action research), in: Zedler, P., Mosewre, H. (eds.): Aspekte qualitativer Sozialforschung (Aspects of Qualitative Research), Leske/Budrich, Opladen: p. 79-93.

Krüger, H., Klüver, J.. Haag, F. (1975): Aktionsforschung in der Diskussion, (action research in discussion), Suhrkamp, Frankfurt.

Kuhn, T. S. (1967): Die Struktur wissenschaftlicher Revolution (The structure of science revolution), Suhrkamp, Frankfurt.

Lewin, K. (1963): Feldtheorie in den Sozialwissenschaften (Field theory in social science), Huber, Bern.

Mayring, P. (2002): Einführung in die Qualitative Sozialforschung (Introduction to qualitative social science research), 5. Auflage, Beltz, Weinheim und Basel.

McDonagh, J., Coghlan, D. (2001): The art of clinical inquiry in information technology-related organizational research, in: Reason, P., Bradbury, H. (Eds.): Handbook of Action Research, London, p. 372-378.

Middel, R., Brennan, L., Coghlan, D., Coughlan, P. (2004): The application of Action Learning and Action Research in Collaborative Improvement within the Extend Manufacturing Enterprise, in: Seuring, S., Müller, M., Kotzab, H., Rainer, G.: Research Methodologies for Supply Chain Management (eds.), Physica, Heidelberg, p. 365-380.

Moser, H. (1977): Methoden der Aktionsforschung (Methods of action research), Kösel, München.

Müller, M., Seuring, S., Goldbach, M. (2003): Supply Chain Management – Neues Konzept oder Modetrend? (Supply Chain Management – New Concept or Fashion Trend?), in: Die Betriebswirtschaft, 63(4): 419-439.

Oquist, P. (1975): Erkenntnistheoretische Grundlagen der Aktionsforschung (science theoretical basics of action research), in: Moser, H., Ornauer, H. (eds.): Internationale Aspekte der Aktionsforschung (International aspects of action research), Kösel, München: p. 25-50.

Otto, A., Kotzab, H. (2001): Der Beitrag des Supply Chain Managements zum Management von Supply Chains – Überlegungen zu einer unpopulären Frage (The Contribution of Supply Chain Management to the Management of Supply Chains – Thoughts on an unpopular Question), in: Zeitschrift für betriebswirtschaftliche Forschung, 53(3): 157-176.

Pannirselvam, G. P., Ferguson, L. A., Ash, R. C., Siferd, S. P. (1999): Operations Management Research – An Update for the 1990s, in: Journal of Operations Management, 18: 95-112.

Popper, K. R. (1971): Logik der Forschung (Logic of Research), fourth edition, Mohr, Tübingen.

Schein, E. H. (1999): Process Consultation Revisited, Building the Helping Relationship, Addison-Wesley, Reading, MA.

Scudder, G. D., Hill, C. A. (1998): A review and classification of empirical research in operations management, in: Journal of Operations Management, 16: 91-101.

Seuring, S. (2001): Supply Chain Costing – Kostenmanagement in der Wertschöpfungskette mit Target Costing und Prozesskostenrechnung (Supply Chain Costing – Cost Management in Supply Chains with Target Costing and Activity-based Costing) Vahlen Verlag, München.

Sievers, B. (1979): Organisationsentwicklung als Aktionsforschung. Zu einer sozialwissenschaftlichen Neuorientierung der betriebswirtschaftlichen Organisationsforschung (Organisational development as action research), in: Hron, A., Kompe, H., Otto, K.-P., Wächter, H.: Aktionsforschung in der Ökonomie (action research in economy), Campus-Verlag, Frankfurt/Main, New York: p.111-133.

Vollmann, T. E., Cordon, C. and Raabe, H. (1998): "Das Management von Lieferketten" (The Management of Supply Chains), International Institute for Management Development, London Business School, Wharton Business School (Eds.), The MBA-book: Mastering Management, Schäffer-Poeschel, Stuttgart: p. 374-381.

Westbrook, R. (1995): Action research, a new paradigm for research in production and operations management, in: International Journal of Operations & Production Management, 15 (12): 6-20.

Wood-Harper, T. (1985): Research methods in information systems: using action research, in: Mumsford, E., Hirschheim, E. (eds.): Research Methods in Information Systems, Elsevier, Amsterdam: p. 169-191.

The Application of Action Learning and Action Research in Collaborative Improvement within the Extended Manufacturing Enterprise

Rick Middel, Louis Brennan, David Coghlan, Paul Coughlan

1	Introduction	366
2	The Extended Manufacturing Enterprise	367
3	Action Learning	368
4	Action Research	368
5	Research Base	369
6	Action Learning and Action Research in the EME	370
7	Discussion	375
8	Conclusions	378
9	References	379

Summary:
Increasingly organizations have to identify and implement improvement initiatives in an inter-organizational context. Implementing collaborative improvement is fraught with difficulties that encompass a wide array of intra- and inter-organizational change issues and working practices. In order to overcome these difficulties, explicit attention should be paid to the accumulation and development of knowledge and to the long-term development of a capability for learning and continuous improvement between organizations. This paper describes the application of an Action Learning and Action Research approach in collaborative improvement within an Extended Manufacturing Enterprise in the Netherlands.

Keywords:
Action Learning, Action Research, Collaborative Improvement, Extended Manufacturing Enterprise

1 Introduction

Market developments, including intense international competition, fragmented and demanding markets and diverse and rapidly changing technologies (Teece et al., 1997), have created new imperatives for competition, moving increasingly from the level of the individual organization to networks of disparate companies. Within these networks companies have to focus on collaborative efforts and initiatives to continuously improve and change the current processes and work practices in order to keep pace with the external dynamics in the business environment. Therefore, the individual company is becoming an insufficient entity to identify improvement projects (Harland et al., 1999) and, accordingly, companies have to identify and implement improvement initiatives in an inter-organisational context, leading to the concept of collaborative improvement.

There is an increasing need to understand and to develop knowledge on the improvement and learning processes that take place at the inter-company level (Boer et al., 2000). Consequently, the concept of continuous improvement, which by now is a consolidated concept in the context of stand-alone companies, has been transferred and extended to the level of 'collaborative' continuous improvement, leading to the concept of collaborative improvement. Collaborative improvement (CoI) is defined as: "a purposeful inter-company interactive process that focuses on continuous incremental innovation aimed at enhancing the Extended Manufacturing Enterprise overall performance" (Cagliano et al., 2002).

The key to collaborative improvement is learning and development (Boer et al., 2000). However, the process of cultivating collaborative improvement across disparate companies within a network is fraught with difficulties that encompass a wide array of intra- and inter-organizational change issues and working practices. Therefore, companies have to apply and to use approaches that enable them to tackle these difficulties of inter-organizational change. One approach designed to tackle real problems and to develop a capacity to learn is 'action learning'. Although action learning is a widely adopted approach by managers in their own companies, it can provide a useful approach for managers and companies in an inter-organizational setting as well (Coughlan & Coghlan, 2004). While managers and companies engage explicitly in action learning cycles, researchers can use, in parallel, an action research methodology to generate actionable knowledge on collaborative improvement in the extended manufacturing enterprise.

This paper will focus on application of the action learning and action research approach in collaborative improvement within an extended manufacturing enterprise participating in the CO-IMPROVE Project. The combination of action learning and action research have been fundamental in the EU research project CO-IMPROVE (Collaborative Improvement Tool for the Extended Manufacturing Enterprise, G1RD – CT2000 – 00299). In 2001, the CO-IMPROVE project started with the objectives to develop a business model, supported by a web-based software system, and action learning based implementation guidelines to support the design, implementation and ongoing development of collaborative improvement and learning in the extended manufacturing enterprise. In the paper, we will introduce firstly the concept of the extended manufacturing enterprise. Secondly, we will discuss the concepts of action learning and action research and its application within the context of an extended manufacturing enterprise. Finally, we will discuss and reflect in detail on the process of action learning and action research and experiences of the researchers. As a piece, the paper contributes to the design and implementation of future action learning and action research initiatives in extended manufacturing enterprises.

2 The Extended Manufacturing Enterprise

Due to changing market and competitive demands, individual companies have found it necessary to focus on their core business in order to remain competitive, while, at the same time, developing relationships with other firms with complementary competences (Rockhart & Short, 1990; Nohria & Eccles, 1992). In order to cope with the market changes and to stay competitive within today's market environment companies have to identify and to implement improvement initiatives in the inter-organisational context. Today's competition takes place less between individual companies than between supply chains consisting of multiple, collaborating organizations (Christopher, 1992; Fine, 1998).

The concept of extended manufacturing enterprise (EME) is rooted in supply chain management literature. This relates to the overall set of relationships from the "supply network" of a focal company (Lamming, 1993; Harland, 1996). A supply network can be defined as a body of advanced relations characterized by an integrated strategy and management policy that the focal company maintains with a limited set of its suppliers (Bartezzaghi & Sassatelli, 2001). The EME (Busby & Fan, 1993) is defined in terms of manufacturing companies that co-operate closely to maximize the benefits of the business they are involved in. Here the suppliers are viewed as a part of the principal company, the so-called system integrator. Both the concepts of supply networks and EME are based on the notion of collaboration between companies, that is, working together, over an extended period of time, for the benefit of both (Ring & Van de Ven, 1992).

3 Action Learning

The key to Continuous Improvement and Collaborative Improvement is development and learning (Boer et al., 2000). Two related components are involved in learning: The first involves the accumulation and development of a core knowledge base – the "core competence" – which differentiates the organization from others and offers the potential for competitive advantage (Bessant et al., 2003). Acquiring this competence is not simply a matter of purchasing or trading knowledge assets, but the systematic and purposive learning and construction of a knowledge base (Teece, 1998; Prahalad & Hamel, 1994). The second is the long-term development of a capacity for learning and continuous improvement across the whole organization (Bessant et al., 2003). The learning process does not stop at the boundaries of the single organization, and, consequently, learning and competence development are relevant in an inter-organizational setting. This recognition places a greater emphasis on mechanisms and approaches towards the long-term development of a capacity for collaborative improvement and learning in an inter-organizational setting. In response, action learning can provide a useful methodology for the development of a capacity for learning as part of the CoI process. Although the concept of action learning (AL) originated at an interpersonal level there is clear potential for their application in CoI and inter-organizational learning (see also Bessant & Tsekouras, 2001).

AL is an approach to the development of people in organisations, which takes the task as the vehicle for learning (Pedler, 1996; Revans, 1998; Weinstein, 1999; Yorks et al., 1999). In AL, the starting point is the action and through implementation and reflection this becomes learning-in-action. AL has six distinct interactive components (Marquardt, 1999): a problem; the group; the questioning and reflective process; the commitment to taking action; the commitment to learning; the facilitator.

4 Action Research

Action Research (AR) is a cyclical process of diagnosing, action planning, action taking, evaluating and specifying learning (Lau, 1999). Action research focuses on research in action, rather than research about action, in which members of the studied system actively participate in the cyclical process. Several broad characteristics define action research (Eden & Huxham, 1996; Coghlan & Brannick, 2001; Coughlan & Coghlan, 2002):

- Research in action, rather than research about action;
- Participative;
- Concurrent with action;
- A sequence of events and an approach to problem solving.

The research reported in this paper was undertaken through an AR approach where the researchers were both managing the project and studying at the same time (Coghlan & Brannick, 2001; Coughlan & Coghlan, 2002). The AR approach was simultaneously applied with AL, which was to allow the researchers to interact with the EME as the companies engage themselves in the process of learning in action.

The AR approach was adopted to facilitate and to stimulate the development of a capability for improvement and learning process within the EME. As stated by Westbrook (1995) a main contribution of action research to learning, which is not available to other methods, is that when participants involve themselves in change experiments, they engage in non-trivial learning, and they think and reflect seriously on what they are doing.

5 Research Base

The focus of the paper is on the application of Action Learning and Action Research within an EME in the Netherlands, comprising of a system integrator and three of its suppliers. The system integrator (SI) is a company, which is specialized in 'Motion Control'-systems for different markets, including the automotive, truck, marine, medical and agriculture market. The company sees itself in a niche market, dominantly automotive and truck.

The suppliers selected by the SI to participate in the CO-IMPROVE project all represent different kinds of relationship and deliver different kind of products. This means that information and communication could pass freely throughout the whole group without running the risk of giving or losing sensitive information to competitors. The underlying reason for the SI to select these suppliers was that the suppliers were perceived as highly involved in collaboration and are dedicated partners that fully support the SI in assembling and delivering the systems of the SI.

Over a period of 1½ years, 5 CoI initiatives between the SI and the suppliers were started in the area of quality, (change) order management, and manufacturing. The CoI initiatives were multi-disciplinary and required the involvement of different functional departments from all the companies, such as purchasing, engineering, sales, quality, and production.

A specific CoI initiative between the SI and one of the suppliers (hereafter the Supplier) concerned a quality problem with a product (hereafter SUP), which was supplied by the supplier to the SI. The SUP had caused severe problems in the final products of the SI due to the fact that the SUP could collapse during function. The project team comprised of people from purchasing, sales, engineering and quality. It was recognized that the supplier was not able to optimise technically their processes to prevent the malfunctioning of the SUP. Therefore, the participants engaged themselves in a systematic process of problem solving in order to retrieve additional information and suggestions to solve the problem with regard the SUP. The problem solving happened in a very open and constructive way, trying to find the underlying causes and how these could be solved. An improvement plan was developed, assigning different tasks and responsibilities to project members with due dates. Regular face-to-face meetings were used to share information, discuss the process and progress of the initiative, reflect and evaluate, synthesize learning. The meetings kept momentum in the CoI initiative, created an atmosphere for direct communication and honesty, and increased the awareness of the benefits of CoI and learning. As the process unfolded over time, a researcher facilitated the entire CoI process. The outcomes of the project and the learning achieved were:

- New material composition of the SUP, reducing cost and increasing quality for the SI and reducing internal scrap rate of the supplier by 33%;
- Increased (awareness of need to) information sharing and communication as part of the CoI process;
- Recognition that openness, trust, goals sharing and mutual understanding are required to allow actual collaboration and to finalize efforts in CoI to effective results.

6 Action Learning and Action Research in the EME

6.1 Action Learning in the EME

The application of the concept of action learning in the CO-IMPROVE project was envisaged as an integrated set of actions to be executed in learning networks. A program was designed based on an AL framework (Marquardt, 1999) and built around a structure of regular workshops. Here participants would meet in a group, discuss and reflect on the progress of the particular change initiative on which they were working and then follow up on the learning from that meeting in the day-to-day enactment of attempted solutions to the problem.

Briefly, the AL approach was put in place in the EME over a period of 18 months through a cycle of 15 workshops. These workshops were organised on a monthly basis. The workshops were aimed at engaging companies in collaborative improvement activities, involving processes of diagnosing, fact-finding, implementation and evaluation of improvement actions. Moreover, the process of action learning emphasised the importance of a structured questioning and reflective process within the EME. The workshops were scheduled according to a fixed format of the agenda. Within the agenda slots were scheduled for the CO-IMPROVE project, CoI initiatives on dyad and EME level and incentives. These slots had the objective of stimulating and triggering discussion and action to identify and to select CoI projects, to learn from experiences of others within the project, to link the meetings in order to keep momentum in the CoI initiatives, and to synthesize learning.

In more detail, the six components of Marquardt's framework (1999) underpinning the CoI initiatives are as follows.

1. A problem

The focus was on immediate operational issues in terms of product and process improvement, pro-active and creative improvement opportunities and improvement of the collaboration between system integrator and suppliers.

2. The group

The AL group was comprised of the SI and the three suppliers. The group met 15 times over an 18-month interval. During the meetings at least two representatives of the SI and one representative of each of the suppliers were present and participated actively in open group discussions.

3. The questioning and reflective process

Monthly EME workshops were used to monitor each improvement initiative and facilitate a reflective process. The workshops aimed at engaging companies in collaborative improvement activities, involving processes of diagnosing, fact-finding, implementation and evaluation of improvement actions. The results of the improvement activities were presented and discussed in plenary to evaluate and to reflect on the process and progress in order to identify experiences, observations and learning moments.

A reflective document was used to structure the process of improvement and to facilitate a reflection on the process and progress of improvement projects between the companies in order to learn from their experiences, observation and reflection. Evaluation and reflection was not an integral part of the improvement process and, therefore, the participating people/companies skipped the evaluation/reflection process and continue with daily activities (priorities) after an improvement project. The reflective document and process of action learning emphasized the importance of a structured questioning and reflective process. Using this document people/companies within the EME began to see the importance and benefits of evaluation and reflection.

Enactment of the process of AL began to emerge through iterations of workshops. In the beginning of the CO-IMPROVE project the questioning and reflective process was planned, because evaluation was, at that time, not a part of the way-of-working in previous (collaborative) improvement projects. The SI constantly emphasized the need and importance of evaluation and reflection and sharing the lessons learned with the members in the EME. As the project continued, the participants saw benefits of the questioning and reflective process and it became an integral part of the collaborative improvement activities.

The expand PDCA was the basis for the improvement initiatives. The improvement initiatives and the questioning and reflective process were structured in alignment with the PDCA-cycle. Company visits and factory tours were used to sharpen the focus on the emerging issues within the EME.

4. The commitment to taking action

The commitment of the AL group was to taking the necessary strategic and operational steps to engage in collaborative improvement initiatives. The premise underlying this commitment was that no real learning takes place unless and until action is taken. The commitment to action was reflected in a schedule of meetings to support and to facilitate the questioning and reflective process. In each meeting explicit attention was given to the progress and process of each improvement initiative, during a number of phases within each meeting:

- Collaborative improvement action planning and evaluation
- Presentation and reflection plenary on the process and progress of the project
- Practical, reflective and challenging discussion on the issues arising in the improvement activities

5. The commitment to learning

In the meetings explicit focus was given to learning during the meetings through presentations and discussions in plenum and the diffusion of knowledge, experiences and lessons as part of the collaborative improvement initiatives. The attention towards learning was planned through a reflective questioning process in order to increase the awareness of the concept and benefits of a structured process of collaborative improvement and learning.

6. The facilitator

Within the AL group members of the University of Twente and Trinity College Dublin facilitated the AL process. The facilitators acted primarily as learning coaches, coordinating the meetings and keeping learning to the forefront of the agenda.

6.2 Action Research

- Organizing for Research and Action

As the definitions of AR and AL indicate, there are common features in both approaches. Both share the same values, are based on the same learning cycle, and focus on learning in action (Coghlan & Coughlan, 2003). However, the divergence between AR and AL is in the focus and outcome. AR goes beyond the focus on learning and seeks to contribute to theory (Coghlan & Coughlan, 2003).

Overall, CO-IMPROVE was a research project that encompassed three EMEs (one of which was the Dutch EME) and four research institutions. Accordingly, the action research process was organized to work with concurrent projects centered in three locations. The action research was focused on how the action learning approach established the usefulness and usability of the business model and the technical model through a sequence of actions across the different settings (Coghlan et al., 2004). For the action researchers, this objective was achieved through a series of action research cycles (Coghlan & Brannick, 2001; Coughlan & Coghlan, 2002). Each cycle involved a process of diagnosing, planning, taking action and then fact-finding about the results of that action in order to plan and take further action. As CO-IMPROVE was using action research to create and maintain the learning networks as learning systems the emphasis was on a process of proactive engagement and not simply reactive adjustment (Chisholm, 1998).

In CO-IMPROVE, Researchers, external to the participating companies, organized and facilitated the efforts of each company learning network. These researchers were organized also as a researcher learning network and collaborated to apply their collective knowledge of continuous improvement to develop the CO-IMPROVE approach. The researchers' efforts were supplemented occasionally by outside consultants, academics who have researched the area, or managers with relevant experience.

There were three levels in the researcher learning network (Coghlan et al., 2004):

1. The local researcher network in each country.
   The local researcher networks engaged in action learning with their local company network, and action research on the development of the project from their local perspective.

2. The workpackage researcher network.
   The ongoing development and application of the business and technical models and the action learning process were each the responsibility of the institutions who were leading the workpackages dealing with these three elements.

3. The project researcher network.
   The project researcher network encompassed the three local researcher networks and the three workpackage researcher networks.

The researcher learning network met three times over a five-month period prior to the start of action learning phase of CO-IMPROVE. In the first two meetings, the Dublin researchers led workshops on action research and action learning in order to achieve a common understanding of the action learning and action research imperatives. The third meeting focused on detailed preparation of the assignments for each company network and of the tracking of what would go on within each company learning network.

- **Data Gathering, Documentation and Reflection**

As with the other two local researcher learning networks, the Dutch network gathered, documented and made sense of data with respect to their respective research area for the duration of the action learning process. Data were gathered through:

- Instrumentation (documentation from assignments)
- Minutes and notes of company network meetings
- Minutes and notes of researcher meetings
- Researcher journaling (This refers to the personal notes of researchers who kept a record of their own observations and reflections, thoughts and feelings and personal learning through the process).

The data gathered, documented and reflected on by the researchers were fed to the various company teams who kept an overall watching brief of the progress of their area of responsibility.

- **Structures for Communication**

Consistent with the three levels in the researcher learning network, there were different structures for communication (Coghlan et al. 2004):

The local researcher network
Each company network meeting was preceded and followed by a local researcher meeting which engaged in the action research cycle, of diagnosing, planning action, taking action and evaluating action with respect to the implementation of and research on the 3 themes - the business model, the technical system and the company action learning process. The purpose of these meetings was to

- Gather, document and make sense of data with respect to each research area with respect to their respective company learning network for the duration of the action learning process
- Review the feedback generated from assessments of practice and performance in each company learning network.
- Develop and outline the process being used to set and to communicate objectives for the change initiative to management in the network partners and to consider the degree of conditionality in their buy-in.

Action Learning and Action Research in Collaborative Improvement 375

- Develop and outline the plan for transitional steps from stage to stage so as to minimize possible deterioration of company performance, company motivation and quality of research data.
- Resolve issues that might arise
- Develop a position paper on the development, application process, usefulness and usability of the business and technical models and the action learning approach in each company learning network.

As outlined earlier, the work of these local teams was facilitated through, development, customization and application of assignments at company network meetings, minutes and notes of company network meetings, minutes and notes by individual researchers of on-site meetings with members of the company learning network between company network meetings and researcher journaling.

The researcher network for each workpackage met at each partner meeting and engaged in the action research cycle, of diagnosing, planning action, taking action and evaluating action with respect to the implementation of and research on the 3 themes in the three company learning networks. The work of researcher network for each workpackage was also facilitated through development of assignments for application at company network meetings, minutes and notes of company network meetings, minutes and notes by individual researchers of on-site meetings with members of the company learning network between company network meetings and researcher journaling.

The project researcher network met at partner meetings where all local and workpackage researcher networks presented reports on the progress of their action research across the three company networks, and the development of the business and technical models and the action learning process. The work of the project researcher network was facilitated in part through writing position papers on the action learning approach in each company learning network.

7 Discussion

Central elements in this work reported in this paper have been collaborative improvement, action learning, and action research. The remainder of this section will focus on a discussion of the latter two elements.

7.1 Action Learning

In general, the EME provided the opportunity to implement and test an AL approach in an inter-organizational setting. The design of the AL approach was built around a structure of regular meetings. Through the AL approach the companies within the EME developed an increased awareness of the concept and benefits of collaborative improvement, recognized the importance of a structured process towards improvement and learning, and provided a setting of reflection and evaluation with a high degree of openness and trust.

The companies within the EME focused on real day-to-day issues and concerns that have been identified by them AL engaged the companies in explicitly learning in collaborative improvement initiatives. During each meeting presentations were given with regard to the progress and process of an improvement initiative, which were discussed and reflected on in plenum at the meetings. Explicit attention was given to the diffusion of knowledge, experiences and lessons learned as part of the collaborative improvement initiatives. The process drew on a wide range of interventions – self-assessment instruments, documents, presentations at meetings, feedback by other participants, factory tours and coaching. The way the facilitators structured the AL process and the different roles they played during the process enabled the companies to keep learning to the forefront of the agenda.

Prior to the AL approach, reflection and evaluation was not performed due to operational priorities within the EME. Consequently, in the beginning of the AL approach, learning was not an integral part of collaborative relationships and CoI initiatives. The situation improved gradually over time, but participants were constantly struggling with balancing operational priorities and learning as part of CoI. Facilitation by the SI and the action researchers was perceived as essential.

Initially, there was no mutual understanding of the concept of CoI, which had a negative effect on the level of openness between the companies and resulted in political behavior of the suppliers towards the SI. The suppliers had the impression that this was another way of implementing cost reduction and quality programs. The first part of the AL approach paid particular attention to creating a shared vision on CoI and a sense of direction.

Another challenge that faced the participants was the diffusion of learning externally to the other companies in the EME and internally in their own organization.

7.2 Action Research

The AR approach provided the Dutch EME with identifiable benefits in terms of the identifying and synthesizing experiences, observations and learning moments. The companies in the EME developed and improved their capability for inter-organizational collaboration, not only through engaging in CoI initiatives, but also through having the willingness to collaborate, communicate and share information, and to understand each others position and develop a sense of direction. Reflection on and evaluation of the process of improvement was not a common behavior within the companies of the EME. This was mainly due to high priorities placed on operational activities. The action researchers facilitated and stimulated evaluation and reflection of the CoI process, acquiring an EME perspective with regard to learning, and, consequently, contributing to the actionable knowledge and development of a capability of collaborative improvement and learning.

By applying the AR approach as a problem-solving tool, companies were able to start solving problems systematically. The approach allowed the researchers to be part of the CoI initiatives with access to rich and detailed information. This access yielded in-depth insight on and development of an understanding of the organization and management of CoI. As understanding of the process of CoI developed, several insights emerged in relation to managing and organizing CoI that might not have emerged otherwise:

1. Companies need to understand each others' positions and to create a shared sense of direction
2. A learning environment can be created in which companies can and do, openly, communicate and share information
3. Trust and commitment have to be created among the companies as part of the collaborative relationship and CoI initiatives
4. The SI should have an active and committed role with regard to CoI initiatives and learning
5. Assessment tools help identify and implement CoI initiatives
6. Project management tools and frequent workshops keep momentum and progress in the CoI initiatives and create a sense of urgency
7. Facilitation by action researchers is required in the process of CoI and learning

The networks of researchers in CO-IMPROVE were engaging in both action learning and action research. With respect to action learning, their task was to implement the action learning workpackage on the application of the business model and technical system in the company learning networks. They did this through the questioning and reflective process in inter-institutional, international and inter-disciplinary networks.

Clearly in action research contexts where a single EME is being studied in action, the organizing of multiple concurrent networks of researchers, as in the broader CO-IMPROVE project, does not apply. Yet, in such single EME situations, the enactment of cycles of action and reflection on the action learning process in order to develop actionable knowledge still remains central. Activities such as the recording of events, the writing and presentation of reflection papers and the joint exploration of shared or divergent meaning and interpretations are essential to the development of actionable knowledge.

8 Conclusions

Action learning has provided a useful methodology for the development of a capacity for learning as part of the collaborative improvement process. Through its enactment as an integrated set of actions to be executed within the EME, AL has contributed towards a continuous process of learning and reflection in (inter-) organizational practice.

The action research approach stimulated and supported the inter-organizational improvement process and the EME through a structured cyclical process. The approach has been efficient and effective for both the researchers and companies. From the perspective of the researchers, it has allowed in-depth insight into and development of an understanding of the process of collaborative improvement in order to generate actionable knowledge. From the perspective of the companies, it has allowed the companies to experience the relevance of reflecting and evaluating upon activities performed as part of inter-organizational work practices.

The suitability of AR to applied fields has been highlighted by Nasland (2002) in the specific case of logistics since it strives to advance both science and practice. However many of his observations in relation to logistics and AR are also applicable to supply chain management (SCM). Problems in this field are often unstructured, real- world problems. AR is a research approach for tackling real world, managerial and organizational problems such as obtain in SCM (Nasland, 2002) and it can contribute to research as well as practice. Given the crucial role of relationships within SCM, the approach underlying AR - that the foundation for understanding lies in interpreting relationships (Nasland, 2002) - is especially congruent with the collaborative improvement needs of SCM. The application of AR has the potential not only to provide insight around relationships but also to re-enforce and to enhance relationships.

The application of AR in this study is within the EME. Such networks are an increasingly important approach to organizing the supply chain. Given the technical, organizational and managerial aspects of such networks, there is a need to understand and to develop knowledge beyond the physical transaction aspects of the chain to encompass behavioral aspects including goal setting and relationships. Such a need has been previously emphasized by Halldorsson & Aastrup (2003) in relation to logistics enquiry. In common with logistics, SCM operates within a context with each enactment of the supply chain appearing in a specific context. As argued by Halldorsson & Aastrup (2003) in the case of logistics, to understand and explain supply chains, we must deal with their specific context. As described above, AR is ideally suited to meeting these requirements.

9 References

Bartezzaghi, E., Sassatelli, M. (2001): Migliorare le reti di fornitura: sviluppo delle competenze e delle opportunità tecnologiche (Improving supply networks: development of competences and technological opportunities), Franco Angeli editore.

Bessant, J., Kaplinsky, R., Lamming, R. (2003): Putting supply chain learning into practice, in: International Journal of Operations & Production Management, 23 (2): 167- 184.

Bessant, J., Tsekouras, G. (2001): Developing learning networks, in: AI and Society, 15: 82-98.

Boer, H., Nielsen, L. B., Nørretranders, T., Gertsen, F. (2000): CI changes: from suggestion box to organisational learning, Continuous Improvement in Europe and Australia, Aldershot, Ashgate Publishing Ltd.

Busby, J. S., Fan, I. S. (1993): The extended manufacturing enterprise: its nature and its needs, International journal of technology management, 8 (3,4,5): 294-308.

Cagliano, R., Caniato, F., Corso, M., Spina, G. (2002): "Fostering Collaborative Improvement in Extended Manufacturing Enterprises: A Preliminary Theory", in Smeds, R. (ed.): Continuous Innovation in Business – Processes and Networks, Espoo, Finland, Helsinki University of Technology: p. 131-143.

Chisholm, R. (1998). Developing Network Organizations: Learning form Practice and Theory, Addison-Wesley, Reading.

Christopher, M. (1992): Logistics and Supply Chain Management, Pitman Publishing, London.

Coghlan, D., Brannick, T. (2001): Doing Action Research in Your Own Organization, Sage, London.

Coughlan, P., Coghlan, D. (2002): Action Research for Operations Management, in: International Journal of Operations & Production Management, 22 (2): 220-240.

Coughlan, P., Coghlan, D., Brennan, L. (2004): Organizing for Research and Action: Implementing Action Researcher Networks, in: Systemic Practice and Action Research, 17 (1): 37-49.

Coughlan, P., Coghlan, D. (2004): Action Learning: towards a framework in inter-organizational settings, in: Action Learning: Research and Practice, 1 (1): 43-61.

Dotlich, D., Noel, J. (1998): Action Learning, Jossey-Bass, San Francisco.

Eden, C., Huxham, C. (1996): Action Research for the study of organizations, in: Clegg, S., Hardy, C., Nord, W. (eds.): Handbook of Organization Studies, Sage Publications, London, p. 526-542.

Fine, C. (1998): Clockspeed: Winning Industry Control in the Age of Temporary Advantage, Perseus Books, Reading, Mass.

Halldorsson, A., Aastrup, J. (2003): Quality criteria for qualitative inquiries in logistics, in: European Journal of Operational Research, 144: 321-332.

Harland, C. M. (1996): Supply chain management: relationships, chains and networks, in: British Journal of management, 7, Special Issue, Mar: S63-S81.

Harland, C. M., Lamming, R. C., Cousins, P. D. (1999): Developing the Concept of Supply Strategy, in: International Journal of Operations & Production Management, 19(7): 650-673.

Lamming, R. C. (1993): Beyond Partnership: Strategies for Innovation and Lean Supply, London, Prentice Hall.

Lau, F. (1999), Toward a framework for action research in information systems studies, in: Information Technology & People, 12(2): 148-175.

Marquardt, M. (1999): Action learning in action, Palo Alto, CA, Davies-Black.

Näslund, D., (2002): Logistics needs qualitative research – especially action research, in: International Journal of Physical Distribution and & Logistics Management, 32 (5): 321-338.

Nohria, N., Eccles, R.G. (1992): Networks and Organizations: Structure, Form and Action, Harvard Business School Press, Boston.

Pedler, M. (1996): Action learning for managers, Lemos & Crane, London.

Prahalad, C., Hamel, G. (1994): Competing for future survival, Harvard Business Press, Boston, MA.

Revans, R. (1998): ABC of Action Learning, Lemos & Crane, London.

Ring, P. S., Van De Ven, A. H., (1992): Structuring cooperative relationships between organizations, in: Strategic Management Journal 13 (7): 483-498.

Rockhart, J, Short, J. (1990): The networked organization and the management of interdependence, in: Scott-Morton, M. (ed.): The Corporation of the 1990s, Oxford University Press, New York: p. 189-220.

Teece, D. J., Pisano, G., Shuen, A. (1997): Dynamic Capabilities and Strategic Management, in: Strategic Management Journal, 18: 509-533.

Teece, D. (1998): Capturing value from knowledge assets: the new economy, markets for know-how, and tangible assets, in: California Management Review, 40 (3): 55-79.

Weinstein, K. (1999): Action Learning: A Practical Guide. Gower, London.

Westbrook, R. (1995): Action Research: a new paradigm for research in production and operations management, in: International Journal of Operations & Production Management, 15 (12): 6-20.

Yorks, L., O'Neil, J., Marsick, V. (1999): Action Learning: Successful Strategies for Individual, Team and Organizational Development, Berrett-Koehler, San Francisco.

Integrating Environmental and Social Standards into Supply Management – An Action Research Project

Julia Koplin

1	Introduction...	382
2	Methodology of Action Research	383
3	Outline of the Research Project	388
4	Action Research as Applied in the Project...	390
5	Conclusions..	394
6	References..	395

Summary:
Companies are perceived as important actors in the drive for sustainability. Linked to this and in response to increasing demands from various stakeholder groups, companies start to look at their supply chain to enhance their overall sustainability profile. Reasons for these two major issues can be identified: (1) focal companies are held responsible for environmental and social problems caused by their suppliers, which becomes more and more important as (2) an increasing share of value is created at the supplier level. In response to such demands, companies have to find ways to incorporate environmental and social aspects into their supply (chain) management. Therefore, environmental and social standards are set up in supply management by amending the purchasing processes. This paper presents an approach to integrate social and environmental standards extensively into supply management at a focal company. Therefore, action research (AR) was used as the research methodology to identify the required changes of the sourcing structures and present possible options for the company to do so.

Keywords:
Sustainability, Environmental and Social Standards, Purchasing, Action Research

1 Introduction

Today's companies are confronted with the growing trend towards internationalization. Globalization creates interaction with many different suppliers to acquire raw materials and preliminary products (horizontal supplier structure), and each first tier supplier often depends on a multilevel supplier chain for their own production (vertical supplier structure). Such a structure makes it difficult for a company to handle the whole supplier network, and thus increases the complexity of purchasing (Monczka et al., 2002; Harland et al., 1999).

Additionally, companies play an important role for the environmental and social development of our world in the context of sustainability (Ulrich, 1977: 1ff; Schaltegger & Sturm, 1994: 11). Therefore, they have to include environmental and socials standards in their management strategies (European Commission, 2002: 5). Focal companies have to ensure the manufacture of products without creating environmental damage, facilitating degrading labor conditions, or causing social problems in their supply chains (Myers & Stolton, 1999; Seuring & Goldbach, 2005).

This fact represents a significant risk to a company's public reputation and their attractiveness on the sales market, because they have to take responsibility for their suppliers in front of the media and critical non-governmental organizations (NGOs) (Scherer et al., 2002). Directly cohesive with these changes, inhumane social conditions are discussed, especially in developing countries (Kraus, 1997; Lal, 1998). Therefore, it is useful to integrate environmental and social standards in supplier relations ex ante (European Commission, 2002: 5). Firms have to think about new criteria for supplier selection and evaluation, means of implementation, and realization of environmental and social requirements as well as control mechanisms and compliance stimuli.

This problem situation creates the question of: How will a potential strategy for integration and control of environmental and social standards in the context of an automaker's supply management appear?

Against this background, the paper first presents some theoretical basics on what AR means. Afterwards, it describes the design process of a concept for integrating environmental and social demands into supply management by using AR. This provides insights into how the theoretical basics were transformed into practice within the project. In chapter four, the final results and issues are analyzed, while some conclusions are presented in closing.

2 Methodology of Action Research

The models of learning, developed by Kurt Lewin (1963), can be seen as the basis of AR. It derives from the notion that analyzing social systems requires a special approach appropriate to the originalities of the systems in detail. Here, we talk about tangible social needs, problems and solutions. Therefore, it is important to understand the total situation rather than abstracting some measurable variables (Westbrock, 1995: 9). In comparison to traditional (positivistic) research, there are changes in the relations between (Coughlan & Coghlan, 2002: 224): (1) theory versus practice, (2) theory versus empiricism, and (3) researcher versus researched objects. The next sections will show these differences.

2.1 Objective and Specifics

The basis of every AR method is the practical implementation of the process results and the changing intervention in practice as science at the same time (Coughlan & Coghlan, 2002: 220). So there is a double purpose for AR, not only concentrated on the verification/search for theoretical cognitions but also one oriented towards social needs for problem solving. The main objective of AR is finding scientific fundamentals for change in corporate situations (Lewin, 1963: 204). The result is a double legitimating constraint inside and outside the science system and confronted with divergent relevance criteria and value preferences (Sievers, 1979: 120). The center stages take the common learning process of the action researcher and the research object in the context of all day working, learning and self reflection processes (Haag et al., 1972: 42). This is the precondition for this research to have a real influence on social changes.

There are some specific characteristics for AR processes. A first one is the new collective operation system between science and practice with a determined time horizon (Clark, 1976 ; Miles, 1968). In this system, the researcher plays the role of a participating moderator who collects ideas, shows problems, and asks for argumentation clusters. In doing so, transparency is a very important condition for everybody to understand the process which lives as a result of the knowledge and the abilities of all participants and the ongoing collective learning process (Kompe, 1979: 60). Therefore, it is necessary to break with the traditional distance between researcher and objective (second characteristic) and implement interaction from both sides. The researcher tries to be an active part of the system. Therefore he has to work or live together with the object over a longer time, but at the same time he/she is not allowed to lose his/her identity as a scientist completely (Johnson et al., 1999). This is the only possible way to develop real action perspectives abutted to the determined social verity (Moser, 1975: 169). Another characteristic is an authority-free communicative situation used for the generation of theory. Therefore the objectives, the conformity, the action process, and the used instruments must be determined together with all participants, and must be revised constantly during control and modulation processes.

The following table shows a summary of the AR characteristics in comparison to the traditional research.

Characteristics	Traditional Research	Action Research
Objective	Description and explanation of the reality	Action orientation for changing the reality → **Learning process**
Role of the Researcher	External observer, not engaged in the research events	Logistical separation of knowledge production (science) and knowledge execution (design) → **Participation**
Relation Researcher – Research Object	Subject-object-relation: external objective observer defines meaning of the situation	Subject-subject-relation: all concerned people together define the sense orientation and reflection of the situation (dissolving the distance) → **Interaction**
Theory Generation	Evaluation of theories on the basis of data	Data are the basis for the discourse of action orientation (authority free dialog) → **Communication**
Design – Research Process	Sequential: survey, evaluation and interpretation	Circular, iterative learning process: definition of problems and objectives, formation of an action plan, realization, evaluation and modification if necessary (Revision) → **Discourse**

Table 1: Action Research in Comparison to Traditional Research

2.2 Research Process

Every AR project has the character of a panel experiment which concentrates on two main points: the intended changes of the practice and the cooperation process between researcher and researched object (Coughlan & Coghlan, 2002: 224). At the beginning there is always a practical problem which has to be solved in a special target way. This is the crucial factor for the design of the process flow depending on the existing circumstances (Mayring, 2002: 51). Because of different conditions (communication, background, problem understanding and interests) for participants in the process, pre-decisions about the following cooperation have to be checked (investigation) before starting with the active part of the project (entry). Subsequently, the variables will be collected, evaluated, and prepared along with the structures and processes accessed (data collection, data feedback and diagnostic). These are the basis of the interpretation and the understanding within the scope of the discourse process to find expedient action recommendations. As a next step, the development of specific action tasks, the determination of responsibilities, and the definition of the evaluation approach (action planning) is needed to implement the changing strategies (implementation). At the end of the process, the results and changes achieved have to be measured and analyzed (Sievers, 1976: 10).

Table 2 summarizes the different steps of the whole process. It shows the concept of the AR phase model. Sometimes there can be some minor modifications, depending on the particular project and the author.

Research Step	Predominantly...	Content
Investigation	Research	First orientation and pre-decision about the following cooperation
Entry	Action	Development of a common working relation and of a contract; first problem orientation; selection of methods for data collection and feedback
Data collection	Research	Analysis of organization variables und processes
Data feedback	Action	Return of the prepared data basis to the client system for discussion und diagnosis
Diagnostics	Research	Access to the situation, the problems and deficits of the systems
Action planning	Action	Development of specific action plans, which include decisions about who will achieve the plan and how the success can be measured
Implementation	Action	Management of acquired changing strategies
Evaluation	Research	Evaluation of the effectiveness / ineffectiveness for the implementation – continuation of the project is possible

Table 2: Phase Model of Action Research (Sievers, 1979: 124)

In spite of these structures, there is still a set of flexibilities for the research because it is possible to arrange the single step in a circular way. This means that if there is any kind of problem during the process, it is possible to feed return to a preliminary, already completed phase and start with the process at that point again. At this point the model takes on a higher complexity (Sievers, 1979: 125). So ultimately, AR consists mainly of three different parts: the collection of information, the discourse, and practical actions. Each research step can be associated to one of these three parts.

2.3 Quality Criteria

For qualitative research, it is necessary to evaluate the used processes on the basis of certain quality criteria. A special set of standards are developed to measure the quality of the results of the research. The quality criteria for AR are different from the classical quality criteria of quantitative research (objectivity, validity, reliability). And, they also differ from the quality criteria for qualitative research originated from Mayring (Mayring, 2002: 144). They apply to the methods of communication between the participants and methods for the interpretation of the results for the discourse as the second and main part of the whole process. In doing so, four different conditions can be differentiated: communication as understanding, intervention as influence, transparency as monitoring, and relevance as remarkableness (Gruschka, 1976: 147). There are three different quality criteria for each of these conditions, which are listed in Table 3.

Condition	Quality Criteria	Content
Communication	Empathy	Understanding of other people or situations
	Mutuality	Accepting of exchange and mutual dependency situation (Concernment)
	Rationality	Legitimization / justification of decisions
Intervention	Ability for intervention	Involvement into real situations and validity of own responsibility
	Feedback	Fast back coupling of information and interpretations to all parties
	Recognition	Validity and acceptance of results because of the communication process
Transparency	Controllability	Understandability of scientific theories, communication and interpretation
	Comprehensibility	Publication of methods, rules, approaches and individual steps
	Changeability	Possibility for revision of existing orientations
Relevance	Relevance of the situation	Interests of the parties for theories, communication and interpretation
	Relevance of the objective	Relevance of the scientific orientation for the realization of the aimed target system
	Relevance of the practice	Ability of transfer by scientific methods and approaches into a target perspective

Table 3: Quality Criteria of Action Research (Gruschka, 1976: 147)

Verbal communication plays an especially important role for AR. Communication in this context consists of four different steps which have to be completed before selecting an operation strategy for the desired changes. Only then is it possible to give reasons for the conclusion. The first step (mutual understanding) includes the exchange of opinions, collecting information and problems. This is the requirement for controversial interpretations about the cases on both sides, which will be discussed in a context of sensible compromise about common sense structures and possibilities of operation for future practical changes. The fourth and last step is systematic decision making that assures the action orientation of the research. The final step is the selection of a strategy for changes in the social situation and the explanatory statement. But it is very important that the researcher has no distorting influence on the research process, which has to be reflected and assured by the discourse, where the fulfillment of the different quality criteria must be checked and evaluated by all participants (Gruschka, 1976: 154).

2.4 Research Methods

Because of the close link between the collection of information and the discourse process, research methods take on a new function in the context of AR. Reality shall be found by systematical argumentation, so research methods are used to realize claims of participation and to expand the competence of operation. For the constitution of research methods, the researcher is allowed to take on a higher level of engagement in the process (Moser, 1977: 25). For AR, all methods can be divided into three different categories: the creation of situations, the acquisition of existing action, and the refurbishment of determinants and processes of operations of the contemporaries. Which category a method belongs to is related to the relation the method defines to its object (Moser, 1977: 28).

For the presentation of several useable methods for collecting information, Moser (1977) uses a two-dimensional matrix. The vertical dimension identifies knowledge of facts, knowledge of specific events, and the knowledge of norms/rules as different types of information. Against this, the horizontal dimension shows three different positions a researcher can take: (a) The researcher is absent from the panel, and the data will be recorded with appropriate instruments (instrumental enquiry); (b) The researcher is a member of the panel (physical attendance); (c) The researcher has contact to people on the panel but does not participate in the events (survey of the panel). The following table shows adaptive research methods for every combination of the different types of dimensions (Moser, 1977: 24).

Some of these methods are not new, but used for traditional empirical research such as questionnaires, interviews, etc. as well. This is because all these approaches are not founded upon a special science. Instead, they represent action frames which originally trace back to all day operations. For this reason, it is not possible for scientific methodologies to revert to an unlimited number of methods. But, depending on methodological basic assumptions, action frames of everyday life gain different significance when using them as research methods (Moser, 1977: 26). Overall, it is important to apply different methods which have a mutual control function depending on the project's objectives and content.

		Kind of Involvement		
		Absence from the panel	Presence at the panel	Survey of the panel
Knowledge derived from	Facts	• Statistical enquiry of socio-economical data • Standardized/open questionnaires • Analyses of content • Quasi-experiment • Informal tests	• Quasi-experiments • Structured/unstructured observation	• Standardized/open interviews • Survey of experts • Analyses of content • Analyses of literature • Analyses of sources • Analyses of documents
	Events	• Analyses of content for repeating events • Interviews for rating of events by self/external assessment	• Recording of processes with media for observation • Protocols • Process reflection with fixation in written form • Crisis experiments	• Survey of affected people's assessment • Survey of experts • Analyses of documents • Analyses of literature • Interpretations of sources
	Norms / Rules	• Sociometry • Analyses of content • Quasi-experiments • Standardized/open questionnaires • Semantic differential	• Structured/unstructured observation • Quasi-experiment • Crisis experiments • Group-dynamic reflection • Role playing	• Standardized/open interviews • Rating of experts • Role playing • Analyses of literature • Interpretations of sources • Analyses of documents

Table 4: Research Methods of Action Research (Moser, 1977: 26)

3 Outline of the Research Project

The research project was a collective project between the University of Oldenburg (research team of two people) and a multinational company (different departments of the entire group). Both partners worked together at the same level in different constellations. Along with a reunion of all parties thereto (workshops), there were informal meetings for the core project team consisting of three people from the company side and the research team.

The main research focus applied to the development process of a realizable solution. Objectives, the process and solutions are dependent on the whole research situation (participants etc.). The design of a process has a great influence on the results and vice versa. It is a continuous process with permanent changes in the context of the problem and objective definition including the resulting specification of needed operations. To meet this challenge, it was important to have a good documentation of all individual research parts. Only with a detailed documentation it is possible to implicate changes of the process and their impacts on the final results of the entire research.

Overall, the project was made up of four different research units along a time period of eighteen months:

- preliminary analysis (literature review),
- six discourse workshops,
- review of the current purchasing structures (internal interviews), and
- involvement of first tier-suppliers (survey/supplier workshop).

The preliminary analysis took place before the discourse-oriented main part of the project started. Main topics for these enquiries were: (1) challenges (chances/risks) for globally acting companies which result from environmental and social aspects inside the supply chain associated with sustainability, (2) standing, proliferation and contents of existing environmental and social standards as well as discovering the most recognized standards, and (3) best practice and negative examples of other companies and industries. Based on this analysis, an overview of the current research status for sustainable development in supply chains was established as the starting point for the first internal workshop.

The six workshops were used to congregate all relevant people involved in the project. The first workshop familiarized the participants with the topic, and the results of the preliminary analysis were shown. In every workshop the current statuses of the ongoing research were discussed, and further actions were determined. Each person took part in the decision process, and together the design and the used research methods were chosen to develop a realizable implementation concept by using the know-how of the practitioners to ensure feasibility of the developed solution.

The review of the current situation of the company was initiated to understand the company's sourcing structures and processes and to identify weak points related to environmental and social standards. The overall supply management system comprises four different phases: the normative level, early detection, the purchasing process, and monitoring and supplier development. Therefore, nine interviews with experts of the respective company departments were carried out. These statements were collected and analyzed to identify possibilities and needs for changes. From them, different solutions could be generated as norm strategies, and were discussed at the workshops to identify a suitable solution.

The integration of automobile suppliers was carried out by a survey in written form, as well as a direct involvement of five selected suppliers into a supplier workshop. The survey of 378 suppliers (mainly located in Germany) included questions about the cognition and importance of sustainability and the realization of environmental and social standards in their own companies and their supply chains. The rate of return consisted of 111 completed questionnaires that showed a picture of the current situation in the automobile supplier industry. This helped achieve an impression of the need for regulations of environmental and social aspects in the context of outsourcing processes (Koplin et al., 2004). For the discussion of the provisional concept, five suppliers were chosen to take part in a supplier workshop to get feedback for the planned changes of the requisitions for suppliers and to discuss corporate solutions.

The following chapter will reflect the processes of the project from the scientific perspective. It will show the implementation of the issues, structures and quality criteria of AR into the project.

4 Action Research as Applied in the Project

This research project was based on the analysis of organizational structures at a multinational company which constitutes a social system. The research team of the University of Oldenburg (scientists) and its company partner (practitioners) were equal partners within a collective operation system. The main objective was the reduction of environmental and social problems in global supply chains by implementing requirements and standards into purchasing structures of a multinational company. This problem represents a tangible social need as the initial situation of the research. Concepts like sustainable development, purchasing, and supply chain management are the scientific fundamentals for the aspired changes of the environmental and social situation in supply chains.

To realize these practical changes to a social system, the existing purchasing structures were analyzed, and weak points were shown. The project tried to find a way to integrate environmental and social requirements and standards into the purchasing structures that caused changes in the system:

- development of additional criteria for supplier selection,
- new classification sets supplier evaluation,
- new responsibilities and tasks during the purchasing process,
- extension of the early detection system towards social factors,
- additional audits including environmental and social categories,
- implementation of internal information systems for supply chains.

4.1 Single Stages of the Process

All three parts of AR were taken into account in the research project. The first part, the collection of information, took place during the preliminary and attendant analysis, including studies about the challenges for companies as a result of developments over the last years in the context of globalization, building worldwide environmental and social standards to achieve transparency about their postulations (regarding content), as well as the exploration of the best practical examples and companies which were charged with environmental and social violations inside their supply chain due to missing guidelines. On the other hand, information about the own situation of the company, and existing sourcing structures and processes (including the defaults for suppliers) were gathered via expert interviews with the company's departments.

Research step	Predominantly	Research project
Investigation	Research	Meeting: development of a project description with shared objectives
Entry	Action	Meeting: reformulation of the project plan - specification of several steps, identification of appropriate research methods and feedback cycles, preparation of the first workshop
Data collection	Research	Preliminary analysis: environmental and social standards, chances and risks for companies, best practice concepts
Data feedback	Action	1st workshop: introduction, definition of problems and objectives, review of the internal situation, discussion and next steps
Diagnostics	Research	Interviews: internal with experts about purchasing structures, processes, weak points und options for solutions
Action planning	Action	Meeting: evaluation of the current situation, analysis of weak points, formulation of possible objective dimensions and options for solution strategies
Implementation	Action	2nd workshop: back coupling to data feedback, discussion of weak points, objective dimensions and solution strategies, following involvement of affected employees for acceptance and motivation to realize future action plans
Evaluation	Research	

Table 5: Project Classified into Action Research Process Structures

The second part, the discourse, was the central instance of the scientific process for the critical question about the sense of norms and facts. Therefore, knowledge stocks are necessary, which admit appropriate and informative argumentations. There are different sources for knowledge stocks: work day knowledge, operating knowledge of institutions, theoretical (academic and philosophic) knowledge and systematical enquiries in terms of empirical methods (Moser, 1977: 66). All these forms of knowledge were used in the project. Work day knowledge came from the people in the different departments of the company from the experiences of the job. The operating knowledge from institutions came from the contact of the researched objects with the company as a social institution. Theoretical knowledge includes e.g. the academic knowledge of the researcher acquired from studies of existing models and concepts in literature. And systematical inquiries were collected during the project, for example by a survey of company suppliers.

As a result of the practical actions, the supplier platform on the Internet was expanded regarding environmental and social information as enlarged criteria for supplier selection. Every supplier had to fill out a self disclosure to show its status. For the evaluation, a new classification set was established. Furthermore, new responsibilities and tasks in the context of job descriptions were distributed to several people and a special ad hoc expert team for environmental and social audits was founded. We now have some fundamental changes for the company's operations directly originating from the project. The entire research process can be arranged into the pattern of the AR phase model as shown in Table 5.

4.2 Research Methods Used

For the project, not all research methods mentioned in chapter 2.4 were used. As already shown, research methods of AR can be characterized into three categories: the creation of situations, the acquisition of existing action, and the refurbishment of determinants and processes of operations of the contemporaries. For the first category, research methods are used which construct situations that lead to actions as main sources of information for a project. Here, two minimum conditions exist: the results of the analysis have to be discussed with concerned people (feedback), and the researcher has to be honest and is not allowed to cheat on the researched object by means of the research methods (threat to reliability). In the context of the project, none of these methods were used because a special situation already existed and actions could be derived from it, so there was no need to create a new situation.

For the next category, the acquisition of existing action, it is important to acquire natural performance or rather to belay aspects of this natural performance on the basis of interviews. Here, it is important to acquire own appraisals and evaluations of the respondents. Their decision making and responsibility is assumed. Different methods belong to this category, and some of them were included into the project. Structured or rather unstructured observations took place the entire time, including during the workshops and project team meetings. For the understanding of the structures and processes, non-standardized interviews were conducted with different departments of the company and suppliers, combined with surveys of experts. Protocols were made for documentation of the process for each meeting, workshop etc., and there was a process reflection with fixation in written form afterwards.

For the refurbishment of determinants and processes of operations of the contemporaries as the third category, it is no longer possible to generate data from a direct observation and interviews; experiences and knowledge are second hand. The analysis concentrates on representational references which serve as an explanation for human behavior. References can be differentiated into two dimensions. The local dimension includes information about parallel events elsewhere and the temporal dimension covers events from the past. Research methods of this category are: analyses of literature, analyses of sources, and analyses of documents, which all played a main role in the context of the project for the refurbishment of the scientific foundations and concepts, and achieving an overview of the structures and processes of the company. The analysis of content played a role in the composition of individual points of views in the protocols.

4.3 Conformance with Quality Criteria

For the reputation of a research program, it is very important to assess the results on the basis of the quality criteria. Table 6 shows the realization of AR quality criteria in the range of the described project.

Condition	Quality criteria	Research project
Communication	Empathy	Establishing a core team of the project made of researchers and practitioners
	Mutuality	Continuous workshops with all participants
	Rationality	Collective decisions of the researcher and the research partners
Intervention	Ability for intervention	Analyzing the existing outsourcing structures
	Feedback	Continuous workshops with all participants
	Recognition	Consideration of internal research results
Transparency	Controllability	Explanation of all used research methods
	Comprehensibility	Discussion of single steps in the project with the research partners
	Changeability	Workshops as a platform for change proposals and new ideas
Relevance	Relevance of the situation	Research objects are directly struck by the structural changes
	Relevance of the objective	Connectivity of the integration concept
	Relevance of the practice	Looking for the practicability when developing the concept

Table 6: Realization of the Project's Quality Criteria

5 Conclusions

This paper has indicated that it is possible to apply action research as an applicable methodology for empirical research in the context of supply management. In this context the function of the project researcher showed similarities to a consulting activity in the field of business management. The objective of changing current social situations is more focused than the generation of new scientific implications for already-existing concepts, so it is important not to lose the balance between both sides. The researcher has to try to keep a kind of impartiality towards the researched object, although there is a certain dependency on the company. It is also important to power the discourse process between all participants at all times because the praxis often has time restraints and does not care for too much reflection. Obstacles must often be overcome at the beginning. The only effective way therefore is a learning process on both sides to gain trust and understanding.

The project also showed some problems which came up during the process and which can be responsible for the failure of such a project. These should be kept in mind for further research design by AR. Using AR makes it initially impossible for a research project to define an accurately planned time table because of the constant reengineering and modifying of the research process. This results from the discourse with the researched objects. Together they try the most adequate process structures to achieve the hoped-for solutions. Besides that, a relatively long-term uncertainty concerning the project results overshadow the whole process. Therefore, continuous back coupling of the findings to the affected people is a responsible idea, and results in changes that last until the end of the project. Further, it is important to attend to the involvement of all researched objects in the whole process. If some of these objects miss several parts of the projects, results will be unrolled again and verified partial results will be re-discussed; this situation takes up valuable time. Finally, another important point for the researcher is the reflection of the question of panel access. He/she has to ask: How intensively can researched objects (processes and people) be analyzed? This is important for AR. The close cooperation between researcher and the researched object is possible only if they know each other and a faithful and constructive relationship exists between both.

6 References

Clark, A. W. (1976): The Client-Practitioner Relationship as an Inter-System Engagement, in Clark, A. W. (ed.): Experimenting with Organizational Life. The Action Research Approach, Plenum, New York, London: 119-133.

European Commission (2002): Communication From The Commission concerning Corporate Social Responsibility: A business contribution to Sustainable Development, COM (2002) 347/1 of 02/07/2002, Brussels.

Coughlan, P., Coghlan, D. (2002): Action Research for Operations Management, in: International Journal of Operations & Production Management, 22(2): 220-240.

Gruschka, A. (1976): Ein Schulversuch wird überprüft – Das Evaluationsdesign für Kollegstufe NW als Konzept Handlungsorientierter Begleitforschung (The Design of Evaluation for Colleges NW as a Concept of Action-orientated Accompanying Research), Athenäum, Kronberg.

Haag, F., Krüger, H., Schwärzel, W., Wildt, J. (eds.) (1972): Aktionsforschung: Forschungsstrategien, Forschungsfelder und Forschungspläne (Action Research: Research Strategies, Research Fields and Research Plans), Juventa, München.

Harland, C. M., Lamming, R. C., Cousins, P. D. (1999): Developing the Concept of Supply Strategy, in: International Journal of Operations & Production Management, 19(7): 650-673.

Johnson, P., Duberly, J., Close, P., Cassell, C. (1999): Negotiating field roles in manufacturing management research - The need for reflexivity, in: International Journal of Operations & Production Management, 19(12): 1234-1254.

Kompe, H. (1979): Kritischer Rationalismus versus Aktionsforschung: eine wissenschaftstheoretische Einschätzung (Critical Rationalism versus Action Research: A Scientific Theoretical Assessment); in: Hron, A., Kompe, H., Otto, K.-P., Wächter, H.: Aktionsforschung in der Ökonomie, Campus, Frankfurt a.M., New York: p. 49-75.

Koplin, J., Beske, P., Seuring, S. (2004): Zur Umsetzung von Umwelt- und Sozialstandards in der Automobilindustrie - Ergebnisse einer Umfrage (Implementation of Environmental and Social Standards in the Automotive Industry), in: Dangelmaier, W., Kaschula, D., Neumann, J. (eds.): Supply Chain Management in der Automobil- und Zulieferindustrie, ALB-HNI-Verlagsschriftenreihe, Paderborn: p. 391-400.

Krüger, H., Klüver, J., Haag, F. (1975): Aktionsforschung in der Diskussion (Discussion of Action Research); in: Soziale Welt: 1-30.

Kurz, R. (1997): Unternehmen und Nachhaltigkeit (Enterprises and Sustainability); in: Ökonomie und Gesellschaft, Jahrbuch 14: Nachhaltigkeit in der ökonomischen Theorie, Campus, Frankfurt a.M.: p. 78-99.

Lal, D. (1998): Social Standards and Social Dumping; in Giersch, H. (ed.): Merits and Limits of Markets, Springer, Heidelberg: p. 255-274.

Lewin, K. (1963): Field Theory in Social Science, Tavistock, London.

Mayring, P. (2002): Einführung in die qualitative Sozialforschung (Introduction to the Qualitative Social Research), 5. überarbeitete und neu ausgestattete Auflage, Beltz, Weinheim, Basel.

Miles, M. B. (1964): On Temporary Systems, in: Miles, M. B. (ed.): Innovation in Education, Bureau of Publication, Teachers College, Columbia University, New York: p. 437-490.

Monczka, R., Trent, R., Handfield, R. (2002): Purchasing and Supply Chain Management, South-Western, Cinsinnati.

Moser, H. (1975): Aktionsforschung als kritische Theorie der Sozialwissenschaften (Action Research as a Critical Theory of Social Science), Kösel, München.

Moser, H. (1977): Methoden der Aktionsforschung. Eine Einführung (Methods of Action Research. An Introduction), Kösel, München.

Myers, D., Stolton, S. (eds.) (1999): Organic Cotton – From Field to Final Product, Intermediate Technology, London.

Schaltegger, S./ Sturm, A. (1994): Ökologieorientierte Entscheidungen im Unternehmen (Ecological orientated Decisions at Business), Haupt, Bern et al.

Scherer, A. G., Blicke, K.-H., Dietzfelbinger, D., Hütter G. (2002): Globalisierung und Sozialstandards: Problemtatbestände, Positionen und Lösungsansätze (Globalisation and Social Standards: Problems, Positions and Solutions); in Scherer, A.G., Blicke, K.-H., Dietzfelbinger, D., Hütter G. (eds.): Globalisierung und Sozialstandards, Hampp, München, Mering: p. 11-21.

Seuring, S., Goldbach, M. (2005): Managing Sustainability Performance in the Textile Chain, in: Schaltegger, S., Wagner, M. (eds.): Sustainable Performance and Business Competitiveness, Greenleaf Publishing, Sheffield, forthcoming Spring 2005.

Sievers, B. (1979): Organisationsentwicklung als Aktionsforschung. Zu einer sozialwissenschaftlichen Neuorientierung der betriebswirtschaftlichen Organisationsforschung (Organizational Development as Action Research. For a social scientific Reorientation of the Business Organizational Research); in: Hron, A., Kompe, H., Otto, K.-P., Wächter, H. (ed): Aktionsforschung in der Ökonomie, Campus, Frankfurt a. M., New York: p. 111-133.

Ulrich, P.(1977): Die Großunternehmung als quasi-öffentliche Institution : eine politische Theorie der Unternehmung (The Large-Scale Enterprise as a Quasi-Public Institution – a Political Theory of Enterprises), Schäffer-Poeschel, Stuttgart.

Westbrock, R. (1995): Action research: a new paradigm for research in production and operations management; in: International Journal for Operations & Production Management, 15(12): 6-20.

Supply Chain Diagnostics to Confront Theory and Practice – Re-Questioning the Core of Supply Chain Management

Günter Prockl

1   The Core of Supply Chain Theory and Realities of Practice 398
2   Exploring a Set of Hypotheses on Supply Chain Management 400
3   Gaining Data – Involving the Stakeholders 407
4   References.. 410

Summary:
This paper illustrates the basic approach, structure and development path of a diagnostic instrument that integrates existing approaches of systemizing, structuring and thus elaboration of the core of supply chain management (SCM). The main purpose of this computer-aided tool is the quick indication of weak spots within supply chain enterprises. But this self diagnostic is not the focus of this paper. More interesting is the side effect of gaining feedback from diagnostics sessions. While answering diagnostic questions, users are confronted in a systematic way with concrete challenges and principles of SCM. Their industries, supply chain stages as well as the answers are documented in standardized data records. So the tool can provide useful data regarding the state of implementation and differences in key challenges for different players in different supply chains. Separate studies on potentials, obstacles and realization of SCM principles as well as existing scientific publications on design principles, interviews with industry experts, and the experiences of the concerned consulting and research institutions have been used as input in the development process of the self diagnostic instrument.

Keywords:
Supply Chain Diagnostics, Boot-Strapping, Principles, Key Challenges, Root Causes

1 The Core of Supply Chain Theory and Realities of Practice

1.1 Supply Chain is Not Supply Chain and Player is Not Player

Since Oliver & Webber (1982) coined the concept and the term, supply chain management has seen rapid advances, especially in recent years, and is now an established concept of the scientific community as well as of most practitioners. It is apostrophized as a kind of meta competence of successful business management, and a great number of literature on concepts, potentials or technical support has been published. Apart from this predominantly popular literature, less work has been finished towards the scientific collection, critical consolidation and systematization of this multitude of models, design recommendations or single principles, thus addressing the question on the emerging nucleus of supply chain management. Though there are some initial and useful taxonomies and systematic collections of supply chain concepts and ideas available as well as initial preliminary results of international Delphi studies[1], the critical and systematic confrontation of theory and practice still seems to be missing.

Additionally, most recommendations and suggested potentials address supply chain management in general. But an increasing number of authors provide convincing arguments for the need of a more differentiated view on what is the right supply chain. Fisher (1997) separates products into functional and innovative products and uses this distinction to argue for two different archetypes of supply chains: the efficient supply chain and the responsive supply chain; each with a different set of specific challenges. Fine (1998) uses product architecture to separate supply chains into modular and integral supply chains. Christopher (1998) differentiates between lean and agile supply chains depending on demand stability. Lee (2002) or Sheffi (2004) combine different views towards more hybrid approaches. All approaches together show that there is no such a thing as the "one perfect supply chain." Theory on supply chain design should reflect this.

Furthermore, players across even the same supply chain may also have different views on what is the right supply chain for them. The supply chain efforts of fast-moving consumer goods are almost exclusively focused on the area downstream from producers to retail. The area upstream has hardly been recognized at all until now (Prockl, 2000: 57). Midsized companies, when asked about the benefits of supply chain management or efficient consumer response, provide answers that are different to those of big players. Studies show that not all supply chain players show the expected results (Heckmann et al., 2003; also Prockl et al., 2004: 32-33).

---

[1] See for example http://legacy.csom.umn.edu/AHill/SCMtenR2/

While the basic theoretical core elements of supply chain management may thus emerge gradually, the next question on the differentiation of supply chain management concept towards different supply chain types or different supply chain actors seems almost totally unaddressed. Insights on the weight of different supply chain challenges for different positions in the chain, different chain types or different actors are lacking.

1.2 Need for Hypothesis and Empirical Data from Practice

Keeping these introductory thoughts in mind, the danger of dividing theoretical rigor and practical relevance is once more apparent (Anderson et al., 2001; Nicolai, 2004). If research on supply chain management asks for both rigor and relevance, then attempts to bridge this gap between theoretical rigor and practical relevance seem to demand meeting at least two requirements (see also Weick, 2001: 72, 74; Starkey & Madan, 2001: 3-4). First there is a need for a confrontation of theory and practice in a straightforward as well as systematic way that is itself interesting and helpful for practitioners. Second, practice of supply chain management should neither be seen as a homogeneous whole, nor should theory reflect the idiosyncrasies of individual cases. Instead, the theory needs to be separated for different supply chains including different supply chain echelons and different types of supply chain players.

One opportunity for such an approach, as outlined in this paper, has been provided by a joint project of university researchers together with business consultants to develop a rapid diagnostic toolset for supply chain management. The main aim of the computer-aided instrument is the quick diagnostics and indication of weak spots within enterprises in a supply chain. Such diagnostics sessions can be run by managers of the respective companies themselves or more commonly in first meetings between the companies and the involved researchers and consultants.

However, the diagnostics itself are not the focus of this paper. Yet, within the context of this paper the two requirements of confronting practice with theory as well as gaining empirical feedback from the diagnostics sessions will be addressed. By answering the diagnostics questions, the users provide empirical feedback on exploratively-gained supply chain challenges and principles. By asking for the industry and supply chain stage of the company as well as the standardized documentation of all answers in a data record, the diagnostics instrument can provide useful empirical data regarding the state of implementation and differences in key challenges for different players in different supply chains.

The following two sections describe first the approach used to explore the hypothesis on supply chain management that are incorporated into the diagnostic tool. Then the structure of the tool and the process of a typical diagnostics session are sketched to illustrate how the diagnostic tool can work as a data machine for relevant feedback from practice.

2 Exploring a Set of Hypotheses on Supply Chain Management

2.1 Combining Top-Down and Bottom-Up Approaches – Bootstrapping of Theory and Practical Experience

One of the major challenges of the project was to create a toolset that is based on science as well as practical experience and that is itself interesting, helpful and easy to use. Therefore, from the beginning a strong emphasis had to be put on the basic structure of the tool, allowing it to take different industry specifics into account later. Furthermore, the tool does not target specific measures but tries to provide a more qualitative system of indicators on relevant hot spots in the users' companies or supply chains. To get better indications of such hidden problems without the opportunity to detail questions (as during an interview) on given answers, it seemed more appropriate to encircle problems by providing bundles of different diagnostic questions that address different views of a problem and thus may show some intended redundancy. The elaboration of these question sets and their sound structuring around core issues of supply chain management played one of the most prominent roles within the project. For this task, a combined approach of top-down and bottom-up analysis seemed most appropriate (Figure 1).

- **Top-Down: Driven by Principles**

On the one hand, such a search for indicators on hidden opportunities within supply chains may be based on relevant principles of supply chain management and, respectively, principles of flow systems design. Such principles and recommendations can be found, although they are distributed throughout the relevant literature. The task was then to identify, condense and evaluate such principles and transform them towards diagnostic questions. Additionally, to structure the questions along the supply chain, so-called topics had to be defined that express concisely the conformity or non-conformity to the related principle.

- **Bottom-Up: Driven by Experience**

On the other hand - besides the more theoretical principle-based approach - the search on indicators may also be related to actual problems observed in daily practice and the related typical solutions to tackle those problems. By requisitioning these typical problems regarding their typical underlying root causes, core issues (now in the sense of key challenges that have to be mastered in supply chain management) could be defined.

The single steps of this approach, referred according to a statistical method as "bootstrapping," are sketched below. But before this, the basic paths "top-down" and "bottom-up" are introduced in some more detail.

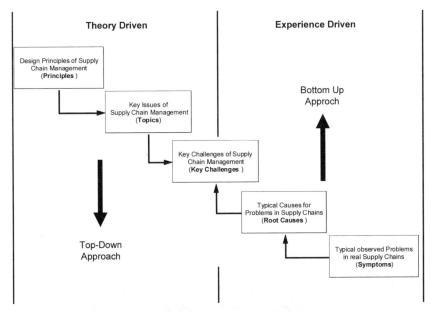

Figure 1: "Bootstrapping" Approach to Combine Theory and Practice

2.2 "Top-Down"- The Good Supply Chain in Theory

Supply chain management gained ample attention in recent years - also as topic of scientific discussion. It seems that the scientific community agrees widely on the basic objectives and the basic levers of supply chain management. Typical, frequently-mentioned objectives include increasing customer value by reducing lead times and reducing costs (Bhattacharya et al., 1996: 39-48; Cavinato, 1991: 10-15; Towill, 1996), and thus finally increasing the success of all companies involved (Stevens, 1989: 3; Cooper et al., 1997: 2; Bechtel & Jayaram, 1997: 16; Christopher, 1998; Klaus, 1998: 23; Kotzab, 2000: 34; Brewer, Speh, 2000: 75). The primary lever is seen as the design and alignment of all activities in the whole supply chain - i.e. across company borders - towards this ultimate goal of customer (consumer) orientation (e.g. Jones & Riley, 1985: 17; Stevens, 1989: 3; Bowersox, 1997: 181-189; Christopher, 1998: 23ff.; Klaus, 1998; Prockl, 2001). Closely related to this is the belief that overall, better coordination of the activities and thus more effectiveness as well as efficiency may be realized by sharing data and joint planning (e.g. Bowersox, 1996: 102) across the total supply chain. In addition to a necessary joint awareness for the objectives of the total supply chain and for the required means to realize these objectives across company borders, the following major tasks of supply chain management seem to be emerging (Prockl, 2001: 42; Delfmann, 1998: 71; Klaus, 1998: 434ff.; Fine, 1998: 105ff.):

- The active configuration of the supply in terms of breaking down and allocating all the activities, tasks, functions, processes and competencies on to different actors in the chain to exploit competitive edges by advantages of locations, specialization and centralization and goal oriented bundling of core competencies;
- the active design of coordination decisions regarding the transfer, control and communication processes between the allocated actors. The chain must mobilize the actors continuously towards the total objectives as well as integrate the actors who are distributed geographically and organizationally into an altogether "optimal" complex. This integration task is basically done by formal organizational means, the application of (information) technology as well as socially oriented interventions into the organizations' routines;
- the permanent re-alignment of the established structures to secure the advantages and thus the sustainable competitiveness of the supply chain. The design and re-design of the supply chain thus becomes a continuous "meta-core competency" of the companies involved (Prockl, 2001: 43; Fine, 1998: 221). In addition to the configuration/allocation and the coordination/integration, the adaptation/development of the supply chain is the third major task of supply chain management.

But supply chain management also incorporates many older concepts and ideas under the umbrella of a new and handy "language" (Klaus, 1998: 436). This makes it much more difficult to define - beyond these basic ideas - which elements and design recommendations really represent the core of supply chain management and which contribute significantly to companies' success. Prockl (2001) provides one approach by adapting Giddens (1984) structuration theory and trying to characterize the phenomenon of supply chain management via its "structural properties," i.e. the proposed and typical standard solutions and related patterns of action.[2] This work provides about 900 design recommendations for supply chain management from different scientific sources, and arranges it to sets of principles essentially structured around the basic ideas and task of supply chain management (Prockl, 2001). Slightly modified in its structure and supplemented by additional, current sources, this systematic collection of principles and ideas of supply chain management could be used as the theoretical starting point to define step-by-step key issues of supply chain management.

Table 1 shows in excerpts some elements of this work. In the third column, some first proposals of such key issues are presented. These issues are then mirrored on

---

[2] For the concept of "structural properties" and the basic thoughts of the structuration theory see Prockl (2001: 16-20) and constitutive Giddens (1984).

experiences and requirements of the practitioners (see 2.3 Bottom-Up) and are refined step-by-step to hypothesize on relevant key challenges of supply chain management.[3]

Core Tasks of SCM	Basic Concepts of SCM[4]	Illustration of Some Topics in SCM
Task 1: Configuration/ Allocation	<ul><li>Flow oriented differentiation, segmentation</li><li>Modularization</li><li>Outsourcing</li><li>Postponement</li><li>Mass customizing</li><li>Capacity harmonization</li></ul>	<ul><li>Segmentation of the supply chain according to customer and demand requirements</li><li>Category management</li><li>Combination of product and service policies; Make2Order vs. Make2Buy</li><li>Network strategy assessment</li><li>Strategic decision structures; Joint vision</li><li>Supply chain technology strategy</li><li>Strategic network planning (Cross docking, Transshipment)</li><li>Encapsulation of related activities (focused factory; modular production)</li><li>Modular/integral product architecture;</li><li>Proximity, Local sourcing</li><li>"Interface" reduction (Single/Modular sourcing)</li><li>"Interface" design (System supplier; One-Stop Shopping)</li><li>Process ownership and consignation arrangements</li><li>Outsourcing of non-core competencies (3PL/4PL)</li><li>"Warehouse Postponement" (e.g. Centralization of slow movers etc.)</li><li>Postponed manufacturing, Assembly and merging</li><li>Postponed transportation (Drop shipments)</li><li>Capacity/Stock harmonization; Joint capacity planning; Synchronized production</li></ul>

Table 1: Core Tasks, Basic Concepts and Topics in Supply Chain Management (Part 1)

---

[3] A similar effort to define the core of supply chain management via sets of principles is currently taken in a Delphi study. See http://legacy.csom.umn.edu/AHill/Scmten/R2.

[4] A deeper discussion of most of these improvement concepts can be found in Prockl (2001: 101ff).

Core Tasks of SCM	Basic Concepts of SCM	Illustration of Some Topics in SCM
Task 2: Coordination/ Integration	<ul><li>Compressing/ Speeding of the supply chain</li><li>Leveling and capacity adjustments</li><li>Early sharing of information and data</li><li>Collaboration, Partnering, Trust</li><li>Adequate formal organization, esp. contract design</li><li>Joint monitoring</li><li>Permanent and early error prevention</li></ul>	<ul><li>Cross company planning and control</li><li>Technical standards, EDI, CPFR etc.</li><li>Process-/operation standards</li><li>Information sharing and monitoring</li><li>Data integrity (Master Data Alignment)</li><li>ERP/SC-Planning software</li><li>Integrated real-time processing (Tracking & Tracing) alerting, Event management</li><li>Cross functional teams; Ad-hoc teams; Cross training</li><li>Collaborative product development (concurrent engineering)</li><li>Strength of bonds, Contracts</li><li>Aligned measurement systems, Gain sharing, Open book, Incentive systems, Bonus/Penalty</li><li>Scorecards, Performance Measuring/Management</li><li>Self management/organization, responsibilities</li><li>Partnering, Win-Win, Cultural proximity</li><li>Commitment within and across the SC</li><li>Origin oriented cost accounting</li><li>Just in Time, Pull, Replenishment</li></ul>
Task 3: Adaptation/ Development	<ul><li>Development and scalability</li><li>Open standards</li><li>Agility</li></ul>	<ul><li>Open scalable technologies</li><li>Adaptive business processes</li><li>Supplier development programs</li><li>Benchmarking und technology exchanges</li></ul>

Table 1: Core Tasks, Basic Concepts and Topics in Supply Chain Management (Part 2)

2.3 "Bottom-Up"- The Problems Shown in Practice

The top-down approach formulates in a more or less normative way the objectives, tasks and principles that, when applied, should secure the "good" supply chain. In contrast to this, the bottom-up works form the other side and start with the identification and description of typical weaknesses and problems in practice. By asking systematically for the underlying reasons of these problems, key issues may be defined, but now from the bottom up. Such approaches of detecting problems in individual analysis and the classification of such problems with standard root causes and standard solutions based on past experiences is the core business of the classic consulting companies. Figure 2, taken from a company presentation of Booz Allen Hamilton, clearly illustrates this approach.

Together with additional studies (e.g. Heckmann, 2003; see also Prockl et al., 2004), this preparatory work of the consultants was to identify typical weaknesses, ask for their underlying causes, and group them according to typical root causes for problems that could be included within the project as second starting point – this time from the viewpoint of the practitioners.[5]

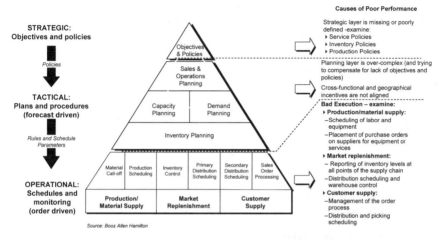

Figure 2: Problems, Typical Causes of Poor Performances and Consulting Issues

2.4 Structuring Principles, Key Challenges, Root Causes and Symptoms

The outlined bootstrapping method was realized in a partly iterative process composed of the basic steps specified in the sections below. These single steps may be further classified into a preparation stage and a realization stage (see Chapter 3). In the preparation stage discussed in this chapter, the identification, collection, grouping and consolidating of the material from the different sources came to the fore. Simple Excel tableaus served as technical support. The following steps were executed:

- **Step One: Defining the Basic Structure and the Relevant Elements**

First, the elements of the both approaches (top-down and bottom-up) were combined into an overall structure, and in some iterations a first matching of the more inductively deduced topics of supply chain management with the deductively investigated root problems of the practitioners were done. The structural link of

---

[5] For the roles of consultants in academic research see also Robey & Markus (1998).

both directions was realized by sets of hypotheses on what is important and relevant for supply chain management today: these are called the "key challenges".

- **Step Two: Collect and Arrange Material from Primary and Secondary Sources**

The developed framework was filled with further material. In this stage, redundancy and gaps still were accepted consciously. To keep the survey feasible and thorough, the project team agreed to focus on some core industries: "Automotive," "Communications, Media," "Fast Moving Consumer Goods," "Pharmaceuticals" and "Chemicals." But not only these industry sources on design recommendations and on typical problem challenges in supply chain management were investigated. The used material collection and evaluation included own surveys and reports from different projects, publication of organizations like Odette published project reports, supply chain models (e.g. SCOR, ECR, VICS), questionnaires, checklists, and whitepapers.

- **Step Three: Formal Consolidation**

The classifications and groupings were checked formally, and entries with very similar content but differently expressed were consolidated. Some redundancies were eliminated in this stage.

- **Step Four: Asking Industry Experts**

In step four, the preliminary key challenges were listed in the form of hypotheses. Each challenge was then attached to a scale (high, medium, low relevance). Then industry experts were confronted with the hypotheses to generate first rankings and estimations on the relevance of single challenges. This feedback was used for further alignment and consolidation of the key challenges.

- **Step Five: Grouping and Consolidation**

In numerous loops, the material collection was then condensed and thinned out systematically, and the remaining gaps were more tightly focused and filled. To do this, the project team members elaborated their individual proposals. Then in group meetings, the proposals were compared, discussed intensively and aligned. Due to a lot of material referring to chain awareness, this large group was split into three smaller groups so that the following six basic principles could build the backbone of the diagnostics instrument.[6]

- "Create Supply Chain Awareness",
- "Create Demand Transparency across the Chain",
- "Align Supply Chain to Products and Customers",
- "Configure Network (Structure)",
- "Integrate Operations (Process)",
- "Develop Supply Chain (Adaptation)".

---

[6] See also chapter 2.2, and for the structure of principles, challenges, questions see 3.1.

- **Step Six: Preparation for Programming**

In the last step of the preparation stage, the results were implemented into an access database used as a basis for the succeeding programming - widely independent of operation systems. Within the database, the single elements were identified by a hierarchical number system. Each data record represents a symptom for possible problems already in the form of a question sentence. Each such question is linked with a referring root cause, the key challenges, and additionally to the evaluation in a diagnostics session regarding how it relates to the levels of strategy, tactics and operations, and to five more factor analytical views on "Products and Innovation," "People and Soft Factors," "Technology and Investment," "Organization and Processes," and "Performance Measuring and Monitoring."

3 Gaining Data – Involving the Stakeholders

3.1 Informing, Challenging and Asking

The major intention that the tool is to provide diagnostics has put some requirements on the questionnaire. On the one hand, e.g. the length of a typical supply chain, the different areas involved, or the mix of strategic and operational aspects demand as many questions as possible. Additionally, the questions should be asked as precisely and least-suggestively as possible. On the other hand, the number and the length of the questions should be limited to a minimum, keeping required time to answer the questions low. Along with the programming for these reasons, a lot of effort was put into the wording of the questionnaire.

But even more important than the wording was the creation of a structure that actively involves the user into the data generation process. The user should not get only a promise of a diagnostics and a kind of an evaluation after the end of the session, but should be informed and challenged with the theoretical core of supply chain management during the answering session. Thus, he should ideally learn about supply chain challenges and be kept curious regarding the next questions. As shown in Figure 3, the two important objectives are combined in this approach. Picking the key challenges as a central theme was not only helpful to combine top-down and bottom-up approaches for the development of the tool, but also supported the actual application of the instrument to meet the necessary balance between asking about facts and problems and informing the user and keeping him curious.

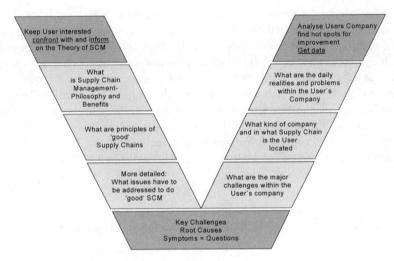

Figure 3: Basic Thoughts on the Structure of the Tool

This idea was implemented into the tool by a catalogue of 90 questions that are grouped around root causes, the root causes around key challenges, and the key challenges around the six basic principles of supply chain management (Figure 4). In the diagnostic sessions, a set of three questions is always related to one root cause and presented simultaneously on one screen. The questions themselves are phrased concisely, but the user additionally gets some text on the same page regarding key actions and common risks related to the root cause, thus explaining the background of the problem that is addressed by the questions in more detail.

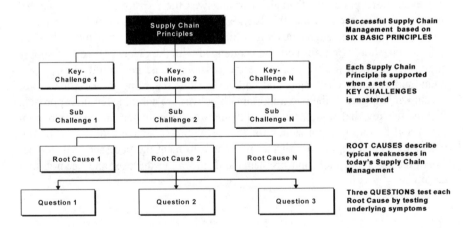

Figure 4: Basic Structure of the Diagnostic Tool

3.2 Basic Structure of a Diagnostic Session

The course of a diagnostics session consists of five basic steps, shown in Figure 5. First step of the diagnostics is the identification of the user. By choosing a name, the user may save his proceedings, with the option to interrupt and resume a diagnostic session later. Also, different users from the same company might run different sessions and compare individual results. In the identification procedure, the user is also encouraged to select his/her supply chain industry and supply chain stage and to provide some more data e.g. size and revenue of the specific company. In non-anonymous sessions e.g. run by the consultants, this information may also be entered by the consultants.

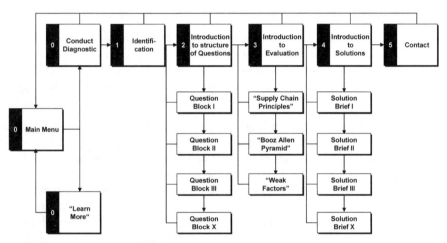

Figure 5: Basic Course of a Diagnostic Session

After identification, the users obtain an overview and introduction regarding the questions and opportunity to answer the single question blocks one after the other or to answer single selected question blocks. The latter might be of specific interest when different users e.g. purchasing, production, sales share the answering task. After answering the questions, the users may proceed to the evaluation. The evaluation of the diagnostics is not the focus of this paper, so only a short outline of the basic functions is given here. There is the opportunity to analyze from three different views. The evaluation of key challenges shows which of these seem mastered by the users' company and which might be at risk. Another view separates into strategic, tactical or operational aspects, and finally, there is the opportunity to check if specific company factors like products, human resources, organization technology or performance monitoring are on track. An introduction to possible solutions and the opportunity to get into contact to the tool providers are the final steps, but not of interest in this paper.

3.3 Using the Data

"The academic's job is to understand how an idiosyncratic individual world comes to be seen as a universal world and how vested interests work to convey this definition of universality." (Weick, 2001: 74). From a more methodological point of view, the tool seems to address the major suggestions for bridging the relevance-rigor gap by supporting not only demanded self-reflection of researchers, but including real reflection from practitioners early on as well (Weick, 1999):

- Not only researchers but also the other stakeholders (Starkey & Madan, 2001) of research, the practitioners, are actively involved in the research process. Thus, by the confrontation of the elaborated theoretical core of supply chain management with the real needs of practice, critical feedback could be generated - not only collected - helping to make this core more robust.
- On the other hand, involvement of practitioners provides direct benefits for this group. The systematic grouping and presentation of important supply chain issues may help practitioners detect gaps and future opportunities and thus enter undeveloped fields beyond the pure reflection of their current typical problems.

Of special interest within the context of this paper is the opportunity to evaluate answers on how different industries and different supply chain stages might provide interesting insights regarding the still-open question on how to differentiate the supply chain for different industries and players. Users directly identify their supply chain industry and stage and provide feedback on their actual hot spots and unsolved problem areas. Later versions of the tool could use this "micro" input to differentiate the challenges step-by-step closer to the needs of different industries or different types of companies. The structural requirements for this are already embedded within the tool.

4 References

Anderson, N., Herriot, P., Hodgkinson, G. (2001): The practitioner-researcher divide in Industrial, Work and Organizational (IWO) psychology: Where are we now, and where do we go from here?, in: Journal of Occupational and Organizational Psychology, 74: 391-411.

Bechtel, C., Jayaram, J. (1997): Supply chain management: A Strategic Perspective, in: The International Journal of Logistics Management, 8(1): 15-34.

Bhattacharya, A., Coleman, J. L., Brace, G. (1996): The Structure conundrum in Supply chain management, in: International Journal of Logistics Management, 7(1): 39-48.

Bowersox, D. (1997): Integrated Supply chain management: A Strategic Imperative, in: Council of Logistics Management (CLM) (ed.): Annual Conference Proceedings, Oakwood: p. 181-189.

Bowersox, D., Closs, D. (1996): Logistical Management - The Integrated Supply Chain Process, McGrawHill, New York.

Brewer, P. C., Speh, T. W. (2000): Using the Balanced Scorecard to Measure Supply Chain Performance, in: Journal of Business Logistics, 21(1): 75-94.

Cavinato, J. L (1991): Identifying interfirm total cost advantages for supply chain competitiveness, in: International Journal of Purchasing and Materials Management, 27(4): 10-15.

Christopher, M. (1998): Logistics and Supply chain management, second edition, Financial Times, Harlow.

Cooper, M. C., Lambert, D. M., Pagh, J. D. (1997): Supply chain management: More than a new name for Logistics, in: The International Journal of Logistics Management 8(1): 1-14.

Croom, S., Romano, P., Giannakis, M. (2000): Supply chain management: An analytical framework for critical literature review, in: European Journal of Purchasing & Supply Management, 6(1): 67-83.

Delfmann, W. (1998): Organisation globaler Versorgungsketten (Organization of global Supply Chains), in: Glaser, Horst (ed.): Organisation im Wandel der Märkte, Gabler, Wiesbaden: 61-89.

Fine, C. (1998): Clockspeed - Winning Industry Control in the Age of Temporary Advantage, Perseus Books, Reading.

Fisher, M. (1997): What is the Right Supply Chain for Your Product, in: Harvard Business Review, 75(2): 105-116.

Giddens, A. (1984): The Constitution of Society, Polity Press, Cambridge.

Heckmann, P., Shorten, D., Engel, H. (2003): Supply chain management at 21 – The Hard Road to Adulthood, Booz Allen Hamilton, New York.

Jones, T. C., Riley, D. W. (1985): Using inventory for competitive advantage through Supply chain management, in: International Journal of Physical Distribution & Logistics Management, 15(5): 16-26.

Klaus P. (1998): Supply chain management, in: Gabler Lexikon Logistik, Gabler, Wiesbaden: p. 434-441.

Kotzab, H. (2000): Zum Wesen von Supply chain management vor dem Hintergrund der betriebswirtschaftlichen Logistikkonzeption – erweiterte Überlegungen, (To the character of Supply chain management on the background of the business logistics conception – extended thoughts) in: Wildemann, H. (ed.): Supply chain management, TCW Verlag, München: p. 21-47.

Lee, H. L. (2002): Aligning Supply Chain Strategies with Product Uncertainties, in: California Management Review, 44(3): 105-119.

Nicolai, A. T. (2004): Der "trade-off" zwischen "rigour" und "relevance" und seine Konsequenzen für die Managementwissenschaften (The tradeoff between rigour and relevance and the consequences on management science), in Zeitschrift für Betriebswirtschaft 74(2): 99-118.

Oliver, R. K., Webber, M. D. (1982): Supply chain management: logistics catches up with strategy, Reprint in: Christopher, M. (eds.): Logistics – The strategic issues, Chapman & Hall, London: p. 63-75.

Prockl, G. (2001): Supply Chain Management als Gestaltung überbetrieblicher Versorgungsnetzwerke – Eine Verdichtung von Prinzipien zur „Strukturation" und Ansätze zur theoretischen Hinterfragung (Designing of extended Supply Chains – Consolidation of principles for the structuration and approaches for a theoretical re-questioning), Hamburg.

Prockl, G., Reinhold, A., Buss, D. (2004): Supply Chain Diagnostics, in: Logistik Management, 5(4): 27-40.

Robey, D., Markus, M. L. (1998): Beyond Rigor and Relevance: Producing Consumable Research about Information Systems, in: Information Resources Management Journal, 11(1): 7-15.

Sheffi, Y. (2004): Demand Variability and Supply Chain Flexibility, in: Prockl G., Bauer, A., Pflaum, A. (ed).: Entwicklungspfade und Meilensteine moderner Logistik – Skizzen einer Roadmap (Developmentpaths and milestones of modern logistics – drafts of a roadmap), Gabler, Wiesbaden: p. 85-117.

Starkey, K., Madan, P. (2001): Bridging the Relevance Gap: Aligning Stakeholders in the Future of Management Research, in: British Journal of Management 12(Special Issue): p. 3-26.

Stevens, G. C. (1989): Integrating the Supply Chain, in: International Journal of Physical Distribution and Logistics Management, 19(8): 3-8.

Towill, D. R. (1996): Time compression and supply chain management – A guided tour, in: Logistics Information Management, 9(6): 41-53.

Weick, K. E. (1999): Theory Construction as Disciplined Reflexivity: Tradeoffs in the 90s, in: Academy of Management Review 24(4): 797-806.

Weick, K. E. (2001): Gapping the Relevance Bridge: Fashion Meet Fundamentals in Management Research, in: British Journal of Management, 12(Special Issue): 71-75.

A Logistics and Supply Chain Approach to Seaport Efficiency – An Inquiry Based on Action Research Methodology

Khalid Bichou, Richard Gray

1	Introduction	414
2	Action Research in Ports and Logistics: Relevance and Applications	415
3	AR Project: Description, Methodology and Analysis	420
4	Conclusion: Criteria for Methodological Rigor and Testing	425
5	References	426

Summary:
Most practical and theoretical approaches to port performance measurement are reducible to three broad categories: physical indicators, factor productivity indicators, and economic and financial indicators. However, an integrative supply chain approach is seldom adopted, although a change process towards supply chain integration is taking place in practice and new appropriate performance measurements are required. Action research enables researchers to participate in this change process, although it requires a close relationship and collaboration between practitioners and researchers. The technique used in the approach described in this paper was to present port managers and other experts with a model of port performance appropriate to the role of ports in a logistics and supply chain context.

Keywords:
Supply Chain Management, Seaports, Action Research, Performance Measurement, Benchmarking

1 Introduction

Increasing recognition of seaports as logistics centers requires them to be conceptualized from a logistics and supply chain management (SCM) perspective. The essence of logistics and SCM is an integrative approach to the interaction of different processes and functions within a firm extended to a network of organizations for the purpose of cost reduction and customer satisfaction (Stank et al., 2001). The contemporary role of ports often extends from providing services to ships and cargo at the traditional sea/land interface, to being a good location for value-added logistics services and standing as a perfect networking site where members of different supply chains can meet and interact. However, despite their logistics and supply chain potentials, a valid curriculum for port logistics and channel management has yet to be developed and successfully applied.

The conceptualization of ports from a logistics and supply chain approach has proven to be constructive on more than one level, including recognizing and integrating the multi-institutional and cross-functional dimensions of ports. This is particularly the case for measuring port efficiency. The logistics approach regularly adopts a cost trade-off analysis between functions, processes and even supply chains (Rushton et al., 2000), and this could be beneficial to port efficiency by directing port operations towards relevant value-added logistics activities. Similarly, supply chain partnership between port members and other market players in international logistics suggests that the issues of performance and competitive benchmarking should be examined at the level of the supply channel rather than at the level of the firm or the industry. There are many techniques for measuring port performance, but despite a plethora of indicators, a problem arises when one tries to apply them to multiple port operations or across a range of ports and terminals. There is no tradition or background of accumulated literature on ports to accommodate an integrated logistics approach, let alone an integrated supply chain approach. Nevertheless, a change process towards such integration is taking place in practice and new performance measurements are required. This study seeks to adopt an approach that incorporates, through an action research (AR) procedure, existing measures of port efficiency, the association of ports with logistics and SCM, and appropriate measures of logistics and supply chain performance. The objective is to show that through conceptualizing ports from a logistics and SCM approach, it is possible to suggest a relevant framework of port performance measurement. Much of the paper will underline the usefulness of AR and its methodological justification in overcoming major impediments against applying valid procedures relevant to supply chain research in general and port logistics and channel management in particular.

2 Action Research in Ports and Logistics: Relevance and Applications

2.1 Basis and Features of Action Research

AR was originally established in the USA, and traces its roots back to the 1940s with the first conscious use of the technique made by Kurt Lewin, a social psychologist who was concerned with applying social science knowledge to solve social problems such as conflict between groups in wartime (Lewin, 1946). Many have followed by applying the approach to other areas, such as in the fields of business manufacturing (Swe & Kleiner, 1998), education (Cohen & Manion, 1980; Howell, 1994), nursing (Smith et al., 2000), and, more recently, management and organizational development (Edmondson, 1996; Ellis & Kiely, 2000).

The basis of AR is the combination between research and intervention with the intent of improving practice and generating relevant theoretical knowledge. The interplay between theory and practice is a key factor of AR methodology (Peters & Robinson, 1984). Another feature of AR is the influence of critical theory, whereby change is the main research subject and the researcher participates in the change process (Checkland & Scholes, 1999). Another advantage of AR over traditional survey approaches is that the latter tend to be past-oriented or 'snapshots' (Näslund, 2002), whereas AR is a forward-looking process with implications beyond the immediate project, hence the importance of analytic generalization in AR. Thus, the method is most suitable for technique development or theory building than for hypothesis testing (Westbrook, 1995).

The validity of AR stems from a spiral process of planning, action, observation, and reflection; this distinguishes it from both the empirical-analytical and interpretative-research approaches (Carr & Kemmis, 1983; Kemmis & Taggart, 1988). This process is often expressed in the literature as a five-step cycle, namely problem identification, planning for intervention, explicit implementation, evaluating the action, and retroactive reflection (Carson et al., 2001).

Whether AR is an approach or a method is still a debatable issue, but the controversy surrounding AR mostly concerns its rather broad label with many varied uses of the terminology, e.g. action research, action science, research action, etc. (Coghlan & Brannick, 2001). Suojanen (2001) identifies four trends in AR: education-oriented focusing on learning improvements; project-oriented directing the research object; research-oriented seeking theory generation; and action-oriented emphasizing the practical application of scientific theories. Gummesson (2000) distinguishes four types of AR for business studies: societal, management, real-time, and retrospective. In marketing, Perry and Gummesson (2004) suggest three forms of AR, namely project action, action learning and case research. However, the interplay of the theoretical system and practical system in AR is extensive enough to allow flexible interpretation, but also provides valid applications for different problem-scenarios. The use of diverse procedures is typical of the critical AR, and thus AR is claimed to be an approach rather than just a method.

2.2 Problematical Issues in Port Logistics and SCM Research

The literature on port efficiency is almost totally quantitative and is known to be extremely vast in scope and nature. But although many analytical tools and instruments exist, a problem arises when one tries to apply them to a range of ports and terminals. Similarly, although extensive literature has addressed theories and practices in logistics and SCM, little has emerged on performance measures, especially in linking operations, design, and strategy within the multi-firm and cross-functional context. A detailed review of the literature on port performance, logistics and SCM measurements is provided by Bichou & Gray (2004).

On the one hand, ports are very dissimilar, and even within a single port, the current or potential activities can be broad in scope and nature, so that the choice of an appropriate tool of analysis is difficult. Organizational dissimilarity constitutes a serious limitation to enquiry, not only concerning what to measure but also how to measure. Furthermore, the concept of efficiency is vague and proves difficult to apply in a typical port organization extending across different types of industries and services. The major obstacle against adopting valid and generalizable-type port performance measurements probably refers back to the complexity of the port business at more than one level, viz:

- Organizational differences: Issues of ownership (public vs. private), social arrangements (labor and manpower), institutional status (landlord/tool models where ports own and develop the infrastructure but lease it to the private sector, vs. service models where the role of ports extends from a simple landlord owner to a commercial operator for cargo-handling and intermodal activities), etc.
- Operational differences: Types of cargo handled, serviced ships, operated terminals, etc.
- Physical and spatial differences: Location, access, connectivity, capacity, etc.
- Legal and regulatory differences: Trade and transport policy, administrative procedures, safety and security regulations, environment, etc.

On the other hand, inquiries involving logistics and SCM are often confronted with the obstacles of channel design and identification. The problem with SCM is that it is usually perceived at the level of the firm, which raises the question of: Whose perspective or interests are to be considered? SCM advocates close cooperation for the benefit of all supply chain partners, but this is not always evident in typical supply chain research. In a similar vein, access to the diverse, sometimes conflicting, supply chain members is not always guaranteed, and even when it takes place, there is little confidence about the accuracy and reliability of the information /data collected, and much less on their interpretation and analysis.

Another common feature in logistics and port research is the influence of the positivist paradigm, with survey, simulation, and modeling quantitative techniques being the most predominant methods. Various studies have confirmed this trend and stressed the lack of publications in logistics that are based on case study and AR methodologies (Mentzer & Kahn, 1995; Ellram, 1996). Many criticize logistics researchers for conducting research within a narrow methodological domain and for being 'one-dimensional' (Monieson, 1981; Hopper & Powell 1985). However, the main features of logistics and SCM are the interdisciplinary, multi-functional, and cross-institutional dimensions. Empirical quantitative research is not always relevant to logistics and supply chain problems (Näslund, 2002), nor to multi-firm seaport aggregate performance. The main criticism stems from the difficulty in understanding and interpreting the results provided by quantitative techniques (Van Maanen, 1982), and that these latter are mostly past oriented or 'snapshots.' This explains why in many research fields, including logistics and SCM, academia is usually following rather than leading the commercial world (Cooper et al., 1997). It also justifies the alleged gap between theory and practice in SCM, with little interest from practitioners in projects applying traditional quantitative techniques. This is more noticeable in research associated with port and supply chain performance, where most measurement techniques originate from innovations in the work place, rather than through academic research.

It seems therefore that there is a methodological difficulty in conducting valid and reliable research in port efficiency and in supply chain performance. In particular, the association of ports, SCM and performance measurement is likely to imply some research limitation, with the major difficulties being identified herein:

- Multi-firm dimensions: Identifying and accessing the wide range of members working in and across port supply chains (shippers, ocean carriers, port operators, logistics providers, freight forwarders, public authorities, etc.).

- Multi-functional dimensions: Recognizing and minimizing differences of operational/strategic viewpoints in a traditional port setting often typified by institutional fragmentation and conflict over channel control and management.

- Multi-disciplinary dimensions: Understanding the interdisciplinary scopes of port research and SCM, the first extending across manufacturing, trade and service industries, while the second intersects wide subjects ranging, inter alia, from engineering and operational research to marketing and quality management.

AR combines practical needs for developing performance and the collective intentional learning involved in it, and thus could be used at the same time for both practical development and scientific studies. It also adopts a systems thinking approach, hence allowing a neutral and objective perspective to boundary-spanning and dynamic problem-situations. This could be particularly beneficial to logistics and supply chain research where the interaction between the practical and theoretical worlds is not always obvious, just like the synchronization between multi-institutional and cross-functional interactions along the supply chain. There is much evidence for this point of view in the context of port efficiency, as well as in research associating ports with logistics and supply chain performance.

2.3 Action Research and its Relevance to Port Logistics and Supply Chain Performance

Conventional applied research in ports and shipping usually focuses on pure theoretical analysis, with little or no involvement of the industry. Most traditional projects on operational management and policy in shipping have not employed AR methods, and have instead insisted on stand-alone modeling, survey and interview-type research without engaging practitioners in the process of inquiry and analysis (NRC, 1983; Walton & Gaffney, 1991). It is not surprising to witness that the findings of such research were usually ignored by the industry and have, more dramatically, resulted in a certain form of distance and polarization of various industry groups (ocean carriers, ports, intermediaries and international logistics providers, etc.) from the research and the academic world. However, it could be convincingly argued that the shipping and port industry offers one of the best cases for AR and participation. Aspects of cultural exchange, external diffusion and practical innovation are key features of the maritime business, hence creating a real potential for reciprocal flows between theory and practice. Such awareness has been taking place in the last two decades or so by shifting from pure applied research projects to promoting participatory AR studies, such as manning innovation, organizational change, and strategic port planning (Roggema & Smith, 1981; UNCTAD, 1995).

In a similar vein, research on port performance and benchmarking needs a different approach that complements, if not replaces, the conventional quantitative methods biased towards institutional fragmentation, external disintegration, and pure theoretical knowledge. The latter limitation also applies to research on logistics and supply chain performance, usually lacking valid practical evidence and industry recognition. AR is an alternative analytical method capable of responding to both theoretical and practical interests of researchers and practitioners. Näslund (2002) considers that AR could contribute to developing research within an applied field such as logistics, and can also help practitioners in solving real world problems. Consequently, action researchers strive to advance both science and practice (Foote, 1991). Furthermore, the main criteria of methodological rigor, namely internal validity, external validity, and reliability can also be satisfied by using AR methodology (Gill & Johnson, 1991).

Yasin's (2002) findings from an extensive literature review indicate that the main focus in benchmarking is on practical knowledge for practitioners; either by learning from others' outstanding performances, or through creating them with others. Thus the basic aim of benchmarking and performance measurement seems to be similar to that of AR. The external dimension is yet another parallel between AR and benchmarking analysis. On the one hand, the interplay between internal and external dimensions is embedded in the basis of AR methodology. On the other hand, benchmarking seeks to assess performances in relation of what is achieved in the real external world, rather than referring to internal and ideal (theoretical) performances such as in frontier analysis and optimum efficiency. Another similarity between the two methods relates to the aspects of critical reflection, with most studies in the field evidencing the close intersection between the AR cyclical-process of evaluation and learning, and the benchmarking stages of continuous learning and improvement (Zairi & Whymark, 2000a, b; Kyrö, 2004). Furthermore, the particularity of AR, being a future-oriented approach, would prove helpful in overcoming the major impediment of conventional past-oriented research methods. In the context of performance measurement, this could be beneficial in directing the research approach and methodology towards the study of future performances rather than investigating historical ratio measures.

Another strong reason for applying AR to logistics and supply chain problems is the predominance of the systems approach in both contexts. AR is intimately connected to systems thinking where researchers should look primarily for patterns of behavior and interrelationships rather than just cause-and-effect relationships as found in positivism (Checkland, 1993). Senge (1990) states that system thinking can help organizations learn to better understand interdependency and change, and thereby deal more effectively with the forces that shape the consequences of our actions. Modern logistics is based on holistic and systemic thinking and uses multi-disciplinary and cross-functional approaches. SCM adopts a systems approach to business by viewing the channel as a single entity rather than a set of fragmented parts or functions. The aim is the integration and convergence of intra-firm and inter-firm operational and strategic capabilities along the supply chain (Holmberg, 2000). The systems approach, in opposition to the managerial approach, allows a neutral and objective perception of a problem's definition and investigation, and there is strong evidence that this approach is also relevant to operational problems in international shipping and logistics (Taylor, 1976; Robinson, 1976; Evans & Marlow, 1990). The systems approach would prove particularly helpful in the context of port operations and management through overcoming the obstacles of channels' identification and conflicting attitudes among the myriad of actors and operators in the port business.

3 AR Project: Description, Methodology and Analysis

In the previous sections, we stressed the need for a participatory framework of research and action in the context of port efficiency, logistics, and SCM. The methodology adopted for this study works within the AR paradigm, and as explained above, there is much evidence of the relevance of AR methodology in the contexts of port logistics and supply chain performance. AR is undertaken by using an appropriate intervention technique analogous to experimentation (Argyris, 1993) and requires a close relationship between practitioners and researchers, made possible in the research described in this paper when one of the authors undertook a short-term appointment with the World Bank. In this context, the researcher not only acted as a facilitator or coordinator, but his role was extended to monitoring the entire project. The ultimate aim of the project was to develop a valid framework for port performance measurement capable of overcoming cross-functional and multi-institutional complexities in ports, and in particular the conflicting operational standpoints in a typical port supply chain configuration. The role and status of the World Bank ensured a neutral perspective regarding problem identification, research, and action. On the other hand, the involvement of a wide range of interest groups, in addition to the primary research subject of ports, has proven to be particularly helpful in ensuring analytical generalization and knowledge creation. Although the overall research was much wider, it is not fully reported in this paper, which restricts discussion to the AR element of the research. The results of the full study can be found in Bichou & Gray (2004). The following sections show how AR has been planned and implemented in the context of the research-subject (ports) and in relation with other selected panels and focus groups.

3.1 Research Design and Procedure

AR is a research strategy, i.e. a methodology, and should not be confused with the methods of data collection and analysis, nor with subsequent stages of testing and measurements. The technique used in this study is to present port managers and a panel of experts and academicians with an interim model of port performance for examination and assessment by them (see Figure 2), leading to an improved model.

The initial model is the result of a diagnostic work undertaken through an online questionnaire designed exclusively for port managers in order to investigate both their perception of logistics concepts and the methods used by them to measure port performance and efficiency. In some cases, surveys were conducted through face-to-face interviews or administered over the telephone. Figure 1 depicts the different stages of the AR methodology adopted in this study, and shows how a

A Logistics and Supply Chain Approach to Seaport Efficiency   421

successful AR project can generate continuous learning and expert knowledge, and ultimately lead to analytical generalization and theory building.

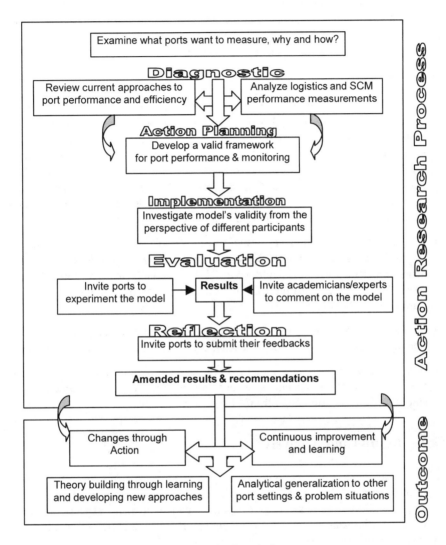

Figure 1: Stages of Research and Framework of Analysis

In a typical AR process, the diagnostic work corresponds to the stage of problems identification, while the development of the model and its submission to ports for experimentation relates respectively to the phases of action planning and action taking (or implementation). At this stage, the research process is expanded to include other interests, clustered into two main focus groups, so as to comment on the relevance and feasibility of the model. The resulting improved model was resubmitted exclusively to port managers (25 ports) in terms of a second AR round-cycle of implementation, evaluation and reflection, leading to a final model. Both the initial and improved models are embedded within an action/improvement inter-related cycle evolving around implementation, evaluation, and reflection. The latter stages are vital for learning in an AR process.

Time and budget constraints have shaped the scope and nature of the research, including the number of AR cycles and the size of port participants. The latter, together with the joint partnership between the researcher and the World Bank, raise concerns about the ethical perspective of the approach, but the involvement of a wide range of interest groups prevails over these difficulties. Indeed, panels were carefully selected to reflect the wide variety of organizational, operational and managerial features of world ports, but also to allow collaborative interaction between the theoretical world and the profession. For the purpose of data collection, analysis, and results, port participants are clustered in this paper in terms of a group panel although they constitute the main subject of inquiry:

- Ports Panel (1): 45 employees drawn from a sample of 60 ports worldwide, of which 35 ports have completed projects financed by the World Bank. Continents represented by the sample were: for World Bank financed ports (Africa, Asia, Central and Latin America, Europe); for other participant ports (Australia, Europe, Asia, North America).
- International Institutions Panel (2): 14 employees of international institutions (mainly World Bank) drawn from a sample of 17 originating from 11 countries.
- Academics and Consultants Panel (3): 14 academics and other experts: drawn from a sample of 17 academics, 3 consultancy firms, and 3 independent (freelance) consultants originating from 11 countries.

3.2 Results and Analysis

Figure 2 depicts a model applying logistics and SCM concepts to port performance measurement. The model was sent to and discussed with port participants to assess its validity and feasibility. Responses varied in many aspects, although most port participants considered the model valid as a 'first initiative' that looks at port efficiency from the perspective of logistics and SCM.

Almost all port participants have measured efficiency in a way similar to that of performance A in the model. However, about half (53%) mentioned the problems of accountability and process continuity in performance monitoring. Members of the port community disagree on which firm should bear the responsibility and authority to collect data, measure, and assess the overall port performance. Some ports do not know where their logistics process (or activity sequencing) starts and particularly where it ends, simply because many activities are at the interface between the port area and the outside world (e.g. industrial parks). For further aspects of performance monitoring, continuous improvement of internal processes through total cost and trade-off analyses appealed to most ports, and in particular the use of a TCA/ABC combination to assess port's aggregate efficiency.

With respect to channel organization (stages 6 to 11 in figure 1), 87% of participants admit difficulty in undertaking a channel orientation, and that in most cases they do not participate in the design and management of channels. Some ports attribute these limitations to the lack of reliable data and information, while others relate this to the complexity of channels and the confusion that surrounds their categorization. Nevertheless, nearly all ports appreciated the concept of channel integration and close collaboration with other members.

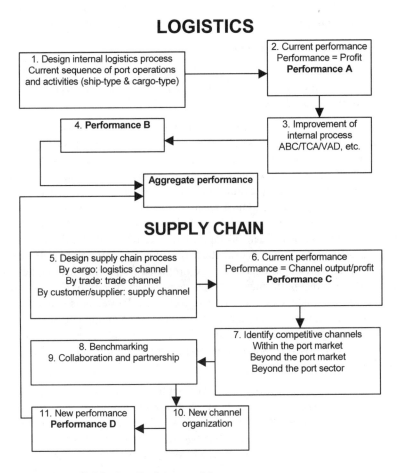

Figure 2: Interim Model for Port Performance Measurement

Performance measurement through SCM was even more difficult to understand and apply. Most participants could not compute quantitatively the overall channel output (performances C and D), nor were they able to use and apply some of the proposed techniques of analysis such as process benchmarking. In their comments on the measurement of supply chain performance, 19 ports (42%) approved the method, 9 (20%) considered it impossible or too difficult to implement, and 17 ports (38%) remained undecided about the validity and practicability of the proposed techniques. Such a high proportion of undecided responses suggests that many ports are unfamiliar with the concepts of SCM.

It appears therefore that most ports are already aware of their logistics and supply chain potential, but they lack proper understanding of the concepts and techniques to apply them in a performance measurement context. A second AR round with 25 ports using an improved model confirmed these results. The final model, the outcome of the AR study, and its contribution to theoretical generation are reported in both Bichou & Gary (2004) and a World Bank published report (2003).

- **Responses from other panels**

The association of panels 2 and 3 aimed originally to involve the outside world and complement the initial model's diagnostic work undertaken during the first AR cycle of planning and action.

For panel 2, all respondents supported the application of a logistics and supply chain approach to port efficiency. They particularly valued the concept of activity sequencing or internal process mapping (stages 1 to 4), and consider it innovative in the context of port operational efficiency. Similarly, the proposal to design, manage and improve supply chain processes in which ports are active members (stages 5 to 11) appealed to almost all participants (93%) with only one respondent questioning the relevance of the whole approach. This reflects a frequent criticism of conventional financial metrics where, for example, the original cost and profit estimates of most World Bank port projects carried out between 1950 and 1990 were lower than expected. The proposed framework has the advantage of computing the real performance by sequencing port operations (Performance A) and continuously improving them (Performance B). Participants suggest training assistance and guidance, part of a continuous process of improvement and learning prior to applying the performance model, but stress the need to 'quantify' and generalize the proposed techniques beyond container-related activities to all types of ships and cargo movement.

For panel 3, the response rate was lower, with more than half of the responses commenting on aspects other than those primarily requested, e.g. the model's design and presentation. Respondents largely (83%) supported the contents and objectives of the proposed model, but two key conditions prior to applying or generalizing the proposed model emerged from this group. On the one hand, there was a requirement to quantify the proposed techniques of performance measurement. In order to assess performances C and D, it is essential to provide the port manager with quantifiable and visible ratios and formulae capable of designing, correlating and computing the contribution of both individual and aggregate channel output. On the other hand, the different concepts and procedures introduced in the proposed model should be both further detailed and simplified. Port managers are not very familiar with logistics and SCM concepts, nor are they willing to apply them without a clear and detailed description.

The feedbacks from participants in panels 2 & 3 have greatly helped in improving the initial model, particularly with regard to the prerequisites of quantifying and simplifying the proposed techniques and procedures prior to implementation and further generalization. Participants from these groups also called for critical reflection and continuous improvement through participatory research and action.

4 Conclusion: Criteria for Methodological Rigor and Testing

Empirical research in logistics and SCM is primarily confronted with the problems of context definition, interdisciplinary scope, and lack of accessibility. This is particularly the case with port research, often typified by diverging attitudes and conflicting operational viewpoints. The inquiry subject of this paper aims at conceptualizing the port system from the perspective of logistics and SCM, and suggesting a valid framework of performance measurements capable of reflecting the logistics scope of port operations and management. It describes a successful implementation of the AR methodology on the subject of ports, especially with regard to participatory research and theory generation, proven by the high response rate and the adoption by the project's participants of many of the research results and findings (Bichou & Gray 2004; World Bank, 2003).

However, the application of AR in a port supply chain context raises a number of questions related to the validity and reliability of the methodology. Among the most debatable issues in AR are the degree of involvement of the researcher as an observer and active participant, and the risk of an impartial and biased role. Although many authors tried to differentiate the AR researcher's role from the consultant's task, there is no clear-cut differentiation between the two roles, especially in ports and logistics research. The logic of theory generation and testing is equally important in an AR context, given that such aspects are not always achieved in a single AR study. Another important issue is the applicability and generalization of theories and concepts generated from a particular AR sample to other contexts and in serving as valid benchmarks for other research problems. The basis of AR is the combination between theory and practice as well as the benefit of generalization, but this advantage is not always obvious in a world-port perspective where operational and managerial differences may obstruct any attempt to export a particular AR-led port concept to other port situations. The association of logistics and SCM with port performance creates a unique set of priorities (channel design and management, overall performance measurement, collaborative arrangements vs. channel conflict and fragmentation, etc.) that distinguishes it from previous traditional AR contexts such as those found in manufacturing, nursing, and education; and thus relevant AR methods and procedures need to be reconsidered. There is no established tradition of using and testing the AR methodology in supply chain research, let alone in the fields associating ports with SCM. By adopting a structured approach centered on AR methodology and involving a wide range of interest groups, the authors tried to ensure a valid and reliable inquiry given a number of research constraints. The inquiry subject of this paper stands as a first initiative, and further investigations and testing of the AR methodology in the context of port logistics and SCM are required.

5 References

Argyris, C. (1993): Knowledge for Action: Changing the Status Quo, San Francisco: Jossey-Bass.

Bichou, K., Gray, R. (2004): A Logistics and Supply Chain Management Approach to Port Performance Measurement, in: Maritime Policy and Management, 31(1): 47-67.

Carr, W., Kemmis, S. (1983): Becoming Critical: Education, Knowledge and Action Research, Deakin University Press, New York.

Carson, D., Gilmore, A., Gronhaug, K., Perry, C. (2001): Qualitative Research in Marketing, Sage Publications, London.

Checkland, P. (1993): Systems Thinking, Systems Practice, John Wiley & Sons, New York.

Checkland, P., Scholes, J. (1999): Soft Systems Methodology in Action, Wiley, London.

Coghlan, D., Brannick, T. (2001): Doing Action Research in Your Own Organization, Sage Publications, London.

Cohen, L., Manion, L. (1980): Research Methods in Education, Croom Helm, London

Cooper, M., Lambert, D., Pagh, J. (1997): Supply Chain Management: More than a New Name for Logistics, in: The International Journal of Logistics Management, 8(1): 1-14.

Edmondson, A. (1996): Three Faces of Eden: the Persistence of Competing Theories and Multiple Diagnoses in Organizational Intervention Research, in: Human Relations, 49(5): 571-95.

Ellis, J., Kiely, J. (2000): Action Inquiry Strategies: Taking Stock and Moving Forward, in: Journal of Applied Management Studies, 9(1): 83-94.

Ellram, L. (1996): The Use of the Case Study Method in Logistics Research, in: Journal of Business Logistics, 17(8): 93-138.

Evans, J., Marlow, P. B. (1990): Quantitative Methods in Maritime Economics, Fairplay, London.

Foote, W. (1991): Participatory Action Research, London: Sage Publications.

Gill, J., Johnson, P. (eds.) (1991): Research Methods for Managers, Paul Chapman Publishing, London.

Gummesson, E. (2000): Qualitative Methods in Management Research, Sage, Thousand Oaks.

Holmberg, S. (2000): A Systems Perspective on Supply Chain Measurements, in: International Journal of Physical Distribution and Logistics Management, 30(10): 47-68.

Hopper, T., Powell, A. (1985): Making Sense of Research into the Organizational & Social Aspects of Management Accounting: A Review of its Underlying Assumptions, in: Journal of Management Studies, 25(5): 429-65.

Howell, F. (1994): Action Learning and AR in Management Education and Development: a Case Study, in: The Learning Organization, 1(2): 15-22.

Kemmis, S., Taggart, M.R. (1988): The Action Research Planner, Deakin University, Victoria.

Kyrö, P. (2004): Benchmarking as an Action Research Process, in: Benchmarking: An International Journal, 11: 52-73.

Lewin, K. (1946): Action Research and Minority Problems, in: Journal of Social Issues, 2(4): 34-46.

Mentzer, J. T, Kahn, K. (1995): A Framework of Logistics Research, in: Journal of Business Logistics, 6(1): 231-250.

Monieson, D. (1981): What Constitutes Usable Knowledge in Macro-Marketing? in: Journal of Macro-marketing, 1, Spring: 14-22.

Näslund, D. (2002): Logistics Needs Qualitative Research – Especially Action Research, in: International Journal of Physical Distribution & Logistics Management, 32(5): 321-338.

National Research Council -NRC- (1983): Requirements for a Ship Operations Program, National Academy Press: Washington D.C.

Perry, C., Gummesson, E. (2004): Commentary: Action research in marketing, in: European Journal of Marketing, 34(3/4): 310-320.

Peters, M., Robinson, V. (1984): The Origin and Status of AR, in: Journal of Behavioral Science, (20)2: 113-24.

Robinson, R. (1976): Modeling the Port as an Operational System: a Perspective for Research, in: Economic Geography, 52(1): 71-86.

Roggema, J., Smith, M. H. (1981): On the Process of Organizational Change in Shipping, in: Proceedings of Ergo-sea 81, Nautical Institute, London.

Rushton, A., Oxley, J., Croucher, P. (2000): The Handbook of Logistics and Distribution Management, London: the Institute of Logistics and Transport, Kogan Page, London.

Senge, P. (1990): The Fifth Discipline- The Art and Practice of the Learning Organization, Currency Doubleday, London.

Smith, P., Masterson, A., Basford, L., Boddy, G., Costello, S., Marvell, G., Redding, M., Wallis, B. (2000): AR: a Suitable Method for Promoting Change in Nurse Education, in: Nurse Education Today, 20(7): 563-70.

Stank, T. P., Keller, S. B., Closs, D. J. (2001): Performance Benefits of Supply Chain Logistical Integration, in: Transportation Journal, 41(2/3): 32-46.

Suojanen, U. (2001): Action research, also available at: www.metodix.com, 31.01.2005.

Swe, V., Kleiner, B. (1998): Managing and Changing Mistrustful Cultures, in: Industrial and Commercial Training, 30(2): 66-70.

Taylor, A. (1976): System Dynamic in Shipping, in: Operational Research Quarterly, 27: 41-45.

United Nations Conference on Trade and Development -UNCTAD- (1995): Strategic Port Pricing, UNCTAD, Geneva.

Van Maanen, J. (1982): Introduction in Varieties of Qualitative Research, Sage Publications, London.

Walton, R. E., Gaffney, M. E. (1991): Research, Action, and Participation: The Merchant Shipping Case, in: Whyte, W. F. (ed.): Participatory Action Research, London: Sage Publications, p. 99-126.

Westbrook, R. (1995): Action Research: New Paradigm for Research in Production and Operations, in: International Journal of Operations & Production Management, 15(12): 6-20.

The World Bank (2003), Logistics Port Performance: Guidelines and Recommendations, available at http://www.worldbank.org/transport.

Yasin, M. M. (2002): The Theory and Practice of Benchmarking: Then and Now, in: Benchmarking: An International Journal, 9(3): 217-243.

Zairi, M., Whymark, J. (2000a): The Transfer of Best Practices: How to Build a Culture of Benchmarking and Continuous Learning -Part 1, in: Benchmarking: An International Journal, (1): 62-78.

Zairi, M., Whymark, J. (2000b): The Transfer of Best Practices: How to Build a Culture of Benchmarking and Continuous Learning -Part 2, in: Benchmarking: An International Journal, 7(2): 146-167.

Part 5
Modelling Supply Chains

Supply Chain Management Research Methodology Using Quantitative Models Based on Empirical Data

Gerald Reiner

1	Introduction	432
2	Supply Chain Management Research	432
3	Developments in Quantitative Modeling	434
4	Discrete Event Simulation Modeling in Quantitative Research	437
5	Aspects of Mixed Methods Research	440
6	How to Conduct and Document Research with Quantitative Models Based on Empirical Data	441
7	Conclusion	442
8	References	443

Summary:
Various papers have been published that define requirements for theory development in operations management or try to connect the knowledge generated along the different research lines. Here, we define the scope of supply chain management research and its relationship with operations management research. We show how quantitative model-driven research - especially under consideration of empirical data and simulation models - can be conducted in supply chain management research because this research type holds great potential for advancing theory. Furthermore, we illustrate our ideas via some selected research examples.

Keywords:
Supply Chain Management, Quantitative Models, Empirical Data, Simulation Models

1 Introduction

One of the main difficulties in research methodology in the field of supply chain management research is that empirical theory building quantitative empirical research is still in its infancy. Therefore, opinions existing on what is "good" quantitative empirical research differ. In particular, the present paper will provide some ideas and concepts to overcome this problem and will describe how empirical quantitative model-driven research can be conducted as this type of research offers great opportunity for further advancing supply chain management theory.

First, in Section 2 the scope of supply chain management research and its relationship with operations management research will be defined. In Section 3, this paper will give an overview of quantitative model-driven research methodologies in supply chain management. In general, quantitative model-based research can be subdivided into empirical and axiomatic research as well as into descriptive and normative research. In particular, some reference papers of each research type will be mentioned.

Furthermore, the importance of discrete-event simulation models (Section 4) and aspects of mixed model research (Section 5) will be discussed. Section 6 will describe how to conduct "good" empirical quantitative model-driven research. Finally, Section 7 will summarize major findings and further ideas.

2 Supply Chain Management Research

In recent years, supply chain management was widely discussed in the management and scientific literature. However, it is not clear whether supply chain management itself can be established as a management concept with a long-term impact on theory and practice. Müller et al. (2003) summarized three supply chain management criteria that are used in literature, i.e.:

- Supply chain processes have to fulfill customer requirements.
- The focus of supply chain management is on the management of the flow and transformation of goods, the flow of information and that of funds from the raw material stage (extraction) to the end user (Handfield, 2002).
- Supply chain processes are company-spanning.

The following presentation describes our supply chain management research point of view. We think that this viewpoint fits very well with empirical quantitative model-driven research which is the core topic of this paper.

The following presentation describes our supply chain management research point of view. We think that this viewpoint fits very well with empirical quantitative model-driven research which is the core topic of this paper.

The main objective of problem-solving methods in supply chain management is to reduce uncertainties. Sources of uncertainty are, e.g., the forecast horizon (i.e., uncertainty that is related to forecasting over a long period of time), input data (i.e., biases and errors of input data), administrative and decision processes, and inherent uncertainties (Van der Vorst et al., 1998). In the context of supply chain management, improvements to the communication and information exchange between the supply chain partners occupy a key position. Various management concepts such as, for example, Vendor-Managed Inventory (VMI), Continuous Replenishment Program (CRP), and Collaborative Planning, Forecasting, and Replenishment (CPFR) take this circumstance into account. These methods differ in the visibility of the whole supply chain (Barratt & Oliveira, 2000). The dilemma is that centralized planning is not always possible or suitable and that, thus, the decentralized coordination of supply chains leads to difficulties. Topical research studies compare the benefits of information sharing with cycle time reduction. The results obtained show that in some supply chain settings, e.g., the reduction in cycle time can have a greater impact on supply chain performance than information sharing (Cachon & Fisher, 2000). From operations management it is known that the cycle time of a process is composed of a capacity term, a utilization term and a variability term (Hopp & Spearman, 1996). The cycle time variability is due to the variability of the process times as well as to the flow variability. From the managerial point of view, this variability is of major importance, being the main factor that influences the parametrisation of a process, e.g., what right utilization is so as to satisfy customer requirements. In principle, there is a set of levers to attack variability, i.e.:

- Reduce demand variability, e.g., through improved forecasting, everyday low-price strategy (no price volatility), and incentives to affect arrival patterns;
- reduce delivery cycle time, e.g., increased safety capacity (scale and speed);
- reduce variability in delivery cycle time, e.g., standardized operating procedures, better training, and synchronized flows;
- reduce supply variability, e.g., reliable suppliers, better forecasts, and reservation.

In general, one can reduce uncertainty by information sharing, lead time reduction, etc., but it is not possible to avoid uncertainty. In this respect, an important management lever is inventory management. On the one hand, different types of inventory are necessary to buffer against demand volatility, operational and supply uncertainties but, on the other hand, inventory is sometimes the result of inefficient management of the supply chain processes. Therefore, inventory management is a focal point of managing supply chain processes.

Traditionally, in the course of the management of supply chain processes, inventory management is challenging because it directly impacts both cost and service. Uncertain demand and uncertain supply and/or production lead times make it necessary to hold inventory at certain positions in the supply chain to provide adequate service to the customers. As a consequence, increasing supply chain process inventories will increase customer service and revenue, but it comes at a higher cost. Therefore, the management of supply chain processes has to resolve this trade-off by identifying possibilities to decrease inventories whilst simultaneously improving customer service. A well-known management reactive lever in this respect is risk pooling by different types of centralization or standardization, e.g. central warehouses, product commonalities, postponement, and modularization strategies. In this way and by combination of these concepts, it is usually possible to reduce inventory costs to a large extent.

The core of supply chain management research are the management of company-spanning processes that offer additional aspects for process improvement. Furthermore, customer requirement and customer satisfaction play a key role in this context. Traditionally, the concept of customer focus (orientation) has been heavily researched from a marketing perspective, but it has not yet received the necessary attention from the operations and supply chain management fields. The problem is that the emphasis of existing research in marketing has been on the identification and measurement of customer requirements and satisfaction, having virtually left untouched the connection to processes. In the context of supply chain management, this is not sufficient. It is necessary to extend the customer focus to company-spanning processes (supply chain processes), too. The optimization of the flows of goods, information and funds is not limited to one's own organization but concerns each firm involved in fulfilling a customer order.

3 Developments in Quantitative Modeling

Here, an overview of developments in quantitative modeling will be given that is primarily based on an article of Bertrand & Fransoo (2002). In the beginning, quantitative modeling in operational research was very much oriented towards solving real-life problems in operations management and not towards developing scientific knowledge. In the 1960s, a strong academic research line appeared that worked on more idealized problems. This research actively built scientific knowledge in operations management. However, in the last three decades, much of this knowledge has lost its empirical foundations. Recently, the need to develop explanatory and predictive theory has come to the forefront.

Quantitative model-driven research can be divided into two different classes. The first class is primarily driven by the idealized model itself and is called the axiomatic research approach. This approach deals with the strict process of theorems and logical proofs (e.g., mathematical models) (Meredith et al., 1989). In this context, axiomatic quantitative research using simulation is an interesting aspect as it captures empirical data (no analytical solutions are possible) and thereby gains scientific relevance. Furthermore, simulation models are a linking bin to the second class of quantitative model-based research.

The second class of model-driven research is determined by empirical findings and measurement. Here, the primary task of the researcher is to make sure that there is a model fit between observation and action in reality. The model is more or less not idealized. Betrand & Fransoo (2002) pointed out that the methodology of quantitative model-driven empirical research offers a great opportunity for further advancing theory. Quantitative empirical research is still in its infancy. Thus, different opinions exist about what is good quantitative empirical research as compared to quantitative axiomatic research. In particular, quantitative model-based empirical studies generate models of causal relationships between control variables and performance variables. This logical positivist/empiricist approach isolates the phenomenon from the context for logical analysis. These models are then analyzed or tested.

The research type used can be descriptive or normative. Descriptive empirical research is interested in creating a model that describes the causal relationships that may exist in reality and leads to improved understanding of the process mechanics, e.g., systems dynamics research (Forrester, 1961), and clockspeed in industrial systems (Fine, 1998). In this sense, simulation is more than a faction of axiomatic quantitative research and can be used in the second class of model-based research, too.

A further type is the normative empirical quantitative research that is interested in developing policies, strategies and actions so as to improve the current situation. There is a wide spectrum of literature about the validation and verification of models. The problem is that so far the verification procedure is not very strong. It is very hard to assess which changes in performance are due to the specific improvement tested and which are due to other changes. However, this form of research is the most complete one (see Bertrand & Fransoo, 2002), and the research cycle is conducted in its entirety (Mitroff et al., 1974):

- Conceptualization,
- Modeling,
- Model solving,
- Implementation.

In many cases, this research is based on research work published earlier that belongs to the axiomatic quantitative research type and where the scientific knowledge for the modeling and model solving parts have already been developed.

Furthermore, operations management and supply chain management research faces the problem that a well-defined methodological framework for identifying and measuring the relevant characteristics of real processes (not idealized) is missing. No objective, situation-independent and generally accepted procedure exists. Of course, each research work deals with this problem somehow. But this is always done in a subjective, situation-dependent way that often is not explicitly reported. As a consequence, it is difficult to judge its scientific value for advancing theory (Bertrand & Fransoo, 2002).

In the context of quantitative model-driven empirical research, measurement occupies an important position. A problem is that in the field of supply chain management, primarily measures are used that more or less come from operations management. Consequently, these measures are usually focused on one company only and do not take into account the company-spanning aspects. Therefore, supply chain management measures have to be used that fulfill this requirement, e.g., the bullwhip effect (see Reiner, 2004).

3.1 Examples - Descriptive Empirical Quantitative Research

Sterman (1989) reports an experiment (which is known as the "beer game") regarding the management of a simulated inventory distribution system which contains multiple actors, feedback, nonlinearities, and time delays. The interaction of individual decisions with the structure of the simulated firm produces aggregate dynamics that systematically diverge from optimal behavior. In particular, Sterman describes and explains what is called the bullwhip effect (i.e., the first law of supply chain dynamics) which states that, in the supply chain, the magnitude of demand volatility a company faces increases upstream.

Also, Fine (2000) presents a good example of descriptive quantitative research in the field of supply chain management. In the past decade, he studied the dynamics of supply chains of fast-clockspeed industries (e.g., internet services, personal computers) with the main objective to identify robust principles for supply chain design. He identified supply chain design as the core competence of an organization. The clockspeed amplification hypothesis (second law of supply chain dynamics) states that the industry clockspeed a company faces increases the further downstream it is located in the supply chain. To gain this insight, he analyzed different stages of a supply chain. In the personal computer industry, e.g., he studied computer manufacturers, semiconductor manufacturers and semiconductor equipment suppliers. These insights help to understand the unprecedented clockspeed experienced in our economy during the last decade and to peer into the future as well. In particular, they help in identifying and understanding clockspeed accelerators and decelerators.

3.2 Examples - Normative Empirical Quantitative Research

Bertrand & Fransoo (2002) describe different examples of normative empirical quantitative research as regards the field of operations management. Jammernegg & Reiner (2004) give an example of a three-stage supply chain (supplier network). This research deals with the opportunities and challenges for improving the performance of supply chain processes by the coordinated application of inventory management and capacity management. The approach is illustrated by a supplier network in the telecommunications and automotive industries. By using discrete-event process simulation it is demonstrated how the coordinated application of methods from inventory management and capacity management results in improved performance measures of both intraorganizational (costs) and interorganizational (service level) objectives.

4 Discrete Event Simulation Modeling in Quantitative Research

We already discussed above the difficulties of normative empirical quantitative research. In particular, it is very hard to assess which changes in performance are due to the specific improvements provided and which to other changes. Quantitative empirical research has to be designed to test the validity of quantitative theoretical models and problem solutions with respect to real-life data. The model-driven empirical research takes advantage of the high number of published axiomatic quantitative research projects. In particular, the empirical observations are driven by hypotheses that are based on the theories that are developed earlier in primarily axiomatic research projects. Therefore, the usage of simulation models (i.e., discrete-event simulation models) could be an opportunity to support this research type. In particular, in the field of supply chain management simulation there is also a possibility to handle the high complexity of supply chain management research caused by the analysis of multiple stages.

Kleijnen & Smits (2003) mentioned that discrete-event simulation is very important in supply chain management research. Also, they present examples of papers in the area of supply chain management research that use this simulation type.

This kind of simulation represents individual events and incorporates uncertainties. In detail, with discrete event simulation models a system is modeled by defining the events that occur in the system, and describing the logic prevailing at such times. These events are processed in a chronological order and simulated time is advanced from one event to the next. Thus, inventory queuing, manufacturing, business process and supply chain process analysis problems are among the types of situations addressed (Evans & Olson, 2002).

The evaluation of existing process designs and the comparison of alternative configurations require concrete values of different performance measures. In case of existing processes, these values could be obtained from the supply chain partners' performance measurement systems. However, in many instances the desired performance measures are not provided by these systems. In case of alternative process configurations, the values of performance measures are never a priori available as existing data. If not available, these values can be calculated, estimated, or obtained by simulation. The possibility of exact calculations is limited by the complexity of the problem, and estimation usually is too imprecise. Therefore, dynamic, stochastic computer simulation can be utilized to deliver the required input for the evaluation of supply chains. As already mentioned, risk is an essential factor for the supply chain process evaluation. Stochastic simulation can deal with random variables and generates not just mean values of performance measures, but it also gives useful information about their probabilistic distribution. For an overview of the use of simulation in supply chain management, refer to Wyland et al. (2000).

There is a general consensus amongst researchers that the process presented in Figure 1 should be undertaken for the purpose of discrete-event simulation modeling. Law & Kelton (2000) define this typical simulation process. It should be started with step 1 for formulating the problem; then the objectives of the study should be determined and the specific issues to be considered identified. Second, data should be collected (if it exists) based on the objectives of the study. Step 3 is the validation of the data. Subsequently, step 4 is the construction of a computer model based on a conceptual model. Step 5 consists in carrying out the pilot run and step 6 in conducting the verification and validation. Steps 7 through 10 are the design of experiments, production runs for providing performance data on the systems design of interest, output analysis considering statistical techniques for analyzing the output of the production runs, and the implementation of the best alternative. The main defining feature of this methodology is the collection of tangible data to produce tangible results based on a sequential process (Eldabi et al., 2002). Therefore, discrete-event simulation is a typical quantitative research method. However, under specific circumstances, this research method could also be used for qualitative research; refer to Eldabi et al. (2002) for a more detailed discussion.

The following example introduces a procedural model that uses discrete-event simulation modeling and helps to improve customized supply chain design (Reiner & Trcka, 2004). Starting points for the analysis of an existing supply chain are changes in the supply chain strategy or in the corporate strategy of a supply chain partner, or a continuous improvement cycle (e.g., every year). To analyze different improvement alternatives, it is necessary to establish a target system for supply chain evaluation. At this level of the analysis, it is essential that all data of the whole supply chain network be available. The analysis of the supply chain design can be carried out on the basis of historical data (e.g., of the last year). This includes the collection of logical data (e.g., process flow diagrams), point of sale (POS) data, as well as order policies (parameter: reorder point, service level ó safety stock), production strategy (make-to-stock, make-to-order, batch size, service level), and the number of elements in the supply chain. In case one partner in the supply chain has problems in sharing information because of its restricted information-sharing policy, the analysis can be carried out on the basis of historical data.

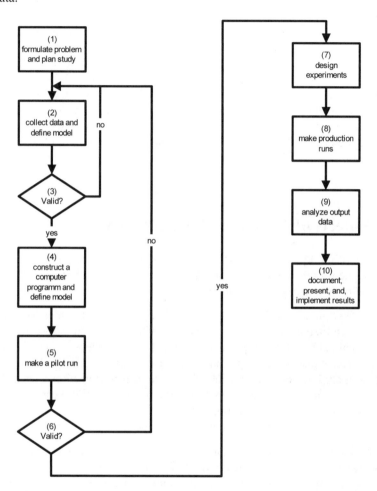

Figure 1: Simulation Study (Law & Kelton, 2000)

The next step consists in building a simulation model of the whole supply chain. It contains a base case process flow model (logical data) and numerical data, stochastic behavior of uncertain indicators as well as disturbing events and information flow. After the validation has been effected, the simulation environment can be used to evaluate different supply chain design alternatives. Thus, the next step is the identification of design alternatives. This includes the design of experiments (DoE), i.e. the range of each decision variable (such as the variation of the number of elements in the supply chain, batch size, reorder points, or target service level) and company-specific processes as well as supply chain process alternatives (e.g., process flow model). After running these experiments using simulation (with sufficient replications), the effects of changes in the setup of a product-specific supply chain design on the overall work in process, fill rate (service level), bullwhip effect measures and times (e.g., cycle time), which are the key supply chain indicators for some industries, can be studied in detail. It is obvious that there are dependencies between these key supply chain indicators and other performance measures (cost, quality, flexibility). The market winners must be selected out of this set of performance measures. The market winner performance measure triggers the evaluation of supply chain design alternatives, which should provide decision support for the reorganization of supply chain processes. If the results obtained are not satisfactory, the design alternatives have to be refined and simulated again.

5 Aspects of Mixed Methods Research

Krajewski (2002) pointed out that academics should get ahead of current practice and lead the way for improved, more effective operations in the future. This thrust will require linking, e.g., quantitative and qualitative research.

The so-called mixed methods research combines theoretical and/or technical aspects of quantitative and qualitative research within a particular research project (Rocco et al., 2003). This research type is widely used in the social and behavioral sciences. But it also offers opportunities in operations and supply chain management research. For example, the field of operations management has been characterized by a dominant positivist epistemology over the last 50 years while other business fields - such as marketing, organizational behavior, and finance -have matured through the scientific theory-building process.

Voss et al. (2002) show that case method research studies can be used for different types of research purposes such as exploration, theory building, theory testing and theory extension/refinement. One good example of mixed methods research is exploration. In many research projects (e.g., quantitative models based on empirical data), exploration based on case method research is needed to develop research ideas and questions. A further example is theory testing. When case study research is employed for theory testing, it is typically used with survey-based research in order to achieve triangulation (this is the use and combination of different methods to study the same phenomenon so as to avoid sharing the same weaknesses).

6 How to Conduct and Document Research with Quantitative Models Based on Empirical Data?

Model-based quantitative empirical supply chain management research projects should contain sections dealing with the following issues (Bertrand & Fransoo, 2002; Kleijnen & Smits, 2003; Eldabi et al., 2002):

- A high-quality research project should start with a "good" research question. Exploration (based on case method research) would be a possibility to support this research step.

- Next, it is necessary to review the relevant (e.g., axiomatic research) literature. The natural outcome of the literature review is to show what is known about the research question.

- The next step is the identification of the basic assumptions concerning the supply chain processes underlying the theoretical models or problems.

- Researches should identify the kind of supply chain process and the type of decision regarding this process, to which the basic assumptions are assumed to apply. Examples of supply chain processes that may be studied are assembly-to-order versus make-to-order (see Jammernegg & Reiner, 2004), buyer's market for the supply chain final product versus seller's market, etc.

- Objective criteria must be developed for deciding whether or not a real-life supply chain process belongs to the class of processes considered and for identifying the decision system in supply chain processes that represents the decision problem under study.

- From the basic assumptions, this step derives hypotheses about process behavior. Process behavior refers to phenomena that can be objectively measured or observed in the supply chain process.

- It is necessary to develop an objective way to do the measurement or to make the observation. Here, the problem is that no formalized construct exists for variables. Furthermore, there is no generally accepted way of measuring if variables exist. Therefore, in quantitative model research based on empirical data, researchers must develop their own way of measuring, and they have to document this carefully. In particular, it is necessary to know how to influence and measure the relevant characteristics of a process. Thus, it is necessary to develop a conceptual model that defines the relevant variables of a system under study, the nature of their relationship, and their measurement.

    In this context, one option is to design a simulation model that explains how the supply chain performance metrics react to environmental and managerial control factors. The type of simulation (e.g., systems dynamics, discrete-event simulation) depends on the kind of research question to be answered by the model; refer to the examples given in Section 3.

- The next step is the application of the measurement and observation systems, the collection of documentation, and the statistical interpretation of the results. The experiment design used cannot be determined in an arbitrary way. The experiments analyzed result from observations of a real-life system where variables cannot be manipulated at will. Therefore, only realistic alternatives are suitable for conducting experiments.

  If you perform the analysis using a simulation model, it is first necessary to validate this model. Second, the simulation model can be used to provide insight into the behavior of the supply chain and delivers the critical control factors. In quantitative model-based research, empirical data restrictions (see above) have to be taken into account. Hence, it is not possible to optimize the critical control factors. In contrast, it is more important and feasible to find robust solutions when considering real alternatives.

- The final step in quantitative model research based on empirical data is the interpretation of research results related to the theoretical models or problems that were tested. The results are the confirmation of the theoretical model in relation to the decision problem and to the process considered, or a rejection and suggestion for improving the theoretical models.

7 Conclusion

We have shown how quantitative model-driven research - especially when considering empirical data and simulation models – could be conducted in supply chain management research. In particular, we have illustrated our ideas using some research examples.

Managerial relevance is of increasing importance in the field of supply chain management research. Quantitative model-driven empirical research deals with real-life data as well as situations and offers, therefore, the potential for fulfilling the managerial relevance requirement. In detail, empirical model-driven quantitative research has a high potential for addressing more practically relevant problems (e.g., complexity). Furthermore, this type of research is able to validate empirically axiomatic (operational research) models in real-life supply chain processes (Bertrand & Fransoo, 2002).

The most complete form of research is normative quantitative model-driven research based on empirical data. Here, the problem is that the verification process is not strong. Furthermore, it is hard to assess which changes in performance are caused by a specific improvement alternative tested and which by other facts. In this context, the use of discrete-event simulation model approaches would represent an interesting opportunity, as they are able to take uncertainties into account.

In this article, a few mixed methods research approaches have been discussed. Do such approaches have potential in supply chain management research? This question should be an issue for further methodological developments.

Quantitative model-driven empirical research in the field of supply chain management is already more or less accepted by the scientific community. Some top research journals (e.g., Management Science, Journal of Operations Management, International Journal of Production Economics, Production and Operations Management) support the publication of this type of research. However, continuous improvement of research methodology is still necessary to convince the remaining critics.

8 References

Barratt, M., Oliveira, A. (2000): Exploring the enablers and inhibitors of collaborative planning, forecasting and replenishment (CPFR), e-Supply Chain Research Forum, Cranfield Centre for Logistics and Transportation, Cranfield School of Management.

Betrand J. W. M., Fransoo J. C. (2002): Modelling and simulation: Operations management research methodologies using quantitative modeling, in: International Journal of Operations & Production Management, 22(2): 241-264.

Cachon, G. P., Fisher, M. (2000): Supply chain inventory management and the value of shared information, in: Management Science, 46(8): 1032-1048.

Eldabi, T., Irani, Z., Paul, R. J., Love, P. E. D. (2002): Quantitative and qualitative decision-making methods in simulation modelling, in: Management Decision, 40(1/2): 64-73.

Evans, J. R., Olson, D. L. (2002): Introduction to Simulation and Risk Analysis, 2nd edition, Prentice Hall, Upper Saddle River, New Jersey.

Fine C. H. (1998): Clockspeed: Winning Industry Control in the Age of Temporary Advantage, Perseus Books, Cambridge.

Fine C. H. (2000): Clockspeed-based strategies for supply chain design, in: Production and Operations Management, 9(3): 213-221.

Forrester J. W. (1961): Industrial Dynamics, MIT Press, Cambridge.

Handfield, R. (2002): Writing the ideal paper for JOM: a new editor's perspective, in: Journal of Operations Management, 20(1): 10-18.

Hopp, W. J., Spearman, M. L. (1996): Factory Physics - Foundations of Manufacturing Management, Irwin, Chicago.

Jammernegg, W., Reiner, G. (2004): Performance management of supply chain processes by coordinated inventory and capacity management, Proceedings of the 13th International Symposium on Inventories (ISIR), Budapest.

Kleijnen, J. P. C., Smits, M. T. (2003): Performance metrics in supply chain management, in: Journal of the Operational Research Society, 54(5): 507-514.

Krajewski, L. (2002): Reflections on operations management research, in: Journal of Operations Management, 20(1): 2-5.

Law, A. M., Kelton, W. D. (2000): Simulation Modeling and Analysis, third edition, McGraw-Hill, Boston.

Meredith J. R., Raturi A., Amoako-Gyampah K., Kaplan B. (1989): Alternative research paradigms in operations, in: Journal of Operations Management, 8(4): 297-326.

Mitroff, I., Betz, F., Pondy, L. Sagasti, F. (1974): On managing science in the systems age: two schemas for the study of science as whole systems phenomenon, in: Interfaces, 4(3): 46-58.

Müller, M., Seuring, S., Goldbach, M. (2003): Supply Chain Management – Neues Konzept oder Modetrend (Supply Chain Management – New Concept or Fashion Trend?), in: Die Betriebswirtschaft, 63(4): 419-439.

Reiner, G. (2004): Supply chain performance measurement with customer satisfaction and uncertainties, in: Spengler, T., Voß, S., Kopfer, H. (eds.): Logistik Management – Prozesse, Systeme, Ausbildung (Logistics Management – Processes, Systems, Education), Physika-Verlag, Heidelberg: p. 217-234.

Reiner, G., Trcka, M. (2004): Customized supply chain design: Problems and alternatives for a production company in the food industry - A simulation based analysis, in: International Journal of Production Economics, 89(2): 217-229.

Rocco, T. S., Bliss, L. A., Gallagher, S., Perez-Prado, A. (2003): Taking the Next Step: Mixed Methods Research in Organizational Systems, in: Information Technology, Learning and Performance Journal, 21(1): 19-29.

Sterman, J. D. (1989): Modeling Managerial Behavior: Misperceptions of Feedback in a Dynamic Decision Making Experiment, in: Management Science, 35(3): 321-339.

Van der Vorst, J. G. A. J., Beulens, A. J. M., De Wit, W., Van Beek, P. (1998): Supply Chain Management in Food Chains: Improving Performance by Reducing Uncertainty, in: International Transactions in Operational Research, 5(6): 487-499.

Voss, C., Tsikriktsis, N., Frohlich M. (2002): Case Research in operations management, in: International Journal of Operations & Production Management, 22(2): 195-219.

Wyland, B., Buxton, K., Fuqua, B. (2000): Simulating the supply chain, in: IIE Solutions, 32(1): 37-42.

Of Stocks, Flows, Agents and Rules – "Strategic" Simulations in Supply Chain Research

Andreas Größler, Nadine Schieritz

1	Usage and Utility of Strategic Simulations	446
2	Stocks and Flows? Or Agents and Rules?	451
3	…or Both?	457
4	References	458

Summary:
Simulation offers a middle ground between pure formal modeling, empirical observation and experiments for strategic issues in supply chain research. Although simulation models are formally specified, they are not limited to analytically solvable equation systems. Additionally, simulation approaches provide the possibility to include estimations of not easily measurable "soft" factors. The inclusion of such variables increases the real world relevance of simulation studies, similar to empirical investigations. Thus, strategic simulation experiments try to combine the clarity and generality of mathematical modeling with the practical relevance and external validity of empirical research.

The approach is demonstrated by a combination of system dynamics and agent-based simulation, two approaches that achieved high significance for the modeling and simulation of socio-economic systems. With the help of a simulation prototype we are able to test the stability of supply chain structures under different levels of uncertainty regarding future events, particularly changing demand.

Keywords:
Supply Chain Management, Simulation, System Dynamics, Agent-Based Modeling

1 Usage and Utility of Strategic Simulations

1.1 Modeling and Simulation as Research Methodology

Supply Chain Management (SCM) is one of the most popular management concepts these days. However, research in the field mostly concentrates on conceptual literature, reports on anecdotal evidence about various SCM techniques and tools, or tackles purely operational issues. The lack of supply chain research addressing strategic problems is often caused by methodological difficulties. For instance, empirical research is difficult to conduct in supply chains because it implies observing and surveying all companies within a given chain; mathematical modeling approaches are frequently restricted to binary supplier-customer relationships and require many unrealistic assumptions due to growing mathematical complexity. Few studies use experiments to investigate human behavior modes in supply chains because, for example, multi-person activities (which SCM usually comprises) are difficult to handle in experiments.[1]

Simulations offer a middle ground (or "third way"; Axelrod, 1997) between pure formal modeling and empirical observation and experimentation. Methodologically, they share a characteristic feature with classical experiments: the possibility to alter one variable and hold all other variables fixed (Conway et al. (1959) understood simulations as statistical experiments). Although simulation models are formally specified, they do not require specific mathematical forms that are analytically solvable. For example, relations in a supply chain can be modeled without paying attention to the question of whether the resulting set of equations can be solved analytically and whether an optimal solution exists, because simulations proceed step-for-step using numerical approximation methods. Additionally, some simulation approaches provide the possibility to include estimations of difficult-to-measure (and "soft") factors. This characteristic allows the inclusion of all important parameters based on real world data or on estimates from actors within supply chains.

In the context of this paper we define strategic situations as characterized by: (1) high detail complexity (many variables that are highly interconnected); (2) high dynamic complexity (non-linearities and time delays that dilute cause-effect relationships); (3) decisions that are based on the mental models of decision makers

---

[1] However, the literature reports on some experiments that used supply chain contexts but did not aim at finding out about supply chain issues. In these cases, the supply chain context is utilized for more general investigations in human decision making in complex environments (e.g., Sterman, 1989; Senge, 1990). We will not discuss these studies in this paper. See also Steckel et al. (2004), who used an experimental setting in a simulated context to examine supply chain issues such as the effects of the length of cycle times or information sharing.

(i.e. on perceptions, estimations, heuristics and simplifications); (4) many "soft" factors (e.g. image, politics).

While these characteristics make strategic decisions very difficult, such decisions are nevertheless usually very important at the same time. Therefore, trial-and-error decision making is rather dangerous. Simulations that support decision making in the strategic area are called "strategic simulations." Strategic simulations try to combine the clarity and generality of mathematical modeling with the practical relevance and external validity of empirical research. A drawback is that strategic simulations do not necessarily provide optimal solutions or make it easy to find such solutions. Furthermore, the development and the analysis of strategic simulation models is – at least partially – still more an art than a technique, depending heavily on the skills, experience and creativity of the modeler.

In principle, modeling and simulation make it possible to examine the dynamic behavior of supply chains. Feedback loops, time delays and accumulations are a few of the most prominent structural causes of counter-intuitive dynamic behavior. Even relatively simple supply chain structures lead individuals to systematically make sub-optimal decisions due to the chain's inherent feedback loops (e.g. between orders and incoming goods) and delays (e.g. order processing times). The (negative) effect of feedback loops and delays on decision makers' performance has been demonstrated in various studies (Brehmer, 1992; Dörner, 1996). Simulation experiments allow for systematic investigations of cause-effect relationships that are separated by space and time, extreme conditions, and situations which cannot be observed in reality because of the costs or risks involved. Another reason for the use of simulations is the possibility to replicate the initial situation (Pidd, 1993). Finally, modeling and simulation are sometimes seen as the primary way towards scientific progress due to the inherent complexity of reality that makes direct conclusions from empirical observations questionable (McKelvey, 1999).

1.2 System Dynamics and Agent-Based Simulation

According to Parunak et al. (1998) many computer-based models developed in the field of SCM use system dynamics (SD), an approach for modeling and simulating systems with the help of ordinary differential equations. However, the field of agent-based simulation (ABS) has attracted more and more attention among researchers from a wide range of different fields, leading (among other applications) to a number of agent-based supply chain models. In this section, both simulation methodologies, SD and ABS, are described in general before focusing on supply chain-related studies applying one or the other approach in the next section.

SD is a simulation methodology that employs continuous handling of time and an aggregate view on objects to model and analyze dynamic socio-economic systems. Many of its basic concepts stem from engineering feedback control theory. The mathematical model description is realized with the help of one or many ordinary differential equations. "The expressed goal of the system dynamics approach is understanding how a system's feedback structure gives rise to its dynamic behavior." (Richardson, 1991: 299) The structure consists of multiple interacting feedback loops as basic building blocks of the methodology. Together these feedback loops represent the policies and continuous processes underlying discrete events (Forrester, 1961). Feedback loops consist of stock (state) and flow (change) variables. Besides feedback loops, accumulation and delays are major constituting features of SD models (Forrester, 1968). Due to elaborated diagramming techniques, SD models can be rather easily inter-subjectively communicated and developed in groups (Vennix, 1996).

In SD, supply chain modeling and simulation is as old as the discipline itself. In 1958 Jay W. Forrester, the founder of the field, modeled a four-level downstream supply chain (Forrester, 1958). By simulating and analyzing this model, Forrester examined "…many current research issues in supply chain management […] including demand amplification, inventory swings, the effect of advertising policies on production variation, de-centralized control, or the impact of the use of information technology on the management process" (Angerhofer & Angelides, 2000: 342). The focus on feedback loops and time delays makes SD a valuable tool for the investigation of supply chains. One important advantage of SD is the possibility to deduce the occurrence of a specific behavior mode because the structure that leads to systems' behavior is made transparent. The drawback of using a traditional SD model of a supply chain is that the structure has to be determined before starting the simulation. For instance, if a flexible structure is to be modeled, every possible participant has to be included into the model and linked to its potential trading partners in advance, thus increasing model complexity.

ABS represents systems as comprised of multiple idiosyncratic agents: "…much of the apparently complex aggregate behavior in any system arises from the relatively simple and localized activities of its agents" (Phelan, 1999: 240). In other words, phenomena result from the behavior of agents which are one level below these phenomena; global system control does not exist (Jennings et al., 1998). Therefore the basic building block of a system is the individual agent—in the supply chain case, usually a company. In contrast to SD, agent-based modeling is a bottom-up approach (Bonabeau, 2002). The dynamics of the system arise from the interactions of agents, whereby the behavior of an agent is determined by its "cognitive" structure, its schema. "Different agents may or may not have different schemata…and schemata may or may not evolve over time. Often agents' schemata are modeled as a set of rules, but schemata may be characterized in very flexible ways." (Anderson, 1999: 219)

In agent-based modeling a consistent understanding of the concept and its terms does not exist. This is contrary to SD which has a definite starting point in Forrester's early work. Therefore, it is more difficult to derive common definitions. For instance, the concept of "agency" is not well-defined (Rocha, 1999). However, researchers have at least agreed on some features that an agent should possess: situated in an environment, reacts to this environment, acts autonomously, tries to achieve certain objectives, and socially interacts with other agents. Agent-based modeling can be assumed to be a reasonable methodology for the examination of supply chains, because in a supply chain, a number of individual companies interact with each other using specific internal decision structures. The structure of ABS models is highly flexible and can adapt to changing conditions, which is an advantage of agent-based modeling in many cases. Using this feature, dynamically changing supply chain structures can be modeled. A disadvantage is found in that agents' behavior frequently cannot be explained in detail because most agents are constructed as black-box systems and/or determine their behavior with the help of "non-transparent" schemata (e.g. by applying genetic algorithms, artificial neural networks, etc.).

Because of the relatively complementary characteristics of SD and ABS, some concepts for combining the approaches have been developed (e.g. Scholl, 2001; Schieritz & Milling, 2003). The approach of combining the two methods was also implicitly suggested by scholars from the agent-based approach: Phelan claims that agents' rules are to be modeled by using algorithms that enable the agent to adapt to its environment over time by feedback mechanisms (Phelan, 2001). More explicitly, when explaining an agent's internal schema, Choi et al. (2001) compare these schemata with the notion of mental models, i.e. an individual's set of norms, values, beliefs and assumptions (Senge, 1990).

1.3 Simulation Studies in the SCM Literature

This section reviews some examples of simulation studies in supply chain research. We start with studies employing SD modeling, proceed with those that use agent-based methodology, and finally present articles which describe combined approaches.

Angerhofer & Angelides (2000) present a literature review on the use of SD in supply chain modeling. They construct a portfolio consisting of the paper category (theoretical, practical and methodological) on one axis and the research area on the other axis and classify papers into this portfolio. As research areas in SCM that can be investigated with SD they identify: inventory management, demand amplification (e.g., the bullwhip effect; Lee et al., 1997), supply chain design and reengineering, and international SCM.

Towill (1996) focuses on the support function of SD when supply chains are to be reengineered. He presents various forms of diagrams that have been successfully used in supply chain modeling and reengineering. He proposes an integration of SD modeling and conventional business reengineering methods.

Akkermans et al. (1999) use qualitative SD techniques (causal diagramming) to study issues in international supply chain management. Following SD tradition, they focus on the feedback loops created by variables from the supply chain domain. An emphasis of the paper is on the identification of virtuous and vicious loops connecting these variables.

Anderson et al. (2000) present a SD model to investigate upstream volatility (or, the bullwhip effect) in the machine tools industry. By a series of simulation experiments they test several hypotheses about the nature of the bullwhip effect, e.g. how production lead times affect the entire supply chain.

Milling & Größler (2001) present a SD model of the well-known "beer distribution game" (Jarmain, 1963). Within this model of a four-tier supply chain, they conduct simulation experiments concerning the influence of shortened information delays and the availability of point-of-sales information at different stages of the chain.

Parunak (1998) uses ABS to examine dynamic effects in supply chains. Based on a four-tier supply chain model, various SCM topics are investigated, for instance demand amplification. The paper provides rich quantitative detail for the simulation runs and results.

Van der Pol & Akkermans (2000) base their usage of agent-based modeling for studying supply chains on the observation that most real world supply chains do not possess a central controlling instance. ABS can therefore be used to find out how favorable behavior emerges from the interactions of the supply chain members, which can generate success for the entire supply chain—without demanding a central process control.

Parunak et al. (1998) compare agent-based modeling and SD with the help of a case study from SCM. They describe an agent-based and a SD model of a supply chain and discuss which conclusions can be drawn from each of the two models. By doing so, they want to achieve guidelines for choosing either of the two simulation approaches.

Akkermans (2001) uses terminology from the agent-based modeling approach to describe a supply network in a SD simulation environment. The individual agents only differ "in the degree in which they base their relative preferences for customers and suppliers either primarily on their short-term performance towards the agent in question, or mainly upon the intensity of long-term relationships, or on both" (Akkermans, 2001: 9). He finds that, in general, the agents choosing customers and suppliers based on short-term performance achieve better results. Moreover, the relative preferences for a specific customer or supplier become fixed over time, i.e. a stable supply network emerges.

Schieritz & Größler (2003) use a combination of SD and ABS to study the connection between timeliness and volume of shipments and the development of stable supplier/buyer relationships. The focus of the paper, however, is on methodological aspects of an integration of SD and ABS and the presentation of a working prototype.

2 Stocks and Flows? Or Agents and Rules?

2.1 The Hammer and the Nail – Using the Right Tool for the Right Problem

The discussion in sections 1.1 and 1.2 of the paper as well as the examples discussed in section 1.3 have shown that each of the two approaches (SD and ABS) has its characteristic features that make it suitable for the investigation of different classes of problems, and that both have been applied to a wide range of problems in the field of SCM.

However, the question regarding which kind of problem requires the application of what approach is mostly neglected in literature. As mentioned above, Parunak et al. (1998) compare SD and ABS with the goal of finding criteria for choosing the appropriate approach for a given SCM problem. However, their conclusion seems to be rather biased; a fact that can be observed for many scholars of the ABS approach and that might be explained by their attempt to establish their relatively new approach (Schieritz, 2004):

"ABMs [agent-based models] are better suited to domains where the natural unit of decomposition is the individual rather than the observable or the equation, and where physical distribution of the computation across multiple processors is desirable. EBMs [equation-based models] may be better suited to domains where the natural unit of decomposition is the observable or equation rather than the individual…ABM is most appropriate for domains characterized by a high degree of localization and distribution and dominated by discrete decisions. EBM is most naturally applied to systems that can be modeled centrally, and in which the dynamics are dominated by physical laws rather than information processing." (Parunak et al., 1998: 12)

If one accepts this statement, then the SD approach not only becomes superfluous for the analysis of strategic supply chain problems, but for the investigation of most socio-economic questions as well. Of course, the fact that the consequence is drastic cannot be a reason for rejecting Parunak et al.'s conclusion. With this in mind however, their opinion also contrasts with the variety of successful SD applications in the field of supply chain management as well as many other areas of social systems. It also contradicts Forrester's (1961) definition of the approach, which considers socio-economic systems to be information-feedback systems and SD an approach for modeling those systems. Forrester's introductory supply chain example is neither modeled centrally, nor are the dynamics dominated by physical laws. Instead, the dynamics are a result of delayed and distorted information exchanged between the participants of the supply chain.

The seemingly very catchy argument to choose a simulation approach according to the "natural unit of decomposition" of the domain under consideration appears weak when examined more thoroughly. The "natural unit of decomposition" depends on the level of aggregation the modeler chooses for the analysis of a given problem. From an application/problem-oriented point of view, every problem can be analyzed from an aggregated as well as a disaggregated view; it is however difficult to judge in advance which of the two will result in better insights (Sawyer, 2001). The "natural" unit of decomposition is therefore not as "natural" as it seems to be at first glance.

From a methodological point of view, one could argue that the "natural unit" is the agent in the ABS approach (Jennings et al., 1998) and the feedback loop in the SD approach (Forrester, 1968): Just like an agent-based model is always composed of individuals (that also can be companies), a SD model is always composed of feedback loops. Like the agents, the feedback loops are then composed of a number of variables: Parunak et al.'s "observables". The SD way of assembling a system is a result of the focus on policies instead of individual decisions. This different degree of abstraction often leads to a higher level of aggregation of a SD model compared to an agent-based model.

The problematic nature is intensified by the fact that the higher level of aggregation of a SD model is only a tendency (a fact that is also mentioned by Parunak, 1998), not a hard rule. Taking again Forrester's (1961) bull-whip example, he develops a four-tier supply chain by explicitly modeling every supply chain member, and every company; the overall system behavior is then a result of the interaction of the four members—an agent-based version of the model would probably have the same degree of aggregation. The chosen level of aggregation is adequate for an explanation of the problem and its causes; therefore disaggregating the model would only add more detail, and by that increase the complexity and prevent the user from gaining new insights.

Because it is difficult to identify absolute selection criteria, the task of choosing an appropriate simulation methodology still is an intuitive decision that depends a lot on the prior experience of the modeler. With the next two sections we want to give an idea of what we "feel" to be the differences between SD and ABS concerning their application domains. Instead of modeling one problem with both approaches the way Parunak et al. did (in such a case the chosen problem will always be more appropriate for one approach leading to a worse performance of the other one), we present an example of a combination of both approaches, each applied to that part of the problem where we consider its strengths to be best expressed.

2.2 Agents and Rules – Modeling Structural Emergence

A problem area where a combination of the features of both simulation approaches is helpful for efficient analysis is the investigation of supply network structures resulting from the interaction of (partly) independent companies. Following an integrative approach, a supply chain can be modeled with two levels of aggregation (Figure 1) where the macro level can be related to the agent-based approach, whereas the micro level is mainly modeled using SD.

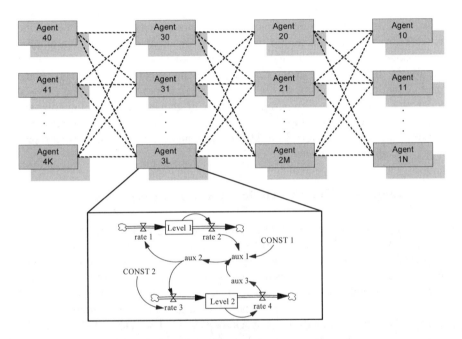

Figure 1: Macro and Micro Level of a Supply Chain

The macro level shows a network of agents that are potential supply chain participants. Every link between two agents can be interpreted as a potential customer-supplier relationship. Which of the relationships becomes active is determined during the simulation run: At any specific point during a simulation run, the structure of the supply chain is determined by the interactions between the agents that in turn result from the implementation of the agents' policies (the micro level) as well as the state of the environment.

Supply network structures as phenomena emerging from the interactions of the participating companies (instead of being expressed by macro equations) are analyzed using an agent-based model where structural changes can be implemented very efficiently, especially when a high number of agents are involved. A SD representation of the macro level would have the following two implications (both made us choose agents for this level):

(1) When deciding for a disaggregated representation as depicted in Figure 1 (meaning that every company is explicitly modeled), model complexity super-proportionally increases with the number of companies involved in the supply network, as every company has to be linked to every potential exchange partner in advance. Moreover, it is not possible to change model structure during the simulation run, meaning companies cannot enter or exit the market.

(2) The use of an aggregated representation requires the knowledge of macro equations that express the development of network structures. In such a case, the network structure is characterized by a number of variables (e.g. stability, number of exchange partners) and the interrelationship is modeled between those variables and others that influence them (e.g. external demand, ordering policies). If the macro equations are known, such a model can result in a very clear and easy-to-understand and -communicate representation of the problem. If, however, the effect of the individual companies' policies on the overall network structure is unknown and cannot be found out by e.g. case studies, a valid aggregated representation is difficult to achieve.[2]

2.3 Stocks and Flows – Modeling Complex Decision Making

A company's policies represent the internal structure or schema of that company; they are implemented on the micro level (the agent level) and are responsible for the structural changes on the macro level. In our approach, SD is used to model the more complex policies, whereas the simple, mechanical ones are modeled using discrete rules. As soon as policies reach a critical level of complexity, and decisions are not based on simple rules, the structural representation of causal relations as well as the focus on feedback loops and delays renders SD suitable for policy modeling. Policies do not only change when triggered by external events, but might change continuously in the cognitive schema of the agents. SD is designed to model such continuous decision making processes (Forrester, 1961).

In the simulation model described in the following, the internal structure of an agent can roughly be divided into four sub-structures: ordering, production, shipping and evaluation. Whereas the first three can be assigned to the ABS approach, the last one – due to its complexity – is modeled using SD.

Ordering sector: Every company uses the same order policy: As soon as the inventory level falls below the safety stock, an order is placed with the preferred sup-

---

[2] The last comment results in the conclusion that a disaggregated model can also be used to support the construction of its often simpler aggregated counterpart.

plier. The order size is determined by the inventory level (material on stock plus material ordered and not yet received), the safety stock level as well as a fixed maximum inventory level. The safety stock level is not fixed; it changes as customer order forecasts change.

Production sector: A very simple production process is assumed. Whenever unfulfilled customer orders exist or the amount of finished goods on stock falls below a certain level (which again is influenced by customer order forecasts), the company produces the amount necessary to fulfill the orders and bring the finished goods inventory back to its safety level. Different production stages and the resulting variations in production time are not taken into account explicitly, but they are represented by using a third order Erlang distribution for production time. As soon as customer orders are backlogged, maximum production capacity is utilized; in times of in-stock production capacity utilization is reduced.

Shipping sector: The companies only ship complete orders. They are then transported to the customer without any delay; in case enough goods are in stock, an order can be filled immediately. Shipping does not take place in a first-come-first-serve manner, as the best customers (being the high-volume customers) are preferred.

Evaluation sector: Contrary to the relative simple decision rules applied in the three sectors that have been described so far, the policy used for selecting an appropriate supplier is more complex in that it involves a higher number of interconnected parameters as well as a lot of "soft" variables. The evaluation sector can be interpreted as a company's mental model of its suppliers whose performance is continuously rated. It consists of a number of evaluation models like the one depicted in Figure 2; a company holds as many evaluation models as potential suppliers exist.

An agent's final supplier selection criterion—Ttrust—is modeled as a level variable (indicated by a rectangle in the diagram in Figure 2) that integrates the difference between the inflow and the outflow. The range of values of the variable Trust lies within [-1,1]. The trust decay rate reflects the degree to which an agent values the past performance of its suppliers. The inflow (respectively outflow) trust change rate is determined by two sub-criteria: Order Volume and Time Order Placed. Together with Order Variance and the two switches (Open Order Switch and No Open Order Switch) they are the input data of the model (input and output data are marked with gray circles). In order to enable comparability between the two different supplier evaluation criteria—waiting time and volume—the value of these two variables is transformed into an attractiveness measure with the help of the functions Wt Effect Table and Volume Effect Table. The higher the number of supplies received from one supplier, the higher the absolute value of the Trust Coefficient for this particular supplier—all other variables being of constant value. The behavior of the delivery time is opposite: the higher the delivery time, the lower the absolute value of the Trust Coefficient. As soon as the delivery time exceeds a critical value, its effect becomes negative, which leads to a negative Trust Coefficient. The effect of the Trust Coefficient on the trust change rate depends on the current Trust state. A Trust Coefficient greater than actual Trust will lead to a positive trust change rate and therefore to an inflow in the level Trust. However, trust evaluation only takes place when a company is waiting for an order to be filled (the Open Order Switch is 1). In every other case, only the outflow from the trust level is active.

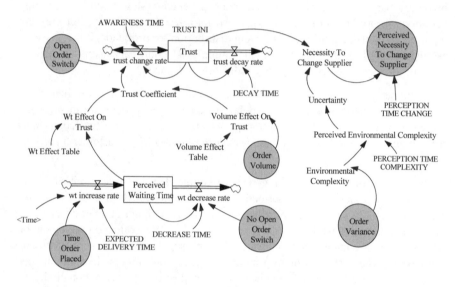

Figure 2: Potential Evaluation Sector in System Dynamics Notation

The second level variable, Perceived Waiting Time, represents the way a company perceives delivery delays: Every deviation of the delivery time from the expected delivery time is accumulated. By this, the exponentially increasing annoyance resulting from increasing delays is modeled. As long as a customer is waiting for its order to arrive, the No Open Order Switch equals zero; only after all orders are delivered does the annoyance start to decrease. However, as long as Perceived Waiting is not zero, a further delivery delay is amplified because of the still- existing annoyance from earlier shipments.

A company evaluates the importance of a relationship based on trust according to the existing environmental conditions. A higher environmental complexity – modeled by a higher Order Variance – results in a higher uncertainty which reduces the willingness of a company to change its supplier. As soon as the Perceived Necessity To Change Supplier, which equals a delayed Necessity To Change Supplier, exceeds a threshold, the company is willing to change its suppliers.

However, whether a change actually takes places depends on the company's perception of the other suppliers in the market. Perceived Necessity To Change Supplier and Trust are the output variables of the evaluation sector.

The structure described above represents the internal structure of all agents that are not located at the end points of the supply chain. They are called Producers in the following. Final Customers and Raw Material Suppliers are structured similarly; however, Final Customers are missing a production and shipping sector; Raw Material Suppliers do not contain an ordering and evaluation sector.

3   ...or Both?

The intention of the last paragraphs was to shed at least some light on the problem of deducing appropriate application areas from features of the two simulation approaches SD and ABS. This was achieved with the help of an integration of the two simulation methods and their application to the problem areas they fit best. The following paragraph now aims at the presentation of a problem area that we identified as possessing features that require an integrative approach: the emergence of supply chain structures. It introduces some simulation results of the model explained above and continues with a possible supply chain question that could be analyzed with the help of such a model.

The simulation model was implemented using the software AnyLogic.[3] It is a multi-paradigm simulation tool that allows for an integration of the paradigms SD and ABS by offering a wide range of different modeling tools like stock and flow diagrams, table functions, discrete and continuous state-charts, algorithmic representations etc. Figure 3 shows a screenshot of a simulation result including the AnyLogic user interface.

The prototypical supply chain displayed in Figure 3 consists of four tiers and ten organizations. External demand from the market (complexity of the environment) is constantly set to 50 units/simulation period. The behavior graphs in the small boxes depict trust variables linked to the potential suppliers of an agent. Trust influences the stability of a supplier-buyer relationship according to a company's internal model described above. The stability is indicated by the lines between supply chain members: The thicker a line, the more stable the particular relationship. Therefore, the overall supply chain structure emerges in the course of the simulation as a result of the members' individual policies in a given environment (market demand). With the experimental setting shown in the figure, the effects of environmental complexity on the development of trust and ultimately supply chain

---

[3] See www.xjtek.com/anylogic/ for a list of features, limitations, computational requirements etc. of this software. Equations are available from the authors.

structures can be studied. More specifically, the dynamics of many, autonomously acting agents can be simulated by the integrated approach, and supply chain structures that originate in their interaction can be observed.

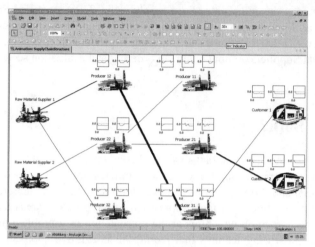

Figure 3: Screenshot of Integrative Supply Chain Simulation Using AnyLogic

AnyLogic allows for an easy duplication of agents. Therefore, the number of potential members of the supply chain can easily be increased. This could even be done dynamically, e.g. when buyers experience long delivery times from all suppliers in the supply chain, they may look for a new partner which then enters the supply chain. In a similar vein, a supplier not trusted by any of its customers might leave the supply chain completely. Furthermore, the schemata of the agents can be varied in order to investigate the effects of different evaluation policies. It might be an interesting question to find out what effects are caused by the combination of, for instance, tolerant buyers and opportunistic suppliers. Another point for further research that is only touched upon in this paper is to study what effects an increase in external complexity (e.g. caused by demand fluctuation) has on the stability and viability of the supply chain structure. Finally, more sophisticated agents' schemata may certainly also be implemented. For example, more criteria other than just trust can be incorporated in the selection of suppliers.

4 References

Akkermans, H. A. (2001): Emergent Supply Networks: System Dynamics Simulation of Adaptive Supply Agents, Paper presented at the 34th Hawaii International Conference on System Sciences, Hawaii.

Akkermans, H. A., Bogerd, P., Vos, B. (1999): Virtuous and Vicious Circles on the Road Towards International Supply Chain Management, in: International Journal of Operations and Production Management, 19(5/6): 565–581.

Anderson, P. (1999): Complexity Theory and Organization Science, in: Organization Science, 10(3): 219–232.

Anderson, E. G., Fine, C. H., Parker, G. G. (2000): Upstream Volatility in the Supply Chain: The Machine Tool Industry as a Case Study, in: Production and Operations Management, 9(3): 239–261.

Angerhofer, B. J., Angelides, M. C. (2000): System Dynamics Modeling in Supply Chain Management: Research Review, in: Joines, J. A., Barton, R. R., Kang, K., Fishwick, P. A. (eds.): Proceedings of the 2000 Winter Simulation Conference: p. 342–351.

Axelrod, R. (1997): Advancing the Art of Simulation in the Social Sciences, in: Conte, R., Hegselmann, R., Terna, P. (eds.): Simulating Social Phenomena, Springer, Berlin: 21–40.

Bonabeau, E. (2002): Predicting the Unpredictable, in: Harvard Business Review, March 2002: 109–116.

Brehmer, B. (1992): Dynamic Decision Making: Human Control of Complex Systems, in: Acta Psychologica, 81: 211–241.

Choi, T. Y., Dooley, K. J., Rungtusanatham, M. (2001): Supply Networks and Complex Adaptive Systems: Control versus Emergence, in: Journal of Operations Management, 19(3): 351–366.

Conway, R. W., Johnson, B. M., Maxwell, M. L. (1959): Some Problems of Digital Systems Simulation, in: Management Science, 6(1): 92–110.

Dörner, D. (1996): The Logic of Failure, Metropolitan Books/Henry Holt, New York.

Forrester, J. W. (1958): Industrial Dynamics: A Major Breakthrough for Decision Makers, in: Harvard Business Review, 36(4): 37–66.

Forrester, J. W. (1961): Industrial Dynamics, MIT Press, Cambridge.

Forrester, J. W. (1968): Principles of Systems, MIT Press, Cambridge.

Jarmain, W. E. (ed.) (1963): Problems in Industrial Dynamics, MIT Press, Cambridge.

Jennings, N. R., Sycara, K., Wooldridge, M. (1998): A Roadmap of Agent Research and Development, in: Autonomous Agents and Multi-Agent Systems, 1: 7–38.

Lee, H. L., Padmanabhan, V., Whang, S. (1997): Information Distortion in a Supply Chain: The Bullwhip Effect, in: Management Science, 43(4): 546–558.

McKelvey, B. (1999): Complexity Theory in Organization Science: Seizing the Promise or Becoming a Fad?, in: Emergence, 1(1): 5–32.

Milling, P., Größler, A. (2001): Management von Material- und Informationsflüssen in Supply Chains: System-Dynamics-basierte Analysen (Management of Material and Information Flows in Supply Chains: System Dynamics-based Analyses), Working Paper Series, Faculty of Business Administration, Mannheim University, No. 2001-01.

Parunak, H. V. D. (1998): The DASCh Experience: How to Model a Supply Chain, in: Proceedings of the Second International Conference on Complex Systems.

Parunak, H. V. D., Savit, R., Riolo, R. L. (1998): Agent-Based Modeling vs. Equation-Based Modeling: A Case Study and Users' Guide, Proceedings of Multi-agent Systems and Agent-based Simulation: 10–25.

Phelan, S. E. (1999): A Note on the Correspondence between Complexity and Systems Theory, in: Systemic Practice and Action Research, 12(3): 237–246.

Phelan, S. E. (2001): What is complexity science, really?, in: Emergence, 3(1): 120–136.

Pidd, M. (1993): Computer Simulation in Management Science, 3rd edition, John Wiley, Chichester.

Richardson, G. P. (1991): Feedback Thought in Social Science and Systems Theory, University of Pennsylvania Press, Philadephia.

Rocha, L. M. (1999): From Artificial Life to Semiotic Agent Models – Review and Research Directions, Los Alamos, http://www.c3.lanl.gov/~rocha/ps/agent_review.pdf, 13/07/2004.

Schieritz, N., Größler, A. (2003): Emergent Structures in Supply Chains – A Study Integrating Agent-Based and System Dynamics Modeling, in: Sprague, R. H. (ed.): Proceedings of the 36th Annual Hawaii International Conference on System Sciences, IEEE Computer Society, Los Alamitos.

Schieritz, N., Milling, P. M. (2003): Modeling the Forest or Modeling the Trees – A Comparison of System Dynamics and Agent-Based Simulation, in: Eberlein, R. L. et al. (eds.): Proceedings of the 21st International Conference of the System Dynamics Society, New York.

Scholl, H. J. (2001): Agent-based and System Dynamics Modeling: A Call for Cross Study and Joint Research, Paper presented at the 34th Hawaii International Conference on System Sciences, Hawaii.

Senge, P. M. (1990): The Fifth Discipline – The Art and Practice of the Learning Organization, Currency & Doubleday, New York.

Steckel, J. H., Gupta, S., Banerji, A. (2004): Supply Chain Decision Making: Will Shorter Cycle Times and Shared Point-of-Sales Information Necessarily Help?, in: Management Science, 50(4): 458–464.

Sterman, J. D. (1989): Misperceptions of Feedback in a Dynamic Decision Making Experiment, in: Management Science, 35(3): 321–339.

Towill, D. R. (1996): Industrial Dynamics Modelling of Supply Chains, in: Logistics Information Management, 9(4): 43–56.

Van der Pol, J. M., Akkermans, H. A. (2000): 'No one in the driver's seat': An Agent-based Modeling Approach to Decentralised Behaviour in Supply Chain Co-ordination, Pre-Prints 11th International Working Seminar on Production Economics, 3: 621–643.

Vennix, J. A. M. (1996): Group Model Building: Facilitating Team Learning Using System Dynamics, Wiley, Chichester.

Analysis of Supply Chain Dynamics through Object Oriented Simulation

Francesco Casella, Giovanni Miragliotta, Luigi Uglietti

1 Introduction 462
2 The Bullwhip Effect: Determinants and Triggers 462
3 Object-Oriented Modeling with Modelica 465
4 The "Supply Chain" Modelica Library 469
5 First Evidences on SC Modeling with Modelica 472
6 Concluding Remarks 473
7 Appendix: The "Supply Chain" Modelica Library 474
8 References 476

Summary:
This paper stems from a cross-fertilization research project aimed at exploring to which extent modeling methodologies and tools that are used in engineering fields could be suitable to solve management problems. A powerful object-oriented modeling language used in those contexts, Modelica, is carefully presented, and its most innovative features are discussed. Then, a very demanding management problem, namely that of understanding Supply Chain Dynamics and controlling the Bullwhip Effect, is addressed. A prototypal application of Modelica is presented in order to evaluate the capability of this language to be applied in the field of Supply Chain Dynamics analysis.

Keywords:
Modelica, Bullwhip Effect, Supply Chain Dynamics, Object Oriented Simulation

1 Introduction

Supply Chain Dynamics is a well established research topic. Introduced by J. W. Forrester in 1961, Supply Chain Dynamics deals with complex supply chains, and with those phenomena which arise due to the non-linear nature of relationships within the chain. A well known effect of Supply Chain Dynamics is the Bullwhip Effect (BE): many scholars have deepened this subject, resorting to analytical models or, more frequently, to simulation models. Despite such research effort, this matter is still unclarified: on one hand there are some limitations in the currently available explanations, while on the other hand there is no agreed view concerning the effectiveness of proposed management levers. In order to contribute to this research field, this paper introduces and tests a new simulation approach, derived from physics and traditional engineering sciences, whose potential could be relevant for innovative investigation in this field.

In this regard, Section 2 will present the state-of-the-art knowledge concerning the Bullwhip Effect, by illustrating a framework which could help newcomers, academicians and managers better understand this phenomenon. Section 3 will be devoted to introducing a new modeling and simulation approach of complex systems: This approach has been "borrowed" from physics and traditional engineering sciences, and relies on Modelica, an innovative language whose most valuable features will be carefully discussed.. Then, Section 4 will be devoted to presenting a prototypal application of Modelica to the simulation of a supply chain: A description of the model architecture, objects, links and functions will be given, so that the reader can understand how this language can be applied. Section 5 will describe the results of a small test performed on a sample supply chain. Finally, Section 6 will draw some concluding remarks concerning the validity of this modeling approach, and its most feasible future development.

2 The Bullwhip Effect: Determinants and Triggers

The first academic description of this phenomenon is usually ascribed to (Forrester, 1961), whose pioneering work on demand fluctuations' amplification was included in the classic production planning and control textbook by (Buffa & Miller, 1979). By expanding the original definition of (Burbidge, 1984), we can now define the BE as a supply chain phenomenon revealed by an increase in the variance of the demand signal[1] as it is transmitted from retailers to suppliers. This topic has captured much attention from researchers and practitioners worldwide; following the classification in (Miragliotta, 2004), the overall body of knowledge can be fairly divided into three main streams.

---

[1] Other measures (e.g. seasonality coefficient, coefficient of variation) are seldom used.

The first stream has a strong empirical focus, and aims at measuring and at giving empirical evidence of the existence of this phenomenon in real supply chains. Various metrics are used to detect and to measure the BE, the variance ratio being the most used one. The variance ratio is defined as the ratio between the demand variance at the downstream and at the upstream stages; when this ratio is greater than 1, then we have bullwhip at that stage. For a more complete list of metrics, please refer to (El-Beheiry et al, 2004). Regarding the empirical evidence, the BE has been observed in several industries, from automotive to chemistry, from grocery to consumer electronics. According to some "guru" estimates, the BE is worth US$ 100 billion in the US alone (1997 figure, see Lee et al., 1997b), but this may be a conservative guess since there are scores of ways in which demand variability can disrupt profitability, many of which are often neglected. Actually, this research stream has somehow lost importance as managers and researchers worldwide have become aware of the BE, and do not ask for evidence anymore.

The second stream in literature concentrates on the causes of the BE. In this regard, it is possible to distinguish two schools of thought. The first one, which is mainly fostered by academics with a strong background in Systems Theory, is focused on the "systemic" nature of the supply chain, and reflects an holistic perception of the causes; the second one, in opposition, is much more oriented towards single aspects which could generate the BE, and therefore is much closer to operations managers' attitudes.

Within the first school, as we expected, the most accredited author is J. W. Forrester: in his works, he always drew attention on feedbacks, and on the non-linear nature of supply chains, as the main cause for the BE. The same opinion is shared by (Sterman, 1989) and by (Senge, 1990), who ascribed the BE to a lack of "system thinking." This first school, therefore, is quite in favor of ascribing the BE to the irrationality of the decision makers, where the concept of rationality is defined as the ability of the decision maker: 1) to perform a complete and correct alternatives' generation and 2) to perform a correct alternatives' evaluation, resorting to a suitable utility function.

Conversely, within the second school, the focus is kept on single elements which may cause the BE. In this regard, many researchers have tried to provide an explanation for the BE, for instance time delays, or incorrect demand forecasts, etc. In 1997, (Lee et al., 1997a) presented a paper which is fairly considered to be the ultimate one, highlighting four causes: demand processing (in conjunction with long lead times), order batching, price fluctuations and (rationing and shortage) gaming. (Lee et al., 1997b) proposed another interesting contribution to this topic, since they demonstrated that, while reacting to any of the four causes above, the strategic interaction of two rational supply chain actors can generate the BE. Therefore, this second school of thought is much different from the first one, since the BE is not seen as the irrational answer to a complex and not perfectly understood system, but as a rational reaction to well perceived factors.

The third stream in literature concentrates on remedies for the BE and reflects the duality discussed above. On the one hand, following the "systemic school," some authors suggest to invest in training programs in order to increase managers' ability to perceive, understand and properly react to the non-linear, feedback oriented nature of supply chains (cf. Senge & Sterman, 1992). On the other hand, coherently with operations managers' attitude, other authors suggest a more punctual list of remedies. For instance, (Lee et al., 1997a) proposed a set of levers to be used to prevent the insurgence of the BE, which are divided into three main areas: Information Sharing, Channel Alignment and Operational Efficiency. These remedies sounded interesting, and much research has been carried out in order to measure their effectiveness. Nevertheless, as highlighted in (Miragliotta, 2004), the picture if far from being consolidated: for instance, the various papers test very different business environments, and resort to different response variables. Also, the most commonly studied lever, i.e. Information Sharing, has no agreement on its operationalisation (sell-out data, retailer's inventory data, etc.). As a consequence, managers have no precise courses of actions to follow, since no fair comparison is available, nor decisive priorities among the different levers, nor significant conclusions on return on investments, and the scientific debate around the best therapy is still open.

Recently, the scientific debate about the causes of the BE has also been reopened. (Miragliotta, 2004) questioned the four causes pointed out by (Lee et al., 1997a). In his opinion, there is a certain heterogeneity between them: It may be true that delays and shortage gaming generate the BE, but these two causes certainly don't act at the same level. Delays, for instance, could depend on the inherent nature of the production process, while shortage gaming is a result of a managerial decisions. A similar problem is true for the mechanism through which those factors generate a BE: Some elements (e.g. price fluctuations) just prompt a variation in final demand, while others (e.g. the batching process) will cause demand variance to increase whatever the starting signal. (Miragliotta, 2004) thus proposed to separate different layers and different mechanisms which may cause a BE. With regard to the layers, he distinguished:

- The first layer, which includes the model of the supply chain's physical structure (production, transportation, etc.), of its state variables and environmental variables;
- The second layer, which includes the model of those systems (forecasting, accounting and performance measurement) which are used by managers to "reconstruct" the state of their business;
- The third layer, which includes the rules, heuristics, algorithms etc. used to manage the supply chain, its inventories, production activities and so on.

Each of these layers' acts may contain elements which can create and/or amplify a demand fluctuation, and each of them should to be considered separately. Second, the author introduced the following distinction:

- Triggers: those factors which create the variance in the demand signal. For instance, a price promotion is a trigger, since it creates a sudden peak in demand, but it doesn't imply *per se* a BE if the supply chain is endowed with proper control mechanisms;
- Determinants: those factors which, given a demand signal characterized by a certain variance, amplify the signal's variance as it is transmitted along the chain. For instance, batching is a determinant.

By mixing these two paradigms, the taxonomy in Table 1 is obtained. In this taxonomy, determinants and triggers are associated to each layer, and therefore a more rigorous portrait of the BE phenomenon is achieved. Moreover, it contains elements to reconcile the two school of thoughts, and to renew and rejuvenate the scientific debate about the causes of the BE.

	Determinants	Triggers
Physical layer	(Linear gain) Quantity Batching Delay + feedbacks	Exogenous demand shocks Process uncertainty
Reconstructing layer	Delay and errors: – in forecasting – in performances measurement	
Control layer	Batching decisions: – Quantity – Frequency Delay (in the control model) Irrational decision making	Price promotions Shortage gaming

Table 1: Taxonomy of BE Determinants and Triggers (Miragliotta, 2004).

In order to explore the suitability of Modelica in modeling complex supply chains, we decided to tackle the subject of BE; hence a supply chain model has been designed to recreate the BE. While doing this, the taxonomy above was to decide which factors should be included in the model, and eventually develop a test bed which could be useful for a subsequent validation of the taxonomy itself.

3 Object-Oriented Modeling with Modelica

3.1 Modelica at a Glance

The modeling and simulation of complex dynamic systems plays a key role in many fields of science and engineering when it is required to understand the behavior of existing systems, or to design them for optimal performance. A typical example is that of control systems, where the overall performance depends in complex ways on the interaction between the plant sub-systems and the control system dynamics. In many cases, the dynamics of such systems can be described by algebraic, differential, and difference equations:

- $f(x, dx/dt, y, z) = 0$
- when <event> then $g(x, y, z, old(z)) = 0$

where x are the continuous state variables, z the discrete state variables, y the remaining variables of the model, f and g suitable vector functions. A modular approach is usually followed to build the overall system equation, i.e. a complex system is described by the aggregation of simpler sub-systems.

The Modelica language (Fritzson, 2003; Modelica Association, 2003) was introduced in 1997 to support the modeling of complex dynamical systems according to object-oriented principles. So far, Modelica has mainly found applications in engineering domains; nevertheless it is the authors' opinion that it can be very promising in other disciplines dealing with dynamic systems, such as management science. The features of the object-oriented approach and of the Modelica language, which are more relevant to this field, are now summarized.

1. Declarative Approach

The majority of modeling languages (and of simulation environments in general), follows a procedural approach, i.e., each sub-system has certain inputs and outputs, and the sub-system model is basically an algorithm to compute the outputs given the inputs. Contrastingly, Modelica adopts a declarative approach: each sub-system is described by the equations which correlate its internal and boundary variables, without bothering about how they will be eventually solved. A Modelica compiler or interpreter can then analyze the model of a complex system resulting from the aggregation of its sub-systems, determine how the equations can be solved (numerically and/or symbolically), and automatically produce the corresponding simulation code. This is a key feature, as it makes it possible to concentrate on the modeling task, rather than on how to actually compute the model variables at each time step. The result is a more elegant and compact system description. To take one example, the Modelica model of an electrical resistor will contain only the equation $V = R*I$, which states how the voltage and the current are tied together. Depending on how the resistor is connected to other components, the current will be computed as a function of the voltage, or vice-versa.

2. Encapsulation

This is a key concept of the object-oriented approach, meaning that different objects can interact only through rigorously defined interfaces, regardless of their internal details. In the context of dynamic system modeling, this means that different objects must be connected by standard interfaces, or *connectors;* moreover, it should always be possible to connect any two objects with compatible interfaces, as long as this is physically meaningful. The connection of two objects usually models a physical connection: an electrical contact in the case of electrical systems, a welding in the case of mechanical systems, or a client-supplier relationship in the case of supply chains.

In the Modelica language, connectors are defined by a set of variables, each characterized by an additional attribute, either *flow* or *effort*. In electrical systems, for example, connectors contain a voltage and a current; the voltage is an *effort* variable, which means that when two or more objects are connected, all the corresponding voltages must be equal; the current is a *flow* variable, which means that when two or more objects are connected, the sum of all the currents (positive when entering the component) is equal to zero[2]. Note that connecting objects actually means generating additional equations, which are then added to the set of equations of the sub-systems.

The model equations use the connector variables as boundary conditions (e.g. the voltage V of the resistor model is the difference between the voltage variables on its two connectors). Consequently, according to the declarative approach, the connector variables are neither input or output variables *per se*. This feature is essential to provide a truly object-oriented approach to physical system modeling, since it allows writing each model in a way which is independent on the specific models it will be connected to. Referring again to the resistor example, the model $V = R*I$ is always the same, regardless of the fact that it is connected to a current source, to a voltage source, or to any generic circuit. It is however possible to declare connector variables as inputs or outputs when this is actually the case; for example, control systems have clearly defined input and output signals.

3. Structuring complex models

According to the object-oriented methodology, complex systems are described by first defining basic entities, and then by using them to compose more complex ones; this is accomplished resorting to modularity and inheritance.

The modularity feature allows to use simpler models as building blocks. In our case, for instance, the marketplace model is defined by a collection of company models, connected by client-supplier relationships; each company, in turn, is described by other models (e.g. assembly line, warehouses, etc.). Conversely, when a family of models shares some common features, inheritance can be used to describe them more efficiently. A parent model is first defined, containing the common attributes; child models are then defined by inheriting from the parent model and adding their own specific features. In our case, for instance, a base company model is first defined, containing all the basic parameters, and the finite part warehouse models. Two child models are then derived to describe companies with

---

[2] Other examples of connectors are given here. Mechanical: displacement (effort) and force (flow). Hydraulic: pressure (effort) and flow rate (flow). Economical: price (effort) and quantity of exchanged good (flow).

or without suppliers; each one adds his own specific equations, while only the former one adds the required raw material warehouse models.

4. Textual modeling

The Modelica language is a purely *textual* language: Any Modelica model is a plain-text file, easily read by both humans and computers. It is possible to add a graphic layer to help the building of complex models, but the model behavior is entirely specified by the text layer. It is then always possible to inspect models, or to share them with others, without bothering about obscure or proprietary file formats, as happens in other simulation environments.

3.2 Why Use Modelica for Supply Chain Modeling?

Modelica has been mainly used for engineering applications; as far as the author knows, this is its first application in the field of production economics and business management. There are many factors which make the use of this language attractive in this field, in particular for theory-building purposes.

(Disney et al., 2004) listed the approaches used until now to study the SC Dynamics: management games (such as the Beer Game), analytical models, statistical models, simulation studies and control theory models (both s and z-transform). As a matter of fact, if one is willing to develop a quantitative model of a supply chain, high analytical skills are required. For instance, consider the APIOBPCS model in (Disney & Towill, 2003): This is a simulation model based on difference equations, but even reading the model could be a difficult task. Moreover, the selection of the proper simulation language and tool could be cumbersome, since the choice is between only commercial software or tailor-made applications. In this regard, Modelica offers interesting perspectives.

First of all, the language definition is not proprietary (it is maintained by the non-profit Modelica Association); moreover, it is quite stable: It has not been modified substantially since its first release, and has now reached a state of maturity. Currently, software packages are available to translate Modelica models into simulation code (e.g., Dymola, MathModelica, OpenModelica); some of them are commercial, while others are free; more of them are likely to appear in the future. Besides being directly used for automatic code generation, Modelica can also be thought of as a high-level specification language for complex dynamic systems; the corresponding simulators code could then be hand-coded with any suitable programming language or simulation tool.

The possibility of writing models in a declarative way allows the specification of models in a more compact and readable way. As a matter of fact, the application discussed in this paper does not fully exploit this potential, as the developed models and the corresponding connectors are basically causal, i.e., it is easy to identify input and output variables, and to rewrite all the equations as assignments and algorithms. Future developments, however, could use this feature more heavily. For example, it could be possible to include the price formation mechanisms in a very elegant way. Each player in the market could have its price-demand (or price-supply) curve represented as an equation, while the connectors to the other players could contain the quantity of exchanged goods (flow variable), and the price (effort variable). Connecting two or more such players would implicitly generate the equations which determine the market clearing price.

These object-oriented features allow the organization of complex models in a conceptually clear way by using modularity and inheritance, as will be shown in the next section. It is also easy to fully publish the models used for simulation case studies, thus allowing the validation (or falsification) of the results by peers.

4 The "Supply Chain" Modelica Library

4.1 Introduction

The focal object of the Supply Chain library is the Company. The aim of this section is to illustrate the structure and the functioning of its components; the reader is strongly encouraged to refer to the code listed in the Appendix, in order both to get a feeling on Modelica, as well as to understand the model's details.

The generic Company offers various Finite Products (FPs) and uses different Raw Materials (RMs); for each kind of FP and RM, a separate warehouse is designed in order to monitor stock and availability levels. Each warehouse is assigned to a (FP or RM) manager, who decides how much to deliver and how much to replenish, by issuing delivery orders, production orders to the assembly line, or purchase orders to raw material suppliers. The capacity of the assembly line is shared among FPs; more than one supplier is available for each RM. A more detailed description of each components is provided in the following paragraphs; it should already be evident how the elements located at the Physical level (e.g. production delays and batches ⇒ Assembly Line) have been decoupled from those at the Control level (e.g. ordering levels ⇒ Managers). All models considered here are discrete-time dynamic systems; the TimeFrame object provides an event generator clock which triggers the state transitions in all the other models.

In order to build a supply chain, various companies must be connected so as to exchange information (forecast and order data) and goods. This happens through a standard connector, named ProdStream, which is used to link RM warehouses on the buy side with FP warehouse on the sell side: The corresponding flow of information and goods is dynamically decided by the managers. Effort variables carry the information signals (forecast + orders), while flow variables describe the flow of goods, so that the algebraic sum of items leaving and entering the companies at each time step is zero. A Consumer model has been created to generate forecasts and actual orders for retailers' FPs. This model is simply connected to two signal generator blocks, and includes some supplementary features in order to record the supply chain's service level (e.g. late deliveries).

4.2 Company

The company is the object used to build Supply Chain models. Each company may deal with n_FP finite products and n_RM different raw materials: No constraints are set to these numbers, and only a single-level bill of material is allowed. The base Company object contains parameters and variables common to all company models, an array of FP warehouse and of assembly line models (one for each FP type), but no relevant equations are included, except for those needed to link all of its components (e.g. the FP warehouses with the Assembly lines).

The Company object is specialized into two types: with and without suppliers. This distinction has been introduced to model the upstream company in the supply chain, which has no constraints on raw material availability; furthermore, the company with supplier is featured by an array of supply quotas, so that each RM can be bought from different suppliers, with given percentages. Each of the two child models, CompanyWithSuppliers and CompanyWithoutSuppliers inherits all the variables, parameters, objects and equations of the parent model, and adds its own ones. The model of these specialized companies includes all the equations needed to process the requests coming from the various FP managers by taking into account the production batch size, the priority of different FP competing for the available production capacity, and the available raw materials. All this information is used to transform such requests in released production orders (ProdStart variables in the model) and to track the production backlog.

4.3 Assembly Line

The AssemblyLine object models the manufacturing process. It is characterized by two parameters: a fixed processing time and an actual scrap rate (which may differ from the estimated one, used by the managers to issue production orders). This component, therefore, has only to reproduce the functioning of a real manufacturing resource. In order to explicitly monitor the WIP and its completion level, an array of pipelined production items (PipeLine) has been used, so that the status of the production orders, from their start to the completion, is observable. To understand the model code, note that the all the involved variables are discrete, i.e. they only change their values when the clock trigger is activated, and that the operator pre(x) returns the previous value of x before the event takes place.

4.4 FP (and RM) Warehouse and Manager

For the sake of simplicity, let's concentrate on the FP. Warehouse and Manager objects are strictly related each others.

The Warehouse_FP object controls and monitors the inventory for the considered FP, and issues production orders to the Company object. The stock control mechanism implemented is the standard "order up to" policy, with fixed order intervals equal to one period, but other policies can be easily implemented. A certain set of equations is used to compute the inventory and the availability level, which has to consider on-hand inventories, past orders, and detected forecast errors. On the basis of this information, plus other relevant parameters such as the "up to" level and the estimated scrap rate of the production process, the Warehouse_FP object computes the Production Order for its FP, and submits it to the Company object, which will decide if and when to pass it to the assembly line, as described above. The FPManager object is responsible for aggregating and synchronizing demand forecasts of the same good coming from different customers with different horizons, for aggregating actual orders, for deciding what has to be delivered to each customer, and for monitoring the related backlog.

A similar setting has been adopted for RM Warehouse and Manager; their model obviously reflects various differences related to the computation of inventory, availability, backlog, raw material consumption and purchase orders to be issued on the basis of agreed market shares.

4.5 Building an Actual Instance of Company

The objects presented in the previous sub-sections allow instances of companies to be built with any number of suppliers, customers, RMs, and FPs, by specifying the connections between the ProdStream interfaces of the company and the corresponding FP and RM managers. For example, the C2 object (see the Appendix) models a very simple company with no suppliers, and a single product sold to a single consumer. The model extends the CompanyWithoutSuppliers model, as well as the Interface0S1C object (not listed in the Appendix), which provides the graphic layer and a ProdStream connector named customer1. The manager models are then added. Finally, the flow of goods and information they manage between the warehouse and the customer interface is modeled by connecting the CustomerSide connector of the warehouse and the customer1 connector of the company to the corresponding interfaces of the FP manager. A similar approach could be followed for the supplier side, if present, by inheriting from CompanyWithSuppliers. Also, in case the same good is sold to many customers, it would be possible to model a priority-based dispatching policy by suitably connecting one manager to every customer interface. Details are, however, outside the scope of this paper.

5 First Evidences on SC Modeling with Modelica

Figure 1 illustrates a simple supply chain model built with Modelica. The Dymola software was used to compile the model and perform the simulation.

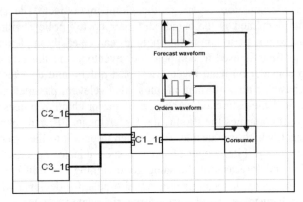

Figure 1: The Simulated Supply Chain: 1 Retailer, 2 Suppliers, 1 Consumer

The C1_1 company acts as a retailer, with a single FP, serving a single customer whose demand is unknown, and whose delivery lead time is equal to zero. A demand forecast is therefore needed in order reduce the FP stock. C1_1 has two suppliers, namely C2_1 and C3_1, supplying two different RMs, both of which are needed to produce the FP. RM inventories are pulled resorting to a "fixed interval, order up to" policy. Processing time is 1 period for C1_1 and 2 periods for its suppliers, while the batch size is set to 10 for everybody.

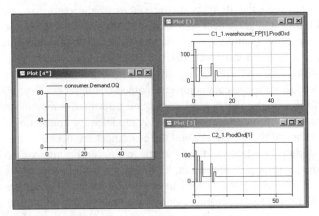

Figure 2: Production Orders at C1_1 and C2_1 when TR.C1_1=100

As depicted in Figure 2, a perturbation in final demand was introduced, without overcoming the maximum throughput rate of C1_1 (set to 100 items/period). Such demand peak produced a strong perturbation in the production orders, and hence production process, of each company. Then the throughput rate of C1_1 was reduced to 40 items/period and we observed a more regular behavior, with the BE still being evident, as depicted in Figure 3.

Even though a limited amount of testing has been conducted, in our opinion Modelica appears to be a suitable methodology for supply chain simulation. Please note that the library presented in the Appendix, including the graphical part, was developed in about 5 days.

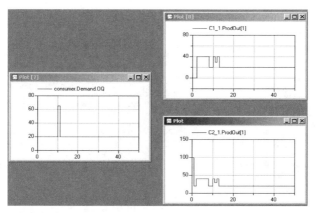

Figure 3: Production Orders at C1_1 and C2_1 when TR.C1_1=40

6 Concluding Remarks

This paper presented how Modelica, a well-acknowledged modeling language for traditional engineering applications, can be usefully applied to the study of Supply Chain Dynamics. Modelica is easy to learn and, as illustrated in the paper, it has powerful and distinctive characteristics which may ease the development and the sharing of innovative research. A first application of Modelica to the task of studying the dynamics of complex supply chains has been described, so that newcomers to this language may become a little more familiar with it and with its usage. This prototypal application was intended to study the Bullwhip Effect. In this paper, a very simple supply chain was simulated, but all the objects needed to build much more complex models have been developed and illustrated as well. The outcomes of this prototypal application are quite encouraging, since the model was easily built, and a bullwhip-prone environment was quickly simulated and observed. As a future development of this research path, the taxonomy discussed in Section 2 will be tested so as to assess its validity from an empirical point of view as well, while additional model features will be added. Furthermore, a "downsizing" of the model for educational purposes is under evaluation.

7 Appendix: The "Supply Chain" Modelica Library

```
package SupplyChain

model TimeFrame
  parameter Real startTime=0;
  inner parameter Real clockPeriod=1.0;
  inner output Boolean clock "Clock for the model";
equation
  clock = sample(startTime, clockPeriod);
end TimeFrame;

connector ProdStream
  Real FQ "Forecasted Quantity";
  Integer DLT " Delivery Lead Time";
  Real OQ "Ordered Quantity";
  flow Real SQ "Supplied quantity";
end ProdStream;

model Consumer "Consumer Model"
  extends InterfaceIcon;
  parameter Integer DLT "Delivery Lead Time";
  discrete Real stockout "Stockout";
  outer Boolean clock;
  outer Real clockPeriod;
equation
  when clock then
    Demand.OQ = OQ.signal[1];
    Demand.FQ = FQ.signal[1];
    Demand.LT = LT;
    stockout = pre(stockout) + Demand.SQ -
       Demand.OQ;
  end when;
end Consumer;

partial model Company "Base company model"
  parameter Integer n_FP=1 "Number of finite parts warehouses";
  parameter Real SR_est[n_FP]=ones(n_FP)
     "Estimated scrap rates";
  parameter Real SR_act[n_FP]=ones(n_FP)
     "Actual scrap rates";
  parameter Integer PLT[n_FP](min=ones(n_FP))
     "Processing Lead Times";
  parameter Real OL_FP[n_FP]
     "Finite Part Order Levels";
  parameter Real BS[n_FP] "Batch size";
  parameter Real PC "Production Capacity";
  parameter Real CC[n_FP] "Capacity consumption";
  discrete Real ProdOut[n_FP] "Production Output";
  discrete Real ProdStart[n_FP] "Production started now";
  discrete Real ProdOrd[n_FP] "Production Order";
  discrete Real backlog[n_FP] "Production Backlog";
  Warehouse_FP warehouse_FP[n_FP](
     PLT=PLT,
     OL=OL_FP,
     SR_est=SR_est) "Finite part warehouses";
  AssemblyLine assemblyLine[n_FP](PLT=PLT,
     SR_act=SR_act);
  outer Boolean clock;
  outer Real clockPeriod;
equation
  ProdOut = warehouse_FP.ProdOut;
  ProdOut = assemblyLine.ProdOut;
  ProdOrd = warehouse_FP.ProdOrd;
  ProdStart = assemblyLine.ProdStart;
end Company;

partial model CompanyWithoutSuppliers
  extends Company;
  discrete Real PO[n_FP] "Production order
     (auxiliary variable)";
  discrete Real PS[n_FP] "Production started now
     (auxiliary variable)";
  discrete Real BL[n_FP] "Production backlog
     (auxiliary variable)";
  discrete Real PC_AV "Available production
     capacity";
algorithm
  when clock then
    PO := ProdOrd;
    BL := pre(backlog);
    PC_AV := PC;
    for k in 1:n_FP loop
      PS[k] := ceil((PO[k] + BL[k])/BS[k])*BS[k];
      PS[k] := min(PS[k], PC_AV/CC[k]);
      PS[k] := floor(PS[k]/BS[k])*BS[k];
      PC_AV := PC_AV - PS[k]*CC[k];
      BL[k] := max(0, BL[k] + PO[k] - PS[k]);
    end for;
    ProdStart := PS;
    backlog := BL;
  end when;
end CompanyWithoutSuppliers;

partial model CompanyWithSuppliers
  extends Company;
  parameter Integer n_RM=1 "Number of raw
     material warehouses";
  Warehouse_RM warehouse_RM[n_RM](OL=OL_RM)
     "Raw material warehouses";
  parameter Real OL_RM[n_RM] "Raw Material
     Order Levels";
  parameter Real UC[n_RM, n_FP] "Utilisation
     coefficients (RM x FP)";
  discrete Real RMCons[n_RM] "Raw material
     consumption";
  discrete Real RMInv[n_RM] "Raw material
     inventories";
  discrete Real PO[n_FP] "Production order
     (auxiliary variable)";
  discrete Real PS[n_FP] "Production started now (auxiliary
     variable)";
```

discrete Real BL[n_FP] "Production backlog (auxiliary variable)";
discrete Real PC_AV "Available production capacity";
discrete Real Inv_AV[n_RM] "Available raw material inventory";
discrete Real PP[n_RM] "Potential production given every RM";
equation
  RMCons = warehouse_RM.RMCons;
  RMInv = warehouse_RM.Inv;
algorithm
  when clock then
    PO := ProdOrd;
    BL := pre(backlog);
    PC_AV := PC;
    Inv_AV := pre(RMInv);
    for k in 1:n_FP loop
      PS[k] := ceil((PO[k] + BL[k])/BS[k])*BS[k];
      for n in 1:n_RM loop
        PP[n] := Inv_AV[n]/UC[n, k];
      end for;
      PS[k] := min(PS[k], min(PC_AV/CC[k], min(PP)));
      PS[k] := floor(PS[k]/BS[k])*BS[k];
      PC_AV := PC_AV - PS[k]*CC[k];
      Inv_AV := Inv_AV - PS[k]*UC[:, k];
      BL[k] := max(0, BL[k] + PO[k] - PS[k]);
    end for;
    ProdStart := PS;
    backlog := BL;
    RMCons := UC*PS;
  end when;
end CompanyWithSuppliers;

model AssemblyLine "Assembly line model"
  parameter Integer PLT(min=1) "Processing Lead Time";
  parameter Real SR_act "Scrap rate (actual)";
  discrete Real ProdStart "Production starting now";
  discrete Real ProdOut "Production output";
  discrete Real PipeLine[PLT - 1] "Production pipeline";
  outer Boolean clock;
equation
  when clock then
    if PLT == 1 then
      ProdOut = ProdStart*SR_act;
    else
      ProdOut = SR_act*pre(PipeLine[PLT - 1]);
      PipeLine[1] = ProdStart;
      PipeLine[2:PLT - 1] = pre(PipeLine[1:PLT - 2]);
    end if;
  end when;
end AssemblyLine;

model Warehouse_FP
  discrete Real Inv "Inventory";
  discrete Real Avail "Availability";
  discrete Real ProdOrd "Production Order";
  discrete Real ProdOut "Production Output";
  discrete Real HistoryOfProdOrd "History of Production Orders";
  discrete Real HistoryOfProdOut "History of Production Outputs";
  parameter Integer PLT(min=1) "Processing Lead Time";
  parameter Real OL "Order level";
  parameter Real SR_est "Estimated Scrap rate";
  ProdStream CustomerSide;
  outer Boolean clock;
  outer Real clockPeriod;
equation
  when clock then
    HistoryOfProdOrd = pre(HistoryOfProdOrd) + pre(ProdOrd);
    HistoryOfProdOut = pre(HistoryOfProdOut) + pre(ProdOut);
    Avail = pre(Inv) + HistoryOfProdOrd - HistoryOfProdOut;
    ProdOrd = max(0, OL - (Avail - CustomerSide.FQ))/SR_est;
    CustomerSide.SQ = min(pre(Inv) + ProdOut, CustomerSide.OQ);
    Inv = pre(Inv) + ProdOut - CustomerSide.SQ;
  end when;
end Warehouse_FP;

model FPManager "Finite Part Manager"
  parameter Boolean LastOne=true "True if there are no further downstream FPManagers";
  parameter Integer PLT(min=1) "Processing Lead Time (should be equal to the corresponding value in the WarehousePF model)";
  discrete Real backlog "Dispatching backlog";
  outer Boolean clock;
  outer Real clockPeriod;
  ProdStream CustomerSide;
  ProdStream InputSide;
  ProdStream ResidualSide;
equation
  when clock then
    InputSide.OQ = CustomerSide.OQ + pre(backlog) + ResidualSide.OQ;
    InputSide.LT = 0;
    CustomerSide.SQ = min(CustomerSide.OQ + pre(backlog), InputSide.SQ);
    backlog = pre(backlog) + CustomerSide.SQ + CustomerSide.OQ;
    InputSide.FQ = ResidualSide.FQ + delay(CustomerSide.FQ, (CustomerSide.LT - PLT + 1)*clockPeriod);
    if LastOne then
      ResidualSide.OQ = 0;
      ResidualSide.LT = 0;
      ResidualSide.FQ = 0;
    else
      InputSide.SQ + ResidualSide.SQ + CustomerSide.SQ = 0;
    end if;
  end when;
end FPManager;

model Warehouse_RM
  parameter Real OL "Order level";
  discrete Real Inv "Inventory";
  discrete Real Avail "Availabilty";
  discrete Real RMCons "Raw material consumption";
  discrete Real BackRM "Raw material backlog";
  ProdStream SupplierSide;
  outer Boolean clock;
  outer Real clockPeriod;
equation
  when clock then
    Inv = pre(Inv) + SupplierSide.SQ - RMCons;
    Avail = pre(Inv) + BackRM;
    BackRM = pre(BackRM) + pre(SupplierSide.OQ) - pre(SupplierSide.SQ);
    SupplierSide.OQ = max(OL - Avail, 0);
    SupplierSide.FQ = SupplierSide.OQ;
    SupplierSide.LT = 0;
  end when;
end Warehouse_RM;

model RMManager "Raw Material Manager"
  parameter Real PurchaseShare(min=0, max=1) "Note: sum of PurchaseShares for the same product should be 1";
equation
  SupplierSide.SQ + WarehouseSide.SQ = 0;

```
SupplierSide.LT = WarehouseSide.LT;         extends InterfaceOS1C;
SupplierSide.FQ = WarehouseSide.FQ*         FPManager ManagerP2(LastOne=true,PLT=PLT[1]);
  PurchaseShare;                              equation
SupplierSide.OQ = WarehouseSide.OQ*           connect(ManagerP2.InputSide,
  PurchaseShare;                                    warehouse_FP[1].CustomerSide);
end RMManager;                                connect(ManagerP2.CustomerSide, customer1);
                                            end C2;
model C2                                    end SupplyChain;
  extends CompanyWithoutSuppliers(n_FP=1);
```

8 References

Buffa, E. S., Miller, J. (1979): Production-Inventory system: planning and control, 3rd ed., Irwin, Boston: p. 411-418.

Burbidge, J. L. (1984): Automated Production control with a simulation capability, Proceedings of IFIP Conference, WG 5-7, Copenhagen: p. 1-14.

Disney, S. M., Naim M. M., Potter A. (2004): Assessing the impact of e-business on supply chain dynamics, in: International Journal of Production Economics, 89: 109-118.

Disney, S. M., Towill D. R. (2003): The effect of Vendor Managed Inventory dynamics on the Bullwhip Effect in supply chains, in: International Journal of Production Economics, 85: 199-215.

El-Beheiry, M., Wong, C. Y, El-Kharbotly, A. (2004): Empirical quantification of the bullwhip effect, in: Proceedings of the Thirteenth Working Seminar on Production Economics, 3: 259-274.

Forrester, J. W. (1961): Industrial dynamics, MIT Press, Cambridge.

Fritzson, P. (2003): Principles of Object-Oriented Modeling and Simulation with Modelica 2.1., Wiley, London.

Lee, H. L., Padmanabhan, V., Whang, S. (1997a): The Bullwhip Effect in Supply Chains, in: Sloan Management Review, 38(3), 93-102.

Lee, H. L., Padmanabhan, V., Whang, S. (1997b): Information distortion in a supply chain: the Bullwhip Effect, in: Management Science, 43(4): 546-558.

Miragliotta, G. (2004): The Bullwhip Effect: a survey on available knowledge and a new taxonomy of inherent determinants and external triggers, in: Proceedings of the Thirteenth Working Seminar on Production Economics, Igls, (Austria), 3: 259-274.

Modelica Association (2003): Modelica Language Specification, ver. 2.1. Available on http://www.modelica.org/.

Sterman, J. D. (1989): Modeling managerial behavior: misperception of feedback in a dynamic decision making experiment, in: Management Science, 35: 321-339.

Senge, P. M. (1990):The Fifth Discipline, Doubleday, New York.

Senge, P. M., Sterman, J. D. (1992): System Thinking and Organisational Learning, in: European Journal of Operational Research, 59 (3): 137-145.

The Potential of Cooperative Game Theory for Supply Chain Management

Jörn-Henrik Thun

1 The Relevance of Stability, Trust and Rationality for Supply Chain Management 478
2 Analyzing Supply Chain Management with Game Theory 479
3 Analyzing Supply Chain Structures with Cooperative Game Theory 485
4 Concluding Remarks 489
5 References 489
6 Appendix 491

Summary:
In this paper Supply Chain Management will be analyzed in the light of Game Theory. The aim of the paper is to show the applicability of Cooperative Game Theory as methodology for analyzing supply chains. A main characteristic of a supply chain is cooperation. The success and sustainability of cooperation depends on the stability as constituting element. Cooperation can be analyzed with Cooperative Game Theory. The Shapley-Value is used as algorithm to allocate the profit among the cooperating partner. But for supply chains the structure is relevant. The Myerson-Value takes the structure of a game into account when formulating a specific allocation rule. Cooperative game theory can be applied as methodology for Supply Chain Management contributing an allocation algorithm.

Keywords:
Supply Chain Management, Cooperation, Cooperative Game Theory, Shapley-Value, Myerson-Value

1 The Relevance of Stability, Trust and Rationality for Supply Chain Management

In recent years supply chain management has evolved as one of the most important fields of operations management. As a concept for coordinating information and material between companies, supply chain management has a significant potential in creating competitive advantage for the companies involved. The great potential of supply chain management for competitiveness has often been mentioned in the literature (see e.g. Chopra & Meindl, 2001). The main advantages that can be derived from choosing the right supply chain are an improvement in efficiency, e.g. due to high turns of inventory, or an increase in market responsiveness, e.g. by shorter lead time (see Fisher, 1997: 108). Another important benefit is to fight cooperatively against a phenomenon commonly referred to as the "bullwhip" effect which was first observed by logistic executives at P&G concerning disposable diapers (see for the bullwhip effect Lee et al., 1997: 93-102; Forrester, 1958). By sharing information across the supply chain, the bullwhip effect can be mitigated.

Supply chain management is currently a major issue within the academic discussion. Different schools of supply chain management exist that have different opinions about the nature of supply chain management, i.e. the 'Information School', 'Future School' or 'Integration School' (see for a discussion of the different schools Bechtel & Jayaram, 1997). Accordingly, there are plenty of definitions for the terms "supply chain" and "supply chain management."

Christopher defines the supply chain as the "... network of organizations that are involved, through upstream and downstream linkages, in the different processes and activities that produce value in the form of products and services in the hands of the ultimate consumer." (Christopher, 1998: 15) A definition of supply chain management is given by Chopra & Meindl: "Supply chain management involves the management of flows between and among stages in a supply chain to maximize total profitability" (Chopra & Meindl, 2001: 6). Handfield & Nichols define Supply chain management as "... the integration of [..] activities through improved supply chain relationships, to achieve a sustainable competitive advantage." (Handfield & Nichols, 1999: 2) All definitions have more or less (explicitly) in common that supply chains are based on cooperation in order to generate a benefit. Some authors claim that, in the future, competition will take place between supply chains rather than between individual companies. In order to generate advantages, contracts for vertical cooperation are established within supply chains.

In this paper, cooperation will be regarded as a constituting element of supply chains. It can be stated that vertical cooperation, as one possible solution on the continuum between market and hierarchy, builds the basis of supply chain management. Cooperation is defined as the process of coordinating goals and actions of agents. A cooperation functions via the coordination of participating companies, e.g. in order to fight against the bullwhip effect.

Generally, trust is seen as a driving force behind cooperation (e.g. Handfield & Bechtel, 2002). Within the framework of supply chain management, trust has an immense potential for improvement. According to a number of authors, trust is the most critical factor of cooperation between companies (see e.g. Poirer, 1999: 46ff.). However, the question arises of which fundamental conditions must be met in a trust-based cooperation for participating companies not to abuse this trust through opportunistic behavior due to the existence of discretionary scope. Therefore, an additional foundation based on rationality seems to be reasonable (Voß & Schneidereit, 2002).

2 Analyzing Supply Chain Management with Game Theory

2.1 Introduction to Game Theory

Despite the fact that it has been widely discussed in the academic literature, there is still a lack of applied rational methodologies analyzing supply chain management. There is a shortage of concepts for profit allocation which are essential for the sustainability of supply chains. Although cooperative game theory has been discussed extensively, little has been written from a strategic perspective (Stuart, 2001: 189). In the following, cooperative game theory will be discussed concerning its great potential to act as a rationality-based foundation for strategic supply chain management. "Cooperative Game Theory has great potential in SCM applications since cooperation to improve SC performance is the key issue in many SC applications" (Cachon & Netessine, 2004).

Often, game theory is equated with non-cooperative game theory including the popular concept of Nash's equilibrium, where players maximize their own payoff regardless of the possible overall outcome of the game. But, in terms of supply chain management, the different players strive collectively to maximize the global benefit. For this analysis, there is a need for a different view: Cooperative Game Theory. Contrary to non-cooperative game theory, agents can cooperate with each other based on binding agreements in order to generate a stabile conjoint outcome.

In terms of cooperative game theory, the aspect of stability is closely related with the allocation of profits in cooperation. Surprisingly, there is a lack of algorithms or heuristics to allocate the benefits of supply chain management. So there is a need for an allocation algorithm taking the specific properties of cooperation into account. An allocation algorithm has to fulfill several requirements. For example, it has to provide a stable solution. The stability of cooperation depends mainly on the payoff for each player, thus no inducements exist that let supply chain partners abandon cooperation. Furthermore, the allocation algorithm calculating the payoff should consider the bargaining power of a supply chain partner. Additionally, the allocation algorithm must be based on axioms to suffice rational conditions.

The shapely value is a solution concept based on an axiomatic framework, which assigns each cooperative game an exact allocation regarding the contribution of each player for the coalition success. Adapting the Shapley-value to the properties of supply chain cooperation, an allocation algorithm for supply chain management can be identified.

It has to be explored whether or not game theory can provide a rational foundation of supply chain management. Within the framework of game theory, decision problems, including several agents, are analyzed. "Game theory can be defined as the study of mathematical models of conflict and cooperation between intelligent rational decision makers. Game theory provides general mathematical techniques for analyzing situations in which two or more individuals make decisions that will influence one another's welfare" (Myerson, 1991: 1).

The basics of game theory were established by von Neumann & Morgenstern (1947). Often, within games of non-cooperative game theory, equilibrium points result which are not pareto-efficient due to defection (see Nash, 1951; Axelrod, 1984). The well-known prisoner's dilemma is such an example (see Luce & Raiffa, 1957: 95). Under certain assumptions, individuals can create advantages by cooperation. Accordingly, cooperation can be regarded as reasonable despite the assumption of individual rationality (see Axelrod, 1984). A discussion of the process of how cooperation evolves will not be done here in order to instead focus on the allocation of profits in supply chains. Coalition theory seems to be a suitable approach for the analysis of this question, as discussed in the next section.

Coalition theory is part of cooperative game theory. Within the framework of coalition theory, situations are analyzed in which two or more players cooperate in a coalition to reach their goals; a coalition can be defined as every non-empty set of players (see Myerson, 1991: 418). Contrary to non-cooperative game theory, it is supposed that participating players can commit themselves to a specific action or strategy because of the existence of exogenous mechanisms such as binding contractual agreements – as constituting characteristics of cooperative game theory; thus, individualistic-cooperative behavior can be assumed. "The key assumption that distinguishes co-operative games from non-cooperative games is this assumption that players can negotiate effectively" (Myerson, 1991: 419). This distinction between cooperative and non-cooperative game theory was first made by Nash. He distinguished between games with and without the possibility for players to communicate and to make agreements, i.e. to negotiate effectively (see Nash, 1951: 286). This is not a restrictive assumption, since it can be seen as the common procedure in supply chain management, e.g. in the form of contracts.

Furthermore, for many cooperative games, it is assumed that players can transfer their profits between each other via site payments without any transaction losses. Such games are called TU games. Again, this assumption holds for supply chain management. In summary, coalition theory has two basic assumptions for TU games:

1. Existence of binding agreements
2. Transferable payments between players

It is the aim of supply chain management to create additional value for the companies participating in the cooperation, which is emphasized by Christopher who defines supply chain management as the "... management of relationships in order to achieve a more profitable outcome for all parties in the chain" (Christopher, 1998: 18). Following Chopra & Meindl, it is the objective of every supply chain "... to maximize the overall value generated" (Chopra & Meindl, 2001: 5). Whether and how the overall profit derived from cooperation is divided between participating companies is an important problem of supply chain management. This leads to the question of a reasonable allocation algorithm. Coalition theory generates solutions for the acceptance of an efficient and rational profit allocation by all participants of a coalition. For this, the solutions have to fulfill several requirements.

2.2 Formal Description of a Cooperative Game

In the following the formal basics of cooperative game theory are described. Firstly, N denotes the set of all players. Secondly, $v(\{i\})$ is the value which can be created by player i on its own. Accordingly, player i must receive at least $v(\{i\})$. This requirement is linked with the property of super-additivity. Following the property of super-additivity, each coalition creates a value which is greater than the sum of the values of the sub-coalitions constituting this coalition. For two disjoint sub-coalitions T and S out of N, the following equation must hold:

$$v(T \cup S) \geq v(S) + v(T).$$

According to the property of super-additivity, no coalition can increase its profit by dividing into two disjoint sub-coalitions. For the extreme case, the following equation must hold: $v(S) = v(T) = 0$; but, $v(T \cup S) \geq 0$. Correspondingly, the conjoint payoff of two sub-coalitions must be at least as much as the sum of the payoffs of each coalition. In the context of supply chain management, this can be described as the required payoff that a value chain must create at least for system generation and system stability.

There are situations where the sequence of the companies is essential. In general it might be stated that the cooperation of two companies linked with each other is more valuable for the supply chain than any other cooperation because collaboration between those companies is more efficient, e.g. Just-in-Time relationships can be established between a manufacturer and its first-tier supplier. In situations where the coalition is determined by a logical restriction such as the unidirectional flow of material within a supply chain, a chain axiom might become relevant. The chain axiom applies to the characteristic function of a coalitional game (Thun, 2003). It is an additional condition that must be fulfilled. For an example of three companies, it can be formulated as follows:

$$v(\{i;j\}) \geq v(\{i;k\}) \land v(\{j;k\}) \geq v(\{i;k\}), \forall j=i+1, i<j<k \in N$$

The chain axiom implies that a coalition of companies which are directly linked creates a higher value than any other coalition. Due to the fact that it will be considered in the characteristic function, the calculation of the Shapley-value itself is still possible, although the result is different for a particular company.

2.3 The Shapley-Value and Its Axioms

The Shapley-value is a concept of cooperative game theory assigning each coalitional game a unique solution based on an axiomatic foundation (see Shapley, 1953: 307–317; Myerson, 1991: 436ff; Roth, 1988: 1–27). The four axioms founding the concept – also called fairness axioms – will be explained to discuss their applicability for supply chain management (see for the axioms Myerson, 1991: 437f.).

The so called pareto-axiom guarantees that the value of a coalition equals the sum of all payoffs the different players receive. The entire available value is allocated as it is done within the framework of the core (see Gillies, 1953; Shapley, 1990). A distribution following the Shapley-value must be pareto-efficient. Assuming pareto-efficiency as a reasonable criterion for the core, it should analogously build the foundation for the Shapley-value.

The axiom of symmetry requires that allocations do not depend upon the identities of players, but instead upon the value they create for the coalition. Two players, i and j, creating the same value for a coalition K must receive the same payoff. For supply chain management, this seems to be reasonable because, for profit allocation, the contribution of a company should be relevant. It has to be mentioned that other factors might have an impact on the allocation. However, in terms of a rationality-based analysis, the contribution of each player seems to be the most appropriate criterion, although the identification of the precise contribution of each company and the definition of the values of the different sub-coalitions will be difficult.

The axiom concerning unessential players guarantees that players, who do not contribute any value to a coalition – so-called 'dummy' players – will not be considered when allocating the coalition profit. A player who contributes the same value to a coalition as he would create acting on his own should receive exactly this payoff. Concerning supply chain management, the consideration of a company contributing nothing more than its own value to a coalition does not make sense.

With the axiom of additivity, the Shapely-value has the property that a payoff received by a player from a composed game equals the sum of payoffs the player would receive from the independent sub-games. This axiom expresses that a company must get as much out of one particular coalition as it receives from two sub-coalitions of that coalition. Basically, it can be stated that the axioms of the Shapley-value hold true for supply chain management and build a reasonable foundation; thus, they can be applied for an allocation algorithm within a supply chain.

The Shapley-value is the only allocation algorithm satisfying all mentioned axioms. The Shapley-value Φ considers the value $[v(K) - v\{K - \{i\}\}]$ a player i contributes to all possible coalitions that can be created by set N. It is calculated according to the following formula:

$$\Phi_i(v) = \sum_{K \subseteq N-i} \frac{(K-1)!\,(N-K)!}{N!} [v(K) - v\{K - \{i\}\}]$$

The first term can be interpreted as a likelihood for the access of player i. The second term of the equation is the added value by the entry of player i. Osbourne and Rubinstein define that term as the marginal contribution of player i (see Osbourne & Rubinstein, 1994). Thus the entire term is something like an 'a-priori-expectation' of a player and expresses the average bargaining power of player i. The calculation of the shapely-value for player i results from the determination of the added value the coalition receives via the admission of this player over all n! permutations. The sum of all added values leads then to the Shapley-value of player i.

It has to be considered that the Shapley-value does not have to be within the core of a coalitional game and, as a consequence, does not have to be stable. However, for convex games, the Shapley-value is always within the core (see Myerson, 1991: 436ff.). For allocations according to Shapley's approach, it is guaranteed that a coalition can neither be attacked by defection of sub-coalitions nor be blocked effectively by the grant coalition due to the pareto-axiom.

In the following section, an example will illustrate the application of the Shapley value in the field of supply chain management. Given are three companies U1, U2 und U3. Conjointly, they can create a coalition value of $100. If only company U1 and U2 decide to collaborate, they can earn $70. Company U1 and U3 can reach only a value of $60 without company U2. If company U2 and U3 form a coalition, their conjoint value will be $80. Additionally, no company is able to generate a benefit alone. The following characteristic function results for the cooperative game. The characteristic function consists of the set of possible constellations of coalitions and assigns each coalition a value without making any allocation between the players within the coalitions:

$$v(\{1; 2; 3\}) = 100, v(\{1; 2\}) = 70; v(\{1; 3\}) = 60;$$
$$v(\{2; 3\}) = 80; v(\{i\}) = 0; i \in \{1;2;3\},$$

whereas v represents the profit of a particular coalition. The cooperative game fulfils the property of super-additivity, since v (S) = v (T) = 0, but v (T $\cup$ S) $\geq$ 0.

For the given example, the question arises how the profit of the coalition should be allocated. Table 1 gives an overview of the particular permutations of the three companies of the supply chain with the corresponding Shapley-values. The Shapley-value in the first row of Table 1 is calculated as follows: Company U1 cannot generate any profit on its own. By the admission of company U2, the conjoint profit rises to $70, thus U2 contributes $70 by its access. If the coalition will be completed by company U3, company U3 still contributes $30 to the overall profit of $100. If company U3 will join the coalition before company U2, the benefit created by company U3 is $60. Company U2 then contributes $40 to the overall profit (see second row in Table 1).

	Contribution to the coalition		
Permutation	U1	U2	U3
$U_1; U_2; U_3$	0	70	30
$U_1; U_3; U_2$	0	40	60
$U_2; U_1; U_3$	70	0	30
$U_2; U_3; U_1$	20	0	80
$U_3; U_2; U_1$	20	80	0
$U_3; U_1; U_2$	60	40	0
Σ	170	230	200
$\Phi_i(v)$	28.33	38.33	33.33

Table 1: Calculation of the Shapely-Values

The Shapley-values show that company U2 should get more of the overall coalition profit than the other two companies. Company U1 receives $28.$\overline{3}$; Company U3 gets $33.$\overline{3}$. The Shapley-value is depicted in Figure 1.

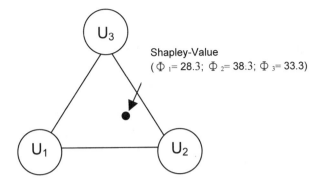

Figure 1: The Shapley-Value

3 Analyzing Supply Chain Structures with Cooperative Game Theory

Although the identification of the precise overall value of a supply chain coalition and the disclosure of the real contribution of a company will be difficult, game theory has a significant potential for the rational foundation of cooperation within the framework of supply chain management (Cachon & Netessine, 2004). Based on its concepts, game theory can contribute value implications to the discussion of supply chain management and can give fruitful hints for the design of cooperation.

If a supply chain is regarded as cooperation, the Shapley-value can be calculated as long as the chain property is considered. There is no impact of the positioning of the particular company in a chain, since the characteristic function has been set up considering particular relationships of companies following the chain axiom. For instance, in a n-tier chain there will be no impact if the particular company is at the end or at the front of the supply chain. The relationship to other companies within the supply chain needs to have been considered in the characteristic function. According to the symmetry axiom, the relevant aspect for the calculation of the Shapley-value is the contribution of a company to the supply chain. Sometimes it might not be reasonable to integrate a company into supply chain activities. Following the axiom of unessential players, they will not be put into consideration when calculating the allocation algorithm.

Many games of game theory imply that either all players will play non-cooperatively or they will cooperate altogether. This assumption is critical for some situations in terms of supply chain management. If material flow comes into play, the approach of a universal cooperation is inappropriate. Myerson provides a framework of partial cooperation structures (Myerson, 1977: 225-229). In this analysis, a set of players N and a set of unordered pairs of distinct members of N, called links, are given, whereas $n : m$ denotes the bilateral agreement between player m and player n. Any cooperation structure can be represented by these links. Contrary to the approach of Shapley, not all links must exist following this analysis. This is based on the idea that two players, although not in direct contact, may effectively cooperate with each other by cooperating both with the same mutual player or being connected by the cooperation graph (Myerson, 1977: 226). The question is, how will the outcome of a game depend on the cooperation structure? This is done by mapping cooperation graphs to allocation vectors, whereas $Y_n(g)$ represents the payoff of player n. The graph g determines the value each player will receive. An allocation rule might give player 2 more in $g_a = \{1:2, 2:3\}$ than in $g_b = \{1:3, 2:3\}$, because in g_a player 2 might play a more essential role. However, it should be guaranteed that $\sum_{1-3} Y_n(g_a) = v\{1,2,3\} = \sum_{1-3} Y_n(g_b)$ meaning that all profit will be allocated between the cooperating players. An allocation rule for a super-additive game is stable if

$$Y_n(g) \geq Y_n(g \setminus m : n) \wedge Y_m(g) \geq Y_m(g \setminus m : n),$$

Whereas the term "$\setminus m : n$" indicates that there is no link between player m and n in the cooperation graph. Accordingly, a stable allocation rule has the property that two players must have a benefit from the bilateral agreement.

In the following it is assumed that an allocation algorithm must satisfy the property of equitableness, which means for instance applying the equal-gains principle: Two players will benefit equally from cooperating with each other.

$$Y_n(g) - Y_n(g \setminus m : n) = Y_m(g) - Y_m(g \setminus m : n),$$

According to this allocation algorithm, an example is given for a super-additive game (A game is super-additive if $v(S \cup T) \geq v(S) + v(T), \forall S,T \subseteq N \wedge S \cap T = \emptyset$). Let $N = \{1, 2, 3\}$ with the characteristic function v:

$$v(\{1; 2; 3\}) = 100, v(\{1; 2\}) = 70; v(\{1; 3\}) = 60, v(\{2; 3\}) = 80,$$
$$v(\{i\}) = 0; i \in \{1 ;2 ;3\},$$

whereas the last term expresses that a player on its own will not generate any additional value (see for a detailed example Aumann & Myerson, 1988: 179). The different coalition structures are depicted in Figure 2.

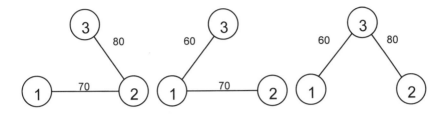

Figure 2: Coalition Structures

The allocation rule Y for this cooperative game is as follows:

$$Y(\emptyset) = (0,0,0),\ Y(\{1{:}2\}) = (35,35,0),\ Y(\{1{:}3\}) = (30,0,30),$$
$$Y(\{2{:}3\}) = (0,40,40),\ Y(\{1{:}2,\ 1{:}3\}) = (55,25,20),$$
$$Y(\{1{:}2,\ 2{:}3\}) = (18.\overline{3}, 58.\overline{3}, 23.\overline{3}),\ Y(\{1{:}3,\ 2{:}3\}) = (16.\overline{6}, 26.\overline{6}, 56.\overline{6}),$$
$$Y(\{1{:}2,\ 1{:}3,\ 2{:}3\}) = (28.\overline{3},\ 38.\overline{3},\ 33.\overline{3}).$$

The results imply that a player, due to the missing link between the others, receives the highest value as 'focal' player. His unique positioning within the game is essential for the outcome of the game. $Y(g^N)$, i.e. all links are established, leads to the same result as the Shapley-value. Accordingly, Myerson's approach can be regarded as a refinement of the Shapley-value for particular cooperation structures, taking missing links into account (see for a model based on the Myerson-value which considers the cost of establishing links Slikker & Von den Nouweland, 2000).

In the following, two specific outcomes of a game with four players will be examined assuming that both chain structures have the same characteristic function.

$$v(\{i\}) = 0,\ v(\{i{;}j\}) = 40\ |\ j=i+1\ \wedge\ v(\{i{;}j\}) = 0\ |\ j\neq i+1,$$
$$v(\{i,j,k\}) = \begin{cases} 60,\ j=i+1, k=j+1 \\ 40,\ \text{other} \end{cases},$$
$$v(\{i;j;k;l\}) = 80\ \forall\ i<j<k<l \in \{1;2;3;4\}.$$

For $Y_1(1{:}2;\ 2{:}3;\ 3{:}4)$ the following situation results:

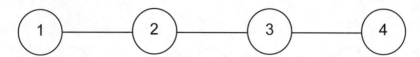

Figure 3: Alternative Chain Structure I

For $Y_2(2:3; 2^*:3; 3:4)$ the following situation results, whereas player 2* is a player similar to player 2.

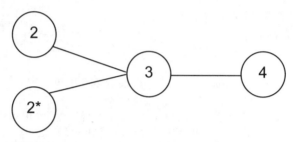

Figure 4: Alternative Chain Structure II

The allocation rule divides the benefit generated by the coalition as follows: $Y_1=(10.8\overline{3}, 29.1\overline{6}, 29.1\overline{6}, 10.8\overline{3})$ for the first structure and $Y_2=(10.8\overline{3}, 10.8\overline{3}, 41.\overline{6}, 16.\overline{6})$ for the second structure. The Myerson-value reflects the symmetry of the players in the first structure. The middle players will receive the same and the outer player will receive the same. Additionally, the middle players, i.e. the players having more direct linkages, will receive more than the other players from the coalition according to the allocation rule due to their property of connecting linkage instead of the property of dependency linkage of the outer player. This aspect becomes more important in terms of chain structure 2. Player 3 receives more than the sum of the rest of the players due to his property of dominant linkage. This is because of player 3's ability to enable the chain structure. Furthermore, an outer player of the alternative chain structure I will receive as much as a symmetric player of the alternative chain structure II. But analyses using cooperative game theory are not limited to these structures. With the allocation rule for supply chain structures introduced in this paper, many other chain structures can be analyzed in terms of profit allocation.

4 Concluding Remarks

In this paper, the aspect of profit allocation within supply chain management has been discussed in the light of game theory. The Shapley-value has been introduced and analyzed concerning its contribution to supply chain management as an allocation algorithm. The analyses show that cooperative game theory has a great potential to explore cooperation within supply chain management. In order to consider direct linkages within a supply chain, a chain axiom is added to the axiomatic framework of the Shapley-value. To take the particularities of a supply chain, i.e. the supply chain structure, into consideration, the calculation of the Shapley-value has been refined by Myerson's approach of an allocation rule based on existing links.

5 References

Aumann, R. J., Myerson, R. B. (1988): Endogenous formation of links between players and of coalitions. An application of the Shapley value, in: Roth, A. E. (ed.): The Shapley value: Essays in honor of Lloyed S. Shapley, Cambridge et al.: p. 175-194.

Axelrod, R. (1984): The Evolution of Cooperation, New York.

Bechtel, C., Jayaram, J. (1997): Supply Chain Management – A Strategic Perspective, in: The International Journal of Logistic Management, 8(1): 15-34.

Cachon, G., Netessine, S. (2004): Game theory in Supply Chain Analysis, in: D. Simchi-Levi, S. D. Wu and Z.-J. Shen (eds.): Handbook of Quantitative Supply Chain Analysis: Modeling in the eBusiness Era: International Series in Operations Research and Management Science. Kluwer: p. 13-66.

Chopra, S., Meindl, P. (2001): Supply Chain Management – Strategy, Planning, and Operation, Upper Saddle River.

Christopher, M. (1998): Logistics and Supply Chain Management: Strategies for Reducing Cost and Improving Service, Second Edition, London.

Fisher, M. L. (1997): What is the Right Supply Chain for Your Product?, in: Harvard Business Review, (March-April) 1997: 83-93.

Forrester, J. W. (1958): Industrial Dynamics: A Major Breakthrough for Decision Makers, in: Harvard Business Review, 36(4): 34–66.

Gilles, D. B. (1959): Solutions to general non-zero-sum games, in: Tucker, A. W. and Duncan, R. Luce (eds.): Contributions to the Theory of games: Volume IV, Princeton: p. 47-85.

Handfield, R. B., Bechtel, C. (2002): The role of trust and relationship structure in improving supply chain responsiveness, in: Industrial Marketing Management, 31(4): 367-382.

Handfield, R. B., Nichols, E. L. (1999): Introduction to Supply Chain Management, Upper Saddle River.

Lee, H. L., Padmanabhan, V., Whang, S. (1997): The Bullwhip Effect in Supply Chains, in: Sloan Management Review, 38(3): 93-102.

Luce, D. R., Raiffa, H. (1957): Games and Decisions: introduction and critical survey, New York.

Myerson, R. B. (1977): Graphs and Cooperation in Games, in: Mathematics of Operations Research, 2(3): 225-229.

Myerson, R. B. (1991): Game Theory – Analysis of Conflict, Cambridge und London.

Nash, J. F. (1947): Equilibrium Points in n-Person Games, in: Proceedings of the National Academy of Sciences, 36: 48-49.

Nash, J. F. (1951): Noncooperative Games, in: Annals of Mathematics, 54: 286-295.

Osbourne, M. J., Rubinstein, A. (1994): A Course in Game Theory, 4th ed., Cambridge/MA and London.

Poirer, C. C. (1999): Advanced Supply Chain Management, San Francisco.

Roth, A. E. (1988): Introduction to the Shapley value, in: Roth, A. E. (ed.): The Shapley value: Essays in honor of Lloyed S. Shapley, Cambridge et al.: p. 1-27.

Shapley, L. S. (1953): A value for n-persons games, in: H. W. Kuhn, Tucker, A. W. (eds.): Contributions to the Theory of Games II, Annals of Mathematics Studies, Vol. 28, Princeton University Press, Princeton/NJ: p. 307-317.

Shapley, L. S. (1990): On Balanced Sets and Cores, in: Ariel Rubinstein (eds.): Game Theory in economics, New York: 453-460.

Slikker, M., von den Nouweland, A. (2000): Network formation models with costs for establishing links, in: Review of Economic Design, 5: 333-362.

Stuart, H. W. Jr. (2001): Cooperative Games and Business Strategy, in: Chatterjee, K., Samuelson, W.F. (eds.): Game Theory and Business Applications, New York et al.: p. 189-211.

Thun, J.-H. (2003): Analysis of cooperation in supply chains using game theory, in: Spina, G. et al. (eds.): One World - One View of OM? The Challenges of Integrating Research & Practice, Vol. II, Padova: p. 323-332.

Von Neumann, J., Morgenstern, O. (1947): Theory of Games and Economic Behavior, Princeton.

Voß, S., Schneidereit, G. (2002): Interdependencies between Supply Contracts and Transaction Costs, in: Seuring, S., Goldbach, M. (eds.): Cost Management in Supply Chains. Springer, Berlin: p. 225-274.

6 Appendix

	Y (1:2; 2:3)			Y (1:2; 1:3)			Y (1:3; 2:3)		
	1	2	3	1	2	3	1	2	3
123	35	50	15	50	35	15	10	20	70
132	10	75	15	50	20	30	30	20	50
213	35	50	15	50	35	15	10	20	70
231	10	50	40	65	20	15	10	40	50
312	10	75	15	50	20	30	30	20	50
321	10	50	40	65	20	15	10	40	50
Σ	110	350	140	330	150	120	100	160	340
$\overline{Y}$	18.3	58.3	23.3	55	25	20	16.6	26.6	56.6

	Y_1(1:2; 2:3; 3:4)				Y_2(2:3; 2*:3; 3:4)			
	1	2	3	4	1	2	3	4
1 2 3 4	20	30	20	10	10	10	40	20
1 2 4 3	20	20	40	0	10	10	40	10
1 3 2 4	10	40	20	10	20	0	40	20
1 3 4 2	0	40	20	20	20	10	40	10
1 4 2 3	20	20	40	0	10	10	40	20
1 4 3 2	0	40	20	20	10	10	50	10
2 1 3 4	20	30	20	10	10	10	40	20
2 1 4 3	20	20	40	0	10	10	40	20
2 3 1 4	10	30	30	10	0	20	40	20
2 3 4 1	10	30	30	10	10	20	40	10
2 4 1 3	20	20	40	0	10	10	40	20
2 4 3 1	10	20	40	10	10	10	50	10
3 1 2 4	10	40	20	10	20	0	40	20
3 1 4 2	0	40	20	20	20	10	40	10
3 2 1 4	10	30	30	10	0	20	40	20
3 2 4 1	10	30	30	10	10	20	40	10
3 4 1 2	0	40	20	20	10	10	40	20
3 4 2 1	10	20	30	20	10	10	40	20
4 1 2 3	20	20	40	0	10	10	40	20
4 1 3 2	0	40	20	20	10	10	50	10
4 2 1 3	20	20	40	0	10	10	40	20
4 2 3 1	10	20	40	10	10	10	50	10
4 3 1 2	0	40	20	20	10	10	40	20
4 3 2 1	10	20	30	20	10	10	40	20

$Y_1 = (10.8\overline{3}, 29.1\overline{6}, 29.1\overline{6}, 10.8\overline{3})$ $Y_2 = (10.8\overline{3}, 10.8\overline{3}, 41.\overline{6}, 16.\overline{6})$

Modeling the Effect of Product Architecture Modularity in Supply Chains

Juliana H. Mikkola

1	Introduction	494
2	Mathematical Modeling as Research Methodology	495
3	Product Architecture Modularity	497
4	Modularity at the Supply Chain Level	498
5	Modularity at the Focal Firm Level	501
6	Conclusion and Discussion	506
7	References	506

Summary:
This paper proposes mathematical modeling as an alternative research methodology for analyzing complex systems. The process of deriving a mathematical model is explored through the complexities of product architecture modularity in supply chains. Two model settings are analyzed: (1) supply chain and (2) focal firm. At the supply chain level, 'modularization characteristic curve' is applied to assess the impact of degree of supplier-buyer interdependence on modularization. At the focal firm level, the 'modularization function' is applied to measure the degree of modularization embedded in product architecture designs. In order to illustrate how the models can be applied, the case of Chrysler Jeep WIPERs is presented.

Keywords:
Supply Chain Management, Product Architecture Modularity, Modeling Methodologies

1 Introduction

Supply chain integration has recently gained increasing attention, as the parties of the supply chain (i.e. suppliers, focal company, and customers) are demanding more flexibility, agility, and cost efficiency. The integrated supply chain increases the proliferation of product offerings in the market, making supplier networks more complex than the traditional supply chain. However, a high degree of supply chain integration is not necessarily desirable in all situations (Bagchi & Skjoett-Larsen, 2003). These factors impose enormous pressure on a firm's strategic policy decisions in supply chain and technology management regarding supplier-buyer relationships, component outsourcing, and product architecture designs. There is a need for more research to explore how supply chain management (SCM) is performed under different situations (Mouritsen et al., 2003).

Many researchers have mentioned that there is little consistency in the use of the term 'SCM' and little evidence of clarity and its meaning (Harland, 1996; Ellram, 1991; Otto & Kotzab, 1999). A handful of researchers have made an effort to make the definition of SCM more precise. For instance, in an attempt to consolidate the academic and practitioners' approach to SCM, Otto & Kotzab (1999) identify the following general principles for managing supply chains: compress; speed up; collaborate, cooperate; integrate; optimize; differentiate, customize; modularize; level; and postpone. On the other hand, Harland (1996) distinguishes four main uses of the term 'supply chain management': (1) internal supply that integrates business functions involved in the flow of materials and information from the inbound to the outbound end of the business; (2) SCM as the management of supply relationships; (3) SCM as the management of inter-business chains; and (4) SCM as strategic management of inter-business networks.

This paper suggests ways to model the effect to product architecture modularity in SCM. The assessment is divided into two levels of analysis: the supply chain level and focal firm level. At the supply chain level, the assembly of complex systems is dependent on many tiers of suppliers, and hence the degree of supplier-buyer interdependence is emphasized as an important factor. A conceptual function called the *'modularization characteristic curve'* (Hsuan, 1999a) is used as the basis for the data collection. The modularization characteristic curve is shaped by two variables: opportunity for modularization and interface constraints. Opportunity for modularization represents the opportunities for mixing and matching of components to create product variety. Interface constraints represent the aggregate effect from interface compatibility effects, component customization, value inputs, and supplier-buyer interdependence. The function provides the foundation for analyzing the effect of supplier-buyer interdependence on product architecture modularity in supply chains. At the focal firm level of analysis, product architecture modularity is concerned with the fundamental relationships shared between components and respective interfaces. At the focal firm level of analysis, a mathematical model called *modularization function* (Mikkola & Gassmann, 2003), is derived to analyze the degree of modularization in a given product architecture; it has the following variables: components, interfaces, degree of coupling, and substitutability of new-to-the-firm (NTF) components across product families.

One of the main focuses of this paper is to describe the processes that took place in order to formulate different models to investigate the complexities embedded in product architecture designs and how these models can be used to analyze the implications of product architecture modularity on supply chain management. The paper is organized as follows. In the following section, the rationale behind mathematical modeling is discussed. Next, a literature review on product architecture modularity is presented, followed by a discussion of modularity with respective research methodologies at two levels: the supply chain level and the focal firm level. The case of Chrysler Jeep's windshield wipers controllers is presented to illustrate how the two models can be applied to analyze the impact of product architecture modularity on supply chain and new product development management. The paper concludes with discussions and proposals for future research.

2 Mathematical Modeling as Research Methodology

The mathematical modeling approach to problem solving is prevalent in engineering and natural sciences but can be extended to explain business phenomena. Mathematical models allow us to predict the outcome of an action, and theoretically evaluate various dynamic properties of complex problems, without incurring expensive and timely field studies. Once the model is derived, simulation, sensitivity, optimization, and trade-off analysis can be easily carried out. With the development of mathematical models, variables must be explicitly defined. This serves as a framework for proper collection of empirical data.

Many problems in business, economics, and life sciences deal with aggregates of things, which clearly are discrete rather than continuous in nature. Although derivatives, and hence differential equations, are meaningful only for variables that change continuously, sometimes functions that take on only discrete values can be treated as if they actually have derivatives and satisfy differential equations. Whether such an approach is justified depends simply on how well a solution of the mathematical formulation of the problem describes the phenomena being studied. If all sets of observed data confirm themselves satisfactorily with the mathematical solution, and if the solution predicts results which are borne out by further experiments, then the mathematical formulation of the problem constitutes an acceptable mathematical model of the real-world problem. Otherwise, the model must either be rejected or refined into one that is more appropriate (Wylie & Barrett, 1982).

Mathematical modeling also has its limitations. One drawback is that the analysis is confined to the limited number of variables allowed by the function. Mathematical models can become extremely complex as the number of additional variables is added to the formulation of the function. Hence, the selection and estimation of variables is one of the most difficult tasks and must be done carefully. Having obtained the solution, it must be interpreted in the context of the original problem. The research design behind deriving a mathematical model to measure the degree of modularization embedded in product architectures is illustrated in Figure 1.

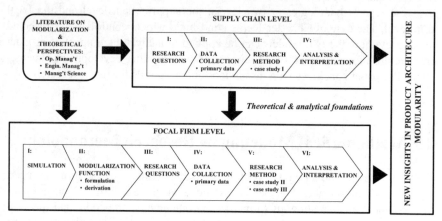

Figure 1: Research Design

The inquiry into the phenomenon of product architecture modularity started with a comprehensive literature review on modularization, operations management, engineering management, and management science. At the supply chain level of analysis, the focus was to investigate how modularization impacts supplier-buyer interdependence and vice-versa. This investigation led to the formulation of the first set of research questions. An exploratory study was then initiated by collecting primary data of Chrysler Jeep's windshield wipers controllers (WIPERs). Then the analysis and interpretation of the data was conducted, from which new insights (both theoretically as well as empirically) were gained. It also served as a foundation to analyze modularization at the focal firm level.

In order to gain better understanding about the dynamic issues of product architecture modularity with respect to the degree of supplier-buyer interdependence, simulations were performed (Hsuan, 1999b). At this stage, several possible mathematical functions were tested (i.e. linear equations, exponential functions, and logarithmic functions) in order to get a shape of the function that best described the non-linear characteristic of modularization. The simulations also allowed me to analyze the effects of components and respective interfaces independently of supplier-buyer interdependence effects. It was only after the confidence gained from the simulation exercise that the *modularization function* was formulated and derived; later it was validated with WIPERs and Schindler Elevators (refer to Mikkola & Gassmann (2003) for details about this case).

3 Product Architecture Modularity

Modularization is an approach for organizing complex products and processes efficiently (Baldwin & Clark, 1997) by decomposing complex tasks into simpler portions so they can be managed independently and yet operate together as a whole. Through standardization of interfaces, modularization permits components to be produced separately, or 'loosely coupled' (Orton & Weick, 1990; Sanchez & Mahoney, 1996), and used interchangeably in different configurations without compromising system integrity (Flamm, 1988; Garud & Kumaraswamy, 1993, 1995; Garud & Kotha, 1994). Modularization strategies are closely associated with product architecture choices in terms of the constituent components and how these components are linked with each other.

Product architectures can range from integral to modular. Integral architectures are designed with maximum performance as a goal, hence enhancing knowledge sharing and interactive learning as team members rely on each other's expertise in designing the architecture. With integral product architectures, firms may be able to customize their products to satisfy each customer's particular needs, although customized components tend to be more expensive than standard components. As the interfaces of the customized components become standardized, costs are significantly reduced, as changes to product architecture can be localized and made without incurring costly changes to other components.

Contrary to integral product architectures, modular product architectures are used as flexible platforms for leveraging a large number of product variations (Gilmore & Pine, 1997; Meyer et al., 1997; Robertson & Ulrich, 1998), enabling a firm to gain cost savings through economies of scale from component commonality, inventory, and logistics. It also allows a more rapid introduction of technologically improved products. Some of the motivations for product change include upgrade, add-ons, adaptation, wear, consumption, flexibility in use, and reuse (Ulrich & Eppinger, 1995). Product variants often are achieved through modular product architectures where changes in one component do not lead to changes in other components, and physical changes can be more easily varied without adding tremendous complexity to the manufacturing system. Outsourcing decisions are often made concurrently with the design of modular product architectures, and specialization of knowledge is gained through division of labor.

4 Modularity at the Supply Chain Level

There is an increasing pressure for firms to constantly search for better ways to integrate NPD capabilities with other organizational and SCM capabilities. Competition exists when more than one supplier is involved. How a firm chooses to decompose its product architectures and how much novelty to introduce to the next generation architectures have a critical role in the global trend of supplier reduction. Furthermore, suppliers are gaining more bargaining power with the increasing state-of-the-art technology and process complexities embedded in their components. Concurrent to supplier base reduction and intensifying commercialization strategies, some firms are also increasing component sharing across product platforms to manage product families and design flexibility responsiveness on a global scale. It has been argued that the best way to achieve product variety and speed is through modular product configurations (McCutcheon et al., 1994).

4.1 Model Setting – Supply Chain Level

At the supply chain level of analysis, the focus is on the forces shaping the opportunities of modularization at different levels of the supply chain (i.e. component, module, sub-system, and system levels), and how the degree of supplier-buyer interdependence influences component outsourcing. Product architecture modularity is examined through the lenses of the 'modularization characteristic curve' (Hsuan, 1999a), which is shaped by two variables: Opportunity for Modularization (y-axis) and Interface Constraints (x-axis), as shown in Figure 2. Interface constraints represent the aggregate effect from interface compatibility effects, component customization, value inputs, and supplier-buyer interdependence:

$MOD = f(\text{interface constraints}) = f(COMP; CUST; VALUE; SBINTERD)$

- Opportunity for modularization (MOD) represents the opportunities for mixing and matching of components to create product variety. From the system's perspective, the opportunity for modularization varies according to the interface constraints imposed by the system, which is the aggregate effect of the following elements: interface compatibility effects, component customization, value inputs, and degree of supplier-buyer interdependence.

- Interface compatibility effects (COMP) refer to the degree to which component interfaces are specified and standardized. Mixing and matching is possible when interface compatibility effects are minimized.

- Component Customization (CUST) refers to the degree of component customization. Customized components, as opposed to standard components, are usually dedicated to a particular application. Hence, commonality sharing and substitutability of these components are often limited. Component customization hinders the potential for mixing and matching.

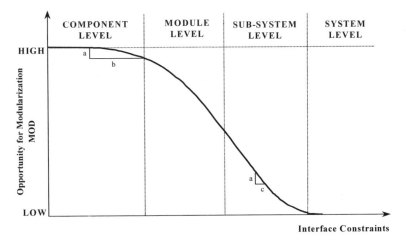

Note: *a* represents a change in opportunity for modularization.
b and *c* represent changes in interface constraints.

Figure 2: The Modularization Characteristic Curve

- Value inputs (VALUE) refer to the value-adding inputs that differentiate the buyer's final system from competitors' systems. The relevance of added value is relative to the structure of supply chains and the number of levels or tiers. First-tier suppliers play a more prominent role in creating value inputs, as they are more willing to invest in product and process developments and are also responsible for coordinating the required supply of inputs from the second-tier and lower-tier suppliers. Parts supplied by the key suppliers often have high strategic value.

- Supplier-buyer interdependence (SBINTERD) refers to the degree of supplier involvement in product development leading to capabilities of benchmarking, trust development, and creation of inter-firm knowledge. Supplier involvement in product development can be characterized by the degree of functional specification and detailed engineering responsibilities carried out by the supplier in the form of a supplier proprietary part, a detailed controlled part, or a black-box part, depending on the proprietary sensitivity of the component and the degree of supplier involvement in design and manufacturing (Mikkola, 2003b). The nature of partnerships can broadly be assumed to vary from one extreme, an arm's-length relationship, to the other extreme, a strategic partnership.

4.2 Example: Chrysler Jeep's WIPERs

This example compares two product architecture solutions of WIPERs, solid-state and silent-relay, of the first generation of the Chrysler Jeep Grand Cherokee when it was introduced in 1993. The data collection took place between 1991 and 1993, from the start of the development date to full production date. For this analysis, COMP, CUST, and VALUE variables were kept constant while SUBINTERD varied from arm's-length relationship (f_0) to strategic partnerships (f_n). The analysis is summarized in Figure 3.

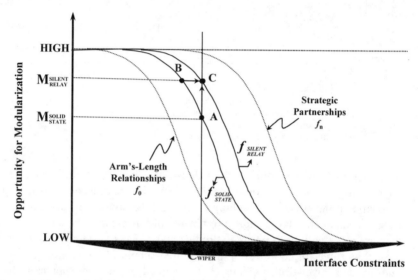

Figure 3: Characteristic Curve Analysis of WIPERs (Hsuan, 1999a: 207)

The characteristic curves for solid-state and silent-relay WIPERs are represented by $f_{SOLID-STATE}$ and $f_{SILENT-RELAY}$ respectively. The solid-state WIPER is represented by point A in the characteristic curve $f_{SOLID-STATE}$ with $M_{SOLID-STATE}$ opportunity for modularization corresponding to C_{WIPER} interface constraints. The subsequent silent-relay WIPER (with same C_{WIPER} interface constraints) is represented by point C in the characteristic curve $f_{SILENT-RELAY}$ with $M_{SILENT-RELAY}$ opportunity for modularization. Point B is an intermediate stage indicating the changes in the solid-state WIPER's product/input characteristics as well as supplier management practices before the realization of the silent-relay WIPER. The improvement in the supplier-buyer partnership towards a strategic partnership is indicated by the shift of point B (in $f_{SOLID-STATE}$) to point C (in $f_{SILENT-RELAY}$). The silent-relay WIPER provided a higher opportunity for modularization ($M_{SILENT-RELAY}$) in Motorola's manufacturing processes, and allowed Chrysler to use the same module in other Jeeps. The improved opportunity for modularization (from $M_{SOLID\text{-}STATE}$ to $M_{SILENT\text{-}RELAY}$) enabled by the silent-relay WIPER is indicated by the shift of point A to point C.

The motivation behind developing the characteristic curve is to build a model that: can be modeled mathematically; shows the non-linear relationship of modularization at different levels of the supply chain and; allows researchers to theoretically test and speculate the dynamics of modularization with respect to the variables mentioned above. The exploratory case study of the WIPERs triggered a curiosity to investigate how components and interfaces would impact product architecture configurations for the focal firm. For instance, simulations of various mathematical functions were tested in order to get a function that best matched the non-linear properties of the characteristic curve. It was only after the confidence gained from the simulation exercise that the modularization function (described in the next section) was formulated and derived.

5 Modularity at the Focal Firm Level

At the firm level of analysis, product architecture modularity is concerned with product architecture design strategies. If we want to understand why some product architectures are more modular (or integral) than others, first we need to understand how components and respective interfaces are arranged. Product configurations and their related variations are rooted in the product architecture designs, while the way in which components can be disaggregated and recombined into new configurations (without losing functionality and performance) is based on the level of modularization in product architectures. The constituent components, which can be standard or unique (referred to as the new-to-the-firm (NTF) components), and how they are linked to one another, determine the performance and cost benefits of present and future generations of product architectures. Using standard components minimizes investment, exploits economies of scale from production volume, and preserves organizational focus. NTF components, on the other hand, have the potential to maximize product performance, minimize the size and mass of a product, and minimize the variable cost of production (Ulrich & Ellison, 1999). The integration of NTF components into product architectures also prevents imitation by the competitors, thus creating competitive advantages for the firm, at least in the short run. But too many NTF components may delay product development lead time and increase the technological complexity of the product architecture.

5.1 Model Setting – Focal Firm Level

Most of the studies on modularization are exploratory. One of the challenges faced by research in modularization is the difficulty with the operationalization of various dimensions into measurable or testable hypotheses. There are few quantitative metrics available to measure product architecture modularity (cf. Ulrich & Pearson, 1998; Fisher et al., 1999; Collier, 1981). Statistical methodologies seem to be the preferred approach in many economic organization and strategy literatures. However, in operationalizing modularization, statistical methods may not capture the intrinsic characteristics of product architectures, which are often firm specific. Data accessibility and collection may also present a problem since product architecture related information is often proprietary. Because product architectures are firm specific, hence distinct from other similar product architectures, it is also interesting to know why and how they are different. One way to understand the complexity of product architecture designs is through a mathematical modeling approach in which systematic analysis is possible. *Modularization function* (Equation 1) is a mathematical model that measures the degree of modularization embedded in product architectures:

$$M(u) = e^{-u^2/2Ns\delta} \qquad \text{(Equation 1)}$$

The following key factors define the degree of modularity [$M(u)$] with respect to the number of NTF components [u] embedded in a given product architecture: components [N and n], degree of coupling [δ], and substitutability [s]. Please refer to Mikkola & Gassmann (2003) for the derivation of the *modularization function*.

Components, N, u - The selection of components reflects strategic choices made by firms. Although there are many ways of categorizing components, firms typically distinguish between two types of components: standard (n_{STD}) and new-to-the-firm (u). The total number of components in a given product architecture is N. The classification of components, and other information such as cost and quantity are normally indicated in bill-of-materials (BOM). Standard components refer to components that have been used in previous or existing architectural designs by the firm (i.e. carried over components) or components that are available from a firm's library of components (i.e. qualified components). Product architectures comprised of standard components are often considered modular product architectures. NTF components (u), on the other hand, are components that are introduced to the firm for the first time. The use of NTF components is strategic because their integration into product architectures makes imitation more difficult for the competitors, thus creating competitive advantages for the firm, at least in the short-run. But too many NTF components may delay product development lead time and increase the technological complexity of the product architecture, as a system achieves greater functionality by the strong interdependence shared among components (Schilling, 2000).

Interfaces, k - Interfaces are linkages shared among components embedded in product architectures. The degree to which interfaces become standardized and specified defines the compatibility between components, hence the degree of modularization. Standard components have well-specified and standardized interfaces. Conversely, interface specifications and hence interface compatibility issues of NTF components with other components are not well understood. Consequently, introduction of NTF components into product architectures reduces modularity freedom. Interface specification of NTF components is also dependent on technological innovation available in the market or whether it is feasible for the firm to develop them.

Degree of coupling, $\delta(n;k)$ - Degree of coupling can be treated as a proxy for the degree of tightness shared among the components. A component that is dependent on many other components (e.g., many interfaces) for functionality would impose a high degree of coupling. We can imagine that product architectures with a high degree of coupling may not be easily decomposed. Product architectures with a high degree of coupling among the components exhibit high 'synergistic specificity' (Schilling, 2000; Schilling & Steensma, 2001), as the strong interdependence shared among components inhibits recombination, separability, and substitution of components, hence preventing the architecture to shift into a more modular one.

Substitutability factor, s (product families; k) - Substitutability factor denotes the substitutability of NTF components across product families. Garud & Kumaraswamy (1995) use the term 'substitution' to suggest that technological progress may be achieved by substituting certain components of a technological system while reusing others, hence taking the advantages of economies of substitution. This has great implications for technological systems that are modularly upgradable. Economies of substitution exist when the cost of designing a high-performance system through the partial retention of existing components is lower than designing the system afresh (Garud & Kumaraswamy, 1993). Another aspect of substitutability is component sharing (i.e. using the same version of a component across multiple products) which is a product-based strategy that depends on the fact that families of similar products have similar components (Fisher et al., 1999).

The modularization function is interpreted as follows. A given product architecture has N components that is the sum of standard components [n_{STD} or $N - u$] and NTF components [u]. The specific ways in which components are linked through interfaces [k] create a certain degree of coupling [δ], which is approximated as the average number of interfaces per component. The impact of substitutability of NTF components in product architecture modularity is captured through the 'substitutability factor' [s], which is estimated as total number of families that the NTF components are used in, divided by the average number of interfaces required for functionality [k_{NTF}]. A perfect-modular product architecture [$M(u) = 1.0$] does not have any NTF components. NTF components that can be used across product families have a higher substitutability factor (hence benefiting from economies of substitution, reusability, and commonality sharing) than NTF components that are dedicated to one specific product family, hence increasing the degree of modularization. The modularization function shows that the combined effect of the variables varies exponentially with any set of NTF components. Every time the composition of NTF is altered (such as with incremental innovations) the degree of modularity also varies. In many cases, the introduction of NTF components requires changes to other parts of the product architecture as well, hence changing the values of N and δ. If we simply assessed the degree of modularity based on the number of components (be they standard or NTF) and ignored the effects of interfaces (captured in δ and s), we might overlook the impact of interfaces on product architecture modularity. The systematic analysis of product architecture modularity of a given system involves the following steps:

1. Define product architecture and its boundaries.
2. Decompose the product architecture into sub-circuits, so that each one of the sub-circuits can be assessed independently.
3. Assess the substitutability factor of the NTF components, s - total number of families that the NTF components are used in, divided by the average number of interfaces required for functionality.
4. Count the total number of components comprising the product architecture, N. This can be accomplished by looking at the product's BOM.
5. Count the number of NTF components, u.
6. Compute the degree of coupling, δ - average number of interfaces per component.
7. Plug these values into the modularization function (Equation 1) to find out the degree of modularization inherent in the product architecture.

5.2 Example: Chrysler Jeep's WIPERs (Continued)

The analysis involved two levels of aggregation: (1) module and (2) windshield wipers system. The assessment started with the detailed design (module level), in which schematics, BOMs, and other proprietary engineering data were analyzed. In this process, the total number of components (N), the number of NTF components (u), and the degree of coupling (δ) are determined. Then the same process is repeated with the windshield system, in which the substitutability factor (s) is added to the final calculation of $M(u)$. The summary of the findings is:

Solid-State WIPER	Silent-Relay WIPER
u = 19 components	u = 17 components
N = 60 components	N = 57 components
s = 0.33 components/interface	s = 1.00 components/interface
δ = 9.85 interfaces/component	δ = 9.94 interfaces/component
$M_{solid\text{-}state}$ = **0.40**	$M_{silent\text{-}relay}$ = **0.77**

The WIPER requires three interfaces for functionality: wiper switch, wash pump, and motor. While the solid-state WIPER is only compatible with Grand Cherokee Jeeps (substitutability factor, $s = 1/3 = 0.33$), all three families of Jeeps (Grand Cherokee, Cherokee, and Wrangler) can use the silent-relay WIPER ($s = 3/3 = 1$). The solid-state WIPER has 60 components ($N = 60$), of which 19 ($u = 19$) are NTF components. Similarly, the silent-relay WIPER has 57 components with 17 NTF components. The comparison of modularization functions of the WIPERs is shown below (Figure 4).

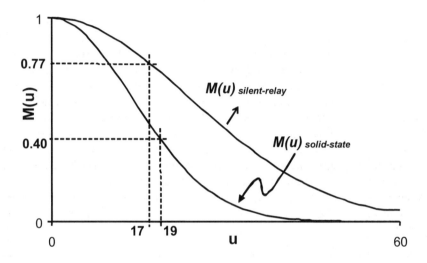

Figure 4: The M(u) of Solid-State and Silent-Relay WIPERs

The silent-relay WIPER has a higher degree of modularization ($M_{silent-relay} = 0.77$) than the solid-state WIPER ($M_{solid-state} = 0.4$). Given the relatively similar values of interface constraints ($\delta_{solid-state} = 9.85$; $\delta_{silent-relay} = 9.94$), the main factor that made the silent-relay WIPER more modular is its higher substitutability factor and lower NTF component composition. Notice how the modularization gap increases as the number of NTF components increases, implying that product architectures can achieve higher levels of modularity by reducing the number of NTF components. Similarly, modularity can also be improved by designing product architectures with a higher substitutability factor, if the NTF component composition remains constant.

6 Conclusion and Discussion

This paper presented ways to model the effect of product architecture modularity in supply chains at two levels of analysis: the supply chain level and the focal firm level. At the supply chain level, the 'modularization characteristic curve' was applied as a framework to analyze the impact of degree of supplier-buyer interdependence on modularization. At the focal firm level of analysis, a mathematical model called 'modularization function' was applied to measure the degree of modularization embedded in product architectures. The application of both models was illustrated with Chrysler Jeep's windshield wipers systems.

Both models can be used as a tool to investigate other issues related to the management of product architecture modularity in supply chains. For instance, with the increasing focus on supply chain integration, many high-tech firms are increasing their outsourcing activities, not only in terms of services and production, but in terms of new product development activities as well. The literature often emphasizes the impact of the initial stages of NPD on the overall performance of the development projects (Khurana & Rosenthal, 1998; Wheelwright & Clark, 1992; Bacon et al., 1994; Ulrich & Eppinger, 1995). The initial stage includes planning, concept development, and system level design. Platform design strategies and related sourcing strategies are often devised during this stage. The extent to which a system can be decomposed with well-specified and standardized interfaces determines whether component outsourcing is a viable strategy, which has a tremendous impact on when to involve and collaborate with suppliers in NPD (Mikkola, 2003b).

Challenges associated with outsourcing are aggravated by the increasing customer demand for product individualization and customization at an affordable cost. Many high-tech firms are dealing with this challenge by devising platform strategies to best meet their customer needs while keeping a hold on the firms' core capabilities. Firms have to carefully decide which NPD activities to outsource to suppliers. Depending on the technological complexity of the activity, firms also have to consider what kinds of relationships they should nurture with the selected suppliers. Other areas worth researching include the implication of product architecture modularity with respect to mass customization and postponement strategies in shaping the supply chain.

7 References

Bacon, G., Beckman, S., Mowery, D. Wilson, E. (1994): Managing product definition in high-technology industries: A pilot study, in: California Management Review, (Spring): 32-56.

Bagchi, P. K., Skjoett-Larsen, T. (2003): Integration of information technology and organizations in a supply chain, in: The International Journal of Logistics Management, 14(1): 89-108.

Baldwin, C. Y., Clark, K. B. (1997): Managing in an age of modularity, in: Harvard Business Review, 75(5): 84-93.

Christensen, C. M., Rosenbloom, R. S. (1995): Explaining the attacker's advantage: Technological paradigms, organizational dynamics, and the value network, in: Research Policy, 24: 233-257.

Collier, D. A. (1981): The measurement and operating benefits of component part commonality, in: Decision Sciences, 12(1): 85.

Ellram, L. M. (1991): Supply chain management: The industrial organization perspective, in: International Journal of Physical Distribution & Logistics Management, 21(1): 13-22.

Fisher, M., Ramdas, K., Ulrich, K. (1999): Component sharing in the management of product variety: A study of automotive braking systems, in: Management Science, 45(3): 297-315.

Flamm, K. (1988): Creating the Computer: Government, Industry and High Technology, Bookings Institution, Washington, DC.

Garud, R, Kotha, S. (1994): Using the brain as a metaphor to model flexible production systems, in: Academy of Management Review, 19: 671-698.

Garud, R., Kumaraswamy, A. (1993): Changing competitive dynamics in network industries: An exploration of Sun Microsystem's open systems strategy, in: Strategic Management Journal, 14: 351-369.

Garud, R., Kumaraswamy, A. (1995): Technological and organizational designs for realizing economies of substitution, in: Strategic Management Journal, 16: 93-109.

Gilmore, J. H., Pine, B. J. (1997): The four faces of mass customization, in: Harvard Business Review, 75(1): 91-101.

Harland, C. M. (1996): Supply chain management: Relationships, chains and networks, in: British Journal of Management, 7(Special Issue): 63-80.

Hsuan, J. (1999a): Impacts of supplier-buyer relationships on modularization in new product development, in: European Journal of Purchasing and Supply Management, 5: 197-209.

Hsuan, J. (1999b): Modularization in New Product Development: A Mathematical Modeling Approach, in: Working Paper 99-4, Copenhagen Business School Press, Department of Industrial Economics and Strategy.

Khurana, A., Rosenthal, S. R. (1998): Towards holistic "front ends" in new product development, in: Journal of Product Innovation Management, 15: 57-74.

McCutcheon, D. M., Raturi, A. S., Meredith, J. R. (1994): The customization-responsiveness squeeze, in: Sloan Management Review, 35(4): 89-99.

Meyer, M. H., Tertzakian, P., Utterback, J. M. (1997): Metrics for managing research and development in the context of the product family, in: Management Science, 43(1): 88-111.

Mikkola, J. H. (2003a): Modularization in New Product Development: Implications for Product Architectures, Supply Chain Management, and Industry Structures, Ph.D. Thesis, Copenhagen Business School: Samfundslitteratur, Copenhagen.

Mikkola, J. H. (2003b): Modularity, component outsourcing, and inter-firm learning, in: R&D Management, 33(4): 439-454.

Mikkola, J. H., Gassmann, O. (2003): Managing modularity of product architectures: Towards an integrated theory, in: IEEE Transactions on Engineering Management, 50(2): 204-218.

Mouritsen, J., Skjøtt-Larsen, T., Kotzab, H. (2003): Exploring the contours of supply chain management, in: Integrated Manufacturing Systems, 14(8): 686-695.

Orton, J. D., Weick, K. E. (1990): Loosely coupled systems: A re-conceptualization., in: Academy of Management Review, 15: 203-223.

Otto, A., Kotzab, H. (1999): How supply chain management contributes to the management of supply chains, in: Larsson, E., Paulsson, U. (eds.): Proceedings of the 11th Annual Conference for Nordic Researchers in Logistics: p. 213-236.

Robertson, D., Ulrich, K. (1998): Planning for product platforms, in: Sloan Management Review, (Summer): 19-31.

Sanchez, R., Mahoney, J. T. (1996): Modularity, flexibility, and knowledge management in product and organisation design, in: Strategic Management Journal, 17(Winter Special Issue): 63-76.

Schilling, M. A. (2000): Toward a general modular systems theory and its application to interfirm product modularity, in: Academy of Management Review, 25(2): 312-334.

Schilling, M. A., Steensma, H. K. (2001): The use of modular organizational forms: An industry-level analysis, in: Academy of Management Journal, 44(6): 1149-1168.

Trienekens, J. H., Hvollby, H. H. (2001): Models for supply chain reengineering, in: Production Planning & Control, 12(3): 254-264.

Ulrich, K. T., Ellison, D. (1999): Holistic customer requirements and the design-select decision, in: Management Science, 45(5): 641-658.

Ulrich, K. T., Eppinger, S. D. (1995): Product Design and Development, McGraw-Hill, New York.

Ulrich, K. T., Pearson, S. (1998): Assessing the importance of design through product archeology, in: Management Science, 44(3): 352-369.

Wheelwright, S. C., Clark, K. B. (1992): Revolutionizing Product Development: Quantum Leaps in Speed, Efficiency, and Quality, The Free Press, New York.

Wylie, C. R., Barrett, L. C. (1982): Advanced Engineering Mathematics, McGraw-Hill, New York.

Heuristics in the Multi-Location Inventory System with Transshipments

Lars Magne Nonås, Kurt Jörnsten

1 Introduction 510
2 Model Setup 511
3 Solution Methodology 514
4 Numerical Results 517
5 Conclusions 522
6 References 523

Summary:
When managing inventory systems with multiple locations, the inherent uncertainty of demand in many cases results in some locations having a shortage of inventory while others have a surplus inventory. One popular action against the costs of not having supply meet demand is the use of transshipments between the locations. We consider a multi-location inventory system with transshipments. Transshipments are allowed as recourse actions occurring after demands are realized and before they must be satisfied (in order to reduce the cost of shortage and surplus inventory). We examine the effect on the expected profit from using an ordering policy based on a greedy transshipment policy. While this policy is optimal for two and three locations, our numerical results show that it is near-optimal for medium sized problem instances. The main advantage of this policy is that the computational complexity is significantly reduced compared to a policy based on an optimal transshipment policy. A greedy transshipment policy would also be much easier to implement in practice.

Keywords:
Inventory System, Transshipments, Greedy Heuristics

1 Introduction

Henry Ford's insight on how to manage an efficient supply chain was one of the main reasons why his famous Model T Ford was such a success. However, his philosophy of providing the car in "...any color you want, as long as it is black" stands in sharp contrast to today's competitive market. Due to an increased global competition in today's market, your supply chain must not only be cost efficient, but also enable you to satisfy customer preferences both with regard to lead time and product variety. In the last couple of decades, the number of products offered on the market has exploded. At the same time, product lifetime has decreased drastically. The combination of these two trends has caused increased inaccuracy of demand forecasts, leading to the firms facing an increased demand uncertainty. Further, as a response to higher pressure on costs, firms tend to source more from low cost countries such as those in the Far East, resulting in longer lead times. An effect of this is that firms are less responsive to demand uncertainty. Correspondingly, one of the major challenges in many industries is making supply meet demand (see Fisher et al., 1994). Several strategies and initiatives to achieve this have gained increasing popularity with firms. This paper studies one such strategy, namely transshipments.

Transshipments can be defined as the practice of shipping stock horizontally in the supply chain, i.e. between locations at the same echelon level. Herer et al. (2002) view transshipments as a tactical solution towards both a lean and agile supply chain. The possibility of receiving transshipments from other locations in the network reduces the optimal safety stock factor for each location. Also, because of the close proximity of the locations collaborating in a distribution network, transshipments are assumed to be much faster than the ordinary replenishments, thus reducing the waiting time for the customer in case of a stock-out. Transshipments are especially helpful in a periodically reviewed inventory system. This is because transshipments prior to the next ordering cycle will reduce the cost of shortage and surplus inventory. Tagaras (1989) shows how transshipments not only reduce cost, but also increase the service level.

Among the first to study transshipments were Krishnan & Rao (1965). They analyzed a multi-location model where the locations were identical both in the cost parameters and in their demand. Robinson (1990) extended their model to a two-location model with non-identical cost parameters. He also introduced an LP-based heuristic for the non-identical multi-location model. Tagaras (1989) defined a set of assumptions that led to the optimality of complete pooling (see section 2.2). Herer & Rashit (1999a) and Herer & Rashit (1999b) examine non-traditional cost structures for the two-location model. Rudi et al. (2001) solve the non-identical two-location model in a more compact and intuitive way than Robinson (1990), while they also examine the non-cooperative transshipment model. Nonås & Jörnsten (2004) show how to solve the three and four location model in an analytical way. Herer et al. (2001) use a gradient search heuristic based on Infinitesimal Perturbation Analysis (IPA) for the non-identical multi-location model. Other recent work on transshipments includes Dong & Rudi (2000), Tagaras (1999), Tagaras & Vlachos (2002), Diks & de Kok (1996), and Evers (2001).

Tagaras & Cohen (1992) claimed that "Future research in this area should focus on systems with more than two pooling locations" and that "a simple heuristic for providing near-optimal solutions appears to be a more attractive alternative for practical applications." We propose the use of a greedy transshipment policy. The simplicity of the greedy allocation makes it very easy to implement in practice, without any costly or time-consuming operations for the managers. This paper is mainly motivated by the results of Nonås & Jörnsten (2004). They show that a greedy transshipment policy is optimal for two and three locations. Also, they characterize the conditions on the cost structure for which a greedy transshipment policy is optimal for a multi-location model. The main contribution of this paper is to provide a simple heuristic supported by convincing numerical results. Note however that an optimal transshipment policy will always perform better (if implemented correctly), but as the number of locations in the distribution network increases, the computational complexity becomes intractable. Thus the greedy transshipment policy is only appropriate when the optimal transshipment policy is too complex.

2 Model Setup

2.1 Notation

Consider the following real life problem where we have n stores selling a seasonal product. Before the season starts, and long before the realization of demand at the start of the season is known, store i has to order large quantities, Q_i, of the product to fill up the store to meet the coming demand, D_i. The joint distribution of demand is assumed to be known and continuous.

Store i sells at unit revenue cost r_i. The stores procure the product at unit ordering cost c_i $(r_i > c_i)$. If store i has not managed to sell all their products $(D_i < Q_i)$ at the end of the season, the surplus inventory will have a per unit salvage value of $s_i > 0$ for store i. There will be an opportunity to sell it back to the factory, or they can put it on sale for under cost $(s_i < c_i)$ after the season has finished. This might lead to increased storage expenses, but this can be included in the per unit salvage value. When the season has started, and store j has ran out of the product in the warehouse $(D_j > Q_j)$, it will be possible to transship products from another store i with a surplus inventory of the product $(D_i < Q_i)$ in order to try to satisfy the demand at store j. The transshipment cost per unit is denoted by τ_{ij}. We will assume that the customers are willing to wait for the transshipment T_{ij} i.e. the lead time is negligible. Otherwise, the loss of goodwill due to the delay can be included in the transshipment cost. Furthermore, we assume negligible fixed transshipment costs in our model formulation. To see the effect of fixed costs on a two-location model formulation, see Herer & Rashit (1999a). Transshipments will be considered as a recourse action occurring after demand realization, but before this, demand must be satisfied in order to optimize profit.

2.2 Parameter Assumptions

In our model we will employ a transshipment policy known as complete pooling. This transshipment policy can be described as follows (Herer & Rashit, 1999b): the amount transshipped from one location to another will be the minimum between (a) the surplus inventory of the sending location and (b) the shortage inventory at the receiving location. Accordingly, transshipments will take place until all locations either have a surplus inventory or they all have a shortage inventory. The optimality of the complete pooling policy is ensured under the so-called triangle inequalities (1)-(3) (which we will denote as the complete pooling assumptions).

(1) $\quad r_j - \tau_{ij} \geq s_i \quad i,j = 1,...n.$

(2) $\quad r_i \geq r_j - \tau_{ij} \quad i,j = 1,...n.$

(3) $\quad s_i \geq s_j - \tau_{ij} \quad i,j = 1,...n.$

Inequality (1) implies that it is always beneficial to transship from a location with excess inventory to a location with an inventory shortage. This is because the revenue at the receiving location minus the transshipment cost, $r_i - \tau_{ij}$, outweighs the salvage value, s_i, at the shipping location. Further, it is neither preferable to transship between two shortage locations by inequality (2), nor between two surplus locations by inequality (3). In addition, to ensure that it is not beneficial to order indirectly from another location (instead of the factory), we consider only the cases of

$$c_i + \tau_{ij} \geq c_j \quad i,j = 1,...n.$$

Similar assumptions are often made in the literature on transshipments (e.g. Tagaras, 1989; Robinson, 1990; Herer & Rashit, 1999a) and are also common in practice.

2.3 Model Formulation

In this section we formalize the problem. We consider the case where inventory choices in each location are centrally coordinated. If the retail stores were to cooperate (e.g. because they were all owned by the same company), it would be of common interest among the stores to maximize aggregate profit. We can write the maximum expected aggregate profit of n locations as

$$\max_Q \pi = \max_Q \left(\sum_{i=1}^{n} -c_i Q_i + E\overline{K}(Q,D) \right)$$

where $\overline{K}(Q,D)$ is the maximum income given order quantities and realized demands. Since the realization of demand is not known ahead of the season, we need to determine the expectation of this expression. For notational convenience we define T_{ii} as the amount sold at location i from the inventory at location i. Due to the complete pooling policy, all transshipments are sold at the receiving location. This allows us to write the maximum income as

$$\overline{K}(Q,D) = \max_{T_{ij}} \sum_{i=j}^{n} \left[\sum_{j=1}^{n} r_j T_{ij} - \sum_{j=1}^{n} \tau_{ij} T_{ij} + s_i \left(Q_i - \sum_{j=1}^{n} T_{ij} \right) \right]$$

subject to

$$\sum_{j=1}^{n} T_{ij} \leq Q_i \quad , i = 1,\ldots,n$$

$$\sum_{j=1}^{n} T_{ji} \leq D_i \quad , i = 1,\ldots,n$$

$$Q_i \geq 0, \quad T_{ij} \geq 0 \quad , i,j = 1,\ldots,n$$

The first term on the right hand side of (6) can be recognized as the income from all that is sent from location i and sold at location j. The second term is the corresponding transshipment costs, and the third term is the salvage value from the surplus inventory at location i. Constraints (7) and (8) say that you cannot sell more quantity than you have, nor can you sell more than the demand at the location. By extracting $s_i Q_i$ from $\overline{K}$, program (5) can be reformulated as

$$\max_{Q} \pi = \max_{Q} \left(\sum_{i=1}^{n} -(c_i - s_i) Q_i + EK(Q,D) \right)$$

where

$$K(Q,D) = \max_{T_{ij}} \sum_{i=j}^{n} \sum_{j=1}^{n} (r_j - \tau_{ij} - s_i) T_{ij}$$

subject to

$$\sum_{j=1}^{n} T_{ij} \leq Q_i \qquad , i = 1,\ldots,n$$

$$\sum_{j=1}^{n} T_{ji} \leq D_i \qquad , i = 1,\ldots,n$$

$$Q_i \geq 0, \quad T_{ij} \geq 0 \qquad , i,j = 1,\ldots,n$$

This stochastic π program is jointly concave in the decision variables (see Robinson (1990). Thus, the first order conditions give an optimal solution, which allow us to determine the optimal order quantum.

3 Solution Methodology

In order to characterize an optimal behavior of an inventory system, one has to know the optimal ordering and transshipment policy. The optimal order policy is known to be an order-up-to S policy (for our single period problem there will of course only be one order cycle), where S depends on the transshipment policy. However, the optimal transshipment policy for more than four locations is not known for a general cost structure. We propose a greedy transshipment policy which is simple and easy to compute. The simplicity of the greedy allocation makes it very easy to implement in practice, without any costly or time-consuming operations for the managers. Also, our numerical results show a near-optimal performance of the policy.

The term "greedy" refers to the most beneficial transshipment T_{ij} in the distribution network, i.e. the one with the largest corresponding value of $r_j - \tau_{ij} - s_i$. For each iteratively greedy choice of transshipment, in order to maximize the K program, it is assumed that either the surplus inventory is emptied or the shortage inventory is satisfied (due to the complete pooling assumptions).

Nonås & Jörnsten (2004) have shown that a greedy transshipment policy will always be optimal in a distribution network with less than four locations. They have also characterized necessary and sufficient conditions of the cost structure for which a greedy allocation is optimal for n locations.

The complexity of the π program increases significantly when the number of locations increases. For more than four locations the optimal transshipment policy is not known, thus one has to use some kind of heuristic. Herer et al. (2001) report a solution time of their heuristic of between two and three hours for up to seven locations. This heuristic is a gradient search-based heuristic where they use IPA in order to estimate the gradient in each step. Basically this means that they are solving a *huge* number of transshipment problems (corresponding to our K program) in *every* gradient step. By using a greedy allocation, the solution time would be dramatically reduced. In fact, every transshipment problem in every gradient step can then be solved in linear time by sorting the cost parameters *once*. For a detailed treatment on how to estimate the gradient using IPA see Herer et al. (2001).

We introduce some new policies based on a greedy allocation of transshipments. For comparison reasons we also define the newsvendor policy and an optimal policy (respectively Policies 1 and 5 below). Note that the policies, which will later be used in our numerical examples, are ordered according to their increasing computational complexity.

Policy 1: Determine the order quantum by not taking into account the possibility of transshipments. Hence, dividing the problem into n newsvendor problems.

Policy 2: Determine the order quantum by not taking into account the possibility of transshipments (ex-ante). Combine the resulting order quantum with a greedy allocation of transshipments in order to satisfy the physical demand realization (ex-post).

Policy 3: Determine the order quantum by taking into account the possibility of a greedy allocation of transshipments (ex-ante). Combine the resulting order quantum with a greedy allocation of transshipments in order to satisfy the physical demand realization (ex-post).

Policy 4: Determine the order quantum by taking into account the possibility of a greedy allocation of transshipments (ex-ante). Combine the resulting order quantum with an optimal allocation of transshipments in order to satisfy the physical demand realization (ex-post).

Policy 5: Determine the order quantum by taking into account the possibility of an optimal allocation of transshipments (ex-ante). Combine the resulting order quantum with an optimal allocation of transshipments in order to satisfy the physical demand realization (ex-post).

To evaluate the different policies we could compare the actual order quantum with the optimal one. Note however that Policies 1 and 2 differ only in the actions performed in order to satisfy the physical demand realizations, hence they will use the same order quantum. This is also the case for Policies 3 and 4. A comparison based on the expected profit from following the policies would probably be more appropriate. Denote π_i as the profit from following Policy i.

Proposition 1. We have that $\pi_5 > \pi_4 > \pi_3 > \pi_2 > \pi_1$.

Proof. From the complete pooling assumptions it follows that all transshipments made will be beneficial. This means that even though we only use a greedy allocation of transshipments in order to satisfy the demand realization, we will have $\pi_2 > \pi_1$. Since the first order conditions of the π program resulting from Policy 1 do not take into account the possibility of a greedy allocation of transshipments in the recourse stage, these conditions will only be suboptimal. The corresponding conditions resulting from Policy 3 will be optimal for the case of a greedy allocation in the recourse stage, thus we will have $\pi_3 > \pi_2$. Since both Policies 3 and 4 use the same order quantum, and an optimal allocation of transshipments in order to satisfy the demand realization never will be outperformed by a greedy one, we will have $\pi_4 > \pi_3$. We will also have $\pi_5 > \pi_4$ since a greedy allocation never will perform better than an optimal one (per definition). Q.E.D.

Define the percentage profit deviation between policies i and j as

$$P_{ij} = \frac{(\pi_j - \pi_i)100}{\pi_j}$$

Since the expected profit for using Policy 5 cannot be found for more than four locations, we have to approximate the profit. In our numerical results we have used a gradient-based approach that Tayur (1995) suggested for a similar problem. This gradient-based approach has not worked well previously because it was expensive to calculate the gradient. Tayur managed to reduce the computing costs by using IPA combined with an efficient way of solving the K problem (see Fu & Hu, 1997) for different gradient estimations techniques including IPA). Note that even if the transshipment policy of the K problem is not optimal, the Tayur approach can still be used as long as it preserves the continuity of the cost function (Herer et al. (2001)). We have therefore chosen to approximate the profits π_i for $i = 1,...,5$ using the Tayur approach. These approximations will also be used for the calculations of P_{ij}. Note that we will use the notation $\pi_i(m)$ for the approximation of π_i using m demand observations.

4 Numerical Results

The demand observations for the examples in this section were all generated from a normal distribution with a mean of 500 and a standard deviation of 150. Even though we have set the correlations coefficient to zero, the gradient-based approach used for approximating the profit allows for covariance structure in the demand distribution. The motivation for these numerical results is to measure the performance of the different policies. We are particularly interested in the performance of a greedy allocation of transshipments in the recourse program K compared to an optimal allocation of transshipments. Even though the Tayur approach has reduced the computing costs of calculating the gradients, these computing costs are still heavy when the number of locations is large. Tayur (1995) concluded that only medium sized problem instances could be solved in reasonable time with his approach for his related problem of computing optimal inventory levels for components that can be used in different products. Although Herer et al. (2001) claim that they can solve large problems with the approach given by Tayur, the computation time is still very expensive.

- **Discretization of demand distribution**

Regardless of which approaches we use to approximate the optimal order quantum, these approximations will depend on how well we are able to approximate the demand distribution. By discretizing the demand distribution, errors will inevitably occur. Unfortunately, according to Tayur (1995), there are no theoretical results that can connect the amount of discretization required to be within a given error bound of the optimal solution. To show the difference in accuracy for an increasing number of demand observations, Table 1 compares the profit $\pi_5(30{,}000)$ with $\pi_5(m)$ for $m \in \{100;\ 1000;\ 10{,}000\}$.

	Number of demand observations (m)		
n	100	1000	10,000
2	0.3065	0.0605	0.0047
3	0.2909	0.1595	0.0011
4	0.6139	0.1209	-0.0003
5	0.2913	0.2155	0.0030
6	0.1390	0.0804	0.0027
7	0.1195	0.0750	0.0023
8	0.1521	0.0436	0.0008
9	0.3461	0.0537	0.0011
10	0.1055	0.1244	0.0013

Table 1: Average Percentage Sub-Performance of $\pi_5(m)$ Compared to $\pi_5(30{,}000)$

Each entry in Table 1 shows the average percentage under-performance obtained using 500 problem instances with different cost structures. For all except two cases, an increase of demand observations resulted in an increase of expected profit. This shows that a finer discretization usually leads to a solution closer to the optimum. Due to a very long solution time when we used 30,000 demand observations, all the results in this section have been obtained by using 10,000 demand observations if not stated otherwise.

- **Cost parameters**

The performance of a greedy heuristic strongly depends on the cost parameters. Hence, we wanted to measure the worst case performance of our greedy-based policies. However, to simulate a cost structure that results in a worst case performance is not an easy task, as not even the optimal solution is known for n locations. In order to determine in which way a greedy-based heuristic is affected by the cost parameters, we examined Policy 3 more closely, since this policy is "all greedy." Tables 2 and 3 compare Policies 3 and 5, and show the effects of increased differences between the cost parameters r_i, s_i and τ_{ij} for $n = 4$. The entries of the tables are the average of P_{35} from 2000 problem instances resulting from different cost structures. The cost parameters for each of the locations were picked at random from the given intervals of the tables. Table 2 relates to cost structures where the total expected order quantum is below the total expected demand, i.e. $r_i - c_i \ll c_i - s_i$. For these cost structures there will be an incentive not to order too much because the upside of selling a product is much lower than the downside of not selling a product. Accordingly, Table 3 relates to cost structures where the total expected order quantum is above the total expected demand, i.e. $r_i - c_i \gg c_i - s_i$. Note that since cost parameter c_i is not a part of the K program, the differences between the ordering costs will not affect the greedy heuristic and has therefore not been examined.

As expected, we can see from Tables 2 and 3 that $P_{35} = 0$ when the transshipment costs are identical across the locations, which means that the greedy heuristic will be optimal in these cases. The tables also show that an increase in differences in the cost parameters r_i, s_i and τ_{ij} will lead to an increase of P_{35}. Note that the more expected profit from transshipments T_{ij} $(i \neq j)$ relative to transshipments T_{ii}, the worse are the performances of the greedy heuristic. This is because the error caused from the greedy heuristic in the K program will be magnified. This "magnifying effect" can be seen by recognizing that P_{35} is much larger for Table 2 than for 3. This implies that a greedy heuristic performance is much better for cost structures where $r_i - c_i \gg c_i - s_i$ than for cost structures where $r_i - c_i \ll c_i - s_i$.

$P_{35}, n=4, c=100$		τ		
r	s	30-30	25-35	20-40
120-120	10-10	0	0.0066	0.0130
	5-15	0	0.0089	0.0151
	0-20	0	0.0107	0.0171
115-125	10-10	0	0.0094	0.0156
	5-15	0	0.0136	0.0181
	0-20	0	0.0177	0.0219
110-130	10-10	0	0.0119	0.0205
	5-15	0	0.0199	0.0248
	0-20	0	0.0259	0.0301

Table 2: Average Percentage Deviation in Profit between Policies 3 and 5, P_{35}, for $r_i - c_i \ll c_i - s_i$.

$P_{35}, n=4, c=100$		τ		
r	s	30-30	25-35	20-40
190-190	80-80	0	0.0011	0.0022
	75-85	0	0.0016	0.0027
	70-90	0	0.0021	0.0033
185-195	80-80	0	0.0015	0.0025
	75-85	0	0.0024	0.0031
	70-90	0	0.0033	0.0041
180-200	80-80	0	0.0018	0.0031
	75-85	0	0.0032	0.0040
	70-90	0	0.0045	0.0052

Table 3: Average Percentage Deviation in Profit between Policies 3 and 5, P_{35}, for $r_i - c_i \gg c_i - s_i$.

- **Performance of the policies**

In order to measure the performance of the policies characterized in Section 3, Table 4 shows average percentage deviation in profit from using Policy 5 instead of policies 1, 2, 3 and 4. The profit from each of the policies was averaged from a solution set of 500 problems where the cost parameters vary across the locations. Due to the considerations regarding the cost parameters we chose the cost structures from Table 2 where the total optimal order quantum is below the total expected demand ($r_i - c_i \ll c_i - s_i$). In particular we picked the cost parameters r_i, s_i and τ_{ij} from the largest intervals given in Table 2. These cost parameters are chosen to simulate a worst case performance of the greedy based heuristics. Note that the resulting cost structures will be totally unrealistic, but are chosen because they will magnify any errors caused in the K problem.

n	P_{15}	P_{25}	P_{35}	P_{45}
2	13.9135	2.1276	0	0
3	19.1728	4.3179	0	0
4	21.8171	5.8939	0.0330	0.0012
5	23.6305	7.2642	0.0722	0.0014
6	24.8359	8.2312	0.1277	0.0169
7	25.8250	9.0976	0.1496	0.0038
8	26.5822	9.7600	0.1861	0.0026
9	27.2658	10.5169	0.2188	0.0054
10	27.7060	10.9394	0.2550	0.0102

Table 4: Average Percentage Deviation in Profit from Using Policy 5 instead of Policy i, P_{i5} ($i = 1,...,4$).

As noted in Section 3, the computational complexity of policy i ($i = 1,...,5$) increases as i increases. From Proposition 1 we have that $\pi_i < \pi_j$ for $i < j$, which means that there is a relationship between the complexity of the policy and the performance of the policy. Due to the especially large increase of computational complexity of Policy 5, the improved performance should be significant in order to justify the substantial increase in computations involved. Using Policy 5 instead of the newsvendor model (Policy 1) results in significant improvement (as seen from P_{15} in Table 4) with more than 20% increase of profit for more than four locations. Even though transshipments are allowed after demand realizations in Policy 2, the performance of Policy 2 is still rather poor compared to Policy 5. However, Policies 3 and 4 show a much better performance. While Policy 3 averages less than 0.3% from Policy 5, Policy 4 averages less than 0.02% from policy 5 for up to 10 locations. Thus the performance of the policies can be divided into two categories: the policies which do not take into account the possibility of transshipments when determining the order quantum, and those which do. This is in line with Tagaras (1999) who recognized the substantial benefit from accounting for the possibilities of transshipments when determining the order policies, while also showing that the type of transshipment policy "does not affect significantly the system's performance."

Note that the deviation in profit compared to Policy 5 increases strictly (in Table 4) for Policies 1, 2 and 3 as the number of locations n increases. Even though one could expect a similar behavior from Policy 4, we were not able to show any such strict relations. To further investigate the performance of Policy 4 we need to use much larger sets of demand observations. However, limitations on the problem size restrict us in doing this. Nevertheless, keeping in mind that we are simulating an unrealistic worst case scenario for a greedy heuristic, the performance of Policy 4 is very convincing. For the two and three location model, the performance of Policy 4 is even optimal. For small and medium sized problem instances, a greedy allocation can be used as an initial policy in the gradient search of the Tayur approach. For large sized problem instances, Policy 4 can be suggested if the Tayur approximation is not satisfactory with respect to solution time. Note that for large sized problems you would use a gradient search procedure with a *huge* number of transshipment problems to be solved in *every* gradient step. Thus, the solution time would be dramatically reduced if a problem were identified to satisfy the necessary conditions on the cost structure for a greedy allocation to be optimal. This is because every transshipment problem in every gradient step could then be solved in linear time by sorting the entries of the cost matrix *once*. Even though the cost structure does not fulfill the necessary condition for a greedy allocation to be optimal, our numerical results have shown a convincing performance of the greedy-based heuristics.

The average calculation time for ten locations with the above-mentioned parameters on an Origin 200 with a 180 MHz MIPS processor was 3 and 30 minutes for Policies 4 and 5, respectively. Note also that the number of feasible solutions for the large number of LP problems that had to be solved in Policy 5 increases exponentially as the number of locations increases. In contrast, the corresponding greedy problems in Policy 4, given an initial sorting of the cost parameters, will be solved in linear time. Thus one can expect a relative increase of computational savings as the number of locations increases.

- **Effects of risk pooling**

To motivate the need for efficient heuristics further, Table 5 shows the average profit per location, $\pi_5(30000)/n$, when the number of locations n increases. Table 5 also shows the corresponding average order quantum per location $\frac{\sum_{i=1}^{n} Q_i}{n}$. As expected, $\pi_5(30000)/n$ increases as n increases (as opposed to the newsvendor model where each location is considered separately). This is due to the effect known as *risk pooling*. The risk of shortage or surplus inventory at location i, with the extra costs this incurs, are pooled between the locations. The benefit of risk pooling is an incentive for large firms to centralize the decision of order quantum and to take into account the possibility of transshipments. Hence, from an economical point of view, there will be an interest in determining heuristics to solve large sized models in reasonable time. Note however, that the marginal increase in $\pi_5(30000)/n$, due to the effect of risk pooling, decreases as n increases. This is because the optimal order quantum at each location will converge to the mean of the demand distribution as n increases. When n increases, the common pool to draw upon to avoid surplus and shortage inventory will increase. This leads to an optimal order quantum closer to the mean of the demand distribution (since the safety stock for each location can be reduced). Hence, $\pi_5(30000)/n$ also will converge because of this upper bound of the optimal order quantum. Note that the entries in Table 5 were found using a cost structure that results in an average order quantum below the expected demand, $\frac{\sum_{i=1}^{n} Q_i}{n} < E(D)$. This is why $\frac{\sum_{i=1}^{n} Q_i}{n}$ in Table 5 increases towards the expected demand as n increases. For cost structures where $\frac{\sum_{i=1}^{n} Q_i}{n} > E(D)$, we will have a decrease towards the expected demand in $\frac{\sum_{i=1}^{n} Q_i}{n}$ as n increases.

n	$\frac{\sum_{i=1}^{n} Q_i}{n}$	$\pi_5(30000)/n$
2	394.42	6071.92
3	408.88	6266.15
4	419.16	6375.66
5	425.44	6450.09
6	431.37	6497.04
7	434.53	6535.56
8	438.22	6562.88
9	441.47	6589.42
10	444.04	6608.37

Table 5: Relationship between $\frac{\sum_{i=1}^{n} Q_i}{n}$ and $\pi_5(30000)/n$

5 Conclusions

We propose a greedy transshipment policy for a multi-location inventory system with transshipments. The simplicity of the greedy allocation makes it very easy to implement in practice, without any costly or time-consuming operations for the managers. Our numerical examples show a near-optimal performance of this heuristic while the solution time is drastically reduced. We suggest therefore the use of an ordering policy based on a greedy transshipment policy for large problem instances where the computational complexity is intractable. A greedy transshipment policy can also be used in initial operations for the search of an optimal order quantum in order to make the search more efficient. Also, given that the cost structure satisfies the necessary conditions for a greedy allocation to be optimal (which can be checked in advance, see Nonås & Jörnsten, 2004), large computational savings can be achieved while still retaining the optimal performance of the system.

6 References

Diks, E. B., de Kok, A. G. (1996): Controlling a divergent 2-echelon network with transshipments using the consistent appropriate share rationing policy, in: International Journal of Production Economics, 45: 369-379.

Dong, L., Rudi, N. (2000): Supply Chain Interaction under Transshipments, Working paper, University of Rochester, Rochester, NY 14627, U.S.A.

Evers, P. T. (2001): Heuristics for assessing emergency transshipments, in: European Journal of Operational Research, 129: 311-316.

Fisher, M. L., Hammond, J. H., Obermeyer, W. R., Raman, A. (1994): Making supply meet demand in an uncertain world, in: Harvard Business Review, 72(3): 83-93.

Fu, M. C., Hu, J. Q. (1997): Conditional Monte Carlo: Gradient Estimation and Optimization Applications, Kluwer Academic Publishers, Dordrecht.

Herer, Y., Rashit, A. (1999a): Lateral Stock Transshipments in a Two-location Inventory System with Fixed Replenishment Costs, Department of Industrial Engineering, Tel Aviv University.

Herer, Y., Rashit, A. (1999b): Policies in a general two-location infinite horizon inventory system with lateral stock transshipments. Department of Industrial Engineering, Tel Aviv University.

Herer, Y., Tzur, M., Yücesan, E. (2001): The Multi-location Transshipment Problem. Faculty of Industrial Engineering and Management, Technion, Haifa 32000, Israel.

Herer, Y., Tzur, M., Yücesan, E. (2002): Transshipments: An emerging inventory recourse to achieve supply chain leagility, in: International Journal of Production Economics, 80: 201-212.

Krishnan, K., Rao, V. (1965): Inventory Control in N Warehouses, in: Journal of Industrial Engineering, 16: 212-215.

Nonås, L. M., Jörnsten, K. (2004): Optimal Solutions in the Multi-Location Inventory System with Transshipments. Working Paper, Norwegian School of Economics and Business Administration, Bergen.

Robinson, L. W. (1990): Optimal and approximate policies in multiperiod, multilocation inventory models with transshipments, in: Operations Research, 38: 278-295.

Rudi, N., Kapur, S., Pyke, D. (2001): A Two-location Inventory Model with Transshipment and Local Decision Making, in: Management Science, 47: 1668-1680.

Tagaras, G. (1989): Effects of Pooling on the Optimization and Service Levels of Two-Location Inventory Systems, in: IIE Transactions, 21: 250-257.

Tagaras, G. (1999): Pooling in multi-location periodic inventory distribution systems, in: Omega, 27: 39-59.

Tagaras, G., Cohen, M. (1992): Pooling in Two-Location Inventory Systems with Non-Negligible Replenishment Lead Times, in: Management Science, 38: 1067-1083.

Tagras, G., Vlachos, D. (2002): Effectiveness of stock transshipment under various demand distributions and non-negligible lead times, in: Production and Operations Management 11 (2):183-198.

Tayur, S. (1995): Computing optimal stock levels for common components in an assembly system. Working paper, Carnegie Mellon University, Pittsburgh.

Contract Typology as a Research Method in Supply Chain Management

Alejandra Gomez-Padilla, Jeanne Duvallet, Daniel Llerena

1 Introduction 526
2 Studied Variables 527
3 Application Case 531
4 Conclusion 536
5 References 537

Summary:
In this paper we present the methodology of research that has been the base of our work. The main objective is to study contractual relations; this is the reason why we talk of a contract-oriented research methodology. Through bibliographical research, assistance to workshops and industrial contacts, we identified the basic elements that are the basic issues for understanding and describing a contractual relation. After explaining why we chose these elements, we will describe them as well as their characteristics. We also show how we describe a relation between an upstream and a downstream company. Then we present a mathematical model of this relationship.

Keywords:
Contract Typology, Supply Chain Management, Economic Model

1 Introduction

1.1 Context

The purpose of the present work is to propose a contract-oriented research methodology in order to analyze a supply chain dyadic relationship. The upstream company is a supplier of products for the downstream one. The downstream company orders a certain quantity of products that will be consumed according to the final market demand.

The study of contracts can be tackled from several perspectives. One of these perspectives is the temporality of the decisions concerning the contract. The decisions that companies are meant to take are classified as strategic, tactical and operational. Strategic decisions are those that influence the long term evolution of the company. Regarding a contract, this concerns first of all the decision of establishing a contractual relation or not. Non-exhaustive examples of strategic decisions would be: future buying options, management of transaction-specific investments, cost analysis of transactions, intellectual propriety, reselling licenses, commercial agreements, cooperation dynamics, technological evolution, change rate fluctuation, legal instances and relational exchanges. All this will be defined during the negotiation process. Our attention is not focused on this, but on the elements which articulate the tactical contract decisions. These tactical decisions will influence the operational decisions of the company.

When we began our study of contracts, we found it necessary to frame the different situations found to differentiate them and to properly situate our work. We have identified and analyzed the main elements, considered implicitly and explicitly, to be able to model different contractual situations. These elements, which can eventually become modeling variables, are the result of bibliographical research (theoretical and case study oriented literature), seminar and conference assistance as well as discussion with industrial contacts.

The elements studied are: 1) time horizon of the analysis; 2) the number of different products exchanged; 3) the information: which information the upstream company shares with the downstream company and vice versa; 4) the characteristics of the demand the downstream company faces; 5) the way financial flows take place, that is, the type of contract to which companies have to adjust their exchanges; 6) the considered costs; 7) the physical flow between the companies, that is, the quantity of products that they are exchanging; 8) the frequency of delivery of these products, or delivery splitting; and 9) the flexibility of quantity delivery in terms of physical flow.

1.2 Organization of the Document

In part 2, the identified elements are analyzed, presenting their definition and the different situations which may be observed. We accord special attention to the financial flows, which are determined by the type of contract and are the main issue and initial purpose of our research.

We demonstrate in part 3 how this typology was used as a starting point to describe the context in which our research will proceed. We describe some contracts using the typology developed and explain with three examples the importance of the contract for the performance of the supply chain. We illustrate then how to pass from this description to a model. With this part we explain how the variables are an important background to reference and describe the dyadic relations in a supply chain. We show how this contract typology can serve as a methodology for analyzing supply chains, describing them, and modeling different situations. Finally, in part 4, we present our conclusions and perspectives.

2 Studied Variables

2.1 Time Horizon

The time horizon refers to the number of periods considered. We distinguish between two types of time horizons: mono-period and multi-period. When there is only one period, the problem is known as "news vendor problem." When there are multiple periods, they can be definite (limited) or indefinite.

The time horizon determines how long the decisions taken are going to impact the companies. There is an issue particular to the mono-period situation: It means that there are no stocks, so there are no products remaining from preceding periods, and unsold products cannot be used in the future (though they can eventually be scrapped). This situation has been studied (among others) by Cachon (2004) and Larivière (2002). The multi-period situation can be for a specific number of periods or for an unspecified number. When the number of periods is specified, this is usually in order to accomplish a specific objective. This situation has been studied by authors such as Anupindi & Bassok (2002), and Bassok & Anupindi (1997). When the number of periods is not specified it is known as a steady state situation, such as the one studied by Tsay (1999) among others. In a model, the multi period situation is represented in terms of k periods.

2.2 Number of Products

The number of products refers to the quantity of different products that are to be exchanged between the two companies. We consider as different products those having different characteristics. Contracts can be either mono-product or multi-product, with the number of products being a source of flexibility in the exchanges when one product can be substituted by another. Usually the approaches are mono-product. An interesting multi-product approach is the one studied by Anupindi & Bassok (2002). Products are modeled as variables whose sum serves to attain a certain objective.

2.3 Information Exchange

Information is defined as the available data. There is some information that is known to the upstream company and some to the downstream one. The question is: Which information is to be shared, and/or, which company has to share its relevant information? Two situations can be observed: 1) both companies share their information and, 2) at least one of the companies shares its information. The first situation is said to be symmetric and the second asymmetric. Depending on the available information, each company is going to make decisions, so it would be easy to think that the more information available, the more the decisions made will help to achieve the objectives fixed by the company.

Information is a very complex issue to which several authors have oriented their research. Chen (2004) has studied and classified the upstream and the downstream information. Lee & Whang (2000) reviewed the types of information shared. Gallego & Ozer (2002) presented different models of the use of demand information and inventory policies, and Lee et al. (2000) proved that information sharing provides significant inventory reduction and cost savings to the manufacturer. Jacot (1996) has done a review of the importance of information for a company. The information is a situational issue, so it is to be studied on a case-by-case basis.

2.4 Demand

The demand is the need for a particular product or component (APICS, 1998). From our bibliographical review, we classified the demand according to its accuracy. Two situations exist: 1) when the demand is deterministic (no uncertainty as to the forecasted demand) and 2) when the demand is stochastic (uncertainty is explicitly considered). Deterministic demand it given as a constant, whereas stochastic demand requires a distribution function to describe it. Demand is a important aspect of supply chain management, so most of the authors touch upon it in one way or another (Corbett & Tang, 2002; Gallego & Ozer, 2002; Weng 1999).

2.5 Type of Contract

A contract is a statement of the rights and obligations of each party to a transaction or transactions (Penguin Dictionary of Economics, 2003), in which the involved parties agree to perform or not perform specific acts or services. It may be oral or written. We center our attention on contracts according to the activated financial flow in terms of price and the reasons for the exchanges. We have identified seven different types of contracts:

- Wholesale price: The price for each product is fixed previously and will not change.

- Quantity discount: The price for each product is digressive according to the quantity of products exchanged.

- Buy back: The downstream company pays a fixed price per unit, but the upstream company must pay a certain quantity for the unsold units.

- Revenue sharing: The downstream company pays a fixed price per unit and then must give the upstream company a percentage of its revenue, which are the proceeds from the sale of the units to its clients.

- Quantity flexibility: The downstream company pays a fixed price per unit and, after the sales, the upstream company refunds this price for the minimum quantity between a percentage (fixed by the contract) of the units the downstream company bought and the unsold units.

- Sales rebate: The downstream company pays a fixed price per unit, but the upstream company offers a rebate for the units bought over a threshold fixed by the contract.

- Capacity reservation: The downstream company agrees to buy a certain number of units and the upstream company agrees to provide them. If the final order is for a lesser number of units, the downstream company is obliged to pay anyway for the agreed units. If the final order is for more units than agreed upon, the price demanded by the upstream company will also be higher.

The prices are fixed depending on the type of contract, and the contract determines the financial flow or transfer between the companies. Some authors who describe different contract modalities are Anupindi & Bassok (2002), Cachon (2004), Harland (1996), Lariviere (2002), Reve (1990) and Tsay (1999). The contracts are represented in a model as a function of the exchanged quantities.

2.6 Costs

The costs are defined as the expenses which the company incurs, other than acquisitions, in order to provide a certain product to a client, including the penalties for not providing the said product. The costs can be described, according to our dyadic case, as the financial flows between the companies or to a third party. In an analysis, we can decide either to not consider any costs at all, or if costs are considered, we must decide which costs ought to be considered. Considered cost may be represented in a model as a parameter or as a function according to the specific situation studied. Some authors who consider costs in their analysis are Cachon & Zipkin (1999), Lariviere (2002) and Tsay (1999). The costs that we have identified are:

- Stock: The cost of holding inventory.
- Stockout: The cost of running out of inventory to satisfy the demand. The goodwill cost and the backlog cost, when existent, are also part of this cost.
- Production: The cost of modifying products or components in order to have a final product in accordance with the specifications of the clients.
- Salvage: The cost (or gain) for removing, selling, scrapping or any other way of giving use to an unsold product that will not be stocked to be sold in the future.
- Capacity creation: The cost of reserving resources to produce a certain number of units.

2.7 Quantity Per Order

The quantity per order refers to the number of units the downstream company orders. There are three possibilities: 1) Constant: the downstream company orders the same quantity every time it passes an order; 2) Minimal: the downstream company orders a quantity of products to comply with the contract (in terms of physical or financial flow); 3) Unique: the downstream company can order any quantity without constraints. The quantity affects the logistical service in terms of the frequency and splitting of delivery, vehicle routing and capacity, inventory control and production systems. Point 2.9 concerns the flexibility that can exist regarding the agreed quantity. This point, as well as the next two, have been developed, among others, by Anupindi & Bassok (2002), Bassok & Anupindi (1997) and Tsay (1999). The quantity per order is usually modeled as a decision variable.

2.8 Delivery Splitting

Delivery splitting is the division of the committed quantity into groups of deliveries. There are two possibilities for the shipping of units to the downstream company: 1) un-split or 2) split deliveries. In the second case, the number and quantity per delivery should be defined. The number of deliveries can be fixed or not. The delivery quantity may be fixed (the same number of units per delivery) or can be fixed throughout the duration of the contract as long as the downstream company has received the complete order by a certain date. Delivery splitting can be a decision (constant), a result of the quantity per order (variable) or a result of the time horizon (constant or variable according to the case).

2.9 Quantity Flexibility

This point refers to how the quantity agreed to in the contract can be modified during the contractual relation. This issue is modeled by establishing boundaries to zero, minimum or maximum quantities, or to infinity. We found three situations:

- No flexibility: when the agreed upon quantities cannot be modified.

- Min, Max: when the quantities can be modified as long as they stay within a fixed range of values. The minimum and maximum quantities accepted can be established as a percentage of the quantity originally agreed upon.

- Min, ∞: when the engaged quantities can be modified as long as they respect a minimal boundary. There is no maximum level because the upstream company has no supply constraints.

The elements used to analyze the contractual relations between the two companies according to our contract typology are represented schematically in figure 1. This figure is used to present in short the previously developed elements.

3 Application Case

3.1 News Vendor

The news vendor is a well known problem in management science and operations research; we use it here as an example to describe a contractual relation. Consider a person who sells newspapers: This person orders a certain quantity of newspapers from his supplier, the printing company, according to how many newspapers he expects to sell that day. The newspaper distribution department has the possibility to supply as many journals as he requests. He is then confronted with the decision as to how many newspapers he must order to satisfy demand. If he orders too many, at the end of the day he will be left with unsold newspapers that he won't be able to sell the next day; on the other hand, if he doesn't order enough, he won't be able to satisfy demand and consequently he won't have as much revenue as he could have had if he had ordered more.

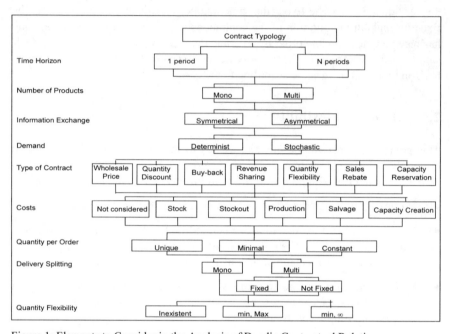

Figure 1: Elements to Consider in the Analysis of Dyadic Contractual Relations

Using our research methodology to analyze this situation, we can describe this as a case with a time horizon of one period, exchanging one product, with asymmetric information (the news vendor only knows his own information – buying and selling price–, while the newspaper company knows, besides this information, its own costs), the newsboy faces a stochastic demand, wholesale price contract, without explicit consideration of the costs, for a unique quantity, where the delivery frequency is constant and with no quantity flexibility. This is shown in figure 2.

Since we are mostly interested in the contractual relation, we are going to describe with more attention what happens between the newspaper company and the news vendor if we consider three contracts: wholesale price, buy back and sales rebate.

If the contract is one of a wholesale price, then the newspaper company will fix a price, and the news vendor will pay that amount per journal he has ordered. If the demand is higher than his order, he will not have sold as many as he could have, and if the demand is lower, then he will have lost the amount paid per unsold newspaper. This is the situation that we have already described using the identified elements to analyze a supply chain.

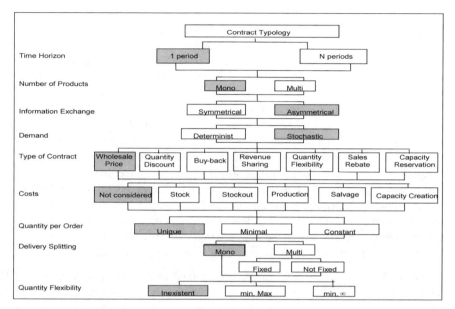

Figure 2: Classic News Vendor Problem Represented According to the Contract Typology

Consider now the situation where the buy back contract exists between the two: The newspaper company will be obliged to buy the unsold journals, usually for a lower price than the one at which they were sold to the news vendor, at the end of the day. Under this situation, the news vendor will have an interest in ordering more newspapers than under a wholesale price contract since he is sharing with the newspaper company the loss associated with the unsold newspapers.

On the other hand, if the contract were in the form of a sales rebate: The newspaper company offers a certain price for each newspaper up to a certain quantity. If the news vendor buys a number of newspapers that exceed this quantity, the price will be lower for the excess newspapers. In this way, the news vendor is encouraged to buy more newspapers at the discounted price that the newspaper company offers him for buying more, no longer sharing with him the loss for unsold journals.

In the three cases we have described, we offer evidence of the fact that, even though the only element that changes is the type of contract, each example of the supply chain would have a different performance.

As we said at the beginning of this section, the news vendor model is a classical problem of study in several disciplines. One of the main implications of this model is that there is no stock. When we move on to a problem were stock exists, we pass automatically to a problem of n-periods. In the next paragraph we will describe an n-periods situation.

Suppose that there are two companies, Company A and Company B. Company A produces envelopes and supplies them to Company B, which sells them to its clients. Company B has to order a certain number of boxes each week containing the envelopes, depending on its demand forecast. The boxes ordered are to be delivered once per week, and Company A can supply all the boxes ordered by Company B. When there are boxes that were not sold during one week, they will be stocked to be sold for the next week. The fact of stocking implies some expenses for Company B. Companies A and B know the production costs of A, the conditions of the contract between them, the price over the final market, the stocking cost and the demand forecast. B pays A a fixed amount per box. Using our research methodology to analyze this situation, we recognize that the problem is one in which the time horizon is of n-periods, with the exchange of one product, with symmetric information, facing stochastic demand, using a wholesale price contract, with consideration of stock and production costs, for a unique and different quantity per period, where the delivery frequency is constant with no quantity flexibility. We show in figure 3 the representation of this situation.

In our work we found it useful to use this method of description to classify and analyze the relations between companies. After typifying a contractual relation between two companies which are members of a supply chain, we found it necessary to create a model so that we could represent some of the elements. This will permit us to measure the performance, in our case in economic terms, since it is this aspect of the relation which interests us.

3.2   Model

The purpose of our model is to measure the performance of two companies by calculating the profit for each member of the supply chain. In this section we explain how each element from section 2 can be represented. To do so, we will present how the profit of the members of the chain is modeled. Consider then the situation presented in the last paragraphs at point 3.1 and shown in figure 3: Company A supplying a product to Company B. We consider an n-period situation, with Company B facing a demand characterized by an identical F distribution function and f density function in each period. We are in a steady state situation, so we don't need to differentiate each k period. All instances are independent of the period. The quantity of boxes that Company B has to order is q, in order to satisfy a base stock. We define Q as the boxes that Company B has available at the beginning of each period (base stock); this is, the ordered boxes q, plus the boxes in stock. The decision variable for Company B is Q, so its sales and its stock are expressed as functions of this available quantity. The expected sales and stock are represented by S(Q) and I(Q) respectively. The expected financial flow between the companies or transfer for supplying the ordered boxes to Company B is T(q). The market price of each box is P, the cost for Company B of holding in stock one box is h and the cost for Company A of producing one box is c. The expected benefit for Company B is equal to the expected revenue made by the sold boxes minus the cost of the expected inventory it has to hold for the next period minus the expected financial transfer to Company A for the ordered boxes. The expected benefit for Company A is equal to the expected financial transfer minus the cost for Company A of producing the q boxes ordered by Company B at the k period.

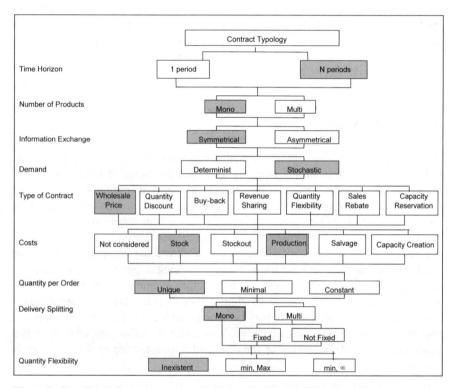

Figure 3: Case Example represented According to the Contract Typology

If we define π_B (Q) as the expected benefit of B (distributor), π_A (Q) as the expected benefit of A (supplier) in any period, we can represent them as:

$$\pi_B (Q) = P\, S(Q) - h\, I(Q) - T(q) \qquad (1)$$

$$\pi_A (Q) = T(q) - c\, q \qquad (2)$$

The financial flow of each company depends on the contract. In a wholesale contract, the expected transfer is T(q)= w q , the wholesale price w at which each box is sold to Company B times the quantity of boxes ordered for that period. The benefit of the companies is then:

$$\pi_B (Q) = P\,S(Q) - h\,I(Q) - w\,q \qquad (3)$$

$$\pi_A (Q) = w\,q - c\,q \qquad (4)$$

We have so far shown how to consider most of the elements shown in 2: time horizon, number of products, demand, type of contract, costs and quantity. There are three elements not yet discussed in this model: information exchange, delivery frequency and quantity flexibility. The information exchange is mostly a strategic issue. If either of the companies has information concerning the other, they can apply pressure, mostly through changes in the price w, so that the other company takes certain actions that will be more convenient. The delivery frequency and the quantity flexibility are restrictive elements, adjusted if needed as constraints.

4 Conclusion

We have presented here a research methodology consisting of framing the contract-oriented research. In this work we identified the elements to be considered, the forms they can take, and their importance. We showed how these elements can be the basis for modeling different situations. This contract typology-based method of analysis can be useful in terms of global comprehension of the supply chain. It can first of all be used to make a general description of the situation and the conditions of work in dyadic relations. It allows the comprehension of the mechanisms that represent the frame of their exchanges. Secondly, it can also be useful as a basis for modeling different contractual situations. It can help to understand the influence in the model of each identified element. This typology can also help to distinguish elements that may become variables and that have an important role in terms of the economic objective. This research method can also serve as a guideline to identify in which of the analyzed issues a more in-depth survey is necessary.

The future trends of research for the present paper are basically three: survey, simulation and case study. A survey directed towards companies in order to analyze their contractual practices will help to understand when and why certain decisions are taken. The survey should be ideally done for several industrial sectors. Another trend will be to pursue the study by simulation, after modeling the situations in which the analysis must be deepened; this will imply the use of empirical data. Finally, continuing with a case study, it will be possible to have a complete picture of a particular situation. An interesting case study would be for the electronics sector and the retailing industry. These two types of business are found to be relevant for this approach.

The originality of our approach is its capacity to simultaneously highlight all the elements that describe dyadic contractual relations from a tactical perspective. It is methodology oriented since it can be useful as a basis for a qualitative as well as for a quantitative description and analysis of a supply chain. The main contribution of this document is to present a research methodology in supply chain management based on framing the relation between two companies according to the contract between them, highlighting the main issues.

We thank the two anonymous reviewers of this paper for their comments and suggestions. We would also like to thank CONACYT (Mexico) for its financial support.

5 References

Anupindi, R., Bassok, Y. (2002): Supply Contracts with Quantity Commitments and Stochastic Demand, in: Tayur, S., Ganeshan, R., Magazine, M. (eds.): Quantitative Models for Supply Chain Management, Kluwer, Dordrecht: p. 197-232.

APICS (1998): Cox, J. F. III, Blackstone, J. H. Jr. (eds.): APICS Dictionary, ninth edition, The Educational Society for Resource Management, Alexandria, USA.

Avenel, E., Caprice, S. (2001): Vertical Integration, Exclusive dealing and product line differentiation in the Retailing Sector, INRA Cahier de Recherche 2001-16, Press Book of the National Institute for Research in Agronomy, Toulouse.

Bassok, Y., Anupindi, R. (1997): Analysis of supply contracts with total minimum commitment, in: IIE Transactions, 29(5): 373-381.

Cachon, G. P. (2004): Supply Chain Coordination with Contracts, in: De Kok, A. G., Grave, S. C. (eds.): Handbooks in Operations Research and Management Science, 11: Supply Chain Management: Design, Coordination and Operation, Elsevier, Amsterdam: p. 229-340.

Cachon, G. P., Zipkin, P. H. (1999): Competitive and Cooperative Inventory Policies in a Two-Stage Supply Chain, in: Management Science, 45(7): 936-953.

Chen, F. (2004): Information Sharing and Supply Chain Coordination, in: de Kok, A. G., Grave, S. C. (eds.): Handbooks in Operations Research and Management Science, 11: Supply Chain Management: Design, Coordination and Operation, Elsevier, Amsterdam: p. 341-422.

Corbett C. J., Tang, C. S., (2002): Designing Supply Contracts: Contract Type and Information Asymmetry, in: Tayur, S., Ganeshan, R., Magazine, M. (eds.): Quantitative Models for Supply Chain Management, Kluwer, Dordrecht: p. 269-297.

Croom, S., Romano, P., Giannakis, M. (2000): Supply Chain Management: An Analytical Framework for Critical Literature Review, in: European Journal of Purchasing and Supply Management, 6(1): 67-83.

Croxton, K. L., Garcia-Dastugue, S. J. (2001): The Supply Chain Management Process, in: The International Journal of Logistics Management, 12(2): 13-36.

Gallego, G., Özer, Ö. (2002): Optimal use of Demand Information in Supply Chain Management, in: J. Song, D. Yao, (eds.): Supply Chain Structures: Coordination, Information and Optimization, Kluwer, Dordrecht: p. 119-160.

Harland, C. M. (1996): Supply Chain Management: Relationships, Chains and Networks, in: British Journal of Management, Special Issue, 7: 63-80.

Jacot, J. H., Micaelli, J. P. (1996): La Performace Economique en Entreprise (The Economical Performance in the Enterprise), Hermès, Paris.

Lambert, D. M., Cooper, M. C. (2000): Issues in Supply Chain Management, in: Industrial Marketing Management, 29: 65-83.

Lambert, D. M., Cooper, M. C., Pagh, J. D. (1998): Supply Chain Management: Implementation Issues and Research Opportunities, in: International Journal of Logistics Management, 9(2): 1-19.

Lariviere, M. A. (2002): Supply Chain Contracting and Coordination with Stockastic Demand, in: Tayur, S., Ganeshan, R., Magazine, M. (eds.): Quantitative Models for Supply Chain Management, Kluwer, Dordrecht: p. 233-268.

Larson, P. D., Rogers, D. S. (1998): Supply Chain Management: Definitions, Growth and Approaches, in: Journal of Marketing Theory and Practice, Special Issue, 6 (4): 1-5.

Lee, H. L., Whang S. (2000): Information Sharing in a Supply Chain, in: International Journal of Technology Management, 20(3/4): 373-387.

Lee, H. L., So, K. C., Tang, C. S. (2000): The Value of Information Sharing in a Two-level Supply Chain, in: Management Science, 46(5): 626-643.

Penguin Dictionary of Economics (2003): Bannock, G., Baxter, R. E., Davis, E. (eds.): Penguin Dictionary of Economics, 7.th Edition The Penguin Books, London.

Reve, T. (1990): The Firm as a Nexus of Internal and External Contracts, in: Aoki, M., Gustafsson, B., Williamson, O. (eds.): The Firm as a Nexus of Treaties, Sage Publications, London: p. 133-161.

Tan, K. C. (2001): A framework of supply chain management literature, in: European Journal of Purchasing and Supply Management, 7: 39-48.

Tsay, A. A. (1999): The Quantity Flexibility Contract and Supplier-Costumer Incentives, in: Management Science, 45(10): 1339-1358.

Weng, Z. K. (1999): The power of coordinated decisions for short life cycle products in a manufacturing and distribution Supply Chain, in: IIE Transactions, 31(11): 1037-1049.

Load Dependent Lead Times – From Empirical Evidence to Mathematical Modeling

Julia Pahl, Stefan Voß, David L. Woodruff

1 Introduction 540
2 Load Dependent Lead Times – Empirical Evidence 541
3 Models Including Load Dependent Lead Times 544
4 Conclusions 552
5 References 553

Summary:
As organizations move from creating plans for individual production lines to entire supply chains it is increasingly important to recognize that decisions concerning utilization of production resources impact the lead times that will be experienced. In this paper we give some insights into why this is the case by looking at the queuing that results in delays. In this respect, special mention should be made that it is difficult to experience related empirical data, especially for tactical planning issues. We use these insights to survey and suggest optimization models that take into account load dependent lead times and related "complications."

Keywords:
Supply Chain Management, Load Dependent Lead Times, Lead Times, Tactical Planning, Aggregate Planning

1 Introduction

Let us define the lead time as the time between the release of an order to the shop floor or to a supplier and the receipt of the items. Lead time considerations are essential with respect to the global competitiveness of firms, because long lead times impose high costs due to rising WIP (work in process) inventory levels as well as larger safety stocks caused by increased uncertainty about production prerequisites and constraints. Despite this, considerations about load dependent lead times are rare in the literature. The same is valid for models linking order releases, planning and capacity decisions to lead times, and take into account factors influencing lead times such as the system workload, batching and sequencing decisions or WIP levels.

Present practice for manufacturing supply chains is dominated by the use of material requirements planning (mrp) with its inherent problems. Many companies do not use adequate planning tools at all. Accordingly, problems arise when fixed, constant or "worst case" lead times are assumed at an aggregate planning level, e.g., to have enough "buffer time" to securely meet demands. In order to meet due dates there is also a tendency to release jobs into the system much earlier than necessary, leading to very high WIP levels and, therefore, longer queuing (waiting times) causing even longer lead times. This overreactional behavior becomes a self-fulfilling prophecy and is addressed in the literature as the *lead time syndrome* which results from the fact that the relationship between WIP, output, workload and average flow times is ignored (Zäpfel & Missbauer, 1993; Tatsiopoulos & Kingsman, 1983). Moreover, most mrp and enterprise resource planning (ERP) models implement sequential planning algorithms which neither consider uncertainties nor resource and production flow constraints of raw material, WIP and finished goods inventory (FGI), leading to suboptimal or infeasible production plans (Caramanis & Ahn, 1999).

Another fundamental problem of manufacturing and production planning models is the omission of modeling nonlinear dependencies, e.g., between lead times and the workload of a production system or a production resource. This happens even though there is empirical evidence that lead times increase nonlinearly long before resource utilization reaches 100% (Asmundsson et al., 2003; Karmarkar, 1987); see Figure 1. This may lead to significant differences in planned and realized lead times. There is a lack of models allowing the analysis of behavior of lead times and WIP levels considering the facility workload under variable demand patterns like seasonal demand. In addition, it seems likely that queuing tends to be correlated so that a machine failure at one point of the system will cause queuing at other stations which leads to the presumption that lead time distributions tend to be fat-tailed and skewed. However, to the best of our knowledge there is no comprehensive (empirical) work on this topic currently available. Furthermore, it seems that there is no model which analyzes load dependent lead times in the context of stochastic demand evidently prevailing in practice.

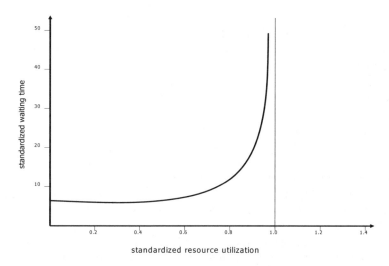

Figure 1: Nonlinear Relationship between Waiting Time and Resource Utilization
(Voß & Woodruff, 2003: 162)

It is necessary to examine the problem of lead time dynamics at individual links to better understand the effects and the modelling requirements and complexities at the aggregate planning level for the entire supply network. The aim of this paper is to demonstrate, based on empirical evidence obtained by a survey and interviews recently executed and briefly sketched in the next section, the need for aggregate planning models with the following features: being able to take into account the nonlinear relation between lead times and workload, while remaining tractable to be adapted to complex production systems and supply chains. The remainder of this paper is organized as follows. In Section 2 we point out the empirical evidence of load dependent lead times by means of the results obtained from interviews and a survey recently executed. Then we survey methods and models dealing with load dependent lead times and examine indirect approaches, aspects of queuing theory, and introduce so-called clearing functions in Section 3. The paper concludes with some remarks and suggestions for future research directions.

2 Load Dependent Lead Times – Empirical Evidence

Production planning is a complex issue especially in the context of variable demand patterns or stochastic demand. In numerous production environments demand quantities are not known at the beginning of the production planning process. As a result it is difficult to create forecasts of (highly) variable demand patterns. Production uncertainties and unforeseen events such as machine breakdowns, unavailability of production resources, illness of workers, etc. raise the instability of the production process with queues building up in front of machines resulting in increased WIP and FGI levels and consequently in raised lead times. Therefore, production processes in such environments tend to become somewhat hectic with overtime in peak situations leading to unbalanced utilization of production resources. This is especially true for the food (or semiconductor) industry which also has to account for various deteriorating rates of their production material, which is another complication issue of (load dependent) lead times. As a result, the forecast quality is very important in tactical (and operational) production planning since it prevents precipitated releases of jobs (orders) in the production process and, therefore, should be linked with aggregate production planning and order release control. Nevertheless, there is a lack of practical and useful tools for tactical production planning which permits companies to account for variable demand and unforeseen events causing load dependent lead times. This is one of the principle outcomes of our survey and interviews with companies from different industrial sectors such as transportation, logistics and inventory, aerospace, industry automation and mineral oil, and the chemical industry.

The study includes enterprises of various sizes producing different types of products with very different product life cycles including base polyols, load cels, indicators/ transmitters, software, IT- and logistic services and satellite launchers. These companies face diverse demand patterns and environmental challenges they have to take into consideration in the overall production planning process, especially with regard to the planning of resources and their utilization levels. Many companies face variable (seasonal) and not easily predictable demand for their foremost products. This seems to be the main uncertainty in the production process, because further potential precarious factors such as, e.g., the cooperations with supply chain partners and delieveries from supply chain partners are not validated as highly impacting the production process. This is due to the fact that, e.g., the launcher business has very long production cycle times (the production of one launcher like Ariane 5 or Vega takes on average 2.5 years). Here, problems concerning the cooperation of supply chain partners are not very critical in terms of time compared to other branches like the automotive industry where JIT production is mainly implemented and late deliveries of components cause the whole production process to stop. Nevertheless, late deliveries of important components for, e.g., a launcher also cause the whole assembly process to stop which leads to great financial losses not only because of idle times of production resources and very expensive WIP waiting in the queue, but also because of the costs for the client associated with the delay (lost profits of satellite services). Other companies do not experience supply chain cooperation problems due to long endurance with few supply chain partners, leading to a stabilized and well defined work flow.

Usually medium or large organisations are characterized by a large number of supply chain partners and more or less complex production processes. The range of surveyed companies and their production systems cover synchronized facilities, job shops and make-to-order-systems with different core objectives in tactical production planning as, e.g., maximizing resource utilization in order to avoid idle times (mostly in synchronized production facilities), minimizing lead times or cycle times (this holds true for make-to-order situations) and minimizing WIP and FGI levels. Only a few companies use specific tools for tactical production planning such as SAP R/3, SAP APO (APO SNP for tactical production planning and APO PP/DS for operational production planning). The survey confirms the prevailing use of mrp-based systems together with estimated lead times (or planned lead times) leading to the problems outlined above. Most of the companies experience rising lead times due to machine breakdowns as well as rising WIP levels and consequent queuing in front of machines. Nevertheless, because of the unavailability of data sets (surveys) which are necessary to execute a detailed empirical analysis, it is not clear whether this occurs before reaching 100% utilization, but despite the lack of information, queuing theory emphasizes the impact of resource utilization on load dependent lead times.

The main goals in tactical production planning of the surveyed companies consist in minimizing lead (or cycle) times, as well as WIP and FGI inventory levels, and maximizing resource utilization in order to avoid idle times. For this purpose some of them use, e.g., some "worst case lead times" in order to have enough buffer time at certain (critical) points in the production system and to secure that demands can be met. Others implement estimates of lead times derived from historical data of the production system, which gets problematic when production processes change. Consequently, the underlying data for estimated or planned lead times is neither reliable nor useful in order to achieve the mentioned objectives. However, companies are aware of the fact that decisions on the workload in the production system (and of single resources), on scheduling and sequencing, and on lot sizing and setup times are key factors influencing (load dependent) lead times. To summarize, they lack models (included in comprehensive, usable and useful software tools) providing them with, e.g., "if-then"-analysis in order to better understand the impact of decisions of resource utilization levels, and not only for one single machine or production resource, but even for the whole supply chain network, and furthermore, in order to permit them to use better estimates of lead times. Until now useful models did not exist which provide production planners with necessary information about the lead times which will be experienced in case of diverse resource utilization levels.

As mentioned above, load dependent lead times are the result of production planning processes and should not be an input factor for production planning and scheduling. Moreover, the surveyed companies state the interest in models which take into account load dependent lead times and their impact on the performance of production. Thus it is necessary to analyse the nonlinear relationship of resource utilization and lead times, as well as influencing factors in more detail in order to integrate them in aggregate production planning. Finally, the integration of supply chain partners in an overall supply chain network tends to precede in the right direction by connecting the participants through information system tools, e.g., the same production planning software or linking them together by add-ons in order to guarantee real time information of their production process and those of the supply chain partners. Nevertheless, this is still an ongoing process.

3 Models Including Load Dependent Lead Times

Load dependent lead times are primarily considered in the framework of capacity planning models and order release control mechanisms. Traditional models aim at "filling time buckets" which represent the available capacity of a production system in discrete time periods, while linear programming models are typically employed using hard capacity constraints which ignore the phenomenon that in asynchronous systems, prevailing in practice, queues build up long before 100% resource utilization is reached. Furthermore, they do not impose costs until the capacity constraint is violated, i.e., the constraint only tightens in case of 100% utilization (Karmarkar, 1989). Moreover, these models neither account for WIP and other lead time related cost factors that increase with queues and delays and accordingly with longer lead times (Karmarkar, 1993; Zipkin, 1986), nor do they include WIP costs and lead time consequences of capacity loading which can have significant effects on the performance of the production system.

3.1 Indirect Approaches

There are several ways to address problems associated with load dependent lead times. Some authors do not directly consider the difficulty of modeling nonlinear dependencies of lead times and workload, but try to solve the problem indirectly by influencing parameters that have an effect on lead times such as decisions on job release policies, influences of the demand side, changes in production plans or by smoothing demand variability, e.g., by implementing a make to stock policy, or shifts (away) from bottlenecks in order to increase capacity. Other approaches concentrate on lot sizing as an influencing factor or on production system characteristics as well as employing queuing theory as an analytical method.

3.2 Aspects of Queuing Theory

Analysis of production system performance and important key factors like throughput, WIP levels and load dependent lead times are frequently executed in the context of queuing theory due to the fact that a large percentage of lead times are waiting times. It has been shown that 90% of the total flow time is due to transit times, where 85% consists of waiting (queuing) time, 3% of quality control, and 2% of transportation time; only 10% is due to value added processing operations (Tatsiopoulos & Kingsman, 1983). Queuing network models highlight the relationship between the capacity, loading and production mix as well as the resulting WIP levels and effect on lead times (Karmarkar, 1987) and provide important information on the causes of congestion phenomena. Furthermore, they show that delays predominantly depend on the service variability, i.e., the processing time of a resource, the variability of the arrival rate of work at a resource and the current workload as well as scale effects with major delays near the maximum capacity usage (Srinivasan et al., 1988).

Congestion phenomena are inherent problems of production systems complicating the planning process. They emerge at different and frequently changing times and places which are hardly predictable. Therefore, it is crucial to better understand the reasons for congestion phenomena like the limited capacity of a machine (resource) to respond to demand variation over time (Lautenschläger, 1999) and to account for them in aggregate planning models. The literature on queuing and congestion phenomena is multitudinous; see, e.g. (Chen et al., 1988; Karmarkar, 1987, 1989; Spearman, 1991; Suri & Sanders, 1993; Zipkin, 1986). Spearman (1991) develops a cyclic closed queuing network model with three parameters, viz. the bottleneck capacity, the "raw processing time" (i.e., increasing failure rate processing time, IFR) and a congestion coefficient which specifies a unique throughput/WIP curve in order to analyze the dependency between mean cycle time (synonymously used for "flow time" in many references) and WIP for the whole production system, i.e., single resources and their processing times are not considered. The model indicates a relationship between mean cycle time and WIP level and can be used to predict the average cycle time in exponential as well as in IFR closed queuing networks. Chen et al. (1988) provide a network queuing model for semiconductor wafer facilities which points out that congestion and delays are due to variability in the operating environment. So this variability has to be smoothed in order to obtain shorter production cycle times.

It is useful to start with a queuing model in order to obtain some approximations for the key parameters or objective functions to be implemented in an aggregate planning model (Buzacott & Shantikumar, 1993).

3.3 Indirect Integration of Load Dependent Lead Times

There are only a few approaches which try to integrate load dependent lead times directly into mathematical programming models. For instance, Zijm & Buitenhek (1996) developed a manufacturing planning and control framework for a machine shop which includes workload oriented lead time estimates. For this purpose they suggest a method that determines the earliest possible completion time of arriving jobs with the restriction that the delivery performance of any other job in the system will not be adversly affected, i.e., that every job can be completed and delivered on time. Their aim is to determine reliable planned lead times based on workload which guarantee that due dates are met and can be implemented at a capacity planning level, serving as input for a final detailed capacity scheduling procedure that also takes into account additional resources, job batching decisions as well as machine setup characteristics. Their framework is partly based on the work of (Karmarkar, 1987; Karmarkar et al., 1985). Missbauer (1998) focuses on the hierarchical production planning concept in which all partial problems can be included (e.g., aggregate production planning, capacity planning, lot sizing, scheduling etc.), but which avoids the problems of a comprehensive model, e.g., problems of data procurement, limited computational storage space, CPU times that are too long for calculation etc.

Graves (1986) studied the dependencies between production capability, variability (uncertainty) of the production requirements, and level of WIP inventory in a tactical planning model and analyzes to which extent the job flow time (or WIP inventory) depends on the utilization of each resource of a job shop or production stage. He further concentrates on analyzing the interrelationship of flow time and production mix. For this purpose he employs a network model where multiple routings of jobs are possible so that the lack of a dominant work flow renders production control, which aims at reducing the variance of planned lead times. In addition, he uses a queuing model that includes flexible production rates of resources which can be set by a tactical planning model in order to smooth the work flow and to avoid the overload of resources. Moreover, he implements a control rule at each resource that determines the amount of work performed during a time period which is a fixed portion α_j of the queue of work at j remaining at the start of the period at a specific resource j: $P_{jt} = \alpha_j Q_{jt}$ $\forall j,t$ with P_{jt} denoting the production of resource j in time period t, α_j a smoothing parameter with $0 < \alpha_j \leq 1$ and Q_{jt} the queue of work at j at the beginning of time period t. This parameter α_j is called "proportional factor" by Missbauer (1998) and "clearing factor" by Graves (1986), because it indicates the quantity of jobs (orders) which can be cleared or finished (and passed to another station) in one time period. Here, the clearing factor implies infinite capacity since the resource is able to complete the fixed portion α_j even when the workload (WIP) is infinitely high. The major drawback of this model is the employment of a linear function and consequently the omission of the nonlinear relationship of WIP and lead times. Nevertheless, Graves (1986) seems to be the first reference accounting for the dependency between lead times and workload and giving a practical aid on how to set planned lead times in, e.g., mrp models considering the workload of the production system.

3.4 Clearing Functions

Taking up the idea of Graves and integrating it in a model with so-called "clearing factors" $\alpha(WIP)$ which are nonlinear functions of the WIP yields a clearing function of the following form (Karmarkar, 1989; Srinivasan et al., 1988):

$$Capacity = \alpha(WIP) * WIP = f(WIP)$$

where f represents the clearing function which models capacity as a function of the workload. The clearing factor specifies the fraction of the actual WIP which can be completed, i.e., "cleared," by a resource in a given period of time (Asmundsson et al., 2003). Missbauer (1998) calls this function "utilization function."

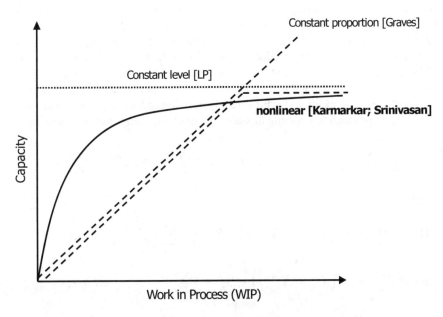

Figure 2: Different Clearing Functions (Karmarkar, 1993)

Figure 2 depicts some possible clearing functions where the constant level clearing function corresponds to an upper bound for capacity as mainly employed by linear programming models. This implies instantaneous production without lead time constraints since production takes place independently of WIP in the production system. The constant proportion clearing function represents the control rule given by Graves (1986) which implies infinite capacity and hence allows for unlimited output. In contrast to the nonlinear clearing function of Karmarkar and Srinivasan et al., the combined clearing function in some region underestimates and in others overestimates capacity. Moreover, the nonlinear clearing function relates WIP levels to output and lead times to WIP levels which are influenced by the workload of the production system (Karmarkar, 1993) and, therefore, is able to capture the behavior of load dependent lead times. By applying Little's Law, the clearing function can be reinterpreted in terms of lead time or WIP turn. Additionally, the slope of the clearing function represents the inventory turn with lead times given by the inverse of the slope (Karmarkar, 1989). Asmundsson et al. (2003) combine aspects of queuing theory with the clearing function concept by employing a clearing function of the above given form and by defining the performance of a resource (work center) as dependent on the workload using a G/G/1 queuing model.

In order to develop the clearing function, two approaches can be found in the literature to date. The first is the analytical derivation from queuing network models and the second an empirical approximation using a functional form which can be fitted to empirical data. Because of the large amount of detail in practical systems the complete identification of the clearing function will not be possible, so we have to work with approximations. Asmundsson et al. (2002) integrate the estimated clearing function in a mathematical programming model where the framework is based on the production model of (Hackman & Leachman, 1989) with an objective function that minimizes the overall costs. It is assumed that backorders do not occur and that all demand must be met on time. We concentrate on this model as an example for the direct integration of load dependent lead times in aggregate production planning models. The model is then stated as follows:

$$Min \sum_t \left[\sum_n \left[\sum_i (\phi_t^n X_{it}^n + \varpi_{it}^n W_{it}^n + \pi_{it}^n I_{it}^n + \rho_{it}^n R_{it}^n) \right] + \sum_j \theta_{jt} Y_{jt} \right]$$

subject to :

$$W_{it}^n = W_{i,t-1}^n - \frac{1}{2}(X_{it}^n + X_{i,t-1}^n) + R_{it}^n + \sum_{j \in A(n,i)} Y_{jt} \qquad \forall n, t, i$$

$$I_{it}^n = I_{i,t-1}^n + \frac{1}{2}(X_{it}^n + X_{i,t-1}^n) - D_{it}^n - \sum_{j \in B(n,i)} Y_{jt} \qquad \forall n, t, i$$

$$X_{\bullet t}^n \leq f_{nt}(W_{\bullet t}^n) \qquad \forall n, t$$

$$X_{it}^n, W_{it}^n, Y_{jt}, I_{it}^n, R_{it}^n \geq 0 \qquad \forall n, t, i, j$$

where $\phi_t^n X_{it}^n$ denotes the costs of the total amount of production over the latter half of period t and the first half of period $t+1$, represented by X_{it}^n, with ϕ_t^n referring to the corresponding unit costs at node n in period t. The WIP costs and the FGI costs of item i at node n at the end of period t are denoted by $\omega_{it}^n W_{it}^n$ and $\pi_{it}^n I_{it}^n$, respectively, with ω_{it}^n and π_{it}^n being the corresponding unit costs and W_{it}^n and I_{it}^n representing the WIP and the inventory, respectively. Likewise, the costs of releases of raw material of item i at node n during period t are represented by $\rho_{it}^n R_{it}^n$ with unit costs ρ_{it}^n and finally the transfer costs on arc j during period t are given by $\theta_{jt} Y_{jt}$ with corresponding unit costs θ_{jt}. $X_{\bullet t}^n$ is the production quantity and $W_{\bullet t}^n$ the WIP level summarized over all items i.

The first two constraints denote the flow conservation for WIP and FGI, which is different from classical models since inventory levels at each node in the network are connected with the throughput rate. ($A(n,i)$ / $B(n,i)$ represent a set of transportation arcs contributing to inflow / outflow of item i at node n.) In contrast to Ettl et al. (2000), the nonlinear dynamic is incorporated in the clearing function and thus not included in the objective function, but modeled as a constraint of the model. Furthermore, the planning circularity which is one of the most significant shortcomings of mrp systems is overcome by not modeling the lead time explicitly in the mathematical program. Consequently, there is no need to employ fixed and / or estimated lead times ignoring the nonlinear relationship between lead times and WIP. Instead, they are calculated using Little's Law:

$$L_{it}^n = \frac{W_{it}^n}{X_{it}^n}$$

where L_{it}^n denotes the expected lead time for the last job of item i which arrived before the end of period t. We are also interested in deriving the lead times for single items i in order to consider multiple product types with different resource consumption patterns. For that purpose we assume the standard case of FIFO processing for which the following relationship holds:

$$\frac{X_{it}^n}{X_{\bullet t}^n} = \frac{W_{it}^n}{W_{\bullet t}^n}$$

Taking this relation and multiplying the production quantities X_{it}^n with their so-called resource consumption factor ξ_{it}^n which defines the capacity consumption per unit produced for item i at node n, we derive a new variable Z_{it}^n of the following form:

$$Z_{it}^n = \frac{\xi_{it}^n X_{it}^n}{X_{\bullet t}^n} = \frac{\xi_{it}^n W_{it}^n}{W_{\bullet t}^n} \qquad \forall n, t, i$$

By implementing this variable Z_{it}^n we obtain the clearing function for each item i which is called the partitioned clearing function:

$$\xi_{it}^n X_{it}^n \leq Z_{it}^n f\left(\frac{\xi_{it}^n W_{it}^n}{Z_{it}^n}\right) \qquad \forall n, t, i$$

with the following properties of Z_{it}^n:

$$\sum_i Z_{it}^n = 1 \qquad \forall i,n,t$$

$$Z_{it}^n \geq 0 \qquad \forall i,n,t$$

The partitioned clearing function is depicted in Figure 3.

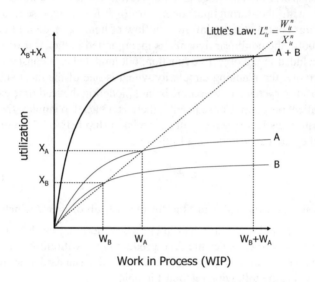

Figure 3: Clearing Function for Products A and B (Asmundsson et al., 2002)

In order to relax the assumed priority rule (FIFO) we only suppose that Z_{it}^n satisfies the properties stated above, but has an arbitrary functional form. With this formulation Asmundsson et al. (2002) succeed in integrating the nonlinear relationship between WIP and lead times in a mathematical model. The second goal is to transform this model in a tractable form which allows even the relatively large planning problems to be dealt with. For this reason we use a linear programming formulation by representing the partitioned clearing function through a set of linear constraints. To be more precise, the clearing function is approximated by the convex hull of straight lines which is possible because of its concavity:

$$f_{nt}(W_{\bullet t}^n) = \min_c \{\alpha_{nt}^c W_{\bullet t}^n + \beta_{nt}^c\} \qquad \forall n,t$$

The individual lines of the items are denoted by the index c. The β coefficients represent the intersection with the y-axis and indicate the capacity splitting (sharing) across the items while the α coefficients represent the slope of the clearing function. Applying this formulation to the partitioned clearing function leads to the following form:

$$Z_{it}^n \left(\frac{\xi_{it}^n W_{it}^n}{Z_{it}^n} \right) = Z_{it}^n \cdot \min_c \left\{ \alpha_{nt}^c \frac{\xi_{it}^n W_{it}^n}{Z_{it}^n} + \beta_{nt}^c \right\} = \min_c \left\{ \alpha_{nt}^c \xi_{it}^n W_{it}^n + \beta_{nt}^c Z_{it}^n \right\}$$

Replacing the former capacity constraint of the original nonlinear mathematical programming model with nonlinear lead time and capacity dynamics gives the complete linearized formulation:

$$Min \sum_t \left[\sum_n \left[\sum_i (\phi_{it}^n X_{it}^n + \varpi_{it}^n W_{it}^n + \pi_{it}^n I_{it}^n + \rho_{it}^n R_{it}^n) \right] + \sum_j \theta_{jt} Y_{jt} \right]$$

subject to:

$$W_{it}^n = W_{i,t-1}^n - \frac{1}{2}(X_{it}^n + X_{i,t-1}^n) + R_{it}^n + \sum_{j \in A(n,i)} Y_{jt} \qquad \forall n,t,i$$

$$I_{it}^n = I_{i,t-1}^n + \frac{1}{2}(X_{it}^n + X_{i,t-1}^n) - D_{it}^n - \sum_{j \in B(n,i)} Y_{jt} \qquad \forall n,t,i$$

$$\xi_{it}^n X_{it}^n \le \alpha_{nt}^c \xi_{it}^n W_{it}^n + Z_{it}^n \beta_{nt}^c \qquad \forall n,t,i,c$$

$$\sum_i Z_{it}^n = 1 \qquad \forall n,t$$

$$X_{it}^n, W_{it}^n, Y_{jt}, I_{it}^n, R_{it}^n, Z_{it}^n \ge 0 \qquad \forall n,t,i,j$$

The approximation of the partitioned clearing function is depicted in Figure 4.

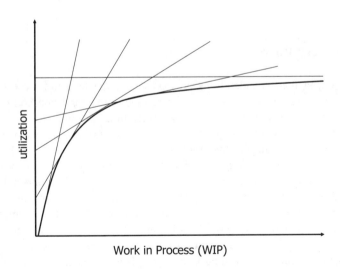

Figure 4: Linearization of the Partitioned Clearing Function

Advantages of this approach lie in the fact that the marginal cost of capacity and the marginal benefit of adding WIP are strictly positive, because of the fact that the constraints are always active as opposed to classical models where, e.g., the capacity constraint is only active at 100% utilization. However, this is only likely to be the fact at the bottleneck of the production system (Asmundsson et al., 2002). In order to examine the relevance and performance of this approach the authors consider an example of a simple single stage system with three products, which gives very good results. Furthermore, the sensitivity of the estimated clearing function to diverse shop floor scheduling algorithms, different demand patterns and techniques of production planning using a simulation model is analyzed. To summarize, the clearing function model reflects the characteristics and capabilities of the production system better than models using fixed planned lead times (like mrp) and derives realistic and robust plans with better on time delivery performance, lower WIP and system inventory (Asmundsson et al., 2003). In addition, the model captures the effects of congestion phenomena on lead times and WIP and, therefore, the fundamental trade-off between anticipatory production to account for possible demand peaks and just in time production to avoid higher costs due to preventable FGI. Finally, the releases generated by the partial clearing function model are smoother and lead to enhanced lead time performance. Moreover, interactions between clearing functions and shop floor execution systems such as the dependency of load dependent lead times on the various priority rules have to be analyzed more closely. This is a circularity, because clearing functions are dependent on the employed scheduling policy and, therefore, on the result of the scheduling algorithm. Moreover, the schedules are dependent on the release schedule and consequently on the planning algorithm.

4 Conclusions

We have seen that considerations on load dependent lead times are rare in the literature to date which is also true for aggregate planning and control models. This is particularly noteworthy, because reflections on lead times are essential with respect to the global competitiveness of firms. Furthermore, we have seen the importance to account for the nonlinear relationship between lead times and workload of production systems and further influencing factors such as product mix, scheduling policies, batching or lot sizing, variable demand patterns, deterioration etc. Analytical (queuing) models emphasize the nonlinear relationship between lead times and workload which is included only in a few mathematical planning models. Additionally, there is a lack of models which analyze load dependent lead times in the context of stochastic demand and uncertainties evidently prevailing in practice. The approach of modeling clearing functions in order to account for load dependent lead times as outlined in this paper is considered very promising and will be implemented in a stochastic framework by using queuing models with the purpose of integrating the problem of variable demand patterns, and in order to analyze the behavior of load dependent lead times. This will be used as a starting point for more sophisticated modelling of production systems where we try to model single production units (resources, workstations, etc.) as queuing models in order to derive their specific clearing functions. Furthermore, it has been stated that load dependent lead times mainly arise due to congestion phenomena which are pervasive problems of production systems, complicating the planning process by emerging at different and frequently changing times and places which are hardly predictable due to various factors like machine breakdowns, variable demand patterns or deteriorating items. For future work we shall develop approaches for aggregate production planning which take empirical values of the probability of machine breakdowns into account as well as the other mentioned causes of congestion phenomena. This can be achieved by applying, e.g., a learning algorithm which allows for learning the behavior of production units (resources or workstations) as well as the overall system behavior, and including this information into aggregate production planning. Information on downtimes is rarely considered or integrated in mathematical models. It is not even considered in the latest and sophisticated supply chain management software like SAP APO. This will be a subject for further research.

5 References

Asmundsson, J., Rardin, R. L., Uzsoy, R. (2002): Tractable Nonlinear Capacity Models for Aggregate Production Planning, Working Paper, School of Industrial Engineering, Purdue University, West Lafayette.

Asmundsson, J., Rardin, R. L., Uzsoy, R. (2003): An Experimental Comparison of Linear Programming Models for Production Planning Utilizing Fixed Lead Time & Clearing Functions, Working Paper, School of Industrial Engineering, Purdue University, West Lafayette.

Buzacott, J. A., Shantikumar, J. G. (1993): Stochastic Models of Manufacturing Systems, Englewood Cliffs, New York.

Caramanis, M. C., Ahn, O. M. (1999): Dynamic Lead Time Modeling for JIT Production Planning, Proceedings of the IEEE International Conference on Robotics and Automation, Detroit, MI, May 10-15, v2, 1450-1455.

Chen, H., Harrison, M. J., Mandelbaum, A., van Ackere, A., Wein, L. M. (1988): Empirical Evaluation of a Queuing Network Model for Semiconductor Wafer Fabrication, Operations Research, 36(2): 202-215.

Ettl, M., Feigin, G. E., Lin, G. Y., Yao, D. D. (2000): A Supply Network Model with Base-Stock Control and Service Requirements, Operations Research, 48(2): 216-232.

Graves, S. (1986): A Tactical Planning Model for Job Shops, Operations Research, 34(4): 522–533.

Hackman, S. T., Leachman, R. C. (1989): A General Framework for Modeling Production, Management Science, 35(4): 478-495.

Karmarkar, U. S. (1987): Lot Sizes, Lead Times and In-Process Inventories, Management Science, 33(3): 409-418.

Karmarkar, U. S. (1989): Capacity Loading and Release Planning with Work-In-Process (WIP) and Lead Times, Journal of Manufacturing and Operations Management, 2(2): 105-123.

Karmarkar, U. S. (1993): Manufacturing Lead Times, Order Release and Capacity Loading, in: Graves, S., Rinnooy Kan, A., Zipkin, P. (eds.): Logistics of Production and Inventory, Handbooks in Operations Research and Management Science, Vol. 4, Amsterdam: p. 287-329.

Karmarkar, U. S., Kekre, S., Kekre, S. (1985): Lotsizing in Multi-Item Multi Machine Job Shops, IIE Transactions, 17(3): 290-297.

Lautenschläger, M. (1999): Mittelfristige Produktionsprogrammplanung mit auslastungsabhängigen Vorlaufzeiten ("Tactical Production Planning with Workload Dependent Forward Production Times"), PhD Thesis, TU Darmstadt.

Missbauer, H. (1998): Bestandsregelung als Basis für eine Neugestaltung von PPS-Systemen ("Inventory Control as a Basis for a New Concept for PPS-Systems"), Physica, Heidelberg.

Spearman, M.L. (1991): An Analytic Congestion Model for Closed Production Systems with IFR Processing Times, Management Science, 37(8): 1015-1029.

Srinivasan, A., Carey, M., Morton, T. E. (1990): Resource Pricing and Aggregate Scheduling in Manufacturing Systems, Working Paper, GSIA, 1988 (Revised December 1990).

Suri, R., Sanders, J.L. (1993): Performance Evaluation of Production Networks, in: Graves, S., Rinnooy Kan, A., Zipkin, P. (eds.): Logistics of Production and Inventory, Handbooks in Operations Research and Management Science, Vol. 4, Amsterdam: p. 199-286.

Tatsiopoulos, I.P., Kingsman, B.G. (1983): Lead Time Management, European Journal of Operational Research, 14(4): 351-358.

Voß, S., Woodruff D.L. (2003): An Introduction to Computational Optimization Models for Production Planning in a Supply Chain, Springer, Berlin.

Zäpfel, G., Missbauer, H. (1993): New Concepts for Production Planning and Control, European Journal of Operational Research, 67(3): 297-320.

Zijm, W. H. M., Buitenhek, R. (1996): Capacity Planning and Lead Time Management, International Journal of Production Economics, 46-47: 165-179.

Zipkin, P. H. (1986): Models for Design and Control of Stochastic, Multi-Item Batch Production Systems, Operations Research, 34(1): 91-104.

Recovery Network Design for End-of-Life Vehicles

Heinz Ahn, Jens Keilen, Rainer Souren

1 Introduction 556
2 Challenges for the German Automotive Industry 556
3 A Decision Support Tool for Recovery Network Design 558
4 Possible Enhancements 569
5 References 570

Summary:
The design, configuration, and optimization of recovery networks have become more important than ever for certain industries. This paper focuses on the specific requirements posed on the German automotive industry. One of the significant regulations concerning this industry lies in the necessity of having to provide an area-wide collection network for the retrieval of all disused vehicles. In a joint project with a major car producer, an optimization tool was generated for solving facility location problems with regard to the positioning of different participants of the automotive recovery network. In order to validate the network structure, an additional simulation tool was developed making it possible to eliminate unfeasible networks. The simulation processes empirical capacity data of the networks' participants. The main focus of the paper aims at the description of the simulation tool and its interactions with the optimization tool.

Keywords:
Recovery Network Design, Automotive Industry, End-of-Life Vehicles, Recycling, Simulation Tool

1 Introduction

According to the Federal Ministry for the Environment, Nature Conservation and Nuclear Safety, approximately 3.7 million private cars are deregistered and decommissioned in Germany every year. The "ELV Ordinance" passed on July 2002 defines the responsibility for an ecologically sound treatment of this enormous number of end-of-life vehicles (ELVs) to be taken by the automotive industry. Especially, it allocates the associated costs to this industry.

The paper first gives a brief description of the developments in legislation necessary to understand the resolving difficulties and required advancements for the automotive industry. The introduction is followed by the presentation of a decision support tool for the German automotive industry; it has been developed in 2002 at the Chair of Operations Research and Logistic Management at the Aachen University under the direction of Prof. Dr. H.-J. Sebastian. The "toolkit" enables the generation and design of an area-wide and cost reducing recovery network for the retrieval of ELVs having to be recycled according to the guidelines of the ELV Ordinance. It consists of two main elements: An optimization tool based on a generic algorithm and a complementary simulation tool. While the optimization tool is characterized as far as necessary, the simulation tool will be described in detail. The underlying empirical data is kept anonymous.

2 Challenges for the German Automotive Industry

2.1 Review of the Developments in Legislation

The basis of all recent legislative developments on behalf of environmental awareness in Germany lies in the "Closed Substance Cycle and Waste Management Act" of 1996 (Dyckhoff et al., 2004a: 23). One enhancement made was the German "Ordinance on the Disposal of End-of-life Vehicles and the Adjustment of Provisions under Road Traffic Law" put into force on April 1998. On June 2002, the "Law Governing the Disposal of End-of-life Vehicles (ELV Act)" was issued to transpose the Directive 2000/53/EC of the European Parliament and the Council of September 2000 on ELVs into German law (for a more detailed description of the European development on ELV directives, see Wallau, 2001: 103ff.; also see le Blanc et al., 2004). The modified ordinance, now called "German Ordinance on the Transfer, Collection and Environmentally Sound Disposal of End-of-life Vehicles" (ELV Ordinance; AltfahrzeugV), came into force on July 1st 2002.

The main topic of this ordinance is the product responsibility which states that the car producers are required to take back all old vehicles of their particular make. Additionally, the automotive industry is obligated to provide an area-wide network of certified collecting points, enabling the last car owner to access a collecting point within a 50 kilometer radius. Collecting points can be located at car dealers, specially established collecting centers or certified dismantlers, as long as they fulfill the requirements listed in the ELV Ordinance, Annex, §2. The modifications in EU Regulations and in the ELV Ordinance foresee the obligation of the automotive industry to retrieve and recycle or dispose of every single car of their make produced after January 2002, as well as all vehicles over fifteen years of age.

The procedures of recycling the ELVs and the predefined recycling ratios are also regulated by law. By January 2006 (January 2015), 85% (95%) of the ELVs' empty weight will have to be recovered and reused, while 80% (85%) of the materials will have to be recovered and recycled (§ 5 Disposal Obligations of ELV Ordinance). Furthermore, a minimum level to which the disassembly process of components needs to be realized is defined in the ELV Ordinance. It mainly consists of removing the batteries and other hazardous substances (the detailed requirements and listings can be found in the ELV Ordinance, Annex, §3.2.2.1).

2.2 Consequences for the German Automotive Industry

The requirements stated by legislation can easily be met if the costs are disregarded. Ecologically speaking, it is possible to recycle almost 100% of an ELV. From the economic standpoint, however, this would not be reasonable. Several consequences for the future environmental policy of the automotive industry are obvious. Resulting from the ELV Ordinance, three main categories of necessary progress can be identified:

- **Vehicle Design**

The first improvement already being realized is the design of new vehicles taking the future disassembly process into account during early development stages. Vehicles consisting of components that on the one hand are composed of a low material-mixture and on the other hand allow an easy dismantling at the end of a vehicle's utilization are being implemented (Dyckhoff et al., 2004b: 20ff.). These provisions facilitate meeting the recycling quotas and minimizing the required costs. However, the fruits of these precautions made today can at the earliest be harvested in ten to fifteen years, when the vehicles produced nowadays will have to be recycled. The main problem in the next two decades will be the treatment of vehicles that were *not* designed with regard to future recycling.

- **Monitoring**

The second major improvement refers to the configuration of a monitoring system providing the automotive industry with correct numbers and percentages on retrieved and recycled vehicles – or more precisely on the reused weight percentages of the ELVs. The shredder companies represent one of the weak spots in this constellation. Most of these shredders in Germany do not only treat ELVs. As input they also handle steel girders, scrap metal, kitchen equipment and other metallic items. This makes it difficult to determine the coherency between ingoing and outgoing material flow and therefore complicates the verification of the compliance to the recycling quotas. The ELV Ordinance also determines to which extent the provision of information and documentation has to be realized.

- **Recovery Network**

The third and from our viewpoint most interesting challenge can be found in the obligation of having to provide an area-wide recovery network for the retrieval of all ELVs. According to the ELV Ordinance, each automotive producer must take back and recycle all vehicles of his specific make. By law, the last owner of a vehicle should be given the opportunity to return it to either a certified collecting point or a certified dismantler within a 50 kilometer radius. All transportation costs exceeding the 50 kilometers are to be covered by the automotive industry. Consequently, the design of this recovery network is a fundamental requirement for the automotive industry today.

3 A Decision Support Tool for Recovery Network Design

3.1 Network Configuration

In order to understand the difficulties involved with designing a recovery network, the "supposed-to-be" network and the corresponding problems are described in the following. Four kinds of actor groups representing the reverse supply chain are distinguished (see Figure 1). The initial actor group can be identified as the last owners of ELVs. In the terms of optimization and simulation, they are regarded to be the source of the ELV emergence. These last owners are to be provided with the possibility of transporting their ELVs to a member of the second actors group within a 50 kilometer radius. The second group is represented by certified collecting facilities (e.g., certified car dealers) and dismantlers. If this possibility does not exist, the respective ELV is to be retrieved from the last owner and taken to the nearest collecting facility at the expense of the car producer. Consequently, the producers are interested in configuring a network of collecting facilities which minimizes the transportation costs by providing an area-wide coverage.

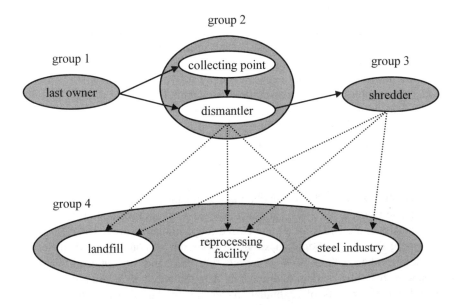

Figure 1: Reverse Supply Chain of End-of-life Vehicles

Every ELV has to be disassembled according to the ELV Ordinance at a certified dismantler. Thus, those vehicles returned to a collecting point – where pre-handling is prohibited in Germany – need to be transported to the nearest dismantler. Here, the cars are drained and dismantled in compliance with the ELV Ordinance. Then, the car wrecks are squeezed for easier transportation to the shredders. This third actor group is responsible for the shredding of the wrecks and for transporting the resolving three fractions to the different participants of the fourth actor group. The first fraction is the shredder light fraction; it contains foams, plastics, etc. having to be disposed of in landfills. The second fraction leaving the shredder is the non-ferrous fraction requiring recycling processes at different reprocessing facilities. The third fraction contains different kinds of ferrous materials which can be reused by the steel industry.

The most important issue from the standpoint of the car producers is to minimize the network costs concerning the groups 1 to 3 in Figure 1. The resolving tasks can be summarized as follows:

- positioning of additional collecting facilities,
- determining the dismantlers to be used,
- setting the transport routes to be taken.

3.2 Towards Combining Optimization and Simulation Procedures

For solving problems which are similar to the described one, a combination of optimization and simulation procedures has already been proposed in literature. For example, Schultmann et al. (2003) analyze the configuration of a closed-loop supply chain for spent batteries in Germany. Their approach "combines an optimization model for planning a reverse-supply network and a flow-sheet process model that enables a simulation tailored to potential recycling options for spent batteries in the steel-making industry" (Schultmann et al., 2003: 57; concerning such a sequential approach, see for example also Latre & Rodriguez, 2002). One of the main differences with regard to our problem lays in the fact that the locations of collecting containers (facilities) for spent batteries are already known, leading to a traveling-salesman-problem/vehicle-routing-problem.

Both an optimization and a simulation possess advantages as well as disadvantages (e.g., see le Blanc et al., 2004, for a mere closed-loop optimization procedure, and Fleischmann et al., 2003, for a mere closed-loop simulation procedure). However, combining the two methodologies makes it possible to compensate their deficits and concentrate on their positive aspects. On one hand, an optimization is not capable of handling random and dynamic data the way a simulation can. On the other hand, the results of a simulation depend on the quality of the input information as well as on the capabilities and the comprehension of the user; here, an optimization procedure generates the best solution possible with regard to the objective function and the restraints, and it can help the user to better understand the background of his problem.

3.3 The Optimization Tool

The challenge of establishing an area-wide recovery network for the retrieval of ELVs refers to a multi-level facility location problem. Against this background, the optimization part of the developed toolkit is based on a binary coded genetic algorithm (GA) which generates such a network with regard to certain premises (for solving similar problems with MILP, see Fleischmann et al., 2004: 72ff.). The GA is explained in detail by Schleiffer et al. (2004).

Dividing the considered area into zip code areas and assigning each ELV to the center of one of these areas, the algorithm generates the total number of necessary – already existing and virtual – facilities as well as the location of the virtual facilities. With respect to the regarded costs, a trade-off between the costs for establishing new facilities and the costs for additional transportation has to be considered. In order to enhance the number of generated networks, the assumption was made that all facilities possess unlimited capacities. Consequently, the optimization provides the required capacities of the individual facilities necessary for coping with the forecasted ELV emergence. Last but not least, the optimization generates the transportation routes to be taken and the overall network costs.

In a case study, the optimization was applied to a specific car producer. To obtain the necessary data was difficult. For each zip code area, historic data on vehicles of his make had to be determined representing the number of cars deregistered. One major problem was to eliminate all cars which merely had been sold abroad. Furthermore, information on the capacities of existing dismantlers and shredders had to be collected for the simulation presented in the following. Obtaining these data and converting them into a consistent form turned out to be very time intensive.

3.4 The Simulation Tool

The optimization tool generates the optimal network of facilities for a certain input scenario. However, since it is possible to integrate existing facilities or exclude them from the input set, the solution will only be the optimum for that specific input set, but not necessarily for the overall optimum network. Furthermore, neither the real facility capacities nor the development of the emergence of the ELV over time are taken into account.

Pointing out that simulation based tools consider the dynamics of the regarded system (Simchi-Levi et al., 2000: 33), a "simulation-add-on" has been developed to verify a generated network configuration with regard to dynamic stability. By including the existing and required capacities, it becomes possible to determine the maximum utilization percentages of the participants in the network. Consequently, the necessary additional facilities as well as superfluous actors can be identified.

As simulation software, Arena Professional Edition Version 5.0 by Rockwell Software Inc. has been chosen. After the implementation of the modules necessary for running the simulation, the user is able to handle this software easily. The input and the output of the simulation tool can be altered to some extent and analyzed in familiar Microsoft applications. It is possible to enhance existing and develop new "drag and drop" modules for building a simulation by making use of Visual Basic programming. In our scenario, the focus lies on the verification of the utilization capacities making it necessary to consider the process times and especially the material flow. Arena contains exactly these features for implementing process and flow-orientated simulations. The software is equipped with an animation platform allowing the user to visualize the proceedings during the simulation run and to present the results.

In the following, the simulation tool will be described, beginning with the required input for the simulation tool and its modules. In the second step, the three different module types corresponding to the three main categories of actors in the recovery network (collecting point, dismantler and shredder) will be presented according to their implementation and functions. In the final step, the output and contribution of the simulation tool will be determined.

1. Necessary Input Information for the Simulation Tool

The simulation tool requires three kinds of input information subdivided according to the data origin and possibilities of altering the information. The first category can be identified as external data taken from a database or other preset data files. This information is read in at the beginning of the simulation run and cannot be altered unless the user possesses access to the database and makes manual changes before the simulation starts. The corresponding data consist of process times, the coordinates of all five digit zip code areas in Germany and a set of data files containing distance matrixes from one zip code area to another. Their configuration and usability will be specified closer in the following.

The second category of input information represents the output of the optimization tool. The data corresponds to the ELV emergence with reference to the amount (per year) and the point of occurrence (zip code area) as well as the existing capacities of the actors (which are, however, not used in the optimization process). They can not be directly altered by the user. Depending on the configuration of the chosen scenario for the optimization tool, the results are also read in from the simulation tool. The simulation tool now contains the information on actors to be set and on their capacities. In addition, the ELV emergence as to numbers and location of origin (zip code area where they are to be generated during the simulation run) is known. This information can be acquired since the optimization tool generates results with regard to the required capacities. These are equal to the amount of ELVs to be handled by the corresponding actor (required capacity for actor x = emergence of ELVs in zip code area of x). Making use of the information from the distance matrix, it is possible to determine the closest delivery destination for each actor and the approximate transport times. This distance matrix consists of 8350 data files (one file for each zip code area in Germany). Each file represents a matrix with the distances from one zip code area to all of the others.

The third category of information must be manually entered by the user in predefined user forms in order to set up the simulation. It includes data concerning the database and data files, whether to show the animations, which actor categories are to be considered, and additional information for each actor category described in detail in the following chapters. As soon as all information has been given, the user can start the simulation run, and the results can be saved in an Excel sheet. These results will be described in more detail in chapter 3.2.3.

2. The Modules

The previous paragraphs have shown that the core of the simulation tool consists of the modules representing the actors and their behavior. They are now described in detail. The modules implemented correspond to the three major actor categories (collecting point, dismantler and shredder).

- **The Collecting Point (CP)**

The purpose of installing CPs lies in fulfilling the provision of an area-wide recovery network. The CPs' mere function is to gather the ELVs. They are legally prohibited to execute any measures of pretreatment (see ELV Ordinance, Annex, § 2.1.2; this regulation refers to Germany only). After being collected, the ELVs are conveyed to a nearby dismantler.

In the simulation tool, the CPs act as the source that generates a part of the ELV entities. In reality, cars are taken to a CP by the last owner who would then be considered as the source. From the simulation's point of view, thousands of entities (cars) would have to be generated at thousands of different locations (8350 zip code areas in Germany) and then transported to the collecting facilities. However, the optimization tool already generates the information on the amount of ELVs and their destinations where they are to be collected, making it sensible to create the entities directly in the CP modules. With regard to the toolkit as a whole, the optimization tool provides a recovery network guaranteeing area-wide coverage on the basis of the required capacities of each CP; these capacities determine the number of ELVs to be generated in the individual CPs. While the optimization tool calculates the transportation costs for the regarded network configuration, the purpose of the simulation tool is to verify the utilization of the network.

The information necessary for the CP module to function properly and the respective sources are the following:

- zip code (Opt. Tool),
- zip code coordinates for positioning on the visualized map (data files),
- ELV emergence = required capacity (Opt. Tool),
- capacity, if available (Opt. Tool),
- delivery destination (distance matrix),
- delivery time (distance matrix and calculation),
- delivery strategy (user form).

The delivery strategy is one of the options the user must key in at the beginning of the simulation. He can choose between two alternatives: The entities (ELVs) can be transferred to the nearest dismantler in periodic intervals (after x days), or a transfer is initialized as soon as a predefined number of vehicles are in storage.

After the simulation tool has generated the CP network according to the user's specifications and the input from the optimization tool, the user can either start the simulation run or make predefined changes regarding the settings of the individual CP modules. The user form (delivery strategy), visualization in the model and the operand (individual configuration of a specific CP) can be seen in Figure 2.

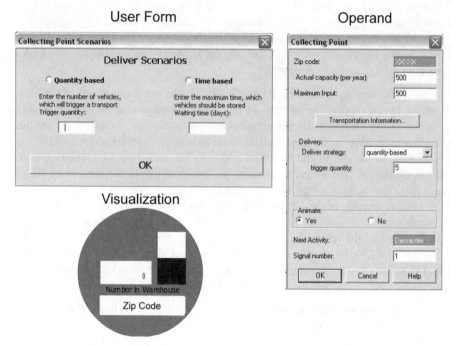

Figure 2: Collecting Point

Inside of the CP, entities representing the collected ELVs are generated randomly throughout a year according to a discrete function varying their generation (= one simulation run). The maximum sum of entities created in each CP is limited to the ELV emergence according to the capacities given by the optimization tool. After being generated, the entities enter a queue and wait for either a specified time period to pass (user defined) or until the predefined quantity is reached. As soon as they are released from the queue, they are batched to the predefined number of ELVs per transport (truck capacity) and sent to the nearest dismantler (delivery destination).

- **The Dismantler**

The second group of actors, respectively modules, represents the bottleneck of the network (this fact was confirmed by several simulation runs). Every single car is obligated to pass through a dismantler where it is drained, dismantled and finally squeezed for better transportability. The fluids and components to be extracted during draining and disassembly are specified in the ELV ordinance, Annex, §3.2).

At the point of entry two different input streams can be identified. Firstly, the dismantler can function as a CP. Should the last owner return his vehicle directly to a dismantler which is closer than any other CP, the module functions in the same way as the CP module and generates the appropriate entity number according the information from the optimization tool and the random discrete function. In this case, the module serves as an entity source as well. The second incoming stream describes the delivered entities from nearby CPs.

The information necessary for the dismantler module to function properly and the respective sources are the following:

- zip code (Opt. Tool),
- zip code coordinates for positioning on the visualized map (data files),
- direct ELV emergence in this zip code area (Opt. Tool),
- capacity, if available (Opt. Tool),
- disassembly scenario (user form),
- process times (database),
- delivery destination (shredder sheet),
- delivery time (shredder sheet and calculation).

Considering the disassembly scenario, the user has two options. Scenario one restricts the depth of disassembly to dismantling the mandatory components as stated in the ELV Ordinance. In the second scenario, the user possesses the possibility to include additional components for disassembly from a predefined list in the user form (see Figure 3). Depending on the chosen scenario, the module extracts the process times necessary for disassembling the specific components from the database before the simulation run. These process times are then embedded in a function generating random operating times. In contrast to the CP module, the delivery destination and time can be retrieved from a different data file. Since 39 different existing shredders were identified in Germany at the time of enquiry, a data file was generated containing the minimum distances from each zip code area to the nearest shredder.

After the simulation tool has generated the network of dismantlers according to the user's specifications and the input of the optimization tool, the user has the option to interact and alter individual dismantler configurations via the operand window (see Figure 3). He can, for example, change the dismantling list.

After either being generated or having entered the dismantler module from a CP, the ELV entity goes into a queue where it waits for an idle resource for the initial inspection process. It then enters a second queue where it waits for the draining process to take place. During draining, all pre-assigned components, as for example oils and gasoline, are extracted. These new entities representing the extracted materials are then counted and, for the time being, disposed of.

After draining, the main ELV entity is again queued and waits for dismantling. This dismantling process occurs on different stages depending on the predefined dismantling depth. For each of the five stages, the corresponding components to be dismantled were implemented according to an exemplary dismantler analyzed before. In all stages, the disassembled parts are represented by new entities as in the draining process. Most of the dismantlers squeeze the pre-treated car wrecks for easier storage and transportation. The same occurs inside of the dismantler module.

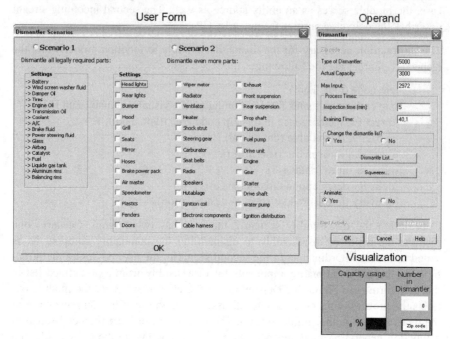

Figure 3: Dismantler

- **The Shredder**

The function of the shredder in the recovery network is to shred the dismantled ELVs into three output fractions. One of the major problems of assuring the compliance to the recycling quotas occurs with regard to this specific actor. Nevertheless, the aim of the toolkit lies in the design of an area wide recovery network and in minimizing the costs. Consequently, the shredders are merely analyzed with respect to their utilization ration and therefore also function as a drain where the entities are disposed of.

The required information to grant the ideal functioning of the shredder module can be summed as follows:

- zip code (Opt. Tool),
- zip code coordinates for positioning on the visualized map (data files),
- capacity, if available (Opt. Tool).

The capacities had to be converted to ELV wrecks per day and base on existing data of actual capacities (as far as they are known).

After the shredders are placed according to their coordinates, the only input the user can alter is the capacity of each individual shredder (see Figure 4).

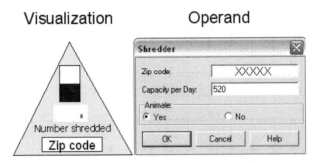

Figure 4: The Shredder

Now the simulation is completely implemented, contains all the necessary data and can be started.

3. Results and Contributions of the Simulation Tool

The output of the simulation tool results in new information respectively new input for the optimization tool. More specific, the simulation tool provides the user with information on the utilization of the actors' capacities in form of Excel sheets including every single participant. The information to be extracted from the simulation run is the following:

- Do any participants exist that are superfluous in the sense that they possess a utilization ratio of an average 50% or less?
- Do any participants exist that are faced with a capacity overload defined by a utilization ratio of an average more than 110 %?
- Does the network configuration suffice for the handling of the number of vehicles estimated?

If the answer to one of the first two questions is "YES", the corresponding participants have to be identified. In the first case, these actors are to be excluded from the set of possible participants in the optimization tool, and a new optimization run will have to be initiated in order to generate a new, better network configuration. In the second case, it is necessary to identify a nearby facility in order to compensate for the missing capacities and include this facility in the optimization run. These two steps have to be repeated until the third question can be answered with "YES".

In order to make the results more conceivable, Figure 5 shows an abstract of the results of a simulation run. Two dismantlers are over-utilized by far; the resolving measures are to identify these two dismantlers (zip code) and to integrate nearby dismantlers into the input set of the optimization tool. Furthermore, two dismantlers have an utilization ratio lower than 50%; they can be excluded from the input set. After that, the optimization tool will be run again.

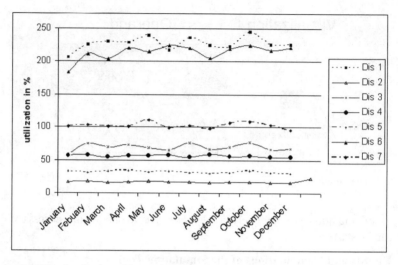

Figure 5: Utilization Ratios of Several Dismantlers

The two individual tools were implemented to form a unit and consequently to interact. In the first step, one begins by keying in the necessary information for starting the optimization tool. On this basis, a "first" and – regarding its input – optimal solution can be generated. The resulting network is then verified dynamically by the simulation tool. In order to do so, the necessary input data for the simulation tool is read in. Additional information depending on the chosen scenario and disassembly range can be directly entered by the user. The simulation tool then generates the specified network including the extra data and runs through the scenario for an entire year. Subsequently, the results in the form of utilizations of the participants are generated, requiring further analyses. The interactions between the two tools as well as the additional external information are shown in Figure 6.

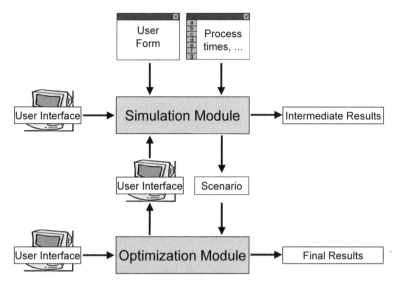

Figure 6: Interaction between the Tools

4 Possible Enhancements

The goal of the described project was to provide the automotive producer with a decision support tool enabling him to design a recovery network for the retrieval and sound recycling of end-of-life vehicles. The presented toolkit is capable of generating and offering different solutions depending on the specific scenario to be defined by the user. Thereby, it already contains provisions for further improvement. Concerning the simulation tool, it is possible to include other actors (e.g. reprocessing facilities) as well as to vary the scenarios and the resulting information. Additional information on the material flow of the dismantled components can be derived after some miner modifications. Although the toolkit was implemented with regards to the zip code system an the actual legal specifications of Germany, the modules can be modified in order to consider the specific information regarding different countries and changes in legislation.

5 References

Dyckhoff, H., Souren, R., Keilen, J. (2004a): The Expansion of Supply Chains to Closed Loop Systems – A Conceptual Framework and the Automotive Industry's Point of View, in: Dyckhoff, H., Lackes, R., Reese, J. (eds.): Supply Chain Management and Reverse Logistics, Springer, Berlin et al.: p. 13-34.

Dyckhoff, H., Keilen, J., Souren, R. (2004b): Konzeptionelle Grundlagen kreislaufgerechter Produktinnovationen in der Automobilindustrie (Fundamental Concepts of Closed-Loop Product Innovations in the Automotive Industry), in: Schwarz, E. (ed.): Nachhaltiges Innovationsmanagement (Sustainable Innovation Management, Gabler, Wiesbaden: p. 361-380.

Fleischmann, M., Bloemhof-Ruwaard, J. M., Beullens, P., Dekker, R. (2004): Reverse Logistics Network Design, in: Dekker, R., Fleischmann, M., Inderfurth, K., Van Wassenhove, L. (eds.): Reverse Logistics – Quantitative Models for Closed-Loop Supply Chains, Springer, Berlin et al.: p. 65-94.

Fleischmann, M., van Nunen, J. A. E. E., Gräve, B. (2004): Integrating Closed-Loop Supply Chains and Spare-Parts Management at IBM, in: Interfaces, (33): 44-56.

German Law Governing the Disposal of End-of-life Vehicles (End-of-life Vehicle Act - AltfahrzeugG) of 21. June 2002 (Federal Law Gazette I number 41 page 2199 of 28 June 2002), Federal Ministry 28 June 2002 for the Environment, Natur Conservation and Nuclear Safety Division WA II 3.

Latre, L. G., Moreira Rodriguez M. T. (2002): Sequential Approach to Production Planning in Multisite Environment, in: Proceedings of the 15th Triennal World Congress on Automatic Control, Barcelona.

Le Blanc, H. M., Fleuren, H. A., Krikke, H. R. (2004): Redesign of a Recycling System for LPG-Tanks, in: OR Spectrum, (26): 283-304.

Ordinance on the Transfer, Collection and Environmentally Sound Disposal of End-of-life Vehicles (End-of-life Vehicle Ordinance – AltfahrzeugV), Federal Official Gazette, Year 2002 Part I No. 41, published in Bonn on 28 June 2002.

Schleiffer, R., Wollenweber, J., Sebastian, H. J., Golm, F., Kapoustina, N. (2004): Application of Genetic Algorithms for the Design of Large-Scale Reverse Logistic Networks in Europe's Automotive Industry, in: Proceedings of the 37th Hawaii International Conference on System Sciences (HICSS'04): p. 1-10.

Schultmann, F., Engels, B., Rentz, O. (2003): Closed-Loop Supply Chain for Spent Batteries, in: Interfaces, (33): 57-71.

Simchi-Levi, D., Kaminsky, P., Simchi-Levi, E. (2000): Designing and Managing the Supply Chain – Concepts, Strategies, and Case Studies, The McGraw-Hill Higher Education, Boston et al.

Wallau, F. (2001): Kreislaufwirtschaftssystem Altauto – Eine empirische Analyse der Akteure und Märkte der Altautoverordnung in Deutschland (Recycling Management for ELVs – An Empirical Analysis of the Actors and Markets of the ELV Ordinance in Germany), DUV, Wiesbaden.

Modeling and Integrated Assessment of Mass and Energy Flows within Supply Chains

Jutta Geldermann, Martin Treitz, Hannes Schollenberger, Otto Rentz

1 Introduction 572
2 Methodology Approaches for Mass and Energy Flow Management 573
3 Multi Objective Pinch Analysis (MOPA) 576
4 Conclusions 582
5 References 582

Summary:
For an integrated assessment of mass and energy flows the specification and detailed mapping of the technical requirements and the material properties is essential. Integrated process design of supply chain structures aims at a holistic approach to process design and operations planning, since changes in materials and operating states influence the whole supply chain. The combination of methods of process integration and Operations Research (OR) in Multi Objective Pinch Analysis (MOPA) allows the consideration of a variety of economic and environmental process attributes for an integrated technique assessment. Consequently, the focus here will be the development of a method for optimizing inter-enterprise plant layout planning in dynamic mass flow networks.

Keywords:
Mass and Energy Flow Management, Supply Chain Structures, Multi Objective Pinch Analysis (MOPA)

1 Introduction

Significant changes in supply chain structures (e.g. due to market dynamics) especially challenge small and medium-sized enterprises (SME). With recent technical improvements (e.g. in the field of VOC[1] recovery in waste gas) and governmental initiatives for recycling (e.g. IPPC Directive (EC, 1996)), supply chains are no longer a linear arrangement of processes ending at a final consumer; but there is an increasing shift towards recycling and utilization of by-products in other supply chains. Therefore waste, emissions and pollution must be reduced and efficiency increased in order to decrease the consumption of resources. In general five different approaches for handling waste streams are identified by (Sarkis, 2003) as suitable for supply chains: reduction, reuse, remanufacture, recycling and disposal. Using these, material cycles can be closed within the supply chain network and resource consumption can be reduced. Improving the resource efficiency is one of the key elements towards a sustainable development.

A recent literature review on reverse network design models (in le Blanc et al., 2004) reveals that most of the case studies on reverse network design and optimization deal with remanufacturing (e.g. electronic equipment) rather than reprocessing (e.g. wastewater streams). However, the focus is primarily on the system performance at the operational level, with rather limited views on single issues, while more comprehensive approaches are rare (Georgiadis & Vlachos, 2004).

While the reuse of production scrap (mostly cuttings or defective products) is required foremost in the manufacturing industry, chemical process engineering in contrast must consider a multitude of by-products with various material properties. Especially the conversion of harmful substances into useful products is a traditional field for mass and energy flow management and process engineering in chemical supply chains. Integrated analysis of different process systems can provide valuable insight into, and also identify improvements in the financial and environmental performance of industrial supply chain systems (Türkay et al., 2004). In this context a supply chain covers all processes which are necessary to produce the final product.

The multi-criteria analysis of different investment alternatives to great extent depends on the input materials and their properties as well as the specific technical application. The focus of the analysis in this paper is not on the information flows along the supply chain and issues concerning transportation or organization of materials, but on the technical interdependencies that can be used to assess further techno-economic-environmental optimization potential. Consequently, the utilization of the technical scope for process improvement (material consumption, operating states, plant variants etc) and its effects on the upstream and downstream supply chain network or industrial park must be considered. The economic selec-

---

[1] VOC volatile organic compounds: e.g. solvents used in the coating process.

tion of an appropriate technology is based on the technical requirements and therefore an integrated approach, discussed in the following, is needed.

Identifying a resource efficient operating state and recommending modifications to the subsequent process layout is the aim of the Multi Objective Pinch Analysis method introduced in this paper. Using the pinch analysis approach (see section 3.1) for the evaluation of energy, water and solvent streams, theoretical minimal consumption values can be calculated as targets for the subsequent process layout design. The trade-off between the different input resources must be analyzed in a multi-criteria analysis (see section 3.3) and aggregated in a metric for resource efficiency based on the regional context.

2 Methodology Approaches for Mass and Energy Flow Management

2.1 Practical Applicability

Promoted by various initiatives, cleaner production strategies are being applied increasingly throughout Europe, with the aim of raising efficiency and preventing environmental damage. Closed loop approaches for the whole supply chain, life cycle assessment (LCA) criteria for products and connected processes (Hunkeler et al., 2003) and techno-economic assessment methods are used to improve environmental performance. However, these approaches are still maturing in industrializing countries, where evolving financial institutions do not value the extra environmental and social benefits cleaner production processes provide. Consequently, an applicable and practical approach is needed that considers both the technical requirements of the production processes and the impacts caused.

In general, there are various approaches and terminologies aimed at the environmental improvement of production processes at the plant and firm level, the inter-enterprise level and even the global level. For example, the research field of *Industrial Ecology* endeavors to study "…flows of materials and energy in industrial and consumer activities and effects of these flows on the environment and the influences of economic, political, regulatory, and social factors of the flows, and the transformation of resources" (White, 1994). Hence, Industrial Ecology considers different scopes of application on the firm, inter-enterprise and global level, thereby incorporating various methodological approaches.

However, apart from *Industrial Ecology* (Graedel & Allenby, 2003) various other approaches exist for incorporating different levels of firm, process, or product assessment, such as *Cleaner Production* (UNEP, 1994), *Eco-Efficiency* (Fussler, 1999; Lehni, 2000), the *Zero-Emission* concept (Suzuki, 2000), supply chain management based concepts (*Green Supply Chain Management* (Sarkis, 2003), *Environmental Supply Chain Management* (Nagel, 2000) and *Integrated Chain Management* (Seuring, 2004b), etc.). Depending on the definition, these approaches might be mutually exclusive or even aid or overlap one another, however, a discussion of the different approaches and their common and differing features is not the intent of this paper (see Seuring, 2004a).

These approaches may be based on different objectives and levels (product, firm inter-enterprise or regional level), and might differ in the application of various methods, but they share the common challenge of applying methods for identifying practically applicable solutions. Or according to (Seuring, 2004b): "Sustainable development is widely accepted as a guiding principle in business. Still, this principle needs to be transformed into business practices".

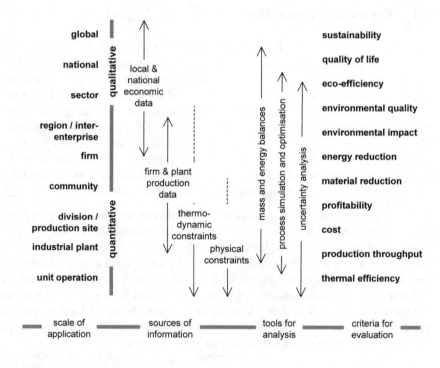

Figure 1: Conceptual Framework; Adapted from (Diwekar & Small, 2001)

Consequently, different sources of information and different available methodologies exist depending on the scale of the application (cf. Figure 1).

Moreover, different criteria prevail depending on the research target. Broad schemas, such as sustainability on a global level, breakdown to narrower criteria such as thermal efficiency on the level of unit operations. The diverse evaluation criteria on the various scales of application comprise different attributes with partially conflicting objectives, which necessitate a multi-criteria decision analysis. Therefore, a process-based approach which considers the different available unit operations is discussed in this paper.

2.2 Technical Scope for Optimization

The assessment of technical applications is driven by the difficulty of identifying comparable alternatives and comparable system boundaries (Rentz, 2004). In contrast to end-of-pipe emission reduction measures, which can be implemented downstream in the process, process integrated measures involve the reengineering of the complete process across the supply chain, making the assessment (e.g. estimation of the investment) very complex since all required parameters (e.g. sulfur concentration) for process changes must be considered (Rentz, 1995). The desulfurization of coal at the mining site (increasing the calorific value and lowering the transportation cost per kWh) vs. an end-of-pipe approach implementing a flue gas desulfurization plant (better sulfur collection efficiency and at the same time emission reduction of further pollutants) is discussed in (Rentz, 1995). Figure 2 illustrates the relationship between material input, energy input, production output and emissions through the operating state of the system.

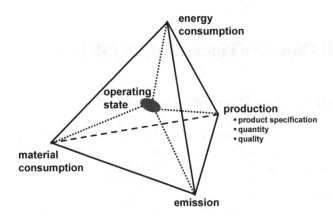

Figure 2: Polyhedron of the Operating State (Rentz, 1995)

For example the coating of metal or plastic parts using solvent-based vs. water-based coatings significantly influences the energy consumption in the corresponding drying step and hence the layout of the heating and waste gas system. Furthermore, changes in process parameters or input materials affect the whole supply chain: Constantly changing solvent concentrations at the paint producer from adjusting paint viscosity for instance influences the investment decision of a waste gas cleaning system at the coating workshop due to the resulting different solvent emission concentrations. Through the analysis of process streams within a supply chain or within an industry park significant improvements may be realized (Wietschel, 2002). For example a combined wastewater treatment system could have a more stable chemical oxygen demand (COD) value and hence a more effective and economical process could be implemented. This could be a viable option especially in industrializing countries where obligations from environmental legislation might be of a lower imperative. These examples show that further optimization potential can be identified using an inter-enterprise approach based on an analysis of the technical applications (Frank, 2003; Tietze-Stöckinger et al., 2003).

The techno-economic-environmental process improvement profits from an insight of the optimization potential in order to assess the different technologies. Here, the assessment of environmental aspects of production processes is a difficult task, especially due to the required evaluation of cross-media aspects. Transmedial problem shifting from one environmental medium to another (e.g. from air into water) must be taken into account (Rentz et al., 1998; Rentz, 1995). The underlying methodology used to measure the optimization potential is the Pinch Analysis, which is introduced in the next chapter and extended with a multi-criteria analysis to the Multi Objective Pinch Analysis (MOPA).

3 Multi Objective Pinch Analysis (MOPA)

3.1 Pinch Analysis Methodology

The pinch analysis provides a consistent assessment method for different mass and energy flows within a company, industry park or throughout the supply chain network. Originally, the pinch analysis was developed for the design of heat exchanger networks, aimed at determining the best possible use of energy (Linnhoff & Flower, 1978). Today, problems addressing wastewater minimization (Wang & Smith, 1994; Thevendiraraj et al., 2003) and VOC recovery from waste gas streams (Dunn & El-Halwagi, 1994; Zhelev & Semkov, 2004) can also be solved applying the pinch approach. The algorithms for solving the design problems have been developed further in the past years. Some case studies have been solved by applying algorithms from the field of Operations Research, for example the transport algorithm (Cerda et al., 1983; Geldermann et al., 2004b; Geldermann et al., 2004b).

The energy pinch analysis is a systematic approach for the minimization of lost energy. In its first step the maximum of energy usable for heat recovery is calculated (Umeda et al., 1979). Hot and cold process streams are combined to form composite curves. A minimum temperature gradient ΔT_{min} must be set representing the driving force of the heat transfer. Heat can be exchanged between the hot and the cold streams of the investigated system. Further heating or cooling required by the system is provided by additional utilities (Linnhoff & Flower, 1978).

The pinch analysis for VOC or multicomponent VOC recovery is applied in a similar way to the energy pinch. Since the separation of waste gas is usually carried out via thermal condensation the problem can be transformed into a heat exchange problem (Dunn & El-Halwagi, 1994). The necessary temperature intervals are obtained using phase diagrams which are defined by the chemical properties of the employed solvents (VOC) (Geldermann et al., 2004a). In the first step a total recovery of consumed solvents is considered. In a subsequent step, a feasible economic solution is obtained through a techno-economic assessment of available technologies which must then be translated into an adapted design, resulting in a new pinch analysis.

Besides energy and VOC recovery, the pinch analysis is also used to determine possible water and wastewater savings. Both single or multiple parameter problems can be addressed. In the case of a single parameter, the mass transfer of the contaminant from the rich to the lean stream is considered (equivalent to the hot and cold streams of the energy pinch). The transfer is described as being linear which is a good assumption for diluted streams (e.g. water used for washing). The water pinch considers concentration-mass load curves. The composite curve represents the "worst" water quality acceptable. The freshwater curve describes the water supply of the system. Both curves match at the pinch point and the obtained slope defines the minimum water flow rate needed (Wang & Smith, 1994).

Practical problems often require the inclusion of several parameters. For the translation of the problem into a single parameter one, aggregation to one target value (e.g. Chemical Oxygen Demand - COD) is necessary. If this is not possible, an iterative process is used to find the overall pinch for all "water-based" flows of the system (Koufos & Retsina, 2001). Additionally, methods addressing the problem of several aqueous streams relevant for one operation, including water losses, have been developed (Hallale, 2002).

More information on pinch analysis and its different areas of application can be found in (Linnhoff et al., 1979; Cerda et al., 1983; Dunn & Bush, 2001; Hallale, 2002).

3.2 Inter-Enterprise Approach

Pinch analysis can also be applied in an inter-enterprise approach considering different supply chain or industry park structures. Recently, a new approach has been presented using pinch analysis for aggregate planning (Singhvi & Shenoy, 2002). Therein, the time-material production relationship is used to determine two composite curves: one demand and one production curve. By including outsourced production and a different client on the demand side, the link to the supply chain is realized and more than one production site is depicted (Singhvi et al., 2004).

Besides product flows, a linking of various production sites can also be realized on the basis of process streams. The advantage of this approach is a possible linking of processes with differing outcomes (e.g. bicycle coating and spirits production). Thus, the combined activities can, but not necessarily must, come from one supply chain.

For the implementation of pinch analysis, the considered processes must be treated as one system. The procedure for the calculation of the savings potential is the same as in the case of an intra-enterprise problem. The result is used as a target for the process design which then results in a shared use of the utilities necessary for fulfilling the requirements of, for example heating and cooling, and which cannot be satisfied on the basis of the process streams. Furthermore, through the linking of process streams from several sites the stream properties can be improved in order to comply with specific technical, chemical or economic requirements. For example, the combination of waste gas streams from process steps emitting solvents (i.e. VOC) may lead to an increased solvent concentration. As a consequence, other technical options for waste gas cleaning and/or solvent recovery may become economically feasible.

3.3 Multi Objective Approach

Multi Objective Pinch Analysis (MOPA) consists of a combination of pinch analyses with different targets (energy, wastewater, volatile organic compounds, etc.) and a following multi-criteria analysis. A set of optimal solutions is delivered, which span the solution space based on the current status. Identifying practically applicable solutions requires detailed economic and technological information (e.g. prices; type of heat exchanger; exchanger surface; type of VOC-condenser; capacities; water treatment systems, etc.). The determination of the preferences is complex since it involves much technical expertise.

MOPA can be illustrated by the seven modules presented in Figure 3. Starting with a process analysis of the company, the industry park or the supply chain (depending on the system boundaries), a process model is developed mapping the various process streams and defining the data requirements. In a second step a technology screening compiles all required information on Best Available Techniques (BAT) and emerging technologies to describe the process model and different technology options with characteristic figures (cf. module 3 in Figure 3). The optimization module (cf. module 4 in Figure 3) is based on the pinch analysis and is solved using the Transport Algorithm from Operations Research found within the Optimization Toolbox of MATLAB. A set of optimal solutions is delivered, which spans the domain of considered technology combinations and peaks at the current status. In a multi-criteria decision process the preferences, according to the different resources, conclusively determine the selection of a set of technologies for consideration. The specific technologies implemented in the subsequent process design (cf. module 5 & 6 in Figure 3) eventually define the savings that can be realized.

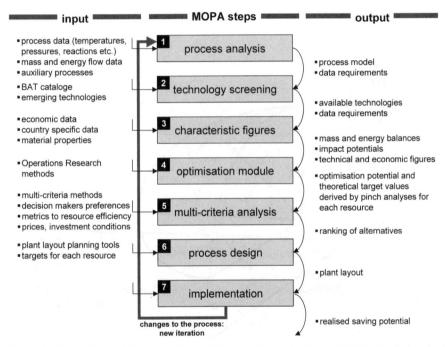

Figure 3: The Different Modules of Multi Objective Pinch Analysis (MOPA) (Treitz et al., 2004)

Using the pinch analysis, target values (water$_{Pinch}$, energy$_{Pinch}$, VOC$_{Pinch}$, etc.) can be identified (cf. Figure 4) for the subsequent process design of the streams, given the set of fixed process parameters (e.g. temperature intervals) in a Multi Objective Pinch Analysis. The theoretical point of simultaneous minimal water, energy and VOC consumption is the origin of the analysis and becomes the basis for the considered improvement potential (e.g. water$_{potential}$ = water$_{current}$ − water$_{Pinch}$). When considering a 3-dimensional problem the solution space is bounded by the lower limit of the theoretical pinch point and by the upper limit of the current status (water$_{current}$, energy$_{current}$ and VOC$_{current}$), since only process improvements need be considered. Obviously, options exist in which one criterion is worse than in the current process status, but only if one or more criteria are improved at the same time. Weights of the different resources can be defined and with them the distance to the new origin (reflecting the potential) can be derived by a modified Euclid norm as the metric of the system (a detailed mathematical description of the metric is given in (Treitz et al., 2004)). Depending on the weights the maximal acceptable limits for each criterion can be calculated. These upper limit points span the pareto surface of the current status and define the maximal acceptable limits of each criterions consumption. Consequently, the space looks similar to an eighth of a sphere (all criteria equally weighted) or an ellipsoid prolongated in the direction of the less weighted criteria.

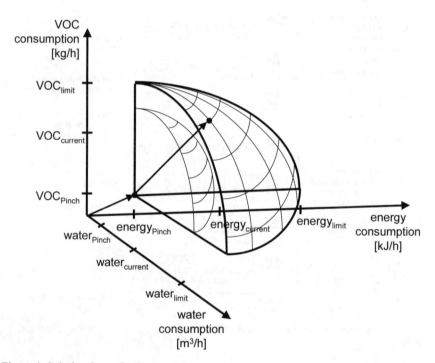

Figure 4: Solution Space for Resource Improvement

Naturally, technological options exist, which are further outside, but these would reflect a worse overall resource efficiency within the system boundaries and need not be considered. Techniques for consideration lie within the compact domain.

The decision on the choice of practically applicable techniques is difficult and driven by a multi-criteria decision problem. To some extent the optimal target values can be realized at the same time, but there are also trade-offs. For example the recovery of VOC requires energy. Consequently, the point of maximal VOC recovery (i.d. VOC_{Pinch}) will require more energy than the point of minimal energy consumption identified using pinch analysis. Therefore, pareto surfaces nested inside the domain exist illustrating the distance to the new origin.

Additionally, further criteria such as investment, operating costs, and quality attributes extend the dimension of the given problem. From a techno-economic point of view the set of available technologies must be compared. Each technological option is represented as a point in the domain. The simultaneous consideration of different mass and energy flows demands a techno-economic assessment of the reasonable process alternatives, using multi-criteria methods such as PROMETHEE (Brans et al., 1986) in MOPA, that consider detailed quantitative and qualitative information (e.g. prices; quality; type of heat exchanger; exchanger surface; type of VOC-condenser; capacities; water treatment systems, etc.). The mathematical formulation of the problem allows the depiction of further constraints (e.g. technical restrictions and/or chemical behavior of the involved substances). The specific technologies implemented in the subsequent process design eventually define the savings that can be realized. In an iterative process the new design can then be evaluated by MOPA. Depending on the system boundaries: processes, sites, supply chains and inter-enterprise problems can be evaluated.

In order to calculate optimization potentials for each selected company two kinds of information are necessary. On the one hand, process related information (process parameters for each identified process step, parameters of auxiliary processes), on the other hand data for the characterization of the company (annual production figures, growth rates etc.). The figures to be gathered are technical and economic ones. The basic concept, especially in case of the process parameters, is to characterize substance flows (mainly solvent, water and energy) by its absolute figure and its economic value through direct measurements, indirect measurements (calculations based on measurements), data derived from technical data sheets, data from identical processes of another company, data derived from comparable processes. The information of the supply chain must be included in order to gather consistent data. For example the customer of painted plastic parts must be included to know beforehand the exact production schedule for that day (especially in just in time production). Also the paint producer must be included in order to receive afterwards an analysis of the specific solvents used and their concentrations in that specific batch.

4 Conclusions

This paper presents an techno-economic approach for modeling and integrated assessment of mass and energy flows in supply chains stressing the importance of considering the technical scope. Multi Objective Pinch Analysis (MOPA) in particular considers the special technical requirements of resource efficiency improvement and inter-enterprise solutions, especially since the definition of realistic abatement options, amongst other things, also specifies that technology and country specific parameters must be considered. Through an comprehensive analysis of process streams within a supply chain or within an industry park significant improvements can be realized. In this context the Multi Objective Pinch Analysis is introduced to operationalize different criteria on different scales. Hence, a systematic approach can be used within the company, its supply chain and within a regional context. Independent of the target value to be minimized (water, energy, VOC etc.), the pinch analysis calculates, in a first step, the overall savings potential of the studied process. The obtained value represents the target for the subsequent design step. The final achievable savings are defined by the selected technological option which must also consider technical and chemical constraints. The layout planning is driven by the trade-off between investments and operating costs, and the constant search for an economically feasible solution. By defining the available domain of possible improvements and a metric for resource efficiency, a multi-criteria analysis can help identify the eligible techniques. The methodology is applied in case studies in Chile and China, which show high optimization potentials.

This work is part of the project „PepOn: Integrated Process Design for Inter-Enterprise Plant Layout Planning of Dynamic Mass Flow Networks" funded by the VolkswagenStiftung. This opportunity is greatly appreciated.

5 References

Brans, J. P., Vincke, Ph., Marshal, B. (1986): How to select and how to rank projects: The PROMETHEE method, in: European Journal of Operational Research, 24: 228-238.

Cerda, J., Westerberg, A., Manson, D., Linnhoff, B. (1983): Minimum utility usage in heat exchanger network synthesis - A transportation problem, in: Chemical Engineering Science, 38 (3): 373-387.

Diwekar, U., Small, M. J. (2001): Process analysis approach to industrial ecology, A handbook of industrial ecology (11), Edward Elgar, Northampton: 114-137.

Dunn, R. F., Bush, G. E. (2001): Using process integration technology for CLEANER production, in: Journal of Cleaner Production, 9(1): 1-23.

Dunn, R. F., El-Halwagi, M. M. (1994): Optimal design of multicomponent VOC-condensation systems, in: Journal of Hazardous Materials, 38 (1): 187-206.

EC (1996): Council Directive 96/61/EC concerning integrated pollution prevention and control, pp. Official Journal L 257: 0026-0040.

Frank, M. (2003): Entwicklung und Anwendung einer integrierten Methode zur Analyse von betriebsübergreifenden Energieversorgungskonzepten (Development and application of an integrated analysis of inter-company energy supply), Universität Karlsruhe (TH), Karlsruhe.

Fussler, C. (1999): Neue Wege zur Ökoeffizienz (New Path to Eco-Efficiency), in: Weizsäcker, E., Seiler-Hausmann, J. (eds.): Ökoeffizienz – Management der Zukunft (Eco-Efficiency), Birkhäuser Verlag, Berlin.

Geldermann, J., Schollenberger, H., Rentz, O. (2004a): Integrated Scenario Analysis for Metal Surface Treatment, International Journal of Integrated Supply Management, 1 (2): 219-235.

Geldermann, J., Treitz, M., Rentz, O. (2004b): Integrated Technique Assessment based on the Pinch-Analysis Approach for the Design of Production-Networks, in: European Journal of Operational Research, *in press*.

Georgiadis, P., Vlachos, D. (2004): The effect of environmental parameters on product recovery, in: European Journal of Operational Research, 157: 449-464.

Graedel, T., Allenby, B. R. (2003): Industrial Ecology, Prentice Hall, Upper Saddle River.

Hallale, N., 2002: A new graphical targeting method for water minimisation, in: Advances in Environmental Research, 6: 377-390.

Hunkeler, D., Saur, K., Finkbeiner, M., Schmidt, W.-P., Jensen, A. A., Strandorf, H., Christiansen, K. (2003): Life Cycle Management, SETAC Publications, Pensacola.

Koufos, D., Retsina, T. (2001): Practical energy and water management through pinch analysis for the pulp and paper industry, in: Water Science and Technology, 43 (2): 327-332.

le Blanc, H. M., Fleuren, H. A., Krikke, H. R. (2004): Redesign of a recycling system for LPG-tanks, in: OR Spectrum, 26: 283-304.

Lehni, M. (2000): Eco-efficiency - creating more value with less impact, World Business Coucil for Sustainable Development.

Linnhoff, B., Flower, J. R. (1978): Synthesis of Heat Exchanger Networks: I, Systematic Generation of Networks with Various Criteria of Optimality, American Institute of Chemical Engineering Journal (AIChE), 24: 633.

Linnhoff, B., Manson, D., Wardle, I. (1979): Understanding heat exchanger networks, in: Computers and Chemical Engineering, 3: 295-302.

Nagel, R. N. (2000): Environmental Supply Chain Management versus Life Cycle Analysis Method Eco-Indicator '95: A Relative Business Perspective versus an Absolute Environmental Perspective, IEEE, Delft University of Technology.

Rentz, O. (1995): Integrierter Umweltschutz (Integrated Environmental Protection), in: Junkernheinrich, M., Klemmer, P., Wagner, G. R. (eds.): Handbücher zur angewandten Umweltfoschung, Handbuch zur Umweltökonomie (Handbooks for Applied Environmental Research, Handbook on Environmental Economics), Analytica, Berlin: p. 64-69.

Rentz, O. (2004): Zum Problem der wirtschaftlichen Auswahl von Entstaubern (On the problem of economic dust-removel), in: Haasis, H.-D., Spengler, T. (eds.): Produktion und Umwelt (Production and the Environment), Springer, Heidelberg: p. 33-37.

Rentz, O., Geldermann, J., Jahn, C., Spengler, T. (1998): Vorschlag für eine medienübergreifende Bewertungsmethode zur Identifikation der „Besten verfügbaren Techniken„ BVT im Rahmen der Arbeiten der Europäischen Kommission (Proposal for an integrated approach for the assessment of cross-media aspects relevant for the determination of 'Best Available Techniques' BAT in the European Union), Studie im Auftrag des Umweltbundesamtes Berlin, Karlsruhe.

Sarkis, J. (2003): A strategic decision framework for green supply chain management, in: Journal of Cleaner Production, 11(4): 379-409.

Seuring, S. (2004a): Industrial Ecology, Life Cycles, Supply Chains: Differences and Interrelations, in: Business Strategy and the Environment, 13: 306-319.

Seuring, S. (2004b): Integrated chain management and supply chain management comparative analysis and illustrative cases, in: Journal of Cleaner Production, 12(8-10): 1059-1071.

Singhvi, A., Madhavan, K. P., Shenoy, U. V. (2004): Pinch analysis for aggregate production planning in supply chains, in: Computers and Chemical Engineering, 28: 993-999.

Singhvi, A., Shenoy, U. V. (2002): Aggregate Planning in Supply Chains by Pinch Analysis, Transaction of the Institution of Chemical Engineers 80 (A): 597-605.

Suzuki, M. (2000): Realisation of a Sustainable Society - Zero Emissions Approaches, GRATAMA Workshop, The United Nations University, Osaka.

Thevendiraraj, S., Klemes, J., Paz, D., Aso, G., Cardenas, G. (2003): Water and wastewater minimisation study of a citrus plant, in: Resources, Conservation and Recycling, 37: 227-250.

Tietze-Stöckinger, I., Fichtner, W., Rentz, O. (2003): Entwicklung und Einsatz eines optimierenden Stoffflussmodells für die strategische Planung der betriebsübergreifenden Entsorgung (Integrated Chain Management for Disposal), in: Inderfurth, K., Schenk, M., Wäscher, G., Ziems, D. (eds.): Logistikplanung und Management, Tagungsband zur 9. Magdeburger Logistiktagung, Marburg: p. 30-45.

Treitz, M., Schollenberger, H., Bertsch, V., Geldermann, J., Rentz, O. (2004): Process Design based on Operations Research: A Metric for Resource Efficiency, Clean Environment for All: 2nd International Conference on Environmental Concerns: Innovative Technologies and Management Options, Xiamen, P.R. China.

Türkay, M., Oruc, C., Fujita, K., Asakura, T. (2004): Multi-company collaborative supply chain management with economical and environmental considerations, in: Computers and Chemical Engineering, 28: 985-992.

Umeda, T., Harada, T., Shiroko, K. (1979): A Thermodynamic Approach to the Synthesis of Heat Integration Systems in Chemical Processes, in: Computers and Chemical Engineering, 3: 273-282.

UNEP Division of Technology, Industry and Economics, (1994): International Declaration on Cleaner Production, Paris,
online, www.uneptie.org/pc/cp/declaration/pdfs/english.pdf, (03.02.2004)

Wang, Y. P., Smith, R. (1994): Wastewater Minimisation, in: Chemical Engineering Science 49 (7): 981-1006.

White, R. (1994): Preface, in: Allenby, B. R., Richards, D. (eds.): The Greening of Industrial Ecosystems, National Academic Press, Washington DC: p. v-vi.

Wietschel, M. (2002): Stoffstrommanagement (Integrated Chain Management), Verlag Peter Lang, Frankfurt (Main).

Zhelev, T. K., Semkov, K. A. (2004): Cleaner flue gas and energy recovery through pinch analysis, Journal of Cleaner Production, 12: 165-170.

Socrates Thematic Network to Enhance European Teaching and Research of Operations as Well as Supply Chain Management

José A. D. Machuca, Rafaela Alfalla Luque,
Macarena Sacristán Díaz, Gerald Reiner

1   Introduction 588
2   Importance of the Thematic Network 589
3   Objectives and Tasks of the Thematic Network 590
4   Contact Us 591
5   References 591

Summary:
The EurOMA-sponsored THENEXOM network has been approved by the European Commission through its Socrates Community Action Program. THENEXOM's short-term goal is to analyze the present state of Operations and Supply Chain Management in European Universities and to identify strengths and weaknesses in order to instigate the use of better practices. A census will be drawn up of OM teachers throughout the 24 countries (and 27 universities) making up the network. Furthermore, a survey will be taken of the teaching staff, content and methods employed. The network's medium-term aim is to tighten links between teaching, research and business practice.

Keywords:
Thematic Networks, Production/Operations Management, Supply Chain Management, Service Operations Management, Teaching, Research

1 Introduction

THENEXOM (European Thematic Network for the Excellence in Operations and Supply Chain Management, Education, Research and Practice) is a thematic network supported by EurOMA (European Operations Management Association) and was established in October 2003 through the European Commission's Socrates Community Action Program.

The THENEXOM network activities include mainstream operations management, supply chain management, and service operations management.

Operations management (OM) is concerned with how organizations produce goods and services and, in particular, with the tasks, issues and decisions of operations managers who are in charge of making sure that the design, production, and delivery of products is taking place effectively. Common topics studied in the OM field include, among many others, operations strategy, product & process design and development, capacity management, location and layout, quality management and continuous improvement, production planning, MRP/ERP systems, just-in-time / lean production, and inventory systems.

Supply chain management (SCM) is concerned with the management of logistical flows (material, information, money) and with the set of management practices used to design, plan, and control these flows in order to achieve seamless integration of the network of suppliers feeding an operations system. Typical SCM topics are supply chain design (logistics network configuration, flow design, integration, etc.), coordinated product and supply chain design (variety management, modularity, postponement, etc.), procurement, supplier management, information management, reverse logistics, or environmental issues.

Service operations management (SOM) focuses exclusively on the service industry and on the difficulty of designing, planning, and controlling operations when an operations system output is intangible, co-produced and involves emotions and experiences. Common topics studied in the SOM field are, among others, service operations strategy, design and management quality, internationalization and globalization of a service company and world class service companies, selection and design of service, selection and design of service delivery systems, technology in services and new technologies, layout in service companies planning, scheduling and control of service operations, management of demand and medium and short-term capacity, operations queue management, yield management, human resource planning and scheduling, or measurement of customer satisfaction.

2 Importance of the Thematic Network

There is a need to bring academics together to exchange ideas on OM, SCM and SOM, because within European institutions there is a lack of knowledge regarding the understanding of individual countries' OM, SCM, SOM, and their sub-disciplines. In addition, given that people with knowledge in OM, SCM and SOM must satisfy the needs of a vast number of companies in many geographical locations, the usefulness of this type of information will increase if comparative data between countries/regions is generated to give a wider perspective of this subject.

The current situation with regard to OM, SCM and SOM teaching in European universities is unclear as well. Teaching is undertaken in polytechnics, universities, engineering schools, management departments, business schools, etc. The classification of work done in environments such as OM, SCM and SOM is based on the nature of the topics addressed and on the background/profile of the person doing the work. A review of the characteristics of journals where academics publish their work and the list of required readings in doctoral programs shows the same diversity (Vastag & Montabon, 2002). A similar broad scope is found in courses, research methodologies and teaching techniques used at different levels. An extensive review of the bibliography by the University of Seville has revealed only a few studies on these topics. Many of those found refer to the USA and only touch on some aspects of OM teaching. An in-depth study of OM teaching needs to be undertaken at the European level (Alfalla & Machuca, 2003). Thus, there is an urgent need for such studies to discover whether an adequate capacity to meet an increasing demand for well-trained professionals in the field exists on the European level.

The thematic network under consideration will undertake in-depth studies in order to build a true picture of the situation of OM, SCM and SOM education in Europe. It will use this information to study collaborative means of improvement, and begin the process of achieving global excellence in this field at European universities. The creation of this network for mapping and sharing varied knowledge can serve teachers and researchers to better understand their positions, discover areas where work is done which could complement theirs, and create new international teaching and research networks in the field. Only with adequate data is it possible to determine whether European universities are responding adequately to companies' training needs in this important field of management. Only in this way can possible deficiencies in the educational system be highlighted, which should facilitate the implementation of the necessary corrective measures. For this reason, links with companies will be searched for, and future surveys will try to map their needs in the OM, SCM and SOM fields.

3 Objectives and Tasks of the Thematic Network

The first aim of the thematic network is to bring together academics in European higher education institutes to identify the European map of OM, SCM and SOM university education. The network will try to find deficiencies in their causes, and will try to to locate and promote best practice content, teaching and assessment methods in OM, SCM and SOM courses, as well as enhance and develop a European dimension in this field. The network will assess innovation in OM, SCM and SOM teaching methods and materials and disseminate the wider application of good practice across Europe and beyond in both the academic and commercial environment. A medium-term additional aim of the network is to establish links between education, research and practice (i.e., companies) in the field in order to reduce imbalances between these three pillars of company competitiveness. Over the first project period, the tasks fulfilled by the network were:

1. A census was undertaken of OM, SCM and SOM teachers in participating countries to determine the "capacity" for the "production" of graduates with knowledge in OM, SCM and SOM. Thus it was determined which institutions were teaching OM, SCM and SOM courses; which academics were teaching graduates; the level and type of training these academics have; and their experience and background. Given the depth and scope that this study required, the identification of these teachers was a major objective demanding considerable effort, since no official source exists.

2. A survey of OM, SCM and SOM teaching was designed in the participant countries to capture data on the quantity and quality of knowledge imparted to OM, SCM and SOM students on how the teaching of OM and SCM is planned and developed and on how the quality of OM, SCM and SOM learning is monitored.

3. The network was enlarged. New members were searched for among representatives from other universities, companies, research centers, and governmental and entrepreneurial institutions so as to increase the European dimension and make the network more relevant to the needs of companies. In compliance with EU recommendations, strategic connections are being sought with America and Asia to expand aforesaid objectives and actions throughout the world.

4. A network design improvement process was undertaken, setting up a core membership of 8 partners to manage this process. This is to ensure that the network evolves over time.

5. The creation and population of an electronic knowledge database was started which, when completed, will include data on European institutions and individuals involved in the fields of OM, SCM and SOM; a listing and description of the topics covered in OM, SCM and SOM courses; a description of the teaching and methodological techniques; and related research lines.

6. Four network meetings were organized and undertaken. 30 academics from the participant countries were involved and observers from other institutions and countries were invited.

7. Five meetings of the core group were organized and held to discuss, among other things, network issues such as scientific aspects, evaluation aspects, network evolution aspects, etc.

4 Contact Us

The network's goals and objectives are of great interest to scientific and business communities in the fields of operations management and supply chain management. For this reason, we encourage you to contact us.

FOR FURTHER INFORMATION, CONTACT THE COORDINATING INSTITUTION

Dr. José A. D. Machuca (Coordinator),
Dr. Macarena Sacristán Díaz (Assistant Coordinator),
Dr. Rafaela Alfalla Luque (Assistant Coordinator),
Universidad de Sevilla, F.C.E.E., Avda. Ramón y Cajal, 1,
41018 Sevilla. España (Spain),
Website: www.thenexom.net,
E-mail: thenexom@us.es, Tel.: +34 954557627, Fax: +34 954557570

5 References

Alfalla Luque, R., Machuca, J. A. D. (2003): An empirical study of POM teaching in Spanish universities (II): Faculty profile, teaching and assessment methods, in: International Journal of Operations and Production Management, 23(4): 375-400.

Vastag, G., Montabon, F. (2002): Journal Characteristics, Rankings and Social Acculturation in Operations Management, in: Omega, The International Journal of Management Science, 30(2): 109-126.

Editors

Prof. Dr. Herbert Kotzab

Born 1965 in Vienna, Austria. 1984-91 studies in Business Administration at the Vienna University of Economics and Business Administration (WU-Wien), 1991 to 1992 assistant to the CEO of Velux-Austria, 1992 - 1996 lecturer and Ph.D. student at the Department for Retail Marketing at the Vienna University of Economics and Business Administration, 1996 to 1999 senior lecturer at this department, 1999 to 2001 assistant professor, 2001 to 2005 associate professor for International Supply Chain Management at the Department of Operations Management at the Copenhagen Business School (CBS), since 2005 full professor at the Department of Operations Management at the CBS. In 1998 visiting scholar at the Center for Transportation Studies at MIT.

Dept. of Operations Management, SCM-Group,
Copenhagen Business School, Solbjerg Plads 3, 2000 Frederiksberg, Denmark
Tel.: +45 3815 2450   Fax.: +45 3815 2973
Email: hk.om@cbs.dk

PD Dr. Stefan Seuring Dipl.-Bw., M. Sc. Chem., M. Sc. Env. M.

Born 1967, studies in Business Administration Chemistry, and Environmental Management in Germany and UK, 1995-98 research assistant at Faculty of Environmental Technology, University of Paderborn (D). In 2001 completion of PhD at the University of Oldenburg (D). 1998-2001 lecturer, since April 2001 senior lecturer at the Department of Production and the Environment, Faculty of Business, Economics and Law, University of Oldenburg (D). Research carried out in close co-operation with major companies from various sectors, specially chemistry and textiles.
Research interest: supply chains, cost management, environmental management.

Supply Chain Management Center, Institute for Business Administration,
Carl von Ossietzky University Oldenburg, 26111 Oldenburg, Germany
Tel. +49 441 798 4188   Fax: +49 441 798 5852
Email: stefan.seuring@uni-oldenburg.de, http://www.uni-oldenburg.de/scmc

PD Dr. Martin Müller Dipl.-Kfm.

Born 1969, 1990-1995 studies in Business Administration at the University of Frankfurt (D). 1995-2000 research assistant at Faculty of Business Administration at the University of Halle-Wittenberg (D). PhD-thesis in 2000, since 2001 senior lecturer at the Department of Production and the Environment, Faculty of Business, Economics and Law, University of Oldenburg (D). In 2000 granting of L.V. Kantorovic-Research Prize at Institute of Business Management Halle (D). Research interests: organisational theory, environmental management, supply chain management.

Supply Chain Management Center, Institute for Business Administration,
Carl von Ossietzky University Oldenburg, 26111 Oldenburg, Germany
Tel. +49 441 798 4187   Fax: +49 441 798 5852
Email: martin.mueller@uni-oldenburg.de, http://www.uni-oldenburg.de/scmc

Dr. Gerald Reiner Mag.

Born 1970, studies in Business Administration in Vienna (A). 1996-98 research assistant at the Department of Industrial Information Processing, Vienna University of Economics and Business Administration (A). Since 1999 Univ.-Assistant at the Department of Production Management, Vienna University of Economics and Business Administration (A).
Research interests: supply chain management, quality management, operations management, performance measurement.

Department of Production Management,
Vienna University of Economics and Business Administration.
Pappenheimgasse 35/3/5, 1200 Wien, Austria
Tel. +43 1 31336 5631   Fax: +43 1 31336 5610
Email: gerald.reiner@wu-wien.ac.at, http://prodman.wu-wien.ac.at

Authors

Rafaela Alfalla Luque

Assistant Professor of Production and Operations Management at the University of Sevilla in Spain, where she has taught for the past ten years in the area of Operations Management. Her Ph.D. is also from the University of Sevilla. She is member of GIDEAO (Research Group in Computer-Aided Business Management). She has participated in a number of research projects sponsored by the European Union.

Research interests: teaching operations and supply chain management..

Dpto. de Economía Financiera y Dirección de Operaciones
Univ. de Sevilla, Fac. de CC. Económicas y Empresariales
Avda. Ramón y Cajal, 1. 41018 Sevilla, Spain
Tel. +34 954 55 64 56 Fax. +34 954 55 75 70
Email: alfalla@us.es, http://www.us.es/defdo

PD Dr. Heinz Ahn Dipl.-Kfm.

Born 1965, studies in Business Administration at the Aachen University (RWTH), 1993-1997 lecturer and Ph.D. student at the Chair for Environmental Management and Industrial Controlling, 1997-2004 senior lecturer at this chair as assistant professor. Since April 2004 representative of the Chair for Operations Research and Logistic Management at Aachen University.

Research interests: environmental management, management control, multi criteria decision making.

Chair for Operations Research and Logistic Management,
Aachen University (RWTH), Templergraben 64, 52056 Aachen, Germany
Tel.: +49 241 80 96209   Fax.: +49 241 80 92179
Email: ahn@lut.rwth-aachen.de, http://www.lut.rwth-aachen.de

Dr. Jan Stentoft Arlbjørn M.Sc.

Born 1970, studies in Business Administration at University of Southern Denmark (1991-1996) and Ph.D. student at University of Southern Denmark from 1996 to 1999. Since 2000 he has worked as external lecture at University of Southern Denmark with teaching activities in logistics, supply chain management and operations management for masters students. He is employed at his own managing consulting company – ARLBJØRN CONSULT – with strategic and operational consulting activities within demand and supply chain management. Previously he has worked as director in LEGO Company's global supply chain and at Dandy A/S and Gumlink A/S as supply chain change agent and ERP project manager.

Research interests: supply chains, philosophy of science and research methodologies.

ARLBJØRN CONSULT, 7120 Vejle Ø, Denmark
Tel.: +45 2088 7191
Email: jan@arlbjorn.dk

Ozlem Bak MBA, M.A.

Born 1973. She received a MA. in European Union Economy, an MBA in European Management program in Germany and United Kingdom. 2002-1996 worked in Multinational Automotive Corporations and on project management for companies in professional sectors. She is a member of Strategic Operations Management Centre, taught seminars in Operations Strategy and Management at University of East Anglia, and currently teaches in University of Greenwich, United Kingdom. Her principal research interest is in the area of manufacturing operations management and especially on the value-shifts within automotive supply chains. Lecturer in Marketing and Operations Management.

Research interests: supply chain management, value creation, marketspace, transformation.

Business School , University of Greenwich,
Maritime Greenwich Campus , Park Row, Greenwich,
London SE10 9LS United Kingdom
Tel. +44 (0)20 8331 9106 Fax: +44 (0)20 8331 9005
Email O.Bak@greenwich.ac.uk,
http://www.gre.ac.uk/schools/business/index.html

Dr. Chuda Basnet

Born 1948 in Nepal. Received Bachelor's degree in Mechanical Engineering in 1973; 1973-1978 Production Engineer; 1978-1985 Aircraft Maintenance Engineer; 1985-1987 Master's degree in Industrial and Management Engineering; 1987-1991 PhD in Industrial Engineering and Management at Oklahoma State University, USA; Senior Lecturer at the management school of Waikato University since 1991.

Research interests: manufacturing modeling, supply chain management.

Department of Management Systems,
The University of Waikato, Private Bag 3105, Hamilton, New Zealand
Tel.: +64 7 838 4562   Fax: +64 7 838 4270
Email: chuda@waikato.ac.nz, http://www.mngt.waikato.ac.nz/systems/

Khalid Bichou M.Sc. (WMU), M.Sc. (Plymouth), B.Sc. (ENA)

Born 1974, studied Public Economics and Finance, ENA (Morocco/France). 1993-2002 various positions in the maritime and port industry in Morocco. 2001-2004 research and consultancy assignments in Europe and North America, including for UNCTAD and the World Bank. 1999 MSc in Port Operations and Management from WMU (S). 2002 MSc in International Logistics from University of Plymouth (UK). 2004-present: Research Associate at the Ports Operations and Technology Centre (PORTeC) at the Centre for Transport Studies of Imperial College London. Research interests: port functional and strategic benchmarking, logistics and sc applications in ports, shipping & intermodal transport operations.

Centre for Transport Studies,
Imperial College London, London SW7 2AZ, United Kingdom
Tel +44 020 7594 6111   Fax +44 020 7594 6102
Khalid.bichou@imperial.ac.uk, http://www.ic.ac.uk/cts

Sakun Boon-itt M.Sc.

Born 1973, 1996-1999 studies in Manufacturing Systems Management at Southern Methodist University, USA. Since 1999, lecturer at the Department of Industrial and Operations Management, Thammasat University, Thailand. Currently, he is a PhD candidate in management of technology in the School of Management, Asian Institute of Technology in Thailand.
Research Interests: supply chain management, operations management.

Dept. of Industrial and Operations Management,
Faculty of Commerce and Accountancy, Thammsat University,
2 Prachan, Rd. Pranakorn, Bangkok, Thailand 10200
Tel. +66 2 5106021   Fax: +66 2 9478912
Email: st029196@ait.ac.th

Dr. Louis Brennan B.E. M.Eng.Sc., MBA, M.Erg.S.

Dr. Louis Brennan is a member of the School of Business Studies at the University of Dublin, Trinity College, where he teaches International Business and Operations Strategy. He has held academic positions in a number of schools in Asia, Europe and the United States. His research work has appeared in a variety of journals, books and conference proceedings.
Research interest: supply chain management, global business & technology management, culture & operations management

School of Business Studies,
University of Dublin, Trinity College, Dublin 2, Ireland
Tel. +353 1 6081993
Email: brennaml@tcd.ie, http://www.tcd.ie/Business_Studies/

Prof. Dr. Francesco Casella

Born 1969, 1988-1994 studies in Electronic Engineering at Politecnico di Milano. 1996-1999 PhD. student in Control Systems at the Department of Electronics and Information Sciences, Politecnico di Milano. 1999-2001 Post-doc researcher. Assistant professor at Politecnico di Milano since 2001.
Research interests: power plant modelling, control and management, object-oriented modelling and simulation of industrial systems.

Dipartimento di Elettronica e Informazione,
Politecnico di Milano,
Via Ponzio 34/5, 20133 Milano – Italy
Tel. +39 02 2399 3465   Fax: +39 02 2399 3412
Email: francesco.casella@polimi.it

Dr. Richard Chivaka B. Com (Accounting)., M. Sc. Accounting & Finance

Born 1972, did Bachelor of Commerce in Zimbabwe, MSc in Accounting & Finance in Manchester, UK. Lectured at the National University of Science & Technology, Zimbabwe from 1997 to 2000. Joined University of Cape Town, South Africa in 2000. In 2003 completed PhD at the University of Cape Town.. 2000-2002 lecturer, since January 2003 senior lecturer in the Department of Accounting, Faculty of Commerce, University of Cape Town.
Research interests: cost management and supply chain management.

Department of Accounting, Faculty of Commerce,
University of Cape Town, Private Bag Rondebosch, Cape Town, South Africa
Tel. +27 21 650 4391   Fax: +27 21 689 7582
Email: rchivaka@commerce.uct.ac.za

Dr. David Coghlan B.A., Bacc. Theol., M.Sc., S.M., M.A.

Dr. David Coghlan is a member of the School of Business Studies at the University of Dublin, Trinity College, where he teaches organisation development and action research. He has published over 60 articles and book chapters. He has published several books, including The Dynamics of Organizational Levels (co-authored with Nicholas Rashford) in the Addison-Wesley OD series (1994); Doing Action Research in Your Own Organization (with Teresa Brannick), 2nd edition, Sage: London, 2005 (1st edition, 2001); Changing Healthcare Organisations (with Eilish Mc Auliffe) Blackhall: Dublin 2003; Managers Learning in Action (co-edited with T. Dromgoole, P. Joynt, & P. Sorensen), Routledge: London 2004.

Research interests: Organisation development, action research, clinical inquiry, reflective practice, action learning, practitioner research, doing action research in one's own organisation.

School of Business Studies, University of Dublin, Trinity College,
Dublin 2, Ireland
Tel. +353 1 6082323
Email: dcoghlan@tcd.ie, http://www.tcd.ie/Business_Studies/

Prof. Dr. Paul Coughlan B.E., MBA

Associate Professor of Operations Management at the University of Dublin, School of Business Studies, Trinity College, Ireland where, since 1993, he has researched and taught in the areas of operations management and product development. In June 2004, he chaired the 11th International Product Development Management Conference at Trinity College. He is President of the Board of the European Institute for Advanced Studies in Management, and a Country Representative on the Board of the European Operations Management Association. He is a Director of Magnetic Solutions Ltd., a Dublin-based process equipment manufacturer which started as a Trinity College campus company.
Research interest: continuous improvement of practices and performance in product development and manufacturing operations, action research, action learning.

School of Business Studies,
University of Dublin, Trinity College,Dublin 2, Ireland
Tel. +353 1 6082327
Email: coughlnp@tcd.ie, http://www.tcd.ie/Business_Studies/

Dr. Donna F. Davis B.A. Mgmt, MBA

Born 1950 in Tennessee, U.S. 1979 to 1999 senior administrator at Maryville College (Tennessee), completed studies in Management in 1983 at Maryville College, 1990 to 1993 Master of Business Administration with a Marketing concentration at the University of Tennessee, 1999 - 2003 PhD student and research assistant in the Marketing & Logistics Department at the University of Tennessee, associate director of the Forecasting and Supply Chain Management Forum and member of the forecast audit team. Research conducted with major global firms in various industries.
Research interests: supply chain management, brand management, information management.

Area of Marketing,
Rawls College of Business, Texas Tech University, Lubbock, TX 79409, USA
Tel.: 011 806 742 3238   Fax: 011 806 742 2199
Email: ddavis@ba.ttu.edu

Prof. Dr. Jeanne Duvallet

Born 1957, studies in Applied Mathematics at Ecole Normale Supérieure (Paris). 1983 – 1993 assistant professor at Department of Mathematics at the Toulouse and Pau Universities, PhD-thesis in 1986, and since 1993 associate professor at the Institut National Polytechnique of Grenoble. Member of the laboratory GILCO (Gestion Industrielle, Logistique et Conception) and develop research program with members of the Grenoble Applied Economics Laboratory.
Research interests: supply chain management, economic modelisation, simulation.

Laboratoire G.I.L.C.O.,
INPG – ENSGI, 46 avenue Felix Viallet, 38031 Grenoble Cedex 1, France
Tel. +33 4 57 46 32   Fax: +33 4 57 47 93
Email: jeanne.duvallet@gilco.inpg.fr

Dr. Jutta Geldermann Dipl.-Wi.-Ing.

Born 1968. Diploma in Industrial Engineering (University of Karlsruhe (TH)). PhD in Business Administration. Scientific assistant and head of the working group "Technique Assessment and Risk Management" at the French-German Institute for Environmental Research (DFIU/IFARE), University of Karlsruhe (TH), Germany. She has conducted and managed numerous research projects on production planning, mass and energy flow management, determination of Best Available Techniques (BAT), and multicriteria decision making.

French-German Institute for Environmental Research (DFIU/IFARE),
University of Karlsruhe (TH), Hertzstr. 16, 76187 Karlsruhe, Germany
Tel. +49 721 608 4583   Fax: +49 721 758909
Email: jutta.geldermann@wiwi.uni-karlsruhe.de, http://www-dfiu.wiwi.uni-karlsruhe.de/

Prof. Dr. Cristina Gimenez M.Sc.

Born 1972, studies in Business Administration at Universitat de Barcelona (Spain), 1989-1996, MSc in Logistics and Supply Chain Management by Cranfield University (UK), 2000, and Ph.D. in Business Administration by Universitat de Barcelona (Spain), 2002 (Ph.D thesis: "Competitive Advantage through Supply Chain Management"). Assistant professor (part time) at Universitat de Barcelona, 1996-2002, and since 2002 assistant professor (full time) at Universitat Pompeu Fabra. Member of GREL (Research Group in Business Logistics, IET, UPF). Research carried out in close co-operation with major companies from various sectors, especially fast moving consumer goods manufacturers and grocery retailers.
Research interests: supply chain management, e-scm, e-procurement, operations management.

Departament d'Economia i Empresa, Universitat Pompeu Fabra
Ramon Trias Fargas 25-27, 08005 Barcelona, Spain
Tel. +34 935 422 901   Fax: +34 935 421 746
Email: cristina.gimenez@upf.edu, http://www.econ.upf.edu/~gimenez/

Prof. Dr. Susan L. Golicic BS Chem. Eng., MBA

Born 1967 in Detroit, Michigan, U.S. 1985 to 1989 completed studies in engineering at Wayne State University (Detroit), 1990 to 1995 radiological engineer (Knolls Atomic Power Laboratory and Scientific Ecology Group), 1995 to 1997 Master of Business Administration with a Logistics and Operations concentration at the University of Tennessee, 1997 to 1999 Materials Supervisor and Logistics Analyst (DaimlerChrysler), 1999 - 2003 PhD student and research assistant in the Marketing & Logistics Department at the University of Tennessee, associate director of the Forecasting and Supply Chain Management Forum and member of the forecast audit team. Research conducted with major global firms in various industries.
Research interests: supply chain management, business to business relationships, logistics strategy.

Department of Marketing, Lundquist College of Business,
University of Oregon. Eugene, OR 97403-1208, USA
Tel.: 011 541 346 3320   Fax: 011 541 346 3341
Email: sgolicic@uoregon.edu

Alejandra Gomez-Padilla M.Sc.

Born 1976, 1994-1998 studies in Industrial Engineering at the Instituto Tecnológico y de Estudios Superiores de Occidente (Mexico), 1999-2001 Master in Science in Industrial Engineering with option on Productics at the Ecole Polytechnique de Montreal, from 2001 to present, PhD candidate at the laboratory Gestion Industrielle Logistique et Conception (GILCO) from de Institut National Polytechnique de Grenoble, France. 1998-1999 production and product engineer for a company in the electronics sector.
Research interests: supply chain management, logistics, inventory control.

GILCO / ENSGI / Institut National Polytechnique de Grenoble,
46, avenue Félix Viallet; 38031 Grenoble Cedex, France
Tel.: +33 476 57 43 26   Fax: +33 476 57 46 95
Email: gomez-padilla@gilco.inpg.fr, http://gilco.inpg.fr/~gomez

Dr. David B. Grant MBA, M.Sc.

Born 1963 in Barrie, Ontario, Canada. Bachelor of Commerce and MBA studies at the University of Calgary, MSc by Research (with distinction) and PhD studies at the University of Edinburgh. Received the James Cooper Memorial Cup PhD Award in 2003 from the Chartered Institute of Logistics and Transport (UK). Lecturer in marketing and logistics at the University of Calgary (1990-98) and the University of Edinburgh (2000-02). Lecturer in logistics in the School of Management and Languages at Heriot-Watt University (2003-date). Business experience includes retail management, corporate banking account management, corporate seminar facilitation and presentations, and management consulting.
Research interests: logistics customer service and satisfaction, supply chain relationships.

Logistics Research Centre, School of Management and Languages,
Heriot-Watt University, Esmee Fairbairn Building, Edinburgh UK EH14 4AS
Tel: +44 (0)131 451 3527   Fax: +44 (0)131 451 3498
Email: D.B.Grant@hw.ac.uk, http://www.sml.hw.ac.uk/logistics/david.html

Dr. Richard Gray M.Sc.

Born 1943. 1977 MSc Cranfield University, 1981 PhD Cranfield University (European logistics). 1999 Fellow of Chartered Institute of Transport. 1999 Fellow of Institute of Logistics and Transport. 1979 to 2004 Successively Lecturer, Senior Lecturer and Principal Lecturer, University of Plymouth. 1990-1996 Head of Division of Shipping and Transport, University of Plymouth. Author of four books, editor of two books, author of many papers. Series editor of the Plymouth Studies in Contemporary Shipping and Logistics. Consultant in logistics for industry and government. Before entering academic life worked in international freight forwarding and export distribution.
Research interests: international logistics, supply chain management.

Centre for International Shipping and Logistics,
Faculty of Social Sciences and Business,
University of Plymouth, Drake Circus, PL4 8AA Plymouth, UK
Tel. +44 (0) 1752 232442   Fax: +44 (0)1752 232853
Email: rgray@plymouth.ac.uk

Dr. Andreas Größler Dipl.-Wirt.-Inf.

Born 1967, studies in Management Information Systems in Germany and Greece. 1995–2000 research assistant, Faculty of Business Administration, Mannheim University, Germany. In 2000 completion of PhD about the effectiveness of gaming simulations. Since October 2000 assistant professor at the Department of Industrial Management, Faculty of Business Administration, Mannheim University.

Visiting researcher at universities in Bergen, Norway and Nijmegen, The Netherlands. Member of the Policy Council of the International System Dynamics Society.
Research interests: rationality and success, manufacturing strategy, complexity, system dynamics.

Industrieseminar der Universität Mannheim, Schloss,
68131 Mannheim, Germany
Tel. +49 621 181 1583   Fax: +49 621 181 1579
Email: agroe@is.bwl.uni-mannheim.de, http://is.bwl.uni-mannheim.de

Prof. Dr. Edeltraud Günther

Born 1965, Study of Business Administration from 1984 to 1989 at the University of Augsburg. 1989 to 1994 research assistant at the Chair of Accounting and Control at the University of Augsburg and completion of a Dr. rer. pol. 1994 to 1996 research assistant and project leader in the department of economy of the Bavarian Institute of Applied Environmental Research and Technology GmbH (BIfA), Augsburg. Since 1996 Professor of Business Administration, esp. Environmental Management at the Dresden University of Technology. August 2001 to February 2002 Visiting Professor of Commerce, McIntire School of Commerce, University of Virginia, Charlottesville, U.S.A.
Research interests: sustainable procurement, environmental performance measurement, deceleration as a strategy for implementing time ecology, emission trading, environmental-oriented economic instruments.

Department for Business Management and Economics,
Professorship of Business Administration, especially Environmental Management,
Dresden University of Technology, 01062 Dresden
Email: bu@mailbox.tu-dresden.de, www.tu-dresden.de/wwbwlbu/homepage.html

Prof. Dr. Árni Halldórsson M.Sc.

Born 1970 in Reykjavik, Iceland. M.Sc. Logistics & Innovation, Copenhagen Business School (CBS) 1997. PhD candidate and lecturer at CBS from 1998, finished 2002. Assistant Professor on inter-organizational issues in operations management at the Department of Operations Management at CBS from 2002. In 2000, a visiting scholar at the Center of Logistics Management, University of Nevada, Reno. External lecturer at the Reykjavik University, Iceland.
Research interests: interorganizational relationships; SCM; logistics competencies; third party logistics; research process; reverse logistics.

Dept. of Operations Management, SCM-Group,
Copenhagen Business School, Solbjerg Plads 3, 2000 Frederiksberg, Denmark
Tel.: +45 3815 3815   Fax: +45 3815 2440,   Email: arni@cbs.dk

Prof. Dr. Alan Harrison MA MSc(Oxon) PhD CEng FIEE

Born 1944, studied chemistry at Oxford University and followed a career in manufacturing industry with Procter and Gamble, BL and GEC. Having been converted to academic life, joined Warwick Business School in 1986 as a senior research fellow studying the application of Japanese management methods to UK manufacturing. Completed his doctorate in enablers and inhibitors to material flow at Cranfield School of Management, which he joined in 1996.

Researched supply chains in automotive, aerospace and grocery sectors. Extended his research base from applications of just in time to limitations of this approach, and recent work has been concerned with developing capabilities for enhanced customer responsiveness. This has resulted in such publications as Creating the Agile Supply Chain (Institute of Logistics and Transport, 1999) and the establishment of the Agile Supply Chain Research Club at Cranfield.

Research interests: customer responsive supply chains, supply chain integration including technical, behavioural and key performance measures.

Supply Chain Research Centre, Cranfield School of Management,
Cranfield, MK43 0AL, United Kingdom
Tel: +44 1234 754121   Fax: +44 1234 751712
e-mail: a.harrison@cranfield.ac.uk

Harlina Suzana Jaafar BBA (Transport), M. Sc. Transport

Born in 1966 in Malaysia. Studies in Business Administration, majoring in Transport in 1986-90 at MARA University of Technology, Malaysia and Transport at Cardiff University, Wales, UK in 1992. She is currently a lecturer at the Faculty of Business and Administration, MARA University of Technology, Malaysia since 1992. Under the scholarship of MARA University of Technology, Malaysia, she is now conducting a doctoral research at the Business School, Loughborough University and expected to complete in 2005.

Research interests: relationship marketing in third party logistics, logistics management, road and rail freight transport.

The Business School, Loughborough University,
Loughborough, Leicestershire LE11 3TU, United Kingdom
Tel. +44 (0) 1509 223 239   Fax: +44 (0) 1509 223 960
Email: H.S.Jaafar@lboro.ac.uk, http://www.lboro.ac.uk

Prof. Dr. Kurt Jörnsten

Born 1948 in Sundbyberg, Sweden. 1980 PhD in Optimization Linköping Institute of Technology, Linköping, Sweden. 1983 Docent in Optimization Linköping Institute of Technology. 2001 Honorary Doctor Stockholm School of Economics, Stockholm, Sweden. Former affiliations: Associate Professor in Optimization,

Department of Mathematics Linköping Institute of Technology, from 1983 full professor, Senior Researcher Chrisitan Michelsen Institute for Science and Intellectual Freedom 1985-1988. Adjoint Professor Molde College, Molde Norway 1990- Adjoint Professor, Department of Mathematics, Aarhus University, Aarhus, Denmark 2001-.

Research interests: quantitative methods in supply chain management, cooperative and non-cooperative game theory, pricing in deregulated markets.

Dept. of Finance and Management Science,
The Norwegian School of Economics and Business Administration,
Helleveien 30, 5045 Bergen, Norway
Tel.: +47 55959552
Email: Kurt.Jornsten.@nhh.no

Prof. Dr. Stig Johannessen M.Sc.

Born 1962 in Trondheim, Norway. MSc in biophysics from the Norwegian University of Science and Technology (NTNU). Studies in organizational development, strategy and management. Worked in the pharmaceutical industry and also as a manager of a small company before joining the Department of Industrial Economics and Technology Management at NTNU in 2000 as Research Fellow. Has since conducted research on organizational complexity theory, strategy and management of logistics oriented organizations. Lecturer in strategic management and strategic logistics at NTNU. Ph.D. in 2003. From January 2004 associate professor of organization and management at the Program for Management and Organizational Studies, University College (HINT) in Levanger, Norway.

Research interests: organizational dynamics, strategy processes, logistics and SCM, organizational complexity theory, methodology.

Program for Management and Organizational Studies,
University College of Nord-Tröndelag (HINT),
Röstad, 7600 Levanger, Norway
Tel: +4792035007, Fax: +4774022501,   Email stig.johannessen@hint.no

Jens Keilen Dipl.-Kfm.

Born 1972, studies in Business Administration at the Aachen University (RWTH) in Germany, 1996-2001. 2001 thesis at University of Maryland, USA. Since 2002, Research assistant at the Chair for Environmental Management and Industrial Controlling, Aachen University (D).

Research interests: supply chain management, environmental management, closed loop management.

Chair for Environmental Economics and Industrial Controlling
Aachen University (RWTH), Templergraben 64, 52056 Aachen, Germany
Tel. +49 241 80 96576   Fax: +49 241 80 92179
Email: keilen@lut.rwth-aachen.de, http://www.lut.rwth-aachen.de

Ines Klauke Dipl.-Kffr.

Born 1975. Study of business administration at the Dresden University of Technology from 1993 to 2000. Since 2000 research assistant at the Professorship of Business Administration, esp. Environmental Management, Department of Business Management and Economics at the Dresden University of Technology. Projects: Multiplier-Effects and Implementation of the Eco-Audit according to EMAS II in Academic Facilities (at the Example of the TU Dresden), Potentials of a Sustainable Procurement and Instruments for Implementation (NaBesI).
Research interest: sustainable procurement, environmental management.

Department for Business Management and Economics,
Professorship of Business Administration especially Environmental Management
Dresden University of Technology, 01062 Dresden; Germany
Email: bu@mailbox.tu-dresden.de, www.tu-dresden.de/wwbwlbu/homepage.htm

Julia Koplin Dipl.-Oec.

Born 1978 in Nordhausen, Germany. 1997-2002 studies in Business Administration and Economics at the University of Oldenburg (D), 2000-2001 distance studies in Business Administration at the University of Northern Colorado (USA), 2001-2002 student research assistant in a project conducted by the University of Oldenburg in cooperation with the IKW (German Detergent Manufacturers Association), 2002-2004 research assistant at the Department of Production and the Environment, Faculty of Business, Economics and Law, University of Oldenburg (D). Since 2004 PhD student at the Volkswagen AG.
Research interests: sustainable development, purchasing & supply chain management, stakeholder theory.

Volkswagen AG, Group Research, Environmental Strategy,
Letter box 1774/3, 38436 Wolfsburg, Germany
Tel. +49 5361 9-38728   Fax: +49 5361 9-72960
Email: julia.koplin@volkswagen.de

Prof. Dr. Marie Koulikoff-Souviron M.A. English (Hons.)

In 1982 M.A. English (Hons) was awarded by the Université de Nice. In 1984 Business Degree obtained from CERAM Sophia Antipolis (France). 1984 to 1999 with Dow Corning Heath Care Business Europe in Sophia Antipolis, France; Latest position as Product Line/Supply Chain Manager. In January 2003: PhD on

Supply Chain Relationships and People Management awarded by Cranfield School of Management. Since 2003 Associate Professor at CERAM Sophia Antipolis for Logistics and Supply Chain Management. Visiting lecturer in supply chain management and research methodology with several institutions.

Research interests: supply chain relationships & people management, case studies.

CERAM Sophia Antipolis European School of Business, Rue Dostoïevski BP085, 06902 Sophia Antipolis Cedex, France
Tel. +33.493.953217   Fax: +33493.953217
Email: marie.koulikoff@ceram.fr, http://www.ceram.edu

Prof. Dr. Rudolf O. Large

Born in 1962, studies in Physics, Industrial Engineering and Business Administration, 1984-1990, Research assistant at the Technical University of Darmstadt (Germany), 1990-1995, and doctoral degree in Business Administration, 1995. Practical work in purchasing management. Professor at the Anhalt University of Applied Sciences, 1996-2003. Since 2003 professor at the HTW Saarland – University of Applied Sciences. Teaching experience in Finland, Romania, Hungary and Poland. Habilitation at the Technical University of Darmstadt (Germany), 2003.

Research interests: purchasing management, logistics, strategic management.

Department of Business Administration, HTW Saarland – University of Applied Sciences, Waldhausweg 14, 66123 Saarbrücken, Germany
Phone +49 681 5867 579 Fax: +49 681 5867 504
Email: rudolf.large@htw-saarland.de, http://www-bw.htw-saarland.de

Prof. Dr. Daniel Llerena

Born 1965, studies in Economics at the Louis Pasteur University (Strasbourg, France). 1991-1996 research assistant at the Theoretical and Applied Economics Research Center of the Faculty of Economics and Management (Strasbourg), PhD-thesis in 1996, since 1997 associate professor at the Pierre Mendes France University (Grenoble, France). Research carried out in close co-operation with Industrial Engineering School of the Institut National Polytechnique of Grenoble.

Research interests: supply chain management, industrial organization, environmental economics.

Grenoble Applied Economics Laboratory (G.A.E.L.),
Université Pierre Mendés France, BP 47, 38040 Grenoble, France
Tel. + 33 4 76 82 59   Fax: + 33 4 76 54 55
Email: daniel.llerena@upmf-grenoble.fr

Prof. Dr. José A.D. Machuca

Full professor of Operations Management. Director of GIDEAO Research Group. Coordinator of THENEXOM, Socrates European Thematic Network for the Excellence in Operations and Supply Chain Management Education, Research and Practice. Board member of EurOMA. Formerly Head of Department (Finance and Operations Management, US) and Vice-dean (Faculty of Economics and Business Science, US); Vice-president of the System Dynamics Society and member of POMS Board. Director of research projects within the European Union and national frameworks.

Dpto. de Economía Financiera y Dirección de Operaciones,
Univ. de Sevilla, Fac. de CC. Económicas y Empresariales,
Avda. Ramón y Cajal, 1. 41018 Sevilla, Spain
Tel. +34 954 55 76 10 Fax. +34 954 55 75 70,
Email: jmachuca@cica.es

Prof. Dr. Teresa M. McCarthy B.A. Retail, MS Human Ecology

Born 1961 in Boston, Massachusetts, U.S. 1979 to 1983 completed BS in Retailing at the University of Massachusetts, 1985 to 1998 Retail Buyer (Bonwit Teller) and Director of Inventory Planning and Control (Ross Stores) in New York, 1996 to 1998 Master of Science in Human Ecology with a Textiles concentration at the University of Rhode Island, 1998 to 2003 PhD student and research assistant in the Marketing & Logistics Department at the University of Tennessee, associate director of the Forecasting and Supply Chain Management Forum and member of the forecast audit team. Research conducted with major global firms in various industries.
Research interests: supply chain, collaborative forecasting, demand management, demand planning.

Department of Management and Marketing,
College of Business and Economics, Lehigh University,
Bethlehem, PA 18049, USA
Tel.: 011 610 758 5882   Fax.: 011 610 965 6941
Email: tem3@lehigh.edu

H.G.A. (Rick) Middel Ir.

Ir. Rick Middel is a PhD student at the Faculty of Business, Public Administration and Technology at the University of Twente. He studied Industrial Engineering and Management at the University of Twente (NL). From 2002 till 2003, he was a research assistant at the Department of Technology and Organisation at the University of Twente (NL).

Research interests: continuous improvement, collaborative improvement, action learning, action research.

Department of Technology and Organisation, Faculty of Business,
Public Administration, and Technology, University of Twente,
P.O. Box 217, Enschede, The Netherlands
Tel. +31 53 4894537
Email: h.g.a.middel@bbt.utwente.nl, http://www.bbt.utwente.nl/leerstoelen/OB

Prof. Dr. Juliana H. Mikkola

Born 1963, 1982-1987 studied Electrical Engineering at the University of Houston, U.S.A., 1991-1993 studied M.B.A. at St. Mary's University, U.S.A., 1987-1993 worked as design engineer and team leader at Motorola's Automotive and Industrial Electronics Group, 1993-1994 worked as executive trainee at Motorola's Corporate Office, 1995-1998 worked as Research Assistant at Helsinki School of Economics (HSE), 1998 received Licentiate Degree from HSE, 2003 received PhD degree from Copenhagen Business School (CBS). Since 2003, Assistant Professor at CBS, Department of Operations Management.

Research interests: supply chain management, new product development, modularization and platform management, mass customization, portfolio management of r&d projects.

Dept. of Operations Management, SCM-Group,
Copenhagen Business School, Solbjerg Plads 3, 2000 Frederiksberg, Denmark
Tel.: +45 3815 2441   Fax: +45 3815 2440
Email: jh.om@cbs.dk

Dr. Giovanni Miragliotta

Born 1973, studies in Industrial Economics & Management, manufacturing and plant engineering at Politecnico di Milano, Italy. In 2003, completion of PhD in Management Engineering. 1998-2002 lecturer and contract teacher for various teaching and educational institutions, both undergraduate and corporate level. Since January 2003, senior lecturer at the Department of Management, Economics and Industrial Engineering at Politecnico di Milano. Since 1998, free-lance consulting in operations management for major Italian and Multinational businesses.

Research interests: supply chain management and supply chain costing, inventory management, production planning and scheduling, industrial dynamics.

Department of Management, Economics and Industrial Engineering,
Politecnico di Milano, Via Giuseppe Colombo, 40, 20133 Milano, Italy
Tel. +39 02 2399 2785   Fax: +39 02 2399 2700
Email: giovanni.miragliotta@polimi.it

Prof. Dr. Eric Molleman

Born 1956, studies in Social and Organizational Psychology, 1974-1980. Member of the supporting staff of the University Hospital Groningen (NL), 1980-1990. PhD-thesis in 1990 at the University of Maastricht (NL). Assistant professor Human Resource Management from 1990-1997 at the Faculty of Management and Organization, University of Groningen (NL). From 1997-2000 associate professor and since 2000 full professor at the same faculty.
Research interests: work design, teamwork, interdependencies.

Faculty of Management and Organization,
University of Groningen, P.O. box 800, 9700 AV Groningen, The Netherlands
Tel. +31 50 363 3846   Fax: +31 50 363 2032
Email: h.b.m.molleman@bdk.rug.nl
http://www.bdk.rug.nl/medewerkers/h.b.m.molleman/

Romy Morana Dipl.-Kffr.

Born 1964, vocational business training in international wholesale trade, 1986-94 studies in Business Administration and Environmental Research at Technical University of Berlin and Humboldt University of Berlin 1994-2000 lecturer for economics and environmental management at Technical University of Berlin, Since 2002 scholar of Heinrich Böll Foundation and doctoral candidate at Supply Chain Management Center, Institute for Business Administration, Carl von Ossietzky University Oldenburg.
Research interests: close-loop supply chain management, environmental management.

School of Process Sciences and Engineering,
Technical University of Berlin, 10623 Berlin, Germany
Tel. +49 30 314 214 11   Fax:+49 030 314 211 314
E-mail: morana@gruen-der-zeit.de

Dr. Axel Neher Dipl.-Kfm.

Born 1969, studies in Business Administration at the University of Marburg (D). 1995-98 research assistant at the Department of Logistics, University of Marburg, PhD Thesis in 1998. Since 1999 Assistant Professor at the Faculty of Business Administration and Economics, University of Marburg.
Research interests: supply chain management, performance measurement, environmental management

Department of Logistics,
University of Marburg, Am Plan 2, 35037 Marburg, Germany
Tel. +49 6421 282 3916   Fax: +49 6421 282 3745
Email: neher@wiwi.uni-marburg.de, http://www.wiwi.uni-marburg.de

Lars Magne Nonås M.Sc. Inf.

Born 1974 in Bergen, Norway. 1994-2001 studies in Mathematical and Natural Sciences at the University of Bergen. Since 2002 Ph.D. student at the Department of Finance and Management Science at the Norwegian School of Economics and Business Administration. During 2000-2001 student assistant at the Norwegian School of Information Technology.
Research interests: supply chain management, inventory management, transshipments.

Department of Finance and Management Science,
Norwegian School of Economics and Business Administration
Helleveien 30, 5045 Bergen, Norway
Tel. +47 55 95 92 86   Fax: +47 55 95 96 50
Email: lars.nonas@nhh.no

Marian Oosterhuis M.Sc.

Born 1979, studies in Business Administration at the University of Groningen (NL), 1997-2002. From 2002-2003, junior researcher at the University Hospital Groningen, research by order of Dutch Ministry of Public Health. PhD Candidate at the Faculty of Management and Organization, University of Groningen, since November 2003. Ph.D. research on 'Behavioral barriers in supply chain management'.
Research interests: supply chain management, organizational behavior.

Faculty of Management and Organization,
University of Groningen, P.O. box 800, 9700 AV Groningen, The Netherlands
Tel. +31 50 363 4783   Fax: +31 50 363 2032
Email: m.j.oosterhuis@bdk.rug.nl

Julia Pahl Dipl.-Kffr.

Born 1975, studies in Business Administration at the University of Hamburg. Since 2003 external Ph.D. Student at the Institute of Information Systems (Wirtschaftsinformatik) in Hamburg.
Research interests: supply chain management; supply chain planning; tactical production planning.

Institute of Information Systems (Wirtschaftsinformatik)
University of Hamburg, Von-Melle-Park 5, 20146 Hamburg, Germany
Email: julia.pahl@esa.int

Dr. Günter Prockl Dipl.-Kfm., M.A. Economics (USA)

Born 1967. Studies in Business Administration in Germany and Economics in USA. 1996 - 2001 Fraunhofer Application Center for Transport Logistics and Communications Technology. Since 1997 Director Supply Chain Management. In 2000 Doctor Thesis on Supply Chain Management. Since 2001 additionally Assistant of the Editors Board of the Scientific Journal LOGISTIKmanagement. Since 2002 Senior Lecturer Friedrich-Alexander University Erlangen-Nürnberg, Department of Business Logistics and Director Supply Chain Management at associated Fraunhofer Center for Applied Research on Technologies for the Logistics Service Industries (ATL).
Research interests: supply chain management, information technology, innovation.

Institute for Business Administration, esp. Logistics,
Friedrich-Alexander-University, 90403 Nuremberg, Germany
Tel. +49 911 5302 454   Fax: +49 911 5302 460
Email: guenter.prockl@logistik.uni-erlangen.de; prockl@atl.fraunhofer.de
http://www.logistik.wiso.uni-erlangen.de; http://www.atl.fraunhofer.de

Prof. Dr. Himangshu Paul

He is a Professor of Operations Management in the School of Management, Asian Institute of Technology in Thailand where he served. Professor Paul had taught at National University of Singapore, North Carolina State University and University of Canterbury, New Zealand. He holds a Doctor of Engineering degree in Systems Engineering and Management from Asian Institute of Technology.
Research interests: operations management, total quality management and management of technology.

School of Management,
Asian Institute of Technology, Khlong-Luang, Patumthani, Thailand 12120
Tel.: + 66 2 5246143   Fax: + 66 2 5162126
Email: hpaul@ait.ac.th

Dr. Mohammed Rafiq B.A.(Hons) Econs., MBA

He holds an Honours degree in Economics from the University of Essex, as well as MBA and PhD from the University of Bradford. He is currently a Senior Lecturer in Retailing and Marketing at the Business School, Loughborough University. He is also the Programme Director for the BSc (Hons.) Retail Management degree and the BSc (Hons.) Retail Management (Automotive) degree at Loughborough. Previously, he has held posts as Lecturer in International Marketing at Trent University, Nottingham, and Research Associate at Warwick Business School.

Research interests: retail assortment and store image, ethnocentrism and internationalisation strategies, internal marketing, relationship marketing in third party logistics.

The Business School, Loughborough University,
Loughborough, Leicestershire LE11 3TU, United Kingdom
Tel.: +44 (0) 1509 223 397   Fax: +44 (0) 1509 223 960
Email: M.Rafiq@lboro.ac.uk, http://www.lboro.ac.uk

Prof. Dr. Otto Rentz

Born 1944. Studies in Economics and Industrial Chemistry, Master's Degree in Economics, PhD in Industrial Chemistry, Habilitation in Industrial Production and Economics. Director of the IIP and the French-German Institute for Environmental Research, University of Karlsruhe (TH).

French-German Institute for Environmental Research (DFIU/IFARE),
University of Karlsruhe (TH), Hertzstr. 16, 76187 Karlsruhe, Germany
Tel. +49 721 608 4460   Fax: +49 721 758909
Email: otto.rentz@wiwi.uni-karlsruhe.de, http://www-dfiu.wiwi.uni-karlsruhe.de/

Prof. Dr. Macarena Sacristán Díaz

PhD in Business Administration. Associate professor at the University of Seville (Spain), where she has been lecturing since 1992 at the Department of Finance and Operations Management. Her quality of teaching has received official recognition. Co-author of a book, she has been published in related journals at both international and national levels. Secretary of the First World Conference on POM (POMSevilla2000). Assistant co-ordinator of the Socrates European Thematic Network for the Excellence in Operations and Supply Chain Management Education, Research and Practice (Thenexom).
Research interests: advanced manufacturing technology, performance measurement, supply chain management.

Dpto. de Economía Financiera y Dirección de Operaciones,
Univ. de Sevilla, Fac. de CC. Económicas y Empresariales,
Avda. Ramón y Cajal, 1. 41018 Sevilla, Spain
Tel. +34 954 556 968 Fax. +34 954 557 570
Email: macarena-sd@us.es, http://www.us.es/defdo

Nadine Schieritz MBA

Born 1975. 1994-2001 studies in Industrial Engineering at Karlsruhe University, Germany; 2001 Diplom. 1998/99 studies in Business Administration at Central Connecticut State University, USA; 1999 MBA. Since August 2001 research assistant at the Department of Industrial Management, Faculty of Business Administration, Mannheim University, Germany.
Research interests: supply chain management, agent-based simulation, system dynamics.

Industrieseminar der Universität Mannheim, Schloss,
68131 Mannheim, Germany
Tel. +49 621 181 1585   Fax: +49 621 181 1579
Email: nadines@is.bwl.uni-mannheim.de, http://is.bwl.uni-mannheim.de

Hannes Schollenberger Dipl.-Geoökol.

Born 1974. Diploma in Geoecology (University of Bayreuth). Scientific research assistant in the working group "Technique Assessment and Risk Management" at the French-German Institute for Environmental Research (DFIU/IFARE), University of Karlsruhe (TH), Germany.
Research interests: production planning, substance flow analysis, techno-economic assessment of process changes under new environmental legislation, metal coating, time and motion studies.

French-German Institute for Environmental Research (DFIU/IFARE),
University of Karlsruhe (TH), Hertzstr. 16, 76187 Karlsruhe, Germany
Tel. +49 721 608 4584   Fax: +49 721 758909

Pornpen Setthakaset B.Sc.

B.Sc. (Accounting) from Assumption University, Bangkok, Thailand; P.G.Dip. in Management Systems from Department of Management Systems, Waikato Management School, The University of Waikato, Hamilton, New Zealand; and currently studying for Master of Logistics Management at Sydney University, Sydney, Australia.
Research interests: supply chain management, logistics management, third-party logistics.

6/18-22 Purkis Street, Camperdown, NSW 2050, Australia
Tel. +61 2 95190152,   E-mail: pset4332@mail.usyd.edu.au

Prof. Dr. Rainer Souren Dipl.-Kfm.

Born 1966, studies in Business Administration at the Aachen University (RWTH), 1991-1996 lecturer and PhD student at the Chair for Environmental Management and Industrial Controlling, 1996-2003 senior lecturer at this chair as assistant professor. Since December 2003 professor for Production and Information Management at Bremen University.

Research interests: environmental management, closed loop management, production and logistics management.

Institute for Production and Information Management,
Bremen University, PO Box 33 04 40, 28334 Bremen
Tel.: +49 421 218 2011   Fax: +49 421 218 4271
Email: souren@uni-bremen.de, http://www.wiwi.uni-bremen.de/prodwi

Dr. Christoph Teller

Born 1972 in Wolfsberg, Austria, 1992-1998 studies in Business Administration at the Vienna University of Economics and Business Administration; 1998-2002 PhD Student, research assistant and lecturer; from 2002 Assistant Professor at the Department of Retailing and Marketing (Vienna University of Economics and Business Administration).

Research interests: retail marketing and retail logistics, supply chain partnering.

Department of Retailing and Marketing,
Vienna University of Economics and Business Administration,
Augasse 2-6, 1090 Vienna, Austria
Tel.: +43 1 313 36 46 21   Fax.: +43 1 313 36 717
Email: christoph.teller@wu-wien.ac.at

Wolfgang Teller MBA

Born 1965 in Wolfsberg, Austria, 1983-1988 studies in Business Administration at the Vienna University of Economics and Business Administration, 1988-1996 general manager of a textile retail chain, since 1996 general manager of a CRM software development company.

Research interests: retail marketing, customer relationship management, Internet based marketing research.

Michael Ircher Consulting and Software Development
Griesstrasse 14, 9400 Wolfsberg, Austria
Tel.: +43 664 3020401   Fax: +43 4352 5559921
Email: castor@ircher.com

Dr. Jörn-Henrik Thun Dipl.-Kfm.

Born 1973, 1993-98 studies in Business Administration at Mannheim University in Germany, 1998-2002 research assistant and lecturer at Faculty of Business Administration, Mannheim University, Germany. In 2002 completion of PhD at Mannheim University. In 1999 research visitor at Creighton University, Omaha, Nebraska/USA. Since April 2003 senior lecturer at the Department of Industry and Operations Management, Faculty of Business Administration, Mannheim University. Research mainly carried out within the international "High Performance Manufacturing"-Project.
Research interests: operations management, supply chain management, high performance manufacturing.

Industrieseminar der Universität Mannheim,
Schloss S 212, 68131 Mannheim, Germany
Tel. +49 621 181 15 84   Fax: +49 621 181 15 79
Email: thun@is.bwl.uni-mannheim.de, http://is.bwl.uni-mannheim.de

Martin Treitz Dipl.-Wi.-Ing.

Born 1975. Diploma in Industrial Engineering (University of Karlsruhe (TH)). Scientific research assistant in the working group "Technique Assessment and Risk Management" at the French-German Institute for Environmental Research (DFIU/IFARE), University of Karlsruhe (TH), Germany.
Research interests: integrated process design, techno-economic assessment, multi-criteria decision making, operations research, mass- and energy flow management.

French-German Institute for Environmental Research (DFIU/IFARE),
University of Karlsruhe (TH), Hertzstr. 16, 76187 Karlsruhe, Germany
Tel. +49 721 608 4406   Fax: +49 721 758909
Email: martin.treitz@wiwi.uni-karlsruhe.de,
http://www-dfiu.wiwi.uni-karlsruhe.de/

Dr. Luigi Uglietti

Born 1974, studies in Industrial Economics & Management, manufacturing and plant engineering at Politecnico di Milano, Italy. Since 2002, PhD student in Management Engineering. 2001-2004 lecturer for various teaching and educational institutions, undergraduate level.
Research interests: human factors management, production planning and scheduling, simulation.

Department of Management, Economics and Industrial Engineering,
Politecnico di Milano
Via Giuseppe Colombo, 40, 20133 Milan, Italy
Tel. +39 02 2399 2814   Fax: +39 02 2399 2700, Email: luigi.uglietti@polimi.it

Prof. Dr. Dirk Pieter van Donk

Born 1961, studies in Business Administration and Econometrics at the University of Groningen, The Netherlands. Completed his PhD in 1995 and is currently an associate professor in Production Management in the department Design of Production Systems, Faculty of Management and Organization, University of Groningen.

Research interests: supply chain integration, process industry.

Design of Production Systems, Faculty of Management and Organization,
University of Groningen, P.O. Box 800, 9700 AV Groningen, The Netherlands
Tel. +31 50 3637345
Email: d.p.van.donk@bdk.rug.nl, http://www.rug.nl/bdk

Prof. Dr. Taco van der Vaart

Born 1965, studies in Mathematics, 1983-1989. PhD-thesis in 2000 at the University of Groningen, The Netherlands, Assistant professor in Production Management since 1997 at the Faculty of Management and Organization, University of Groningen (NL).
Research interests: supply chain management, integrative practices.

Faculty of Management and Organization, University of Groningen,
P.O. Box 800, 9700 AV Groningen, The Netherlands
Tel. +31 50 363 7020   Fax: +31 50 363 2032.
Email:j.t.van.der.vaart@bdk.rug.nl,
http://www.bdk.rug.nl/medewerkers/j.t.van.der.vaart/

Prof. Dr. Eva Ventura

Born 1958, studies in Economics and Business Administration in Spain, 1975-1982, and PhD in Economics by the University of Minnesota (USA), 1989. Assistant professor at the University of Illinois, 1987-1988, and visiting professor at the Carnegie Mellon University, 1988-1989. Assistant professor at the Universitat Autònoma de Barcelona (Spain) from 1989 to 1991, and assistant professor at the Universitat Pompeu Fabra from 1991 to 1999. Since 1999, full professor at the Universitat Pompeu Fabra. Part of research has been financed by the Institute of Fiscal Studies of Spain, and the official statistics institute of Spain (INE). Member of GREL (Logistics Research Group, IET, UPF).
Research interests: supply chain management, structural equations modeling, small sample estimation, taxation, public spending.

Departament d'Economia i Empresa,
Universitat Pompeu Fabra, Ramon Trias Fargas 25-27, 08005 Barcelona, Spain
Tel. +34 935 421 760   Fax: +34 935 421 746
Email: eva.ventura@upf.edu, http://www.econ.edu/~ventura/

Prof. Dr. Stefan Voß

Stefan Voß, born 1961 in Hamburg, is full professor and director of the Institute of Information Systems at the University of Hamburg. Previous positions include full professor and head of the department of Business Administration, Information Systems and Information Management at the University of Technology Braunschweig (Germany) from 1995 up to 2002. He holds degrees in Mathematics (diploma) and Economics from the University of Hamburg and a Ph.D. and the habilitation from the University of Technology Darmstadt.

Research interests: Quantitative / information systems approaches to supply chain management and logistics including public mass transit and telecommunications. He is author and co-author of several books and numerous papers in various journals. Stefan Voß serves on the editorial board of some journals including being Associate Editor of INFORMS Journal on Computing and Area Editor of Journal of Heuristics. He is frequently organizing workshops and conferences. Furthermore, he is consulting with several companies.

Institute of Information Systems,
University of Hamburg, Von-Melle-Park 5, 20146 Hamburg, Germany
Fax: +49 40 42838 5535
E-mail: stefan.voss@uni-hamburg.de

Dr. Carl Marcus Wallenburg Dipl.-Wi.-Ing.

Born 1973, studies in Industrial Engeneering and Management and in Business Administration at the Universities of Karlsruhe (D) and Gothenburg (Sweden), 2000-2004 research assistant and PhD student, since 2004 assistant professor at the Otto Beisheim Graduate School of Mangement (WHU) in   Vallendar/Koblenz (D). Research carried out in close co-operation with major companies from various sectors, specially logistics service providers.

Research interests: logistics and supply chain management, firm performance and performance measurement, market performance and customer loyalty.

Kühne-Center for Logistics Management,
Otto Beisheim Graduate School of Management (WHU),
56179 Vallendar, Germany
Tel. +49 261 6509 488   Fax: +49 261 6509 479
Email: cmwallen@whu.edu, http://www.whu.edu/control

Prof. Dr. Jürgen Weber

Born 1953, studies in Business Administration at the University of Göttingen (D), 1978-1981 research assistant and Ph.D. student at the University of Dortmund (D), 1981-1986 assistant professor at the University of Nürnberg-Erlangen (D), since 1986 professor for Business Administration at the Otto Beisheim Graduate School of Mangement (WHU) in Vallendar/Koblenz (D). In 1990 visiting professor at the University of Vienna and in 1999 at the Vienna University of Economics and Business Administration. Editor of the "Zeitschrift für Controlling und Management" and the "Zeitschrift für Logistikmanagement".
Research Interests: controlling, management accounting, corporate governace, logistics and telecommunications.

Chair of Controlling and Telecommunications, – Deutsche Telekom AG Foundation Chair –, Otto Beisheim Graduate School of Management (WHU),
56179 Vallendar, Germany
Tel. +49 261 6509 470   Fax: +49 261 6509 479
Email: jweber@whu.edu, http://www.whu.edu/control

Magnus Westhaus Dipl.-Oec.

Born 1977 in Hamm (Westf.), Germany. 1997-2002 studies in Business Administration and Economics at the University of Oldenburg (D), 2002 to 2003 company employee in a logistic service enterprise in Bremen (D). Since 2003 research assistant at the Department of Production and the Environment, Faculty of Business, Economics and Law, University of Oldenburg (D) and assistant lecturer at the University of Applied Sciences in Wilhelmshaven (D).
Research interest: supply chain controlling.

Supply Chain Management Center, Institute for Business Administration,
Carl von Ossietzky University Oldenburg, 26111 Oldenburg, Germany
Tel. +49 441 798 4179   Fax: +49 441 798 5852
Email: magnus.westhaus@mail.uni-oldenburg.de,
http://www.uni-oldenburg.de/scmc

Prof. Dr. David L. Woodruff

David L. Woodruff is Professor of Management at the University of California, Davis. He was Chair of the INFORMS Computing Society, and serves on several editorial boards including INFORMS Journal on Computing, Journal of Heuristics (Methodology Area Editor), Production and Operations Management, and International Journal of Production Research.

Graduate School of Management,
University of California, Davis. Davis, CA 95616, USA
E-mail: dlwoodruff@ucdavis.edu

 **springeronline.com**

Strategy and Organization in Supply Chains

S. Seuring; M. Müller; M. Goldbach; U. Schneidewind (Eds.)

Supply chain management has gained wide importance for companies that produce goods or services. Though it is well understood that shifting from the single company to the whole supply chain triggers the need for reorganization and reengineering, strategic management or organizational theories have not yet been incorporated in supply chain management. This volume addresses the intersection between organizational theory, strategic management and supply chain management. Within the 23 chapters of the book, 35 authors show how new concepts help companies and their suppliers and customers to coordinate efficiently the partners in a supply chain. The concepts and methodologies presented are illustrated with case studies from various industries and logistical services.

2003, 402 p. 90 illus., Hardcover
ISBN 3-7908-0024-4 ▶ € 74.95 | £52.50

Cost Management in Supply Chains

S. Seuring; M. Goldbach (Eds.)

Supply Chain Management and Cost Management are important developments helping companies to respond to increased global competition and demanding customer needs. This title provides insights into new concepts for cost control in supply chains. The frameworks presented are illustrated with case studies from the automotive, textile, white goods, and transportation industry as well as from retailing. Academics will benefit from the wide range of approaches presented, while practitioners will learn from the examples how their own company and the supply chains which they compete in, can be brought to lower costs and better performance.

2002, 435 pp. 109 figs., 26 tabs., Hardcover
ISBN 3-7908-1500-4 ▶ € 74.95 | £57.50

Easy Ways to Order ▶ Springer Distribution Center • Haberstr. 7 · 69126 Heidelberg, Germany • Tel.: +49 (0) 6221 - 345 - 4303
Fax: +49 (0) 6221 - 345 - 4229 • e-mail: SDC-bookorder@springer-sbm.com • or through your bookseller
All Euro and GBP prices are net-prices subject to local VAT, e.g. in Germany 7%. All prices exclusive of carriage charges. Prices and other details are subject to change without notice. d&p · BA 15837